DONATION

DATE DUE

PRINTED IN U.S.A.

A Code of Jewish Ethics

VOLUME 1

You Shall Be Holy

Also by Rabbi Joseph Telushkin

NONFICTION

The Nine Questions People Ask About Judaism
(with Dennis Prager)

Why the Jews?: The Reason for Antisemitism
(with Dennis Prager)

*Jewish Literacy: The Most Important Things to Know About
the Jewish Religion, Its People, and Its History*

Jewish Humor: What the Best Jewish Jokes Say About the Jews

*Jewish Wisdom: Ethical, Spiritual, and Historical Lessons
from the Great Works and Thinkers*

Words That Hurt, Words That Heal: How to Use Words Wisely and Well

*Biblical Literacy: The Most Important People, Events, and Ideas of the
Hebrew Bible*

The Book of Jewish Values: A Day-by-Day Guide to Ethical Living

The Golden Land: The Story of Jewish Immigration to America

*The Ten Commandments of Character: Essential Advice for Living an
Honorable, Ethical, Honest Life*

FICTION

The Unorthodox Murder of Rabbi Wahl

The Final Analysis of Dr. Stark

An Eye for an Eye

Heaven's Witness
(with Allen Estrin)

A CODE OF
JEWISH ETHICS

VOLUME 1

YOU SHALL BE HOLY

RABBI

JOSEPH
TELUSHKIN

BELL TOWER / NEW YORK

Grateful acknowledgment is made to the following for permission to reprint previously published material:

BASIC BOOKS: Excerpts from *Civility: Manners, Morals and the Etiquette of Democracy* by Stephen Carter. Copyright © 1998 by Stephen L. Carter. Reprinted by permission of Basic Books, a member of Perseus Books, LLC.

OXFORD UNIVERSITY PRESS, INC.: Excerpts from *On Apology* by Aaron Lazare. Copyright © 2004 by Aaron Lazare. Reprinted by permission of Oxford University Press, Inc.

Library of Congress Cataloging-in-Publication Data
Telushkin, Joseph
A code of Jewish ethics / Joseph Telushkin.—1st ed.
Includes bibliographical references and index.
Contents: 1. You shall be holy.
1. Jewish ethics. 2. Jewish ethics—Anecdotes. 3. Judaism—Essence,
genius, nature. I. Title.
BJ1285.2.T45   2006
296.3'6—dc22   2005014556

ISBN-13: 978-1-4000-4835-9
ISBN-10: 1-4000-4835-4

Printed in the United States of America

Marbleized paper on endpapers and section openers by
⌂ SAVITRIS Recycled Hand-made Paper & Stationery / www.savitris.com

DESIGN BY BARBARA STURMAN

6 8 10 9 7

First Edition

To my beloved friends, Terry and David Wohlberg,

whose belief in this project
and whose encouragement of its importance
have been so great an inspiration to me.

ACKNOWLEDGMENTS

Perhaps the pleasantest part of completing a book is to have the opportunity to acknowledge publicly those who have helped me.

I cannot overstate my appreciation to my editor, Toinette Lippe. Since I first spoke with her, some four years ago, about the concept of this code, she has fully comprehended what I wanted to do, and played a crucial role in bringing it to fruition. In addition to being a person of broad vision, Toinette is also a wonderful line editor. There are writers I know who resent their editor's pencil, but I am not one of them. Toinette's improvements are so obvious that she makes it easy for me to accept them.

Richard Pine has represented me as a literary agent on fifteen books, and my respect and affection for him grows and grows. Richard knows how to express skepticism and criticism when appropriate, but he is always encouraging, and there are many times when I've needed encouragement. He is, in addition, a person of integrity, loyalty, and enormous talent, and I wish him and his partners, Kim Witherspoon and Michael Carlisle, great success in their newly launched InkWell Management.

Many friends have read parts of this book in manuscript, and have offered suggestions that have greatly improved it.

Rabbi Israel Stein checked every biblical and rabbinic reference cited in the book, and more. He also tracked down the sources of some teachings that were embedded in my memory but which I couldn't locate. In addition, he corrected a number of errors that had crept in, suggested a few sources I had overlooked, and, along the way, offered a concise and penetrating definition of *lashon hara* (see page 332n.). This was an extraordinary effort, and I am very grateful to him.

Dr. Isaac Herschkopf, a psychiatrist and faculty member of the NYU School of Medicine, and the author of *Hello Darkness, My Old Friend*, an important study of anger, read through the entire book, parts of it twice, and repeatedly enriched the manuscript with insights and illustrative anecdotes. Ike also challenged my conclusions on a number of issues, an exercise that forced me to refine my own thinking.

I had the pleasure of meeting Robert Mass through our mutual friend, David Wohlberg. Rob, a lawyer and a keen student of both Jewish and American legal ethics, is an extraordinarily clear thinker. He took several chapters, most notably the section on truth and falsehood, and reorganized the material in a manner that made the Jewish teachings on this very complicated subject so very clear.

My neighbor Rabbi Irwin Kula was among the book's earliest readers, as he has been among the first readers of almost all of my books. Irwin shared with me his contagious enthusiasm and his always sharp insights, but he also noted a number of instances in which I had unfairly characterized positions with which I disagreed, and I am deeply grateful to him for doing so. Irwin, the long-term president of CLAL, the National Jewish Center for Learning and Leadership, which I am proud to serve as a Senior Associate, is now nearing completion of his own first book, and I wish him much success in this new endeavor.

Like Irwin, Daniel Taub has read and critiqued almost everything I have ever written. A fine stylist and writer, with enormous reservoirs of both Jewish and secular knowledge, and a person of keen logic, he will find many of his suggestions incorporated into the book.

Rabbi Dr. Michael Berger of Emory University, currently serving as headmaster of the Yeshiva Atlanta High School, is an extraordinary teacher and a scholar of wide-ranging Jewish knowledge. Over the years, Michael has helped me with careful readings and critiques of my manuscripts. He has done so now once again, and has offered me, as always, important suggestions, while conveying instances in which he thought my analysis of certain sources were overstated.

Rabbi Vernon Kurtz read an early version of several sections of this book and offered a detailed response, along with valuable suggestions and emendations. My friend and fellow shul-goer at Congregation Ramat Orah, Jeff Bogurksy, offered very helpful critiques and comments. I would also like to thank Rabbi Saul Berman, whom I sit near in shul, for many valuable insights he offered me on subjects on which I was writing. I cherish Saul's wisdom and his careful and subtle reasoning. My thanks go as well to the recently ordained Rabbi Sam Finesmith, a man of widespread Jewish knowledge, for his well-thought-out suggestions.

David Szonyi read and edited this book in manuscript, and improved my style repeatedly. Since I wrote *Jewish Literacy* some years ago, David has worked on all of my nonfiction books and, as I have often said, any writer is blessed to have David as a freelance editor.

I have in the past had many occasions to thank my wife Dvorah for her help in reading and improving my manuscripts (and for so much more), and I would like to thank her again for her suggestions and many stylistic improvements. Dvorah is herself a wonderful writer (she is currently completing a novel), with a highly honed literary sensibility. I have also been repeatedly touched by her passionate belief in the importance of this project. What gives me additional *nachas* (pleasure), is that my children have also been involved in reading and reacting to this book. Shira read through large sections of the manuscript, and offered suggestions as to where I needed to amplify, while commenting on points that she didn't think were logically convincing. On one occasion I could not think of an appropriate anecdote to illustrate a point I was making (I had been struggling with this issue for a long time), and Naomi, effortlessly and with great precision, offered me a perfect example. Rebecca and Benjamin commented upon and discussed with me the various subjects on which I was writing, and offered their perspectives on what they felt I needed to emphasize.

There are two additional people who influenced this book profoundly. The first is my lifelong friend Dennis Prager. Over the more than forty years of our friendship, Dennis has influenced me with his uncanny ability to cut through to the core of an ethical issue. We also evolved together, while in our twenties, an understanding of Judaism that, although modified and refined, has guided us both ever since. The second person, Rabbi Abraham Twerski, M.D., is a man I do not know nearly as well, but whom I regard as one of the great treasures of Jewish life today. Rabbi Twerski has now written over forty books. His body of Jewish knowledge is awesome, as is his ability to apply Jewish teachings to a large variety of issues. Most of all, Rabbi Twerski writes in a manner that inspires his readers to want to do good. It was only when reviewing my own thousands of note cards that I came to appreciate fully how much I had learned from him. His influence is felt deeply throughout this book, particularly in the chapter on humility and its section on self-esteem, a topic on which he has such important things to say.

While working on this book, I spent many days in the library of the Jewish Theological Seminary, one of the great research centers in Jewish life. I would like to thank, in particular, reference librarian Leah Schechter Bennett, who always responded in so warm and helpful a manner to my queries, and who helped me to track down many books I needed to check.

I acknowledge with thanks Rabbi Abraham Twerski, M.D., Dennis Prager, Dr. Solomon Schimmel, Rabbi Jack Riemer, and Rabbi Hanoch Teller for granting me permission to quote from their books—works that, I hope, will affect you as they have affected me.

I would also like to thank Stewart Iden for his wonderful computer skills and unflagging energy. He brought order to a manuscript that had been starting to look anarchic.

I also am pleased to thank four other people involved in my professional life: Ruth Wheat is director of the B'nai Brith Lecture Bureau. A dear friend and a woman of unfailing kindness and talent, she has arranged my lectures throughout North America for over two decades, lectures that deal largely with the subjects written about in this and in my earlier books. Ross Fineman, of Ross Fineman Entertainment, a man of enormous warmth and enthusiasm, has represented me with great skill for almost a decade on television and movie projects. Donna Rosenthal, the executive vice chairman of CLAL, is a woman blessed with talent and kindness in equal measures, and I thank her for how easy and pleasant she has always made my relationship with CLAL. I am happy to acknowledge as well, with admiration and friendship, Carolyn Starman Hessel, the director of the Jewish Book Council, a woman who, in my opinion, has done extraordinary, and singularly important work in popularizing Jewish knowledge and study, and in promoting the buying and reading of Jewish books. I am honored to serve on the board of the Jewish Book Council, and to have the opportunity to work with Carolyn.

I also wish to thank my congregation in Los Angeles, the Synagogue for the Performing Arts—its wonderful officers and members alike, particularly Cookie and Lee Miller, Susie and Dan Ross, and Howard Fine—for giving me the opportunity to teach and speak about the subjects that form the core of this book. All of these people, and many more members of the synagogue, are very special to me, but I want to acknowledge that I have never met a person who works with greater devotion and commitment on behalf of a synagogue than Susie Ross.

This publication was made possible by the support of Keren Keshet.

Two other deeply beloved friends, Terry and David Wohlberg, offered me extraordinary support for this project from its inception, and it is to them that I have dedicated this book.

CONTENTS

I
##

THE TASK OF A LIFETIME

WHAT MATTERS MOST TO GOD

BUILDING CHARACTER

II
##

BASIC VIRTUES AND VICES

JUDGING OTHERS FAIRLY

GRATITUDE

GOOD MANNERS AND CIVILITY

III
===

FAIR SPEECH

THE JEWISH LAWS OF FAIR SPEECH

CRITICISM

TRUTH, LIES, AND PERMITTED LIES

IV
===

LEADING A HOLY LIFE

ACTING AS AMBASSADORS OF GOD

V
===

GOD AND ETHICS

GOD AND GOODNESS

Torah Study: The Mitzvah That Equals All the Others

Appendix

A Code of
Jewish Ethics

VOLUME 1

You Shall Be Holy

INTRODUCTION

This book has a simple thesis: God's central demand of human beings is to act ethically. But although what I have just said is clearly and repeatedly reflected in Jewish sources (see chapter 1), over the past centuries the role of ethics in Judaism has been deemphasized. Most significantly, the word "religious" has come to be associated exclusively with ritual observance. Thus, when two Jews are speaking about a third and a question is raised as to the person's religiosity, the response offered is based solely on that person's level of ritual observance ("She keeps Shabbat and Kashrut, she is religious," or "He doesn't keep Shabbat or Kashrut, he is not religious"), from which we may form the peculiar and inaccurate perception that in Judaism ethics are an extracurricular activity and not very important.

Such a perception, so false to three thousand years of Jewish teachings, deeply concerns and upsets me. But, in addition to wanting to write a book that emphasizes the ethical within Judaism, my primary goal in writing *A Code of Jewish Ethics* is to affect you, the reader. I once heard a friend point out that investors in a public company sometimes receive a memo telling them of some deal in which the company is engaged, followed by the comment, "No action need be taken." Though this book is, I hope, informative about many Jewish teachings, it would be very disappointing if you were to conclude after reading it, that "no action need be taken."

To make it easier for readers to incorporate these teachings into their lives, I have gathered in one place, topic by topic, three thousand years of Jewish laws and suggestions on how to improve our character and become more honest, decent, and just people. The subjects dealt with are those we all have to confront in working on our character, among them judging people fairly, expressing gratitude,* asking forgiveness when we have wronged

---

*As to why gratitude is not only ethically appropriate, but a prerequisite for being happy, see pages 96–111.

another, expressing anger without inflicting irrevocable hurt, not speaking unfairly of others, analyzing when, if ever, it is appropriate to lie, and restraining our impulses of envy, hatred, and revenge. The sources cited are as broad as all Jewish literature, starting with the Torah, the Prophets, and the later books of the Bible, going through the Talmud and Midrash, the medieval codes of Jewish law, the teachings of the Mussar and Chasidic movements, and contemporary Jewish scholars. I have also drawn on insights and examples from nonreligious Jewish literature. Thus, a selection from the great Yiddish writer Sholom Aleichem illustrates as well as anything I know the perversity and foolishness of envy (page 305). I have, in addition, cited anecdotes and insights from non-Jewish writers and from contemporary scholars who, though Jewish, were not writing out of a specifically Jewish framework. Thus, the chapter on good manners was influenced by the writings and experiences of Professor Stephen Carter. Dr. Carter, an African-American and a professor at Yale University, is the author of *Civility*, a detailed and compelling examination of why good manners matter so much. In his book, Dr. Carter writes of an act of graciousness, performed when he was a child, that permanently transformed his life for the better (see page 121). Dr. Aaron Lazare, a former professor of psychiatry at Harvard Medical School, and now the chancellor and dean of the University of Massachusetts Medical School in Worcester, has written a detailed investigation of forgiveness, *On Apology*, and his anecdotes and examples, several of which I have cited, have affected and influenced my understanding of both repentance and forgiveness.

The mentioning of anecdotes points to a central feature of *A Code of Jewish Ethics*. Throughout history, morality has generally been taught in two ways, through binding legal rules and principles, and through stories.* Both exert a profound effect. For every nineteenth-century American who passionately opposed slavery because of its unjust violation of the principle that "all men are created equal," there were probably equivalent numbers of Americans who hated it after reading Harriet Beecher Stowe's *Uncle Tom's Cabin*.†

The significance of both rules and stories accounts for an unusual feature of this book: Statements of law are almost invariably followed by anecdotes illustrating how these principles have been, or can be, carried out in daily life. In a certain sense, I would argue that this is how Jewish tradition has long taught

---

*See the discussion of this point in Rabbi Jonathan Sacks's essay, "*Tikkun Olam*: Perfecting God's World," in Marshall Breger, ed., *Public Policy and Social Issues*, page 40.

†Indeed, when President Lincoln met Stowe during the Civil War, he is reputed to have said to her, "So you're the little lady who made this big war" (Eric Foner and John Garraty, eds., *The Reader's Companion to American History*, page 1094).

ethics. Thus, although the Torah contains a large number of laws, 613 to be precise, anyone who has read the Torah and the rest of the Bible knows that it is not a dry legal text. Rather, it is filled with hundreds of stories that serve to illustrate many of the laws it mandates. For example, the Tenth Commandment forbids coveting our neighbor's spouse or possessions, while the Books of Samuel and Kings tell the stories of two kings who coveted, David and Ahab, and the tragedies that ensued (see pages 48–49 and 302). I suspect that these two stories make as great an impact on the average Bible reader as the commandment itself.

Similarly, the Talmud, filled as it is with legal debates and pronouncements, is also filled with anecdotes illustrating how legal principles were practiced in daily life. To cite a poignant example, the talmudic discussion of the laws of martyrdom deeply influenced Jewish behavior, but the story illustrating how Judaism's most famous martyr, Rabbi Akiva, died with the words of the *Sh'ma* on his lips, have provided Jews for almost two thousand years with a powerful example of how a Jew should meet death (see page 469).

However, when codes of Jewish law started to be compiled in the medieval period, a change occurred, and little use was made of illustrative material. Few stories are to be found in the two most important compilations of Jewish law, Maimonides' twelfth-century, fourteen-volume *Mishneh Torah* (perhaps the most frequently quoted work in this book) and Rabbi Joseph Karo's sixteenth-century *Shulchan Arukh*.*

But my own experience, both in researching and teaching issues of Jewish ethics, is that few things make Jewish teachings so immediate and tangible in the lives of students, listeners, and readers as do anecdotes illustrating how people have carried out these teachings. In addition to inspiring people ("That sounds like something I can do"), stories also make the principles easier to remember.

Stylistically, the code is written in the format in which Jewish legal codes have been written since the Mishnah (circa 200 C.E.): chapters and numbered paragraphs. This style was followed a millennium later in the *Mishneh Torah*, and also in the *Shulchan Arukh*. Each chapter of *You Shall Be Holy* covers one portion of a large area of Jewish ethics. For example, the section on repentance contains five chapters detailing, among other things, "How to Repent" (chapter 14), and "Obstacles to Repentance" (chapter 15). Within the chapters, each of the numbered paragraphs deals with a separate and discrete

---

*There is one lesser known, but influential, medieval code, the thirteenth-century *Sefer Chasidim* (*Book of the Pious*), by Rabbi Judah the Pious, which frequently relates anecdotes to exemplify proper behavior; see, for example, page 494.

point. In the chapter on obstacles to repentance, paragraph 1 deals with blaming others, paragraph 2 with rationalizing what we have done, and paragraph 14 with defrauding the public, an offense for which it is generally impossible to fully atone, since if you have stolen from many people you most likely don't know or recall all your victims, and therefore cannot make restitution.

The distilling of the book into separate paragraphs keeps the code's teachings focused, and enables readers to more easily consult the book when looking for ethical guidance from Jewish teachings.

You Shall Be Holy is the first of a projected three-volume code of Jewish ethics that will present in a systematic manner Judaism's ethical teachings on the most important issues that come up in our lives. This first volume deals primarily with issues of character development. But it is not just a book about improving ourselves; refining our own character will affect how we treat others. The second volume, *Love Your Neighbor,* will focus, God willing, on interpersonal relations, and deal with issues such as *tzedaka* (charity), obligations to society's weakest and most vulnerable members; kindness in our daily interactions with others; relations between employers and employees and between Jews and non-Jews; business ethics; treatment of animals; tolerance for those with whom we disagree; and issues of life and death. The third volume will deal with issues of family, friendship, and community.

Because the focus of *You Shall Be Holy* is improving one's character, I have occasionally found it necessary to repeat stories and laws in different sections. Thus a biblical, talmudic, or midrashic episode cited in one chapter is sometimes also found in another, because it is relevant in both. For example, the biblical story of Doeg, an aide to King Saul, reveals both the important talmudic principle that one should not carry out an immoral order, while also illustrating the great destructiveness that can result from speaking *lashon hara* (see pages 31 and 338). The Joseph story, the central motif of the last quarter of the Book of Genesis, communicates many lessons, among them the dangers of unchecked hatred, the animosity engendered by tattling, and, perhaps most important, the theme of repentance (see pages 168, 300, and 336). A midrashic story about Rabbi Yannai is relevant both in the section on judging fairly and that on good manners (see pages 114 and 218).

One final thought: A friend once told me that when he comes across a helpful and insightful parenting book, he reads it over and over, so that he can remember and internalize the strategies described. The same applies to ethical improvement. The material in this book, if it is to become a vital force in our lives, has to be studied again and again, both to remind us how to act and to keep us from reverting to inappropriate behavior. I know that the rereading and studying of this material plays that role in my life. I certainly cannot claim to have fully mastered all the teachings and techniques described in this book, but studying this material inspires me to do much better than I would otherwise. In addition to presenting ethical teachings to live by, my hope is that *A Code of Jewish Ethics* can serve as a work of reference, a book that can be studied alone or in a small group, and that raises questions to ponder and to discuss with others.

Over three thousand years ago, when God revealed himself to Abraham, the first Jew, He told him, "And you shall be a blessing" [in the lives of those with whom you come in contact; Genesis 12:2]. I think it fair to say that if we undertake to incorporate into our behavior the age-old Jewish teachings in this book, we too will become a blessing in the lives of all those with whom we come in contact, and a blessing in our own lives as well.

I

THE TASK OF
A LIFETIME

WHAT MATTERS
MOST TO GOD

———

"Love your neighbor as yourself";
this is the major principle of the Torah.

RABBI AKIVA,
Jerusalem Talmud, *Nedarim* 9:4

1

JUDAISM'S ETHICAL ESSENCE

═══════════

1. In what is perhaps the Talmud's most famous passage, a non-Jew asks Hillel to "convert me to Judaism on condition that you teach me the entire Torah while I stand on one foot." Hillel answers the man, "What is hateful unto you, do not do to your neighbor. This is the whole Torah! All the rest is commentary. Now, go and study" (*Shabbat* 31a).

The four components of Hillel's response go far in explaining the essence of Judaism.

• *What is hateful unto you, do not do to your neighbor.* If we must restrict ourselves to a single principle defining how we should behave, then this is the appropriate guideline. For example, just as when you solicit advice from another, you want the person to give you the advice that will most benefit you, make sure that when you advise anyone, your advice is solely intended to benefit the recipient and is in no way self-serving. Similarly, if you hate people gossiping about your character flaws, then don't gossip about anyone else's.

• *This is the whole Torah!* Hillel emphasizes that not treating others in a manner that we do not wish to be treated is truly Judaism's essence, and not just one of several important principles of behavior. Thus, although belief in monotheism is at the heart of Judaism, if someone believes in God but does not practice Hillel's guideline in his dealings with others, he cannot be regarded as a religious Jew. Indeed, we may question if the God in whom such an individual believes is the God in whom Judaism believes.

• *All the rest is commentary.* This means that all Jewish laws, including the ritual ones, should in some way reinforce, and certainly not negate, ethical behavior. For example, the Shabbat laws prohibiting labor on the seventh day teach that human beings have value even when they are not working. The Fourth [of the Ten] Commandment's prohibition against servants (in the context, it probably meant slaves, i.e., unpaid servants) working on the Sabbath guaranteed that all people, slaves no less than masters, had a weekly chance to rest. The laws of Kashrut ensure that slaughtered animals are killed instantaneously, and effectively forbid Jews from practicing the sport of hunting, an activity that often leads to a slow and painful death for wounded animals.*

• *Now go and study.* Knowing how to act appropriately is often not a simple matter, and can require a lifetime of study.† For example, it is not enough to know that the Bible commands, "Justice, justice you shall pursue" (Deuteronomy 16:20); we also need to study and deduce *in every situation* what constitutes acting justly. Having good intentions is not enough. For example, Immanuel Kant, perhaps the most esteemed philosopher of the past three centuries, argued, on moral grounds, that it was forbidden to lie to a murderer who asked where his intended victim had gone (see page 423). Hillel's principle dictates otherwise. If you would find it unconscionable for someone to answer a murderer truthfully as to your whereabouts, then assume that others (with perhaps the exception of Kant) would agree. Therefore, in such a situation, tell a lie (see pages 424–427). That Hillel intended his summary of Judaism's essence to be taken literally is reflected in the fact that, when the non-Jew accepted this teaching as valid, Hillel converted him.‡

---

*It would be naïve and inaccurate to claim that every Jewish ritual law promotes ethical behavior. It is hard, for example, to extract an ethical upshot to the law against carrying in public areas on Shabbat. However, Hillel's comment, "All the rest is commentary," suggests that we should try to uncover the ethical teachings embedded in many of the ritual laws. For example, the Talmud asks what a person should do if he has enough money for either Shabbat candles or Hanukah candles, but not for both. Which should take precedence? The answer is Shabbat candles, and the reason is ethical, "on account of the peace [Shabbat candles] bring to one's home" (*Shabbat* 23b). Living in a world lit only by fire, the Rabbis realized that, without Shabbat candles, the family members would have to sit in darkness, turning what should be a joyful family day into a gloomy one. The same passage rules that Sabbath candles take precedence over wine for Kiddush for the same reason, "on account of the peace it brings to one's home" (see also Maimonides, "Laws of Hanukah" 4:14).

†American president Lyndon Johnson once said, "A president's hardest task is not to do what is right, but to know what is right."

‡While there is no indication in the Talmud that the non-Jew committed himself to observing Judaism's ritual laws, talmudic commentaries insist that Hillel, a man of unusual perspicacity, was confident that the man would become a fully observant Jew. Nonetheless, this story suggests that the teaching of Judaism to potential converts should focus disproportionately, though not exclusively, on Judaism's ethical teachings.

———

Most parents, including many who regard themselves as committed Jews, take greater pride in their children's intellectual or cultural achievements (and, in the case of girls, in their good looks) than in their kindness. While such parents want their children to be good people, they rarely see becoming ethical as the most important thing that they, and their children, can do.* These parents have priorities different from Hillel's.

———

2. If Hillel had been the only rabbinic sage to define Judaism in ethical terms, we might infer that his definition represented an idiosyncratic view. But this is not the case. A century later, Rabbi Akiva, the leading rabbi of his age, and perhaps the greatest figure—along with Hillel—in the Talmud, taught that the verse "Love your neighbor as yourself" is "the major principle of the Torah" (Jerusalem Talmud, *Nedarim* 9:4). Again, treating others fairly and lovingly is not seen as one worthy act among many, but as the most important act.

THE SIGNIFICANCE OF ETHICS IN THE BIBLE

The Torah

3. Perhaps the Torah's most consequential statement of Judaism's ethical essence is the Ten Commandments (Exodus 20:2–14), the biblical document that is the bedrock of Jewish and Western morality. The Ten Commandments obligate Jews to affirm God (who brought them out of slavery) and to observe the Sabbath (on which day they must make sure that even their animals are not put to work), and ban idolatry.† The Ten Commandments also prohibit murder, adultery, stealing, bearing false witness, taking God's Name in vain (on the ethical implications of this prohibition, see pages 457–458) and covetousness: "Where are all the sacrifices? Why no mention

---

*Even if they do believe that, they rarely act as if kindness and ethical behavior were their highest priority. Thus, compare how rarely we hear parents brag about a child's kindness with how often we hear them boasting about a child's other accomplishments. Indeed, the older a child becomes, the more parental pride tends to focus on issues of material and professional success, and the less on goodness.

†In Jewish law, idolatry is seen as not only theologically but also morally wrong. For one thing, idolaters sacrificed their children to the idols whom they worshipped; see, for example, the story of Mesha, the king of Moab, who, when losing in battle against Israel, offered his firstborn son as a sacrifice (II Kings 3:27). For more on the Bible's moral objections to idolatry, see page 430n.

of Passover or of circumcision?" asks Rabbi Shubert Spero. "The testimony of the Decalogue seems overwhelming: Moral rules regulating relations between human beings are primary. Morality is the essence of Judaism."[1]

4. Even prior to the giving of the Ten Commandments, the Bible underscores the paramount significance of the ethical. Thus the Torah's opening chapter teaches that human beings are created "in the image of God" (Genesis 1:27). In Jewish thought, creation "in God's image" is understood as meaning that human beings are like God, and unlike all other living creatures, in that they know good from evil (see, for example, Genesis 3:5, 22). It is this ability that marks human beings as unique and in God's image.*

5. God explains the mission of Abraham, the first Jew, as being ethical: "For I have singled him out in order that he may instruct his children and his posterity to keep the way of the Lord by doing what is right and just" (Genesis 18:19). Abraham, in turn, understands justice to be a— perhaps *the*—defining characteristic of God. When he fears that God is acting unfairly in planning to destroy the cities of Sodom and Gomorrah, he challenges Him, "Shall not the judge of all the earth act with justice?" (Genesis 18:25).

6. There are three laws in the Torah for the obeying of which God promises either long national or personal life, and all three involve issues of ethics and kindness:

- "Honor your father and mother that you may long endure on the land that the Lord your God is assigning to you" (Exodus 20:11).

- "If along the road, you chance upon a bird's nest . . . with fledglings or eggs and the mother sitting over the fledglings or on the eggs, do not take the mother together with her young. Let the mother go, and take only the young, in order that you may fare well and have a long life" (Deuteronomy 22:6–7). Maimonides explains that the mother bird is sent away, "for the pain of animals under such circumstances is very great" (*Guide to the Perplexed,* part 3, chapter 48).

---

*In addition, while Genesis 1:26 ordains that human beings should "have dominion over the fish . . . the fowl . . . and over the cattle," it pointedly "excludes the dominion of men over other men, who are equally endowed with divine qualities. Any act which disregards the rights of other people constitutes an unlawful exercise of dominion" (Abraham Block, *A Book of Jewish Ethical Concepts,* page 255).

• "You must have completely honest weights and completely honest measures so that you endure long on the land that the Lord your God is giving you" (Deuteronomy 25:15).

7. The medieval Torah commentator Ramban (*Nachmanides*, 1194–1270) notes that the broad but vaguely worded commandment "And you shall do that which is right and good in the eyes of God" (Deuteronomy 6:18) was necessary because the Torah could not issue ordinances that would cover every contingency ("it is impossible to mention in the Torah all aspects of man's conduct with his neighbors and friends"), and so included this general admonition to act ethically to cover cases where there is no specific law.

———

According to the Talmud, this verse mandates that we sometimes even ignore a law if adherence to it will lead to injustice. For example, if a debtor does not pay a debt on time, the creditor may seize his land in payment. If the debtor later comes up with the money owed, the creditor may say to him, "Too late, I prefer to keep the land." Basing itself, however, on the verse "And you shall do that which is right and good in the eyes of God," the Talmud rules that the land must be returned, even if the money was paid after it was due (Bava Mezia 16b).*

Another talmudic passage sees this verse as so fundamental that it claims that the entire Book of Deuteronomy became known as the "Book of the Right" [i.e., the Upright] simply because it contains the verse, "And you shall do that which is right and good in the eyes of God" (Avodah Zarah 25a).

———

The Prophets

8. Some seven hundred years before Hillel's summary of Judaism's essence, the prophet Micah (circa 750–700 B.C.E.) taught that God's primary demand of human beings is to act righteously: "And what does the Lord require of you? To do justice, love mercy, and walk humbly with God" (6:8). Micah does not speak of faith, sacrifices, or other rituals; rather, God's most significant demands are justice, compassion, and humility.

9. Any attempt to downplay the primacy of ethics in the Bible can likewise be disproved by two verses (9:22–23) in Jeremiah:

———

*In his eleventh-century Torah commentary, Rashi notes that this verse is intended to teach people in a dispute to compromise, and not to insist on the letter of the law.

Let not the wise man glory in his wisdom;
Let not the mighty man glory in his might;
Let not the rich man glory in his riches.
But one should only glory in this: That he understands and knows
Me, that I am the Lord, Who exercises mercy, justice and
righteousness on the earth. For in these I delight, says the Lord.*

Jeremiah singles out the three accomplishments on which people tend to pride themselves, and which often cause them to feel superior to others. Thus, highly intelligent people frequently regard those who are less intelligent as their inferiors, while the powerful and the rich often look down upon the powerless and the poor. But what most delights God is mercy, justice, and righteousness. As Jeremiah makes clear, anyone who does not understand this does not "understand and know" God.

———

A moment's reflection reveals how foolish it is to expect God to be impressed with any human being's wisdom, might, or wealth, all of which cannot be compared to God's absolute wisdom, might, and wealth. However, what Judaism does teach is that a person blessed with one or more of these attributes can impress God by using these gifts to achieve ethical ends, i.e., the wise man who teaches and inspires goodness, the powerful person who uses her power to protect the oppressed, and the wealthy person who uses his riches to help those in need. Since God often refrains from interfering directly in this world in order to allow human beings free will, the wise, powerful, and wealthy who act in this manner are doing God's work, and become, in a manner of speaking, God's partners.

Elsewhere in the Book of Jeremiah, the prophet emphasizes that ethical behavior matters more to God than ritual observance. "For I spoke not with your fathers nor commanded them on the day I brought them out of the land of Egypt concerning burnt offerings or sacrifices; but this I commanded them, saying: Listen to My voice, and I will be your God, and you shall be My people" (7:22–23). Therefore, according to Jeremiah, those who rely on bringing sacrifices to the Temple (Judaism's primary ritual activity when the First and Second Temples were standing) to gain God's forgiveness are deluding themselves. They will be forgiven only if they mend their ways, act justly, and refrain from oppressing the stranger, orphan, widow, and all other innocents: "Then will I let you dwell in

———

*Rabbi Aharon Lichtenstein comments on these two verses: "The ethical element is presented as the reason for seeking knowledge of God." ("Does Jewish Tradition Recognize an Ethic Independent of Halakha?" in Marvin Fox, ed., *Modern Jewish Ethics: Theory and Practice*, page 67.)

this place" (i.e., the land of Israel; see Jeremiah 7:3–7). In other words, while God bestowed the Land of Israel on the Jews as an eternal inheritance (see verse 7), their right to dwell in it is contingent on their acting ethically.*

———

10. The Rabbis understood the prophet Isaiah as seeking to discover the essence of Judaism. Thus, in an oft-quoted talmudic passage (*Makkot* 24a), the Rabbis conjecture that Isaiah condensed (or summarized) the Torah's 613 commandments into six principles of behavior:

- practicing righteousness
- speaking truthfully and fairly
- spurning dishonest gain
- refusing bribes
- closing your ears to blood (this obscure wording seems to refer either to not associating with anyone plotting violence, or avoiding any discussions that might lead to violence)
- closing your eyes from seeing [that which might lead to] evil[†]

According to Isaiah, a person who fulfills these six principles, "will dwell on high" (33:15–16); i.e., be rewarded by God.[2]

The Talmud follows this discussion with another passage which insists that Isaiah summarized the whole intent of Torah law in two principles:

- Do justice (i.e., act fairly).
- Perform acts of righteousness (alternatively "charity"; Isaiah 56:1).

———

In addition, Isaiah denounced the tendency to believe that God's favor can be won by those who do evil, and then offer prayers or perform ritual acts: "And when you lift up your hands [in prayer], I will turn My eyes from you. Though you pray at length, I will not listen. Your hands are stained in blood" (Isaiah 1:15). In another passage, which is read in synagogue on Yom Kippur, Isaiah emphasized that, even on fast days, God wishes the main concern of Jews to be righteous and ethical—rather than ritual—behavior: "Is such the fast I desire,

———

*Jeremiah's formulation brings to mind the prophet Isaiah's teaching, "Zion shall be redeemed through justice" (1:27).

†The Talmud understands this, for example, as refusing to look at a member of the opposite sex who is immodestly dressed.

a day for men to starve their bodies? Is it bowing the head . . . and lying in sack-cloth and ashes? Do you call that a fast, a day when the Lord is favorable? No, this is the fast I desire: . . . to let the oppressed go free and to break off every yoke. It is to share your bread with the hungry, and to take the wretched into your home; when you see the naked, to clothe him, and not to ignore your own kin" (58:5–7). Isaiah seems to be offering a radical reinterpretation of Yom Kippur; we fast so that we know what it is to feel hungry.

In the same passage (Makkot 24a), one rabbi suggests that the prophet Habakkuk summarized all 613 commandments in the verse: *"A righteous person will live in [alternatively "because of"] his faith"* (2:4). It is not clear exactly what Habakkuk meant by this teaching; one likely explanation is that the righteous person's faith will motivate him to do God's will even when it is difficult or disadvantageous to do so.

———

11. Amos and Hosea also emphasized the significance of the ethical over the ritual. According to Amos, prayer offered by unethical people actually offends God: "Take away from me the noise of your songs; to the melody of your harps I will not listen. But let justice well up as waters, and righteousness as a mighty stream" (5:22–24).

Hosea teaches that ethical behavior, even when not accompanied by ritual observance, appeases God: "For I desire kindness and not sacrifice, attachment to God rather than burnt offerings" (Hosea 6:6). A rabbinic Midrash comments on this passage: "Says God: The acts of kindness that you do for each other are more precious to me than all the sacrifices offered to Me by King Solomon" (*Yalkut Shimoni, Hosea* #522).

———

In line with this midrashic teaching, Dennis Prager has offered a common-sense proof as to why it makes sense that God values ethical behavior toward others more than ritual behavior directed toward Him. As Prager asks parents, "What gives you greater joy, when your children tell you that they love you, or when you hear them say to their brothers and sisters, 'I love you.'?" Overwhelmingly, parents answer that they derive greater satisfaction from seeing their children act lovingly toward each other. Prager concludes, "I think God is the same way. He regards humankind as His children (see, for example, Malachi 2:10), and so is most happy when He sees His children treating each other well."

———

12. Zechariah also proclaims that God's main concern is that people behave ethically: "Then the word of God came to Zechariah: This is what the God of Hosts said: 'Render true justice, be kind and merciful to one another. Do not oppress the widow, the orphan, the convert or the poor; and do not plot evil in your hearts against one another'" (Zechariah 7:8–10). As the prophet makes clear, it was the Israelites' refusal to obey these injunctions (Zechariah does not mention ritual violations) that prompted God's great anger at them (7:11–12).

13. The last of the prophets, Malachi, teaches that the fair and compassionate treatment of others is the outgrowth of belief in God: "Have we not all one Father? Did not one God create us? Why do we break faith with one another, profaning the covenant of our ancestors?" (2:10). Malachi is not claiming that his teaching—that because God is our Father, all other human beings are our brothers and sisters—is original. Rather, he insists that this is what the covenant, which goes back to Abraham, always intended. Malachi's teaching is consistent with how God wanted Abraham to understand his mission, to "instruct his children and his posterity to keep the way of the Lord by doing what is just and right" (Genesis 18:19).

14. Nothing suggests the primacy of the ethical in the Bible's prophetic books more than an analysis of the sins that the prophets accuse the Jews of having committed. In addition to sins of idolatry (which leads to unethical acts such as child sacrifice; see, for example, Jeremiah 7:31), they are almost all ethical offenses. Thus, one looks in vain for prophetic condemnations of their fellow Israelites for eating bread products on Passover or lighting fires on the Sabbath, though such behavior was outlawed in the Torah. What one does find are condemnations for oppressing the poor (see, for example, Amos 2:7), perverting justice (Amos 5:7), using unjust weights (Micah 6:10–11), accepting bribes (Micah 3:11), lying (Jeremiah 9:4), murdering and stealing (Jeremiah 7:9), adultery (Jeremiah 5:8), swearing falsely (Jeremiah 5:2), not paying workers their wages (Jeremiah 22:13), and disregarding others' property rights (Micah 2:2).[3]

Later biblical books

15. In posing and answering the question "Who will abide in Your tent? Who will dwell in Your holy mountain?" (Psalms 15:1), the Psalmist offers eleven characteristics that define someone worthy of dwelling with God; all involve ethical behavior. They are a person who:

- lives without blame (i.e., lives a blameless life)
- does righteous acts
- speaks the truth in his heart (i.e., acts truthfully, even when the truth is known to him alone, and is disadvantageous in practical terms)*
- does not deceive
- has not done evil to his fellow
- has not borne reproach for [how he has acted toward] his neighbor
- regards a contemptible person as abhorrent
- honors those who fear the Lord
- stands by his oath even when it is to his disadvantage
- never lends money for interest
- does not accept a bribe against the innocent [presumably referring to a judge] (Psalms 15:1–5).†

16. Proverbs also emphasizes (as did Jeremiah, Isaiah, and Amos) that "to do what is right and just is more desired by God than sacrifice" (Proverbs 21:3). On the basis of this verse, the talmudic sage Rabbi Elazar stated: "Giving charity is greater than offering all the sacrifices" (*Sukkah* 49b).

Ethics in the Talmud

17. On the same page on which the Rabbis record Hillel's statement of Judaism's essence, the Talmud proposes that the first question the Heavenly Court puts to someone who has died is "Did you conduct your business affairs honestly?" (*Shabbat* 31a). Another rabbinic source suggests just how significantly the Rabbis regarded business honesty: "One who deals honestly in business, and his fellow men are pleased with him, is considered as if he fulfilled the entire Torah" (*Mechilta, Beshalach* on Exodus 15:26).

The second question is "Did you set aside regular time to study Torah?"; without Torah study, a Jew will not know how to act properly (see page 496). The third question is "Did you try to create a family?" [literally, "Did you try to procreate?]; without descendants, the Jewish people and their mission will come to an end.‡ The fourth question is "Did you hope for the world's re-

---

*For an example of what this means in daily life, see page 412.

†The Talmud understands this Psalm as a summary statement of the Torah's 613 commandments; see *Makkot* 24a.

‡Significantly, these three questions correspond to the three blessings given at the naming ceremony of a Jewish child (girls are named at the first Torah reading after their birth, boys on the eighth day, at the *brit* (circumcision): "May the parents rear this child [son or daughter] to

demption?" In other words, did you try to help bring about *tikkun olam*, the repair and perfection of the world?

18. According to the Talmud, compassion, besides being the hallmark of an ethical person, is *the* defining characteristic of being a Jew: "If someone is compassionate toward others, you can be sure that he is a descendant of our father Abraham, and if someone is not compassionate toward others, you can be sure that he is not a descendant of our father Abraham" (*Beizah* 32b). Sadly, one sometimes meets Jews who, according to this definition, are certainly not spiritual descendants of Abraham.

19. One of the Rabbis' most important teachings, based on a biblical commandment, is the duty to imitate God's deeds (*imitatio dei*; see Deuteronomy 28:9 and 10:12).[4] Yet because of the rabbinic commitment to ethical behavior, the Rabbis limit the traits of God that we should imitate to those that promote kindness and holiness. For example, "Just as the Holy One, blessed be He, is called compassionate, so you be compassionate. Just as the Holy One, blessed be He, is called gracious, so you be gracious. Just as the Holy One, blessed be He, is called righteous, so you be righteous. Just as He is called Holy, so you be Holy" (*Sifre, Deuteronomy* # 49). On the other hand, we do not find in rabbinic literature statements instructing Jews to imitate God's more aggressive attributes. Thus, although the Torah speaks of God as "a jealous God," Jews are never enjoined, "Just as God is jealous, so must you be jealous," or "Just as God is a zealot, so must you be zealots."[5]

20. Though Jewish tradition, and the Jewish people to this day, have long esteemed intellectual accomplishment (that is why, for example, Jews take such pride in the disproportionately large percentage of Nobel Prize winners who are Jewish), intelligence is not, in and of itself, a good thing. Thus intellectual accomplishments can be morally neutral, as is often the case with work done by researchers, or may even be used to support evil; the scientific community in Germany during World War II was filled with people who worked on developing weapons for the Nazis. In contrast, the Talmud teaches that "The purpose of wisdom is to bring about repentance and

---

adulthood imbued with love of Torah and the performance of good deeds, and may they escort him [or her] to the wedding canopy" (the blessing is based on *Shabbat* 137b). "Love of Torah" corresponds to the question "Did you set aside time to study Torah?"; "May they escort him [or her] to the wedding canopy" corresponds to the question "Did you try to create a family?" and "the performance of good deeds" corresponds, in a general sense, to the question "Did you conduct your business affairs honestly?"

good deeds" (*Berachot* 17a). Thus a goal, perhaps the *primary* goal, of wisdom is to use our intelligence and creativity to discover how to apply the instruction to "love your neighbor as yourself" in every situation.

Conversely, when a smart person uses his God-given intelligence to do something God opposes, he is not only doing something immoral, he is also betraying God (just as a physician who uses his medical knowledge to harm rather than heal is not only committing a crime, but is also betraying those who taught him).

An alternative view

———

A talmudic text suggests that observance of the laws between man and God is more important than observance of Judaism's interpersonal laws.

———

21. The texts already mentioned—with citations from, among others, Micah, Jeremiah, Isaiah, Amos, Hosea, the Psalms, Hillel, and Akiva—focus on the centrality of ethics in Judaism. However, there is a passage in the Talmud that suggests otherwise. In commenting on a verse in Isaiah, "Say of the righteous, when [they are] good, that they shall eat the fruit of their works" (3:10), the fourth-century sage Rava, speaking in the name of Rav Idi, expresses puzzlement at the prophet's words, "the righteous when [they are] good": "Is there a righteous man who is good and a righteous man who is not good?" Rather, Rava explains this verse as meaning that one who is both good to Heaven [i.e., observes Judaism's rituals] and good to man is a righteous man who is good. On the other hand, a person who keeps the laws between people and God, but not Judaism's ethical laws, is "a righteous man who is not good" (i.e., although not ethical, he is still regarded as righteous; *Kiddushin* 40a).

The text's implication is that a person's righteousness is primarily characterized by his behavior toward God; thus a person who observes Judaism's ritual, but not ethical, laws is not doing all that he should, but should still be regarded as a righteous person. Conversely, as the passage continues, one who is good to people, but doesn't keep the rituals, is a *rasha*, an evil person.

Though this passage represents a minority view, within the context of numerous opposing biblical and talmudic passages, its spirit has unfortunately proven influential in Jewish life. Thus, as noted, most people associate religiosity primarily with the performance of ritual rather than ethical acts, although both are mandated by Jewish law, and although a preponderance of Judaism's greatest figures have placed primary emphasis on the performance of Judaism's ethical teachings.

Why has this happened?

Most likely for two reasons:

• Many Jews, out of a desire to keep Jews from assimilating, prefer to emphasize those aspects of Judaism that distinguish Jews from non-Jews. For example, since most non-Jews see acting honestly and being kind to others as the appropriate way to behave, emphasizing Judaism's commitment to honesty and kindness would not necessarily indicate Judaism's uniqueness. However, laws forbidding the eating of shellfish or lighting a fire on the Sabbath do mark Jews off as separate and unique.*

• In general, it is easier to observe ritual laws (though the keeping of them is not necessarily easy) than ethical ones. Ethical commandments, such as the prohibitions against speaking ill of others or judging people fairly (see pages 332–78 and 70–94) are extremely difficult, if not impossible, to observe fully. Thus, some people emphasize the significance of ritual laws to make themselves feel that they are fully observant Jews, rather than putting emphasis on those ethical laws in which they, like everybody else, sometimes fall short.

Ethics in Medieval Writings

22. According to the *Tanna D'Bei Eliyahu* (a midrashic work probably dating from the tenth century), it is people's behavior—not their religion, social class, or gender—that defines them as worthy or unworthy in God's eyes: "I bring heaven and earth to witness that the Holy Spirit dwells upon a non-Jew as well as upon a Jew, upon a woman as well as upon a man, upon a maidservant as well as a manservant. All depends on the deeds of the particular individual" (end of chapter 20).

---

*While it is true that one function of ritual laws is to preserve both the Jewish religion and people (in addition to fulfilling God's commands and creating an atmosphere of holiness), this does not negate the centrality of ethics. After all, Hillel did not answer his non-Jewish questioner with the statement, "Keep the Sabbath. This is the whole Torah! The rest is commentary. Now go and study."

23. Rashi's commentary on Genesis 11:9 asks, "Which was worse, the sins of the Generation of the Dispersion [the people who revolted against God by building the Tower of Babel, and who were dispersed throughout the world], or the sins of the Generation of the Flood [Noah's compatriots, who were guilty of violence and other ethical transgressions]?" Rashi notes that, while the Flood Generation committed serious ethical offenses, they did not revolt against God. Yet the Lord destroyed them all in the flood, while the builders of the Tower of Babel, who revolted against God, were dispersed but not destroyed. Why? "The Generation of the Flood were thieves and fought among themselves. It is for this reason that they perished. The Generation of the Dispersion, on the other hand, treated each other with love and friendship, as it is written, 'And the whole earth was of one language, and of one speech' (Genesis 11:1). This teaches us that dispute [and dishonesty] is despised [by God] and peace is beloved."

Elsewhere in Rashi's commentary, he teaches that "the main accomplishment [literally "offspring"] of the righteous are their good deeds" (Genesis 6:9).

24. The centrality of ethics is a recurring theme in the *Mishneh Torah*, Maimonides' comprehensive and exceedingly influential fourteen-volume code of Jewish law. For example, Maimonides (1135–1204) rules that:

• When it is necessary to violate a Sabbath law to save a life, we should *not* ask non-Jews or children (both of whom are not bound by the Sabbath restrictions) to do the forbidden activities; rather, "Israel's great and wise men" should be called upon to do what is necessary. In that way, people will understand that the laws of the Torah are not arbitrary directives, but are intended to increase "mercy, kindness, and peace" in the world ("Laws of the Sabbath" 2:3).

• The goal of Jewish law is to bring about universal peace: "Great is peace, as the whole Torah was given in order to promote peace in the world, as it was stated (Proverbs 3:17): 'Her ways are the ways of pleasantness and all her paths are peace'" ("Laws of Chanukah" 4:14).

• Dispensing charity is the most important positive commandment in Judaism: "We are to be more particular about the mitzvah of charity than about any other positive commandment. . . . The Jewish people will be redeemed only through charity" ("Laws of Gifts to the Poor" 10:1).

ETHICS IN MODERN TIMES

25. Rabbi Chaim Soloveitchik (1853–1918) of Brisk was among the pre-eminent Talmud scholars of the twentieth century; countless stories are told of his great intellect. Yet when his grandson, the highly renowned Rabbi Joseph Baer Soloveitchik (1903–1993), spoke of his grandfather, it was apparent that both he and Reb Chaim's other descendants found his ethical achievements to be more significant than his intellectual ones: "As a *chesed* personality (practitioner of kindness), Reb Chaim towered above his intellectual personality."[6] Upon Reb Chaim's death, his two sons wrote nothing of his intellectual attainments on his tombstone; the only words they inscribed were *Rav Ha-Chesed* ("Master of Kindness"; the expression can also be understood as a pun and rendered as "Rabbi of Kindness").

Reb Chaim's own teachings make it clear that he believed ethical activities to be our most important responsibility. Thus, when discussing the question "What is the primary function of a rabbi?" he answered, "To redress the grievances of those who are abandoned and alone, to protect the dignity of the poor, and to save the oppressed from the hands of the oppressor."[7]

Rabbi Joseph Soloveitchik, deeply influenced by his grandfather, concluded: "Neither ritual decisions nor political leadership constitute the main task of *halakhic* man. Far from it. The actualization of the ideals of justice and righteousness is the pillar of fire which *halakhic* man follows, when he, as a rabbi and teacher in Israel, serves his community."[8]

———

The great American rabbi Milton Steinberg (1903–1950) said, "When I was a young man, I admired clever people. Now that I am older, I admire kind people."

———

26. When Rabbi Moshe Feinstein (1895–1986), the preeminent twentieth-century expert on Jewish law, was asked what the merit was that caused him to be so revered, he did not point to his phenomenal dedication to Torah study and teaching, or to his meticulous adherence to Jewish rituals. Rather, his response was: "All my life I never knowingly caused hurt to another human being."[9]

27. When Rabbi Abraham Joshua Heschel (1907–1972) marched in a civil rights demonstration with Martin Luther King Jr., and was criticized for not being in synagogue praying, Rabbi Heschel responded, "I'm praying with my feet."

28. In 1935 the Nazis were firmly ensconced in power, and had issued the Nuremberg Laws, stripping German Jews of their citizenship. A short time later, in preparation for Yom Kippur, Rabbi Leo Baeck (1873–1956), the leading Reform rabbi in Germany, wrote a prayer that he sent to his colleagues and that he read aloud on Yom Kippur to his own congregation. The prayer contained a heroic protest against the Nazis' antisemitic attacks: "We pronounce our abhorrence . . . [at] the lies which are turned against us, and the slander directed against our religion and its character." Then Baeck, starting with a series of rhetorical questions, presented a statement of his Jewish credo: "Who has revealed to the world the sense for the purity of conduct, for the purity of family? Who has given to the world, to the attention of mankind, the image of God? Who has shown to the world the command of righteousness, of social responsibility? The spirit of the prophets in Israel, the revelation of God to the Jewish people, has produced all of them."[10]

Rabbi Baeck concluded his prayer with the statement, "We stand before our God . . . we bow to Him, and we stand upright and erect before men." Shortly thereafter Baeck was arrested for offering this prayer. He was soon released; the Nazis, at that time, were still concerned about international opinion and protests. During World War II, Baeck was a prisoner in Theresienstadt.

BUILDING CHARACTER

If one desires to turn himself to the path of
good and be righteous, the choice is his.
Should he desire to turn to the path of evil
and be wicked, the choice is his.

MAIMONIDES,
"Laws of Repentance" 5:1

2

FREE WILL AND HUMAN NATURE:
THE TWO QUESTIONS

═══════

Free will: How much free will do we have?

1. For those who do not believe in God and a soul, human behavior is generally understood as being determined by heredity and environment. This was the belief of Clarence Darrow, the most famous criminal defense lawyer in American history, and perhaps the country's most famous religious skeptic as well: "All people are products of two things, and two things only—their heredity and environment. And they act in exact accord with the heredity which they took from all the past, and for which they are in no wise responsible, and the environment. . . . We all act from the same way."[1]

Because Darrow did not believe in free will, he thought it unjust to punish criminals (Darrow particularly opposed capital punishment for murderers). What moral justification is there for punishing someone for an act he could not resist?

Judaism so opposes the belief that human beings do not have free will that one can state, without exaggeration, that it stands or falls on this issue.[2] If there is no free will, it makes as little sense to have a Torah instructing people how to act as it would to have a law commanding people to run a four-minute mile. For almost all people, such a law would be unjust. If we do not have free will, then Darrow was correct; it would be as unjust to punish people for acting wickedly as it would be for not running a four-minute mile.

In the absence of free will, the Bible's moral judgments make no sense either. Why would the Torah depict Moses as good and Pharaoh as evil if each was solely the product of heredity and environment? True, Pharaoh commanded the drowning of male Israelite infants in the Nile, but why should he be condemned for that, if he was acting on the basis of forces beyond his control?

Judaism teaches that God endowed human beings with free will, which is what enables each person—despite her heredity and environment—to *choose* to do good or evil: "If one desires to turn himself to the path of good and be righteous, the choice is his. Should he desire to turn to the path of evil and be wicked, the choice is his" (Maimonides, "Laws of Repentance" 5:1).*

———

The Midrash teaches that if a person wishes to become a priest (kohen) *or a Levite, he cannot do so, since these roles are passed down by heredity from father to child. But any person, Jew and non-Jew alike, can become a* tzaddik, *a righteous person (Midrash Psalms).*

*Jewish teachings do acknowledge that heredity and environment influence human behavior. The Talmud assumes that people are born with different predilections (including bad ones), such as inclinations toward violence.† And the rabbinic recognition of environmental influences is epitomized by the advice to "stay far away from a bad neighbor" (*The Ethics of the Fathers *1:7). But, and this is Judaism's crucial point, human beings can overcome bad environments. Indeed, two of Judaism's paradigms of moral greatness, Abraham and Moses, were raised in highly imperfect environments; thus, Jewish tradition teaches that Abraham's father, Terah, was an idolater, while Moses was raised in Pharaoh's household.*[3]

———

2. While acknowledging that the lure of sin is powerful, the Torah insists that free will endows people with the strength to resist it. When God

---

*Elsewhere, Maimonides writes ("Laws of Repentance" 5:2) that each person can become as righteous as Moses and as evil as Jeroboam, the Israelite monarch who commanded the Israelites to worship golden calves (see I Kings, chapter 12). Maimonides does not say that each person can become a great leader like Moses, but only that he can become righteous like Moses. In other words, free will applies to ethical behavior, but not to all areas of life (see pages 31–32). The British theologian Rabbi Louis Jacobs has argued that Maimonides' position is overstated even as regards ethical behavior. We cannot expect a child raised among dishonest people, for example, to achieve the integrity of a child raised in an ethical environment. Therefore we should judge people from morally deprived backgrounds on a different scale. For example, a child raised among violent criminals should be given some credit even if he does dishonest deeds, but refrains from violence.

†Many of the talmudic Rabbis assert that human inclinations are influenced by astrology (in the sense that the stars impel, but don't compel). For example, one talmudic view states that people born under the sign of Mars come into the world with a predilection to shed blood. The Rabbis advise these people to become surgeons, ritual slaughterers, or circumcisers (*Shabbat* 156a). Today, most people don't believe that character traits are determined, or even influenced, by the stars under which they were born. But even if one rejects astrology, the Rabbis' insight, that we need to channel negative inclinations into activities that benefit society, remains valid.

sees the enormous hostility Cain feels toward his brother Abel, whom he later murders, He says to him, "Sin crouches at the door, its urge is toward you, yet you can be its master" (Genesis 4:7).* Although we all give in to sin sometimes (see Ecclesiastes 7:20), we can ultimately be its master. In particular, we can avoid the most evil of sins, such as that committed by Cain.

————

Viktor Frankl, the psychoanalyst and Holocaust survivor, concluded that sometimes the only free will that we have is how we choose to meet our death, and how we act in the days and hours preceding it. But some freedom of action always remains: "We who lived in concentration camps can remember the men who walked through the huts comforting others, giving away their last piece of bread. They may have been few in number, but they offer sufficient proof that everything can be taken from a man but one thing: the last of the human freedoms—to choose one's attitude in any given set of circumstances, to choose one's own way."[4]

————

3. Because we have free will, we bear responsibility for the wrong that we do. If a superior orders us to perform a wrongful act, we should disobey, and if we obey, we cannot deny responsibility by blaming the person who issued the order. Since God is on a higher plane than the superior who issued the command, we must follow God's commandments, not immoral ones.

In the Talmud, this principle is known as *ain shaliach le-dvar aveirah*, which literally means, "There is no messenger in a case of sin" (*Kiddushin* 42b). Normally a messenger is not responsible for the content of the message he delivers; responsibility is borne by the one who sent it. But if a messenger is sent to perform an evil act (a hired assassin, for example), he cannot defend himself with the claim that he was only acting at someone else's command. The messenger bears responsibility for the evil he does.

The Bible offers examples both of heroes who refused to follow immoral orders and of others who carried them out:

• Pharaoh ordered the midwives Shifra and Puah to kill all Israelite male babies at birth, but "the midwives, fearing God, did not do as the king of Egypt had told them" (Exodus 1:15–21). Had other Egyptians acted with the same courage, no evil would have ensued. Unfortunately, the other

————

*Even after issuing this warning, God does not deprive Cain of his free will by preventing him from killing Abel.

Egyptians cooperated in Pharaoh's plan to wipe out the Israelites (Exodus 22).

• When King Saul ordered his troops to murder innocent priests in the town of Nob, "the king's servants would not raise a hand to strike down the priests of the Lord." Saul's order would have been thwarted, but Doeg the Edomite stepped forward to follow the order, and murdered eighty-five priests on that day (see I Samuel 22:9–23).

• Joab, the leader of Israel's army, obeyed King David's wrongful order to have Uriah, an army officer, killed in battle (for the reason David gave this command, see page 302). Not only did Joab carry out the order, but he also arranged for other soldiers to die along with Uriah so that less attention would be drawn to Uriah's death (II Samuel 11:14–25).

• The happiest example of resistance to an immoral order involved another of Saul's commands. Just prior to a battle, Saul announced that any soldier who ate before evening (and the completion of the battle) would be executed. His son, Jonathan, did not hear the order, and ate some honey. Saul insisted that Jonathan be executed, but his officers refused to carry out the order—"Never! As the Lord lives, not a hair of his head shall fall to the ground." Finally, Saul relented (I Samuel 14:24–45).

In modern times, the defense offered by Nazi killers such as Adolf Eichmann, "I was just following orders," is, from the standpoint of Jewish law, no defense at all.

4. The acknowledgment that we have free will and bear responsibility for our actions is the essence of human dignity. At the age of Bat and Bar Mitzvah (twelve for girls, thirteen for boys), when a Jewish child assumes the obligations of adulthood, the parents offer the blessing, "Praised be He who has released me from the responsibility for this one's misdeeds" (*Shulchan Arukh, Orach Chayyim, Ramah* 225:2). In other words, Jews thank God that their children have reached the age when they are capable of becoming responsible for their own actions (this is the real meaning behind the blessing, not that parents are celebrating that they are no longer subject to punishment for their children's wrongful actions). Personal responsibility and free will are to be celebrated.

5. While free will applies in the moral sphere, it does not apply in all areas of life. For example, while I have the free will, hence the ability, to act rightly when confronting a moral dilemma, I do not have the ability to become

a great scholar in chemistry (no matter how hard I study) or a great athlete (no matter how much I practice). A talmudic passage teaches that at the moment of conception, "the angel in charge of pregnancy . . . takes a drop [of semen from which a child will be conceived], and sets it before the Holy One, blessed be He, and asks, 'Master of the Universe, this drop, what is its destiny? Will the person who develops from it be mighty or weak, intelligent or foolish, wealthy or poor?' " (*Niddah* 16b).

However, the angel does not ask God whether the person will be wicked or righteous, for this is not determined by God, but by each human being.*

———

The Chasidic teacher Rabbi Zusha of Hanipol used to say, "When I come before the heavenly court and am asked, 'Zusha, why were you not Moses?' I will answer, 'Because I did not have Moses' leadership abilities.' And when I am asked, 'Zusha, why were you not Abraham?' I will answer, 'Because I was not blessed with Abraham's intellectual abilities.' For every such question, I will have an answer. But when I am asked, 'Zusha, why were you not Zusha?' for that I will have no answer.' "

As Reb Zusha's teaching underscores, all of us have limits on our abilities, but we also have capabilities and challenges that we alone can meet.

———

6. Although this talmudic teaching suggests that traits such as wisdom, strength, and wealth are predetermined, a series of questions and answers in *The Ethics of the Fathers* (4:1) suggests that even in these areas, human beings have considerable ability to affect their destiny:

- *Wisdom:* "Who is wise? One who learns from every person." While our intellectual attainments may be restricted by innate limitations, the Rabbis teach that wisdom is available to everyone. From this perspective, the wise person is not the one who has amassed knowledge or who has a high IQ, but the one who keeps seeking to learn more.†

———

*The Talmud also teaches, "Everything is in the hands of God except the fear of God" (*Niddah* 16b). Because God has granted us free will, we can choose, in defiance of God, to do evil, but our doing so does not mean that God desires this evil to occur. Of course, we can argue that because God is all-powerful, He could stop all evil behavior if He wished. But if God did so, we would no longer have free will; we would be permitted to do only what God wanted us to do. This might make for a kinder world, but God did not intend for the world to be populated solely by robots, even angelic ones.

†"The Nobel laureate in physics, Isidor Rabi, was once asked, 'Why did you become a scientist, rather than a doctor, or lawyer, or businessman, like the other immigrant kids in your

• *Heroism:* "Who is a hero? (alternatively, "strong"; the word *gibbor* means both). One who subdues his [evil] inclination." Therefore, all of us, even those with fearful dispositions and weak bodies, have the ability to be heroic and strong several times a day (on the implications of this teaching for daily behavior, see page 54).

• *Wealth:* "Who is wealthy? One who is happy with what he has." We may not be in a position to determine how much money we have, or if we can escape poverty. But if we learn to be satisfied with what we have, we will be happier (and in that sense richer) than those wealthy people who are dissatisfied with what they have.

———

Sometimes strength of character involves subduing even one's good, or kind, inclination. A friend of mine, a doctor, remembers his post-operative and feverish mother begging him, with tears in her eyes, for a glass of water. However, the surgeon had absolutely forbidden her to consume anything by mouth and so, with tears in his eyes, he didn't give it to her.

———

Are human beings naturally good?

7. The Torah has a skeptical view of human nature, although it is by no means hopeless about people's capacity to change and improve. In Genesis, God, disappointed by humankind's propensity for violence and dishonesty, laments, "The tendency of man's heart is towards evil from his youth" (Genesis 8:21). This does not mean that we are born bad or, as certain Christian groups believe, damned (hence the need for baptism), but it also means that we are not born good (and corrupted by society, as Enlightenment thinkers taught). Rather, human beings are born morally neutral, with *strong* inclinations toward evil. Children, for example, are born self-absorbed, and have to be educated toward sharing, empathy, and generosity.*

---

neighborhood?' Dr. Rabi answered: 'My mother made me a scientist without ever intending it. Every other Jewish mother in Brooklyn would ask her child after school, '*Nu?* did you learn anything today?' But not my mother. She always asked me a different question, 'Izzy,' she would say, 'did you ask a good question today?' That difference—asking good questions—made me become a scientist." (Donald Sheff, *New York Times*, 19 January 1988).

*It is rare to hear a mother yelling at a three-year-old child to stop giving his toys away to other children; generous behavior has to be taught. Similarly, children have to be taught not to make insensitive remarks to, or tease, children with disabilities or those who are poor. Rabbi Joseph Soloveitchik recalled a period from his European childhood when his father, a prominent rabbi,

———

The Bible's view is echoed in the writings of the contemporary sociologist James Q. Wilson: "The forces that may easily drive people to break the law, a desire for food, sex, wealth, and self-preservation, seem to be instinctive, not learned, while those that restrain our appetites, self-control, sympathy, a sense of fairness, seem to be learned and not instinctive" (The Moral Sense).

———

8. Because of the Bible's assumption that human nature cannot be relied upon to ensure that people do what is right, Jewish law does not issue general edicts on matters of ethics, such as "Be generous," when it comes to giving to charity. If there were no specific guidelines on how much to donate, many people would regard themselves as having fulfilled this command by giving small sums of money to others in need.* Hence Jewish law speaks of donating between ten and twenty percent of one's net income to charity.

Jewish law prescribes numerous other ethical acts, the practice of which refine our natures and lead us to goodness.† The Jewish view of human nature would seem to be "Do good and you will become a good person in spite of yourself."

Therefore, at the heart of Judaism's teaching on how to improve our character is the *mitzvah* (commandment), the obligatory deed.

———

A medieval Jewish folktale: An ancient king, a contemporary of Moses, heard such extraordinary reports about the Jewish leader that he commissioned an artist to paint Moses so that he could see what this great man looked like. The artist returned with the painting, and the king was shocked, because Moses looked like someone of bad character. The king was puzzled, and set out to see Moses for himself. When he met him, he saw that the painting was accurate. He said to

---

had not been paid for a long time: "I walked around in torn pants. My classmates at *cheder* [elementary school] ridiculed me. Boys are very cruel. Children in general can be very cruel. It appeared funny to them that the rabbi's son should walk around in torn pants" (Aaron Rakefett-Rothkoff, *The Rav*, volume 1, page 262). Obviously, if children were born kind, they would refrain from such behavior without having to be taught.

*An old joke has it that a wealthy miser dies and comes before the Heavenly Court. When his deeds are examined, the angels can find no acts of kindness, and the outlook for the man seems grim. The frightened miser suddenly remembers an incident from years earlier. It was a snowy, freezing day and he saw a beggar in the street shivering in a threadbare shirt. Overwhelmed by pity, the wealthy man dug in his pocket and handed the beggar a quarter. A deep, loud voice is heard in the Heavenly Court: "Give the man his quarter back, and tell him to go to hell."

†For example, if you start to follow the laws about visiting the sick (*bikur cholim*), and do so on a regular basis, it will begin to feel wrong to you not to do so.

Moses, "I don't understand. Your appearance is so coarse and unrefined, yet I know that you have done many great things." Moses answered, "You are right. By nature, I am a person filled with lust and sinful thoughts. Yet by submitting myself to the will of God and His laws, I have refined myself."

In modern times, Rabbi Chaim Soloveitchik, the great Talmud scholar and, as noted in the previous chapter, a man renowned for his kindness, acknowledged that his innate character was harsh, even cruel. According to his grandson, Rabbi Joseph Soloveitchik, Reb Chaim told his family, "Do not think that I am inherently good. My character is actually bad. One must force oneself to develop gracious character traits. A person must transform himself. I have worked hard to uproot any traces of cruelty from myself."[5]

Even those commandments that deal with ritual, as opposed to ethical, matters, can further character development. My friend Dennis Prager told me that when he was six years old, the first words he learned to read in English were "pure vegetable shortening only." He added, "It was good training to learn at the age of six that I couldn't have every candy bar in the candy store."

————

9. Human nature, as the Talmud understands it, consists both of a *yetzer hatov*, a good inclination, and a *yetzer hara*, an evil inclination. However, the Rabbis did not believe that the goal of a good person should be to fully eradicate the "evil inclination," for within it resides the aggressive instincts that prompt so much creativity and achievement. The Rabbis speculate that without a *yetzer hara*, we would not engage in business, build homes, marry, or have children (*Genesis Rabbah* 9:7). For example, our motives for engaging in sexual relations emanate from lust no less than love, but out of such mixed, and somewhat impure, motives something very pure, a new life, emerges.

The Talmud relates that Ezra and the Men of the Great Assembly* wanted to destroy the evil inclination, but were warned that doing so would have catastrophic consequences. They therefore chose to experiment by imprisoning the *yetzer hara* for three days; they then searched for a new-laid egg and could find none (*Yoma* 69b). In other words, all human and animal life will cease if the evil, i.e., aggressive, inclination is eliminated.

10. From Judaism's perspective, therefore, greatness of character is not measured by our not having an evil inclination, but by our success in controlling it. The Talmud taught that "The greater the scholar, the greater his

———

*The 120–man ruling body of the Jewish people during the early days of the Second Temple; in Hebrew it is known as *Anshei Knesset ha-Gedolah*.

evil inclination" (*Sukkah* 52a). The Rabbis believed that when someone has pronounced capabilities, more opportunities, including illicit ones, will be presented to him, and it takes enormous self-control not to act on them. For example, it is a greater moral achievement for a person to build up a business from scratch and remain scrupulously honest than for someone who is always employed by another to engage in no financial chicanery. Similarly, it is a greater act of character for a person of good looks and a sensual disposition not to lead a promiscuous life than for one who is afforded few such opportunities.

11. It is important for us to be aware of our own "evil" inclinations (see pages 54–65), because this enables us to channel even our ignoble inclinations for good. For example, if we know we have a strong need to be admired, we should strive to become well known for doing good deeds. Some people deride philanthropists who donate large sums of money to a university or hospital building campaign and insist that a building be named for them. But such behavior may show a proper amalgamation of both good and "evil" inclinations. The person's *yetzer hatov* is what prompts her to donate money to a good cause, while she has channeled her *yetzer hara*'s desire for acclaim into an activity that is worthy of it.

———

The Bible records that when Boaz met the impoverished Ruth, he acted generously toward her and gave her roasted grain. But, the Midrash comments, "Had Boaz known that the Holy One would cause it to be written of him [in the Bible] that "he handed her roasted grain" (Ruth 2:14), he would have given Ruth fatted calves to eat" (Leviticus Rabbah 34:8). What the Rabbis assumed to be true of Boaz is true of most of us as well. When someone asks us for help, I think many of us would respond more generously if we knew our behavior would be reported in tomorrow's newspaper.

———

12. When given the opportunity to perform one of two possible *mitzvot* (commandments), choose the one that involves overcoming your "evil inclination" (Rabbi Nachman of Bratslav).[6] The Talmud offers this example: If you see two people, one with an animal that needs to be loaded, the other with an animal that needs to be unloaded, first help the person with the burdened animal, since it is unpleasant for an animal to be weighed down by a heavy load. However, if the person with the laden animal is your friend, and

the other your enemy, the Rabbis rule that you should first help your enemy. By doing so, you will overcome your "evil inclination" to ignore someone you don't like (*Bava Mezia* 32b; see also Maimonides "Laws of Murder" 13:13; for a further discussion of the rationale behind this law, see pages 319–320).

In modern terms, if we have the opportunity to help a friend or someone with whom we have a difficult relationship, we should try—at least on occasion—to help the latter first.* It may be that we will also have the chance later to help our friend, and in the meantime we may help transform an enemy into a friend.

3

DEVELOPING GOODNESS

1. Judaism regards improving character as the goal of life. As the Midrash teaches, "The Torah's commandments were not given to mankind for any purpose other than to refine people" (*Genesis Rabbah* 44:1). The Rabbis did not say that it is one of the purposes of the Torah and its commandments to improve our character, but that this is their sole purpose.

The guideline enunciated in this Midrash—"to refine people"—gives each of us a standard for determining whether we are leading a morally successful life. Are we growing in honesty, kindness, and compassion? If we are not more compassionate and empathetic at sixty than we were at twenty, we have lived a failed life.

———

Similarly, the Gaon of Vilna (1720–1797) taught that "the purpose of life is to strive to break bad habits, and improve oneself. Otherwise, what is life for?" (Even Shleimah 1:2). The Gaon's statement suggests that such labor is a task that might take decades. Unfortunately, the need for such vigilance is something that few of us wish to acknowledge. As the early-twentieth-century Mussar rebbe,

---

*We shouldn't act like this all the time both because it would be unfair and because our friends may well conclude that we are disloyal.

Rabbi Yaizel of Navorodock, taught, "A person wants to become a scholar and a leader overnight, and to sleep that night as well."

―――

Techniques for refining our character

2. We become good people not by thinking good thoughts but by doing good deeds again and again, until they become part of our nature.* That is why Maimonides taught that it is better to give needy recipients one gold coin on a thousand different occasions than to give someone a thousand gold coins all at the same time. True, the net good to that one person may equal, or even surpass, the combined good to the recipients of the smaller donations. But for the person who gives the thousand gifts, "if he opens up his hand again and again one thousand times, the trait of giving becomes part of him."[1] Indeed, when we give repeatedly, or do any ethical deed again and again, it becomes part of our character.†

―――

Because of the capacity of deeds to affect character, the Talmud teaches that "a person should always . . . follow the commandments, even if not for their own sake [i.e., but rather for ulterior motives], because, from doing them not for their own sake, one will eventually come to do them for their own sake" (i.e., for right and pure reasons; Sotah 22b). In short, the rabbinic view is that actions shape the heart more than the heart shapes actions.

―――――――――

*This point is famously made by Aristotle (whose writings Maimonides and some other medieval Jewish scholars studied) in his *Nichomachean Ethics*: ". . . men become builders by building and lyre-players by playing the lyre; so too we become just by just acts, temperate by doing temperate acts, brave by doing brave acts. . . . It makes no *small* difference, then, whether we form habits of one kind or of another from our very youth; it makes a very great difference, or rather *all* the difference." In short, people become virtuous by practicing virtues.

†Dr. Isaac Herschkopf, a psychiatrist, notes that we not only become good people by doing good deeds, we become healthy people by doing healthy deeds. Thus, Dr. Herschkopf once had a patient with a dog phobia so severe that she refused to address it; indeed, she stopped seeing the doctor. Several years later she called him; she now had a son and was scared that he would inherit her phobia. Dr. Herschkopf explained that inheritance would come from learning, not from genetics. To avoid her son learning her phobia, the woman came to realize that she couldn't avoid dogs in his presence. So, when a dog came up to her while she was pushing her stroller, she didn't run away. In the doctor's words, "she would stay there, and she would die a thousand deaths, but for her son's sake, she wouldn't move." In the end, her son never developed her phobia, and she, because of her repeated exposure for her son's sake, ended up curing her own phobia.

Sara Levinsky Rigler, a Jerusalem-based writer, tells of coming to the United States to attend her father's funeral. He had not been religiously observant, but when Rigler stood beside his covered body in the mortuary, she "was overwhelmed by the sense that legions of angels were surrounding [him] and escorting his soul to the next world."

Her father, she explains, was a man who devoted his life to acts of kindness. A pharmacist, he often granted loans, many of which he never collected, to people who could not pay for medications. When the neighborhood fell on hard times, he would buy ice cream for young children and counsel teenagers, who didn't have the money to go to a doctor, on health issues. Once a year, on Christmas, he would go to the homes of poor neighborhood women to bring them flowers, doing this until he was seventy-five. Several of the women told Rigler's brother, who accompanied him on these trips, that these flowers were the only thing of beauty they received all year.

During the Six-Day War, Rigler's father borrowed four thousand dollars from the bank and donated it to the United Jewish Appeal's Israel Emergency Fund. Later, in a remarkable act of philanthropy, he took out a second mortgage on his home so that he could make a large contribution toward the building of a Jewish geriatric home.

What did Rigler learn on the day of her father's funeral? "I saw that deeds are all that count—not good intentions, not beliefs, not convictions, not even spiritual consciousness, but deeds. . . . Standing beside my father's body, gazing at his luminous face, I was shocked to realize who he had become by virtue of his deeds alone."[2]

3. When Rabbi Akavia ben Mehalalel was dying, his son was fearful that, once his father died, he would lose his status among the Sages, and he therefore beseeched him: "Father, commend me to your colleagues." When Rabbi Akavia refused to do so, his son asked, "Is it because of some fault you have found in me?" Rabbi Akavia answered: "No. It is your deeds [and not my words] that will endear you [to the Rabbis], and your deeds that will estrange you" (Mishnah *Eduyot* 5:7).

Rabbi Akavia's lesson is difficult for many people—particularly scions of the famous—to absorb. The newspapers reported the arrest of a drunk driver who was the son of a prominent figure in American life. When approached by the police, the young man shouted at them, "Do you know who my father is?"—a re-mark that was simultaneously arrogant, pathetic, and irrelevant.

A rabbinic passage teaches: "A person has three names; the one that his fa-ther and mother call him, the one that his fellows call him [e.g., how people talk about him], and the one he acquires [by the way he acts]. And this last one is better than all the others" (Tanhuma Va-Yakel #1). Thus, Oskar Schindler was a womanizer and a dishonest businessman. But during World War II, when he came to realize the Nazis' murderous intentions, he repeatedly risked his life and employed remarkable ingenuity to save the lives of more than eleven hundred Jews. By changing his ways, Schindler transformed the association people previ-ously had with him and his name. Indeed, since the publication of Thomas Keneally's Schindler's List, *and the release of the movie of the same title, the name Schindler has become a byword for courage and compassion.*

———

4. When trying to improve your character, don't despair and lose heart when you do something wrong, and don't think, "Oh, I'm never going to be any good." We must remember that even imperfect or incomplete improve-ment is far better than none at all.

When the Chaffetz Chayyim, the renowned legal scholar and ethicist, 1838–1933, published his book on the laws prohibiting *lashon hara* (speaking unfairly of others), Rabbi Israel Salanter told him, "If all you accomplish is to evoke one sigh from one reader, then your book is worthwhile." The Chaffetz Chayyim himself cited these words to a businessman who bought all his books with the exception of the volume on right speech. When asked why, the man explained that it was impossible in his business dealings to avoid speak-ing ill of others, and he didn't want to read the book, given that he would ignore or, worse, violate it. The Chaffetz Chayyim insisted that he take the book, telling him that if reading the book "at least evokes a sigh," it was worth it.

5. Cultivate the friendship of people who are both good and wise. From friendships like these, you will learn new ways to help others, while the kind-ness of these people will inspire you to want to become kinder.

Rabbi Aryeh Levine, the twentieth-century Jerusalem *tzaddik,* told his son that, early in life, he came to understand that he couldn't learn how to be a good person from books alone, "but only from the actions of *tzaddikim.*" That is why, even as a young man, Reb Aryeh sought out people known to be righteous, so as to learn from their behavior.[3]

In addition, spending time among good people inspires us with the de-sire to become better. For example, if we spend time in a household where the family members speak to each other in a consistently loving manner, it is likely that we—at least while we are with these people—will also speak in a calmer, more loving, manner than we normally do: "It is in the nature of human beings to be influenced in their opinions and actions by their friends and neighbors. . . . Therefore, a person should strive to become friendly with righteous people, and to stay in the presence of those who are wise, so that one will learn from their actions" (Maimonides, "Laws of Character Development" 6:1).

———

During the 1930s, the philosopher Martin Heidegger was one of Germany's premier intellectuals; he is still regarded, particularly in Europe, as one of the twentieth century's most profound thinkers. But anyone who tried to learn from Heidegger how to conduct his life would have learned that it was appropriate to become a Nazi so that one could become the rector of Freiburg University, as Heidegger did.* His university lectures and classes included the Nazi salute. That is why we must learn how to behave only from those who are righteous as well as intelligent.†

———

Rabbi Chaim Ozer Grodzensky (1863–1940) and his students were once walking together on a bitterly cold Shabbat evening in Vilna when they were stopped by a young man who asked for directions. The man had a severe stutter, and it was clear that he was embarrassed by his disability. The street he was searching for was an obscure one, and reaching it required a twenty-five-minute walk. Despite the great cold, Rabbi Grodzensky insisted on accompanying the man to his destination. After the rabbi and his students took the man there, they started back, and his students asked him why he hadn't just told the man the way, instead of accompanying him. Rabbi Grodzensky explained, "You saw how complicated it was to find this street. We were able to do so only because we know

———

*At his rectoral address, Heidegger declared: "The Fuhrer himself and alone is today and in the future German reality and its law." A short time later, on April 10, 1933, he instructed his deans to dismiss all faculty members of Jewish religion or origin.

†Despite the veneration expressed for Heidegger's brilliance by intellectuals such as Jean-Paul Sartre, Hannah Arendt, Richard Rorty, and George Steiner, Heidegger was, in moral terms, an idiot. Thus, when the anti-Nazi philosopher Karl Jaspers asked him, "How can a man as coarse as Hitler govern Germany?" Heidegger responded, "Culture is of no importance. Just look at his marvelous hands." In 1946, a year after World War II had ended and the horrors of the Holocaust carried out by Heidegger's fellow Nazis had become known, Heidegger wrote, in his *Letter on Humanism,* "Perhaps the distinguishing feature of the present age lies in the fact that wholeness as a dimension of experience is closed to us. Perhaps this is the only evil." The *only* evil? (see the discussion of Heidegger's philosophy and character in Jonathan Glover, *Humanity: A Moral History of the Twentieth Century,* pages 367–376).

this city so well; we even know the shortcuts. But had we told this young man the directions, he would have become confused after a few blocks and then, because of his stutter, would have been reluctant to stop people to ask the way. Indeed, he probably would have tried to find it himself and become lost, a particularly unfortunate thing on a night as cold as this. So instead we accompanied him, which both reassured him and saved him from having to embarrass himself."

————

6. To rework an ancient rabbinic proverb: "It is good for the righteous person, and good for his neighbor."* When moving into a new neighborhood, many of us are most concerned with finding a beautiful house. From Judaism's perspective, it is more important to ascertain the character of the people who live in the neighborhood. This is the environment in which we and our children will live; the people we see on the street are the people with whom we will associate, and the better their characters, the more likely it is that we and our children will grow in goodness.

Similarly, as my friend Daniel Taub suggests, when seeking out a school for our children, we should look not only at the preschool and first grade (which is what most parents do), but also at the higher grades, to see what kind of people the school seems to be producing.

7. Avoid people with bad character and unkind disposition. It is difficult, if not impossible, *not* to learn from, and be influenced by, our neighbors, by those with whom we work, and by all those with whom we spend time. Thus the opening verse in the Book of Psalms hails the person who takes care to avoid all those who exert a bad influence: "Fortunate is the person who doesn't follow the advice of the wicked, who doesn't associate with sinful people, and who doesn't spend time among scoffers."† People of bad character can easily influence us to become like them: "Do not associate with a man of temper and do not come near a man of wrath lest you learn from his ways and endanger your soul" (Proverbs 22:24–25). A wrathful disposition, or any bad disposition, like a disease, is contagious.‡

The contagious quality of bad character helps explain the phenomenon of

————

*Based on the words of the Mishnah, "Woe to an evil person. Woe to his neighbor" (Mishnah *Nega'im* 12:6).

†Scoffers are cynics who make all efforts at goodness seem pointless. They literally *demoralize* people by making attempts at moral behavior seem futile.

‡Studies done in the workplace document that the personality and character of the boss profoundly affect, for good and for bad, employees' behavior. Thus, when a compassionate person

children from "good homes" who suddenly start engaging in self-destructive and/or criminal behavior (e.g., taking and selling drugs). Frequently they have been swayed by bad companions, who often exert a stronger influence than do good ones. That is why it is more common to hear of teenagers who are influenced by their peers to start taking drugs than to hear of those influenced by their friends to stop doing so.

———

The thirteenth-century Rabbi Menachem ha-Meiri understood the rabbinic admonition not to associate with the wicked (The Ethics of the Fathers 1:7) as absolute: "[A person should not say] 'I shall take care not to live in the neighborhood of an evil person because that would involve constant association, but I shall spend time with him occasionally for purposes of business. . . .' Such a person is, therefore, warned not to associate with the wicked, that is, any kind of association."

We suffer from such associations in one of two ways: either by being influenced or by being victimized by the bad person. A criminal defense lawyer I know mounted a vigorous defense on behalf of a client. But when the client, who was indeed a criminal, became dissatisfied with her work, he threw her up against a wall and grabbed her by the throat. Truly, you will suffer if you associate with evil people.*

———

Inspiring ourselves to do good

8. Try to live up to the reputation you aspire to. My grandfather, Rabbi Nissen Telushkin, used to advise people, "Don't be so concerned with being humble that you try to hide from others all knowledge of the good you do. It is good to be known as being something of a *tzaddik*. If nothing else, you'll be afraid to do something bad because you'll fear that it will become known, and will harm your good name."

———

is appointed the number-two person to a boss with a harsh disposition, the mild-mannered person—in his or her desire to please and impress the boss—often becomes a harsher and less kind person. Conversely, "a top manager with a gentler nature softens the edges of more aggressive midlevel managers." Dr. Michelle Duffy, a University of Kentucky psychologist who studied 177 hospital workers, observed that "if there's a strong leader in the group, then that person's behavior is contagious." (Benedict Carey, "Fear in the Workplace: The Bullying Boss," *The New York Times*, 22 June 2004.) As Roslyn Stein, head of the Chicagoland Jewish High School, puts it, "A company takes on the character of its CEO."

*Am I suggesting, therefore, that one should not become a criminal defense lawyer? No, but we should be aware that if we choose this profession we will be spending a large amount of time with many people who have concluded that the Ten Commandments do not apply to them.

———

Maintaining our good name is so important that—at a time when men domi-nated the household—the Rabbis ruled that if a man forbade his wife from help-ing her neighbors (e.g., lending them household items), she could have a court compel him to grant her a divorce. Otherwise the woman would acquire a bad name among her neighbors, and no one has the right to deprive another of her good name (Ketubot 72a). In modern terms, such a provision would apply to a husband or wife who tried to stop their spouse from giving charity or helping others.

———

9. See every act you do as being of great significance. Maimonides sug-gests that we regard ourselves as being equally balanced between good and evil, and the world itself as similarly balanced. Therefore, one good act will tip the balance toward good in our own life and in the entire world. Con-versely, one bad deed will tip the balance toward evil in our personal life and that of the entire world ("Laws of Repentance" 3:4).

For example, when someone comes to you for assistance, imagine that you are the only person who can assist this person; thus, if you help her, she will have what she needs, but if you refrain from helping, no one else will, either.

———

On a societal level, bad behavior tips the balance as well. Criminologists under-stand that if a neighborhood has many broken windows in its buildings, and they are not repaired, crime in the neighborhood, including violent crime, will soon increase; the broken windows and the dilapidated buildings become a sig-nal to offenders that the neighborhood is a place in which disorder is accepted and crime tolerated or ignored. That is why fixing broken windows can tip the balance in the neighborhood toward better, more civil, behavior by its citizens, while ignoring such a seemingly minor detail can start a neighborhood on a path of moral deterioration.[4]

———

10. If you offer personal prayers to God for your own well-being and success, pray for others before you pray for yourself. And don't just pray for someone's good health. Few of us begrudge others their health (in any case, such a prayer is commonly offered during the Torah reading). But if you are worried about your livelihood, pray for someone who also has worries about her financial situation or job security. And if you are anxious about your marriage or relationship, pray for the romantic or marital happiness of someone else before praying for your own.*

Offering these prayers helps us develop greater empathy for others. Often, when we hear of someone else's hardships (e.g., "So-and-so lost his job"), we feel a momentary sense of sympathy and concern, but soon forget about it. But if each morning we spend a few minutes praying for others, their hardships and needs remain fresh in our consciousness. Thus a man who prayed daily for his unemployed friend found that doing so prompted him to make a great effort to help him get work, and eventually he was able to do so.

———

While our motives for offering such prayers should indeed be altruistic, the Talmud also promises a reward to those who do so: "Whoever pleads for Heaven's compassion for someone else, and he needs the same thing himself, is answered first" (Bava Kamma 92a).

When God told Abraham that He intended to destroy the wicked city of Sodom, Abraham repeatedly argued and pleaded with Him not to do so (Genesis 18:16–32). However, when God told Noah that He was planning to destroy humankind, and that Noah should build an ark for himself and his family, Noah neither argued with God nor warned his fellow humans to repent. Instead, he built the ark and seems to have said nothing to others about why he was doing so (Genesis 6:11–7:10). Abraham, in short, spoke to God on behalf of others; Noah, it would seem, did not.

———

11. Cultivate and develop your moral strengths. Commenting on the verse "Follow the path of your heart" (Ecclesiastes 11:9), the nineteenth-century rabbinic scholar Naftali Tzvi Yehuda Berlin (the *Netziv*), taught that each of us must find our own way of serving God. One person carries out his divine service through Torah study, another through prayer, and a third concentrates on charity and acts of loving-kindness. Clearly these are not mutually exclusive, but represent a person's primary focus. There are different ways in which each of us can do good and fulfill our life's mission. When

———

*Offering such prayers is not only a kind thing to do, but also reminds us that there are people we know who are suffering greater, often far greater, difficulties than we are. This awareness can put our own situation into perspective, and guard us against self-pity.

you find the path that most attracts you and for which you seem to have a natural affinity, you should cultivate it.*

Consider such questions as these:

- Do you have an ability to listen to people, console them, and help them come to a right decision at an important and perplexing moment in their lives?
- Do you enjoy making connections between people, helping those looking for work or a partner to find what they need?
- Are you hospitable, the kind of person who enjoys feeding and caring for others, particularly on Shabbat and holidays?
- Do you have the ability to inspire other people to perform acts of kindness?
- Are you a person of means, who cannot only donate to good causes, but influence others to do so?
- Can you teach Torah, and the fundamental values of Judaism, to people who would like to learn about them?

We should first find our way, and then pursue it "with all our heart, with all our soul, and with all our might."[5]

12. Rabbi Shlomo Wolbe, author of *Alei Shur*, suggests that one way to start the process of improving ourselves is to keep a "character journal" focusing exclusively on the area in which we wish to improve. If we are honest and comprehensive in what we record—and we should try to make daily entries—we will soon note patterns in the events that provoke us to act inappropriately. By acquiring such awareness *in advance*, we will be better able to avoid such behavior in the future.†

For example, use the material recorded in your journal to find the periods each day during which you are most apt to say critical things and pass on negative gossip about others. For most people, it is during lunchtime at

---

*See the discussion of this point in *The Tzedakah Treasury* by Rabbi Avrohom Feuer, page 37. For example, if we have a nervous or morose disposition, we should not choose as our particular *mitzvah* visiting the sick (*bikur cholim*). Patients will profit most from visits by those who have calm and optimistic natures.

†Dr. Isaac Herschkopf, a psychiatrist, argues that keeping a character journal is analogous to keeping a food diary, which he regards as the gold standard in weight reduction: "It's amazingly simple, yet completely effective. You write down everything that goes in your mouth, preferably before you eat it. You then write down your weight at the beginning and end of every day. Before long, you can't help but notice the causality. You eat more, you weigh more; you eat less, you

work, or dinnertime at home. Work on not speaking about others, certainly not critically, during those periods.*

Keeping a journal will help us learn to lead the kind of life we want, instead of allowing ourselves to be controlled by emotions and impulses.

———

While we struggle to overcome our weaknesses, we should not delude ourselves into believing that we will always be successful; sometimes we need to learn to work with them. The Gaon of Vilna taught: "A person should not go completely against his nature even if it is bad, for he will not succeed. He should rather train himself to follow the straight path in accordance with his nature."[6] For example, if you have a tendency to be moody, don't pretend to be in a very upbeat mood when you are not (your effort will be transparent, and make those around you uncomfortable); rather, learn not to say anything to others when you are upset that can make them feel responsible for your unhappiness. You might not be able to control what you are feeling, but you can control what you say and how you make the people around you feel.

———

13. When trying to correct a bad trait, temporarily go to the opposite extreme.[7] Although going to extremes is usually counterproductive, sometimes we need to do so for a while to achieve balance. For example:

• If you have a tendency to gossip about other people's faults, for the next week do not allow yourself to say anything bad about anyone.† Instead, find things to praise in others.

• If you are very, perhaps overly, strict with your children, try for one week to be extra lenient.

• If you are stingy, over the next few months, if you donate clothing to an organization that helps the poor, give one or two of your best garments instead of your used, threadbare garments. Similarly, if you

———

weigh less. Soon you realize the pleasure of seeing your weight go down exceeds the momentary pleasure derived from eating the extra doughnut. In thirty years of working with this system, I have never had a single patient who stayed on the food diary who didn't lose weight and keep it off. It really is foolproof, as would be the 'character journal' if adhered to honestly."

*In the course of keeping a journal, you will become aware of other things, for example, the kind of people you are drawn to. Are they compassionate or not? Do they make you feel better about yourself, and do they inspire you to want to be a better person?

†Regarding emergencies, when it is necessary to warn someone about another, see chapter 41.

give food to the poor, give from your best food (*Yoreh Deah* 248:8, and Maimonides below).

———

Rabbi Sholom Schwadron, the renowned Jerusalem maggid *(inspiring lecturer) was known for his generosity to those in need. One afternoon, just before a holiday, a poor man came to his house for assistance, and Rabbi Schwadron's daughter was chagrined to see her father taking out a new and expensive shirt he had purchased on a trip to England. He opened the shirt, showed the man how beautiful it was, and then refolded and rewrapped it. "Take it! Take it!" he said. "You should have a new shirt. Good* Yom Tov *[Happy Holiday]."*

When the poor man left, Rabbi Schwadron's daughter, who was present along with her husband, was upset: "If you had to give him a shirt, why the special shirt from England, the shirt you had bought for your own holiday celebration? Why?"

Rabbi Schwadron went over to his bookcase, took down Maimonides' code of Jewish law, and read aloud from it: "One who wishes to offer a sacrifice [at the Temple] for his own merit should suppress his evil inclination and bring of the best quality there is of the type he is offering. This is the law with everything. If one builds a House of Prayer, it should be more beautiful than his dwelling place. When feeding the hungry, he should give of the best and sweetest food on his table. When dressing the naked, he should offer his finest clothing" ("Laws of Issurei Mizbeach [Things Prohibited for the Altar]" 7:11).[8]

———

A medieval commentator on Maimonides offers an analogy to explain the logic of going to an opposite extreme: If we wish to straighten a bent bamboo cane, we can do so only by bending it in the opposite direction, until it bounces back to the middle. If we try to bend it back only to the middle, it will remain permanently misshapen.[9]

———

14. Avoid even sins that seem minor because, as a rabbinic maxim teaches, "One sin will lead to another" (*The Ethics of the Fathers* 4:2). The Bible offers an illustration of this teaching. King Ahab, in violation of the Tenth Commandment, coveted the vineyard of a man named Navot, which adjoined his winter palace. He offered to buy the land from Navot, but the man refused; the land had been in his family for generations and he didn't wish to part with it. Ahab returned home depressed; he turned his face to the wall and refused to eat. When his wife, Queen Jezebel, a Phoenician princess, learned why he was so upset, she vowed to acquire the field for him. She arranged for two witnesses to offer perjured testimony that Navot cursed both God and king; this was a capital crime and Navot was executed. Then, because those convicted of blasphemy and treason lost their estates as well as their lives, Jezebel rushed to her husband with the happy news: "Come take possession of the vineyard of Navot . . . for Navot is no longer alive; he is dead" (I Kings 21).

What began with Ahab's violation of the Tenth Commandment against coveting quickly led to the violation of the Ninth Commandment (the prohibition against bearing false witness), the Sixth Commandment (forbidding murder), and the Eighth Commandment (outlawing stealing).

Making difficult decisions: two guidelines

15. When confronted with a situation where you are uncertain if what you are intending to do is right, ask yourself one question: "What is motivating me to act in this way, my *yetzer hatov* (good inclination) or my *yetzer hara* (evil inclination)?" Just answering this one question will usually determine the appropriate course of action.

———

Rabbi Abraham Twerski notes that people involved in romantic relationships, along with their families, often withhold information that their potential partner is entitled to know. He cites a case that occurred in the Orthodox world in which a young woman suffered several episodes of mania and depression. Fearing that knowledge of this problem would make it impossible for her to marry, the girl and her family withheld the information from a young man who wished to wed her.

Some months after the wedding, the groom's parents grew alarmed at the girl's depressed behavior, and arranged for her to be seen by a psychiatrist. When her earlier medical history came out, both her husband and in-laws were outraged that such important information had not been disclosed to them. Feeling that the marriage was based on fraud, they went to a Jewish court, a Beit Din. The court agreed, and ordered a divorce.

All of this came about not because the girl and her parents intended to do evil, but rather because they allowed their "evil inclination" to convince them that what they were doing was good. Had the family asked themselves whether it was their yetzer hatov *or* yetzer hara *that was motivating them, they would have understood that it was immoral to withhold information that they would have felt entitled to know had the situation been reversed.*[10]

———

A woman who had several children successfully pressured one of her daughters (once when the woman was in her twenties, and again in her thirties) to break off relationships with two different men who wished to marry her. To this day the mother insists that the men were not good enough for her daughter (though her husband, other relatives, and her unfortunately weak-willed daughter did not agree with her assessment), and that she was motivated only by the highest intention, her love for her daughter. The daughter is considerably older now, and unlikely to get married. She lives near her aged mother, and takes devoted care of her. Is it not possible that the mother's desire to be cared for in her old age influenced her to persuade the daughter to break off relationships that could have brought the young woman considerable happiness and fulfillment?

———

16. Look at your life from the future. As moral educator Michael Josephson teaches: "If you want to know how to live your life, think about what you would like people to say about you after you die—then live backwards."[11]

———

Talk-show host Dr. Laura Schlessinger received a call from Tony, a single man who was raising the two children of his deceased sister and brother-in-law. He was exhausted by the relentless responsibility of raising the children, and part of him wanted to give up; perhaps he should entrust the children to an orphanage or put them up for adoption. Dr. Laura asked him, "If I could project you fifteen years into the future and you could look back at this time in your life, what would you want to see yourself having done?" Tony sighed deeply and, choking back tears, answered, "Continue to help them."[12]

———

Yom Kippur is Judaism's annual confrontation with death. During this twenty-four-hour period, Jews are expected to lead a largely aphysical existence: to eat no food, consume no liquid, and refrain from sexual relations. In addition, many Jews spend the day in synagogue dressed in a kitttel, *the plain white garment that is also the Jewish burial shroud. The goal of this confrontation is to make us feel all those "deathbed regrets" while there is still time to do something about them.*

A prominent theme of Yom Kippur is the focus on how God and our behavior will determine "who shall live, who shall die" in the year ahead. In preparation for Yom Kippur each year, a friend of mine writes two obituaries of himself. In one he sets down an accurate rendering of what he has already done with his life, and in the second he writes an obituary outlining the life he would like to have led.

———

Three guidelines from the Torah

17. One of the Torah's 613 commandments is "You shall be holy" (Leviticus 19:2). In Nachmanides' Torah commentary, he explains that, to achieve holiness, it is not enough to refrain from doing unholy and wrongful acts, although that indeed is a necessary first stage (we can't be holy while stealing, deceiving others, or engaging in a forbidden sexual relationship). But the second stage, to which all people should aspire, is "to sanctify yourself through that which is permitted to you" (*Yevamot* 20a). Thus, if we eat permitted food but "eat like a pig," we have not violated Judaism's dietary restrictions, but we have violated the command to "be holy." Similarly, if we refrain from saying words that could console or inspire another, we have not done anything directly immoral, but we certainly have not obeyed the injunction to "be holy."

To achieve holiness, we must strive to do what is permitted—whether it involves eating, speaking to others, or conducting our business—in a way that is holy.

Therefore, in any given circumstance in which we are uncertain how to behave, we should ask ourselves, "What would the command to 'be holy' bid me do in this situation?"

18. Another verse that offers guidance where there is no definitive Jewish law is Deuteronomy 6:18: "And you shall do that which is right and good in the sight of the Lord." Nachmanides comments, "The meaning of this verse is as follows: First, God tells you to keep the statutes and laws which He has commanded you to. And then He tells you that even with regard to those matters concerning which there is no specific command, you should see to it that you do only that which is good and right in His eyes, for He loves that which is good and right."

Thus, there is no law mandating that we leave a waiter a tip. But waiters' low salaries are based on the presumption that people will offer gratuities. Therefore we must do the "right and the good" and act generously.

For an example of how this verse influences talmudic legislation, see page 14.

19. God represents the ultimate biblical model for character-building. Deuteronomy 13:5 commands that "you should walk after the Lord your God." The Talmud asks, "How is it possible for a person to walk after God? This is what the verse means: You should follow the attributes of the Holy One, blessed be He." The Talmud offers these examples:

- Just as God clothed Adam and Eve in the Garden of Eden (Genesis 3:21), so should we clothe those who lack adequate clothing.

- Just as God visited Abraham when he was weak (recovering from his adult circumcision; Genesis 18:1), so should we visit the sick.

- Just as God buried Moses (Deuteronomy 34:6), so should we help arrange for the burial of the dead (see *Sotah* 14a).*

The best way for us to emulate God is to become a blessing in other people's lives.

———

The prophet Isaiah, speaking in God's Name, says, "And it will be before they call, I will answer" (65:24). We can emulate God in this regard by approaching someone we know to be in need and offering financial or emotional assistance even before that person asks for it.

———

The enduring effects of good character

20. "Righteous people are even greater [alternatively, "more powerful"] after their deaths than in their lives" (*Chullin* 7b). This counterintuitive teaching (we generally assume that after a person's death, his power and influence decline) underscores that people who leave behind a legacy of goodness will affect not only their own generation, but also succeeding ones. For example, shortly after the death of the Jerusalem *tzaddik* Rabbi Aryeh Levine, Simcha Raz collected and published hundreds of stories detailing the creative and compassionate ways in which Reb Aryeh helped so many people. Since its publication, *A Tzaddik in Our Time* has inspired tens of thousands of people who never knew Reb Aryeh to follow his example by finding creative and generous ways to help others.

Here is one of Raz's characteristic stories: At the Etz Chayyim school where Reb Aryeh worked, he noticed a young student walking around in tat-

———

*The Rabbis were selective in enumerating the acts and qualities of God that people should follow. Thus, although the Torah sometimes speaks of God as jealous (e.g., Exodus 20:5 and 34:14) and angry (e.g., Exodus 32:10 and Numbers 11:1), the Talmud does not instruct us to emulate God's jealousy and anger (see page 20). Furthermore, Jewish commentators have always understood words such as "angry" and "jealous" when applied to God as anthropomorphisms (the applying of human attributes to God); God does not experience emotions like human beings, but, as the Talmud, speaking in a different context, puts it, "the Torah speaks in the language of people" (*Berachot* 31b).

tered shoes. Clearly the boy needed a new pair immediately, but Reb Aryeh also knew that the boy's father, a proud man, would take offense if the rabbi simply bought him a pair of shoes. What to do? "During the morning recess, while the youngsters were playing in the courtyard, Reb Aryeh called the boy to his room because, he said, it was time to test the boy on his talmudic learning. The questions he asked were well within the boy's grasp, and the boy answered them. 'Splendid,' said the good rabbi, beaming, 'that was just splendid. For this you deserve a prize.' And there and then he gave the boy a note to a local shoemaker to give the boy some good shoes, for which Reb Aryeh would pay. When the lad went home after school, he took with him another note from the good rabbi to his father, explaining about the 'prize' he had won."[13]

On a more somber note, Rabbi Akiva's heroic declaiming of the *Sh'ma Yisrael*[14] at the moment that he was martyred by the Romans (circa 135 C.E.) has inspired Jewish martyrs, and many other Jews facing death, ever since. Regarding the enduring influence of martyrs such as Akiva, it has been said, "The tyrant dies and his rule is over, the martyr dies and his rule begins" (Søren Kierkegaard).

———

A story on which I was raised: My maternal grandfather, Abram Resnick, acquired an apartment building during the 1920s. When the stock market crashed in 1929, he lost his savings, many of his apartments became vacant, and many of the remaining tenants could pay rent only sporadically.

My mother once went with my grandfather to collect rents, and they knocked on the door of one apartment. Inside, a man was seated with his wife and children. "Mr. Resnick," he said to my grandfather, "we haven't eaten in two days." My grandfather handed my mother several dollars (a large sum of money for them during those difficult times), and told her to go out and buy groceries and basic foodstuffs. My mother returned with bags filled with food.

This incident occurred in the mid-1930s, more than seventy years ago (my grandfather died in 1964), yet this story continues to affect me. It is now known to my children, who heard it from my mother and who, God willing, will continue to be influenced by their great-grandfather's kindness even a hundred years after it happened.

———

At the **Brit Milah** *(circumcision) of his son, S. Daniel Abraham, the prominent businessman and philanthropist, shared with his guests a childhood recollection of his father, Samuel (Simcha) Abraham, who was rushing to catch a train. Along the way, the father passed a young boy who was walking barefoot. He asked him* *why he wasn't wearing shoes, and when the boy said he had none, the father took him into a shoe store, bought him a pair, and then went to get his train. On this day, as Mr. Abraham named his son for his late father, he made it clear that this was a story that had always influenced him, and that he hoped would influence his son as well.*

"When the righteous are born, nobody feels any difference, but when they die, everybody feels it" (Ecclesiastes Rabbah 7:4). *The Rabbis offer as an example Miriam, whose birth was not noticed by anyone outside her family, but when she died, all felt her loss. The Israelites were now grateful for Miriam's leadership in the desert, and for the major role that she played in saving the life of the infant Moses.*

———

4

KNOWING OURSELVES AND GUARDING AGAINST OUR WEAKNESSES

———

1. Because we all have flaws, the most important struggle in which we must engage is with ourselves. As noted, the Rabbis defined a hero not as someone who leads people into battle or who prevails in a fight, but as "one who subdues his [evil] inclination" (*The Ethics of the Fathers* 4:1; see page 32). Thus, while popular culture defines heroism as prevailing over others, the Rabbis define it as prevailing over oneself.

———

The Book of Proverbs offers the most basic biblical teaching on self-control: "One who controls his passions is better than one who conquers a city" (16:32).

John Jay (1743–1829), the first chief justice of the U.S. Supreme Court, expressed a similar thought. After losing the 1792 gubernatorial race in New York (he later served two terms as governor), he wrote to his wife: "A few more years will put us all in the dust, and it will then be of more importance to me to have governed myself than to have governed the state."

———

2. In order to struggle successfully with yourself, you must know your character intimately, and be aware of your faults. To achieve this self-awareness, sit down with pen and paper—this exercise will be painful—and write down what you feel are your most obvious character flaws and weaknesses:

• Am I prone to anger? When I am angry, do I overreact and say or do things that inflict pain on others? Or am I the sort of person who, if asked, will deny that I am angry, yet will treat other people with coldness, disdain, and annoyance?

• Do I judge others fairly, or am I harshly critical (both in what I say and what I think)?

• Am I stingy with my money or my time?

• Do I speak curtly, making people feel that I have no time for them? (This is unkind, even if we are busy.)

• Do I avoid saying or doing what I believe is right because I fear how others will react or what they will think of me? (The question we should ask ourselves is not "What will others think?" but "What does God want me to do?")

• Am I moody? Do I make people around me feel that they are somehow responsible for my moods? Does my unhappiness affect the atmosphere in my home, transforming, often in a matter of minutes, a general feeling of pleasantness and goodwill into one of tension and sadness? (Taking away the good mood of those around us and lowering their spirits is a cruel, even if unintentional, act of aggression.)*

• Do I treat strangers with more consideration than members of my own family?

• Do I take other people's kind behavior for granted, or do I go out of my way to express thanks and help those who have been kind to me?

• Do I blame my wrongful actions and mistakes on others, or do I take responsibility for the wrong I do?

---

*Regarding the contagious quality of unhappiness, Dr. Thomas Szasz observes: "A person cannot make another happy [because happiness has to come from within], but he can make him unhappy. This is the main reason why there is more unhappiness than happiness in the world" (*The Untamed Tongue: A Dissenting Dictionary*, page 233). As regards those whose unhappiness is due to chemical imbalances, see page 124.

- Do I jump to conclusions and blame other people before I know all the facts?

- Am I able to control my impulses, or do I give in to temptation easily?

- Do I bear grudges and remain angry at others for a long time after an argument?

- Am I tardy, and thereby waste other people's time by keeping them waiting?

- Do I rationalize dishonesty with excuses such as "Business is different"?

- When I hear of other people's sufferings or misfortunes, do I find ways to help them, or do I feel sadness in my heart but do nothing?

- Am I jealous of the success of others? Do I begrudge others their good fortune?

Once you have drawn up your list, do not become discouraged even if you find that you have many weaknesses. Drawing up a list is the first and most important step in changing your character for the better.

Next, work on improving one quality at a time (see, for example, pages 263–264 on Rabbi Wolbe). If you try to work on several areas at once, you may become overwhelmed, and give up.

———

When counseling a couple in marital crisis, a rabbi asked each partner to describe his or her flaws, and how they contributed to the marriage's problems. The man acknowledged that he devoted too much time to his work and, even more important, that he had grown up in a family in which women's views were not treated with respect. He realized that he did not spend enough time in serious and intimate conversation with his wife.

When the rabbi asked the wife to describe her weaknesses, she acknowledged only one: "I'm too nice. I don't make enough demands of others, including my husband. I just try to help people, and am hurt when they are not equally nice to me."

Despite prodding on the rabbi's part, she would not admit to other faults, and the marriage ended in divorce.*

---

*The Kotzker rebbe taught, "Deceiving another person is a sin. Deceiving oneself is stupidity."

This woman's lack of introspection and self-awareness reminds one of Rabbi Israel Salanter's observation, "A person can live with himself for seventy years, and still not know himself."

———

The nineteenth-century Chasidic rebbe Chayyim of Sanz asked a man what he would do if he found a wallet with a great deal of money inside it. "I'd return it to the owner immediately," the man said.

"Are you really so sure?" the rebbe challenged him.

When he posed the same question to a second person, the man responded, "I'd keep it. When else will I have an opportunity to get money so easily?"

The rebbe told the man that such behavior was reprehensible.

When he asked the question of a third man, the man responded, "How can I be certain what I'd do? I know that I must return it, but how can I be sure that I would? I pray to God that I would have the strength to overcome my evil inclination and return it."

It was only this last response, combining both the man's awareness of his potential for dishonesty and his desire to do good, that pleased the rebbe.

———

3. Knowing oneself means being self-aware in a balanced way, and neither focusing only on your strengths (the source of arrogance) or only on your weaknesses (the source of low self-esteem). In truth, strengths and weaknesses coexist in all of us: "Anger, generosity, and modesty, for example, can be found together in the same person, much in the same way that tenants of all sorts—unrelated to one another—can be housed in a common building"(Rabbis Za'ev Abramson and Eliyahu Tougher).[1]

To encourage its readers to understand human nature and themselves, the Bible goes out of its way to note flaws even in its greatest figures. Thus, although the Matriarch Rachel has entered Jewish consciousness as the epitome of a loving mother (Jeremiah 31:15), she also had some less attractive features. Early in her marriage, when Rachel was infertile, her response to her situation was a common, but unelevated, one: "And Rachel saw that she was not bearing any children to Jacob, and Rachel envied her sister [Leah, who had many children]" (Genesis 30:1; see further examples of character flaws in biblical heroes on page 150).

Knowing of Rachel's envy should make us aware that we must not deny our faults (as the Bible does not deny those of Rachel), but recognize and work on them, and always be aware of how those negative qualities may influence what we do.*

4. The more conscious we are of our weaknesses, the more we can limit their impact on our lives and the lives of others. For example, if envy causes us to behave badly and judge others harshly, knowing that this is one of our character flaws should help us realize that, when dealing with someone whom we envy, we will probably act unfairly; for example, the bad motives we might attribute to such a person are likely exaggerated or inaccurate.

In contrast, those who lack such awareness are apt to demonize the object of their envy, and justify whatever harm they wish to inflict on the other.

5. We must guard ourselves against our weaknesses. The Rabbis advise us to "make a fence around the Torah" (*The Ethics of the Fathers* 1:1). A fence protects a garden from being violated. This admonition is often applied to matters of Jewish ritual law. Thus, because the Torah forbids lighting a fire on the Sabbath, later Jewish law also forbids even holding a match on Shabbat, since doing so increases the chance that we will use it and violate the holy day of rest.

Once we have identified our weaknesses, we should refrain not only from the forbidden activity itself, but also from any behavior that may cause us to engage in it. For example, a married man attracted to a woman other than his wife should not allow himself to be alone in a closed room with her.†
Had this advice been followed some years ago by an American president who had a proclivity for inappropriate extramarital behavior, it would have saved him from behavior that humiliated him and his family, and almost cost him the presidency.

Regarding the temptation to deceive, the Torah not only prohibits using false weights and measures, but outlaws having them in our possession. The assumption is that their presence will tempt us to use them (just as having a marked deck of cards can tempt a gambler). Therefore we must destroy them

---

*In addition, knowing that a person of Rachel's stature was guilty of envy should also "lessen the guilt feelings of anyone who feels envious of another person" (see Zelig Pliskin, *Growth Through Torah*, page 83, citing his father, Rabbi Shmuel Pliskin). Yet another reason for the Bible's bluntness about its greatest figures' failings is "perhaps to teach us that we too can be good people without being perfect" (*Etz Hayim*, page 72).

†According to traditional Jewish law, *halacha*, a man should not be alone in a closed room with a woman with whom he is forbidden to have relations (unless it is an immediate relative).

"so that they do not become a snare" (*Sefer Charedim,* number 97; see Deuteronomy 25:13–14).

What fences do you need to erect?

6. Unwholesome and bad qualities such as envy, vengefulness, ingratitude, laziness, and self-centeredness are usually deeply rooted. Because such traits can be subdued, although rarely fully conquered, the battle against them can last a lifetime. That is why the Rabbis caution, "Don't trust in yourself until the day of your death" (*The Ethics of the Fathers* 2:5). We need to be watchful all the time. Rabbi Israel Salanter taught, "A person is like a bird. A bird can fly very high, as long as it keeps moving its wings. If it stops flapping its wings [even for a moment], it will fall. So too is it with people."[2] The moment we believe that we have reached such a high spiritual and ethical level that we no longer need to work on ourselves, we are likely to fall.

———

A biblical hero who became a sinner late in life was King Solomon. Although the Bible records that Solomon was the wisest man of his time, under the influence of his foreign wives he started to worship pagan gods in addition to the God of Israel: "In his old age, his wives turned away Solomon's heart after other gods." This king who built the Temple became in his old age a follower of Ashtoreth, the goddess of the Phoenicians, and Milcom, the god of the Ammonites, as well as of the God of Israel (I Kings 11:4–5). *

———

Six common weaknesses to avoid

7. *Insatiability.* The desire for more—more money, more possessions, more acclaim, more sexual partners—is among the most common weaknesses in human nature, and motivates much criminal, wrongful, and unholy behavior. As the Rabbis express it, "No one departs from this world with half his desires gratified" (*Ecclesiastes Rabbah* 1:13).

But we need not be depressed about this ("I'm condemned to a life of frustration and unfulfilled hopes"); indeed, this teaching can serve as a consolation. Since it is natural for most of us to want far more than we have, the

———

*God, who had earlier blessed Solomon with both wisdom and riches, later said to him, "[Because] you have not kept My covenant and the laws which I commanded you, I will tear the kingdom away from you and give it to one of your servants" (I Kings 11:11).

fact that we don't have many things that we desire is not a sign that we are leading a deprived life; it is more likely a sign that we want too much. The first-century Roman philosopher and playwright Seneca cautioned, "I may have less than I hoped for, but perhaps I hoped for more than I ought."[3]

8. *Rationalization*. The ability to use our reason to justify what is wrong is yet another common, and unworthy, human characteristic. In Albert Camus's novel *The Fall*, the protagonist engages in numerous sexual affairs. He has "principles," however, "such as that the wife of a friend is sacred. [But when I was attracted to a woman] I simply ceased quite sincerely, a few days before, to feel any friendship for her husband": that way, he could act in good conscience on his lustful inclination.

The tendency to rationalize applies with equal force in the financial realm. Maimonides notes the Torah law that once a person designates a specific animal to be sacrificed, he is forbidden to substitute another in its place: "One may not exchange or substitute another for it, either good for bad or bad for good" (Leviticus 27:10). The prohibition of substituting "bad for good" makes sense, but what is the logic of prohibiting the substitution of a superior animal for an inferior one, since such a substitution shows God greater honor, not less?

According to Maimonides, this law is a response to the human tendency to rationalize: "If permission would have been given for a person to exchange a superior animal for an inferior one, one [who regretted his vow, will come to] exchange an inferior one for a superior one, declaring that it really is superior. Consequently, the Torah closes the door to such an action, declaring that one can never exchange it, and fining one for doing so. All these provisions are for the purpose of controlling one's inclinations and improving one's character" ("Laws of *Temurah*—Substitutions" 4:13).

More than any other character flaw, rationalization makes repentance and self-improvement impossible. A person who understands that she often gives in to her lower inclinations will at least recognize when she is doing something unethical. Perhaps one day she will be motivated to stop engaging in this behavior. But a person who uses her intellect to rationalize or justify wrong behavior will never be motivated to repent. Why should she?

Therefore, wrong as it is to act immorally, we should not commit the additional sin of convincing ourselves that what we are doing is right. For example, it is preferable to acknowledge to ourselves that "I bought a dress to wear for a wedding, and then returned it, but I know that Jewish law forbids my doing so," rather than "A lot of people do this, and besides, who was hurt by my action?"

9. *Having a greater concern with prevailing in an argument than with being right.* Human nature, with its competitive and sometimes angry spirit, causes many of us to argue and advocate wrongful positions for no other reason than the perverse desire to dispute any assertion made by those we regard as opponents (this is particularly common among religious and political disputants). After all, an assertion is not necessarily false because our enemy says so, or true because our friend does.

In recognition of this tendency, the Talmud legislates that "Two scholars who hate one another must not sit together as judges in the same case" (*Sanhedrin* 29a). Maimonides explains: "For such a thing brings about a perverted judgment. Because of the hatred they bear one another, each will be inclined to prove the other wrong" ("Laws of the Sanhedrin" 23:7).

If Jewish law feels the necessity to impose such a regulation on judges—figures who are held in the highest regard in Jewish tradition—how much more does it apply to the rest of us? Are there people who so annoy or antagonize you that the moment you hear them assert something, your mind starts searching for arguments to refute it? Before we argue with someone we dislike, or with a competitor, we should make sure that we would feel the same way about what he said if it were said by someone whom we like.

———

Many political figures have trouble acknowledging the truth of a statement or the goodness of an action taken by a member of the opposition party, but a fact or a valid argument should be acknowledged as true, whatever its source.

———

10. *Letting pride or stubbornness stop us from acknowledging a mistake.* The refusal to admit an error causes us to persist in wrong and/or foolish behavior. As an old proverb teaches, "One who makes a mistake and doesn't correct it is making a second mistake."

———

The classic biblical instance of a person who refused to acknowledge an error was Jephtah, who led the Israelite troops in combat against Ammon. Prior to going into battle, Jephtah vowed to sacrifice to God "whatever comes out of the doors of my house to meet me when I return safely." Obviously he expected an animal to come out to greet him, but the one who emerged was his beloved daughter. Then, having made a foolish vow, Jephtah made an even more foolish pronouncement: "For I have uttered a vow to the Lord and cannot retract it."

What an absurd statement! Since his vow violated the Torah,* it should, of course, have been retracted or ignored, for it had no validity. It would be as if we vowed to kill someone ("I swear to God I'm going to kill you"), and then declared that although we regretted saying this, we would nonetheless fulfill our oath. An illegitimate act is illegitimate; that we swore to carry it out is irrelevant.

Not only did Jephtah refuse to acknowledge his mistake, but, in the manner of many obstinate people who refuse to admit their errors, he blamed his victim: "Alas, daughter! You have brought me low; you have become my troubler" (see Judges 11:1–12:7).

While it is easy for most of us to feel a sense of superiority to Jephtah, who sacrificed his daughter, many parents steer their children in directions that the young people do not wish to go (for example, forcing a child to attend medical or law school). Then, even when it is clear that the demands they are making are unrealistic, and the child is suffering because of them, the parents don't retract them, but, like Jephtah, persist in their mistake.

———

The Rabbis explain that one of the reasons the Talmud records minority viewpoints is to teach future generations that we should not stubbornly insist that our opinion prevail. After all, the greatest figures of Judaism, such as Hillel and Shammai, did not insist that they were right once their opinions were ruled to be wrong (Eduyot 1:4).

———

11. *Wasting time.* Rabbi Moshe Feinstein came to the United States when he was already an adult, and one of the phrases he heard Americans use, "I have plenty of time," seemed strange and foolish to him. Reb Moshe used to say, "I wish they could give me some of that time. I never have enough of it."

Similarly, Rabbi Israel Stein, a student of Rabbi Abraham Joshua Heschel, recalls that Rabbi Heschel regarded the American expression "to kill time" (as in "I have some time to kill") as particularly odious.

One way to become aware of time, and how not to waste it, is to arrange to do some important activity each day for precisely five minutes. We

---

*The Torah was the first legal code in history both to express abhorrence at human sacrifice and to outlaw it; see Genesis 22; Leviticus 18:21, 20:1–5; Deuteronomy 12:31, 18:10.

should use this time, for example, to study a sacred text, perhaps a portion of the weekly Torah reading, or selections from *The Ethics of the Fathers*. When the five minutes are up, we should force ourselves to review what we have learned. Through this kind of regular activity, even of short duration, we can come to understand concepts with which we were previously unfamiliar.

Alternatively, we should devote the time each day to making contact with someone who would profit from hearing from us. I know a man whose cousin was dying of cancer. He spoke to the cousin often, but their conversations were growing ever more morbid and depressed. Finally, he arranged that each day he and his cousin would tell each other a joke, a reminder that as hard as his cousin's circumstances were, life was not only bad. Of course, he allowed his cousin time to talk about things other than the joke, but in just a few minutes each day the man was able to provide his relative with important emotional support.

————

To use time well, we must avoid saying two things to ourselves:

- *"I have plenty of time." If we do, then it means that there is something empty or missing in our life.*
- *"I have no time at all." This often becomes a rationale for not doing things that we can do.*

————

And, worst of all

12. *Being indifferent to someone else's suffering.* The Talmud records that Rabbi Judah, the editor of the Mishnah, had difficulty feeling compassion for people who were ignorant about Judaism. Once, during a famine, he arranged for food to be made available only to hungry people who were knowledgeable in Torah. When one of his students, who didn't wish to profit from his Jewish learning, went to Rabbi Judah in disguise and pretended to be a total ignoramus, Rabbi Judah refused to give him any food; finally the man begged to be fed as one would feed a dog, and Rabbi Judah relented. After the man departed, Rabbi Judah regretted that he had given food to an ignoramus, but when he learned that it was his own student, he changed his attitude: "Let everyone enter [the storehouse]," he announced (*Bava Bathra* 8a).

It is a common theme in Jewish folklore that a beggar who appears undistinguished, and seemingly unworthy of special concern, is the prophet Elijah in disguise. When someone is in need of help, we should extend it, and not look for excuses not to help.

————

The Passover Haggadah *commands Jews to begin the Seder with the declaration, "Let all who are hungry come in and eat, let all who are needy come in and make Passover." Unfortunately, although we recite these words, most of us ignore its demand, and invite to our Seder only someone who would have a Seder to attend even if she were not invited to ours. However, the* Haggadah *instructs us to invite someone who is hungry and needs our food, or someone who is needy (i.e., alone), and needs our companionship.*

————

Right priorities

13. The Chaffetz Chayyim recalled that once he had passed through a small city where he saw a little girl playing with a doll, and thought, "If I would put this doll away and offer it to this girl twenty years from now, wouldn't she laugh? That which was precious to her as a child would have no value to her at that age. So it is with a person when he ascends to the world of truth. He will feel ashamed over what he considered valuable during his life in this world. For in the world of truth, nothing but Torah [i.e., God's teachings] and good deeds have any value."[4]

Although goodness should be our greatest priority, we often live our lives preoccupied with earning more money than we need, or obsessed with being invited to prestigious social events or knowing prominent people. In the meantime we often ignore real suffering that we could help alleviate.

The one occasion on which people generally appreciate that the highest priority is goodness is a funeral. Every eulogist knows that no one wishes to hear a description of the deceased's luxurious swimming pool and tennis court, or how he kept his car so well polished that you could see your reflection in it. What matters most when we depart this world is the legacy of goodness that we leave behind. Were we loyal friends and fair employers? Did we extend ourselves when others needed help? Were we loving and kind to our spouse? Did we leave our children with a feeling of being loved and appreciated? Did we inspire them to want to do good?

———

The legendary Green Bay Packers football coach Vince Lombardi was most famous for his mission statement about life: "Winning isn't everything, it's the only thing." To which Rabbi Shimon Finkelman has responded, "Winning isn't everything, doing what is right is everything."[5]

———

II

BASIC VIRTUES
AND VICES

Judging Others Fairly

In justice shall you judge your fellow man.

Leviticus 19:15

5

THE IGNORED COMMANDMENT

1. The biblical commandment "in justice shall you judge your fellow man" (Leviticus 19:15) requires judges to be scrupulously fair. They must favor neither the rich nor the poor (Leviticus 19:15). They may not allow one litigant to speak at length and then instruct the other to keep his presentation short (*Shevuot* 30a). And judges are not allowed to listen to the claims of one party without the other being present (*Shevuot* 31a).

2. In addition, the commandment to judge others "in justice" is understood in Jewish law as applying to everyone. Throughout the day, almost all of us make judgments about others, many of which are harsh and unfair. A clerk does not process a request as quickly as we would wish, and we dismiss him—or all clerks or members of the ethnic or racial group to which he belongs—as being unintelligent, lazy, or incompetent. Our child does not immediately do what we ask, and we condemn her (verbally, or just in our minds) for being selfish or never listening to us, although dozens of times a week the child does obey us, even when asked to do something she doesn't want to. Therefore, this verse obligates us to judge righteously, which means to be fair.

Judging with empathy

3. One reason many of us have a higher regard for our own character than that of others is that we judge ourselves by our intentions and others by their acts, especially those acts we find annoying. For example, if we don't visit a friend or relative in the hospital, we usually don't think of ourselves as having done something wrong. Instead, we rationalize, "I really did think of paying a visit; I just didn't have enough time. But I wanted to go." Yet, when we are a hospital patient, and others don't visit, most of us don't spend time devising explanations for the non-visitors' behavior. Instead, we are apt to dismiss them as selfish or "fair-weather" friends. Therefore, in the future,

make an effort to judge others by their intentions when their actions upset you, in the same way most of us judge ourselves when we have done something that has upset another.

———

As we get older, many of us become aware of how often we have hurt the people we love most—our parents, spouses, and children. When confronted by those whom we have hurt, we apologize and explain why we acted as we did. We want them to understand that our intentions were not impure, even though our behavior was wrong.

In short, we should try to use the same criteria for judging others as we use—and want others to use—for judging ourselves: If we judge others harshly, condemning them on the basis of one or two possibly uncharacteristic actions, we deserve to be judged by the same standard. Rabbi Avrohom Ehrman cites a characteristic example: "Did you ever excuse yourself by saying, 'That's the way I am! That's the way I was brought up! It's [very difficult, almost impossible] for me to change! All right, so I'm not perfect. Other people aren't perfect in other ways.' The next time you jump to condemn someone, put yourself in his place and say: 'That's the way he is! That's the way he was brought up! It's impossible for him to change! All right, so he's not perfect. Other people aren't perfect in other ways.'"[1]

———

Commenting on the difficult commandment to "love your neighbor as yourself," the Ba'al Shem Tov, the eighteenth-century founder of Chasidism, taught that just as we love ourselves despite our faults, so too should we love others despite their faults. We should think of some wrong we have done, such as giving less charity than we could have, or not being completely honest in a business dealing or a personal communication. Do we conclude that we are hardhearted and stingy, or fundamentally dishonest? Probably not, for we have worked out rationalizations for why we were justified in acting as we did: "I give enough to charity, and my expenses are so pressing that I can't afford to give more," or "In business, everybody acts this way. I'm actually better than most." Loving our neighbor as ourselves means seeking out rationalizations and excuses for others' behavior in the same way we do for our own.

———

4. Don't rush to reach a negative conclusion about another. Thus, if you see someone of whom you have reason to think well engaging in behavior that seems wrong, don't assume that all that you've thought about the person is wrong, for there may be an explanation for the person's behavior that has

never occurred to you. If and when appropriate, ask the person to explain his behavior. This is exactly what Rabbi Aryeh Levine used to do. Rabbi Levine explained that not jumping to critical conclusions did not come naturally to him. As a young man, he had gone to the funeral of Rabbi Eliezer Rivlin where, to his shock, he saw Rabbi Shmuel Kook, one of Rabbi Rivlin's closest friends, leave the funeral procession, and enter a flower shop to buy a pot. "I thought to myself: Is this how a man should act toward a true friend who has passed away? . . . Could he not give him this last kindness and pay him this last honor? Could he not find some other time to buy the flowerpot? Did he have to buy it right now, during the funeral?"

Reb Aryeh went over to Rabbi Kook, and demanded an explanation. The rabbi answered that, for several years, he had been helping a man stricken with leprosy. The preceding day the man had died, and the doctors had ordered that all his clothes and possessions be burned. Among the man's possessions were a pair of tefillin, and, as Rabbi Kook explained, "I rebelled with all my heart at the thought of the holy tefillin being burned." He therefore reached an agreement with one of the doctors: if the rabbi brought a flowerpot to the hospital before noon, the tefillin could be placed into the pot and buried in the ground, in accordance with Jewish law. In the interim his dear friend died, and that is why he had to cut short his participation in the funeral. "Since then," Reb Aryeh explained, "I firmly resolved to judge every person favorably"[2]

———

Some years ago, a newspaper ran a photograph of new senators taking the oath of office. A few days later the paper received a caustic letter complaining that "the senator from Hawaii doesn't know his right hand from his left." The writer was indeed correct, the senator from Hawaii had taken the oath of office with his left hand. What the writer did not know was that the senator, Daniel Inouye, a recipient of the Bronze Star and the Purple Heart, had enlisted in the army after Pearl Harbor, and had lost his right hand fighting for his country.[3]

A person accustomed to judging fairly would have asked himself, "I wonder why the senator raised his left hand instead of his right," instead of jumping to the conclusion that the man was either foolish or disrespectful.

———

Professor Deborah Tannen, author of You Just Don't Understand, *a study of the different speaking and communication styles of men and women, describes how a female psychologist offered potentially damaging advice because of her rush to judge a style of communicating that differed from her own. On a tele-*

vision program focusing on couples' relationships, a woman in the audience voiced a complaint to the psychologist: "My husband talks to his mother, but he won't talk to me. If I want to know how his day was, I listen to his conversations with his mother." The psychologist—knowing nothing more about the couple than this comment—told the woman, "He probably trusts his mother more than he trusts you."

Tannen notes that what "the psychologist said was perfectly legitimate and reasonable within the framework of talking in women's friendships. The friend with whom you talk daily, telling all the little experiences you had, is your best friend. But how reasonable an interpretation is this from the man's point of view? I would wager that her husband did not think he needed to do anything special to create intimacy with his wife because he was with her every day. But because his mother was alone, he humored her by telling her unimportant little things that she seemed to want to hear. His mother's need to hear such details would make sense to her son because she was alone and needed them as a substitute for the real thing, like watching life from her window. He wouldn't understand why his wife would want or need to hear such talk. Although it is possible that this man trusts his mother more than his wife, the evidence given does not warrant such a conclusion. This therapist was judging the man's way of talking by women's standards."*[4]

———

5. If we are not in a position to ask someone to explain her behavior (it might be too awkward to do so), then we should try to imagine a reasonable explanation for why she might have acted as she did. In *Courtrooms of the Mind: Stories and Advice on Judging Others Fairly*, Rabbi Hanoch Teller suggests that, unless we think up an extenuating explanation, our mind will automatically gravitate to a hostile one. Therefore, we should try to come up with scenarios that can account for behavior that might otherwise appear inexcusable.

———

I was recently sent an anonymous prayer intended to promote judging fairly and charitably:

———

*Dr. Isaac Herschkopf says that he would have advised the woman to address the issue with her husband in a nonconfrontational manner: "Sweetheart, I'm not sure if you're aware of it or not, but you often share information about your day with your mother that you don't share with me."

Heavenly Father,

Help us to remember that the "jerk" who cut us off in traffic last night may be a single mother who worked nine hours that day and who is now rushing home to cook dinner, help with homework, do the laundry, and spend a few precious minutes with her children.

Help us to remember that the pierced, tattooed, disinterested young man who couldn't make change correctly at the register today is a worried nineteen-year-old student who is preoccupied with whether he passed his final exams and with his fear of not getting a student loan for next semester.

Remind us, Lord, that the scary-looking "bum" begging for money in the same spot every day is a slave to addictions that we can only imagine in our worst nightmares.

Help us to realize that the old couple walking so slowly through the store aisles, blocking our shopping cart, are savoring this moment, because they know that, based on the biopsy report she got back yesterday, this may be the last year they will go shopping together.

———

Rabbi Jack Riemer comments that the capacity to make judgments is one of the most valuable gifts given us by God, but it is also one of the most dangerous. "We can use it to distinguish between good and evil, but so often we misuse it by making judgments without knowing enough facts, or without the sympathy and the empathy that we ought to show toward other human beings."

6. If an incident can be viewed in one of two ways, choose the interpretation that yields a more favorable assessment. Rabbi Zelig Pliskin notes that people who look for ways to interpret others' behavior negatively sometimes employ psychological jargon to make their opinion sound well thought out and definitive. Thus, when a person is late, they dismiss his behavior as "passive aggressive." If he arrives precisely on time, he is "obsessive-compulsive." And if he comes early, he "fears disapproval," and is overly concerned with what others think of him.

Rabbi Pliskin offers a fairer model for explaining the behavior of others. "If someone is late, there is the possibility that he was detained through no fault of his own. If someone is punctual, it shows that he is orderly, and has good time management. If someone is early, it shows that he does not want to inconvenience another by causing [people to have] to wait."[5]

The Rabbis teach that a characteristic feature of a wise person is that he "judges a man fairly according to his deeds" (Derech Eretz Zuta 1:1). Thus, when somebody does something commendable, we shouldn't try to explain away the action as having been determined by ulterior motives.* Unfortunately, many of us do this routinely, for example, by dismissing large donations by philanthropists with comments such as, "They just did it to get a big tax write-off." But in fact, although major donors do get large tax deductions, they would still end up with far more money in their own pockets if they made no contributions to charity. Condemning or minimizing philanthropists' idealism for taking advantage of tax policies that have been set up by the government to encourage charitable giving is to judge them unfairly.

Avoiding unfairness

7. Recognize that judging other people favorably and fairly is, for most of us, so difficult that we need God's help to do it. Before beginning his morning prayers, the eighteenth-century Chasidic rabbi Elimelech of Lizhensk would beseech God, "May I see the good traits of others and not their defects."

For at least one day each month—perhaps the first day of the month—try to see only good in all those you meet.

8. "If you see a Torah scholar commit a sin in the evening, harbor no ill thoughts against him in the daytime, for perhaps he has repented" (*Berachot* 19a). Indeed, the Talmud surmises, "for surely he has repented." Jewish law applies this teaching only to sins of a private nature, such as an inappropriate but consensual sexual liaison. However, in cases of financial wrongdoing, such as deceiving or taking unfair advantage of another, a person should not be judged favorably until she makes restitution to her victim.

---

*In some instances, others' ulterior motives are so pronounced and nefarious that they should and must be noted. For example, it is true that the terrorist organization Hamas provides clothing, food, and other forms of aid to many poor Palestinians. But the far more significant truth is that perhaps the primary goal of extending such aid is to gain a political following and to build up the goodwill that then enables Hamas to recruit young people willing to become suicide bombers, and go into Israel to murder as many Israelis as possible. Such behavior reminds one of an oddly worded verse in Proverbs: "Charity exalts a nation, but the kindness of the nations is a sin" (14:34). Such is the case when the kindness is extended to one group in order to bring about the murder of another.

By implication, this teaching should be extended beyond Torah scholars to anyone you know to be a good person, but who has engaged in a private ethical lapse. If an action is uncharacteristic, regard it as such (see paragraph 11).

9. We should not condemn others based on hearsay. In the Bible, God sets an example of how to avoid condemning others without first checking the facts: "The outrage of Sodom and Gomorrah is so great, and their sin so grave, I will go down to see whether they have acted altogether according to the outcry that has reached Me; if not, I will take note." (Genesis 18:20–21). Since God is all-knowing, the words "I will go down to see" are obviously an anthropomorphism. We must try to make sure that we know the whole story before we assume the worst about another, and certainly before we attack him.

———

When the tribes of Reuben, Gad, and half of the tribe of Menashe built an altar at the Jordan River, the other tribes feared they would start their own religion and rebel against God. But before going to war, the priest Pinchas spoke to them, and learned that they were building the altar as a memorial, and not to offer pagan sacrifices. Happily, war was averted (Joshua 22:9–34).

———

Contrary to the example offered by God, King Saul never investigated his suspicion that David intended to kill him. Instead, he launched a war against David that ultimately destroyed his own life, while causing David great misery as well (I Samuel, chapters 18–27, intermittent). Indeed, on two occasions, David had the opportunity to kill Saul, and refrained from doing so. While Saul was impressed for a few hours, within a short time he resumed his campaign to murder David. Because Saul hated David, he refused to judge him fairly, and to "take note" of the clear evidence that David had no intention of harming him.

———

10. Passing on negative information, *lashon hara*, to those who don't need to know it (see pages 332–343) harms the reputation of the one being discussed: "A gossip always seeks out faults in people, and talks of these faults; he is like a fly who always rests on a dirty spot. If a man has boils, the fly will ignore the rest of the body and sit on the boil. Thus it is with a gossip. He overlooks all the good in a person and speaks only of the evil" (*Orchot Tzaddikim*, "The Gate of Slander"). Those who judge others unfairly will almost certainly violate Judaism's strictures against *lashon hara*, and will often commit a far greater sin than the wrong for which they are condemning the other.

Putting things into perspective

11. See each person as a whole. *The Ethics of the Fathers* contains a well-known teaching that is usually rendered as "Judge each person favorably" (1:6). A more precise translation, however, is "Judge the whole of the person (*kol ha-adam*) favorably." In other words, when you assess another, don't reach a conclusion on the basis of one or two negative things you know, but make your judgment on the basis of the person's behavior as a whole.* Therefore, if the person's behavior in a particular instance is wrong, but her overall behavior is good, then that is the way you should think of her. Also, if you hear about someone's misdeeds, take into account that her good deeds may be more significant. As Maimonides writes in his "Laws of Repentance" (3:2), "There are some merits which outweigh many sins."†

12. The talmudic teaching "Don't judge your fellow until you have been in his place" (*The Ethics of the Fathers* 2:4) means that we should judge others in light of their background and the context of their actions. For example, the more difficult and deprived people's lives have been, the more they are to be commended for their achievements, and forgiven for occasional inappropriate behavior. But many of us do the opposite, and make disparaging references to another's deprived or scandal-ridden background. Similarly, if someone acted wrongly when under great personal pressure, we should not rush to condemn her, but rather imagine how we might have acted in such a situation.‡

———

A well-known talmudic passage comments on the seemingly odd wording the Bible uses to describe Noah: "Noah was a righteous man, blameless in his generation" (Genesis 6:9). Why, the Rabbis ask, did the Torah include the words, "in his generation"?

Jewish tradition favors the answer offered by Rabbi Yochanan: "in his generation" emphasizes that only in a generation of moral depravity could Noah be

———

*If the person's general behavior is bad, then that also should form your basis of judgment; see page 92.

†Judging "each person favorably," was obviously not what *The Ethics of the Fathers* intended to say. For example, did the Rabbis expect a woman to judge favorably a man who wishes to marry her, but whose last wife divorced him for beating her, or should an accounting firm judge favorably a convicted embezzler who applies for a job? Only if each of these people has truly repented and changed should he be judged favorably.

‡The same might apply even when one was not acting under great pressure. Thus Joseph Epstein, in an extended meditation on envy, notes, "The crime of accepting insider stock information is one of which, I daresay, more of us would not like to be put to the test" (*Envy*, 72).

regarded as great. But had he lived in another, more moral, age, he would not have been regarded as special. More insightful and fair, I believe, is the often ignored observation of Yochanan's contemporary, Resh Lakish: "If even in his [awful] generation he was righteous, he would certainly have been righteous had he lived in another, more moral, generation" (Sanhedrin 108a).

The Talmud elsewhere relates that Resh Lakish grew up in deprived circumstances. One source claims that as a young man he was part of a band of thieves (suggested by Rabbi Yochanan's words in Bava Mezia 84a), another that he was a member of a circus (Gittin 47a). Because Resh Lakish had been raised in a rougher and less moral environment than Rabbi Yochanan, he could judge Noah more compassionately and fairly; he appreciated the efforts needed to overcome a deprived background. Indeed, as Resh Lakish suggests, if someone like Noah could grow up without a good role model and emerge as a righteous man, how much greater would he have been with support and encouragement.

———

Commenting on the words "Don't judge your fellow until you have been in his place," Irving Bunim, author of Ethics from Sinai, explains, "Only if you can put yourself entirely in the other's place, almost to become the other person for a moment, can you begin to understand and appreciate the forces and pressures to which he was subjected."[6] On occasion, the Rabbis apply this even to the most serious of sins. Thus, when Rav (Rabbi) Ashi made a sarcastic reference to his students about the idolatrous King Menashe, the long-dead monarch appeared to him in a dream that very night. The king posed a difficult question in Jewish law, and when the rabbi couldn't answer it, Menashe did. The amazed sage not only assured the king that he would repeat the teaching in Menashe's name to his students, but then asked him, "Since you are so learned, why did you worship idols?" Menashe replied, "Had you been there, you would have lifted up the bottom of your garment, and run after me [to join me in idol worship];" Sanhedrin 102b).

Even when the matter is not as serious, we often judge others harshly, forgetting that we, too, often act inappropriately in the exact same way. Yehudis Samet, author of The Other Side of the Story: Giving People the Benefit of the Doubt, recounts an incident told her by a woman who had lent a blow dryer to a young woman who lived in a dormitory across the street from her house. The young woman sent it back through another girl, and when the woman's daughter tried to use it, it was broken. As she told Samet, "I was extremely annoyed, as you can well imagine. The girl didn't have the decency to tell me, to apologize, or to offer to pay. I went about my business, but a few times during the day I heard myself saying, 'What a chutzpah!'" (What nerve!).

But the woman, preoccupied with thinking about this incident, suddenly had a memory from her own teenage years: "My friends and I were studying for a test at someone's house. There was a blackout. We lit some candles so that we could continue studying. A few minutes later my friend screeched, 'Look, Esti! The candle!' One of the candles I had lit had fallen into the upholstery and burned a hole in the couch. I felt terrible. But I never did anything about it. Nothing. I didn't talk to the people, I didn't call them . . . and I never offered to pay. Why? Because I was so embarrassed, I just didn't know how to face them. Thinking back, I can hardly believe I did something so irresponsible. With that memory fresh in my mind, I thought sympathetically. I bet that girl is so perplexed that she just can't bring herself to face me—just as I couldn't face those people then."[7]

———

13. Since the Bible teaches that "There is no person on earth so righteous, who will do only good and not sin" (Ecclesiastes 7:20), we should not set standards for others that neither they nor we can meet. All of us occasionally stray from the path, and it is not right to be dismissive of someone because we learn of a sin he has committed (unless it's a wrong of huge proportions), or because he has done something of which we disapprove. We should realize that people can have faults and still be, on balance, wonderful individuals.

———

Some years ago, in California, just prior to an election, the head of one of the political parties released the information that the other party's candidate, Bruce Herschenson, had been seen going to a striptease show. Some of his supporters were so upset at this news that they did not vote for him, and Herschenson lost the election. One such voter, an evangelical Christian, wrote to the talk-show host Dennis Prager: "Some time ago, I received a letter from you requesting that I vote for and support Bruce Herschenson. You mentioned that you had never done this before and that Bruce was of upstanding moral character. Well, the newspapers reported that Bruce had frequented nude girl shows. I have never heard Bruce deny it. Did you know this about Bruce? Or is it untrue, or did it surprise you?" Prager responded that he knew Bruce Herschenson well, and was aware that he had been to a strip show, adding, "So have I, and so has just about every man that I know. Indeed, given the ubiquity of such shows in Las Vegas, and the number of people I know who have seen a show there, I suspect that most of the women I know have been to a strip show." But, Prager concluded, "Many kind, honorable and honest men sometimes go to strip shows, sometimes use curse words in private, sometimes play poker or go to a casino, and sometimes buy sexually explicit material; and the truly dishonorable men and women are those who pry into the lives of honorable people to ruin their good names"[8]

———

14. Judging others fairly often involves overlooking insignificant matters. Reuven Bulka, a rabbi and psychologist, teaches, "There are many ways to break up a relationship. If one looks hard enough, one can always find an insult or unwarranted remark made by a friend, and make this the basis for ending the friendship."[9] On the other hand, if someone repeatedly mistreats or insults us, it is probably a good idea to end the friendship. But we must make sure that this is what the person really is doing; therefore, we should not make such a decision hastily.

15. The Talmud teaches that "a fault that you have, don't go about pointing out in others" (*Bava Mezia* 59b). Often, for example, it is the child who shares a character or personality flaw with a parent whose behavior most provokes the parent's anger. If a parent feels the need to critique this trait in a child, then, to be fair, the parent must acknowledge to the child that she suffers from this, too.* Similarly, if we are going to critique a flaw in another that is a flaw that we ourselves have, we should acknowledge this weakness, both to ourselves, so that we will be less harsh in our criticism, and to the other, so that he will be less defensive in his response.

———

A woman and her brother were left equal portions of their parents' estate. The woman felt this to be unfair, however, since her brother was single while she had three children and high expenses. When the brother insisted that the equal division of the estate was what their parents wanted and was fair, his sister accused him of caring "only about money," and threatened to cut herself and her children off from any further contact with him. Her willingness to divide and possibly destroy the family for the sake of money suggested that she cared far too much about money, the very fault of which she accused her brother.

So, before we speak critically of another, we should ask ourselves if we share in their failing.

———

———

*Dr. Isaac Herschkopf comments: "A great parenting technique is to criticize your own identical flaw without even making reference to your child's. They will know exactly what you're doing

16. "People are not held responsible for what they say when they are in pain [or distress]" (*Bava Bathra* 16b). Therefore, if someone says something nasty to us at a time of sorrow or other hardship, we should be forgiving of such words, and not let this incident cause us to end our relationship with the person. For example, it is common for harsh words to be expressed among siblings in the period following the death of a parent (particularly the last surviving parent) whose care devolved upon the children. Some surviving children feel that they have borne the burden of caregiving, and believe that one or more of their siblings have shirked their responsibilities. At such times we should carefully monitor what we say, be willing to forgive, and give others the benefit of the doubt.

17. Though people are held responsible for what they do, as opposed to what they say, when in pain (for example, the fact that one is suffering does not entitle one to strike another), clearly extreme pain and deprivation can drive good people to acts they would otherwise never commit. Thus, although Hananya, Misha'el, and Azaryah were willing to accept death rather than bow down to a gold statue erected by King Nebuchadnezzar, the Talmud comments that had they been lashed, they would have bowed down (*Ketubot* 33b). Therefore, judge with mercy those who succumb to torture and other forms of duress. As Rabbi Moshe Tendler notes, such a situation often arises among those who are ill: "When an individual is subjected to intense, intractable, pain, his behavior cannot be viewed as an expression of his personality or ethical nature, rather, his experience is superhuman and does not in any way reflect on his personality. When patients suffering from pain have changes in personality, becoming more demanding, less considerate, this is not the patient talking. Pain has a voice of its own."[10]

When it is best not to judge at all

18. We should avoid having strong views and feelings on too many subjects. A friend of mine grew up in a household that suffered from what he called "French's mustard syndrome." Not only did his parents prefer French's mustard to all other brands, but they were convinced that it was objectively superior. While they would never say so explicitly, they believed that those who preferred other brands had inferior taste. When set down so starkly, such a view sounds ridiculous, but many of us hold equally strong views

and why. They will also appreciate the respect you are showing them and will thus be more likely to try and correct their own flaw."

in too many areas. We believe that there's always a good and a bad way to do something, but the truth is there are many areas in which people simply have different preferences, and none is "the best." Thus people may dress in different styles from those we prefer, have longer or shorter hair or wear more makeup than we like, or enjoy different kinds of books or television shows than we do, and this does not entitle us to look down upon them (even if we just do so in our own minds).

In short, there are many areas in which it is not enough to judge fairly; in those areas one simply should not judge at all.

The benefits of judging fairly

19. The Talmud promises a divine reward to those who judge in a merciful manner: "He who judges his fellow man favorably is himself judged favorably [by God]" (*Shabbat* 127b). Conversely, those who judge harshly will be judged similarly: "In the measure with which a man measures, so is he measured" (*Sotah* 8b).

20. The Ba'al Shem Tov taught, "Be careful when you pass judgment on another. It is really yourself whom you may be judging." The prophet Nathan told King David about an injustice committed by a wealthy man who had stolen a beloved lamb from his poor neighbor, and then slaughtered the animal to serve to a guest. The outraged monarch pronounced, "The man who did this deserves to die!" Nathan responded, "You are that man" (II Samuel 12:7; referring to David's sleeping with Bathsheba, the wife of his army officer, Uriah, and then arranging to have Uriah killed in battle; for a further discussion of this episode, see page 302).

———

A friend of mine laughed when he learned that the writer Norman Cousins, who was due to be given an honorary doctorate at a university commencement, had confused the dates and missed the event. Later that night my friend learned that, even as he was laughing, he himself was failing to deliver a lecture that he had entered in his calendar on the wrong date.

I have been annoyed at someone for something he or she has done, only to find myself doing the same, or a similar, thing. Just a day after working on this section, my son left his coat in a hospital room where we had been paying a visit. It took us about a half-hour to return to the hospital, and several times I pointed out to my son how much time his carelessness had cost us. Finally, when we reached the hospital, and the nurse returned his coat, she also gave me back my watch, which, until that moment, I had not realized I had left. My son had hardly been the only one who was careless.

———

A final thought

21. The Chasidic rebbe Wolf of Strikov offered the following guideline for avoiding self-righteousness in our judgments of others: "Remember that you are not as good as you think you are, and the world is not as bad as you think it is."

6

CHALLENGES TO JUDGING FAIRLY

———

1. We should acknowledge virtues even in those whom we dislike, and do so without mentioning any of their bad traits. Many of us find this very difficult. When acknowledging a good quality of a person whom we dislike, we invariably follow it with a list of "buts," and often share a whole litany of complaints against the person.

We should make an effort to acknowledge positive traits in those whom we dislike, and force ourselves not to mention anything negative about them. After all, would we think it fair if someone acknowledged something good that we had done, but then described our weaknesses, faults, and all the things he or she did not like about us?

———

Assyria was a historic enemy of Israel, but when the citizens of its largest city, Nineveh, collectively repented, the Bible recorded this fact in the Book of Jonah, which Jews still read each year during the afternoon Mincha *service on Yom Kippur. As psychologist Solomon Schimmel comments, "How often does a nation preserve in its sacred history a story about the merits and righteousness of its enemies?"*[1]

———

2. Similarly, when angry at a group, keep in mind all that is good about it. Try to recall any good acts performed by the group or by its members, even if you feel that much of what they say or do is wrong. Not doing so will lead you to demonize those with whom you disagree.

The refusal to acknowledge the good in our opponents characterizes many of the arguments between American liberals and conservatives, and many of the denominational conflicts in American Jewish life. In truth, conservatives were more apt to recognize the evil of communism and liberals were more apt to recognize that segregation of, and other discrimination against, African-American people ruined the lives of millions and called into question the justice of our entire society. Yet polemicists in both parties routinely speak and write of their opponents as if everything they advocate were not only wrong, but also motivated largely by selfishness, self-righteousness, and/or stupidity.

A similar situation prevails in the religious conflicts in Jewish life, where representatives of the various denominations often attack each other venomously. Yet, as Rabbi Yitz Greenberg has taught, "I don't care what denomination in Judaism you belong to, as long as you're ashamed of it." Each denomination is committed to *tikkun olam,* the perfection of the world, and since such perfection has not come about, can each movement argue that it's the exclusive fault of the other movements?

———

People who dislike a group often explain away even those qualities of the group that are commendable. For example, Voltaire, the father of the French Enlightenment, was a lifelong opponent of torture, and did everything in his power to influence states and religious authorities to stop its use. Thus, one would have expected him to admire the Jews who, in opposition to the Roman and Christian societies (both of whom regarded evidence extracted under torture as valid)* had effectively forbidden torture by rendering it pointless, since Jewish law did not accept forced, or even voluntary, confessions in capital cases. Unfortunately, Voltaire hated Jews.† Indeed, it is probably fair to say that his hatred of Jews was

---

*The Inquisition, for example, was notorious for the torture it inflicted on suspected heretics.
†In Voltaire's most important work, *Dictionnaire Philosophique,* he defined the Jews as "the most abominable people in the world." In the article on Jews in the *Dictionnaire,* he wrote, "They are a totally ignorant nation who, for many years, have combined contemptible miserliness and the most revolting superstition with a violent hatred of all those nations that have tolerated them. Nevertheless, they should not be burned at the stake." In a 1770 appendix to this entry, Voltaire accused the Jews of having "always sacrificed human victims with their sacred hands" (for a further discussion of Voltaire's antisemitism, from which these examples were drawn, see Dennis Prager and Joseph Telushkin, *Why the Jews,* pages 115–119, and Arthur Hertzberg, *The French Enlightenment and the Jews: The Origins of Modern Anti-Semitism*).

greater than his hatred of torture. He therefore dismissed and ridiculed Judaism's opposition to torture with ill-disguised sarcasm: "What is very odd is that there never is any mention of torture in the Jewish books. It is truly a pity that so gentle, so honest, so compassionate a nation did not know this means of finding out the truth. The reason for this, in my opinion, is that they did not need it. God always made it known to them as his cherished people . . . thus torture cannot be in use with them. This was the only thing lacking in the customs of the holy people."[2]

———

3. Even when we are most angry at someone with whom we are having a conflict, we should acknowledge that our opinion of the person is probably somewhat exaggerated and inaccurate. None of us can be completely fair and balanced when our own interests are at stake.

———

As a rabbi who has performed weddings for couples who subsequently divorced, I know how easy it is for people in love to be "blind" to their partner's flaws, and how much easier it is for those who are divorcing to be "blind" to their spouse's virtues. Indeed, when divorcing couples are negotiating a financial or child custody settlement, it is rare for both sides to act fairly and not exaggerate their former spouses' character flaws and responsibility for the marriage's end.

———

When the renowned seventeenth-century Lithuanian legal scholar, Rabbi Shabbetai ha-Kohen, known as "the Shach," was involved in a financial dispute, a rabbinical court ruled, to his shock, in his opponent's favor. When the Shach challenged the court as to what flaw it had found in his case, one judge pointed to a ruling from the Shach's own commentary on the legal code, the Shulchan Arukh. *The rabbi checked the reference, then acknowledged that in attempting to justify his position, he had not approached the problem objectively, and had overlooked a ruling that he himself had written.[3]*

———

"In forming opinions of a person we usually ignore his overall behavior and consider only whether he is kind to us. This is unfair since the person's relationship with us might constitute a small percentage of his life activity. . . . What we often do, however, is magnify the faults that affect us and minimize or ignore the virtues that affect numerous other people" —Dr. Solomon Schimmel.[4]

———

4. We should refrain from commenting on the character of a person whom we hold in low regard, since we probably won't be fair. When the name of the person comes up in a conversation, we should avoid offering an opinion. As the Talmud comments: "No one can see . . . the merit of one whom he hates" (*Ketubot* 105b). Further, our animosity will perhaps cause us to disparage even the person's good deeds, either by denying that they occurred, or by interpreting them cynically (see *Orchot Tzaddikim,* "The Gate of Hatred").

————

Many years ago, a colleague and I had occasion to interview the late Israeli prime minister Yitzhak Rabin. Before the interview, we spoke with him privately. At one point I asked him something about the Israeli foreign minister at the time, Abba Eban. Rabin refused to be drawn into the discussion, saying, "It is well known that Eban and I did not get along, and it would be inappropriate for me to speak about him."

————

5. If we can't avoid speaking about someone we dislike (for example, if we are in a public controversy with the person), then we should make certain that what we say is fair, even if it is critical. We should prepare our words beforehand, review them with someone else, and refrain from making spontaneous remarks. Unfortunately, this important principle of behavior is often forgotten or ignored when we are most agitated, which is exactly the time when we should take the most care with what we say. For example, during the emotionally charged 1952 debate in Israel over whether or not to accept reparations from West Germany, Menachem Begin, then a Knesset member and a future prime minister, turned to Prime Minister David Ben-Gurion, and said, "I know that you will drag me to the concentration camps [for opposing you on this issue]. Today you arrested hundreds [of violent anti-reparation demonstrators]. Tomorrow you may arrest thousands. No matter, they will go, they will sit in prison. We will sit there with them. If necessary, we will be killed with them."[5]

Begin certainly had the right to make a logical, and also emotional, case as to why it was wrong to accept German reparations. Nevertheless, his claim that Ben-Gurion was, like the Nazis, planning to incarcerate and possibly kill his political opponents in concentration camps, was without any basis. His words constituted an extraordinarily unjust violation of the biblical injunction "In justice shall you judge your fellow man." With a similar lack of fairness, Ben-Gurion, at a public rally years earlier, shortly after Hitler had come to power, referred to Vladimir Jabotinsky, Begin's mentor, as "Vladimir Hitler."[6] Indeed, it is embarrassing, as well as sad, to read of these attacks. Surely there existed a way for two of world Jewry's most significant leaders to make their own positions clear, without branding their opponents as Nazis.

6. When assessing a person who might be less intelligent than you, consider that, "When he acted as he did, he might not have realized the pain his action would cause."

7. Don't condemn children because of their parents' misdeeds. Few people will acknowledge acting in so unfair a manner, yet it is very common in traditional Jewish circles to greatly emphasize *yichus* (lineage) when considering marital prospects for oneself or one's children. Thus, families in which a scandal has occurred often find it difficult to make a match. The Bible repeatedly warns against making a child suffer for a parent's sins. Jeremiah prophesies that a criterion of a better world is that children no longer suffer because of the misdeeds of their parents: "In those days, they shall no longer say, 'parents have eaten sour grapes, and their children's teeth are set on edge'" (Jeremiah 31:29–30).*

How, then, is one to explain the verse, "[God] visits the iniquity of parents upon children and children's children" (Exodus 34:7)?

First, even if God does this, the Torah forbids human beings from acting similarly: "Parents shall not be put to death for children, nor children be put to death for parents: a person shall be put to death only for his own crime" (Deuteronomy 24:16).

----

*The character of the parent is certainly not an infallible indicator of the child's character. There are few more evil figures in the Bible than the Pharaoh of the opening chapter of Exodus, who decreed the drowning of the male Israelite infants. Yet it was this Pharaoh's daughter who, out of compassion, defied her father's decree and saved the life of the infant Moses (Exodus 2:5–10). Later the Bible describes King Josiah, who ruled over Judah from 640 to 609 B.C.E., in superlative terms: "There was no king like him before who turned back to the Lord with all his heart and soul and might, in full accord with the teaching of Moses, nor did any like him arise after him" (II Kings 23:25). Yet Josiah's father was King Amon, a morally debased figure, and his grandfather was King Manasseh, whom the Bible regarded as singularly wicked, and a man who sacrificed one of his sons in fire (II Kings 21:6, 11,16). Conversely, the Bible relates that the priest Eli, a highly righteous man, raised two sons who were scoundrels (I Samuel 2:12–17).

Further, the Talmud explains that visiting "the iniquity of parents upon children" refers only to children who follow their parents' bad example (Sanhedrin 27b). Therefore, if a young person of bad ancestry shows evidence of being a good person, we should give him the benefit of the doubt; God will not punish him or hold his parents' sins against him, and neither should we.

———

8. If we want to judge others fairly, we should pay most attention to their character, not their physical appearance or professional accomplishments. This goes counter to the manner in which many of us assess others—namely, focusing primarily on the person's looks, wealth, and success. The Bible's view is different. Thus, although the matriarch Rebecca was beautiful (Genesis 24:16), what most appealed to Abraham's servant, who was seeking a wife for Isaac, was her great kindness (Genesis 24:18–19). When the prophet Samuel was looking for a successor to King Saul, and was struck by the appearance of one of David's older brothers, God said to him, "Do not consider his appearance or his height, for I have rejected him [as a potential king]. The Lord does not look at the things man looks at. Man looks at the outward appearance, but the Lord looks into the heart" (I Samuel 16:7).

In later Jewish writings, the Talmud emphasizes that, though the first- and early second-century sage Rabbi Joshua was very ugly, he was extraordinarily esteemed both for his scholarship and for his acts of kindness (*Ta'anit* 7a).

———

Because people know that they are judged largely on the basis of their appearance, many people spend far more time working on how they look than on how they behave.

———

Many, perhaps most, people would prefer to be friendly with a prominent person whose character might be lacking than with a good person of more-limited accomplishments. In contrast, the Bible goes out of its way to depict people in the lower ranges of society who act righteously. Thus Rahab, a prostitute, provides lodging and then saves the lives of the two Israelite spies whom Joshua has sent to Jericho (Joshua 2). Similarly, a prostitute is shown as the model of a compassionate mother in the famous case judged by Solomon (I Kings 3:16–28; the other prostitute in the story, not the child's mother, is a cruel woman who would prefer to see the baby killed).

———

9. We should use the same compassionate standard in judging strangers that we use in judging someone close to us. Rabbi Avrohom Ehrman teaches that judging fairly means recognizing that "had we seen this [particular] action or bad quality in a close friend or relative . . . we would . . . find some way to excuse or overlook it. It is only because a stranger is involved that we condemn this action or failing."[7]

Rabbi Irwin Kula notes that for some people the reverse applies; such people judge those closest to them most harshly, and are overly critical of their family members. If you fall into such a category, resolve to treat your family with the same courtesy and fairness you extend to strangers.

10. Do not be tempted to explain another's sufferings and misfortunes as a punishment from God. This was the sin committed by Job's friends, who told him that the sufferings he was experiencing, including the death of his children, severe illness, and the loss of his wealth, could only be explained as punishments from God, against Whom he must have sinned. At the book's end, God rails against Job's friends for speaking so uncharitably, and insists that they beg Job's forgiveness, and ask him to pray for them (Job 42:8).

Blaming people for their suffering is malicious and only increases the victims' suffering. It's bad enough to be suffering, but considerably worse to be told that the suffering is deserved, and is your own fault.

People sometimes blame others in a less mean-spirited but still painful manner. For example, there are those who, when a serious illness befalls someone, are quick to attribute it to the person's psychological makeup; for example, "She keeps everything bottled up inside. That's why she got cancer." The people who say such things obviously hope that they have found the way to avoid such diseases themselves, which they likely haven't.

In a famous passage, the Talmud acknowledges that none of us know why bad things happen to good people and, for that matter, why good things happen to bad people. As Rava teaches: "The length of one's life, children [i.e., whether one has them, or the number of children one has] and livelihood depend not on merit, but rather on fate [or fortune]" (*Mo'ed Kattan* 28a).

———

Rava explains how he reached this conclusion: Two of the great third-century rabbinic scholars, Rav Chisda and Rabbah, were acknowledged to be tzaddikim. *As proof of their righteousness, each one's prayers for rain, when offered on behalf of the community, were accepted by Heaven. Yet, Rav Chisda lived ninety-two years and Rabbah only forty. Rav Chisda witnessed sixty weddings of children and grandchildren, whereas Rabbah's household suffered a large number of premature deaths. And Rav Chisda's household had bread in such abundance that fine flour was offered even to dogs, whereas Rabbah's household survived on bread made out of barley flour (normally used to feed animals), and people still went hungry. In other words, the two rabbis, both* tzaddikim, *differed tremendously in their longevity, the fate of their children, and their financial resources. That is why Rava concluded that these matters were determined by fate, not merit.*

Rava's teaching has long caused me to question the fairness of another well-known talmudic teaching, one that is read quietly in many synagogues during the Friday evening service: "For three transgressions women die during childbirth: because they are not meticulous in observing the laws of menstrual separation, in separating the dough offering, and in lighting the Shabbat candles" (Mishnah Shabbat *2:6).*

Throughout much of Jewish history, we can assume that when a Jewish woman died in childbirth, her good name was questioned by people speculating, even if only in their own minds, as to which of these Jewish laws she might have violated. The Talmud itself fueled such speculation by citing Rabbi Isaac's view: "She sinned with the chambers of her belly [by not observing the laws of menstrual separation]; therefore, she is stricken in the chambers of her belly." Other rabbis follow this with explanations for why death during childbirth is an appropriate and fitting punishment for the other ritual violations as well (Shabbat 31b–32a).

But since far fewer women today die in childbirth than at the time this Mishnah was composed, should we assume that the percentage of contemporary Jewish women who scrupulously observe these laws is far higher than at the time of the Mishnah (circa 200 C.E.)? Hardly. I must admit that I find it hard to reconcile this particular Mishnah with the injunction to judge our neighbor justly.

Indeed, despite this and several similar talmudic statements, contemporary rabbinic scholars generally condemn efforts to explain people's illnesses and deaths from disease as punishments for their behavior. For example, Lord Jakobovits, the late British Chief Rabbi and medical ethicist, criticized religious people who chose to see AIDS as God's punishment of homosexuals (an activity banned by Torah law; see Leviticus 18:22): "We can no more divine why some people endure terrible ills without any appropriate cause than we can comprehend why others prosper though they clearly do not deserve their good fortune. Even less are we justified in being selective, subjecting some scourges to this moral analysis while exempting others—AIDS, yes, but earthquakes, or flood or drought, no."8

———

11. If we find that we often think and speak critically of others, we should get into the habit of asking ourselves, "Am I being fair? And if I'm not, why am I drawn to harsh evaluations of others?"

12. Rabbi Shlomo Zalman Auerbach offered this suggestion on how to assess whether criticism we come across of another is fair: "When I read any sort of criticism of a book, I always look to see if the writer first praises the work and its author, and then comments on, or criticizes, a specific aspect or detail. If he does, I know the criticism is genuine and therefore permissible. But if the piece opens with criticism, and attacks the author and his book, then it is *machloket* (sheer controversy). . . . Only when a person knows the value and importance of his fellow man can he criticize him without descending into controversy."

Obviously there are exceptions to Rabbi Auerbach's advice. A few books are so odious, or otherwise wrong, that one should emphasize their flaws in the same way that pharmacists attach a sticker noting that an item is toxic or otherwise harmful. But such cases are the exception; in general, expressing only criticism of a person or a book makes the critic as suspect as the person or book who, or which, he is criticizing.

Instances in which we have the right to judge another cautiously

13. When we don't know someone, or when something in the person's behavior has struck us as inappropriate, we should regard the person with caution, but should still treat him graciously. This is in line with a dictum of Rabbi Joshua: "Regard all men as if they were thieves, yet honor them as you would honor Rabbi Gamliel." In commenting on the surprising wording of this statement, the Rabbis tell of an incident in which a man asked Rabbi Joshua for hospitality, and the rabbi treated him generously, giving him food and drink. He then took the man up by ladder to his attic, and gave him a bed. When Rabbi Joshua left the attic, he withdrew the ladder. The guest gathered up several valuable items in the attic and wrapped them in a blanket, but when he tried to leave the room, he fell and injured himself. When Rabbi Joshua saw him lying on the floor, surrounded by the stolen goods, the man said, "I did not know that you took away the ladder." Rabbi Joshua replied, "Did you not know that last night I was suspicious of you?" (*Derech Eretz Rabbah,* chapter 5)

Thus, though Rabbi Joshua did not trust the man completely, he treated him generously, yet took steps to guard his property. Presumably, had he been more suspicious, he would not have welcomed the man into his house at all.

When it is appropriate not to judge another favorably

14. Judging fairly does not mean judging naïvely. If someone does many bad, even wicked, things, we are not obliged to devise far-fetched explanations to excuse her behavior.* Indeed, viewing such people favorably can have a negative impact on our own character: "One who gets into the habit of ignoring the acts of wicked people [or trying to explain them away] will begin to condone their practices. . . . We must oppose them and take a stand against them" (Rabbi Simcha Zissel Ziv). Therefore, we should be on guard even when such a person behaves well, for who knows what deceptions she is planning? On the other hand, do not be quick to label someone as bad.

15. We should be suspicious of anyone who becomes violent when angry. Concerning those who tear clothes or break things when angry, the Rabbis say that such a person should be regarded as if he were an idolater, and capable of the worst forms of misbehavior when furious (*Shabbat* 105b; for more on this teaching, see page 256).

———

In 1970 a woman and her two children were bludgeoned to death in North Carolina. There was much speculation among legal authorities as to whether the woman's husband, Dr. Jeffrey Macdonald, a successful physician, was the murderer. For over nine years the police could not find sufficient evidence to indict Macdonald. During this time he continued his medical practice, and most people who knew him believed in his innocence.

However, when Macdonald entered into a relationship with a woman, her ten-year-old son saw a different side of the doctor. On one occasion, when the boy's behavior upset him, Macdonald dangled the boy by his feet over the edge of a dock, threatening to drop him headfirst into the water. A short time later, on a boat, the boy again angered Macdonald, who grabbed him and remarked furiously that when they returned to shore, he would hold him over the front of the boat and crush his skull against the dock. Instead, Macdonald threw the boy into the water, and the mother immediately broke off her involvement with him.

When the boy recounted these two episodes some ten years later to author Joe

---

*Rabbi Jonah Gerondi cautions: "[As regards] one who is mostly wicked . . . judge his actions and speech negatively" (*The Gates of Repentance* 3:218).

McGinniss, he explained that at that moment on the boat, seeing the awful look in Macdonald's eyes, he understood that he must be guilty of the murders; he could see from this incident what the man was capable of doing when angry. Some time after this incident, Macdonald was arrested for, and subsequently convicted of, the three murders.[9]

———

When we have misjudged another

16. If we have misjudged someone, we should go out of our way to do that person a good turn. He might not know why we are acting especially nicely (and there is no reason for us to explain), but our kindness will wipe out the negative feelings we felt, and might also make us more cautious before we misjudge someone else.

———

The priest Eli, standing in the temple in Shiloh, witnessed a woman named Hannah whose lips were moving, but no sounds were coming out of her mouth. Eli jumped to a wrong conclusion, and sharply reprimanded her, "How long will you make a drunken spectacle of yourself? Sober up!" (I Samuel 1:14).

Hannah explained that she was not drunk, but a brokenhearted woman pouring out her heart to the Lord; in fact, she was praying to God to cure her infertility.

Embarrassed that he had suspected someone inappropriately, Eli immediately offered Hannah his blessing: "May the God of Israel grant what you asked of Him" (1:17).

Based on this incident, the Talmud concludes, "One who has unfairly suspected his neighbor is obligated to pacify him and also to bless him" (Berachot 31b).

This incident also teaches us that we should not permit others to judge us unfairly. Hannah understood that remaining silent when accused of having entered the temple drunk would constitute an admission of guilt. Maintaining our good name is important. Further, if we don't correct a person who has falsely accused us—for example, if we just skulk away out of pride—the other person will continue to believe that what he said is true, and might easily share his opinion with others. Therefore, Hannah's telling Eli of his error not only caused him to bless her, but also offered him the opportunity to repent. The Talmud, therefore, notes in its discussion of this event that "one who is suspected of something of which he is innocent should inform the one who accused him of the error he is making" (Berachot 31b).

———

A final thought

17. We should focus our primary, though not our exclusive, efforts on improving ourselves, not others. Rabbi Israel Salanter taught, "When I first began to learn *Mussar* (the Jewish ethical teachings on self-improvement), I would get angry at the world, but not at myself. Later I would get angry at the world and also at myself. Finally, I got angry at myself alone."[10]

GRATITUDE

——

For every breath that a person takes,
he should praise his Creator.

Genesis Rabbah 14:9

7

BECOMING A GRATEFUL PERSON

1. The Hebrew term for gratitude is *hakarat ha-tov,* "recognition of the good [another has done for you]." Grateful people look forward to helping those who have helped them. Thus the Bible tells of a devout and wealthy woman who often welcomed the prophet Elisha to her house. During one of his visits, Elisha had his servant say to her, "You have gone to all this trouble for us. What can we do for you?" (II Kings 4:13). The woman, it turned out, was infertile, so Elisha prayed to God on her behalf, and she conceived.

Elisha's statement to the woman reflects how to acknowledge and repay the generosity of others. He doesn't start by asking, "What can we do for you?" for this might make the woman embarrassed and too timid to ask for anything for herself. So he first emphasizes all the kindness *she* has extended to him: "You have gone to all this trouble for us." By doing so, the woman is made to feel more comfortable requesting something for herself.

2. In addition to being the right thing to do, gratitude is also a prerequisite for happiness.* Consider the mindset of a grateful person: "Look what Sam did for me; he really likes me. Look how Barbara helped me; she really cares about me." At the very moment that we cultivate the feeling of gratitude, we also cultivate a feeling of being loved.

Conversely, what is the mindset of an ungrateful person? "The only reason Sam helped me is to make sure I'll reciprocate when he needs me. Barbara spoke to so-and-so on my behalf so that she can ask me to do something for her." An ungrateful person reveals not only a suspicious and mean-spirited disposition, but how profoundly unloved she feels. Ungrateful people cannot imagine that others care enough about them to be generous with no thought of quid pro quo.

---

*I am grateful to Dennis Prager for this insight.

———

Think of people you regard as ungrateful. You will quickly realize that not one of them is a happy person. How could they be, living in a world which they see as loveless and friendless?

Then think of those people you know who express gratitude even for small favors. Aren't the people who come to mind among the happier people you know?

The emotions most often expressed by the Israelites in the desert are annoyance and ingratitude. Thus, although God supplies them daily with food, the Israelites, angered by their diet's monotony, complain, "We have come to loathe this miserable food" (Numbers 21:5). When the demagogic Korach tries to stir up a rebellion against Moses, most of the people refuse to take sides between Moses—who has devoted his life to helping them—and his rival. The Talmud (Avoda Zara 5a) depicts Moses as calling the Israelites "ungrateful ones, children of ungrateful ones."

As is the fate of ingrates, the Israelites—despite having witnessed more of God's glory and miracles than any nation before or since (the revelation at Sinai, the crossing of the Red Sea, the daily provision of manna)—seem, throughout their sojourn in the desert, to be petulant, untrusting, and unhappy.

———

Cultivating gratitude

3. Gratitude is rooted in remembrance. Therefore we must make a conscious effort to recall how others have helped us; if we don't do this, we will forget. The Bible tells of a great favor Joseph performed for Pharaoh's former cupbearer, when both men were in prison. During a desperate time in the cupbearer's life, Joseph interpreted the man's unsettling, and prophetic, dream, assuring him that he would soon be released from prison and restored to Pharaoh's good graces. Joseph made but one request of the man; when all this came to pass, he should mention to Pharaoh Joseph's unusual ability, and thereby help him gain his freedom also.

Within three days, as Joseph predicted, the cupbearer was freed. Perhaps the man initially intended to help Joseph, but the Bible records: "And the chief cupbearer did not remember Joseph, and he forgot him" (Genesis 40:23). This language is instructive. Because the man did not actively cultivate a remembrance of the favor Joseph had done him, he gradually forgot about him.*

---

*Ecclesiastes also relates a story illustrating the cruelty of ingratitude: "There was a little city and few men in it; and to it came a great king, who surrounded it, and built mighty siege works against it. Present in the city was a poor wise man who saved the city with his wisdom, but nobody remembered that poor man" (Ecclesiastes 9:14–15).

———

A man who spent his childhood in a crowded apartment on New York City's Lower East Side told me that for several years his struggling parents took into their home a cousin's family, who were even poorer than they; the children of both families were crowded into one bedroom. What hurt him, however, was that when the cousin's family prospered and moved out of the house, they limited, and eventually ended, contact with his family. The man tried on several occasions to seek them out, to learn if he and his family had somehow offended them. The other family was formal and polite, but never responded to his queries, nor initiated contact. He concluded that just seeing him and his family reminded these people of the poverty in which they had once lived, and so, to avoid the pain of that remembrance, they decided to cut off all contact with their former benefactors. Understandable? Maybe, but definitely hurtful and the action of ingrates.

As a corrective against forgetting, try each day to remember at least one favor or kindness extended to you.

———

4. Let your gratitude to others last for a long time. A classic American joke tells of a congressman who, when he solicits a constituent's vote, learns that the man is planning to vote for his opponent. "But how can you do that?" the congressman objects. "Don't you remember that time ten years ago when your business burned down, and I arranged for you to get a low-interest loan from the Small Business Administration? And what about the time when your daughter got in trouble with the police overseas, and I arranged for her to be released and sent back to the United States? And the time when your wife was sick, and I helped get her admitted to the special hospital she needed?" The voter answers, "That's all true, but what have you done for me lately?"

"What have you done for me lately?" is the ingrate's question. Judaism's perspective is very different. When King David is on his deathbed, and offers his final words of wisdom and advice to his son and successor, Solomon, he reminds him to "show kindness to the sons of Barzillai of Gilead, and let them be of those that eat at your table, for they befriended me [many years ago] when I fled from Absalom your brother" (I Kings 2:7).*

---

*When Absalom launched a revolt against David, the king was caught unawares and fled for his life. He crossed the Jordan River and took refuge in Gilead, where Barzillai and some other notables supplied him and his followers with all their needs, including lodging and food (II Samuel 17:28–29). Later, after David put down Absalom's revolt, he invited Barzillai to remain with him in Jerusalem, but the eighty-year-old man refused, preferring to remain in Gilead, where he had lived his whole life; instead, David took into his court Chimham, Barzillai's son (II Samuel

The Talmud teaches that "one who learns from his companion a single chapter, a single law, a single verse, a single expression, or even a single letter, should accord him respect" (*The Ethics of the Fathers* 6:3). It was probably in fulfillment of this teaching that, when the third-century rabbi, Rav, learned that his earliest childhood teacher had died, he tore his garment as a sign of mourning (see Palestinian Talmud, *Bava Mezia* 2:11). Some might regard this gesture as excessive. But Rav, mindful that this man had taught him to read and understand basic texts—thereby opening up to him the whole world of Jewish learning—felt that his debt remained very deep.

Remember those who have helped you at different moments in your life:

- family members, teachers, and rabbis who inspired you and believed in you
- friends with whom you are perhaps no longer in touch, who showed you loyalty and warmth
- an employer who gave you a break, perhaps when you were young and inexperienced

Even if these people are no longer in a position to help you, indeed specifically *because* they no longer are in a position to help, you should find a way to make known to them how you feel. After all, a person who expresses gratitude only to those who can help him is manipulative, not grateful.*

———

Treating others with gratitude is not only pleasant for the recipient, it also makes us feel good about ourselves, while forgetting about those who have helped us can later fill us with remorse and shame. The actor Kirk Douglas writes of his embarrassment at realizing how selfishly he had behaved sometimes when he was younger. As he recalls in his memoir, My Stroke of Luck, *"Today I received a fax that reminded me of my faults: 'Dear Mr. Douglas, My father, Paul Wilson,*

19:39); on his deathbed, David instructed Solomon to continue this tradition of gratitude (I Kings 2:7).

*The French essayist La Rochefoucauld (1613–1680) wrote that "we find few guilty of ingratitude to us while we are still in a position to help them" (*Maxims*). A story, probably apocryphal, is told of Andrew Carnegie, the great early-twentieth-century business tycoon. His sister lamented to him that her two sons, who were away at college, rarely responded to her letters. Carnegie assured her that if *he* wrote them he would get an immediate response. He sent off two warm letters to the boys, and told them that he was happy to send along to each of them a check for a hundred dollars (a large sum in those days). Then he mailed the letters, but didn't enclose the checks. Within days he received warm, grateful letters from both boys, who noted at the letters' end that he had unfortunately forgotten to include the check. How likely is it that they would have responded so quickly if the check had been enclosed?

was a friend of yours back in the 40s. I understand that you even lived with the Wilson family when jobs were scarce. My father recently died and amongst his papers we have found old playbills and clippings mentioning you. I would be happy to forward copies if you would like them. Please contact me. Gale Patron."

Mr. Douglas wrote Ms. Patron: "Your fax made me very sad. I loved your father." Indeed, her father had been Mr. Douglas's loyal and generous friend, but *"we lost track of each other when I went to Hollywood, but that's my fault. I know Paul. He wouldn't want to seem to be interfering with my activities. It was really up to me.... When I received your fax, it was like a kick in the ass. Why was I so self-centered? Why did I forget someone who gave me help and friendship when I really needed it? Gale, your father was a great guy, and a gentleman. We had a lot of fun together. Please forgive me for being so self-absorbed that I didn't look up my old friend...."*

Mr. Douglas's words should inspire all of us to recall and reconnect with those who have once helped us, and whom we have let fall out of our lives: *"I felt ashamed. Was it sixty years ago? How time flies when you're thinking only of yourself. I would have liked to see Paul again, to thank him for being such a good friend. But now it's too late."*[1]

Long-term gratitude has characterized the Jewish community's attitude toward "righteous gentiles" who risked their lives to save Jews during the Holocaust. Yad Vashem, the Holocaust memorial museum in Jerusalem, conducts ceremonies to honor such people, and various Jewish organizations, and individuals who were themselves saved, provide financial support to help those saviors who are in financial need.

Similarly, it was Leopold Pfefferberg (in the United States, he changed his name to Page), saved by Oskar Schindler, who persuaded the Australian novelist Thomas Keneally to write the book that became known as Schindler's List. All of this was done in fulfillment of a vow Pfefferberg made to Schindler shortly after the war, that he "would make his name known to the world."[2]

———

5. Remember and acknowledge the good done even by those who later do wrong. By the end of his life, the once modest and lovable King Saul had turned into a paranoid monster (see page 223), but he had not always been that way. When Saul first became king, the Israelite city of Yavesh-Gilead was besieged by Ammon, and King Nachash threatened to gouge out the right eye of every man in the city (see I Samuel 11:2). Within days, Saul mustered an army, attacked Ammon, and saved the people of Yavesh-Gilead. Decades later, when the Philistines killed Saul and three of his sons and put their disfigured bodies on display, the men of Yavesh-Gilead risked their lives by taking down the bodies and giving them a dignified burial (I Samuel 31:11–13).

Bad deeds should be condemned, but never use them as an excuse to forget or ignore the good others have done.*

6. Express gratitude to your family members and friends. Many of us take the people closest to us for granted, and show far greater appreciation to strangers who have done us a favor than to those who have undoubtedly done us hundreds.

If those close to you have made it known that they do not feel appreciated, resolve that—for a specified period of time, perhaps the first week of each month—you will treat your spouse, children, siblings, and parents with the same courtesy and gratitude you extend to strangers.

7. Show gratitude not only to those who help you, but to those who help the people you love. The Bible records that Boaz was especially caring and generous to Ruth. Why? Because Ruth had been very kind to her mother-in-law, Naomi, who was Boaz's cousin (Ruth 2:11–16).

———

Some years ago, Texas senator John Tower was nominated to become Secretary of Defense. The Senate confirmation process became quite sordid when rumors started to circulate (many of which were later shown to be untrue) depicting Tower as a drunk, a womanizer, and corrupt. While most of the Democrats instinctively turned against the Republican Tower (who had started his career as a Democrat), Senator Christopher Dodd, a Democrat, rose to speak in the Senate: "Twenty-two years ago, my father, Senator Thomas Dodd, was on trial before this same Senate. He was accused of financial misconduct. . . . [And there was one senator in particular] who stood up and defended my father and who made sure he was treated fairly, and that man was Senator John Tower. We Dodds don't forget someone who does us a favor. I owe John Tower. I owe him the same fairness and the same careful judgment he showed to my father twenty-two years ago." Later, Dodd broke ranks with his party and voted for Tower's confirmation.†

---

*As to how this point applies to institutions and countries, see pages 107–108.

†See Rabbi Jack Riemer, *The World of the High Holy Days*, volume 1, page 23. Commenting on the incident, Rabbi Riemer notes that during the High Holidays, "the prayer book warns us many times that the sins that we do are recorded and not forgotten, and that they can come back to haunt us years later. But what Senator Dodd did reminds us that the good that we do is also recorded and not forgotten, and that it too can come back to reward us years later."

To remember the good done for us or someone dear to us—even after twenty-two years have passed—is precisely the opposite of the "What have you done for me lately?" mindset.

Rabbi Joseph Soloveitchik (known to his students as "the Rav") was known for being unusually grateful for any favor done to him or his family. Thus, for a period of several months, he traveled to the Bronx from Manhattan every Wednesday to visit a woman who was receiving chemotherapy. Her sole tie to the Rav was that her father had done a kindness for Reb Moshe, Rabbi Soloveitchik's father. When the renowned talmudic scholar, Dr. Louis Ginzberg, of the Jewish Theological Seminary, died, the Rav went to visit the mourning family. The surprised mourners asked him if he knew Dr. Ginzberg, and Rabbi Soloveitchik answered that he had met him once, when Professor Ginzberg paid a shiva call after the Rav's father had died.[3]

———

8. Help not just the person who has helped you, but also her family and friends. Jonathan, King Saul's son, was a loyal friend to David, even though he realized that David's elevation to the kingship would come at his expense. Nonetheless, Jonathan protected David from Saul's wrath, and loved David as he loved himself. Jonathan later died, along with his father and two of his brothers, while battling the Philistines. When David became king, he inquired of his servants, "Is there anyone still left of the House of Saul with whom I can keep faith for the sake of Jonathan?" (II Samuel 9:1).

9. Thank those who work for you, particularly those whose efforts you may take for granted. For example, make known your appreciation to the cleaner who takes care of your house. Don't just make him aware of the things that displeased you. If an editor has improved your manuscript, make sure she knows how grateful you feel for that. Do the same for all those who perform services for you. Make sure they understand how much their help has meant to you.

Thus, when Moses told his Midianite father-in-law Hobab (also known as Jethro) that he and the Israelites were journeying to the land promised them by God, and invited him to come along, Hobab refused, saying he wanted to return to his native land. "Please do not leave us," Moses said. "You know where we should camp in the desert, and you can be our eyes" (Numbers 10:31). Is there any doubt that Hobab left this encounter with the greatest leader of his age feeling understood and appreciated?

One of the many destructive aspects of slavery was that owners grew accustomed to slaves helping them without having to be thanked. The incivility such behavior could engender is reflected in an 1858 statement by South Carolina senator James Henry Hammond, in which he demanded that the citizens of the North acknowledge their subservience to the South: "You fetch and carry for us. One hundred and fifty million dollars of our money passes annually through your hands. Much of it sticks; all of it assists to keep your machinery together and in motion. Suppose we were to discharge you; suppose we were to take our business out of your hands; we should consign you to anarchy and poverty."[4] Decades of treating African-American people without gratitude had certainly had an adverse affect on this senator's character; it would seem that whoever had dealings with him, and was in some way dependent on him, was treated with contempt and threats.

10. Express gratitude to those who help you, but whom you don't see. When checking into a hotel, people tip the bellman who carries up their bags, but most people do not leave a tip for the chambermaid. Because they rarely meet the chambermaid, they feel no need to leave her anything. But it is good for your character (and obviously good for the maid) to acknowledge the good someone has done you, even if you don't meet the person.

11. Minimize the favors *you* have done for others: "If you have done a big kindness for your neighbor, let it be in your eyes a small matter" (*The Fathers According to Rabbi Nathan* 41:11). Otherwise you may walk around in a constant state of annoyance at others: "Look what I did for so so-and-so and he never mentions it." Society functions best when people remember *their* obligations, when those who have been helped remember the favor, and when those who have helped another don't dwell on it.

Many people have trouble expressing gratitude because they don't want to acknowledge how dependent they are on others. Therefore, when we remind people of what we have done for them, we often provoke an annoyed response, even hostility, rather than gratitude. Unfortunately, this is a failing among many parents who remind their children of the sacrifices they made for them.

12. Maximize what others have done for you. "If your friend did you a small favor, let it be in your eyes a big favor" (*The Fathers According to Rabbi Nathan* 41:11). Many of us have a tendency to take for granted or forget what others have done for us.

Unfortunately, we are likely to recall—in great detail—any slight other people have inflicted on us. If you are the sort of person who does this, make an effort to reverse this tendency. Don't take the kindness of others for granted, and be appreciative of each and every favor.

———

When Reb Aryeh Levine was in his eighties, he had difficulty standing. His student, Yaakov David Perlin, would come to his house every day to massage his feet. A few days before he died, Reb Aryeh told a friend, "In the World-to-Come, no less than this one, I won't forget his kindness toward me."

———

13. Repay one person's kindness by being kind to someone else. I read a story of a man whose business was in very difficult straits. His late father's friend offered him a generous interest-free loan. A long time passed before the man was in a position to repay the loan, but when he finally did, the lender refused to accept his check. The man was upset. "I'm not a charity case," he protested. "I always intended to pay you back."

The lender told him, "Many years ago, I found myself in a similar situation, and I also needed a loan. When I went to pay it back, the lender refused to accept the money. I too protested as you did, that I didn't want to be treated as a charity case. The man answered me, 'It was indeed a loan, and you do have to pay it back . . . but not to me. I want you to pay back the loan in the following manner. One day in the future, when you come across a person or a family who needs the money, pass it along . . . as a loan. And when they come to pay it back, explain the terms of the loan to them, as I just explained them to you.'" The lender then added, "The money I gave you was indeed a loan to me, and now it's your turn and obligation to pay it back in the very same manner I paid back my loan. I chose to pay it to you, someday you will pass the money on to someone else."[5]

Sometimes the person who has done us a great favor needs nothing from us in return (other than thanks), but only that we make the same gesture to someone else.

14. Be grateful to institutions that have helped you, not just individuals. The Midrash teaches: "A person must be grateful to a place where he derived some benefit" (*Genesis Rabbah* 79:6). This could apply to a school, for example, that gave you a scholarship and/or provided you with a good education. Help such a school financially, and speak well of it to others.

Gratitude can apply to much larger institutions, even to countries. For example, Jews owe a debt of gratitude to the United States, a society in which Jews have greater rights and status than in any other society in which they have ever lived. We should apply the admonition of Jeremiah to pray for the peace and prosperity of the government (29:7). Indeed, during the weekly Sabbath service, a prayer for the government of the United States is recited in many synagogues.

Here is one version of a recently composed prayer for the American government, written by Professor Ester Fuchs of Barnard College:

> *God, whose rule spans all eternity,*
> *Who commanded all humanity to create just governments:*
> *May God preserve and protect our democracy,*
> *Bless and help the elected and appointed officials of the government of the United States to carry out their duties consistent with the Constitution and the Bill of Rights.*
> *May God put in their hearts devotion to fairness and equality for all who live in our great nation and compassion for the poor and needy among us.*
> *May God inspire them with the courage to defend the few from the tyranny of the many and to use the might of the United States in support of the State of Israel and of other nations that share a commitment to democratic values and human rights.*
> *May this be the will of God, and let us say, Amen.*

Don't be an ingrate

15. When someone has treated you well, don't offer a cynical explanation for that person's behavior. This is the criterion used by the second-century rabbinic scholar Ben Zoma, to distinguish between good and bad guests. The good guest is one who thinks, "How much trouble has my host gone to for me. How much meat he set before me. How many cakes he served me. And all this trouble he has gone to for my sake!" The ungrateful guest regards the situation very differently: "What kind of effort did the host make for me? I have eaten only one slice of bread. I have eaten only one piece of meat, and I have drunk only one cup of wine. Whatever trouble the host went to was done only for the sake of his wife and children!" (*Berachot* 58a).

Many of us go through life as "bad guests," minimizing the good others have done for us, emphasizing their supposed self-interest in doing so, and praising their kind and generous qualities insufficiently. If someone has done us a favor, we should focus on the good done, not on thinking that the person could have done more, or speculating that she had some selfish motive for acting as she did. We should train ourselves to think, "Look what so-and-so did for me. For that I should be grateful."

There are additional, perhaps even more common, ways to be an ungrateful guest. For example, many people leave a home in which they have been entertained and well treated and, even as they drive home, start criticizing and analyzing their host and her family. Such postmortems often involve speculations about their host's marital relationship, wealth, aesthetic sensibilities, taste in food, intelligence, and children's personalities. To do so is to act as a *kafui tovah,* an ingrate, toward those who have spent hours, perhaps even days, preparing and trying to make our time with them as pleasant as possible. If you find it hard not to make critical comments about people who have hosted you, at least refrain from doing so for twenty-four hours. By then, perhaps, your negative comments may be toned down.

16. When someone has helped you, but has perhaps not done all that you requested, focus on what the person has done, not on what he hasn't. Although this would seem to be morally obvious, many people are so caught up with their own wants and needs that they ignore the good done for them. Thus, Rabbi Eliyahu Dessler, one of the great figures of twentieth-century *Mussar,* once received a letter from a student, posing fourteen unrelated questions on a variety of subjects. Rabbi Dessler wrote back a long reply in which he dealt with thirteen of the questions. He soon received a return letter from the student, who not only noted the omission, but expressed no thanks for what the rabbi had written.

Though Rabbi Dessler was a man of great patience, he was pained by the student's behavior: "Not only [was there no word of thanks], but at the beginning of your letter you reminded me that there was one of your questions to which I forgot to furnish an answer . . . Was that the proper beginning [and response] to a letter of ten pages?" He went on to tell the student: "[I mention this] not because I need your thanks, but because of my love for you and concern that you not become a person who denies the good done for him. Recall what I wrote . . . concerning the words of our Sages, 'Whoever denies the good done him by his friend will in the end deny the good *Hakladosh Baruch Hu* (God) has done him as well.' "[6]

———

When the student responded to Rabbi Dessler's rebuke with a letter filled with contrition, the rabbi built up the young man's self-esteem, and made it clear that he totally forgave him: "You are dear and honored in my eyes because you accept rebuke. . . . I enjoyed your letter very much, my precious one."[7]

———

For more on how to criticize fairly and in a manner that will evoke change, see chapter 45.

17. Never take advantage of anyone who has been good to you. A person who violates this principle is labeled in Jewish writings as "one who returns evil for good." Thus, when Mrs. Potiphar tries to seduce Joseph, her husband's handsome servant, Joseph demurs: "My master . . . has entrusted me with everything he owns. . . . He has not kept back anything at all from me, except for you, his wife. How could I do such a great wickedness? It would be a sin before God" (Genesis 39:8–9). In the Bible's view, ingratitude, like adultery, is also a sin against God.

18. Don't point to an institution's imperfections as reasons for not acknowledging the good it has done you. The Talmud teaches, "Cast no mud into the well from which you have drunk" (*Bava Kamma* 92b). Rabbi Joseph Soloveitchik taught that if you studied at a school, even if you come to disagree with the school's approach later, don't "throw mud at it" and condemn it because of those aspects of the institution with which you now disagree.[8]

This dictum is relevant as well for those who have changed their religious orientation. For example, some Jews who grow up Orthodox later leave it for other denominations, while others who grow up Reform, Conservative, or unaffiliated later become Orthodox. Such people often speak with bitterness of the movements in which they were raised, but they should also acknowledge whatever good they gained from their earlier experiences. And those who claim that their experience was entirely negative should reflect on what is perhaps the most unusual of the Torah's 613 commandments: "You shall not abhor an Egyptian, for you were a stranger in his land" (Deuteronomy 23:8). Although the experience of Egyptian slavery included oppression and the drowning of Israelite newborns, the Israelites were commanded not to hate the Egyptians; rather, they were to remember—along with their recollections of slavery—how Egypt originally admitted them (at the time of Joseph), saved them from famine, and treated them with generosity.

If we are commanded to remember the good even when mingled with such evil, then we are certainly obligated to recall the good done for us by institutions and denominations with which we later come to disagree.

———

Professor Noam Chomsky, the MIT linguist and one of the most highly regarded left-wing commentators on politics, often writes of America with venom. During the Vietnam War, he called the Department of Defense "the most hideous institution on earth." In the aftermath of 9/11, Chomsky wrote that the United States was responsible for the great hatred felt toward it by many people throughout the world. The ingratitude expressed by people such as Chomsky for a society that has done so much to spread freedom throughout the world—it is America's freedom that allows Chomsky to express his anti-American venom*—is a profound violation of the Jewish imperative to "be grateful to a place where one derived some benefit" (Genesis Rabbah 79:6). On an even more basic level, had Chomsky's family not immigrated to the United States, he, and they, would probably have been murdered in the Holocaust.

———

When gratitude is not owed

19. If someone does you a favor for selfish reasons (for example, someone who employs a person who is in the country illegally, and who takes advantage of the person's tenuous status to pay her a very low wage),[†] you are not required to feel grateful. Bachya ibn Pakuda, the eleventh-century moral philosopher, wrote of such cases: "If we derived some benefit from a person who had no intention of helping us, our obligation ceases and we owe him no thanks" (*Duties of the Heart*, treatise III, introduction).

20. If people whom you have helped often act ungratefully (and you have reached this conclusion even after giving them the benefit of the doubt), don't go out of your way to help them in the future (this applies to family members as well); there is no shortage of grateful and good people who deserve to be helped, so why expend your efforts on behalf of ingrates?

---

*It has been rightly observed that if you compare America with the rest of the world, it is very impressive. If you compare it to Utopia, it is awful.

†Although such people are commonly referred to as "illegal aliens," I find it offensive to refer to a human being as "illegal," while the term "alien" conveys the impression that such people are creatures from another planet.

As regards gratitude to God, see pages 492–494.

Final thoughts

21. Acknowledge the good while you have it. As a rabbi, I often meet with people who have suffered serious losses, either through the death of a close relative, or owing to an irrevocable decline in health or financial fortunes. In such situations, people sometimes say, "Oh, if things could only go back to being the way they used to be, I would be so happy." Yet I knew these people when things were "the way they used to be," and they weren't so happy, and often complained. A grateful person doesn't express happiness for what he had only when he's lost it. Gratitude consists in acknowledging the good in your life while you still have it.

———

When Rabbi Irving Lehrman was a child in the 1920s, he accompanied his mother to get a bracha, *a blessing, from the Lubavitcher rebbe, who was then visiting the United States (it is a long-standing Jewish tradition to solicit a blessing from a holy person). They stood in line for hours, and when they finally reached the rebbe, he asked her, "How are your children?"*

"Baruch Hashem" *(Thank God), Rabbi Lehrman's mother answered.*

"And how is your parnassah *(livelihood)?"*

"Baruch Hashem."

"How is your family's health?"

"Baruch Hashem."

"So then what kind of bracha *do you want me to give you?" the rebbe asked. She answered:* "Zol nisht farshtert veren" *(It should not be spoiled).*

Such is the attitude of the pious, a sense of appreciation for what they have, instead of a focus on what they are missing.

———

Appreciating what you have

———

"You have the gift of vision. You can see a beautiful spring day, and you can see a smile on a baby's face. You can sit up, stand upright, and [walk]. If a person who is bedridden with a paralyzing, muscle-wasting disease were told, 'If you commit yourself to doing good deeds, you can regain your muscle strength and live an active life,' he would not hesitate for a moment to jump at the

opportunity. . . . Do not take physical functioning for granted. This is a gift that should be cherished."

—Rabbi Abraham Twerski.

———

22. "If you cannot be grateful for what you have received, then be thankful for what you have been spared" (Yiddish proverb): If you are often conscious of what's wrong in your life, post this proverb in a prominent place and reflect on what you have been spared:

- If you do not have serious health problems, are you grateful for your good health?
- If your children do not suffer from special, and perhaps untreatable, conditions, are you grateful for that, or do you take your children's well-being for granted?
- If you have enough money to provide for your family's basic needs, do you, nonetheless, often focus on what you lack?

———

Right now, before you finish this chapter, mark down the many ways in which your life is blessed, and for which you can and should express gratitude to God. One person to whom I presented this challenge offered the following list:

1. *I am in good health and the chronic disease I do have is treatable by medication. I know that had I lived a century ago, before this medication was discovered, I would be long dead. That thought alone spares me from naïvely romanticizing the "good old days"; they would not have been good for me.*
2. *My children have good characters and are intelligent. Some of them have problems in school and problems with self-discipline, but they are kind and lovable people.*
3. *My wife knows my faults and still loves me, and I know her faults and love and cherish her. We each trust that the other truly cares about us, and strives to help when the other is in need.*
4. *In a world filled with poverty, I am able to support my family. My life would be easier and less tense if I earned more money or our expenses were lower, but our basic needs are met, and there is enough money to make donations to charity. I know that when I focus on the additional money I wish I was earning, it makes me*

———

*Angels Don't Leave Footprints, pages 71–72.

anxious and upset, but it is self-destructive to focus on that which I lack rather than on that which I have.

5. *I love my work, and I thank God that I can earn my living doing something that interests and inspires me, and which I think makes the world better.*

6. *I have close friends whom I love and trust. Since my childhood, I have always had deep friendships, and those friendships have made me feel secure, and have helped make my life interesting.*

7. *And, perhaps most important, I believe that there is a God Who knows me, Who cares about me, and Who hears my prayers. If I lost my faith, my life would seem meaningless and goodness purposeless. Fortunately, my faith in a God Who knows and cares about me has grown deeper over the years, and for this I am grateful.*

———

Good Manners
and Civility

Receive every person with a
cheerful expression.

Rabbi Shammai,
The Ethics of the Fathers 1:15

8

WHY GOOD MANNERS MATTER

———

1. An ancient rabbinic text teaches, *kadmah derech eretz et ha-Torah*, "the commandment of good manners [i.e., considerate behavior] preceded the Torah" (*Leviticus Rabbah* 9:3). The Rabbis explain that while the Torah's commandments were revealed and became binding only at the time of the revelation at Mount Sinai, the obligation to act with courtesy and civility toward others originated with Adam and the creation of humanity. God could imagine humankind existing for thousands of years without the Torah, but He could not imagine human beings existing without the need for civility.

———

Derech eretz (literally "the way of the land") is the Hebrew term for good manners and basic civility.[1] Thus the Midrash tells of an episode in which Rabbi Yannai insulted a man and subsequently learned that his victim never repeated negative gossip and exerted great efforts to make peace between those who had quarreled. Ashamed at having insulted so worthy a person, Rabbi Yannai apologized: "That I should have called you a dog, when you possess such derech eretz" (Leviticus Rabbah 9:3; see page 218).

———

2. Good manners consist of far more than saying "please" when asking for a favor, and "thank you" to those who have helped us. It is rooted in a willingness to make sacrifices so that we can live together with others without unnecessary conflict. Good manners means

- not cutting in line even when we are impatient, and might well think that our time is more important than other people's
- offering our seat on the bus or train to one who is older or weaker, even though it is definitely pleasanter to sit than to stand

- treating those with whom we interact, as journalist Ellen Goodman has written, "as if they matter"
- treating even those with whom we disagree with respect and fairness*

Derech eretz also refers to behavior that makes life pleasanter for all people. It means respecting children no less than adults, foreigners no less than Americans, non-Jews no less than Jews, and strangers no less than family (as regards those who find it easy to be polite and gracious to strangers, it means showing equal consideration for family members). It also means acting in a way that makes others feel appreciated and respected. Maimonides writes, "One is obligated to conduct his affairs with others in a gentle and pleasing manner" (commentary on *The Ethics of the Fathers* 1:15).

———

The laws of civility also apply to couples who separate or divorce, although we often hear of separating couples who speak to, and of, each other in a hateful manner. One contemporary observer, Professor Stephen Carter, author of Civility,[†] *has written, "Goodness knows what the incivility with which we conduct our divorces is teaching our children about how to treat those we once loved and no longer love."*[2]

———

3. The basic guidelines for practicing *derech eretz* are set down in one verse in Proverbs, and in two teachings of *The Ethics of the Fathers*:

- In offering a general prescription for how people should behave, Proverbs teaches, "Her ways [i.e., the ways of a life based on Torah] are pleasant ways, and all her paths peaceful" (3:17).
- "Which is the proper way in which a person should act? Whatever brings credit to oneself, and earns one the esteem of others" (*The Ethics of the Fathers* 2:1).
- "If the spirit of one's fellow is pleased with him, the spirit of God is pleased with him" (*The Ethics of the Fathers* 3:10).

---

*As Republican presidential candidate Bob Dole declared concerning President Bill Clinton and Vice President Al Gore, the 1996 Democratic candidates, "they are opponents, not enemies."

†Carter's book, *Civility: Manners, Morals and the Etiquette of Democracy*, examines why civility means so much more than polite manners, and has influenced my understanding of this topic. I have drawn on several examples from this book.

As is the case with all generalizations, there are exceptions. For example, when confronting idolatry, it would be inaccurate to say that the ways of Torah are pleasant and peaceful (it demands the destruction of idolatry in the land of Israel; see, for example Deuteronomy 7:25). Similarly, in an unrighteous society, a person might be popular with his fellow citizens (as Hitler was in Germany for most of his years in power), but not be at all esteemed by God.

Such instances are the exceptions, however. As a general rule, for example, those whose emphasis in teaching Judaism is on its pleasant and gentle ways are acting in the way God intended (as was the case with Hillel; see pages 252–253). However, those whose teachings of Judaism lead to ugly behavior and conflict (e.g., instances in Israel when religious zealots have thrown rocks at drivers on Shabbat) are not acting in a manner that brings people close to God, let alone to their fellow citizens.

4. Another rabbinic teaching, "Who is wise? One who foresees the consequences of his actions" (*Tamid* 32a) offers additional guidance in the practice of good manners. Before we do something, we have to think through how our behavior will affect others. For example, if we double-park, this teaching would mandate that we leave a note on our car informing others where we can be found; otherwise the person whose car we blocked might need to move her vehicle, and have no idea how to reach us. Such behavior seems obvious, yet on the street where I live, cars routinely double-park and I rarely see such a note on a car's front window.

Why bad manners are so damaging

5. Many people believe that the importance of good manners is overrated. For example, some years ago, a judge in New York proposed procedures that would oblige opposing lawyers to act civilly to each other in the courtroom. Raoul Felder, New York's best-known divorce lawyer, ridiculed the suggestion, arguing that it is often proper for lawyers to become pugnacious, and that civility "may not always be the right reaction in an adversarial courtroom. . . . I have never heard a client complain that his or her lawyer was rude."

Perhaps that is true, but, as Professor Stephen Carter asks, is it good for society to exempt entire professions from the obligations of civility? Thus the world of politics is filled with campaign managers who see their primary obligation as diminishing the opposing candidate's reputation, while college campuses contain many radicals who think it right to try to stop those with whom they disagree from expressing their views. And, unlike what Raoul Felder said, bad manners pollute the social environment as surely as DDT and other such chemicals pollute the physical one.

6. So destructive is incivility that the Talmud teaches that 24,000 disciples of Rabbi Akiva died because they did not treat each other with respect (*Yevamot* 62b). Though some people assume that this was a divine punishment for their acting inappropriately, there may be a more natural interpretation. Bad manners, epitomized by a refusal to show one's colleagues honor and respect, causes animosity between people. When Akiva and his disciples joined Bar Kochba's rebellion against Rome, it is possible that this long-brewing ill will made it impossible for them to coordinate their efforts, and this inability made them more vulnerable to Roman attacks.

Is such an analysis far-fetched? Not at all. Even during the Holocaust, the ill will and lack of appropriate civility between competing Jewish groups often delayed the coordination of efforts to resist the Nazis. Thus few people are aware that there were two different armed Jewish undergrounds in the Warsaw Ghetto, one founded by the socialist Zionists, the other by their political opponents, the Revisionist Zionists (Ephraim Zuroff).[3]

———

During the early days of World War II, Leo Baeck, the leading Reform rabbi in Germany (who was later arrested by the Nazis and sent to Theresienstadt), sent Rabbi Frank Rosenthal on a special mission to the Jews in the Lodz ghetto in Poland, outlining a suggestion as to how some Jews could be saved from the Nazi death machine. Rosenthal met with the Jewish leaders there, but they wouldn't listen to him. As historian Leonard Baker writes, "Much of their distrust stemmed from his being a German [as opposed to Eastern European] Jew as well as a representative of the leading Berlin Jew; the Lodz Jews could not forget the offensiveness that they and their fellow Eastern European Jews had met [years earlier] when they had come to Berlin. Rosenthal's mission was a failure."[4]

———

A final thought

7. An anecdote in the Talmud suggests that a lack of consideration for others reveals one to be not only ill-mannered and uncouth, but often dishonest as well. Thus the rabbinic sage Mar Zutra, while staying at an inn, had a silver cup stolen from him. Mar Zutra had no idea who the thief was, but

when he saw a guest wash his hands and wipe them dry on another man's garments, he called out, "That is the [thief], since he has no consideration for another person's property." The man was taken into custody and confessed (*Bava Mezia* 24a). As is often the case, inconsiderate manners often reveal bad character.

9

THE OBLIGATION TO BE CHEERFUL

1. We should greet people whom we see, and go out of our way to be the first to extend the greeting. The Talmud relates that it was said of Rabbi Yochanan ben Zakkai, the most distinguished rabbi of his age, that "no one ever greeted him first, even a Gentile in the marketplace" (*Berachot* 17a). Rabbi Yochanan could easily have stood on ceremony, thinking, "I am a prominent leader and scholar, and more important than most of the people I meet. Therefore they should greet me before I acknowledge them." Instead, realizing that every person he met was also created in God's image, Rabbi Yochanan considered it an honor to be able to greet other images of God.

Just as remarkable, given that Rabbi Yochanan lived at a time when the Romans were oppressing the Jews, and Jewish-Gentile relations were hostile, he extended greetings to non-Jews as well as Jews. It is likely that Rabbi Yochanan, in addition to recognizing the divine image in the non-Jews whom he met, hoped in this way to help improve Jewish-Gentile relations.

———

In large cities where pedestrians pass hundreds of people while walking, the obligation to greet every person whom we pass no longer applies. As Rabbi Chaim Ozer Grodzensky told a young student who moved to Vilna, "When I lived in a small town before I came to Vilna, I was very scrupulous to cheerfully greet every person I met in the street. But since I came to Vilna, I stopped this practice, because in such a big city, it's impossible to greet everyone."[1] Still, it is appropriate to greet those whose eye we catch, and all those whom we know, even if only slightly.

———

2. Scholars, rabbis, and Jewish leaders—individuals who serve as representatives of the Jewish community—have a particular responsibility to be gracious. As Maimonides rules: "A scholar should greet all men before they greet him, so that the spirits of others derive pleasure from him" ("Laws of Character Development" 5:7).

———

When Rabbi Moshe Sherer, the late head of Agudat Yisrael (a century-old international organization, and today one of the major Orthodox organizations in the United States), was a young man, he was assigned to escort the great European sage, Rabbi Elchanan Wasserman, who was visiting New York. On their first morning together, Rabbi Wasserman, who knew no English, asked Rabbi Sherer how to say the Yiddish Gut Morgen *in English. Rabbi Sherer explained to him that the English was almost the same as the Yiddish, "Good Morning." As they waited for the elevator, Rabbi Wasserman paced up and down practicing the expression. When the elevator arrived, he said to the elevator man, "Good morning," and then turned to Rabbi Sherer and said, in Yiddish, "Did I say it right?"*

Rabbi Wasserman understood the particular importance of rabbinic scholars, who exemplify Judaism to many Jews and non-Jews, acting with warmth; in that way, Jews and non-Jews alike will look upon rabbis not as stern figures, but as friendly and approachable.

Similarly, when a rabbinic chaplain at a large New York hospital was speaking to a group of health professionals about Jewish perspectives on medical issues, he cited a ruling of the legal scholar Rabbi Moshe Feinstein. An African-American nurse, upon hearing Rabbi Feinstein's name mentioned, said in a loud voice, "He's a real rabbi." The rabbi was puzzled as to how this nurse, who was not Jewish, was familiar with Reb Moshe. When he spoke to her, he learned that she had helped care for a newborn great-grandchild of Rabbi Feinstein. When the rabbi visited the house, he made a point of seeking her out and thanking her for all she had done for his great-grandchild.

This story reminds us that, although many of us think that others are impressed by our intellectual insights, our elegant clothing, or our wealth and standing, what often most appeal to others are simple acts of kindness and personal attention. As this nurse explained when she called Rabbi Feinstein's family to offer her condolences after his death: "I remember how the Rabbi smiled and wished me a good day. I could see that in his eyes I was important."[2]

———

3. Most people greet wealthy and influential people pleasantly, but the Rabbis' insistence that we "be the first to extend greetings to *every* person

[we] meet," and that we receive "*every* person" with a cheerful expression (*The Ethics of the Fathers* 4:15 and 1:15), mandates that we greet everyone with courtesy and warmth, not just those who are prominent.

———

A Chasidic story tells of two young and unknown scholars and brothers, Rabbis Zusya and Elimelech, who visited Ludmir, Poland, and were in need of a place to stay. Inquiries were made of a wealthy man in the town but, unimpressed by the men's credentials, he did not offer them hospitality. Another man in the town, who was quite poor, took the young scholars in. Over the coming years, the two men became acknowledged figures in the Chasidic world, with thousands of followers. Once, when they returned to the town, the wealthy man insisted on hosting them, but the rabbis insisted on staying with the poor man who had hosted them years earlier: "Nothing has changed in us to make you respect us more than before. What is new are just the horses and the carriage. Take them for your guests, and let us stay with our old host, as usual."[3]

———

4. The talmudic teaching that you should "be the first to extend greetings to every person you meet" should also apply to those who perform services for us. Many of us, for example, never bother to learn the name of the waiter who serves us. It would be better, rather, that when the waiter comes to our table, we ask his or her name and tell him ours. This act of good manners will change the encounter between an anonymous server and patron to an encounter between two cordial, mutually respectful human beings.

———

When I shared this thought with a friend, she said, "I disagree! I can't bear it when the waiter insists on giving his name. It's possible to treat someone like a human being without exchanging names."

That is certainly true, but, in my experience, an exchange of names (many people, even if the waiter tells them his name, don't tell him theirs) usually promotes greater warmth and affability than does anonymity.

A man who had worked as a stenographer in the White House for over thirty years was asked which president he had most enjoyed working for. The man answered Harry Truman, because he was the only president who called him by name.

Yale law professor Stephen Carter has expressed his sense of dismay at the large number of his university colleagues who never bother to learn the names of the people who clean their offices several times a week.[4]

As a general guideline, it would be good for people to treat those whom they

*regard as their social inferiors the way that they would like those who regard
them as their social inferiors to treat them.*

*When a driver came to take Mrs. Feinstein to a physician's appointment,
her husband, Rabbi Moshe Feinstein, greeted the driver warmly. The driver
commented, "In Europe, they would say, 'The wagon driver* (ba'al agolah) *is
here.' In America, they say, 'The car is waiting.' "*

*Reb Moshe answered, "Your comment illustrates a sad fact about this coun-
try. In Europe, no one would ever say, 'The wagon is here.' It was always 'The
wagon driver is here.' The emphasis was on the person. But, here in America, it
is, 'The car is here.' An individual is not given the respect he deserves."*[5]

———

5. In a law that is not widely practiced today, Rabbi Joshua ben Levi
teaches that "when a man sees a [beloved] friend after a lapse of thirty days,
he is to recite the *she-he-chi-yanu* blessing, 'Blessed are You, Lord our God,
King of the Universe, who has kept us alive, preserved us, and brought us to
this day' " (*Berachot* 58b; *Shulchan Arukh, Orach Chayyim* 225:1).

6. One should make a particular point to greet vulnerable, disadvantaged, and insecure people, and to do so in a manner that makes them feel accepted and respected. There are times when each of us feels vulnerable, and a
gracious act at such a moment can affect the recipient's entire life.

———

*Professor Stephen Carter, an African-American, tells of an incident from his
youth, when his parents moved from an African-American neighborhood to a
white one in Washington, D.C. Carter remembers how uncomfortable he was
about the move. Sitting on the front steps of his new house with his brothers and
sisters, "we waited for somebody to say hello, to welcome us. Nobody did. . . . I
knew we were not welcome here. I knew we would not be liked here. I knew we
would have no friends here."*

*But Carter's fears and trepidations were set at ease by one person who, it
turned out, was a religious Jew: "All at once, a white woman arriving home from
work at the house across the street from ours turned and smiled with obvious delight and waved and called out, 'Welcome!' in a booming confident voice I would
come to love. She bustled into her house, only to emerge, minutes later, with a
huge tray of cream cheese and jelly sandwiches, which she carried to our porch
and offered around with her ready smile, simultaneously feeding and greeting
the children of a family she had never met—and an African-American family at
that—with nothing to gain for herself except perhaps the knowledge that she had*

done the right thing. We were strangers, African-American strangers, and she went out of her way to make us feel welcome. The woman's name was Sara Kestenbaum, and she died much too soon, but she remains, in my experience, one of the great exemplars of all that is best about civility. . . . She managed in the course of a single day, to turn us from strangers into friends, a remarkable gift that few have. . . . To this day, I can close my eyes and feel on my tongue the smooth, slick sweetness of the cream cheese and jelly sandwiches that I gobbled on that summer afternoon when I discovered how a single act of genuine and unassuming civility can change a life forever."[6]

———

Martin Buber, the twentieth-century Jewish philosopher who placed great emphasis on the importance of establishing deep, intimate encounters between people (I-Thou as opposed to I-It relationships), often spoke of a tragic incident that shaped his life. While still in his twenties, Buber was at home working on a scholarly manuscript when there was a knock on the door. The visitor seemed somewhat distraught, and Buber, sympathetic to the man but anxious to return to his work, answered the man's questions briefly, but, as Buber later expressed it, "I did not answer the questions which he did not ask." Buber subsequently learned that, just a few days after their brief encounter, the man died, an apparent suicide. From then on, Buber concluded, encounters with people must take precedence even over scholarship and mystical speculation.

———

Receiving people cheerfully

7. Rabbi Shammai teaches: "Receive every person with a cheerful expression" (*The Ethics of the Fathers* 1:15). When I taught this teaching to a friendly but somewhat moody man I knew, he said, "That's ridiculous. If I am in a bad mood, am I supposed to act as though I'm in a good mood?" I answered yes (unless one is in an unhappy mood because of something truly bad that has happened), because the lack of a friendly facial expression or manner might well lead the person whom we are meeting to think that we are upset with her. Each of us has had the experience of being with someone who seemed upset, and leaving the encounter wondering if we had somehow offended that person.

The fact that Shammai felt the need to remind people to receive others cheerfully suggests that this does not come naturally to many people, and is something that we may have to work on. Indeed, several stories in the Talmud suggest that Shammai himself had an irascible disposition (see pages 252–253), in contrast to his contemporary Hillel, who was known for receiving everyone warmly and rarely, if ever, losing his temper. Thus, Shammai, in issuing this guideline, was perhaps reminding himself and others that when someone comes to see us, we should ask ourselves, "Am I acting in a manner that will make this person feel that I am receiving him warmly and cordially?"

If we are aware that we are in a bad mood and find it hard to greet others cheerfully, we should quickly note to the people whom we meet that we are upset about something, so that they won't feel that we're irked at them.

———

That the lack of a smile and a friendly demeanor does often reflect ill will is reflected in Jacob's statement to his wives, Rachel and Leah, when he tells them that they must leave their father Laban's house: "I see that your father's face toward me is not as it has been in the past" (Genesis 31:5).

———

During the Aseret Y'mei Teshuva, *the ten days between Rosh Hashana and Yom Kippur, Rabbi Israel Salanter saw a scholar he knew who had a woebegone look on his face. Rabbi Salanter asked the man why he was so worried.*

The rabbi seemed surprised by the question. "These are the days when God is judging us, and deciding whether or not to inscribe us in the Book of Life. How could I not be worried?"

Rabbi Salanter answered, "But other people will not realize that that is what is bothering you. They might well think you are upset with them. If you want to feel worry in your heart, that's your concern. Your heart is a reshut ha-yachid *(a private domain), and what you feel there is known to you alone. But your face is a* reshut ha-rabbim *(a public domain), and no one has the right to cause damage to public property."*

In another version of this story, after the anxious scholar ignored a question posed to him by Rabbi Salanter, the rabbi set down the thoughts that went through his mind: "Is it my fault that you are a God-fearing man and filled with trembling at the Day of Judgment? What has that got to do with me? Are you not required to answer my questions pleasantly and patiently, because such is the way of goodness and kindness?"[7]

———

8. Because a parent's moodiness can have a profound effect upon her children, it is important for parents to receive their children, in accordance with Shammai's directive, "with a cheerful expression." It is known, for

example, that when parents of young children divorce, the children have to be assured that it is not their fault. Children have a tendency to assume that anything that happens in their orbit is due to, or a reaction to, them; how much more so in the case of moody parents? A child whose father often greets him with a distracted or unhappy look will assume that he has upset his father, or that his father doesn't love or even like him. Children raised in homes like this are often emotionally penalized for life, and come to feel that it is their fault when those around them seem unhappy, and that it is their obligation to make others happy. Human beings, as Dennis Prager has argued, have a moral responsibility to be as happy *as they can be,** and this applies particularly to our interactions with our spouses and children, the people with whom we spend the most time, and the people who are most likely to feel responsible for our bad moods.

If our moodiness is due to a chemical imbalance, and is therefore beyond our control, we have a moral obligation to those who live with us to seek out the drug and/or psychological treatments that can improve our emotional balance.

––––

The Fathers According to Rabbi Nathan *(13:4) teaches: "When a man gives his friend the finest gift in the world, but shows an angry (or stern) face, the Bible regards it as if he had not given him anything. On the other hand, if he receives his friend with a cheerful countenance, Scripture regards it as if he had given him the finest gift in the world." Such words might sound exaggerated, but, in truth, children raised in wealthy homes by parents who are distant, unloving, and who do not receive them cheerfully are often unhappy, as if they truly had been given nothing.*

––––

9. So important is it to cultivate a pleasant facial expression that the Talmud teaches that "the man who shows his teeth to his friend in a smile is better than one who gives him milk to drink" (*Ketubot* 111b). In short, smiles are a powerful form of nourishment and inspiration. The Talmud teaches elsewhere: "If you see a student whose studies are as hard for him as iron, attribute it to his teacher's failure to show him a cheerful countenance" (*Ta'anit* 8a).

––––––––––

*I emphasize the words "as they can be" because some people are naturally happier, calmer, and more easygoing than others. There is not a single standard of happiness to which all people should aspire. But if we have a tendency to focus on problems, and to be often anxious, moody, and pessimistic, then we are obligated for the sake of others to rein in these tendencies.

A student of Rabbi Natan Tzvi Finkel (1849–1927) came to tell the rabbi of his engagement. Rabbi Finkel noticed that the boy's manner of speaking was so solemn that he instructed him to make sure to smile more. If he spoke in so serious a manner to his fiancée, she might be afraid that he was upset with her.

10. Rabbi Menachem ha-Meiri, the medieval talmudist, understood the obligation to welcome others as mandating for example that, even when we resent a visitor's intrusion, we still act as if we are happy to receive him (see his commentary on *The Ethics of the Fathers* 1:15). Such behavior is not hypocrisy but courtesy. Obviously, if the visit is inconvenient, we can, after a few minutes, explain why this is not a good time for a visit. But courtesy demands that, unless the visitor is deliberately interrupting us, we put on a good face. Many people don't do this but appear so agitated that the visitor is made to feel uncomfortable and embarrassed.

If someone makes a habit of arriving without warning, we should talk to her about it, and try to find a solution. But when it is an infrequent occurrence, we should not act curtly or show resentment.

11. The obligation to receive people cheerfully also applies to our dealings with beggars: "One who gives charity to the poor grudgingly loses the merit of the deed, even though he gives much; it is better that he give only one coin with a pleasing countenance" (*Orchot Tzaddikim*, "The Gate of Magnanimity"). While we may feel annoyed at a beggar—most of us are not delighted to be stopped and asked for money—we should not let our facial appearance reflect that annoyance.* While some beggars might not mind, others, humiliated at having to beg, will be further mortified at encountering an angry, grudging look.

Behavior to avoid

12. When we greet someone whom we have not seen in a long time, or who might not know us well, we should never ask the person, "Do you remember me?" or even worse, "What is my name?" Doing so embarrasses the

---

*In traditional Jewish communities, beggars sometimes come to solicit at people's homes as well.

other person, and often forces him to lie; he may respond, "Of course I remember you," even when he doesn't.

Unfortunately, many people pose such questions to those who meet thousands of people in the course of their work and cannot be expected to remember everyone they encounter. In addition to disconcerting the person being questioned, such questions usually end up embarrassing the questioner as well, confirming for him that he must not be very important since so-and-so doesn't remember him. Rather, when we go over to someone whom we are not sure remembers us, we should say, "Hello. I'm Jonathan Brown, and I met you at the speech you gave in White Plains." That way, the other person is immediately put at ease. And that is one of the main points of good manners—to put others at ease.

13. Never ignore a greeting. The Talmud teaches that "one who is greeted by a fellow Jew and does not return the greeting is considered a *gazlan,* a robber" (*Berachot* 6b). Why? Such a person is regarded as having stolen from someone else the pleasure of being greeted. Indeed, if we greeted someone and were snubbed, we would feel hurt; whatever good feelings we had would be taken away from us.

In societies such as the United States, where Jews have equal rights and are treated fairly and equitably by non-Jews, the obligation to return all greetings applies with equal force to Gentiles. Failure to do so is a *Chillul Hashem* ("desecration of God's Name"). A non-Jewish clerk at a store told a friend of mine that whenever he saw a customer who was clearly Jewish (e.g., wearing a yarmulke), he would greet the person with "Shalom," and was hurt that many people ignored his greeting and didn't respond.

———

So important is it to respond to a greeting that Jewish law permits us to interrupt some of the most important prayers, during which it is normally forbidden to speak, in order to return a greeting. If the person who greets us understands that we are praying, and can't break off to return their greeting, then we should not do so. But if he won't understand this, and will be hurt or antagonized, we should respond.*

———

*". . . since if one will not greet him, the other can come to hatred" (Chaffetz Chayyim, *Mishnah Berurah* 66:2). Rabbi S. Wagschal explains: "This does not apply nowadays since we are accustomed to not interrupting in the middle of [praying]" (*Guide to* Derech Eretz, 15).

14. When someone whom we dislike, or with whom we are at odds, greets us, we should return the greeting. And if we see her first, we should initiate a greeting. Rabbi Tzvi Elimelech of Dienov writes that in cases of strife, it is particularly important to offer greetings, since such behavior can hasten reconciliation.[8] Conversely, when we allow our anger at someone to escalate to the point where we can no longer exchange a civil "Good morning," our mutual dislike is likely to grow. The simple practice of good manners can prevent dislike and even hatred from hardening.

———

A friend who lived in a New York apartment building told me that there was an elderly woman in the building who had a mean-spirited disposition; she would yell at the staff and at the children, who nicknamed her "the witch." My friend, who had had some run-ins with the woman, decided to take these rabbinic teachings concerning a cheerful disposition seriously, and went out of his way to greet the woman and ask after her well-being. It took far less time than he had anticipated for her to start responding to him pleasantly. Very soon her manner toward his children—which had always been one of annoyance and unkindness—also improved markedly. Such is the power of greeting others in a cheerful and warm manner.

———

10

BECOMING MORE CONSIDERATE

1. Recognize when the needs of others are greater than your own. The *Sefer Chasidim* offers an example: "A man walking on a narrow road comes across another man carrying a heavy load, walking in the opposite direction. [Even if he has arrived first], the man without the load should step onto the shoulder of the road, even if it is muddy, so that the other man can pass by" (paragraph 551).

In modern terms, if you are hailing a taxi, and see a pregnant woman, someone with young children, or a senior, let that person have the first taxi that comes. Although this seems morally obvious, many people are inflexible in taking a me-first approach.

Similarly, on the highway, we should slow down and let another car into our lane. For some reason, driving brings out a competitive and non-compassionate attitude in many people. We routinely act as if a ten- or twenty-second delay will be catastrophic, and treat the person who is signaling to cut in as if she were, at worst, an enemy or, at best, making an extreme and selfish request.

2. An important and frequently overlooked principle of good manners: Don't be late and don't waste other people's time. As Rabbi Moshe Chaim Luzatto wrote: "Stealing an object is stealing, and stealing time is stealing" (*Mesillat Yesharim* [*Path of the Upright*] 11).

Although people who habitually run late usually see this as a minor flaw, Jewish ethics regards it as a serious offense (as do most people who are kept waiting). Rabbi Abraham Twerski, in his commentary on *Mesillat Yesharim*, notes: "If we have an appointment and do not take the necessary precautions to be there on time, it is more than just a lack of consideration—[we] are stealing the other person's time."[1]

In addition, even when we arrive promptly, we must be careful not to waste other people's time. I once heard someone say, "A man who has taken your time recognizes no debt, yet it is the only debt he can never repay."

———

The Chazon Ish was organizing a minyan for the Mincha [afternoon] service. One of the men told the rabbi that he was happy to stay and pray, but that he would therefore be late for an appointment. Even though the man's departure meant that a prayer quorum would no longer exist, the Chazon Ish insisted that the man leave immediately, saying, "One cannot pray on stolen time."

There are certain professionals—particularly physicians—who "overbook" (out of a desire to go promptly from one patient to another without wasting any of their time), and keep patients sitting in waiting rooms, often for long periods. Many physicians don't do this, but a substantial number do, and they justify their behavior with the argument that doctors cannot be expected to be precise in matters of time because they deal with emergency issues. This is sometimes the case, but if a doctor's office is often filled with waiting patients, the physician should ask himself if he is overbooking in a manner that is causing many people's time to be wasted. If an emergency arises, the doctor's assistant should call patients who have not yet arrived and tell them that there will be a delay, and advise them as to when they should come.

The negative effects of prolonged waits in doctors' offices can go beyond wast-

ing people's time. My friend Rabbi Israel Stein showed me a broken finger that had never properly mended; he explained that he was subjected on several occasions to such long waits in his doctor's office that he got up and left. Was his behavior unwise? Yes, but the doctor and his policy of overbooking also shared in the responsibility.

———

3. When our presence is required at an event that is important to someone else, we should make a particular effort to be on time, or even early. Rabbi Aryeh Levine was asked to officiate at a wedding service, and the driver assigned to bring him was late in picking him up. He told Reb Aryeh that since wedding ceremonies always start later than the time printed on the invitation, he saw no reason to waste the rabbi's time by bringing him early. Reb Aryeh was displeased by the driver's reasoning: "Today, when that [young groom] is getting married, his head is full of worries and concerns. Is it right for me to add another worry to his burdens, to make him wonder . . . why I have not appeared? It would be better for me to waste an hour in the wedding hall rather than cause the bridegroom needless concern over my lateness."[2]

4. Don't describe at length how you are going to help someone; rather, "Say little but do a lot" (*The Ethics of the Fathers* 1:15). The biblical personality who epitomizes this trait is Abraham, who tells the three weary-looking travelers whom he invites to his tent, "Let me fetch a morsel of bread that you may sustain yourselves." When the travelers accept his offer, Abraham and Sarah prepare a large repast consisting of bread, cakes, and meat (Genesis 18:5–8).

This is also good advice in terms of self-interest. When we go on at length, our listeners' expectation can become so elevated that, even if we do a great deal for her, she might still be disappointed. If, however, we promise a little, her expectations will be realistic. Then, when we do more than we promised, she will think of us as a person of integrity and generosity, and be very grateful.

———

When a person talks a lot about something, he deceives himself into thinking that he is doing it, even if he isn't. There is an expression, 'After all is said and done, more is said than done." —Rabbi Moshe Goldberger[3]

———

5. Basing themselves on a verse in Ecclesiastes, "For God will call every creature to account for all their conduct" (12:14), the Rabbis taught that we will be held accountable for doing things that disgust others, even if the act is not, in and of itself, immoral—for example, spitting in the presence of those who find this upsetting (*Chagigah* 5a).* Similarly wrong would be talking about revolting subjects at mealtimes or eating with poor manners, both of which can cause other people to lose their appetite. The criteria here are somewhat subjective; certain acts will repel some people but not others.

Good manners dictate that we also refrain as well from activities that annoy, not just disgust, others. A friend who flies a great deal told me that he has on several occasions been seated next to someone playing solitaire, and the sound of the cards being repeatedly and loudly shuffled prevented him from taking a nap or focusing on what he was reading. One can, of course, argue that my friend should simply ask the other person to shuffle the cards quietly and less frequently, but most of us are uncomfortable making a request like this. Therefore, when we are doing something in a public place (such as speaking on a cell phone), we should ask ourselves, "Is it likely that what I am doing will bother others?" (This question particularly applies when we are in an enclosed space, such as an airplane or restaurant, which others can't leave). If the answer is not obvious, we should check with the people near us. Many people, however, act as if it is the annoyed party's responsibility to ask them to be quiet.

———

A former American president used to summon aides to meet with him while he was sitting on the toilet. It seems that the man, who grew up poor, enjoyed forcing aides, particularly those who had attended Ivy League schools and came from more affluent backgrounds, to look at him in this undignified setting and obey his orders. This is precisely the sort of behavior that the Talmud opposed.

———

6. When complimenting another, be precise in your praise. For example, don't just tell someone that she is good, but say what has impressed you. This enables the person receiving the compliment to feel fully seen and appreciated (when compliments are nonspecific, the person may feel that the words are just a formality). Thus, when Rabbi Yochanan ben Zakkai spoke of his five closest disciples, he specified what was special about each one.

---

*An inelegant example: I am repeatedly shocked when using public facilities—at movie theaters and airports, for example—at how many people don't flush after using the toilet, thereby causing an unpleasant experience for those who follow them.

Rabbi Eliezer was "a cemented cistern that doesn't lose a drop of water" (i.e., he absorbs whatever he has learned and forgets nothing); Rabbi Shimon was "a fearer of sin"; and Rabbi Elazar ben Arach was "an overflowing stream" (that is, an innovator overflowing with new insights).

7. We should notice, compliment, and even bless someone on a new garment she is wearing. The *Shulchan Arukh* rules that we should say to a person wearing a new item of clothing, *Tevaleh ve-techadesh*—"May you live to wear it out and to buy a new one" (*Ramah, Orach Chayyim* 223:6).*

———

Similarly, we should compliment people who have, for example, a new hairstyle. Women in particular often spend considerable time and money trying to make their appearance attractive to others, and receiving a compliment helps make the effort seem worthwhile.

———

8. Many principles of good manners have to do with speech. For example, a wise person does not respond to a question or statement without thought. His listeners can trust that he has considered his reply, and is not speaking impulsively. Also, taking more time makes it less likely that we will say something tactless, hurtful, or incorrect.

9. When someone is speaking, don't interrupt so as to show everyone else that you are familiar with what the speaker is saying. The thirteenth-century *Sefer Chasidim* cautioned: "And when you hear your friend speaking and saying something you already know, don't jump in and interrupt; rather, remain quiet" (paragraph 15). In other words, let others shine.

———

Another reason we should not break in when someone else is speaking is so that we avoid coming to an erroneous conclusion. That is perhaps the reason the Rabbis cited not interrupting another as a characteristic of a wise person (The Ethics of the Fathers 5:7).

———

10. Do not enter another person's house suddenly, thereby catching the person unawares. In modern terms, this means calling ahead. Jewish sources

———

*If the item is a coat or shoes made from animal skins, then the blessing is not extended, presumably because an animal had to suffer or die for the item to be made available.

deduce such behavior from a biblical incident involving God. When Adam ate of the fruit from the forbidden tree, God hid Himself, as it were, at the entrance to the Garden of Eden, and called out to Adam, "Where are you?" (Genesis 3:9). God, the all-knowing, obviously knew exactly where Adam was, but He did not wish to startle him (*Derech Eretz Rabbah* 5:2; see also *Niddah* 16b and *Pesachim* 112a). So, God called out, and gave Adam time to adjust to His presence. We, too, should take care not to startle others.

11. The directive not to startle others applies in one's own home as well: "Rabbi Shimon bar Yochai said: The man who enters [even] his own house . . . unexpectedly, the Holy One hates" (*Leviticus Rabbah* 21:8). Thus, parents should always knock before entering their children's rooms; everyone, children as well as adults, is entitled to privacy.

12. A man's disposition should always be pleasant [and attuned] to others" (*Ketubot* 17a). The Rabbis teach, "One should not rejoice among those who are crying, nor cry among those who are celebrating" (*Derech Eretz Rabbah* 7:7). If our mood is very different from those in our company, we should restrain our behavior or leave.

13. Do not stare at anyone, particularly a guest, while she is eating. Doing so makes the other person self-conscious in two ways: first, she might feel that we are begrudging her the food she is eating; people who are being stared at eat less, or not at all. Second, even if you have good manners, it is difficult to maintain your dignity while eating—particularly foods such as spaghetti or a peach—and being stared at. That is why almost all of us are uncomfortable being watched while eating (see *Shulchan Aruch, Orach Chayyim 170:4*). In general, staring at other people is rude and therefore inappropriate.

14. "Do not regard anyone with contempt . . . for there is no man who does not have his hour" (*The Ethics of the Fathers* 4:3). Throughout history, middle- and upper-class people have often shown poor manners to members of the lower classes, treating them without respect or consideration. The Jerusalem Talmud tells a story about the Roman emperor Diocletian (285–305 C.E.), whose father was a slave. As a young man, Diocletian worked as a swineherd near Tiberias, a city in northern Israel. When he passed the study house of Rabbi Yudan the Patriarch, the local children taunted and tormented him (one can imagine that most Jewish children, particularly in the Land of Israel, were not raised to show respect to swineherds). According to a talmu-

dic tale, when Diocletian became emperor, he summoned the Jewish leaders of Tiberias to his residence and castigated them for the mistreatment he had suffered there years earlier. The Jewish leaders responded rather lamely: "We did insult Diocletian the swineherd, but to Diocletian the emperor we willingly submit." The Talmud, however, gives Diocletian the final word: "Even so, you should not insult the humblest Roman citizen or the lowest-ranking Roman soldier" (Jerusalem Talmud, *Terumot* 8:4).

15. Good manners means treating others as equals. If someone addresses us as Mr. or Mrs., we should speak to them in the same way, and not call them by their first name. Conversely, if someone addresses us by our first name, even if we feel they are being prematurely familiar, we shouldn't call them Mr. or Mrs., thereby embarrassing them.

16. The obligation to act with good manners applies even when we are carrying out a divine command. Rabbi Israel Salanter taught, "It is not uncommon for an energetic individual to rise in the middle of the night [in the days preceding Rosh Hashana, when the early-morning *Selichot* prayers are recited] and make such noise when arising from bed that he wakes the entire household and even the neighbors. . . . He is blissfully unconscious that the loss outweighs his gain."[4] Such behavior is designated in Jewish law as *mitzvah ha-ba'ah be-aveirah*, a commandment (that is, in this case, going to synagogue) that is achieved through committing a sin (depriving other people of needed sleep; see *Sukkah* 30a).

This happens, for example, when we criticize someone so severely that she feels humiliated. If the manner in which we offer the criticism causes more harm than good, then, even if the criticism is justified, it would be better if we remained silent.

People sometimes argue that it is always better to "do [or say] something," rather than remain passive. But it is only better to "do something" if doing so will achieve more good than doing nothing.

Well-mannered children

17. Train your children to have good manners, not only for the sake of those with whom they interact, but for their own sake as well. Children who take things without asking, who receive favors but don't say "thank you," who make a mess in other people's homes and don't clean it up, become disliked. To raise a child to be an unlovable person whose presence is dreaded by others is irresponsible and a form of parental abuse. Well-mannered children have a significantly better chance of succeeding in their lives, both professionally and socially.

———

Professor of education William Kilpatrick writes: "Child-rearing experts never cease to remind us that love is the central ingredient in raising children. And, of course, they are right. But what also needs to be acknowledged by the experts is something they rarely say: It's easier to love children who are lovable. And all things considered, better-behaved children are more lovable than badly behaved children."[5]

———

COMMON SENSE:
A MORAL VALUE,
NOT JUST A
PRAGMATIC ONE

———

Who is wise? One who foresees the
consequences of his actions.

BABYLONIAN TALMUD,
Tamid 32a

11

WHY COMMON SENSE IS SO IMPORTANT

The damaging effects of a lack of common sense

1. Many people regard a lack of common sense as just a personality flaw ("Oh, she's a wonderful person, she just doesn't have common sense; that's why she's always putting her foot in her mouth"). But Jewish law sees it as a character flaw as well; a person who lacks common sense, even if she has good intentions, may well end up advocating or doing terrible things. The Talmud refers to such a person as a "pious fool" (*chasid shoteh*; Mishnah *Sotah* 3:4), and offers as an example a man who sees a woman drowning in the river, and says, "It is improper for me to look upon so immodestly dressed a woman" and thus refuses to rescue her (*Sotah* 21b). As the Mishnah comments about such people, "A pious fool . . . brings destruction on the world" (*Sotah* 3:4).

————

Many people think the Talmud's example is so far-fetched as to be absurd. But several years ago in Saudi Arabia, a fire broke out at a dormitory in a girls' school, and the "pious" Islamic firemen refused to go inside to rescue the students lest they see the girls immodestly dressed. Fifteen young women died.

————

2. Another talmudic passage describes a rabbinic scholar whose priorities were so inflexible and misplaced that he brought about the Temple's destruction. During the first century of the Common Era, a man named Bar Kamtza, because of a personal grievance against several Jewish leaders, purposely made a blemish on a sacrifice that was to be offered on the Roman emperor's behalf at the Jerusalem Temple. The Rabbis considered offering the sacrifice, despite the blemish, for the sake of maintaining good relations with Rome. Rabbi Zechariah ben Avkulas, a leading sage, objected: "Shall people say that blemished animals may be offered on the altar?"

The Rabbis then considered killing Bar Kamtza, lest he incite the emperor by telling him that the Jews refused to offer a sacrifice on his behalf. Rabbi Zechariah again protested: "Shall people say that one who causes a blemish on a sacrifice should be killed?" As the Talmud relates, the sacrifice was therefore not brought, and Bar Kamtza did, in fact, incite the Romans to come and invade Judea.* Rabbi Yochanan ben Zakkai later commented that the behavior of Rabbi Zechariah caused the destruction of the Temple and the exile of the Jews from their homeland (*Gittin* 56a).

What Rabbi Zechariah lacked, of course, was not good intentions but a proper sense of priorities, which is a serious flaw in an individual, and a fatal one in a leader. Of course, in normal times, the Jewish law that forbade the offering of animals with blemishes should be obeyed, but not if obeying it would cause an emperor with unlimited military power to believe the Jews were deliberately insulting him. And, of course, someone who intentionally blemishes an animal should not normally be put to death. But an exception should be made for someone like Bar Kamtza if his purpose was to commit treason and bring about the nation's downfall.

Rabbi Zechariah was a scholar who devoted his life to serving and teaching the Jewish community. Because of his lack of common sense, however, he inflicted greater damage on his people than did almost any of their enemies.

————

A similar misjudgment and lack of appropriate priorities seems to have characterized Mahatma Gandhi, the twentieth-century Indian saint and leader. He held pacifism to be so inviolable a value that he urged British troops to lay down their arms and not fight against Hitler; he advocated that the British people resist the Nazis only spiritually, but permit them to occupy England, take possession of their homes, and allow themselves to be killed if necessary.[1] Gandhi's advice, if followed, would have allowed the Nazis to take over much more of the world and murder far more people than they did.[†]

Billy Graham, the American Protestant evangelist, and a man who, like Gandhi, has done much good (for example, Graham helped broaden evangelical Christians' tolerance toward non-Christians), seems to have understood the Epistle to the Romans' admonition to Christians to obey the authorities (chapter 13)

---

*The Talmud does not explain why the Jews could not pacify the emperor by explaining to him what Bar Kamtza had done.

†Gandhi's advocacy of pacifism did work in India. Part of his lack of common sense was his inability to appreciate the difference between the British, who had a conscience to whom the Indian people could appeal, and the Nazis, who did not. Common sense, therefore, involves making a realistic assessment of your opponents.

as binding even when the authorities are evil.* Thus, on a trip to the Soviet Union, then under Communist rule, Graham urged attendees at a church service to do all within their power to be "better worker[s]" and more loyal citizens of a government that, among other evils, punished people for being religious Christians. Columnist George Will commented at the time, "I pray that some of today's clergy, on the left and the right, will stop acting as though pious intentions are substitutes for intelligence.²

Pious foolishness is, of course, not only the province of some religious thinkers. Immanuel Kant believed so absolutely in the immorality of lying that he even forbade lying to a would-be murderer who asked in which direction his intended victim had gone (see a discussion of Kant's position on lying on page 423).

———

3. A lack of common sense in speech—a failure of tact or sensitivity—is what causes otherwise good people to say things that hurt others. For example, the second-century Rabbi Meir criticized those whose words of consolation cause a mourner more pain than comfort: "A person who meets a mourner after one year and consoles him, to what can he be compared? To a physician who meets a person whose leg has been broken and says to him, 'Let me break your leg again, and reset it, to convince you that my treatment is good' " (*Mo'ed Kattan* 21b).

A similar lack of common sense (if it's not malice) is probably what motivates someone to praise a person in the presence of her enemies, prompting them to start enumerating all the things that they don't like about her, and thereby causing her more harm than good.

———

Rabbi Zelig Pliskin writes of the sad case of an advanced yeshiva student whose wife complained to the student's rabbi about his insensitivity: "She had many complaints, but the central one was that her husband wasn't warm enough toward

---

*Saint Paul's language in commanding obedience to governmental authority seems absolute: "You must obey all governing authorities. Since all government comes from God, the civil authorities were appointed by God, and so anyone who resists authority is rebelling against God's decision, and such an act is bound to be punished" (Romans 13:1–2). Martin Luther, the founder of Protestantism, understood Paul's theology as mandating absolute submission to authority. When peasants asked him, "What shall we do if the authorities do not cease to oppress us?" Luther answered, "If rulers are wicked and unjust, it does not mean that one may rebel against them." Later, when the peasants did rebel, Luther instructed the princes in Germany to "treat the rebels like mad dogs. Beat them, the scoundrels. He does best who throttles them first [i.e., even if he is not directly provoked]. It is good and right that everyone should fall upon them without awaiting a positive command" (cited in Hayim Greenberg, *The Inner Eye*, pages 102–112).

her. She felt lonely and miserable. The fellow wasn't mean or cruel in any way, but was sort of in his own world and tended to ignore her. The [rabbi] spoke to the young man the next day and told him to be more expressive toward his wife. On a practical level he advised him to be more openly affectionate. The fellow dutifully followed his [rabbi's] suggestion, but told his wife, 'I'm doing this because the [rabbi] told me to.' Needless to say, the [rabbi] received another call with a further complaint"[3]

A victim of a well-meaning person who lacked common sense wrote to the ethics advice column I used to write: "At a party a few months ago, when I was barely beginning to come to terms with the news that my two-month-old baby was born with a disability, I mentioned my situation to another guest. She replied, 'You must be a very nice person—I don't believe that God would give such a baby to someone who wasn't good enough to take care of him.'" The person who said these words might have thought she was being kind. But what did the mother feel? "Stunned, hurt, appalled, angry."

As advice to those who say foolish and often painful things, the late Jewish comedian and humorist Sam Levenson noted, "It's not so hard to be wise. Just think of something stupid to say and don't say it."

The indispensability of common sense

4. The story is told of a young scholar who approached the early-twentieth-century rabbi Chaim Soloveitchik* and asked the rabbi to grant him rabbinical ordination (*semicha*). Since ordination is normally given after testing the applicant's knowledge of the *Shulchan Arukh*, the sixteenth-century code of Jewish law, the rabbi began the examination by asking the young man to name the *Shulchan Arukh's* five volumes. Confused, the young student protested, "But there are only four volumes in the *Shulchan Arukh*." "No," the rabbi answered. "There is a fifth, unwritten volume. It is called common sense (*seichel*), and unless you know this volume, your knowledge of the other four volumes will not help you at all." In short, it is impossible to be wise, righteous, kind, a successful leader, and an effective rabbi without common sense.

---

*This story, which may well be apocryphal, is also attributed to other rabbis.

———

*In a similar manner, Rabbi Israel Salanter taught, "The eleventh command-
ment is 'Don't be a fool.'"*

———

Jewish law and common sense

5. Jewish law so values common sense and logic (*sevara*) that the Talmud on occasion relies upon it to decide matters of life and death. As noted
(see pages 213–214), a man informed the rabbinic sage Rava that the governor of his town had ordered him to kill someone or he himself would be
killed. He asked the rabbi what to do. Rava did not root his response in a biblical verse or a rabbinic citation, but in common sense: "What reason do you
see for thinking that your blood is redder [than that of your would-be vic-
tim]? Perhaps his blood is redder" (*Pesachim 25b*).*

It seems to me that common sense dictates that, in such a case, the man
has the right to kill the governor who issued such an order and who is now
threatening his life, but not the governor's intended but innocent victim.

———

*In a talmudic discussion of whether a judge must recuse himself from a case in
which one of the parties is a personal friend, some rabbis try to look to the Bible
for guidance, but the Talmud teaches, "Rather it is logic [which dictates that a
friend is disqualified from acting as a judge]. For what reason is an enemy disqualified? Because his attitude toward the litigant is unfavorable. In regard to a
friend as well, the same concern applies, since his attitude toward the litigant is
favorable" (Sanhedrin 29a). By rooting the law in logic, the Rabbis apparently
wanted to emphasize that God wants human beings to use common sense, in
addition to religious texts, to decide questions of Jewish law.*

———

A final thought

6. It has been rightly said that "common sense is not so common."
Unfortunately, all the knowledge and goodwill in the world are of no avail
unless we have the common sense to know how and when to apply them.

———

*In other words, you are forbidden to kill an innocent person to save your life, for his life is as
valuable as yours.

Therefore, we are all obligated to work on increasing, developing, and applying our common sense.

12

TEN PRINCIPLES OF COMMON SENSE

1. The most important principle of common sense is offered by the Talmud: "Who is wise? One who foresees the consequences of his actions" (*Tamid* 32a). This teaching suggests that we should make every effort to foresee and forestall the harm that may result from an action we take or neglect to take.

Indeed, this principle is already suggested by a law in the Torah: "When you build a new house, you shall make a parapet for your roof, so that you do not bring bloodguilt on your house if anyone should fall from it" (Deuteronomy 22:8). The rationale behind this law suggested to the Rabbis that it be broadened to prohibit keeping anything dangerous in the house. Yet today there are parents who keep loaded guns in their homes, which are found by children who then injure or kill themselves, or others.

The Talmud, basing itself on this verse, rules that it is forbidden to raise a vicious dog or keep a rickety ladder in our home (*Ketubot* 41b). Posttalmudic Jewish law ruled that if we dig a pit or well on our property (not just on public land), we must provide a railing around it or cover it to prevent an accidental fall (*Shulchan Arukh, Choshen Mishpat* 427:7).*

———

Rabbi Israel Salanter was walking with a man who was carrying an umbrella under his arm with its sharp point protruding. Rabbi Salanter warned the man not to do this, since the umbrella might poke people. The man pulled in the umbrella and held it vertically, but when a few minutes later he put it back under his arm, Rabbi Salanter reproved the man and stopped walking with him.

---

*Thus, people who build a railing around their swimming pools to protect young children from falling or jumping in are not only obeying a widely legislated civil law, but are also fulfilling a biblical law, rooted in the commonsense awareness of the possible consequences of our actions.

Many people share powerful prescription medications with others, without knowing whether they are safe for the other person, or what the appropriate dosage for that person is. This, too, violates the talmudic principle of wisdom: to foresee the possible negative consequences of our actions.

————

2. Don't speak when words are unnecessary and can do more harm than good. The Mishnah in *The Ethics of the Fathers* (4:18) teaches, "Do not try to pacify your friend in the hour of his anger." In other words, we should not try to calm someone when he is enraged and needs to express his anger.

The text continues, "nor comfort him while his dead lies before him." We should not try to stop a person from expressing grief in the moments and hours after the death of a close relative or friend, with comments such as "Don't feel bad. He is in a better place now." The deceased might well be in a better place (traditional Jewish theology does believe in an afterlife). Nevertheless, immediately after a person has died, the grief is so palpable that consolation should be postponed until the mourner is ready to hear it.

The text further says, "nor question him in the hour of his vow." For example, if we hear a person who is feuding with another say, "I swear I'll never speak to her again," we should not say something like, "You don't really mean that." Such a comment might cause the person to deepen and confirm her vow: "Yes, you can believe me. In God's Name, I mean it! I will never speak to her again."

What is wrong in all these examples is not the effort to speak to the upset party, but the timing. Thus an angry person can be pacified, but later, not at the moment he is most angry. A grieving person can be consoled with thoughts of afterlife, but not in the hours following death. And a person making a destructive or self-destructive vow can be influenced to annul it, but only when emotions have calmed.

By intervening at the wrong time, a person who lacks common sense brings about the opposite of what she intended: a reinforcement of anger, a deepening of grief, and a recommitment to the destructive vow. Conversely, one who has common sense knows how and when to apply the teaching of Ecclesiastes: "[There is] a time for silence and a time for speaking" (3:7).

The thing to do is to give the person who is upset your full attention and care. Very often, nothing need be said.

3. Don't tempt or test yourself. The Rabbis advise someone who has become a *Nazir* (a type of ascetic; such an undertaking involved, among other things, a commitment to refrain from drinking wine) to "take a circuitous route . . . but do not approach the vineyard" (*Shabbat* 13a). In other words, a *Nazir*—and, by implication, any of us—should avoid temptation. Similarly, "Rabbi Judah said in the name of Rav: 'A man is forbidden to keep in his house a measuring vessel smaller or larger [than the standard measure] even if it is to be used as a chamber pot " (*Bava Bathra* 89b; see also Deuteronomy 25:14). Either we will be tempted to use the measuring vessel to defraud others, or someone else in our house might clean it and use it for measuring. As the talmudic commentator Rashbam notes, the only proper thing to do with an inaccurate measure is to destroy it.

———

A talmudic tale teaches that David was so confident in his moral strength that he challenged God to test him. God agreed to do so, and even told him in advance that He would test him "in a matter of sexual temptation." God then arranged for David to look out the palace window, and see the beautiful but married Bathsheba, with whom he soon sinned. As the Talmud concludes, "A person should never intentionally bring himself to a test, for [even] David, King of Israel, brought himself to a test, and failed" (Sanhedrin *107a*).

———

4. "Don't rely on miracles" (Jerusalem Talmud, *Yoma* 1:4). As the Rabbis teach, "the world follows its natural course" (*Avoda Zarah* 54b); therefore, don't take undue risks, and say things such as "God will protect me." It is a serious violation of Jewish law for a dangerously ill person, in need of food or drink, to fast on Yom Kippur, or for a poor person in need of assistance to refuse to take charity.

Other rabbinic teachings are also based on the presumption that we should rely on common sense in conducting our lives. For example, *The Ethics of the Fathers* advises, "Keep far away from an evil neighbor and do not associate with the wicked" (1:7). If we have such neighbors, or if we associate with bad people, we are likely to be influenced by them. In line with this, Maimonides advocates that if the society in which we live becomes evil, we must move away ("Laws of Character Development" 6:1).

In addition, evil neighbors are likely to harm us. Thus, once Hitler came to power with the support of many millions of Germans, it should have been clear to German Jews that they were living in an incredibly hostile environment, and that they should leave as quickly as possible. As a bitter bon mot of the postwar years expressed it: "The pessimists went into exile, the optimists went to the gas chambers" (that is, in dangerous times, pessimists are realists, and therefore don't rely on miracles).

5. Don't make excessive demands of others; you will only cause them to fail. The Talmud records that Rabbi Joshua protested against those who excessively mourned the destruction of the Temple. The event was catastrophic, but Rabbi Joshua grew alarmed when these mourners told him that they would no longer eat meat, drink wine, or even eat bread and fruit; it was also clear that they thought everybody should follow their example. He therefore offered them advice that has been a mainstay of Jewish common sense ever since: "My children, come and let me advise you. Not to mourn at all is impossible, because of the destruction which has befallen us. But to mourn too much is also impossible, because we are forbidden to impose a decree on the community that the majority will find unbearable" (*Bava Bathra* 60b; see also *Avodah Zarah* 36a).

As the United States learned when it passed a constitutional amendment prohibiting alcohol, unfavorable consequences can result when "a decree [is imposed] on the community that the majority will find unbearable." For one thing, prohibiting people from doing something they like and are accustomed to do, provokes many law-abiding citizens to break the law.

This, in turn, brings about a certain contempt for the law, as people who would previously not have broken a law now do so shamelessly. Furthermore, once people start breaking some laws, they are more likely to start breaking others.

Passage of a truly unpopular law can generate other ills that are as bad, or worse, than the ill being forbidden. For example, Prohibition led to a tremendous expansion of organized crime, which became the suppliers of the forbidden liquor.

Finally, setting unrealistic standards is demoralizing. A highly intelligent woman told me that, as a child, when she came home from school with a 98 on a test, her father would ask her, "What happened to the other two points?" Perhaps the father thought he was being humorous, or perhaps he wished to make sure that his daughter didn't become arrogant, but the message that she picked up was that anything less than perfection was failure.

Couples also often set the bar so high for each other that failure and disappointment ensue. A friend told me that when he used to make romantic comments to his wife, she frequently responded, "It doesn't sound to me like you really mean it. You're just saying it because you think I want to hear it."* After trying to reassure her for years that he meant it, and often getting the same response, he began to comment less, not wanting to be rebuffed and

---

*Dr. Isaac Herschkopf commented, "In effect, she was adversely conditioning behavior she should have been positively reinforcing."

hurt. Needless to say, this did not please his wife either. In short, if we make excessive demands, we will end up with much less than if we make moderate, fair ones.

6. Don't be naïvely overtrusting. The Rabbis claim that among those whose pleas God ignores are people who lend money without witnesses and then, when the borrower denies the loan, cry out to God to help them (*Bava Mezia* 75b). If we are going to lend money like this, then we must be ready to lose it. In short, we should be intelligent enough to anticipate the tricks that can be used against us.

———

A Jewish charity fund gave out interest-free loans for extended periods of time. To ensure that the loans would be repaid, and that the fund would not be depleted, every loan required a guarantor. A rabbi who was unknown to the fund's directors asked for an unusually large loan, and listed his guarantor as God. The head of the fund responded, "In that case, God will have to be your lender as well."

———

An outgrowth of this advice: My mother, Helen Telushkin, used to say, "Not everyone deserves a second chance." Thus, judging people fairly (see chapters 5 and 6) does not mean dismissing all bad behavior as uncharacteristic or inconsequential. If we see someone acting irresponsibly or dishonestly, we should be cautious in our future dealings with that person, and not automatically assume it was a one-time event.

———

7. We should not follow the letter of the law if doing so will lead to the opposite of what the Torah intended. For example, biblical law rules that striking one's parents is forbidden, and a capital crime (Exodus 21:15). According to the rabbinic understanding of this verse, the offense merits a death sentence only if the child draws blood.* Later Jewish law further qualified the law, permitting a child to bleed a parent in a surgical procedure.† Surprisingly, the Talmud justifies this provision on the basis of the verse, "Love your neighbor as yourself." What is the possible connection between bleeding one's parent and loving one's neighbor as oneself? Common sense caused the Rabbis

---

*We have no record of this punishment ever being carried out.

†See *Sanhedrin* 84b, and the discussion of this point in the *Encyclopedia Talmudit*, volume 1, page 212. Bleeding was a procedure used in pre-modern medicine by which supposedly sick blood was drawn from an ill person with the intention of improving the person's health.

to reason thus: Treat your neighbor—in this case, your parent—as you would want to be treated; since you would want your own blood drawn in such a circumstance to improve your health, it is fine to draw your parent's blood for the same reason.

8. Don't be a pious fool. As noted (see page 136), the essence of a pious fool is that he has high-minded but misplaced priorities. Thus the Talmud tells of a rabbi who taught that "the spirit of the pious" is displeased with those who kill snakes and scorpions on the Sabbath, whereupon Rava, the son of Rabbi Huna, retorted, rather, that the spirit of the Sages is displeased with those "pious ones" who oppose killing snakes and scorpions on the Sabbath (*Shabbat* 121b). Because snakes and scorpions endanger life, it is meritorious to kill them even on the Sabbath, and anyone who endangers people's well-being by telling them not to do so brings more misery to the world.

———

Jewish history has no shortage of examples of well-meaning people whose misordered priorities caused them to advocate and adopt self-destructive policies. Thus, in the second century B.C.E., when the Maccabees launched a revolt against Antiochus, the Hellenic king of Syria, a large group of pious Jews, Chasidim, refused to fight on the Sabbath. They believed that doing so, even in self-defense, desecrated the holy day. To no one's surprise, Antiochus's troops quickly wiped them out.

Judah, the leader of the Maccabees, responded to the incident with admirable common sense: "If we all do as our brothers have done . . . then [the Syrians] will soon wipe us off the face of the earth." On that day, the Book of Maccabees records, the Jewish soldiers "decided that, if anyone came to fight against them on the Sabbath, they would fight back, rather than all die as their brothers . . . had done" (I Maccabees 2:40–41).

This has been the universally accepted Jewish law ever since. In 1973, when Egypt and Syria jointly attacked Israel on Yom Kippur, the reserve army—in addition to the standing forces—was immediately mobilized.

———

9. When you have a problem, consult with people you know to be wise: "The more counsel, the more understanding" (*The Ethics of the Fathers* 2:8). Indeed, one reason "it is not good for man to be alone" (Genesis 2:18) is that we are forced to make major life decisions without the counsel of a sympathetic friend. For example, some years ago, a friend did something that hurt

me deeply. I wrote him an angry but, in my opinion fair, letter, then showed it to several friends before I sent it. Two of them told me that one paragraph in the letter was too hurtfully personal. I deleted it. My friend responded to my letter, and apologized. Thus the matter was resolved amicably. To this day I am certain that had I not shown the letter to other people and followed their advice to delete the offensive paragraph, the letter would have been counterproductive and might have ended our friendship.

10. Don't speak about what you don't know, and don't offer advice in areas where you are not qualified. This seems to be obvious, yet many of us violate this dictum, often because of misplaced priorities. Rabbi Abraham Twerski notes that some rabbis are so committed to keeping a married couple together, in defiance both of Jewish law and common sense, that they advise abused women to remain in a marriage. They justify this by appealing to the traditional Jewish value of *shalom bayit* (a peaceful home), telling the abused spouse that Jewish tradition wishes to see a married couple stay together for the sake of this value. In fact, the very term *shalom bayit* suggests that if there is no *shalom* in the *bayit*, there is no home worth preserving. To tell a repeated victim to stay with someone who is abusing them causes the abused spouse much greater suffering than a divorce.

This principle applies to all areas in which people offer advice. Unless we are quite certain that the advice we are offering will improve the quality of life of the other person, we should not offer it.

REPENTANCE

———

As long as the candle is burning,
it is possible to mend.

RABBI ISRAEL SALANTER

13

WHO NEEDS TO REPENT?

1. Everyone needs to repent, for we all do wrongful acts sometimes. As the Bible teaches, "There is not one righteous person on earth who does only good and never sins" (Ecclesiastes 7:20).[1] The Bible underscores this by describing transgressions and even crimes committed by its *greatest* figures:

- Judah arranges to sell his brother Joseph into slavery (Genesis 37:26–27).
- Aaron (acting under pressure) helps the Israelites in the desert erect a golden calf (Exodus 32:2–5).
- Miriam and Aaron speak unfairly and jealously of Moses (Numbers 12:1–10).
- Moses loses his temper and acts so inappropriately that God denies him entry into the land of Israel (Numbers 20:9–12).
- David sleeps with another man's wife, and arranges for her husband to die in battle (II Samuel 11:1–5, 14–17).

An old adage teaches, "Great men have great flaws." But ordinary people do also; the flaws are just more visible in great people. We all commit acts for which we need to repent.

Think of some improper behavior in which you are currently engaged. If nothing comes to mind, reflect on whether you sometimes

- hurt others, including family members, by saying unkind or unfair things, particularly when you are angry
- mistreat people who work for or with you, perhaps by blaming them for something that was not their fault, criticizing them in a tactless, hurtful manner, or rarely expressing praise and gratitude
- mislead or cheat others in financial matters
- flaunt your accomplishments in a way that makes others feel insecure or inferior

• humiliate others (an especially grievous offense if done in the presence of other people)

2. The Rabbis teach that God created repentance even before He created the world (*Genesis Rabbah* 1:4). God knew that He would endow human beings with free will, which they would sometimes misuse. Thus, God needed to provide humankind with a way to atone for and correct wrongful behavior. Without a process such as *teshuva* (repentance), even good people would be overwhelmed by guilt, both toward God, Whose laws they had broken, and toward those whom they had hurt.

———

The ability of repentance to transform one's relationship with God is reflected in the story of one of the Talmud's most unusual characters, Elazar ben Dordai, who traveled all over the world to sleep with prostitutes. It once happened that he was with a prostitute who passed wind. She then commented, "Just as this wind will never return to its place, so will the repentance of Elazar ben Dordai never be accepted."

For some reason—perhaps her unflattering comparison made him realize how repugnant he had become—this strange statement cut through to Elazar's core. He immediately left her presence, went and sat between two hills and mountains, and said, "Mountains and hills, plead with God to have mercy on me."

They replied, "Before we pray for you, we must pray for ourselves, for Scripture says, 'For the mountains shall depart and the hills be removed!'" (Isaiah 54:10).

One by one, he asked heaven and earth, the sun and the moon, and the stars and constellations to intercede for him, but they each explained how they must first pray to God for themselves, to assure their own survival.

Elazar concluded, "Then the matter depends on me alone." He placed his head between his knees, and groaned and wept until his soul departed.

A heavenly voice went forth and said, "Rabbi Elazar ben Dordai has been summoned to the life of the World-to-Come!"

Rabbi Judah the Prince, when he heard of this, wept, and said, "One person may gain the World-to-Come by the toil of many years, and another gains it in one hour [through repentance]. And, it is not enough for those who repent that they are accepted; they are called 'Rabbi' too!" (Avodah Zarah 17a).

Why does this penitent profligate merit the title "Rabbi"? Rabbi Abraham Twerski, who has spent most of his professional career as a psychiatrist treating alcoholics and drug addicts, comments, " 'Rabbi' means 'teacher,' and he taught us an important lesson: A person can always redeem himself."[2]

———

3. Repentance is rooted in the optimistic idea that people can recognize sin, repent, and curtail or minimize their bad behavior. This is the message God conveys to Cain: "Sin crouches at the door . . . yet you can be its master" (Genesis 4:7).* God's assurance that we can overcome evil means that we can learn to resist it, even if we have not done so before.

4. There is a key difference between Jewish and Christian teaching on the effectiveness of repentance. Paul, the dominant formulator of early Christian theology, taught that people are damned for any sins that they commit (Galatians 3:10–13). Since each of us sins at some point, all of us will be damned. That is why, Paul teaches, God had to send Jesus (in Christianity's view, God's son), who allowed himself to be a sacrificial atonement for humankind's previous and future sins.

In contrast, the Hebrew Bible acknowledges that all people will sin (for example, I Kings 8:46, "for there is no man who does not sin"), but that God does not want to punish them for this: "As I live, says God, it is not my desire that the wicked shall die, but that the wicked shall turn from his evil ways and live" (Ezekiel 33:11; see also 18:32). Furthermore, "The evil of the wicked man shall not trip him up on the day he turns from his wicked ways" (Ezekiel 33:12).

Therefore, if you have done wrong, don't despair. The awareness that you can change your behavior and find your way back to God should fill you with a sense of resolve and hope: "Better one hour of repentance and good deeds in this world than the entire life of the World-to-Come" (*The Ethics of the Fathers* 4:17).

———

The Talmud tells of some criminals in Rabbi Meir's neighborhood who caused him so much grief that he prayed that they should die. His wife Beruriah questioned how he could believe that such a prayer was even allowed. "Do you justify it on the basis of the verse [in Psalms 104:35] 'May sinners disappear from the earth, and the wicked be no more'? But the word that means 'sinners' [chotim] can also be read as 'sins' [chatta-im; 'Let sins disappear from the earth,' which is how the biblical verse is generally understood]. Furthermore, look at the end of the verse, 'and the wicked shall be no more.' Once the sins will cease, they will no longer be wicked men! Rather, pray that they repent, and there will be no more wicked people around.' Rabbi Meir did pray for them, and the criminals repented" (Berachot 10a).

---

*Cain chooses to disregard God's advice and murders his brother Abel.

Although praying for others to repent does not usually impel them to do so, this story can still serve as a corrective to the common tendency to pray, or hope, that those who have hurt us will suffer. We should pray rather that these people no longer hurt us or anyone else and, therefore, no longer deserve punishment.

———

5. Repentance helps all who sin, Jews and non-Jews. The Bible's most famous model of repentance is Nineveh, the ancient Assyrian metropolis so filled with evil that God dispatched the prophet Jonah to go there and announced, "Forty days more and Nineveh will be destroyed" (Jonah 3:4). The city's residents believed Jonah, and immediately embarked on a serious program of repentance. When "God saw their deeds, how they were turning back from their evil ways" (3:10), He decided to spare Nineveh from destruction.

Each year on Yom Kippur, the story of Nineveh's repentance is chanted in the synagogue during the *Mincha* (afternoon) service. On the holiest day in the Jewish calendar, Jews learn from the behavior of the non-Jews of Nineveh the power of repentance.

———

The episode of Nineveh reminds us that it is never too late to repent. Elie Wiesel says, "God's will itself may change. Even though punishment has been programmed, it may be canceled. . . . Every human being is granted one more opportunity to start his life all over again."[3]

———

6. The story of Nineveh also teaches that the primary issue in repentance is ethical, rather than theological or ritual, transformation. As the Talmud comments, "The verse does not read, 'And God saw their sackcloth and their fasting,' but 'God saw what they did, how they were turning back from their evil ways'" (*Ta'anit* 16a). What matters most to God is that we stop behaving badly and start to do good.

———

The prophet Zechariah likewise emphasizes the superiority of ethical over ritual transformation. Speaking in God's Name, he dismisses those who fast but who do not transform themselves ethically: "When you fasted and lamented . . . did you fast for My benefit?" Rather, "Thus said the Lord of Hosts. Execute true justice, deal loyally and compassionately with one another. Do not defraud the widow, the orphan, the stranger, and the poor, and do not plot evil against one another" (7:5, 9–10).

———

7. Judaism regards sins against our neighbors as also being sins against God. The late theologian Rabbi Jakob Petuchowski explained: "When I steal the apple in my neighbor's orchard, I have not only wronged my neighbor, but I have also rebelled against the One who said, 'You shall not steal.' That is why, even after I have made restitution to my neighbor, I still have to clear my account with the Creator of the world."[4]

The greatness of those who repent

8. "In a place where a *ba'al teshuva* (a penitent person) stands, even the thoroughly righteous person cannot stand" (*Berachot* 34b). This counter-intuitive teaching of the Talmud—shouldn't the person who has *not* sinned be regarded as superior to the one who has?—is based on the Rabbis' profound and sympathetic understanding of human nature. As the Rabbis teach, "According to the effort is the reward" (*The Ethics of the Fathers* 5:23). It is a much greater achievement for a thief to give up stealing than for someone who has never stolen to refrain from doing so. Similarly, it is a greater accomplishment for someone who loses his temper easily to refrain from yelling when annoyed than for a calm person to do so.

Therefore the Rabbis regarded the penitent's achievement as worthy of the greatest commendation. Maimonides explains: "[The merit of a *ba'al teshuva*] is superior to that of a person who never committed a sin, because the penitent had to exert greater effort in suppressing his [evil] impulse" ("Laws of Repentance" 7:4).*

———

The Rabbis, understanding that sinners could be overwhelmed by a sense of shame, wanted to encourage penitents to retain some feeling of pride. True, it is not a good thing to have been a drug addict, but a recovering addict who has remained drug-free for years—despite numerous temptations—should take pride in this achievement.

———

*Indeed, Maimonides insists that God so appreciates the effort expended by a successful *ba'al teshuva* that such a person is "beloved and desirable before the Creator as if he never sinned" ("Laws of Repentance" 7:4).

When should a person repent?

9. Rabbi Eliezer taught, "Repent one day before your death."

His disciples asked him, "But does a person know on what day he [or she] is going to die?"

Rabbi Eliezer answered, "All the more reason, therefore, to repent today, lest one die tomorrow. In this manner, one's whole life will be spent in repentance" (*Shabbat* 153a).[5]

Don't postpone repentance in the belief that that you will have a chance to do so later. As the Rabbis teach, "A man cannot say to the Angel of Death, 'Wait till I make up my accounts' " (*Ecclesiastes Rabbah* 8:11, commenting on Ecclesiastes 8:8).

———

Implicit in this teaching is that even the elderly should continue to work on their character. If they have fallen out with others, or have certain faults, they should not think, "It's too late to mend fences" or "I am too old to change."* They should keep working on changing and improving themselves.

Rabbi Israel Salanter learned this lesson from a shoemaker whom he saw working late into the night by the light of a flickering candle. When Rabbi Salanter asked the man why he didn't stop working and go to sleep, the shoemaker responded, "As long as the candle is burning, it's possible to mend."[6]

———

10. Hillel's well-known aphorism "If not now, when?" (*The Ethics of the Fathers* 1:14) applies especially to repentance. When we are engaged in immoral behavior that is difficult to give up (such as dishonesty that is profitable, an illicit sexual relationship that gives us much pleasure), it is tempting to postpone repentance again and again. But Hillel's admonition tells us to stop now, as soon as we recognize the wrong we are doing. After all, Hillel does not say, "If not *today*, when?" He says, "If not *now*, when?"

Along the same lines, the sixteenth-century Samuel of Uceda, author of *Midrash Shmuel*, a commentary on *The Ethics of the Fathers*, teaches, "The text does not say, 'If not today, when?' in order to inform us that even today itself is in doubt regarding whether one will survive or not, for at every instant one potentially can die. Therefore, since all one has is the present moment, the text reads, 'If not now, when?' "[7]

---

*I once heard someone say, "The person who is too old to change was probably always too old to change."

Regarding those who postpone their repentance, particularly for sexual sins, until their old age, Rabbi Jonah Gerondi comments in his thirteenth-century Gates of Repentance: "The choicest repentance is that of one's youth, when you subdue your evil inclination while you are yet in possession of your energies." In other words, it is best to repent in your younger years while you still have the strength, and are able—and are probably most drawn—to sin. In a similar vein, Saint Augustine, the fourth-century Church Father, taught, "To abstain from sin when a man cannot sin is to be forsaken by sin, not to forsake it."

A final teaching

11. If you find yourself worrying that some wrong you have done has permanently alienated you from God, remember the Torah's promise that God is always near: "When you are in distress and all these things come upon you in the latter days, if you turn to the Lord your God and hear His voice . . . He will not forsake you nor destroy you" (Deuteronomy 4:30–31).

Maimonides teaches that repentance can effect a *total* reconciliation with God: "Yesterday this person was hated before God, defamed, cast away, and abominable; today, he is beloved, desirable, a favorite and a friend" ("Laws of Repentance" 7:6).

14

HOW TO REPENT

1. Repentance for sins committed against others requires the following actions:

- Acknowledge the wrong you have committed.
- Do what you can to undo the damage you have inflicted, and ask for forgiveness.
- Resolve not to sin in this way again, and carry out your commitment.

Acknowledge the wrong you have committed

2.   The first step is to admit that we have done wrong. If, for example, we have acted dishonestly, we must acknowledge this and not refer to what we did as a "mistake." A mistake is an accident, while a sin is a choice.

———

Dennis Prager elaborates on the important, and often ignored, distinction between "sin" and "mistake": "If my company has paid me to drive to Chicago, and I make a wrong turn and end up in Indiana, I have made a mistake. If my company has paid me to drive to Chicago, and I drive to Indiana in order to shop at a favorite store, I have not made a mistake. I have sinned [by deceiving my employer]. In the first case, I did not do what I intended to do—drive to Chicago; in the second case, I did what I intended to do—drive to Indiana. Mistakes are unintentional; sins are intentional."[1]

———

Some years ago, professional basketball player Latrell Sprewell of the Golden State Warriors became angry at his coach, P. J. Carlesimo, during a practice session, and started to choke him, for which act Sprewell was suspended and later traded. When he subsequently apologized, he said, "I think it's fair to say I had a bad day. . . . That's not me."

But, of course, it was Carlesimo, the victim of the attack, who had the "bad day." The player chose his words to minimize and negate the wrongfulness of his behavior. Dr. Aaron Lazare, a psychiatrist and the author of On Apology, *comments that Sprewell's "explanation compounds the original offense . . . [and] trivializes the gravity of the offense. We all have bad days but we do not go around choking people as a result."**

———

3.   The Hebrew term for acknowledging our wrongdoing is *ha-karat ha-chet,* "recognition of the sin [one has committed]." Without such recognition, we will never repent and improve, for we will feel no need to do so. The medieval *Path of the Righteous (Orchot Tzaddikim)* explains: "If one does not know wherein he has transgressed, how can he regret what he has done?" ("The Gate of Repentance").

Try to think of at least one or two things—and possibly more—you have done that you know are wrong (see, for example, the list on pages 150–51). Even if you are not ready to give up these actions, at least recognize that they

———

**On Apology,* 124. I have drawn several examples from this book.

are wrong. Just reflecting on your actions—even without committing yourself to change—will start to affect your conduct.

————

A non-ethical, but relevant, example of how such recognition can affect us is a food diary. Overweight people who simply write down what they eat will start to lose weight even without going on a formal diet. Awareness alone inevitably affects one's behavior (see footnote on page 46).

————

4. Painful and embarrassing as it might be, we should confess our sins aloud (though not necessarily in the presence of others).* By admitting a sin out loud (instead of just mentally acknowledging a wrong we have committed), we will be less likely to try and rationalize it. Also, we are more likely to be horrified by what we have done, and motivated to atone.

————

The power of verbal confession is borne out by the experience of Alcoholics Anonymous. Realizing that many alcoholics insist that they can control their drinking, attendees at AA meetings start their public remarks with an acknowledgment of their addiction: "My name is John and I am an alcoholic."†

Without such an admission, alcoholics will be much less motivated to stop drinking, since they will continue to believe that they can control their actions. The same applies to a host of people who don't control their behavior, including drug addicts, gamblers, sex addicts, dishonest people, and those who say cruel things when angry. Hence, Narcotics Anonymous, Gamblers Anonymous, and anger management groups.

———————

*Maimonides, "Laws of Repentance" 1:1, basing himself on Numbers 5:6–7. The purpose of this confession is to shock us into righting the wrong we have done. If others are present, we are more likely to try to downplay or rationalize our wrongful behavior. It is usually easier to be honest with ourselves, and about ourselves, when we are alone.

†Even during these public confessions, the speakers maintain some sense of anonymity by giving only their first names; one presumes that that is why the organization has the word "anonymous" in its name. Also, groups such as AA are an exception to the rule of not generally confessing to one's wrongdoings in public; there is less sense of shame at owning up to one's failings at such a meeting, since the people there have all engaged in the same misbehavior. However, it is harder—and sometimes counterproductive—on our ego to confess in the presence of those who have not engaged in similar behavior. Think, for example, of some incident in your life of which you would be embarrassed were it to become known to others. Obviously, it would be harder for you to own up to it in the presence of those who have never done such a thing than in the presence of those who have.

———

From Judaism's perspective, repentance without verbal acknowledgment is invalid: A person may think to herself, "From now on, I shall be honest in my business dealings." Or, "I'll stop berating my child when he can't solve his math problems" ("What's the matter with you? Are you stupid?"). Rabbi Joseph Soloveitchik teaches that such thoughts are commendable, "but as long as they are not expressed verbally, they do not comprise an act of repentance . . . only after confession has been made can repentance be effective."[2] As the Talmud teaches, "devarim she-be-lev einam devarim, thoughts in the heart [that is, thoughts that have not been articulated] are as if they do not exist" (Kiddushin 49b).

———

My friend Dr. Isaac Herschkopf suggests that an important first step in recognizing and acknowledging our sin is to write out what we have done: "I have patients write letters of confession and contrition to those they have wronged, even if they don't send them. Writing out one's sins is incredibly cathartic [and can motivate a person to change]." But this is only a first step.

———

5. We should be specific about the wrong we have done. This is difficult, because we all like to repress unpleasant memories. Nevertheless, we should not engage in such generalizations as "I've been dishonest" or "I haven't been a good husband [or wife] to my spouse." Such generalizations, even if verbalized, allow us to avoid fully confronting the damage and hurt we have inflicted. Instead, we should say (even if only in a whisper), "I was dishonest in my business dealings with Max. I misled him into thinking that the used car I sold him was in better condition than it was, and I charged him $1,500 more than the car was worth. That was an act of deceit." Or, "I've been dishonest with my wife. I cheated on her."

6. We should not rationalize or minimize what we have done. The Bible suggests that God is most apt to forgive sins when the sinner doesn't try to evade responsibility for the wrong he has done. Thus, when the prophet Samuel reproves King Saul for disobeying a divine edict, Saul, instead of acknowledging his guilt, tries to defend his behavior, and God immediately decrees that the kingship be taken from him (I Samuel 15:13–23). In contrast, when the prophet Nathan reproves King David for a most serious offense, and David immediately owns up to his guilt—"I have sinned before the Lord"—he is punished, but then forgiven (II Samuel 12:13–14).

———

King Ahab is a more egregious example than Saul of a monarch who refused to own up to his evil. Ahab's wife, Queen Jezebel, arranged for the execution of Navot, an innocent man, so that Ahab could take possession of his field. But when the prophet Elijah confronted him at the field, and demanded, "Have you murdered and also inherited?" the monarch's first response was not shame or guilt, but anger at Elijah: "So you have found me, my enemy" (I Kings 21:20). *

For several years, a prisoner I had been counseling regarded anyone who reproved him as an enemy.

———

Wrongs committed by a nation against individuals or a whole people must be acknowledged as well. In 2000, Kevin Gover, assistant secretary of the Bureau of Indian Affairs for the U.S. Department of the Interior, made a public admission of the terrible crimes committed by the American government against Native Americans: "We must first reconcile ourselves to the fact that the works of this Agency have at various times profoundly harmed the communities it was meant to serve." Surveying the history of Native Americans under the American government, Gover said, "By threat, deceit, and force, these great tribal nations were made to march one thousand miles to the west, leaving thousands of their old, their young and their infirm in hasty graves along the Trail of Tears." He described in detail the means by which the Indian population was reduced: "the decimation of the mighty bison herds, the use of the poison alcohol to destroy mind and body, and the cowardly killing of women and children." The result was "a tragedy on a scale so ghastly that it cannot be dismissed as merely the inevitable consequence of the clash of competing ways of life." Furthermore, "after the devastation of tribal economies and the deliberate creation of tribal dependence on the services provided by this Agency, this Agency set out to destroy all things Indian," by forbidding the speaking of Indian languages, prohibiting traditional religious activities, and making Indians ashamed of who they were.†

In this model apology, no effort was made to downplay or rationalize the crimes committed against Native Americans.

———

---

*Only after Elijah prophesies the terrible suffering that will come upon Ahab as a divine punishment for his sin does the monarch rend his clothes. He apparently doesn't regret what he and his wife have done, but wants to avoid punishment.

†Cited in Aaron Lazare, *On Apology*, pages 81–83. Should Americans such as myself, whose grandparents did not come to this country until the late nineteenth and early twentieth century, be ashamed of how our country treated the Indians? Yes. As Dr. Lazare explains: "If we can be proud of national accomplishments not of our making, so, too, must we accept shame for national deeds not of our making. . . . [And] just as people take pride in things for which they had

7. Maimonides teaches: "How does one confess? He states, 'I implore You, God. I have sinned, I have transgressed, I have committed iniquity before You by doing the following [list the sin]. Behold, I regret and I am embarrassed by my deeds!'" ("Laws of Repentance" 1:1).

———

Maimonides then instructs the sinner to say, "I promise never to repeat this act again" (he mentions this again in 2:2). There are two possible concerns about a sinner making such a statement:

- *If the sinner repeats the sin, then, in addition to the sin he has committed, he will be adding that of breaking a promise to God.*
- *The fact that we confess the same sins in the* Machzor *(High Holiday prayer book) each year suggests that there are many sins we will probably commit again—although, one hopes, with declining intensity and frequency.*

———

8. Along with an admission of guilt, as Maimonides notes, we should feel ashamed of what we have done. The Talmud believes that such embarrassment constitutes a form of repentance: "Whoever commits a sin and is embarrassed about it, is forgiven for all his sins" (*Berachot* 12b).

Do what you can to undo the damage you have inflicted, and ask for forgiveness

9. "For sins between man and God (such as eating unkosher food), Yom Kippur atones. But for sins committed against another, Yom Kippur does not atone, until one appeases one's fellow" (Mishnah *Yoma* 8:9). Appeasing one's fellow is understood as meaning both that we undo, to the extent possible, the damage we have inflicted, and that we ask for forgiveness. As the Mishnah teaches regarding physical harm, "Even though the offender pays back the damage and fines to the victim, the offense is not forgiven until he asks the victim's pardon" (*Bava Kamma* 8:7).*

---

no responsibility (such as famous ancestors, national championships of their sports teams, and great accomplishments of their nation), so, too, must these people accept the shame (but not the guilt) of their family, their athletic teams, and their nations." Lazare concludes, "Accepting these responsibilities is part of what we mean when we speak of having a national identity" (pages 41 and 84).

*Maimonides rules that as soon as we pay for the damage done to another's property, we receive atonement. But if we physically hurt someone, an act that inflicts greater emotional pain than

The responsibility to undo the damage

In the town of Radin, where the Chaffetz Chayyim lived, an aged Jew fell into an open pit and broke his leg. A resident of the town brought the suffering man into his home and nursed him back to health. Deeply impressed by the kindness extended to the old man, the Chaffetz Chayyim told the host, "I pray that my reward [in the World-to-Come] be as great as yours [for your extraordinarily kind behavior]." The man responded, "I deserve no praise. It was I who dug the pit and left it uncovered."³

One's responsibility to ask forgiveness

The contemporary Mussar teacher Rabbi Yechiel Perr tells of a teacher he had when he was a teenager, who was strict about not allowing students who arrived late to enter the classroom: "If you were brave, you could knock; he might answer or he might not. If he did, he might let you in, or he might not. He might just close the door in your face. He was a wonderful teacher; he just didn't tolerate teenage sloppiness. . . . One Friday, a boy named Pinchas knocked on the door. It was nine-thirty-one. The teacher opened the door, looked out, then closed the door and returned to his class. When the class met again the following Monday, the teacher came in as usual, but before he began the lesson, he spoke to the boys: 'I didn't know that Pinchas is the son of a baker,' he said, 'and that he stays up all night on Thursdays helping his father bake for Shabbat. And, after working the whole night, he goes home, takes a shower, changes his clothes, and then rushes here to class.' He then turned to the boy with tears in his eyes: 'Pinchas, can you forgive me for not letting you into the class on Friday? Can you ever forgive me? I was so wrong.' "⁴

It is never too late to own up. Dr. Aaron Lazare tells of a seventy-one-year-old man, Manny, who was bothered throughout his life by a hurt he had inflicted on a childhood friend, Eddie. A full sixty years after the event, Manny wrote Eddie and recalled the incident. A group of boys had gathered around Eddie, and were taunting him for being a sissy and throwing a ball the way a girl would. When Eddie recognized Manny coming toward him, he said something like "I knew

---

damaging property, we don't receive atonement until we ask for forgiveness ("The Laws of Personal Injury" 5:9).

you would stand by me." But Manny hadn't stood by him, and ended up remaining with the other boys. As he wrote Eddie, "I saw your disappointment in me, as I inflicted such cruelty upon you." Manny concluded his letter, "So now I am apologizing for my behavior then on Wildwood Street. Though I wanted to say these words to you [over the years], I felt that I couldn't. Typing these words has been difficult enough for me. Your loving friend, Manny." He then delivered the letter in person.

Manny wrote to Dr. Lazare: "As Eddie read this letter, I saw his face first register surprise, then a smile slowly spread over his features. We hugged, and he said, 'I love you.' He explained that he had a weak throwing arm throughout his life, which was the reason he threw the way he did." As Manny told Lazare, "One end result of my letter of apology is that I have been released of that haunting image of hurting Eddie." When Eddie died a year and a half after receiving the letter, Manny realized how much peace he felt, a peace that would have been denied him had Eddie died before the apology had been extended.[5]

---

10. Even if we upset somebody only through harsh words, without committing any tangible act of injury, we are still required to seek forgiveness (Maimonides, "Laws of Repentance" 2:9).

11. We should express shame for what we did. When asking for forgiveness, people often say, "I beg your forgiveness for what I did to you." "Beg" is an appropriate word. When we hurt someone, in addition to any damage we inflict, we probably also humiliate that person. By apologizing, or even begging for forgiveness, we place ourselves in a position comparable to that in which we have placed our victim, and therefore become worthy of forgiveness.*

Dr. Aaron Lazare describes how his own embarrassment and expressions of shame healed a patient's hurt: "Several years after [one of my patients] had completed psychotherapy, she left a message for me to phone her. I misplaced the message and consequently failed to phone her. Later, she wrote me a scathing letter informing me that by not returning her phone call, I had failed to respond to her need for me to visit her when she was hospitalized for a potentially serious

---

*I heard this insight from philosophy professor Joshua Halberstam. It is more effective to use the words "I beg your forgiveness" than "I beg your pardon," since the latter expression is so commonly used (for example, when we bump into someone on the street) that the word "beg" no longer connotes anything shameful.

condition [I did not know from the message that she was ill or in the hospital]. She experienced my lapse as both 'abandonment and humiliation.' I was mortified by my lapse and asked to meet with her to offer my heartfelt apology. At the end of our interchange, she looked relieved. I asked her how she understood our current interaction. She told me that my failure to phone had made her feel she was not as important as I was. My apology, she said, made us equals."[6]

————

12. Although the best way to seek pardon is to go to the person you've hurt, confess what you have done, and ask her forgiveness, many people make their apologies too broad (in other words, just as acknowledgment of one's sin must be specific, so, too, must one's apology). For example, many parents, prior to Rosh Hashana, will say to their children, "I'm sorry if I did anything during this past year that hurt you."* Such a general and vague apology is insufficient; it doesn't acknowledge the specific hurt the child has suffered, and it doesn't force the parent to confront what she said or did. It would be preferable to say, "I'm sorry I yelled at you in front of your friends." Or, in a worse case, "I'm sorry I locked you in your room for not listening [parents who do such a thing should strongly consider getting therapy]. It was wrong of me. Please forgive me."

The more specific our acknowledgment of the wrong we have done, the more likely it is that our victim will feel mollified and perhaps even healed.

13. However, there *are* instances when it is unwise to be so specific, because doing so will cause our victim anguish. For example, if we have passed on a reputation-destroying rumor about someone, she will probably be devastated to learn that many people now think ill of her. In such a case, Rabbi Israel Salanter cautions that it is better to say nothing. We are obligated, however, to go to all those we spoke to and try to undo the damage.

————

The Chaffetz Chayyim disagreed with Rabbi Salanter's ruling, arguing that we are obligated to confess to the victim what we have done, even if he did not previously know about it (see Chaffetz Chayyim, "Laws of Lashon hara" 4:12; the exception would be if we knew the listeners had disbelieved us). Rabbi

————

*Dr. Isaac Herschkopf comments, "Such a statement is not even an apology. The minute you include the word 'if,' you are not acknowledging that you necessarily did anything wrong."

Salanter argued, however, that our desire to repent shouldn't give us the right to cause emotional pain to our victim; in other words, there are times when confession might be good for our soul but terrible for the person we have injured.

———

14. After we have requested forgiveness, we should ask the person whom we hurt to pray to God on our behalf. This advice is based on three biblical episodes. In Genesis, King Abimelech, believing the matriarch Sarah to be unmarried, took her to his palace. He learned in a dream that she was Abraham's wife. God then indicated in a vision to Abimelech: "Now, therefore, restore the man's wife . . . and he [Abraham] will pray for you and you shall live" (Genesis 20:7).

Later, when Miriam and Aaron sinned against Moses, and Miriam was punished (it seems that she was the primary offender), Aaron asked Moses to pray for her; after Moses did so, she was soon healed of leprosy (Numbers 12:11–13).

Finally, Job's friends slandered him by insisting that all his sufferings (the death of his ten children, his sickness, and the loss of his wealth) were God's punishment for evil he had done. At the end of the book, God reproved the friends for having spoken so cruelly, then instructed them to pacify Job: "Let Job, my servant, pray for you, for to him I will show favor and not treat you vilely" (Job 42:8).

15. Even when your victim forgives you without your apologizing, you are still required to apologize; if you do not do so, God might not forgive you. This is implied by the wording of the earlier cited talmudic teaching on repentance and forgiveness: "For sins between man and God, Yom Kippur atones. But for sins committed against another, Yom Kippur does not atone, *until one appeases one's fellow*" (Mishnah *Yoma* 8:9; emphasis added). In short, on Yom Kippur, God forgives those who have sinned against Him and repented. God also forgives those who have sinned against their neighbor, but only if they have appeased their neighbor. If they don't, the text implies, God will not forgive them even if their neighbor does so.

The Talmud recounts an incident (*Yoma* 87a) that reinforces this idea. When Rabbi Zeira had been wronged, he would go out of his way to encounter the person who had mistreated him, so as to give him an opportunity to apologize. But why did he do this? Couldn't he have just stayed at home and recited a prayer, such as, "I forgive all those who pained me"

(*Megillah* 28a)?* Apparently, Rabbi Zeira believed that the offender was obliged to appease his victim.

The goal of repentance, therefore, is not just to win forgiveness, but to transform the sinner. Forgiveness granted without an apology by the offender will not normally do this; thus, to win God's forgiveness, we must seek out our victim and beg his forgiveness.

––––

Even when victims of the most terrible crimes extend forgiveness to their assailants (see, for example, pages 201–204), we cannot assume that, in the absence of sincere repentance, God forgives the criminals.

––––

16. "If one sinned and others are now suspected of having committed the offense, one is obligated to say, 'I am the one who did this act,' so as to remove suspicion from those who are innocent" (*Sefer Chasidim*, paragraph 22).

––––

In Victor Hugo's classic novel Les Misérables, *Valjean, the novel's hero and an ex-convict, faces the agonizing decision of whether to turn himself in when Champmathieu, a man who physically resembles him, is tried for offenses attributed by the police to Valjean. Valjean arrives at the courthouse just as Champmathieu is about to be convicted, and interrupts the trial to reveal that it is he, not Champmathieu, whom the police are seeking.*

––––

17. If you hurt someone who died before you sought forgiveness, you should go to the person's grave and say, "I sinned against God, the Lord of Israel, and against this person by doing the following. . . ." (Maimonides, "Laws of Repentance" 2:11); Maimonides also rules that this should take place in the presence of a *minyan*.†

It seems to me that if it will be highly humiliating for a person to say what the sin was (particularly if the sin was not widely known), one should not confess in the presence of other people (just as one would not confess in

––––––––––––

*The Talmud cites this as a prayer offered by Mar Zutra.

†Jewish law traditionally defines a *minyan* as ten or more adult (i.e., over Bar Mitzvah) male Jews; Conservative Judaism rules that a *minyan* may be composed of ten adult Jews, male or female.

public if the victim was alive). Thus, a woman confided to a rabbi that she had long ago committed adultery with a married man, and regretted that she had not sought forgiveness from the man's wife, who knew of the affair, but had died. The rabbi told her of this ruling of Maimonides (the thought of going to the grave with a *minyan* horrified her), and advised her that it would be worthwhile for her to go to the grave of the woman and beg forgiveness, even without others present.

————

The late Israeli chief rabbi, Abraham Isaac Kook, was defamed by many religious zealots during his lifetime; among the things for which they criticized him was his friendship and respect for the nonreligious pioneers, the chalutzim, *who were settling in Palestine, and for his openness to Jews engaging in secular as well as religious studies. Meir Madan, an admirer of Rabbi Kook, recalled that some years after Rabbi Kook's death, on his* yahrzeit, *he and some others of the Rav's adherents were praying together at the Kotel, the Western Wall: "When we finished praying, a young Torah scholar, dressed in ultra-Orthodox garb, approached us. He removed his shoes [in the manner of a mourner] and said in a tearful voice, 'When I was a young boy, people taught me to curse and defame the holy* tzaddik *whose* yahrzeit *is today . . . and I did as they said. Now, however, I understand the severity of my actions. Rightfully, I should prostrate myself at his grave and beg forgiveness, but I cannot do so, for I am a Kohen.** *Therefore, I beg of you, holy assembly'—at this point he fell to the ground and wept bitterly—'that you be my witnesses that I regret what I did and beg forgiveness.'"*

Madan recalls that all those present were in shock and, at first, did not know how to react. Finally, Madan helped the man to his feet and said to him, "You are forgiven; you are our brother." The man thanked them, and walked away, still shedding tears.[7]

————

18. If you have stolen from someone, cheated them, or simply owe someone a debt, and the person dies, then return the money to the heirs. If there aren't any, Jewish law rules that you should give the money to a Jewish court (Maimonides, "Laws of Repentance" 2:11). An alternative—if there are no heirs—might be to distribute the money as charity in the name of the deceased.

———————

*Jewish law forbids *Kohanim*, priests, from going to a cemetery.

The final condition of repentance: Resolve not to sin in this way again, and carry out this resolution.

19. "How is one proven to be a true penitent?" Rabbi Judah asked, and answered: "If the opportunity to commit the same sin presents itself on two occasions and the sinner does not yield to it" (*Yoma* 86b). Maimonides expands on this talmudic teaching: "What constitutes complete repentance? When one is confronted by the identical situation in which he previously sinned and it is within his power to commit the sin again, and he nevertheless does not succumb because he wishes to repent, and not because he is afraid or physically too weak [to repeat the sin]. For example, if he had relations with a woman forbidden to him and, after some time, he is alone with her, still in the throes of his passion [literally, 'in love'] for her, and his virility is unabated, and they are in the same place where they previously sinned; if he [or she] abstains and does not sin, this is a true penitent" ("Laws of Repentance" 2:1).*

———

Many years after Joseph's brothers sell him into slavery, he rises to the second highest position in Egypt, and his brothers, confronted by starvation in the land of Canaan, come to Egypt to buy grain. There they meet up with Joseph, who recognizes them, although they don't recognize him. After several meetings, Joseph levels a false accusation of stealing against his brother Benjamin, telling the other brothers that they can go free but that he will keep Benjamin as a slave.

Judah, who twenty-two years earlier had first proposed selling Joseph into slavery, steps forward and pleads with Joseph to take him as a slave, and to let Benjamin go free. At that moment Joseph, overcome with emotion, sends all the Egyptians out of the room, and reveals himself to his brothers. The fact that Judah, who years earlier had sold his brother into slavery, now offers himself as a substitute for his younger brother is proof to Joseph that Judah's—and by implication his other brothers'—repentance is complete (Genesis 44:18–45:2). Rashi, in his commentary to Sanhedrin *31b, relates the story of Nathan bar Ukva, who was very attracted to a married woman. His desire for her was so great that*

———

*Rabbi Jakob Petuchowski comments: "In other words, *teshuva* is complete only once the *ba'al teshuva* is no longer subject to the same temptation. This, I submit, amounts to nothing less than a total change of personality" (*Studies in Modern Theology and Prayer*, page 21). Alternatively, one can argue that a penitent's personality need not undergo so great a transformation, but just his behavior. Thus, even if you remain attracted to, and tempted by, the same man or woman, but resist the temptation, you are still a valid penitent.

when it couldn't be satisfied, he became sick and was confined to bed. A short time later the woman suffered severe financial losses, and sent word to him that if he helped her, she would consent to his wishes. He complied with her request. Yet when the woman came to him, Nathan, overcome by a sense of the great wrong he was about to do, repented and sent the woman home untouched. Later, when he went out into the street, his face was radiant with a divine light.[8]

————

Additional ways of repentance

20. Use the very limbs or faculty you sinned with in order to do good. The medieval *Gates of Repentance* (1:35) teaches: If your feet ran to do evil, let them now run to do good. If your tongue lied, be exceedingly careful to be truthful, and use your mouth to speak words of loving-kindness. For example, violent hands should be opened in charity, and the troublemaker should become a peacemaker. If you slapped a child, use your hand now to caress him. If you used your brain to deceive others, apply it now to find ways to help others.

21. To compensate for wrongs you have committed, increase your good deeds. For example, give more to charity than you normally do, acknowledging to yourself that the additional money is to help you atone (Maimonides, "Laws of Repentance" 2:4). And while it is always good to expand our observance of both ethical and ritual commandments, we should pay greater attention to the ethical. As Rabbi Nachman of Bratslav taught: "God prefers a person performing commandments which are also pleasing to other people over those which are exclusively between man and his Maker."[9]

22. If you intend to commit a sin, and through circumstances beyond your control you are prevented from doing so, you should still repent. The Talmud rules that if a person ate meat that he thought was pig, but it turned out to be lamb (which is kosher), he should nonetheless repent for his intention (*Kiddushin* 81b). Similarly, if you planned to cheat or deceive someone, and for some reason your plan did not work, you should still repent.

23. The Chaffetz Chayyim suggests that if you spoke *lashon hara* (a mean-spirited truth), and thereby damaged someone's reputation, you should make a special effort to encourage others to observe the Jewish laws of ethical speech. This means refraining from speaking ill of others, except to those who have need of the information (obviously the most fundamental require-ment of repentance in such a case is to seek out those to whom you told the *lashon hara*, and try to undo the damage; for a discussion of the laws of *lashon hara*, see chapters 37–43).

Ways to avoid sinning in the future

24. When you are contemplating doing something wrong, remember that God sees everything. "Think about three things and you will not be overcome by the desire to sin: Know what is above you: an eye that sees, an ear that hears, and all of your actions are recorded in a book" (*The Ethics of the Fathers* 2:1). Most of us act in a law-abiding manner when in the presence of a policeman; religious people should realize that God, though invisible, is always present.

25. Do not put yourself in a situation where you are likely to sin. Some-one who has transgressed sexually, for example, should not allow himself to be alone with a person to whom he is attracted, but who is forbidden to him. A gambling addict should not set foot in a casino, even if it's just to meet a friend. A recovering speaker of *lashon hara* should walk away from people who start to gossip. In general, stay away from any friends or relatives who exert a negative influence on you (for more on this, see pages 178–179).

———

This is the prudent way to act, though the talmudic definition of a true penitent cited earlier—one who encounters the same temptation twice and resists it—might encourage some people to seek out temptation so as to prove themselves true penitents. I believe this to be unwise, and understand the talmudic criterion as applying only if the temptation presents itself on its own—for example, if you accidentally encounter the person with whom you committed adultery—and not that you seek out opportunities to be alone with that person just so that you can prove to yourself that you won't sin.

———

26. Think through the consequences of an action before you do it. Rabbi Abraham Twerski advises: "A simple and good guide to proper behav-ior is to ask yourself, 'Would there ever be a reason why I would have to deny having done what I am about to do?' If the answer is 'Yes," don't do it."[10] The mother of a friend advised him when he had to make an ethically difficult choice: "Imagine that what you choose to do will be published on the front page of tomorrow's newspaper. Would you still do it?"

27. In order to avoid committing a sin again, resolve that you will never lie about what you have done. Thus, when you're tempted to commit this sin, you'll think, "If somebody asks me if I did this, and I tell the truth, I'll get into trouble and be very embarrassed. But if I lie, I'll break the one rule to which I agreed to adhere" (*Pele Yoetz*).[11] Keeping this one rule can restore you to full repentance (for more on this technique, see page 401).

After you have repented

28. Once you have repented for an act, move on with your life and don't dwell on what you did (except in a case where you inflicted an irrevocable hurt, and might still have to go on helping the person). As the Talmud teaches (*Yoma* 86b): "The sins that a person confessed this Yom Kippur, he should not confess on the next Yom Kippur [except if he repeated them during the year]. . . . And if he did not commit the sins again, but still confessed them again, about such a person the Bible says, 'Like a dog who returns to his vomit, so is a fool who repeats his foolishness'" (Proverbs 26:11).

——

My grandfather, Rabbi Nissen Telushkin, offered this analogy to explain the Psalmist's words "Turn away from evil and do good" (34:15). If one is given water filled with salt to drink, one can either remove the salt, an impossible task without sophisticated equipment, or one can add so much fresh water to the salt water that the salt becomes virtually unnoticeable. So, too, my grandfather argued, "One who has sinned should not waste his time aggravating over what cannot be changed, but instead do so many acts of kindness that eventually they will overwhelm the earlier, wrongful acts, and make them seem much less significant."

——

Repentance at the end of life

29. Encourage those who are near death to repent: "If one took ill and is leaning toward death, those at his side should say to him, 'Confess your sins'" (*Shabbat* 32a). The *Shulchan Arukh,* in discussing the *vidui,* the

confessional prayer, describes how to minimize the sick person's fear and terror: "If a person feels death approaching, he should recite the *vidui*. And he should be reassured by those around him: 'Many have said the *vidui* and not died, and many have not said the *vidui* and have died.' And if he is unable to recite it aloud, he should confess it in his heart. And if he is unable to recite it by himself, others may recite it with him or for him" (*Yoreh Deah* 338:1).

What follows is the traditional text of the *vidui* prayer:

> *O my God, the God of my ancestors, accept my prayer and do not reject my supplication. Forgive me all the sins that I have committed in my lifetime. I am ashamed and abashed for all the wrong things that I have done. Please accept my pain and suffering as an atonement and forgive my sins, for against You alone have I sinned.*
>
> *May it be Your will, Adonai, my God and God of my ancestors, that I sin no more. With Your great mercy, cleanse me of my sins, but not through suffering and pain. Send a complete healing to me and to all those who are stricken.*
>
> *I acknowledge to You, Adonai, my God and the God of my ancestors, that my life is in Your hands. May it be Your will to heal me. But if You have decreed that I shall not recover from this illness, I accept the decree from Your hand. May my death atone completely for all the sins and all the transgressions that I have committed before You. Shelter me in the shadow of Your wings and grant me a portion in the World-to-Come.*
>
> *Father of all orphans and guardian of widows, be with and protect my dear family, for my soul is bound up with theirs.*
>
> *Into Your hands do I commit my soul. You have redeemed me, Adonai, O God of truth.*
>
> *Sh'ma Yisra'el, Adonai Eloheinu, Adonai Echad (Hear O Israel, the Lord is our God, the Lord is One).*

——

Despite the odd insistence in the vidui *prayer that all sins are sins exclusively against God, if the dying person has sinned against another person, and has never repented, or has offered an inadequate repentance, she should be strongly encouraged to do so even at this late time. If extending an apology is possible, it should be done. And if offering some sort of recompense for the damage she inflicted is appropriate, that too should be done as well.*

——

Helping those who repent

30. Never embarrass anyone by taunting him with his earlier misdeeds (see Mishnah *Bava Mezia* 4:10). According to Maimonides, "It is an utter sin *(chet gamur)* to say to one who has repented, 'Remember your previous sins'" ("Laws of Repentance" 7:8). It is also wrong to remind anyone of behavior that he now regrets.

———

It is so important to avoid embarrassing penitents that the Torah did not set aside a separate area for the bringing of sin offerings, so that onlookers would not be able to identify the people bringing them (see the discussion of this point in Sotah 32b).

———

Every year during Rosh Hashana and Yom Kippur, a rabbi I know offers several communal aliyot *at his congregation, inviting people in different categories to come up to bless God and the Torah; for example, all those who will have surgery in the coming weeks, or all those who have not had an* aliyah *in a long time. On Yom Kippur, one group he invites for an* aliyah *is those who have a sin that is weighing on them, and who wish to open their hearts to God. But so as not to embarrass or expose those people (a man's wife might wonder, for example, why he is going up for the* aliyah*), he simultaneously invites up all those who have a special request to make of God. He has long noted that this is the* aliyah *for which the most people come up.*

Yet another reason why reminding penitents of their misbehavior is wrong: One motivation for repentance is the desire to restore one's good name. By reminding people of their bad behavior, we make them feel that, no matter how much good they now do, they will always remain associated with the wrong they did. This is demoralizing, and might make a penitent feel that it is not worth changing.

———

31. Don't feel superior to *ba'alei teshuva* (penitents); indeed, we should all be *ba'alei teshuva.* The term *ba'al teshuva* is associated today primarily with formerly non-observant Jews who have undertaken to start observing Judaism's rituals. In the observant world, *ba'alei teshuva* are contrasted with Jews who are FFB ("*frum* [i.e., Orthodox] from birth"). But in the sphere of ethics, all of us need to be *ba'alei teshuva.* How many of us can claim perfection, even near-perfection, in our observance of the commandments "Love your neighbor as yourself" and "Do not go about as a talebearer." Therefore, since we have all committed sins for which we need to atone, it follows that we must all be *ba'alei teshuva*.

A final thought

32. Every night, Rabbi Levi Yitzchak of Berditchev would write down any sins he had committed that day. He would then read the list aloud to himself and say, "Today, I, Levi Yitzchak, did such-and-such. But tomorrow, I, Levi Yitzchak, will not do such-and-such."

While it is hard to improve ourselves in many areas at the same time, we might try this technique for one bad trait at a time, each night monitoring the conduct we are striving to improve.

15

OBSTACLES TO REPENTANCE

1. *Blaming others*. This is perhaps the most obvious and common impediment to repentance; the Bible depicts it as being as old as humankind. Genesis 2:17 tells of the one command God gives Adam: not to eat of fruit of the Tree of Knowledge. The serpent persuades Eve to eat the fruit and she persuades Adam to do the same. When God reproves the couple for violating His edict, Eve defends herself by blaming the serpent, and Adam in turn blames Eve (Genesis 3:12–13).

Do not blame others for your bad behavior.

The Talmud teaches that a person can't exonerate himself with the defense that "I was just following orders" (see Kiddushin 42b). Since God is higher than any human being, one does not have the right to obey a command issued by a human being if it contravenes one of God's commandments (for a further discussion of this principle, see pages 30–31).

---

2. *Rationalizing what we have done*. On Yom Kippur, we confess in the synagogue service, "for the sin we committed *be-oness* (under duress)." Yet, if we were truly forced to commit a sin, there would be no obligation for us to repent (for example, if someone pointed a gun at us, demanding that we eat unkosher food, and we did so; see Maimonides, commentary to Mishnah *Yoma* 8:6).* So why do we repent on Yom Kippur for sins we were "forced" to commit?

The late Israeli philosopher and educator Professor Ernst Simon suggested that there are sins that we claim we were forced to commit, but in truth we were not. For example, many people rationalize their business deceptions by claiming that they were under financial pressure, yet they exaggerate the pressure. After all, there are many people under similar or greater monetary stress who did not engage in deception. As Supreme Court justice Louis Brandeis wrote: "The irresistible is often only that which is not resisted."

———

On occasion, even highly moral people try to rationalize errant behavior. Aaron, under pressure from the Israelites, helped them build the Golden Calf. When his brother Moses reproved him, "What did this people do to you that you brought such great sin upon them?" Aaron refused to accept responsibility: "So I said to them, 'Whoever has gold take it off,' They gave it to me, and I hurled it into the fire and out came this calf" (Exodus 32:24).

Aaron's explanation recalls the words of the American writer Sydney Harris: "We have not passed the subtle line between childhood and adulthood until we move from the passive voice to the active voice; that is, until we have stopped saying, 'It got lost,' and say, 'I lost it.'" Indeed, if you reread Aaron's explanation of how the Golden Calf came into being, his words do, in fact, sound childlike.

———

3. *Believing that the wrong we have done is good*. The most obvious examples of such behavior are terrorists and assassins who murder innocent people and then claim to have done a great act. Concerning people like this, the prophet Isaiah declared, "Woe to those who call darkness light and light darkness" (5:20).

———

John Wilkes Booth, the assassin of President Lincoln, was a man who arguably did greater damage to the United States, both North and South, than any other

---

*Maimonides' enumeration of the order of the texts in the Mishnah is slightly different from ours, and in current editions his commentary is found on 8:8, not 8:6.

person in American history. Yet how did Booth view himself? As a martyr and idealist. While fleeing troops searching for him, Booth wrote in his diary: "After being hunted like a dog through swamps, woods, and last night being chased by gunboats till I was forced to return wet, cold, and starving, with every man's hand against me, I am here in despair. And why? For doing what Brutus was honored for; what made Tell a hero. And yet I, for striking down a greater tyrant than they ever knew, am looked upon as a common cutthroat. My action was purer than either of theirs." Just before he died, Booth said, "Tell Mother I died for my country."

———

4. *Minimizing the wrong.* "If you have done a little wrong to your neighbor, let it seem large in your eyes" (*The Fathers According to Rabbi Nathan* 41:11). You should not dismiss what you have done as inconsequential, but be honest with yourself. If you had been treated in the same way, would you find it upsetting? If so, then you must acknowledge the distress you have caused.

———

Senator Trent Lott of Mississippi, speaking at Senator Strom Thurmond's one hundredth birthday party in 2002, spoke longingly of Thurmond's 1948 presidential campaign to maintain segregation in America. Lott made it clear that he thought America would have been better off if Thurmond had won: "I want to say this about my state [Mississippi]. When Strom Thurmond ran for president, we voted for him. . . . If the rest of the country had followed our lead, we wouldn't have had all these problems" (i.e., racial unrest).

When Lott's comments were publicized and provoked an angry backlash, the senator tried to minimize his comment as "a poor choice of words." When this "apology" was deemed inadequate, he had to apologize yet again and again (a total of four times), but by then it was too late to undo the damage, and he had to resign his position as Senate majority leader.

At the time, President George W. Bush seized the moral high ground and issued a statement that in its directness, comprehensiveness, and lack of self-justification represented a model apology: "Any suggestion that the segregated past was acceptable or positive is offensive and is wrong. Every day that our nation was segregated was a day that America was unfaithful to our founding ideals."[1]

———

5. *Not repenting for something as soon as you become aware of it.* The first time an otherwise honest person does something deceitful, he is very

uncomfortable. If he repents quickly, he is far less likely to transgress again. But, as the Talmud teaches, if "a person sins, and then repeats the sin [one or two more times], it starts to seem to him like a permitted action" (*Kiddushin* 40a).*

Psychologist Stanley Milgram, who devoted much of his career to investigating how otherwise good people come to engage in wrongful behavior, noted the importance of stopping the behavior as quickly as possible. Otherwise people tend to continue in their wrongful behavior rather than saying, "Whatever I have been doing until this point is bad, and now I acknowledge it by breaking it off."[2]

6. *Intending to repeat the offense*. Among those whose repentance is unacceptable is one who says, "I will sin and then repent," or one who says, "I will sin and the day of Yom Kippur will atone for me" (Maimonides, "Laws of Repentance" 4:1). For example, if you speak of others unfairly and repent but don't intend to stop doing so, what is your repentance worth?

———

The biblical Pharaoh epitomizes an insincere penitent. When plagues continue to strike Egypt, he acts as if he were seized by remorse, and summons Moses and Aaron to tell them, "The Lord is in the right and I and my people are in the wrong. Plead with the Lord that there may be an end to God's thunder and the hail. I will let you go; you need stay no longer." A short time later, however, "when Pharaoh saw that the rain and the hail and the thunders had ceased, he became stubborn and reverted to his guilty ways . . . and he would not let the Israelites go" (Exodus 9:27, 34–35).

———

7. *Pointing to worse things done by others*. Many people try to evade responsibility for their own behavior by pointing to the actions of others.[†] True, others may have done far worse things than you have, but that still doesn't excuse your behavior. Imagine how you would feel if, when you pointed to good deeds you had done, others minimized their value by point-

---

*"Habit makes wrongdoing almost necessary to a person, like the natural actions from which it is almost impossible for one to abstain" (Bachya ibn Pakuda, *Duties of the Heart* [*Chovot ha-Levavot*]. Thus, someone who is dishonest cannot imagine how he can earn enough money without cheating.

†Albert Camus, the Nobel Prize–winning French writer, wrote, "To justify himself, each relies on the other's crimes."

ing to others who had done even greater good. Or if they minimized a loss you suffered by pointing to others who had suffered more.

8. *Hypersensitivity to criticism.* People who hate being criticized, and who react defensively when it happens, are unlikely to repent, even when others point out to them what they have done. Therefore, if you find that you become angry at those who criticize you, try to regard your critics as you would a doctor. When your physician gives you his diagnosis, you don't lose your temper. Rather, you are probably grateful, for by knowing what's wrong you can usually start treatment that will make you better.

If criticism is valid, then you can use it to improve yourself. If, out of politeness or through fear of offending you, the person had said nothing, your conduct might well have become more ingrained.

The Gaon of Vilna taught that the reason we are put on earth is to learn how to correct our bad traits. Our critics, if they are fair, help us to fulfill this goal.

For more on how to react to criticism, see chapter 46.

9. *Excessive pride.* Pride is a seldom acknowledged but common obstacle to repentance; it can keep us from owning up to our flaws or admitting that we have done wrong. Yet, if we do not acknowledge what we have done, we will continue on the same path or do something even worse. Therefore we need to cultivate sufficient humility to acknowledge our faults and wrongful behavior.[3]

———

In business, owning up to a mistake enables us to "cut our losses." But some people cannot bring themselves to acknowledge that they have erred. If pride stops us from admitting to our spouse, children, or friends that we were wrong in how we acted toward them, or pride stops us from saying "I'm sorry," then our relationships will deteriorate, and our emotional losses will mount.

———

10. *Peer pressure and bad companions.* Rabbi Yaizel of Navorodock taught: "If a traveler on a ship sailing west regrets having made the trip and turns himself toward the east while remaining on board, he has obviously accomplished nothing. The same is true of a person who tries to mend one of his ways while remaining in the company of those who continue to do the same

bad act."[4] If you want to go in a different direction from the boat, you have to get off. And if you want to change a negative pattern or behavior, make sure to stay away from the people who continue to engage in that behavior and who will influence you to do so as well.

Acts which people think don't require repentance

11. *Bad character traits, such as anger, hatred, and jealousy* (Maimonides, "Laws of Repentance" 7:3). These almost always lead to violations of other fundamental laws. For example, hatred and jealousy make it impossible to fulfill the biblical command to "love your neighbor as yourself" (Leviticus 19:18), while a bad temper causes one to say hurtful things.

Another, perhaps less obvious, bad trait is rejoicing at someone else's suffering or humiliation (Maimonides, "Laws of Repentance" 4:4). Even if you don't express your jealousy or hatred publicly, but just rejoice privately, feelings of happiness at another's misfortune are almost always wrong, and we should regret doing so and repent.

——

Maimonides comments: "A person should not think that repentance is only necessary for those sins that involve deeds such as lewdness, robbery, or theft. Rather, just as a person is obligated to repent for these, so too must he search after the evil qualities he has. He must repent for anger, hatred, envy, frivolity, the pursuit of money, of honor, of gluttony, and the like" ("Laws of Repentance" 7:3).

——

12. *Suspecting the innocent.* Most of us think that as long as we don't voice our suspicions publicly, we haven't harmed anyone. A couple told me that when they couldn't find an expensive dress, they blamed their cleaning woman, suspecting her of misplacing the item or stealing it. When one of their daughters returned home, they learned she had taken the dress to her apartment and had forgotten to return it.

True, they never accused the cleaning woman to her face, but suspecting her and speaking ill of her (as they did between themselves) is still an offense, one that most people are not aware of having violated. "I didn't do her any harm, did I?" they will protest (see Maimonides, "Laws of Repentance" 4:4).

We should learn from this ruling to be careful before we voice complaints and accusations, even among close family and friends. Also, once we're aware that we have misjudged someone, even if that person is unaware of what we have said, we should treat the person, at least for the next few days, with particular kindness. Doing so will largely or completely reverse the negative feelings we felt and perhaps even expressed.

For a fuller discussion of this subject, see chapter 6.

13. *Eating a full meal at a poor person's house.* Someone who eats a large meal at a poor person's house is likely to defend himself by saying, "But she invited me for dinner." However, if you know the woman and her family to be of limited means, exercise your moral imagination and realize that it may be a hardship for them to entertain. Since it might embarrass the family if you decline the invitation, you should eat little without making it apparent why.

A modern application of this suggests that when a fundraiser approaches someone he knows to be of modest or declining means, he should ask for a sum that will not be a hardship for the person to donate, or not solicit a donation at all. This is true particularly if he suspects that the person will, out of embarrassment, give more than he can afford (*Shulchan Arukh, Yoreh Deah* 248:7).

Sins for which we cannot fully repent, even when our intentions are pure

A prerequisite for complete repentance is undoing any damage we have inflicted, but in the following five instances we do not know all the people who have been harmed.

14. *Defrauding the public.* In earlier times, a common such offender was a storekeeper who used false weights and measures. Today, defrauding the public includes stock market manipulation, false or misleading advertising claims, and cab drivers cheating naïve tourists. Since anyone guilty of such crimes does not know the names of most or all of the people he defrauded, there is no way he can compensate them, even if he wishes to repent.

Because Jewish law did not want to discourage and demoralize would-be penitents, the Rabbis suggest that offenders like this should perform deeds that will benefit the general public. Thus the Tosefta, a talmudic source, speaks of the case of penitent tax and custom collectors who, during the Roman period, gouged large sums of money from people.* The Rabbis ruled that if these people wished to repent, they should make an effort to calculate how much they misappropriated, pay back those whom they knew, and devote the balance to public needs, such as digging a well, a ditch, or a water reservoir (*Bava Mezia* 8:26; see also *Beizah* 29a). In modern times, someone who has defrauded the public could donate money to causes such as a school, library, or park, with the hope that some of the victims will benefit.

———

The following scenario is based on the Talmud, and underscores the extent to which someone who has committed a crime is morally responsible for its unintended consequences: A thief broke into a tent in which five men were sleeping, and stole a large sum from one of them. Subsequently the thief, wishing to repent, gathered the five men together and offered to return the money to the victim. But, to the thief's chagrin, all five men insisted that they had been robbed. What should the thief do?

According to the strict letter of the law, he may set down the money and leave, letting the men divide it among themselves. Rabbi Akiva argues, however, that if the thief wishes to repent fully—thereby ensuring that his victim be compensated—he must give the full sum of money to each man. Otherwise the victim will still have a primary grievance against him, because he was short-changed: if not for the thief, the man would still have his money. Therefore, to redress the wrong he has done (even though the other men are acting dishonestly) and attain full repentance, the thief is obligated to make sure that his victim receives all his money back (see Bava Kamma *103b).*

———

15. *Buying from a thief.* Since you don't know from whom the item was stolen, you can't return it, even if you come to regret possessing somebody else's property. Also, by buying from someone who has robbed others, you are encouraging him to continue stealing, and so you bear a measure of responsibility toward his future, as well as his past, victims.

Even otherwise honest people sometimes buy from thieves when, for example, they purchase a pirated videotape. You may argue that you didn't know that the film was copied illegally. But if someone on the street is selling a copy of a recently released film for a fraction of its normal purchase price, you should strongly suspect that the item is stolen, and not buy it.

———

*The Romans would assess a sum to be raised, and whatever the tax officials collected over and above that amount was theirs to keep.

In addition, one might argue that buying goods produced by exploited workers constitutes buying from a thief. You are, in effect, paying money to a company that has underpaid and/or overworked (both forms of thievery) the employees who produced the goods. In the case of exploited child labor, the employer is, in effect, stealing the children's childhood. And again, because you don't know those who were exploited personally, there is no way you can help undo the wrong perpetrated on them.

16. *Not returning a lost object you have found.* Once time elapses, then, even if you want to return the item, it will often be impossible to locate the owner.

17. *Damaging someone's reputation.* A person who has stolen an object usually has a clear memory of what he or she has done, but speaking ill of others is done so often that most people cannot recall the majority of occasions they have done so. Hence, people don't repent of this sin, because they don't recall having committed it. In addition, even if you do recall what you have done and try to undo the damage by speaking to the people to whom you spread the damaging information or comments, they have probably transmitted the information to others, and you will not be able to locate all the people who now have a lowered impression of the person (for more on the unending damage caused by *lashon hara*, see page 337).

18. *Influencing others to do something wrong.* The thirteenth-century rabbi Menachem ha-Meiri (known as "the Meiri") explains that "just as the thief's repentance is ineffectual until he returns what he stole, so is one who caused others to sin incapable of repenting while his teachings exert a negative influence."[5]

The best hope for someone like this is to acknowledge the wrong he has done, and try to influence those whom he encouraged to act badly to repent as well. If he succeeds, his repentance will be complete. Even if he influences just some of those upon whom he exerted a negative influence, that constitutes a higher form of repentance than if he repents alone.

———

In the 1980s and early '90s, Larry Trapp, head of the Ku Klux Klan in Nebraska and an avowed neo-Nazi, used to go on television shrieking about "kikes," "the Jews' media," and "half-breeds," and launch into tirades against African-Americans and Vietnamese. Through the extraordinary work of Cantor Michael Weisser and his wife, Julie, Trapp was brought to an awareness of the great evil of his racist and antisemitic diatribes. In November 1991 he resigned from the Klan and all other racist organizations of which he was a member. Trapp then wrote apologies to the many people he had threatened and abused, and issued a statement saying, "I wasted the first forty years of my life and caused harm to other people. Now I've learned we're one race and one race only." Through repeating statements like this, Trapp hoped to persuade some of the people he had influenced with his earlier attacks to reconsider their views as well.

Shortly after leaving the Klan, Trapp's already fragile health deteriorated. In the last months of his life he converted to Judaism at B'nai Jeshurun, the Lincoln, Nebraska, temple he had once planned to blow up.[6]

———

In the late 1940s, the British Labour Party parliamentarian Richard Crossman published The God That Failed, *a book-length compilation of detailed autobiographical accounts by prominent writers and intellectuals (such as Arthur Koestler, Ignazio Silone, and Richard Wright) who had been communists or supporters of communism, and who had eventually concluded that communism's evils far outweighed any good they may have once thought it had done. Having witnessed firsthand the cruelties and injustices of communism, the writers believed that it was not enough for them to quietly resign from the Communist Party. They wanted to share their insights with others and, by doing so, discourage them from following the false "god" that they had, while challenging those who were still communists to rethink their position. As Arthur Koestler wrote in his* mea culpa: *"Every single one of us knows at least one friend who perished in the Arctic subcontinent of forced labor camps, was shot as a spy or vanished without a trace. How our voices boomed with righteous indignation, denouncing flaws in the procedure of justice in our comfortable democracies; and how silent we were when our comrades, without trial or conviction, were liquidated in the Socialist sixth of the earth. Each of us carries a skeleton in the cupboard of his conscience."**

———

---

*See Richard Crossman, ed., *The God That Failed,* page 71. Koestler concluded his article with a stunning Midrash on a biblical text: "I served the Communist Party for seven years—the same length of time as Jacob tended Laban's sheep to win Rachel his daughter. When the time was up, the bride was led into his dark tent; only the next morning did he discover that his ardors had been spent not on the lovely Rachel but on . . . Leah. I wonder whether he ever recovered from the shock of having slept with an illusion" (pages 74–75).

16

WHEN A GREAT EVIL HAS BEEN DONE

1. A great evil can be defined as an act or series of acts the aim of which is to inflict serious and/or irrevocable damage. The ultimate example is murder, for which it is impossible to win full atonement, since securing the victim's forgiveness, a prerequisite for complete repentance, is impossible. Still, even though one cannot win full atonement, one should do all within one's power to repent.

———

In a rarely discussed and highly provocative talmudic passage, Rabbi Yochanan, speaking in the name of Rabbi Shimon bar Yochai, says that David's dual sin (committing adultery with Bathsheba, then bringing about the death of her husband; II Samuel, chapter 11) was totally out of character for him, as was the Israelites' sin of worshipping the Golden Calf (Exodus, chapter 32). So why did they commit these acts? Rabbi Shimon bar Yochai conjectures that God (in a singular, not-to-be-repeated deprivation of free will) ordained that David and the Israelites commit these sins so as to provide hope to future sinners. Thus, if someone has sinned, and doubts his repentance will be accepted, we should tell him to look at David, whom God punished but forgave. Similarly, if a community commits a sin, we can recommend that they look at the community of Israel, whom God also punished for the Golden Calf, but whose sin was forgiven. Therefore the sinner should understand that he can also repent and be forgiven (Avodah Zara 4b–5a).

Alternatively, we can suggest that God didn't deprive the Israelites and David of free will by ordaining that they commit these sins. Rather, the reason the Bible recorded them, thereby damaging David's and the Israelite community's good names, was to inspire future sinners with the knowledge that no matter how grave your offense (and there are not much graver sins than idolatry, homicide, and adultery), God is still open to your repentance.

———

2. As noted, repentance for murder is inevitably incomplete, because reconciling with one's victim is impossible. Furthermore, murder is *often* a sin that extends even beyond the victim's life span. Thus, after Cain murders

Abel, God says to him, "The blood of your brother cries out to me from the earth" (Genesis 4:10). The word used for blood, *d'mei*, is a plural, so the verse literally reads, "the *bloods* of your brother." From this plural usage, the Talmud deduces that what cries out is not only Abel's blood, but also that of all his future, never-to-be-born descendants (Mishnah *Sanhedrin* 4:5). This is an additional reason why it is impossible to fully atone for murder.

3. One who has murdered and wishes to maximize his atonement, must, therefore, fill his life with a large stream of acts of kindness and, if possible, with acts that save lives.

———

The most powerful story of repentance with which I am familiar is that of Ernst Werner Techow, an antisemitic right-wing radical who, in 1922, along with two other men, murdered Walter Rathenau, Germany's minister of foreign affairs, and a Jew. In the murder's immediate aftermath, Rathenau's heartsick mother wrote a letter to Techow's mother: "Say to your son that, in the name and spirit of him who he has murdered, I forgive, even as God may forgive, if before an earthly judge he makes a full and frank confession of his guilt . . . and before a heavenly judge repents."*

After serving a prison sentence of only five years, Techow was released, and joined the French Foreign Legion. Unlike the Nazis, who came to power in 1933 and had supported Rathenau's murder, Techow underwent a full repentance for his antisemitic beliefs and deeds. He remarked to a nephew of Rathenau's whom he happened to meet, that "just as Frau Rathenau conquered herself when she wrote that letter of pardon, I have tried to master myself. I only wish I would get an opportunity to right the wrong I've done."

In 1940, after France surrendered to Germany, he went to Marseille and helped more than seven hundred Jews escape to Spain with Moroccan passports. For those individuals who lacked money, Techow arranged their escape without payment. Techow's change of heart and his saving of lives comes as close as one can imagine to a model penitence by a murderer.

———

An important, rarely commented-upon story in the Bible suggests that repentance can help even murderers. The account of King Menashe in II Kings (chapter 21) describes him as the most evil Jewish monarch who ever reigned. Menashe put so many people to death "that he filled Jerusalem [with blood] from end to

———

*Mrs. Rathenau's letter is unusual in that it makes forgiveness dependent on full confession of guilt before a judge and the acceptance of punishment, followed by a full repentance before God.

end" (21:16). He also rebuilt pagan temples that his father, the righteous King Hezekiah, had destroyed, and brought an idol into the Temple in Jerusalem. In the words of the Bible, "Menashe led them [the Jews] astray to do greater evil than the [Canaanite] nations which the Lord had destroyed before the Israelites" (21:9).

It is hard to imagine a less likely candidate for repentance. Yet a later biblical book, the Second Book of Chronicles, claims that, when great suffering came upon Menashe (he was deposed by the Assyrians, then shackled and taken to Babylon; II Chronicles 33:11), he turned to God and expressed full contrition for his behavior, whereupon God restored Menashe to Jerusalem, and Menashe destroyed the idolatrous temples he had built and urged his subjects to return to God (II Chronicles 33:12–16).*

————

4. Changing one's first name (see *Rosh Hashana* 16b). Generally, when a person repents of a great evil he has done, and feels ashamed for how he behaved, he wants to start over as a new person. Nothing symbolizes this as much as the taking of a new name. Maimonides writes, "To change one's name, as if to say, 'I am a different person and not the one who sinned'" ("Laws of Repentance" 2:4).

I know of a man who was convicted of murder and, very late in life, when he finally acknowledged his crime, decided to go back to being called by the Hebrew name bestowed on him at birth. That name, which he had not used in decades, seemed unsullied by his later deed. By taking back this name, he wanted to elevate his identity from that of a murderer and to be, so to speak, reborn.† Perhaps also, by taking on a Hebrew—indeed biblical—name, he hoped that he would motivate himself to act better.

————

The impact of symbolic change is reflected in an incident told by Rabbi Aryeh Levine. Reb Aryeh was visiting inmates in an Israeli prison, one of whom, Yona M., had murdered his wife. The morning after his meeting with the rabbi, Yona, for the first time, put on a tallit *and* tefillin *(phylacteries), which Jewish law com-*

---

*The account in II Chronicles certainly supports the notion that God fully accepted Menashe's repentance and forgave him, although many Bible scholars have expressed wonderment as to why the details of Menashe's repentance and return as king to Jerusalem were omitted from the Book of Kings.

†Obviously this is a sensitive issue that must be handled on a case-by-case basis. One does not want a criminal who has committed a violent crime to adopt a new name, leave prison, and hide evidence of his past behavior.

mands adult male Jews to don each morning. Only he did so incorrectly, wrapping the tefillin *for the hand around his right arm, even though Jewish law dictates that a right-handed person, as Yona was, wrap the* tefillin *around his left arm.*

Some prisoners who shared the large cell assumed that Yona was purposely trying to make a travesty of the Jewish ritual. But when a prisoner in the cell questioned him, Yona answered, "After Reb Aryeh spoke with me, I kept thinking all day of what I had done; and I felt so sorry for the terrible crime I committed. Then I just felt a mighty need to pray properly, wrapped in tallit *and* tefillin. *Yet then I thought: But how can I put on holy* tefillin *on my vile unclean hand that killed a human being? You see, though, I found an answer: It was the left hand that did the murder. The right hand is still pure and clean."[1]*

5. In short, repentance always helps. Even if it doesn't bring absolution in this world, it might well do so in the next. The Talmud teaches that just before a person who committed a capital crime was executed, he was instructed to "confess the sin [i.e., for which you are going to be put to death] and all your other sins . . . because one who confesses [and repents of the evil he has done] has a share in the World-to-Come" (Mishnah *Sanhedrin* 6:2).

Atoning for an evil act committed by someone under your command

On March 13, 1997, a Jordanian soldier shot and murdered seven Israeli schoolgirls, aged thirteen to fifteen, while they were on a field trip to Jordan's "Island of Peace," near the northern border between Israel and Jordan. The sense of grief and devastation Israelis felt was overwhelming, and attendance at the seven funerals was huge. It was reported that one of the girls, Adi Malka, knew sign language and was her deaf parents' primary link to the world.

On the day after the funerals, Jordan's King Hussein came to Israel. He went to the homes of each of the bereaved, got down on his knees, and begged forgiveness on behalf of his people. "I feel as if I have lost a child of my own," the king said. "If there is any purpose in life, it will be to make sure that all the children no longer suffer the way our generation did."

An observer in Israel reported: "He won the hearts of this country. He could have easily remained aloof and discounted this crazy soldier as unstable and unrepresentative of the Jordanian army. He would have had every reason to do that. Instead he came here and expressed his deep compassion" (Beth Huppin).

Indeed, Hussein stayed in touch with some of the families until his own death, two years later.[2]

———

17

ROSH HASHANA AND YOM KIPPUR

═══════════

1. Rabbis Byron Sherwin and Seymour Cohen write: "One of the most popular and regularly observed rituals in America is the annual medical checkup. Each year, millions of people are examined, tested, and evaluated in order to determine the state of their physical health and well-being. Often, one fasts in preparation for a variety of tests and procedures. . . . If an illness is detected or if a potential illness is indicated, a modification of one's behavior is required. When sickness is diagnosed, a regimen is prescribed to help restore health. What may be ascertained during the examination period can lead to a change of life-style for the rest of the year, indeed, for the remainder of one's life. During the High Holiday season, Jews undergo a kind of 'spiritual checkup.' Prayer, fasting, and introspection are meant to be catalysts to aid one in evaluating the state of one's spiritual [and moral] health. This process is called *teshuva*, repentance."[1]

2. Because the following exercise is painful, many people may try to find excuses to avoid doing it. Yet this procedure, more than almost any other, can help us prepare for the High Holidays. Start with the sentence, "What I regret having done in the last year is . . ." and list the things you wish you had done differently or not done at all. The list can include such items as these:

- I didn't visit my friend who was sick with cancer.
- I let a friendship drop because it would not help me socially or professionally, and might even hold me back.
- I misled someone in a financial transaction.
- I didn't return a phone call, or several calls, to someone who really needed to talk to me.

- I didn't make an effort to help someone get a job, even though I had a connection that might have helped them.

Rabbi Abraham Twerski—from whom I first learned of this idea—suggests that writing out this personal confession can be more effective and personally meaningful than simply reciting the general confession shared by all in the prayerbook (*al chet*, "for the sin I committed by . . .").[2]

3. Another difficult act, but one that will help cleanse our soul: We should make peace with someone with whom we have had a falling-out, particularly if the person is a family member.

In many families there are people—first cousins or even brothers and sisters—who are not on speaking terms. I urge people to take advantage of the High Holiday period of forgiveness to make at least an initial, even if seemingly superficial, peace with the other party (during the course of the year, the peace may well grow deeper). For one thing, unless your sibling or other close relative is a hard-core criminal or a highly abusive person, it is a great act of disrespect to your parents, whether they are living or dead, to disassociate from close family members. As a parent, I know how important it is to me that my children love and care for each other. Among the greatest tragedies I could imagine would be to learn that my children were no longer on speaking terms. Therefore, the fulfillment of the Fifth Commandment, "Honor your father and mother," mandates that, except in the most extreme instances, we do not break off contact with a close family member.

Also, there is something hypocritical about coming to synagogue on the High Holidays and beseeching God to look upon us favorably and treat us with mercy and forgiveness, if we are unwilling to act that way toward others. The Talmud teaches that God forgives the sins of those who don't hold grudges and who forgive offenses committed against them (*Rosh Hashana* 17a). Only if we act in a forgiving manner toward others do we make ourselves worthy of God's forgiveness.

———

This Jewish tradition, of a holiday devoted to seeking forgiveness and granting it, is one I believe we should try to influence our non-Jewish neighbors to adopt. Perhaps the United States could establish a National Apology Day, during which people would seek out those they had hurt, and ask for forgiveness. Such a day might be scheduled for December, so that people could end one year and start a new one with something approaching a clean slate. By having an annual date when an offender has reason to believe that many others will seek forgiveness and that the hurt parties will be more open to granting it, the embarrassed offender might more easily be ready to approach the person whom she has hurt.

———

4. Perhaps the most famous sentence in the High Holiday liturgy underscores the three acts that Jewish tradition teaches are most likely to secure God's forgiveness: *Teshuvah, tefilah, tzedakah,* "Repentance, prayer, and charity can avert the severity of the evil decree" (from the *Machzor,* the High Holiday prayer book). Engage in all three acts during the days between Rosh Hashana and Yom Kippur.

5. Yet another High Holiday prayer reminds us that "all of your deeds are written down in a book" *(ve-kol ma'asecha ba-sefer nichtavim).* As the Talmud teaches, "When a person comes to his eternal world, all of his earthly actions are enumerated before him" *(Ta'anit* 11a).

6. Jewish tradition encourages us to act with particular piety, kindness, and generosity during the *Aseret Y'mei Teshuva* (the Ten Days of Repentance), the period of time starting with Rosh Hashana, and concluding with Yom Kippur. Many Jews presume that God will reward them in the year ahead if they act righteously during this period. Does such a belief make sense, the notion that if we behave well during these ten days, but do not continue to do so after Yom Kippur, we will fool God into believing that we are worthy of divine kindness?

Rabbi David Woznica speculates that the demands made of Jews during the *Aseret Y'mei Teshuva* have less to do with impressing God than with teaching people how good they can be. Thus, if you were to ask people to make permanent changes in their lives—never again speak a word of *lashon hara;* never again ignore a beggar; always be patient with your family and with those around you; whenever you pray, keep your mind fully focused on the prayer's meaning—most people, realizing that they could not follow such advice forever, would give up in advance, and not even make the effort. But if we ask people—including ourselves—to act this way for just ten days, many will make an effort. In the process, we will not only do much good, but we will also learn that we can be much better people than we thought possible. And such a realization can bring about an improvement in our behavior that will last well beyond the ten days.

So, this year, during the *Aseret Y'mei Teshuva,* make a particular effort to give more money to charity than you normally do, refrain from losing your temper with your family and co-workers, focus with real concentration on your prayers, and try to go for these 240 hours without saying an unkind word about or to anyone.

A final thought

7. One of the best-known prayers recited on Yom Kippur is the confessional prayer known as the *Al Chet*, "For the sin I committed by . . ." On this day, Jews confess repeatedly to forty-four different transgressions. The awareness of how many sins we routinely commit can, however, overwhelm some of us with a sense of guilt and despair. I suggest, therefore, that we also focus on the good things we do, and the good things we can do. Hence, the following—titled "For the Mitzvah We Performed"—is a suggested reading for the Yom Kippur service, which can be read aloud by a congregation or recited and studied individually:

1. *For the* mitzvah *we performed by remembering the good someone did for us even when we were upset with him or her.*
2. *For the* mitzvah *we performed by stopping our child from teasing or humiliating another child, or using a hurtful nickname.*
3. *For the* mitzvah *we performed by standing up for justice when we saw someone mistreated.*
4. *For the* mitzvah *we performed by refusing to buy anything produced by child labor.*
5. *For the* mitzvah *we performed by remembering to express gratitude to anyone who helped us.*
6. *For the* mitzvah *we performed when we heard an ambulance siren and offered a prayer to God on behalf of the sick person inside.*
7. *For the* mitzvah *we performed by knowing embarrassing information about someone and not passing it on.*
8. *For the* mitzvah *we performed when we gave food or money to someone who said he was hungry.*
9. *For the* mitzvah *we performed by donating to charity cheerfully.*
10. *For the* mitzvah *we performed by apologizing to one of our children whose feelings we had unfairly hurt.*

All these things, God, please remember and inspire us to do more acts like these in the year ahead.

11. *For the* mitzvah *we performed by blessing our children on Shabbat and on the Jewish holidays.*

12. *For the* mitzvah *we performed by returning a lost object to its owner.*

13. *For the* mitzvah *we performed by visiting a sick person and offering emotional support to him and his family.*

14. *For the* mitzvah *we performed by helping someone to find work.*

15. *For the* mitzvah *we performed by teaching our children Torah.*

16. *For the* mitzvah *we performed by studying Torah ourselves.*

17. *For the* mitzvah *we performed by reserving our highest praise of our children for when they do kind deeds.*

18. *For the* mitzvah *we performed by hearing a negative rumor about someone and not passing it on.*

19. *For the* mitzvah *we performed by not encouraging our children to make friends with, or date, wealthy people, just because they are rich.*

20. *For the* mitzvah *we performed by refraining from snapping at the person who has chosen to share our life—our spouse.*

All these things, God, please remember and inspire us to do more acts like these in the year ahead.

21. *For the* mitzvah *we performed by forgiving those who hurt us and sought our forgiveness.*

22. *For the* mitzvah *we performed by helping a developmentally disabled person find work.*

23. *For the* mitzvah *we performed by not exaggerating the bad traits of those with whom we disagree or whom we dislike.*

24. *For the* mitzvah *we performed by striving to be punctual even when it was difficult, so as to avoid keeping someone waiting.*

25. *For the* mitzvah *we performed by interacting with non-Jews in a way that brings credit to the Jewish people.*

26. *For the* mitzvah *we performed by accepting responsibility for the wrong we have committed, and not blaming our behavior on others.*

27. *For the* mitzvah *we performed by asking those whom we have hurt for forgiveness.*

28. *For the* mitzvah *we performed by not asking a storekeeper the price of an item when we had no intention of buying there.*

29. *For the* mitzvah *we performed by staying in close communication with our elderly parents.*

30. For the mitzvah *we performed by not serving liquor too gener-ously at social events.*

All these things, God, please remember and inspire us to do more acts like these in the year ahead.

31. For the mitzvah *we performed by not using words like "always" [e.g., "you're always inconsiderate"] and "never" ["you never think before you act"] when we are angry with someone.*
32. For the mitzvah *we performed by not making comments that could inflict irrevocable hurt on someone who has upset us.*
33. For the mitzvah *we performed by restricting our expression of anger at someone to the incident that provoked it.*
34. For the mitzvah *we performed by feeding our pets before eating ourselves.*
35. For the mitzvah *we performed by arranging to donate our or-gans for transplant.*
36. For the mitzvah *we performed by expressing gratitude on an on-going basis to the people we are most likely to take for granted, our family members.*
37. For the mitzvah *we performed by helping someone in an un-happy frame of mind to laugh.*
38. For the mitzvah *we performed by treating our children and spouse with the same courtesy and kindness we extend to guests.*
39. For the mitzvah *we performed by donating the money we did not spend on food on Yom Kippur to a charity that feeds the poor.*
40. For the mitzvah *we performed when we were tempted to do something dishonest, and refrained.*

All these things, God, please remember and inspire us to do more acts like these in the year ahead.

FORGIVENESS

―――

One who overcomes his natural tendencies
[i.e., to hold on to a grudge] and instead
forgives, all his sins are forgiven.

BABYLONIAN TALMUD,
Rosh Hashana 17a

18

WHEN OBLIGATORY, WHEN OPTIONAL, WHEN FORBIDDEN

The importance of forgiveness

1. Because we are often driven by irrational and destructive emotions, such as anger, envy, greed, self-absorption, and indifference, and by less negative emotions, such as a lack of insight into another's needs, we often hurt each other. We are not perfect and must all learn to apologize when we have acted wrongly, and to forgive others who have hurt us. Without apologies and forgiveness, no long-term relationship can endure.

2. Generally, forgiveness should be dependent on the offending party's repentance. Thus, as mentioned, God pardons the city of Nineveh when its inhabitants alter their evil behavior (Jonah 3:10; see page 153). But God does not forgive the city of Sodom (indeed, He destroys it), because its citizens persist in their ways and show contempt for those who act righteously (Genesis 18:20–21; 19:4–9).

3. For many of us, it is not easy to let go of a grievance and to forgive the offender. Perhaps because it is so difficult, the Talmud offers an extraordinary reward and encouragement for forgiving others: "One who overcomes his natural tendencies [i.e., to hold on to a grudge] and instead forgives, all his sins are forgiven" (*Rosh Hashana* 17a). In other words, if we are merciful to those who offend us, then God will be merciful when our behavior offends Him. This promise might, and should, overcome any reluctance to forgive on the part of someone who has been wronged.

When forgiveness is obligatory

4. If the person who has hurt you makes a sincere plea to be forgiven, "it is prohibited for one to be hard-hearted and to refuse his forgiveness . . . [but] one should forgive with a complete heart and a willing spirit" (Maimonides, "Laws of Repentance" 2:10).

But what if you are so angry that you cannot bring yourself to forgive, and certainly feel that you cannot do so "with a complete heart and a willing spirit"? In that case, explain to the person that you are still too upset to grant forgiveness, and that she should come back and ask again in a specified period of time (perhaps two weeks or a month). During this period, work on relinquishing your anger, so that when she returns you can forgive her (for techniques for relinquishing anger, see pages 262–272).

Do this only when someone has hurt you very deeply. Otherwise, try to grant forgiveness the first time it is asked for, particularly if you believe that the request is genuine.

———

According to Rabbi Zelig Pliskin, "When Rabbi Eliyahu Lopian lived in London, someone approached him and requested forgiveness for having sinned against him. Rabbi Lopian asked the man to specify what he had done, but the man refused to do so. 'I will not forgive you until you tell me exactly what you have done,' said Rabbi Lopian. Seeing that he had no alternative, the man reluctantly told Rabbi Lopian what had happened. Upon hearing the person's confession, the rabbi said to him, 'I could easily say that I forgive you. But since what you have done is a truly serious matter, I know that my forgiveness will not be with complete sincerity. I therefore advise you to go home now and come back in two weeks. During this period, I will study Mussar [Jewish texts that deal with ethical self-improvement], and I hope that after two weeks my forgiveness will be sincere.' Two weeks later, the man approached Rabbi Lopian again, and on this occasion the forgiveness was granted."[1]

———

Some years ago in the United States, a woman named Linda Kenney nearly died when, prior to an operation, anesthesia was administered to her improperly. Her husband, understandably, wanted to sue the doctor and the hospital. Then the anesthesiologist wrote the couple a note expressing his contrition and grief. He told her, "Whenever you want to speak to me, I will make myself available. Here is my home telephone number and my beeper number." The Kenneys later learned that the doctor did not inform the hospital or its lawyers of what he was doing. He knew that they would probably have forbidden him to contact the *patient, because acknowledging his responsibility so frankly would put him and the hospital at great risk if the patient sued. The Kenneys were deeply moved by the doctor's letter, and even more impressed when he came to their home and begged forgiveness. The couple ended up not pursuing a malpractice suit, and instead, in conjunction with the doctor, started a group to help both doctors and families deal with the trauma of medical and surgical errors.[2]**

_____

Conversely, my friend Rabbi Hanoch Teller, a deeply pious and highly forgiving person, was severely injured and nearly killed when a driver ran a red light and crashed into his motor scooter. His recovery involved painful physical rehabilitation and took many months. Yet he told me that the greatest pain he experienced was that the driver, who was fully at fault for the accident, never contacted him, let alone asked for forgiveness. Others told him that she was probably advised by her lawyer not to do so. How sad!

_____

5. One who refuses three genuine requests for forgiveness is regarded as cruel and a sinner (Maimonides, "Laws of Repentance" 2:9). After having been rebuffed three times, the offender is not expected to ask again,[†] and is regarded as forgiven by God.

When forgiveness is optional

6. You are not required to forgive those who do not ask you. However, although not obligated, the Talmud records that the rabbinic sage Mar Zutra used to offer the following prayer before going to sleep: "I forgive all those who pained me." Similar prayers by other sages are recorded in the Talmud (see *Megillah* 28a).

_____

In the nineteenth century, Rabbi Abraham Danzig, author of the legal code Chayyei Adam, *composed the* Zakkah *prayer, which is still widely recited right before the beginning of the* Kol Nidrei Yom Kippur *eve service. It reads in part, "I extend complete forgiveness to everyone who has sinned against me, whether*

_____

*One is, of course, not forbidden to pursue a malpractice suit after granting forgiveness, particularly if one faces extraordinary expenses as a result of the injury incurred; see paragraph 9 of this chapter.

†One view in the Talmud even forbids one from doing so, perhaps because too many requests constitutes a self-destructive form of humiliation (*Yoma* 87b); in addition, as my friend Daniel Taub suggests, it is likely to cause the other person to sin yet again by refusing to forgive.

physically or monetarily, or who has gossiped about me or even slandered me."[3]
Many Jews recite a similar prayer before going to sleep at night, as part of the
bedtime Sh'ma ritual: "Master of the Universe, I hereby forgive anyone who an-
gered or antagonized me, or who sinned against me—whether against my body,
my property, my honor, or against anything of mine; whether he did so acciden-
tally, willfully, carelessly, or purposely."[4]

Both of these prayers should be directed toward forgiving those who commit-
ted the kinds of offenses that frequently produce grudges. It is good to release
enmity before going to sleep at night, and doing so will enable us to maintain a
relationship with the person who has upset or offended us. But are we obligated
to forgive those who have done us great harm, particularly in cases where they
haven't even asked for forgiveness? To cite two examples: Is a victim of rape ob-
liged to forgive her rapist? And is a man falsely accused of rape supposed to for-
give his accuser? I cannot think of a reason why.

The Zakkah prayer does withhold forgiveness from one "who sins against me
and says, 'I will sin against him and he will forgive me.'"* There is something
morally wrong, as well as masochistic, in granting forgiveness to those who in-
tend to go on hurting us.

———

7. According to Jewish law, we are not required to forgive one who has
slandered us and damaged our good name (presumably because the damage
will continue even after the offender apologizes; in other words, we are not
required to forgive someone who has inflicted irrevocable damage). Thus the
Talmud teaches that "One who gives his neighbor a bad name can never gain
pardon" (Jerusalem Talmud, *Bava Kamma* 8:7). Yet if the person appears
truly contrite, it is good to forgive him or her.

———

Rabbi Abraham Twerski relates that one Yom Kippur, when Reb Zalman, a noted
Vilna scholar, was still a very young man, he overheard a man ask another for
forgiveness. The latter responded: "You slandered me, and Jewish law rules that I
am not required to forgive a slanderer." The young but already knowledgeable
Reb Zalman said to him: "According to the Talmud (Bava Mezia 30b), Jerusalem
was destroyed because its inhabitants decided disputes according to the strict letter
of Torah law. In other words, as long as Jews treated each other lifnim me-shurat
ha-din ("beyond the letter of the law"), God treated them in a forgiving manner,

---

*For the one other limitation on forgiveness suggested by the author of the *Zakkah* prayer, see
paragraph 9.

and didn't enforce the letter of the law. But when litigants started insisting on strictly enforcing the law, God acted toward them in the same way." Reb Zalman concluded, "You may invoke the law and refuse to forgive this man. But remember, when you ask God to forgive your sins this Yom Kippur, He may treat you as you have treated this man."[5]

———

8. Although you are entitled to demand repayment from anyone who stole from or defrauded you, there are instances when Jewish law encourages victims to forgive their offenders and forgo their financial claims. This is described in the Talmud as *takkanat ha-shavim,* "an amendment to assist would-be penitents to repent" (see *Gittin* 55a), and asks victims to forgo claims when repayment will be financially ruinous for the offenders. This unusual ruling of the Rabbis came about, in part, because of an incident described in the Talmud. A man wished to repent and return an item he had stolen, but his wife said to him, "Fool, if you start returning the things you have stolen, even the belt you are wearing will not be yours." Intimidated by the realization that a full repentance would impoverish him, the man chose not to return anything.

When this and similar episodes became known, the Sages, under the leadership of Rabbi Judah, declared that if a robber repents and offers to restore what he has taken, the owner should not accept, since doing so will discourage robbers from repenting. Therefore, if one does accept payment, "the spirit of the Sages is not satisfied with him" (*Bava Kamma* 94b).

We can presume, however, that the Talmud is referring to relatively minor losses, since it is unreasonable to expect a person to forgo a substantial claim (see paragraph 9, below). Indeed, the newspapers recently reported that a band of thieves, whose crimes had forced a large store to declare bankruptcy, had just been caught. If these thieves were to request the owner's forgiveness, it does not seem to me that the Rabbis would expect him to forgo his claim. Indeed, on the very page that the Talmud records this ruling, the medieval commentary *Tosafot* argues that it applied only to the generation that made this enactment: "But it was not meant to be applied in future generations for, behold, it happens every day that we accept [returned items] from robbers."

Therefore this ruling's applicability needs to be examined on a case-by-case basis. If not demanding restitution makes it more likely that the perpetrator will repent, then it is a worthy act, but not obligatory, to do so.

The Talmud offers a related instance in which a victim may not insist on strict justice. According to Jewish law, the verse in Leviticus mandating that a robber "shall restore what he took by robbery" (5:23) obligates a thief to return, as is, the object he stole. But what if, for example, the robber stole a beam, and then used it as part of a building? Is the thief required to tear down the building so that he can return it? The School of Shammai ruled that this is exactly what he should do: "he must demolish the whole [building] and restore the beam to its owner." The House of Hillel, however, whose judgment prevails, says that the victim can claim only the monetary value of the beam, so as to not place obstacles in the way of penitents (*Gittin* 55a).

This ruling is consistent with Judaism's general commitment to fairness and a realistic assessment of human nature. As Rashi explains in his commentary on this passage, "For if you force him to destroy his dwelling and return the beam to its owner, he will avoid the act of repentance."

9. In cases in which another has caused you *considerable* financial damage, however, forgiveness does not mean that you should feel pressured to forgo your legal claims. Thus, in the *Zakkah* prayer (see paragraph 6, above), the worshipper declares that, although he forgives those who have wronged him, he does not thereby forgo legitimate monetary claims that "I wish to claim and can recover by law."[6]

A final thought about cases in which forgiveness is optional

10. Even in instances in which we find it difficult to grant forgiveness, we should remember that forgiving those who have greatly wronged us—or at least letting go of intense anger—can be beneficial to us, the victims. Holding on to anger and grudges is almost always detrimental to our own well-being. Rabbi Harold Kushner tells of a woman who had been mistreated by her husband and who, ten years after her divorce, could still not surrender her rage. The rabbi counseled her, "For ten years you have been walking around with a hot poker in your hand, ready to throw it at your ex-husband. But you've never had the chance. All you've done is burn your hand."

Therefore it is sometimes worth forgiving not for the sake of the one who hurt us, but for our own. Not letting go of our rage is likely to have the effect of prolonging, not shortening, our suffering.

When forgiveness is forbidden

11. It is forbidden to forgive a crime committed against someone else. This teaching pits Jewish tradition against mainstream contemporary Christian thinking, which considers it a good thing to forgive even murderers, a crime that by definition is directed against someone other than oneself. To cite several examples:

- In August 1997 the Reverend John Miller of Martha's Vineyard, conducting a service in the presence of then President Bill Clinton, held up a photo of Timothy McVeigh, the man who bombed the Murragh Federal Building in Oklahoma City, killing 168 people and injuring hundreds, and instructed his congregants, "I invite you to look at Timothy McVeigh and then forgive him. . . . I have, and I ask you to do so. . . . We as Christians are asked to do so."

- At about the same time, a rabbi in South Africa attended a forum conducted by the South African Truth and Reconciliation Commission. The commission had earlier announced that amnesty would be granted for crimes committed under the apartheid regime if the perpetrators gave a full confession and accounting of their criminal acts. In attendance at the forum that day was a white police officer who confessed that, years earlier, he had ordered that two houses in a black township be set on fire. Seven adults and five children had died in the ensuing blaze. Because of the grant of amnesty, the officer was freed both from punishment and from any legal obligation to the victims' families. "As [the officer] recounted his story," the rabbi recalled, "lamenting how much he regretted his action, audience members began to weep, eventually giving him a standing ovation. I was aghast. 'I'm sorry, but this is ridiculous,' I called out. 'You can't sadistically murder twelve innocent people by burning them alive, and just say "I'm sorry!"'" A Christian participant in the forum immediately attacked the rabbi: "That's because you Jews don't know how to forgive."[7]

- On September 11, 2002, the first anniversary of the attacks on the World Trade Center and the Pentagon by Islamist terrorists, in which over three thousand people were murdered, Pope John Paul II offered the following prayer: "We pray for the victims today, may they rest in peace. And may God show mercy and forgiveness for the authors of this terrible attack."

From Judaism's perspective, no one can forgive a crime committed against another* (see page 201). Only the victim of the crime can grant forgiveness.

---

*In addition, in at least two of the instances cited here, those of Timothy McVeigh and the perpetrators of the attack of September 11, the murderers—or those who sent them—showed no remorse for their crimes. In contrast to these attitudes, Dietrich Bonhoeffer, the Lutheran

Since he or she is no longer able to do so, that means that murder is, by definition, an unforgivable act (see pages 184–185).

Judaism's perspective on not forgiving murderers has long distinguished it from many of the societies among whom the Jews have lived. In the ancient world, for example, it was common for a murderer to pay a ransom to the victim's family, in return for which the family granted absolution. In repudiating this practice, the Torah ruled, "You may not accept ransom for the life of a murderer who is guilty of a capital crime; he must be put to death" (Numbers 35:31). As Maimonides explains, "The soul of the victim is not the property [of his family members] but the property of God" ("Laws of Murder and Preservation of Life" 1:4). Thus, from Judaism's perspective, parents who forgive their child's murderer are behaving as if the child were their property. Just as they have the right to forgive a thief for stealing their television, so too, they imply, they have the right to forgive another for stealing their child's life; according to the Torah and Jewish law, however, they do not.*

The Jewish position on not granting forgiveness to murderers is reflected in the prayer offered at Auschwitz by Holocaust survivor and Nobel Peace Prize winner Elie Wiesel at the fiftieth anniversary of the death camp's liberation (January 26, 1995): "Although we know that God is merciful, please, God, do not have mercy for those people who created this place. Remember the nocturnal procession of children, of more children, and more children, so frightened, so quiet, so beautiful. If we could simply look at one, our hearts would break. But it did not break the hearts of the murderers."

———

The differing attitudes of Jews and Christians on granting forgiveness for serious, particularly violent, crimes is reflected in an incident that Dr. Solomon Schimmel, a psychologist and a religious Jew, relates in his book, Wounds Not Healed, *concerning a Christian woman who nursed back to life a man who had murdered her parents and raped her. The man, shocked by her behavior, asked*

---

minister, theologian, and anti-Nazi activist killed in a concentration camp in 1945, argued against "the preaching of forgiveness without requiring repentance." He referred to such forgiveness as "cheap grace" (*The Cost of Discipleship*, 47).

*I am not suggesting that parents who extend forgiveness in such a case actually do regard the child as "property," but unfortunately they are acting as if they do. What parents might say to the murderer is, "I forgive you for the terrible pain your act has caused *us.*" It's the act perpetrated against another that is not ours to forgive. As Dostoevsky put it in *The Brothers Karamazov*, "I do not, finally, want the mother to embrace the tormentor who let his dogs tear her son to pieces! She dare not forgive him! Let her forgive him for herself if she wants to . . . but she has no right to forgive the suffering of her child."

the woman, "Why didn't you kill me?" She replied, "I am a follower of him [i.e., Jesus] who says, 'Love your enemy.'" A remarkable story, but as Schimmel, writing from a Jewish perspective, asks, "Why, however, is it noble to love and take care of evil people?"[8]

In contrast to this woman's attitude, when the Jewish writer Cynthia Ozick was asked if it was morally appropriate to forgive a penitent Nazi SS officer who had participated in the murder of a Jewish community in Poland, she responded: "'I forgive you,' we say to the child who has muddied the carpet, 'but next time don't do it again.' Next time, she will leave the muddy boots outside the door; forgiveness, with its enlarging capacity, will have taught her. Forgiveness is an effective teacher. Meanwhile, the spots can be washed away. But murder is irrevocable. Murder is irreversible. . . . Even if forgiveness restrains one from perpetrating a new batch of corpses, will the last batch come alive again? . . . Forgiveness is pitiless. It forgets the victim. It cultivates sensitiveness toward the murderer at the price of insensitiveness toward the victim."

And what of the penitent SS officer? "Let the SS man die unshriven. Let him go to hell."[9]

The Jewish view can be summed up as follows: Forgiveness is almost always a virtue, but the taking of an innocent life is an unforgivable offense.

————

12. Murder is not the only crime that is unforgivable; any crime can be forgiven only by the victim. Do those who advocate forgiveness even for offenses committed against others believe that we should forgive someone who, at this very moment, is sexually or physically abusing a child?

————

Those who forgive the perpetrators of crimes against others are not only committing an injustice; unless they are equally forgiving in their own lives, they are also hypocrites. Unfortunately, such hypocrisy is not rare. For example, Dr. Solomon Schimmel was speaking with a Bible scholar who was criticizing Israelis for their unwillingness to forget atrocities committed by Palestinian terrorists. During the conversation, the scholar expressed resentment toward a colleague who, years earlier, had failed to give him due credit for an article he had written. Concluded Schimmel, "I don't think he was even aware of the incongruity between his own inability to forgive a relatively minor offense to his ego some decade or so ago, and his preaching to victims of terror that they should forgive and forget."[10]

————

13. Although the victim of a crime has the right to forgive the perpetrator, it seems to me that the victim, particularly of a serious crime, should generally not ask that the assailant be spared punishment. Thus—to cite a case not drawn from Jewish life—Pope John Paul II forgave Ali Agca, the Muslim fanatic who injured him in an attempted assassination in 1981, but the Pope did not oppose the judicial punishment of Agca, who was sentenced to life imprisonment.

On the other hand, journalist Susan Jacoby writes of a crime that rocked New York City in the 1980s, in which two men raped and tortured a nun, cutting twenty-seven crosses into her body with a nail file. They also used broomsticks and crucifixes in their attack.

The nun refused to testify against the men, hoping that her attitude of forgiveness would inspire her attackers to regret the harm they had done. The public was outraged when the men were not tried either for rape or for aggravated assault, but only for lesser offenses, for which they received light sentences.

The nun's behavior, reflecting an extraordinary capacity to love and forgive, puts one in mind of a Persian proverb, "To spare the ravening leopard is an act of injustice to the sheep." Her unwillingness to testify guaranteed that the men would be out of jail within a few years. This, in turn, could easily have led to another woman being the victim of these men's extreme sadism (I do not know what, in fact, happened). If that had occurred, would the nun have forgiven that act as well? One also wonders if the newly attacked woman would be expected to forgive the nun. And would the nun have felt obliged to ask that woman's forgiveness?

In contrast, Maimonides, in his *Guide to the Perplexed* (one of the seminal works of medieval Jewish philosophy), writes that if the victim of an attack forgives his attacker and then dies, the assailant should still be executed (3:41). This teaching suggests that, even after human forgiveness has been granted, justice requires that the murderer's act be punished.

————

In contemporary society, in which the death sentence is a much more rarely inflicted punishment than during the twelfth century, when Maimonides lived, it is very unlikely, perhaps inconceivable, that someone would be executed after having been forgiven by the victim. But it should be equally inconceivable that the murderer not be punished at all.

————

14. Even though it is forbidden to forgive someone for a wrongful act committed against someone else, if the perpetrator seems sincerely regretful, we should encourage him to make amends to his victim; further, if we are in a position to do so, we should offer to act as the conduit between the perpetrator and the victim.

19

HOW TO FORGIVE

1. "A person should not be cruel when forgiving another" (Maimonides, "Laws of Character Development" 6:6). In other words, once you choose to forgive, don't, for example, talk repeatedly about how much the other person hurt you. If it is important to you that the other person understands how much their action pained you, say it, but only once or perhaps, at most, twice. Then let it go.

2. If a relatively minor offense is committed against you, forgive the offender in a way that conveys the feeling that you do not regard the offense as significant. For example, Rabbi Meir Schlesinger, who had studied under Rabbi Shlomo Zalman Auerbach, was afraid that he had cited ideas learned from Rabbi Auerbach as his own without crediting him (Jewish tradition regards it as a serious wrong to take credit for another's insight). When he asked forgiveness, Rabbi Auerbach assured him that he had no reason to worry: "If you say my thoughts in your name, I am grateful and happy. However, I earnestly request that you not say your thoughts in my name."*

3. Let the person feel your forgiveness by resuming your friendship with her. In the words of an infrequently cited teaching in *The Fathers According to Rabbi Nathan:* "Who is a hero among heroes [alternatively, 'a strong person among strong people']? One who turns an enemy into a friend" (chapter 23). A strong person is not one who prides himself on holding a grudge, but one who relinquishes it. A strong person fights his inclination toward

---

*Cited in Rabbi Hanoch Teller, *And from Jerusalem, His Word*, pages 86–87.

vengefulness; rather, he tries to find a way to reconcile with anyone with whom he has feuded.*

4. Go out of your way to offer those who have hurt you the opportunity to repent. For example, don't avoid the person by not returning his phone calls (unless the wrong done to you was so extreme that you are not required to forgive it, and/or it would be emotionally unhealthy for you to be involved in any contact with him). The Talmud reports incidents in which great rabbinic figures who had been treated badly by others sought out opportunities to enable the offenders to ask forgiveness and reconcile (for an example, see page 165).

5. Strive to let your forgiveness be wholehearted. One way to achieve this is to reflect on some unintended good that resulted from the wrong done to you. As Joseph says to his brothers, "Although you intended me harm, God intended it for good, so as to bring about the present result—the survival of many people" (Genesis 50:20). When others harm us, it frequently forces us to grow in ways we would otherwise not have done. Joseph had been arrogant as a young man, but because of the suffering he endured, he became more humble. And as a result of what his brothers did to him, he was ultimately put into a position at the court of Pharaoh in which he achieved great power and saved many thousands of lives.[†]

Several people have told me of instances in which they were unfairly fired, but went on to become more successful than they would have been in their old jobs. Therefore, if you find it very hard to forgive someone—particularly somebody who has asked for forgiveness—see whether you can find any personal growth or other good that came about because of what happened. On the basis of that, find it in your heart to forgive the person who hurt you, or at least to stop bearing a grudge.

———

A friend who read this suggestion challenged me: "But what if one can perceive of no genuine 'good' that resulted from the evil? For example, if one became a paraplegic after a car accident? In addition, even if some good did result

---

*In fact, this is a concrete example of the more popular answer to the question posed in *The Ethics of the Fathers* (4:1), "Who is a hero? One who conquers his [evil] inclination."

[†]Because his brothers' intention had been malevolent, Joseph was not required to be grateful to them; indeed, that is why he tested them to see if they had repented. But it is certainly easier to feel forgiving toward those who harmed you when their behavior unexpectedly brought you success you would not have achieved otherwise.

certainly the injured party should feel no obligation to forgive the one who brought about the injury."

———

6. Take into account any psychological problems the one who offended you might suffer from or any abuse he experienced, and ask yourself whether those factors might have made him more liable to do the evil he did to you. While these factors do not excuse his behavior, your thinking about them with some sympathy will probably make it easier for you to forgive him.

7. Pray for the person who has sought your forgiveness. When the citizens of ancient Israel repented before the prophet and judge Samuel for their wrongdoings, and beseeched him to pray to God on their behalf, Samuel replied, "Far be it from me to sin against God and refrain from praying on your behalf " (I Samuel 12:19, 23).

Offering such a prayer will also help diminish your animosity and anger against the person who harmed you.

HUMILITY

———

What reason have you for assuming your
blood is redder [than the other person's]?
Perhaps his blood is redder.

Pesachim 25b

20

WHAT HUMILITY IS, AND WHY IT
IS IMPORTANT

1. There are numerous biblical stories about Moses that describe the many fine traits he possessed. Thus, Moses was courageous (he defended a Jewish slave from the Egyptian overseer who was beating him; Exodus 2:11–12), and determined to fight injustice (in Midian, he defended women shepherds from male shepherds who were bullying them; Exodus 2:16–17). Moses was also compassionate (he prayed for the health of his sister Miriam when she was stricken with leprosy as God's punishment for having spoken ill of him (Numbers 12:1–13). Yet nowhere does the Bible refer to Moses as "courageous," "a defender of justice," or "compassionate." Rather, we infer these characteristics from what we are told about him. There is only one virtue that the Bible explicitly ascribes to Moses: "Now Moses was a very humble man, more so than any other man on earth" (Numbers 12:3). That this is the *only* virtue the Torah attributes to its greatest hero is itself the most significant indication of the importance of humility in the Jewish tradition.

2. In the Bible, the virtue of humility is a recurring theme. Abraham speaks of himself as "but dust and ashes" (Genesis 18:27), while the prophet Micah commends one who walks "humbly with God" as fulfilling one of the three most important demands God makes of us (Micah 6:8); the other two are "doing justice and loving kindness." According to Micah, an absence of humility, just like a lack of concern with justice and kindness, is in and of itself proof of a person's lack of religious commitment.

———

Why does Micah speak of walking "humbly with God," and not just of "walking humbly"? Perhaps because if we are certain that God is on our side, we can easily become arrogant and even cruel. Thus, contemporary Islamist terrorists, certain that they are "walking with God," have no compunction about killing innocent people, and even shouting "God is great!" (Allahu akhbar) *as they do so. This is what can happen when one walks "arrogantly [and not humbly] with God."*

In contrast to Abraham, Pharaoh is the epitome of arrogance. He responds scornfully to Moses' appeals, brought on behalf of the oppressed Israelite slaves: "Who is the Lord that I should heed His voice" (Exodus 5:2). Later, when Pharaoh again refuses to heed God's commands, Moses and Aaron, speaking in God's Name, ask him, "How long will you refuse to humble yourself before Me?" (Exodus 10:3).

———

3. Because self-centeredness—and even a measure of arrogance—is natural to many people, Judaism encourages us to make every effort to cultivate humility. In the verse cited above, Moses is not described simply as being "humble," but "very humble." Similarly, *The Ethics of the Fathers* instructs people to be "very, very humble in spirit" (4:4). And Maimonides, normally an advocate of the "golden path" of moderation, rules that, in pursuing a path between arrogance and humility, "one should move away from the one extreme [i.e., of arrogance] and adopt the other [extreme humility]" ("Laws of Character Development" 2:3).

———

If humility is so important, why is it not one of the 613 commandments? That was the question raised by the eighteenth-century rabbi Michel of Zlotchov, a Chasidic rebbe, before his followers. He answered, "Because if a person were to think, 'Now I am fulfilling the commandment of becoming humble,' and would then believe that he was becoming humble, that would be the worst vanity of all." In other words, even humble people need to work on humility. The moment they feel they have fully achieved it, they need to start working on it again.

My grandfather, Rabbi Nissen Telushkin, told me of a man he knew who was a prominent member of a synagogue, and who by all rights should have occupied a seat near the front of the synagogue, yet he chose to sit in an undistinguished seat near the back. However, his eyes would constantly dart around to see if people were taking note of what he was doing. So my grandfather said to him, "It would be better for you to sit in the front of the synagogue and think you should be sitting in the back, than to sit in the back of the synagogue and think you should be sitting in the front."

———

4. What exactly is humility? Does it mean speaking of ourselves as un-accomplished, even when this is not the case? Many of us have ambivalent, even negative, feelings about humility, associating it with characters like Uriah Heep, the shrewd, deceitful clerk in Charles Dickens's *David Copper-field*. By pretending to be "so very 'umble," Heep gained people's trust, and then defrauded them of their money. Thus his name has become a byword for obsequiousness and *false* humility.

In truth, humility is not difficult to define (though it is hard to embody). It means not regarding ourselves as more important than other people, including those who have achieved less than we have. And it implies judging ourselves not in comparison with others, but in light of our capabilities, and the tasks we believe God has set for us on earth. This idea is conveyed in a seemingly immodest teaching of Rabbi Israel Salanter: "I know that I have the mental capacity of a thousand men, but because of that, my obligation is also that of a thousand men."[1] As Rabbi Salanter's statement emphasizes, the very capabilities that can make a person most proud ("I know I have the mental capacity of a thousand men") are also those that should be most humbling. If we have greater wisdom, then we also have a greater responsibility to bring people to understanding and wisdom. If we have wealth, then we have a greater responsibility to help those in need. If we occupy a position of power, we have a greater obligation to help the oppressed. In short, the fact that we have greater abilities than another does not mean that we are greater in God's eyes—another person, for example, might be more accomplished than we are in fulfilling the commandment "Love your neighbor as yourself"—but only that we have greater responsibilities.

Thinking about how much we can do in comparison to what we have done also serves as a corrective against pride and arrogance.

———

A brief meditation from the Orchot Tzaddikim *(The Path of the Righteous) may help those of us who are inclined to take too much pride in our achievements: "All of the good things I do are but a drop in the ocean in comparison to what I ought to do" ("The Gate of Humility").*

Steven Spielberg's Academy Award–winning film, Schindler's List *relates the story of Oskar Schindler, who saved over 1,100 Jews from the Nazis. At the end of the war, when the former prisoners give Schindler a ring emblazoned with the Talmud's words "He who saves one life it is as if he saved an entire world" (Mishnah Sanhedrin 4:5), the film depicts Schindler as starting to weep uncontrollably, realizing that perhaps he could have rescued even more people. It was precisely the awareness of how much good he had done that heightened Schindler's awareness of how much more he might have done.**

———

Three sources of humility

5. *An ongoing awareness of God:* "I am always mindful of the Lord's presence" (Psalms 16:8). Abraham and Moses' constant God-consciousness made them humble, even though they had many reasons to feel proud and superior to others. As Rabbi Avrohom Feuer comments, "When one measures himself against the infinite and eternal Creator, he understands his own relative insignificance. Thus, precisely because Moses achieved such a tangible closeness to God was he [more humble] than any man to have walked the earth. One's greatness as a person depends, perhaps, on the degree to which [one] can truly perceive his Creator's presence and make [this] ultimate yardstick a reality for himself."[2] In contrast, arrogant people are that way precisely because they judge themselves not in relationship to God, but rather in contrast to those who are less accomplished.

———

Rabbi Shmuely Boteach explains Moses' humility through an analogy: "If I were a teacher of nuclear physics in a high school, I could feel that I knew more than most people about my subject. I could feel arrogant because I was knowledgeable in such a difficult field. But if I were invited to work together with Albert Einstein in his laboratory, I would immediately discover that everything I thought I knew was meaningless compared to Einstein's grasp of the subject. I would come to terms with my own inadequacies and stand humbled in the face of true greatness. This is what happened with Moses, but infinitely more so. Because Moses had stood closer than any other to God, he was also the most humble man who ever lived. . . . Having enjoyed the constant and lifelong presence of God, Moses felt [his own knowledge and abilities] to be insignificant. . . ."[3]

———

6. *The awareness that every human being with whom we interact is created in God's image (Genesis 1:27), and therefore is as valuable as we ourselves.* The Talmud records the story of a man who came to Rava, the fourth-century sage, with a most disturbing moral dilemma: The governor of his

———

*The speech delivered by Schindler was written for the film, but was not given in precisely this manner in real life. Nonetheless, the scene is a powerful lesson in humility and goodness.

town had ordered him to murder an innocent person; if he refused to do so, he himself would be put to death. When the questioner asked Rava whether he was permitted to kill the man in order to save his own life, the rabbi answered, "What reason do you have for assuming your blood is redder [than the other person's]? Perhaps his blood is redder" (*Pesachim* 25b).*

Rabbi Simcha Bunim, a Chasidic rebbe, notes that this seminal talmudic ruling conveys an important lesson about humility: "[The fact that we cannot kill an innocent person to save our own lives is based on the presumption that we cannot know] whose life is more important in the eyes of God. If even in so crucial a moment we have no right to deem ourselves superior to another, what right can we possibly have to do so on less critical occasions?"[4]

———

Another ramification of this talmudic teaching: Don't exploit others, as historically was done through slavery, and as is done today by those who overwork, underpay, or otherwise wrong their employees. How can one assume that one's blood is more precious than the blood of those whom one mistreats?

This teaching has implications in far less serious areas than matters of life and death and exploitation. For example, a humble person will not push ahead of someone else in line. Rather, he will think, "What gives me the right to assume that my time is more valuable than his?"

———

7. A less fortunate source of humility is suffering, which can make even self-confident people aware that they are not the masters of their fate. Thus the Torah describes the young Joseph, the favored son of the patriarch Jacob, as a bit arrogant. When Joseph has dreams in which his brothers bow low to him, he relates them to his brothers, thus further inciting and intensifying their hostile feelings (Genesis 37:5–11). But after suffering years of slavery and imprisonment in Egypt, Joseph's manner changes. When Pharaoh says to him, "Now, I have heard it said that you can hear a dream and interpret its meaning," Joseph responds, "It is not I. It is God who will see to Pharaoh's welfare" (Genesis 41:16).

The benefits of humility

8. It is an important prerequisite for finding the truth. The Talmud teaches that Hillel and his disciples' humble manner caused their rulings on

---

*Indeed, by killing another, we may make ourselves less worthy of living than our victim.

matters of Jewish law to be accepted over those of their opponents, the School of Shammai. The School of Hillel studied even those views of Shammai with which they disagreed; indeed, they studied those views first (*Eruvin* 13b). Because humble people don't assume that they possess the full truth, they consider opposing viewpoints. The Mishnah (*Eduyot* 1:12–14) records instances in which the School of Hillel, after considering the views of the School of Shammai, retracted their original positions and acknowledged that Shammai's views made more sense. Thus, by encouraging a person to consider viewpoints other than his own, the trait of humility often leads one to a greater grasp of the truth.

———

One author told me that when he and his co-writer disagreed, they would argue the issue until one side convinced the other. Because they wanted to come to a well-reasoned, accurate conclusion, they took pains not to allow their egos, the source of pride and stubbornness, to dominate.

———

9. Humility also leads us to become more tolerant and accepting. Rashi, Judaism's most important biblical and talmudic commentator, identifies tolerance, along with modesty, as the defining characteristic of humility (see his commentary on Numbers 12:3). Thus, precisely because Hillel and his disciples were not certain that they were entirely in the right, they tolerated opposing views, realizing that, though these views might be wrong in their conclusions, they might still learn something from them. Therefore, a humble person bears no ill will toward those who disagree with him. Such an individual is aware that people have the right to understand the world differently, and that their perceptions might have something to teach him.

———

When a rabbi wrote an apology to the Chazon Ish, the great twentieth-century talmudic scholar, for arguing against a legal ruling the scholar had rendered, the Chazon Ish responded, "Your mention of any possible ill will on my part [because you disagreed with me] is simply not understandable to me. What place is there for ill will? Your words are precious to me."

———

10. Humility brings about a greater sense of inner peace. Because humble people do not see themselves as superior to others, or more deserving, they are less apt to suffer from a sense of entitlement. Instead they feel grateful for all that they do have, and this diminishes envy (a major cause of anxiety and dissatisfaction); after all, envy arises only when we lack what others have and to which we feel entitled as well.

11. So essential is humility to leading a worthy life that the Talmud's response to the query "Who is destined for the World-to-Come?" is "One who is modest and humble" (*Sanhedrin* 88b).

21

CULTIVATING HUMILITY

1. Learn from every person. The Talmud teaches, "Who is wise?" One who learns from every person" (*The Ethics of the Fathers* 4:1). In this statement, wisdom and humility are united. This passage orients us to think in terms of what we can learn from everyone (itself a humbling thought), not just what others can learn from us.

———

When Rabbi Abraham Twerski was in his first months of psychiatric training, he received a call from a friend whose brother was suffering from severe depression. Far too junior to offer any advice himself, Rabbi Twerski put the woman in touch with Dr. L. B. Kalinowski, a renowned scholar who had written a widely used text on the treatment of depression. A week later Dr. Kalinowski called Twerski, informed him that an antidepressant medication had been ineffective in treating the patient, and asked if he thought electroshock treatments might work. "Dr. Kalinowski," Rabbi Twerski said, "you may have the wrong impression. I am not a psychiatrist, but only in my first year of training. The only thing I know about the treatment of depression is what I am learning from your book."

Kalinowski responded, "Yes, I know treatment, but you have a better knowledge of the man's personality."

Under the doctor's prodding, Twerski explained why he thought electro-shock treatment would not benefit this patient, and Dr. Kalinowski accepted his reasoning.

Later, when Twerski told his supervisor how amazed he was to have been consulted by so eminent an authority, the supervisor smiled and said, "The only one who would feel secure enough to ask the opinion of a first-year resident is the man who wrote the book. He is not worried that this would be a reflection on his competence."

As this episode taught Dr. Twerski, "The attitude of taking advice only from someone of prominence and with outstanding credentials is nothing but an ego trip. . . . A person with a healthy ego will have no difficulty accepting counsel from anyone."[1]

———

2. For each person we know, we should identify an area in which he is our superior. Bachya ibn Pakuda's medieval *Duties of the Heart* records that when a great sage was asked, "How did you come to be accepted as the undisputed leader of your generation?" he answered, "Because I never met a person in whom I didn't find a quality in which he was superior to me."

For the next week or so, we should find an area in which each person with whom we come into contact is our superior.* Perhaps she is more likely than us to

- visit the sick
- contribute a greater percentage of income to charity
- speak of others in a more kindly, less judgmental, and fair way
- address others in a manner that inspires confidence and optimism
- express gratitude
- be more devoted to her synagogue or children's school

Once we have identified the other person's superior trait, let this become our immediate association when that individual's name is mentioned (for example, "Oh, yes, Sarah, she's amazing. I saw how patient she is with her children; she never seems to lose her temper"). Then we should remind ourselves to try to emulate her.

Many of us are accustomed to doing exactly the opposite. When speaking about someone we both know, we often discuss the person's faults at

———

*Doing so will also help us fulfill an important talmudic dictum: "If one knows that his friend is greater than he even in only one area, he is obliged to accord him honor" (*Pesachim* 113b).

length, while either ignoring their strengths or mentioning them only briefly and in passing.

———

Focusing on other people's finer qualities is important for those who tend to feel superior to those of lesser intellectual attainments. Thus the Midrash records that, while taking a walk, Rabbi Yannai encountered a man of impressive appearance, whom he assumed to be a scholar. He invited the man to his home and entertained him lavishly. But when he started to speak to the man in areas of Jewish learning, it became apparent that the man was quite ignorant. Later, when Rabbi Yannai asked him to recite a blessing over the wine, the man said, "Let Yannai make the blessing in his own house." At this point, Rabbi Yannai, by now furious at the man's ignorance, said to him, "Can you repeat what I say to you?"

When the man said "Yes," Yannai said, "Then say, 'A dog has eaten Yannai's food.' "

Outraged at the insult, the guest seized Yannai and reproved him for his rude behavior. Yannai, who quickly realized that the man, though ignorant of religious matters, was by no means stupid, asked him, "What merit have you [i.e., what good deeds have you done] that you should eat at my table?"

The man said, "I never heard malicious gossip and repeated it, nor did I ever see two people quarreling without making peace between them."

The now chastened and humbled Rabbi Yannai said, "You have such fine qualities, and I called you a dog" (Leviticus Rabbah 9:3).

To counteract this tendency to look down on those who are less professionally and intellectually accomplished, Rabbi Meir taught, "Be of humble spirit before every person" (The Ethics of the Fathers 4:10).*

———

3. Always cite your sources (*The Ethics of the Fathers* 6:6). Not only is this the fair thing to do—taking credit for someone else's insight is a form of stealing—but it also serves as a reminder to each of us that our wisdom is built upon that of others.†

———

*Dr. Isaac Herschkopf notes that focusing on another person's superior traits is a particularly important technique for a parent who has a child with some unpleasant tendencies. In such cases, many parents ignore the "least favorite" child and focus instead on those of their "favorite" children with easier dispositions. What the parents should do is spend time with the child until they find something about him that they can love and admire. Every child should be his parents' "favorite" in some way.

†My friend Rabbi Robert Hirt has noted the ironic fact that *The Ethics of the Fathers* does not record the name of the rabbi who made this observation.

The late Rabbi Moshe Besdin, an erudite Bible scholar who imparted his insights on the Torah portion to thousands of students, said that he was quoted in many synagogues every Shabbat, but only in New York's Lincoln Square Synagogue, whose spiritual leader was Rabbi Shlomo Riskin, was he quoted by name.

Respect all those you meet

4. Go out of your way to show honor and respect to others. The Talmud teaches that the person most worthy of honor is one who honors others (*The Ethics of the Fathers* 4:1). Rabbi Abraham Twerski says, "The average person undoubtedly thinks that an honorable person is one who receives much honor, whereas the Torah's attitude is the reverse: It is the one who gives honor."[2]

On the eve of Yom Kippur one year, Rabbi Joseph Soloveitchik, the "Rav" of Yeshiva University and one of the greatest rabbinic figures in American Jewish life, traveled to the cemetery to visit his wife's grave. While there, "he was approached by two non-observant Jews. They did not recognize him, but judged him from appearances to be a rabbi. They asked if he would accompany them to their parents' grave and recite a prayer. The Rav obliged. Their brother was also interred in the cemetery, and they asked the Rav if he would accompany them to his gravesite as well. Again the Rav graciously complied. Then, declining their repeated offers for remuneration, the Rav wished them well and returned to his waiting car. A cemetery official had witnessed the entire scene. After the Rav's departure, he approached the two beneficiaries and identified the anonymous rabbi. They were stunned that so great a personage burdened with vast responsibilities, had diverted time and energy to address the needs of two unknown, non-observant Jews. Two weeks later, Maimonides School [which Rabbi Soloveitchik had founded with his wife, Tanya] received a letter, with a thousand-dollar contribution enclosed: "'Please accept our donation in tribute to Rabbi Soloveitchik. We are the two Jews whom he so graciously and affectionately assisted at the cemetery on the eve of the Day of Atonement.'"[3]

---

5. Do not gossip about others' flaws. Rabbi Israel Meir ha-Kohen Kagan (1838–1933), one of Judaism's greatest legal scholars, noted in his book

Chaffetz Chayyim* that one who is truly aware of his faults will be reluctant to speak badly of others. He will realize that his own faults might be even greater than the other person's.

6. Judge others not only by their achievements, particularly if these are not substantial, but also in light of how they are fulfilling their potential. When you are interacting with those who are less accomplished than you are, recognize that they might be fulfilling their potential as much, or even more, than you are fulfilling yours. Even if they aren't doing so, this might be because of psychological or other difficulties; they might still be doing as well as they can.

———

The Talmud records the following prayer, recited by the Rabbis in the Israeli city of Yavneh, to guard against feelings of superiority toward the simple farmers among whom they lived:

"I am a creature, and my fellow man is a creature. My work is in the city, and his work is in the field. I rise early to perform my work, and he rises early to perform his. Just as he does not presume to do my work, so do I not presume to do his. And if you should say that I do much [for Heaven] and he does little, we have learned: Both the one who does much and the one who does little [are equally rewarded], provided that each directs his heart toward Heaven" (Berachot *17a*).

———

Every year, just before Rosh Hashanah, people would come to the home of the Chazon Ish to ask for his blessing and to bless him as well. The rabbi would sit at his desk, people would come in, shake his hand, exchange a few words, and leave. However, the Chazon Ish would honor one man who came every year by standing up when he saw him, and escorting him to the door when he left. When the rabbi's wife asked him why he regarded this man as so special, the rabbi answered, "This young man was born with a reduced potential, and with great effort he has succeeded far beyond everybody's expectations. [He] . . . has lived up to his full potential, and I honor him because of that."[4]

———

————————

*After the publication of this book on the laws of permitted and forbidden speech, its author became known throughout the Jewish world by its title. The Hebrew words *chaffetz chayyim* mean "eager for life." The phrase comes from Psalm 34:13: "Who is the man who is eager for life, who desires years of good fortune? [To achieve this] Guard your tongue from evil, and your lips from deceitful speech."

7. When dealing with those we perhaps regard as less intelligent than ourselves, we should apply the Golden Rule and consider, "How would I like someone smarter than I am to treat me?"

In addition to encouraging us to act in a kinder and more patient manner toward others, this question will remind us that there are many people who are more intelligent than we are. If we don't believe this, all we have to do is think of a subject about which we know very little. A prominent Jewish scholar told me that he has only to think of his ignorance of physics and chemistry or the fact that he has to call in a handyman when there is the slightest leak in his bathroom, to remind himself of how limited his expertise is.

8. We should ask others, particularly those we have helped, to bless us. Many people, when helping someone on a lower socioeconomic rung such as a beggar, say, "God bless you." Such words are kind and appropriate, but so, too, is soliciting the recipient's blessing: "A blessing given by an ordinary person should not be taken lightly" (*Berachot* 7a). It is particularly worthwhile to solicit a blessing from those whom we have helped, and to be pleased and honored—no matter how highly we may regard ourselves and our achievements—with the compliments and/or blessings of any person.

———

A man I know extended considerable financial aid to an elderly widow whom he had befriended. Whenever he had a business project pending, or some matter of family concern, he would ask the woman to bless him. He explained, "She was a person of extraordinary goodness, so I felt, 'Who better than she to offer me a blessing?' Also, I know she felt deeply embarrassed that she needed assistance, so by making it known that I desired her assistance as well, it helped equalize our relationship. And, finally, if I want God to show me mercy and look upon me with love, then who better to have bless me than a person to whom I have shown mercy and love?"

———

If you are prominent

9. Instead of using whatever prominence and influence we have only to advance ourselves, we should use it to help others. Deuteronomy 10:17 describes the Lord as "the God of gods and the Lord of lords," while the next verse tells us that "God executes justice for the fatherless and the widow."

The first verse speaks of God's preeminence, while the second suggests that one of God's greatest concerns is to help the vulnerable.

Similarly, successful people should imitate God by helping "the fatherless and the widow," and all others who are vulnerable. A friend who has achieved considerable fame confided that its greatest benefit is that it makes it easier to do good for others. For example, he knows that if he, as a well-known person, calls someone who is sick, his fame will help the vulnerable person feel better about him- or herself ("the fact that an important person calls me means that I am important"), more so than if the call came from a less prominent person. (This is not fair, but, fair or unfair, this is how the world works.)

We should also use whatever prominence and connections we have to make calls or write letters of recommendation to help people find employment or a better job.

What a different take on fame in a society in which prominent people who are not accorded the respect they take for granted are known to shout, "Do you know who I am?"

———

During the early twentieth century, a terrible fire broke out in the Russian town of Brisk, and many homes were destroyed. Particularly hard hit were shacks belonging to the poor. Although the world-renowned scholar Rabbi Chaim Soloveitchik's house was not damaged, he slept that night in the synagogue along with those who had lost their homes. When the town's citizens asked him why he was doing so, he told them that he would go on sleeping in the synagogue "until everyone has a roof over his head. If I remain in my own house, who knows how long it will take the community to raise the necessary funds to rebuild the homes of all the poor, the widows and the orphans? But if it is known that I too will sleep in the shul *until the work is completed, the fundraising will go much faster." Only after the last home had been rebuilt did Reb Chaim return to his own house.*[5]

———

10. If you occupy a position of authority, study the Torah and the other Jewish sources to remind yourself not to feel superior to those over whom you have power. People who occupy high positions often become arrogant, both because of their power and because of the flattery offered them by subordinates. To counteract this tendency, the Torah ordained that, upon assuming office, a king should write and carry around his own Torah, thereby reminding himself that he is God's servant, and serves at God's wish. The

Torah also notes that this should be done so "that his heart not be lifted above his brothers" (Deuteronomy 17:20).

Sit down periodically, and study or copy Jewish teachings, such as Deuteronomy 17:14–20 or Psalm 82, which remind the powerful that God is above them, and Psalm 15, which reminds us all of how God wants us to act.

————

Saul, Israel's first king, provides the classical biblical example of a humble person who became arrogant and cruel upon gaining power. When he was originally chosen to be king, Saul was a humble man, and unconcerned about his status (I Samuel 10:22). However, once ensconced in power, he was willing to slaughter innocent people to retain his position (I Samuel 22:9–13). That was the case even after Samuel, the prophet who had anointed him, informed Saul that God no longer considered him fit to be king. Had Saul retained the humility that characterized him before he became ruler over others, he would never have acted in such a fashion.

————

11. "One should always speak gently to one's fellow human beings" (*Yoma* 86a). The very act of speaking gently encourages us to regard all those to whom we speak as equals. When we order others about, we tend to think of them as inferiors (that is why speaking in an imperious manner both reflects and reinforces arrogance). We should be particularly careful to speak in a gentle manner to children, employees, and those with whom we disagree. Also, we should use such expressions as "Would you be so kind?" or "Please," when speaking to household help or handymen, the sort of people to whom we may be likely to issue orders.

12. We should not speak about our achievements to others, unless there is a pressing reason to do so. The Book of Proverbs advises, "Let a stranger praise you and not your own mouth" (27:2). Although it is sometimes tempting to flaunt our accomplishments, we should try to refrain from doing so. If we have achieved a great deal and are eager to impress others, restraining ourselves can be difficult. Therefore, we should work on developing this trait one occasion at a time. We should resolve that the next time we are at a social gathering, we will not mention any personal achievement unless it is absolutely germane to the conversation.*

————

*People who brag a lot about their accomplishments reveal a desperate need for recognition, admiration, and praise. Therefore, although braggarts come across as conceited, their boasting

However, when it is important that people know of our abilities and accomplishments (such as at a job interview), we should, of course, make others aware of them. In such a case the Zohar somewhat whimsically punctuates the verse to read as follows: "Let a stranger praise you, but if not? Let your own mouth praise you."

———

The Talmud teaches that one need not keep his or her well-known identity a secret "where he is unknown" (Nedarim 62a). The Sefer Chasidim, elaborating on this point, notes that if a scholar comes to a city where he is unknown and will be ignored, he should start engaging townspeople in conversation so that they will come to appreciate who he is (paragraph 328).

Bragging, which often provokes annoyance and animosity in listeners, can also be self-destructive. The Bible informs us that when Joseph told his brothers of his dreams that they would one day bow down to him, "they hated him even more" [they already despised him for being their father's favorite]. Later it was this boasting that served as the brothers' rationale for plotting his murder: "Let us kill him and see what becomes of his dreams" (Genesis 37:5–11).*

———

13. We should help prepare for the Sabbath, which honors God for creating the world, with our own hands. Even if we are rich and have hired help to do such work, we should make sure to do some of the holiday's preparations personally. The *Shulchan Arukh* warns people not to think, "I will not blemish my honor [by engaging in demeaning labor]" (*Orach Chayyim* 250:1), while the Talmud offers many examples of physical labor engaged in by the greatest sages in preparation for Shabbat (*Shabbat* 119a). Spending just a few minutes before Shabbat honoring God through our own efforts serves as a tangible reminder that there is a God above us. This type of God-consciousness is the most powerful source of humility.

———

often reflects a low sense of self-regard. As Rabbi Shlomo Wolbe writes: "One who craves attention from others has not yet found himself; he is unaware of his true worth. Lacking self-esteem, he depends on the opinion of others. He hungers for their praise, for without their appreciation he feels worthless. When people fail to applaud him, he becomes . . . hostile and angry" (*Alei Shur* 1:43).

*In addition, "When a man boasts, if he is a sage, his wisdom departs from him" (*Pesachim* 66b). Boasting causes us to stop thinking critically about ourselves, and therefore makes us more likely to say or do foolish things.

Cultivating goodness in private

14. Rabbi Nota Tzvi Frankel, the *Alter* ([Wise] Old Man) of the Slobodka Yeshiva, taught, "Do only good, for that is why you were created. But who needs to know about it?" In line with this teaching, we should try to do some act of kindness on a routine basis that remains unknown to others. We should let it remain a secret between us, the recipient of our kindness (if it is an act that cannot be done anonymously), and God.

———

Rabbi Nachman of Bratslav taught, "The way in which a person can tell that he truly wants to serve God is if he has no desire for recognition."[6]

———

15. We should resist the temptation to perform an act, even a good one, just to be praised. If we sense that we are doing something only for that purpose, then, if possible, we should do it privately.

———

Rabbi Eliyahu Chaim Rosen, commenting on the common absence of humility, even among many of those who practice Jewish law, taught, "Why is it that people always choose to be stringent in those areas where others can find out about it?"[7]

A mussarnik, *a Jew who had spent decades trying to improve his character, confided to a disciple on his deathbed that the evil inclination* (yetzer hara) *was still trying to seduce him.*

"How so?" the astonished student asked.

The dying man answered: "He keeps telling me, 'Say the Sh'ma Yisrael *in a loud voice so that when you die, people will say, "What a* tzaddik *(righteous person). He died with the* Sh'ma *on his lips."'**

———

Acknowledge your weaknesses

16. We should cultivate humility by acknowledging what we don't know. The Talmud teaches, "Get your mouth into the habit of saying, 'I don't know,' lest you be led to telling a lie" (*Berachot* 4a). Pride causes many of us to act

---

*According to Jewish tradition, a Jew should make every effort to say the *Sh'ma* ("Hear O Israel, the Lord is our God, the Lord is One") as his or her final words.

as if we are all-knowing. Thus we sometimes give advice when we're not qualified to do so. A humble person knows what he knows, acknowledges what he doesn't, and, when appropriate, says to people, "I'm sorry, but I don't know."

———

Rashi was always ready to acknowledge what he didn't know. For example, Genesis 28:5 describes Laban as "the brother of Rebecca, the mother of Jacob and Esau." Why does the verse describe Rebecca this way, given that this relationship has repeatedly been noted in the preceding chapters? (This is comparable to an American history textbook repeatedly identifying Abraham Lincoln as an American president.) Rashi comments on this odd wording: "I do not know what this comes to teach us."*

Of course he could have said nothing. But had Rashi passed over the verse, people would have assumed that he found no problem with it—which he did—or that he understood why the Torah offered this identification of Rebecca, which he didn't. Instead, Rashi acknowledged that here was a textual problem he couldn't solve (perhaps thereby motivating others to try and solve it).

———

17. We should admit when we have made an error. Out of pride, many people refuse to acknowledge when they are wrong; instead, they invest intellectual energy in trying to defend a position that is incorrect. Thus pride, the source of arrogance, can cause us not only to hold on to incorrect teachings, but to try to convince others of their truth as well. In contrast, Rabbi Joseph Soloveitchik, the Rav, was always willing to accept the truth, from whatever the source, even when it disagreed with what he had thought earlier. Rabbi Haskel Lookstein, a longtime student of the Rav, recalls an instance when the Rav had built up an extended analytic structure to explain an issue in the Talmud. However, toward the end of his explanation, a student noticed a discrepancy between what the Rav was now teaching and something he had taught some months earlier. Gently, and with trepidation, the student asked, "Rebbe, how does this fit in with the analysis that we developed some months ago on a similar subject?" The Rav's eyes opened wide and he said to the student, "You are right, I am wrong. Do you hear, students? He is correct,

———

*This acknowledgment is far from a singular occurrence. Rabbi Berel Wein notes that on seventy-seven occasions in Rashi's Bible commentary, and on forty-four in his Talmud commentary, he uses the expression "I do not know what this means," or a variant thereof (*Living Jewish*, page 241).

I am incorrect. I'll have to go home and relearn the entire subject and present it again tomorrow."[8] Rabbi Lookstein recalls at least two other occasions when the Rav, in response to a student's challenge, acknowledged that he was wrong.

Another student of Rabbi Soloveitchik, Rabbi Shlomo Riskin, recalls an incident when the Rav snapped angrily at a student who had challenged his analysis. When the class ended, the student left the room abashed. The Rav, however, remained in his chair, sunk in thought; after about twenty minutes he looked at Rabbi Riskin, who was still in the room, and said to him, "Who asked the question at the end of the *shiur*? Friedberg? Take me to him." Rabbi Riskin led the Rav to the local dairy diner where the student had gone to eat. "Everyone was shocked when the Rav entered the restaurant, immediately out of respect jumping to their feet. From the corner of my eye I caught Friedberg, eating an omelette. His color had finally returned to his cheeks. His recovery was short-lived, however. The Rav immediately saw him. 'Friedberg.' The hapless student began to tremble. The Rav continued, 'You were right and I was wrong. Because of your question, I'll have to . . . completely rethink my interpretation. Thank you.' "[9] The Rav was perhaps the greatest Talmud scholar of his age, in part because he had the humility to acknowledge the truth when he was wrong.

In Genesis, when Tamar confronts Judah with evidence of a wrongful act he committed—evidence he could easily have suppressed—he immediately acknowledges, "She is more righteous than I" [alternatively, "She is more in the right than I"] (Genesis 38:26).

Maintaining perspective

18. We should minimize our accomplishments in our own eyes. The Rabbis, who regarded study of Torah as the most important act in which to engage, still cautioned scholars: "If you have learned much Torah, do not boast of it, for it was for this very purpose that you were created" (*The Ethics of the Fathers* 2:8). Similarly, if we do a great deal of good, we should remember that perhaps that was why we were born.

In addition, we should maximize in our own eyes the accomplishments and good deeds of others, and appreciate and admire them. Elazar Cohen was the officer in charge of the Israeli army's helicopter squad. During wartime, the squad's job was to fly into the range of enemy fire in order to rescue wounded soldiers.

Cohen once came to Rabbi Aryeh Levine, the Jerusalem saint, and asked for a blessing. To the army commander's shock, Reb Aryeh refused the request.

"But why?" Cohen asked.

Reb Aryeh responded, "Who am I to bless you? I truly believe your merit before Heaven is greater than mine."[10]

———

19. When someone compliments you, do not allow your sense of self to become inflated. "Even if all the world says you are a *tzaddik*, regard yourself as if you were evil" (*Niddah* 30b).

But if you *are* a good person, is it healthy or right to regard yourself as bad, even temporarily? Yes, but only at those times when you begin to think too highly of yourself, such as when you are being praised. During such times, view yourself, if not as bad, then as capable of serious wrongdoing. Also, consider how little good you have accomplished in comparison with how much you could have done. To think like this all the time would be demoralizing, so do so only when you are at risk of developing an inflated ego.

———

Before giving a speech, a prominent Chasidic rebbe would seclude himself in a room, and heap praises upon himself such as, "You are the greatest scholar of our age . . . our most inspiring leader . . . our wisest thinker," so that he wouldn't take such words seriously when they were said by others. When he was once overheard, the rabbi explained, "The words sound ridiculous when I say them to myself, and I want to accustom myself to their sounding ridiculous when said by others."

———

20. We should not pursue honor, or rush to accept it. The Talmud teaches that one who is invited to lead a prayer service should first decline, then be hesitant, and accept the honor only at the third invitation (*Berachot* 34a). Elsewhere the Talmud teaches that "if one pursues honor, honor flees from him" (*Eruvin* 13b).

———

On Rosh Hashanah and Yom Kippur, a cantor—whose head can easily swell at the thought that he is representing many hundreds of people before God—begins the Mussaf *service with the* Hineni *prayer: "Here I stand [before God] deficient in good deeds."*

———

21. We should correct flattery that is untrue; the Talmud forbids a person from accepting praise that is untrue, for reasons of both truthfulness and humility. "If people honor someone on the assumption that he knows two tractates of the Talmud, and he knows only one, he must inform them that he knows only one" (Jerusalem Talmud, *Shevi'it* 10:3). In other words, we should accustom ourselves to refusing honor that is exaggerated or undeserved.

———

22. We should avoid people who flatter us. Rabbi Moshe Chaim Luzzato, author of the eighteenth-century *Mesillat Yesharim (Path of the Upright)*, one of Judaism's most important guides to ethical self-improvement, taught that "it is clearly seen that most officers and kings, and men in positions of influence in general, regardless of their level, stumble and are corrupted by the flattery of their subordinates" (chapter 23, "The Means of Acquiring Humility").

———

23. Don't be concerned about being shown honor by others. For example, if someone does not address you by your title, let it pass, unless you think that the person is doing so to be intentionally disrespectful (as was once common in the American South, where, for many years, African-Americans were addressed by their first names, without being called Mr., Mrs., or Miss).

———

A man was driving in Manhattan's Lower East Side, when he saw his son on the sidewalk. He pulled his car over and called out "Moshe" to the boy. To the man's acute embarrassment, Rabbi Moshe Feinstein, who was also walking down the street, came over to his car and asked him what he wanted. The man explained that he was calling out to his son, and that he would never have addressed Rabbi Feinstein in so familiar a manner. Rabbi Feinstein waved aside the man's apology: "It has been a long time since such things mattered to me."

———

Rabbi Israel Salanter was known to go and visit scholars who came to town, although it was customary for the resident rabbi to wait for the guest to come and visit him. He expressed bemusement at this protocol: "This business of who visits whom first makes no sense to me. What is this? Some kind of childish game with rules."

———

24. Try to ignore personal slights. This is one of the hardest exercises in humility to practice, but the Talmud speaks with particular praise of those who "accept insult and do not mete it out" (*Shabbat* 88b). The thirteenth-century *Sefer Chasidim* tells of an incident in which a member of a community spoke unfairly of a local sage, and the communal leaders wanted to take action against the offender. When the rabbi said that he did not wish to see the man punished on his account, the leaders protested: "But if we do nothing, people will draw the conclusion that it is all right to make scurrilous attacks against rabbis." The rabbi answered, "I'd prefer that you do nothing, and rather let people learn from my behavior that it is best to just ignore meaningless attacks" (see page 363).

However, such rulings and statements should be applied flexibly. Thus, if someone is lying about you, and your good name is at risk of being damaged or destroyed, you should respond to the attackers by making certain that the truth is made known to others (see page 363 in the section on *lashon hara*).

———

Rabbi Aryeh Levine was once ferociously insulted in a synagogue by a religious extremist, who despised him for his friendship with the pro-Zionist chief rabbi, Abraham Isaac Kook. Reb Aryeh left the synagogue without saying a word, and never returned to it.

When another man, who was one of the extremists, subsequently asked Reb Aryeh, "Do you know perhaps why you were punished by that man's act and words of deep insult? Do you know the underlying reason?"

"It may be that I sinned toward God."

"Oh, no," said the other man. "It is because you are friendly with that rabbi" [namely Rabbi Kook; the extremists hated him so much that they wouldn't even utter his name].

"Tell me," said Reb Aryeh, "was I right to keep silent and say nothing?"

"Certainly, that is a very fine quality you have," the other answered, and went on to note that the Talmud praised the trait of accepting insult and not meting it out.

"Well, you should know," said Reb Aryeh, "that I learned this trait from that rabbi" (i.e., Rabbi Kook).[11]

———

Regarding the wisdom of ignoring acrimonious and unfair attacks, Abraham Lincoln, America's greatest, and most bitterly attacked, president, said: "If I were to try and read, much less answer, all the attacks made on me, this shop might as well be closed for any other business." As Lincoln put it, "I do the very best I know how, the very best I can; and I mean to keep doing so until the end. If the end brings me out all right, what is said against me won't amount to anything. If the end brings me out wrong, ten angels swearing I was right would make no difference."

———

25.   When offering personal prayers to God, we should make our appeal dependent on the merit of others, not our own. For example, when Moses beseeched God not to destroy the Jews because of their sin with the Golden Calf, he said, "Remember your servants Abraham, Isaac and Jacob" (Exodus 32:13). Still, a later biblical text credits *him*, not the Patriarchs, as deserving the credit for God's decision to save the Jews: "He (God) would have destroyed them had not Moses, His chosen one, confronted Him in the breach to avert His destructive wrath" (Psalms 106:23; see *Berachot* 10b). When we offer personal prayers to God—something almost all religious people do at least occasionally—we should make our request, at least sometimes, in the name of a parent, grandparent, or someone else who loved us, and who was a very good person.

26.   Even if your children are highly accomplished, do not allow them to be overly praised. Rabbi Moshe Feinstein (1895–1986), the preeminent Jewish legal scholar, was recognized as a Talmud scholar of note at the tender age of eleven. Once, when he entered a room where his father was sitting with some distinguished rabbinic colleagues, the other rabbis stood up in honor of the young scholar. The boy turned red with embarrassment, and his father said, "What are you doing to me? You are destroying my child! You will turn him into a *ba'al ga'avah* [an arrogant person]."

True, it's important for children's sense of self-esteem that parents praise them for their talents and accomplishments. But parents should guard against the *adulatory* compliments often given to children for their academic or athletic achievements, or for their good looks. As Rabbi Feinstein's father noted, you don't want your child to become conceited.

The danger of excessive and inappropriate humility

27.   We should avoid exaggerated humility; among other things, it can damage our good name. Rabbi Chaim Soloveitchik generally disliked issuing

rulings on questions of Jewish law, particularly ritual issues. His grandson, Rabbi Joseph Soloveitchik, explained that because Reb Chaim was familiar with so many different Jewish texts and had an immensely penetrating mind, "he could always find ways to justify different approaches to the same problem." For this reason, when the Jews of Brisk asked him to become the town's rabbi, he accepted on condition that his friend, Rabbi Simcha Selig Reguer, be designated to answer all ritual questions. That way, when a question of law was posed to him, Reb Chaim would feign ignorance and say, "I don't know, go ask Reb Simcha Selig." However, when he heard his son, Rabbi Moshe Soloveitchik, giving people the same response, he said to him, "Listen, my son. When I tell people I don't know, they don't believe me. However, if you start telling people that you don't know, they will believe you. See to it that you answer their questions."[12]

Rabbi Louis Jacobs believes that "self-denigration on the part of a rabbi can be disastrous." He tells of an incident when the scholar Rabbi Shimon Skopf came to Manchester, England, to raise money for his yeshiva in Grodno (Belarus). He was accompanied by another rabbi, an eloquent speaker, who kept praising Rabbi Skopf very highly, whereupon Rabbi Skopf, in his remarks, would say, "Please disregard my colleague's praise. I can learn a little, but I am not the great scholar he makes me out to be." Later, when a wealthy businessman in the city was solicited for a contribution to Rabbi Skopf's yeshiva, he responded, "Why should I give my cash to the yeshiva of a man who publicly admits that he is not a great scholar?" Rabbi Jacobs cites the Gateshead Rav's observation that "If you repeat often enough that you are unworthy, it will not take very long for people to believe it is true."[13]

---

28. Never allow "humility" to serve as an excuse to avoid or evade making important decisions. The late-sixteenth-century *Sefer Charedim (Book of the God Fearers)*, by Rabbi Elazar Azikri, warns scholars and community leaders not to avoid making hard decisions out of fear of rendering a mistaken judgment. *The Ethics of the Fathers* teaches, "In a place where there is no man, be a man" (2:6). In short, we must never let humility prevent, or even paralyze, us from acting.

When King Saul refused to stand up to his own soldiers, fearing that they would resent him, the prophet Samuel reproved him, "You might be small in your own eyes, but you are the head of the tribes of Israel, and God has anointed you as king over Israel" (I Samuel 15:17).

———

29. We should also never let humility either blind us to matters of right and wrong or, worse, become a cover for cowardice, and stop us, for example, from reprimanding or criticizing an evil person or ideology. Such behavior is common among moral relativists who, supposedly guided by a form of humility, say things like "Who is to say our society is better than such-and-such a society?" even when it clearly is (in the sense that it promotes greater freedom, and protects human rights).

22

AVOIDING ARROGANCE

════════

1. If you tend to compare yourself with those of lesser abilities or achievements, remind yourself of your weaknesses. Thus, if you possess great intelligence, recall errors that you have made (perhaps in misjudging the character of others, in an investment, in your understanding of a Jewish text, or perhaps in all three). "Even the finest mind," wrote Rabbi Moshe Chaim Luzatto, "is imperfect and prone to error. Even the most accomplished sage makes mistakes" (*Mesillat Yesharim*, chapter 22).

What have been some of the most significant mistakes that you—as intelligent as you may be—have made?

2. Similarly, if you feel entitled to praise and honor for your accomplishments, think of things you have done of which you would be ashamed were they to become publicly known. Such an exercise, if done honestly, can be quite painful, but also can serve as an important corrective. For example:

- Did you ever tease and humiliate someone, perhaps on an ongoing basis? (If you haven't done so in recent years, perhaps you did so during childhood.)

- Have you betrayed your spouse?
- Have you acted dishonestly, perhaps more than once?
- Have you given another person bad advice so as to benefit yourself?

Each of us has done things that, if known to others, would cause them to regard us more critically. Rabbi Abraham Twerski, whose writings on humility and self-esteem have deeply influenced my own thinking, observes, "If we expect others to praise and honor us, would we expect this from them if they watched a video [of our lives] and knew everything about us? If we will be honest with ourselves, we will admit that the only way we can make a claim to [other people's] honor and praise is that they do not know the entire truth about us."*

3. When we feel superior to another because of a bad trait he has and can't seem to overcome, we should think of some bad trait of our own that we have difficulty overcoming. Do we:

- waste time?
- overeat?
- gossip unfairly?
- say cruel things when we lose our temper?
- give less to charity than we should?

Probably there are things in our life that we should, but don't, change. So we shouldn't rush to criticize others for their failings.

4. Reflect on how much our wisdom depends upon that of others: "There is no sage . . . who will not need to learn from the words of his friends, and very often, even from those of his disciples. How then can he pride himself in his wisdom?" (*Mesillat Yesharim*, chapter 22).

See page 218 on citing one's sources.

5. If somebody else had our abilities (for example, a high IQ), she might be as wise as we are, or perhaps wiser. Thus, feeling superior to others because of an innate ability such as intelligence makes no sense.

Lights Along the Way, pages 289–290. Rabbi Twerski, who has written over fifty books, claims that they are all on the same subject, self-esteem.

6. Remember that good looks and beauty are ephemeral. The *Sefer Chasidim* offers the following meditation to those who pride themselves on their appearance: "Just as snow begins pure white but soon turns into slush, so we, too, despite our great beauty, will become a small heap of worm-eaten matter." Furthermore, the deterioration in our looks generally begins many years before our demise. Therefore, even if we are attractive now, we will probably live for several more decades, during which others, particularly young people, will no longer be impressed by our appearance. Indeed, they might be shocked to learn that we were once regarded as handsome or pretty. So, if we are attractive, we should consider ourselves fortunate, but not superior to others.

———

The Bible reminds us that pride in one's physical appearance can become a person's undoing. David's son Absalom—"in the whole of Israel, there was no man who could be praised for his beauty as much as Absalom"—took excessive pride in his physical appearance, and particularly his glorious head of hair (II Samuel 14:25–26; he would even weigh his thick mane on the rare occasions that he cut it). Later, when he led an unsuccessful revolt against David, Absalom fled on his mule, and his hair got caught in the foliage of a large tree. The mule on which he was riding continued on its way, leaving Absalom dangling from the tree until David's troops, led by David's general, Joab, found him and killed him (II Samuel 18:9–15). The Talmud comments, somewhat metaphorically: "Absalom revolted with his hair . . . therefore, he was hanged by his hair" (Sotah 10b).

———

To cite one example: In high school, pretty girls often become cheerleaders, and receive much acclaim for their good looks. Sometimes they become so focused on physical appearance and so lulled by compliments that they don't bother to develop academic or other skills that will be crucial for success later in life.

———

7. Remember the Persian proverb, "After the game, the pawn and the king go into the same box." A classic Jewish teaching echoes this: All of us come from a drop of semen, and are destined to return to dust, in an earth filled with worms and maggots, whose food we shall become. Therefore, what role is there for feeling arrogant about our wealth or high intelligence, "since the expectation of man [rich and poor alike] is worms" (*The Ethics of the Fathers* 3:1 and 4:4).

The Orchot Tzaddikim *offers the following advice to the self-important: "Think about how many proud men have vanished from the world and have been forgotten as if they never existed" ("The Gate of Pride"). There were many proud people who lived in the eighth century and thought they were of great importance. How many people—if any—can you name who lived in that one-hundred-year period?*

8. Don't become arrogant because of wealth, even if people cater to you or flatter you, and show you great honor. Many wealthy people understandably want to believe that people respect them for *who they are* rather than for *what they possess.* Society itself reinforces this view by treating wealthy people as if they were more important than those who are not rich.* Dr. Solomon Schimmel writes, "The wealthy person may internalize these social attitudes and come to believe that he is indeed more significant than those less well off materially."[1] Wealthy people should therefore reflect on the fact that, unless they are appreciated for reasons other than their wealth, respect for them will vanish quickly if they lose their money. And this could easily happen: "Let one consider the vicissitudes of life. The rich may easily become poor, the ruler subservient, and the honored insignificant. Since a person is thus liable to find himself occupying a station in life that he now looks upon with contempt, how shall he be proud of the good fortune which he never can be sure will last?" (*Mesillat Yesharim,* chapter 23).

Rabbi Chiyya, the talmudic sage, who was particularly conscious of the cyclical nature of life, advised his wife to make sure to be generous to beggars so that "the same may be done to your [i.e., our] children." When his wife reproved him for "cursing" their children with the suggestion that they might one day be very poor, Rabbi Chiyya responded, "There is a wheel which revolves in this world" (Shabbat *151b*).

A New York Times *obituary of a man who was identified as "a celebrated fixture on the international social scene for almost half a century" noted that he had a sharp and rude tongue. "One woman [friend of his] kept a cache of ten- and twenty-dollar bills handy when he was her escort to a restaurant. The money was to placate the staff" (June 9, 1995).* It is difficult to imagine that*

---

*As the famous line in *Fiddler on the Roof* proclaims, "If you're rich, they think you really know."

this man, the heir to a real estate fortune, would have acted as he did if he had not been wealthy and used to being catered to; indeed, if he were someone of less substantial means and social connections, he would probably have been unwelcome at the restaurants where he insulted the staff.

In addition, there is something truly unsavory in being known as a person "whose caustic remarks were often directed at waiters, clerks, and taxi drivers." The man apparently regarded such people as his inferiors, and did not feel the need to control his tongue when speaking to them.

————

9. No matter how accomplished you are, realize the extent to which you depend on others of lower status and earning capabilities for your survival, people whom you may not normally appreciate and may even look down upon. For example, most middle-class people regard sanitation workers as social inferiors. Yet without them we would all face life-threatening diseases and epidemics. Therefore, by what right do we feel superior to anyone who earns his living doing honest work, particularly labor that benefits the community?

————

Dr. Solomon Schimmel, a psychologist and Jewish educator, tells of a highly paid and accomplished business executive he knew who had a serious car accident: "In an instant, the woman's life suddenly depended on a paramedic and a police officer, two people with whom moments before she would have been unlikely to interact in any but a most perfunctory manner." Now she begged them to alleviate her pain, and save her for the sake of her children. "These two men were less educated, economically poorer, and had less power in society than she. But they saved lives. They alleviated pain and suffering. She never did these things. This lesson was a powerful corrective to her pride."[2]

————

Simcha Raz, Rabbi Aryeh Levine's biographer, records that Reb Aryeh used to get up early each morning for prayer: "On his way to the synagogue, he made it a point to greet everyone he met on the street; and he was especially careful to wish a good morning to the street-cleaners, who also rose early to work. Once he

————

*I am not giving the man's name because he also had pleasant aspects to his personality, and it is unfair to identify him only by his negative traits. A friend, however, suggested that when offering an example, it is more effective to mention the person's name, and then make reference to the person's positive traits as well. But my experience is that once you make reference to a person's negative traits, particularly if they are memorable ones, these become people's overwhelming, and often exclusive, association with that person.

told me why he did this: 'I have affection for the street-cleaners. Just look: When everyone is still asleep, they take the trouble to come and clean the streets of Jerusalem, so as to support themselves by their own honest labor. Their work is not respected; they are not esteemed for it; their salary is niggardly. And still they take their pains to do their task faithfully.'"[3]

———

George Orwell, while living among hardworking miners, wrote, "It is brought home to you . . . that it is only because miners sweat their guts out that superior persons can remain superior."[4]

———

10. We should recall the warning of the *Mesillat Yesharim*: "How many different kinds of sickness, God forbid, is a person prone to, which could make it necessary for him to beg others for help and assistance, for a little relief" (chapter 23). Rabbi Abraham Twerski, who is also a physician, comments on this passage: "Medically speaking, all it takes is a minute clot of blood, perhaps only one millimeter in size, to clog a crucial blood vessel to the brain, and instantaneously transform an intellectual genius into a mentally defective person, and a highly praised executive into a virtual vegetable state. With such fragility, how can one possibly be vain?"[5] Thus we should be humble and grateful for what we have, and for every moment that we have it.

A final thought

11. Our propensity to be arrogant, even though we have many areas of weakness, is reflected in a remarkable teaching by the nineteenth-century Chasidic *tzaddik* Rabbi Rafael of Barshad: "When I go to the heavenly court, they'll ask me, 'Why didn't you learn more Torah?' And I'll tell them that I'm slow-witted. Then they'll ask me, 'Why didn't you do more . . . for others?' And I'll tell them that I'm physically weak. Then they'll ask me, 'Why didn't you give more to charity?' And I'll tell them that I didn't have enough money. But then they'll ask me, 'If you were so stupid, weak, and poor, why were you so arrogant?' And for that, I won't have an answer."[6]

23

THE MORAL NECESSITY FOR SELF-ESTEEM

1. You, the person reading these words, are precious. Your worth is not rooted in your wealth, physical attractiveness, or status in society, but derives from the fact that you, like every other human being, are created in God's image (Genesis 1:27). During moments of self-doubt or even self-loathing, which almost all of us experience, remember the divine image inside you, and that God loves you: "Humans are beloved for they were created in the image of God. An extra measure of love is shown them by [God's] making it known to them that they are created in God's image" (*The Ethics of the Fathers* 3:14).

2. A well-known passage in the Mishnah notes that, by originally populating the world with only one person, Adam, God intended to teach that each life is of infinite value: "Therefore was Adam created singly to teach us that he who saves one life it is as if he saved an entire world, and he who destroys one life it is as if he destroyed an entire world." The Mishnah goes on to teach that each person, as Adam's direct descendant, should say, "For my sake was the world created" (*Sanhedrin* 4:5). There is always some special mission for you, something in this world that only you can accomplish.

———

The Chasidic rebbe Simcha Bunim suggested that every person carry around in his or her pockets two pieces of paper. On one—to be consulted when we are feeling smarter, more popular, more generous, or otherwise superior to others— should be written Abraham's words, "I am but dust and ashes" (Genesis 18:27). And on the other—to be taken out when we are suffering from low self-esteem or despair—should be these words from the Mishnah: "For my sake was the world created."

———

3. Self-esteem must include self-love. The Torah's most famous law, "Love your neighbor as yourself" (Leviticus 19:18), commands us to love the people among whom we live. But implicit in "as yourself" is the command to love ourselves. As a rule, if people don't like themselves, they will be less kind to others. For example, has there ever been an abusive parent with a decent self-image? People who despise themselves are more likely to mistreat others than are those with a positive self-image, particularly when their self-image derives, at least in part, from seeing themselves as people of good character.

———

Rabbi Abraham Twerski notes how healthy self-esteem enables a person to heed many important ethical admonitions of the Sages, while low self-esteem discourages one from doing so. People with a healthy self-image

- *are more apt to judge others fairly and favorably, as urged by* The Ethics of the Fathers *(1:6), because, unlike people with low self-esteem, they do not need to disparage others to raise themselves in their own eyes (on judging people fairly, see chapters 5 and 6);*
- *have no need to feel superior or in control; thus they show respect and honor to others rather than demanding recognition (see, for example,* The Ethics of the Fathers *1:10, "Despise lording it over others," and 2:10, "Let your fellow's honor be as dear to you as your own");*
- *tend to associate with the wise and avoid the ignorant, because they don't need to be with people to whom they feel superior (see, for example,* The Ethics of the Fathers *1:4: "Let your house be a meeting place for the Sages");*
- *are likelier to welcome constructive criticism. Because they believe they can improve, such people are usually not afraid to have their weaknesses pointed out to them (as Proverbs 19:20 advises: "Listen to advice . . . in order that you may be wise in the end"[1]).*

———

4. In order to feel self-esteem, we must appreciate our accomplishments. On six occasions in the opening chapter of Genesis, the Bible informs us that God was proud of what He had created. For example, "God saw all that He had made, and found it very good" (see 1:31; see also 1:4, 10, 12, 18 and 21). The text's unusual repetition of this phrase makes it clear that God took pleasure in seeing that His work was good. In contrast, there are many people who seem to feel guilty about, or who are reluctant to take pleasure in, their accomplishments; instead they minimize them so as to make them seem insignificant. Like God, however, we should be pleased to take pleasure in our accomplishments and good works, and be even more pleased knowing that we have reason to believe that those good works are pleasing to God.

5. Humility should not be confused with low self-esteem. People often believe that a humble person is one who has low regard for himself, his character, and his accomplishments, or at least speaks about himself as if he did. (It is this widespread perception that causes many people to regard humility as a pretense, perhaps even a phony virtue; see page 212). But if we have reason to believe that our accomplishments or virtues are of little value, then our being humble about them is no virtue. Rabbi Chaim of Volozhin taught, "A man who has no outstanding qualities or achievements at all, cannot be considered a humble person, even if he humbles himself, for he has nothing to be proud of."[2] As Winston Churchill remarked of a political rival whose humility did not impress him: "He is a modest man who has much to be modest about."

————

A classic Jewish joke mocks the tendency of some public figures to display false humility. In a large congregation on Yom Kippur, as the cantor stands up to start the service, he is suddenly overcome with trepidation. He runs over to the Aron Kodesh, *where the Torah scrolls are kept, and speaks aloud to God: "Lord, I am not worthy to lead this holy congregation in prayer. What am I but dust and ashes?"*

The rabbi, deeply touched by the cantor's words, also runs to the ark and cries out to God, "I am nothing in Your eyes. What have I ever done that is worthy?"

At this point the shammes *(the synagogue assistant) is also moved. He bounds up from his seat, runs to the ark, and calls out, "God, I am a man of no values, a miserable sinner, a nothing."*

The rabbi taps the cantor on the shoulder and says, "Now look who's calling himself a nothing."

————

6. Humility, therefore, should not lead us to become overly self-critical. Rabbi Chaim Reines observed, "It cannot be the aim of ethics to command respect of our fellow man and at the same time preach self-contempt."[3]

7. Rather, humility must be rooted in a true, hardheaded assessment of ourselves. The Chazon Ish noted: "People are mistaken in thinking that humility means to think of oneself as an ignorant boor, even when such is surely not the case. Humility means that a person realizes his true worth. If one is a great Torah scholar, he should know this and conduct himself in a manner commensurate with his true understanding—but he must not seek

honor and glory because of it, for this [accomplishment] is his purpose in life"[4] Thus humility means knowing our strengths but not becoming arrogant because of them.

8. Parents should reserve their highest praise of their children for when they are kind. Doing so will cause our children to feel higher self-esteem and most love themselves when they act generously and sensitively toward others.

The detrimental effects of low self-esteem, and how to avoid it

9. Resist the *yetzer hara* ("evil inclination") when it encourages you to have a low regard for yourself. Rabbi Abraham Twerski notes that "if you're humble because you don't even know your abilities, [that's not humility, that's] just low self-esteem."

Rabbi Twerski's important distinction is between humility, which is rooted in a truthful self-assessment, and low self-esteem, which occurs when a "person has negative feelings about himself that are not warranted by facts." Low self-esteem usually undermines both a person's ability to act (people will not try to achieve things if they believe themselves incapable of succeeding) and emotional well-being (people with low self-esteem often dislike themselves). Thus Rabbi Twerski speculates that unwarranted feelings of inferiority are the work of the *yetzer hara*.

Jewish teachings on the *yetzer hara* generally focus on how it tempts us to commit wrongful actions. But Rabbi Twerski, in a theological insight of extraordinary originality, suggests that it is the "evil inclination" that "gives a person unjustified feelings of inferiority in its attempt to crush him." For example, while some people are enticed by the *yetzer hara* to cheat others or to commit adultery, the "evil inclination" can achieve a similar goal by telling us, "There is no point in your trying to be good. You are a nothing. You cannot achieve anything. [For example], you are too dull to understand Torah, so why bother studying it? You might as well give up and get whatever pleasures you can in this world."*

Twerski's perspective on the "evil inclination" as the cause of feelings of inferiority has significant practical implications. People with a healthy sense of right and wrong learn to recognize the wiles of the *yetzer hara* when it

---

Angels Don't Leave Footprints, pages 19 and 39–40. Elsewhere, Rabbi Twerski comments that "inasmuch as these negative feelings about oneself are not based on reality, they are false and as such cannot possibly be components of humility. As we have seen, the Torah condemns falsehood in whatever shape it comes" (*Lights Along the Way*, page 165).

tempts them to do something immoral. So, too, those with unwarranted feel-ings of low self-esteem must learn to recognize the evil inclination's demoral-izing and untruthful arguments. For example, people should understand that it is the *yetzer hara* which is telling them that they are not smart enough to finish a task of which they objectively are capable. Through such self-understanding they will find it easier to shrug off the evil inclination's argu-ments, just as they would dismiss an inner voice that told them to kill, or just punch, someone who had mistreated them. Resisting the evil inclination is also possible when it tries to make us feel bad about ourselves. As Eleanor Roosevelt, America's most famous first lady and a woman who struggled for much of her life with feelings of low self-esteem, taught, "No one can make you feel inferior without your consent."

10. Low self-esteem can also make us unreasonably fearful. The Bible tells how Moses sent twelve tribal representatives to spy out the land of Is-rael. They were probably people of good intentions, or Moses would not have sent them, but because the spies had a poor self-image, they panicked when they came upon the inhabitants of Canaan: "We looked like grasshoppers to ourselves, and so we must have looked to them" (Numbers 13:33). Thus, when they came back, they advised the Israelites to give up hope of ever liv-ing in Canaan. Contrast their behavior with that of Moses, who, although he was the humblest man of his time (Numbers 12:3), was unintimidated by Pharaoh.

———

The need to derive our sense of self-worth from how we perceive ourselves is under-scored in a parable told in Orchot Tzaddikim *(The Way of the Righteous): "They tell of a certain king who one night, when many men were sitting before him, got up and tended to the fire himself so that it would not go out. When he was asked why he did not order another to take care of it, he replied, 'I arose a king, and returned a king'"* [that is, because I am secure in my sense of dignity and worth, I can undertake to perform what others would consider a menial task].

———

11. "One who does not recognize his strengths and talents is even worse off than one who does not know his flaws, because he is totally unaware of the tools with which he can achieve spiritual growth" (Rabbi Yerucham Levovitz [1874–1936], the *menahel ruchani* [spiritual guide] of the Mir Yeshiva in Poland). We all have weaknesses to overcome, but it is our strengths that will enable us to do so. For example, if we often, and unfairly, lose our temper, but have a strong sense of reason, we can draw on that reason to see that our temper is irrational and disproportionate to the provocation. But if we don't appreciate our ability to reason, we will deprive ourselves of a powerful weapon in learning to control our anger.

———

One can apply Rabbi Levovitz's teaching to a country no less than to an individual. As President Bill Clinton said, "There is nothing wrong in America that can't be fixed by what is right in America."

———

Rabbi Shlomo Zalman Auerbach of Jerusalem, the great twentieth-century Jewish scholar, would visit mourners on the first and second days of shiva *(seven days of mourning), and would initiate conversation with those who were grieving. He did this although only the closest family and friends are supposed to visit mourners during the first three days of* shiva, *and visitors are supposed to wait for mourners to speak first. Rabbi Hanoch Teller, Rabbi Auerbach's student and biographer, explains this unusual departure from Jewish tradition: "He was well aware of how much his presence could contribute to lifting the spirits of the bereaved and bring solace to the mourner. Since he was conscious that he had something significant to contribute, he wished to offer it when it would be needed the most.*[5] *Rabbi Auerbach knew his strengths, and felt no need to refrain from using them out of false humility.*

———

12. Rabbi Abraham Twerski suggests a useful test to discern whether we are governed by true humility or low self-esteem: "A person who is humble because he realizes that he has not fulfilled his God-given potential is stimulated to action to do so. The person with low self-esteem does not feel there is any purpose in trying [because of] his attitude of, 'What's the use? I can't do it anyway.' "[6] In short, humility inspires, while low self-esteem demoralizes.

A final thought on the significance of the Jewish people's self-esteem in the face of antisemitism

13. Jews have traditionally derived a positive self-image from the belief that they are created in God's image, and that they were chosen by God to make His existence and ethical demands known to the world. These beliefs enable committed Jews to maintain a sense of self-esteem in the face of persecution ("If people hate us, there must be something wrong with them, not us"). In contrast, those Jews who are less connected to the Jewish tradition,

and who derive their self-image from how others perceive them, suffer more—particularly in terms of self-esteem—during periods of persecution. In his powerful Holocaust memoir, *Man's Search for Meaning*, Viktor Frankl, a Viennese psychoanalyst incarcerated in Auschwitz and other Nazi camps, writes of how humiliated he felt when a Nazi soldier threw a pebble at him, as if he were an animal, to attract his attention.

But, ideally, our perception of ourselves as Jews, or as human beings, should not be diminished because a vile person treats us with contempt.* In the *Zygelbohm Bukh*, a Holocaust memorial volume, a survivor who came from a traditional Jewish background wrote: "The attitude on the part of the Jewish masses toward the Nazis is like that toward a ferocious beast: There is a fear of the beast, she may kill, she bites, tears pieces out of the human body, one feels pain, but there is not a feeling of being insulted and morally denigrated by the beast."[7]

The awareness that their enemies told—and often believed—lies about them also helped inoculate the Jews against developing a poor self-image. For example, starting in the eleventh century, a libel (popularly known as the "blood libel") that Jews murdered Christians and drank their blood for ritual purposes spread throughout Europe. This lie, which led to the deaths of tens of thousands of Jews, is still current in much of the Arab world.

The Zionist thinker Ahad Ha'am (1856–1927), argued that the blood libel, horrible though it was, provided Jews with one unexpected benefit, in that it helped immunize them against internalizing the world's hostile portrayal: "The [blood libel] accusation is the solitary case in which the general acceptance of an idea about ourselves does not make us doubt whether all the world can be wrong, and we right, because it is based on an absolute lie. Every Jew who has been brought up among Jews knows as an indisputable fact that throughout the length and breadth of Jewry there is not a single individual who drinks human blood for religious purposes. . . . 'But,' you ask, 'is it possible that everybody can be wrong and the Jews right?' Yes, it is possible: the blood accusation proves it is possible."

---

*Unfortunately it often is; I am just arguing that it shouldn't be.

ANGER

———

When a person becomes enraged, [even] if
he is wise, his wisdom deserts him.

BABYLONIAN TALMUD,
Pesachim 66b

24

UNTAMED ANGER

1. Uncontrolled anger is, along with hatred, the most destructive of emotions. The Torah cites several instances of the horrors that ensue when people do not control their rage. For example:

• When God rejects Cain's offering while accepting that of his brother Abel, Cain murders Abel, and then shows no remorse: "Am I my brother's keeper?" he taunts God (Genesis 4:8–9).

• Anger can lead to great evil, even when its cause is righteous. For example, Simeon and Levi, sons of the patriarch Jacob, are justifiably furious at Shechem for raping their sister Dinah. In their rage, however, they murder Shechem as well as "all the males" of his town, men who played no role in Dinah's rape (Genesis 34:25–26). Years later, on his deathbed, Jacob curses Simeon and Levi's unbridled temper: "For when angry they slay men and . . . maim oxen. Cursed be their anger so fierce, and their wrath so relentless" (Genesis 49:6–7).*

2. Rage separates people's minds and hearts from God, and inhibits moral constraints. As the Talmud explains, "When one becomes rageful, God becomes of no consequence to him" (*Nedarim* 22b).

It is also true that angry people often act in a most ungodly way when they believe that they are acting in God's Name (on the assumption that God approves of whatever they are doing).† After the death in 1797 of Elijah, the

---

*The reference to maiming oxen illustrates the extent to which enraged people commit acts of gratuitous violence.

†In 1995, Yigal Amier, an observant Jew, assassinated Israeli prime minister Yitzhak Rabin in the Name of God and the Jewish people, arguing that Rabin's willingness to make territorial compromises with Palestinians made it essential that he die: "If I hadn't done it, I would feel much worse. My deed will be understood in the future. I saved the people of Israel from destruction" (see Michael Karpin and Ina Friedman, *Murder in the Name of God: The Plot to Kill Yitzhak Rabin,* page 28).

Gaon of Vilna, the greatest Jewish scholar of his age, his followers heard reports that the Chasidim (whom the Gaon had opposed) had rejoiced when they heard of his passing. In fury, one of the Gaon's followers went to Russian government officials with a false accusation of treason against Rabbi Shneur Zalman of Liady, a Chasidic leader. The Russians arrested the rabbi and sentenced him to death (his life was eventually spared). His accuser apparently believed that all measures, including false accusations, were justified against someone who deserved to suffer.

We have all said or done things when we were angry that we realized afterward were wrong. One man told me that he prayed to God for the immediate death of his boss when the man told him that his job was being eliminated. Most of us have occasionally responded to bad behavior with disproportionate rage, which is why we all need to learn how to control ourselves when we are consumed with anger (see chapter 4 for techniques for controlling anger).

———

The Talmud tells of an incident in the town of Tiberias in which two rabbis, Elazar and Yossi, became so outraged during a debate over Jewish law that a Torah scroll was ripped up. A third rabbi, Yossi ben Kisma, who was present during the dispute, commented, "I would be surprised if this synagogue does not turn into a house of idol worship." Indeed, that is what eventually happened (Yevamot 96b).

———

The Talmud also records that the distinguished sage Rabbi Sheshet, when angry, used to pour brine, a pickling solution, on his maidservant's head (Shabbat 105b). The Talmud explains that he did so to instill fear in his household so that people would obey him; nonetheless, this is a shocking act by a representative of a religious tradition that regards humiliating another person as akin to killing (see page 276).

———

3. "It is certain that the sins of the angry man outweigh his merits" (*Nedarim* 22b). The Talmud records a tragic instance of a host who, during a time of scarcity, had only three eggs to set before his three guests. While the host was gone from the room, the man's young son entered, and each of the guests gave his egg to the boy. When the host returned, and saw one egg in his son's mouth and the two others in his hands, he became enraged and threw the boy to the ground with such force that the boy died (*Chullin* 94a).*

———

*Obviously, even if the son had in fact stolen the eggs, the father's response would have been equally wrong.

As the medieval *Orchot Tzaddikim* (*The Ways of the Righteous*) observes, "When the spirit of anger asserts itself over man, the trait of mercy flees and cruelty takes over to shatter and destroy" ("The Gate of Cruelty").

———

This incident brings to mind the words of Seneca, the first-century Roman Stoic philosopher, that anger "conquers the most ardent love, and so in anger men have stabbed the bodies that they loved and have lain in the arms of those whom they have slain" ("On Anger"). *

In the aforementioned talmudic tale, the child's mother, upon seeing what her husband had done, went up to the roof and jumped off. The father then committed suicide. The lesson the Talmud derived from this event was that a guest should not give anything from what is set before him to the host's son or daughter without his permission, but that is clearly not the only lesson to be learned from this episode.†

———

4. A contemporary manifestation of untamed anger is "road rage," during which a driver becomes so infuriated at another driver (for example, someone who has cut in front of his car) that he tries to take revenge. These outbursts often lead to accidents, including, not infrequently, the death of the angry driver. The National Highway Traffic Safety Administration has estimated that uncontrolled rage is a factor in 28,000 highway deaths every year.[1]

Have you ever become angry at another driver? Did you drive in a manner that put others, and yourself, at risk? Even if you didn't retaliate, did you fume so much that it became unpleasant for those riding with you?

———

"On the Fourth of July in 1995, a group of teenagers riding in an old Chevrolet on Interstate 17 near Phoenix accidentally swiped a pickup truck during a maneuver to avoid another car. But when they exited the freeway and tried to talk to the driver of the truck, a passenger leaped from it and shot a sixteen-year-old sitting in the Chevrolet's backseat, leaving him a quadriplegic." Concludes Mark Caldwell, author of A Short History of Rudeness: *"Small morals [such as learn-*

---

*Indeed, uncontrolled anger lies behind most instances of child and spousal abuse.
†The first-century Roman historian and philosopher Plutarch offered a poignant observation on the destructive nature of anger: "We who tame wild beasts and make them gentle . . . under the impulse of rage cast off children, friends, and companions, and let loose our wrath, like some wild beast, on servants and fellow citizens" ("On the Control of Anger").

ing to control one's temper] aren't really small if they can tame the passions that lead to this kind of tragedy."[2]

———

5.   Even anger expressed solely through words can destroy relationships, most commonly marriages and friendships. Many people who would never strike someone exercise little if any restraint over their tongues. The Bible depicts both King David and his wife Michal as temperamental and verbally harsh (II Samuel, chapter 6:16–23). When Michal sees David dancing before the Ark in a manner she considers undignified, she rebukes him sarcastically: "Didn't the king of Israel do himself honor today, exposing himself in the sight of . . . his subjects, just like one of the riffraff?" Stung, David lashes out at her: "It was before the Lord who chose me instead of your father and all his family and appointed me ruler over the Lord's people Israel [that I danced]." David's barbed response came only a short time after Michal's father and three of her brothers had been killed in a battle against the Philistines. The next verse records that Michal was childless. It seems likely that after such an exchange (and there might have been many more), David and Michal were never intimate again.

The Bible's point is as clear today as it was in 1000 B.C.E.: If a husband or wife, or two siblings or friends, don't hold their tongues when they are upset, their love is unlikely to survive, no matter how deeply they once cared for each other.

6.   When we are angry, even if we are intelligent and otherwise kind people, we are apt to lose control of our tongues and say unfair things. For example, while the prophet Jeremiah was right to condemn sinfulness in ancient Israel, was he speaking the truth when he said of his fellow citizens, "Oh, to leave my people, to go away from them. For they are *all* adulterers, a band of rogues . . . *every* friend is base in his dealings"? (9:1,3; emphasis added). Isaiah called his fellow Israelites "a people of unclean lips" (6:4), a libel for which the Rabbis claimed the prophet was punished by God (*Yevamot* 49b).

If Jeremiah and Isaiah, people of far greater integrity than most of us, could not be fair or fully accurate when enraged, how likely is it that you and I will succeed? Therefore, when we are angry, we must be careful *not* to say all the angry thoughts that go through our minds.* Otherwise we will say things that we will—and should—regret.

———

*However, if we are in a therapist's office, that is the one place where we should say whatever we are feeling; the expression of our deepest anger will enable both us and the therapist to come to a better understanding of our needs and our fears, and may help us devise ways to exert better self-control.

Many people, when they are angry, say things they don't—in their rational moments—want to see happen. When Noah's son Ham showed him a gross lack of respect, Noah didn't even bother to curse Ham, but he cursed Ham's son, Canaan, that he should become a slave to his brothers (Genesis 9:25). Is it likely that when Noah recovered from his initial outburst of rage, he truly wished to see this fate befall his own grandson?

———

7. An excessive temper is so destructive a trait in a teacher that *The Ethics of the Fathers* declares that "a hot-tempered person cannot teach" (2:5). There are several reasons why this is the case. Bad temper in a teacher makes students reluctant to ask questions (they are afraid of evoking the teacher's wrath), and consequently they may not fully understand what they are taught: "If you see a student whose studies are as hard for him as iron, attribute it to his teacher's failure to show him a cheerful countenance" (*Ta'anit* 8a). Also, angry and overly strict teachers alienate students from Jewish learning (fear is far more likely to evoke hatred than love).

In addition, throughout history, short-tempered teachers have humiliated their students. This is particularly despicable when directed, as it often has been, against people with learning disabilities.

In short, a person with an angry disposition is as unfit to teach as someone unfamiliar with the subject. In both cases, students will not learn, or appreciate, the material properly.

———

The Talmud tells of three non-Jews who were interested in learning about Judaism. Each, on a different occasion, approached the quick-tempered scholar Rabbi Shammai (first century B.C.E.) with questions about the Jewish faith. One, for example, asked Shammai if he could convert to Judaism on condition that he accept all the laws written in the Torah, but not be bound by the Oral Law, the rabbinic understanding of these laws. Infuriated by the questioner's rejection of so important a part of Jewish tradition, Shammai scolded the man, and angrily repulsed him. When a second and third would-be convert asked him a question not to his liking, Shammai, who was a builder, shook the rod in his hand at the men, and drove them away. Each of the men then went to Shammai's contemporary, the gentle Rabbi Hillel, who taught them and converted them to Judaism (for an example of how Hillel responded to their queries, see pages 10–11). Later, the three men concluded, "The angry strictness of Shammai would have driven us out of the world, but the humble gentleness of Hillel brought us under the wings of the divine presence" (Shabbat

31a).* As this passage makes clear, rabbis and teachers have an obligation to be sweet-tempered and pleasant, because they represent Judaism and the Jewish people to the world.

———

The self-destructive effects of anger

8. Excessive anger has a harmful effect not only on others, but also on ourselves. The Talmud teaches, "When a person becomes enraged, [even] if he is wise, his wisdom deserts him" (*Pesachim* 66b). According to the Torah, even Moses acted foolishly when angry. In the Book of Numbers, Moses becomes enraged at the Israelites for their constant whining about water. When God tells him to speak to a large rock, from which God will send water to satisfy the people's thirst, Moses disobeys God's command, and strikes it with a rod, saying, "Listen, you rebels, shall we get water for you out of this rock?" (Numbers 20:10). Although Moses surely did not intend it, the "we" implied that it was he and his brother Aaron (who was standing beside him), and not God, who were responsible for the miracle of the water that gushed forth. His was a dangerous comment, and could have led the Israelites to believe that Moses himself was a god. He paid dearly for his loss of self-control, when God denied him entry into the land of Israel (Numbers 20:12).

Like Moses, many of us hit objects when we are angry.† And, like Moses, many of us also pay dearly for the stupid things we say and do. For example, we may walk out of a relationship that should be preserved, insult another with words that will never be forgotten, or refuse to reconcile with someone with whom we have had a falling out. If our wisdom deserts us when we are enraged, we must learn to hold our tongues, particularly when we are the most angry.

———

Elsewhere the Rabbis teach that "one who comes under the influence of anger will make mistakes" (Sifre, a rabbinic commentary on Numbers 31:21). Difficult as it is to avoid making mistakes when we are thinking clearly, it becomes

———

*The preceding page of the Talmud records that Hillel trained himself never to lose his temper, even when he was asked foolish questions.

†New York Yankees pitcher Kevin Brown, enraged at an umpire's call, punched a wall so hard that he broke two fingers and could no longer pitch during the climax of the 2004 baseball season. Brown, like most pitchers, had learned not to express his anger with his pitching hand. Nevertheless, he couldn't field and therefore couldn't take the mound.

almost impossible to do so when our minds are clouded by anger. How many drivers, furious at the behavior of a passing motorist, miss an exit or, worse, get into an accident?

———

9. A bad temper causes people to lie to us out of fear. Rabbi Chanina ben Gamliel's irascible disposition led to his being served unkosher meat, because his servant feared to tell him that there was no available meat in the house (*Gittin* 7a). This is another reason why it is so unwise for someone in authority, be it a boss, a general, or a parent, to intimidate others with a bad temper. Thus a businessman confided to me that his anger stopped employees from telling him bad news, and his business suffered in consequence.

———

Probably the most common reason children lie to their parents is that they are afraid of what might happen if they tell the truth. Two parents were exasperated by their five-year-old son's tendency to blame others, including ghosts, for mischievous things he did (such as writing with a crayon on the wall). They assured him that they would not get angry at him as long as he told the truth, but would be upset if he lied. After repeated reassurances from the parents, the boy started telling the truth consistently. Two years later, when the mother pressed him as to whether he had taken some important papers off her desk, he said, "Mommy, you know I don't lie anymore."

———

10. Anger makes us unproductive. The Talmud teaches, "When a hot-tempered person loses his temper, he achieves nothing but his anger" (*Kiddushin* 40b–41a). When you become furious at someone, your rage dominates your thinking. It becomes difficult to focus on your work, and on your love for others. Some people wake up in the middle of the night, and cannot fall back to sleep, because they are so enraged. Others waste a good part of their working day in fantasy monologues with the subject of their wrath.

———

Commenting on this talmudic maxim, Rabbi Abraham Grodzensky notes two reasons that anger is generally not beneficial: First, it does not help us, but puts us in a foul mood. Second, the person at whom we are railing usually pays less attention to what we are saying than if we had spoken calmly and tactfully.[3]

———

11. Anger causes our lives to be filled with unhappiness. The Talmud notes, "There are three kinds of people whose lives are not really lives [among whom are] those who are rageful" (*Pesachim* 113b).* In other words, while the victims of our temper may suffer, we do not emerge unscathed: our lives, scarred by rage and bitterness, and by constant irritations and conflicts with others, are no lives at all.

——

A diabetic friend told me that his losses of temper are generally followed by a significant rise in the level of his blood sugars. Doctors have warned him that when his emotions are out of control, his blood sugars will follow suit. In addition, during periods of rage, he will often eat junk food. Indeed, it is hard to imagine that anyone with an angry disposition will be able to maintain strict adherence to a diet.

——

25

DEALING WITH ANGRY PEOPLE

1. As much as possible, avoid associating with people who do not control their tempers, even if they are close relatives. As noted, Jacob was speaking of his own ill-tempered sons when he said, "Into their company let me not come" (Genesis 49:6). Certainly, when you enter into a relationship with someone, observe their disposition. If you choose to marry a temperamental person, this is the environment in which you will spend your life and in which your children will be raised.

——

A woman was dating a man who once punched a wall so hard that he broke several fingers; on other occasions as well he showed totally inappropriate explosions

---

*The same page of the Talmud teaches that among the three people whom God most loves is one who does not display anger.

of anger. The woman ignored these episodes and married him. Later, when he became furious with her, he punched her, in lieu of the wall.

———

2. Realize that anyone whose temper is out of control is capable of terrible things. The Talmud teaches: "One who tears up his garments in his fury, or breaks his vessels in his anger, or who scatters his money in his rage, let him be in your eyes as like an idolater, for such is the way of the evil inclination: today it says to him, 'Do this,' tomorrow it tells him, 'Do this,' until it bids him, 'Go and serve idols,' and he goes and serves them" (*Shabbat* 105b).

The Rabbis regard both paganism and idolatry as motivated in large part by a lack of self-control over one's passions.

Think of your own passions and your own evil inclination (*yetzer hara*). What might happen if you gave in to them? Consider, for example, all the angry thoughts that have entered your mind. Did you act on them or restrain yourself? Once you start to lose self-control (breaking plates, throwing away money), you become capable of moving from self-destructive acts to violence against others.

3. Bad-tempered people not only cause pain, but also influence our behavior negatively. The Book of Proverbs teaches that one should not "befriend a quick-tempered person or go about with one who is hot-tempered, lest you learn from his ways" (22:24–25). As this verse intuits, seeing another's constant explosions, we will begin to think that this is a normal way to behave. Children who grow up in homes where there is shouting are likely to become screamers, and children raised in homes where parents say mean things when enraged are likely to grow up to do so as well.

———

Seneca tells of a boy who studied with Plato and who, upon returning home, saw his father in a towering rage. "I never saw this sort of thing at Plato's," the boy said. But, Seneca wryly comments, "I doubt not that he was quicker to copy his father than he was to copy Plato." And psychologist Solomon Schimmel concludes, "Angry behavior is unfortunately more readily imitated than mildness."[1]

———

4. When dealing with someone who is furious over a hurt he has suffered, we should exercise common sense, tact, and restraint. Rabbi Simeon ben Elazar taught, "Do not try and pacify your fellow in his hour of anger" (*The Ethics of the Fathers* 4:18). In practical terms, this means not trying to calm someone when that person needs to express her fury and is most angry. A comment such as "You don't really mean that" might well reinforce rage rather than assuage it. Instead we should agree with what we can, and gradually calm the person down, if not on the first day, then on the second or third.

5. Nevertheless, we should try to pacify someone if that person is beginning to act precipitously out of anger. The Torah depicts Moses employing such a strategy vis-à-vis God Himself. In Exodus 32, while Moses is on Mount Sinai communing with God, the Children of Israel start to worship a golden calf. Outraged, God says to Moses: "Now leave Me be that My anger may blaze forth against them and that I may destroy them, and make of you a great nation" (32:10). Moses appeases God, "Let not your anger blaze forth against your people . . . turn from Your blazing anger and renounce the plan to punish Your people" (32:11–12).

Moses also employs other strategies to assuage the Lord's wrath. He asks God to remember Abraham, Isaac, and Jacob, and "how You swore to them by Your Self and said to them, 'I will make your offspring as numerous as the stars of heaven, and I will give to your offspring the whole land of which I spoke, to possess forever.'" This plea proves successful: "And the Lord renounced the punishment He had planned to bring upon His people" (32:14).

We should learn from Moses' encounter with God that when someone who is angry is about to shift from venting to engaging in destructive behavior, we should do whatever we can to stop him.

6. When dealing with an enraged person, particularly someone angry with us, we should act as calmly as we can. The Book of Proverbs teaches that calmness can be contagious: "A gentle response pacifies wrath" (15:1). It is hard for someone to continue to shout if we respond gently and in an unruffled way. If we respond to shouting and accusations with more shouting and accusations, the conflict is far more likely to escalate.

7. If someone has reason to be upset with us, we should acknowledge that fact, and ask for mercy. Thus, when Joseph caught Benjamin stealing (in actuality, it was a ruse by Joseph), Judah pleaded for mercy: "Please . . . let [me] appeal to you, and do not be impatient with [me]" (Genesis 44:18).

Rabbi Zelig Pliskin comments, "When you think that what you say will be irritating to the person you are talking to, you can defuse his potential anger by mentioning right at the start that you hope that what you say will not get [him] angry." Most people think of themselves as fair and generous. If we acknowledge their right to be upset, but appeal to them to restrain their anger, they are more likely to be disarmed. But, if we challenge or even deny the other party's right to be upset, we will probably trigger another angry reaction.

26

JUSTIFIABLE ANGER

When it is wrong not to be angry

1. Philo, the first-century Egyptian Jewish philosopher, believed that anger is always inappropriate, and that we should "completely extirpate and eradicate anger from the soul" ("Treatise on the Allegories of the Sacred Law" 3:65). His contemporary, Seneca, the Roman philosopher, argued that anger is an unnecessary emotion, since reason, in combination with other desirable emotions, will always guide one to righteous behavior, whereas anger won't.

However, Philo's and Seneca's reasoning strikes me as unreasonable. For example, those who were infuriated by Hitler, such as Winston Churchill, were more likely to want to fight and destroy him than those who were not particularly angry at Hitler, such as Neville Chamberlain, the British prime minister, and Joseph Kennedy, the American ambassador to England, who advocated making concessions. For that matter, who would want to live in a city whose police department was composed of officers who felt little or no anger toward the murderers, rapists, and pederasts they were trying to catch? As Rabbi Abraham Joshua Heschel has written: "[Anger's] complete suppression in the face of outbursts of evil may amount to surrender and capitulation. . . . The complete absence of anger stultifies moral sensibility."[1]

Justifiable anger in the Bible

2. The belief that anger is always illegitimate continues to be embraced by many religious people. In one instance, a deeply pious woman confided to her therapist that she never allowed herself to become angry because she thought it ungodly to do so. The therapist sent her home with the assignment to read through the Bible and to mark down passages in which God and some of the Bible's heroes become angry. As the woman quickly came to realize, there are times when anger is an appropriate response to others' cruel or otherwise wrongful behavior, and any lesser response is wrong. Among the instances of morally appropriate anger expressed by God and human beings in the Bible are the following:

• *Against those who misuse their talents for evil:* God is outraged at the prophet Balaam for taking money from the king of Moab to curse the Israelites (Numbers 22:22). Balaam was a man of immense spiritual and intellectual capabilities. The fact that he used these gifts in this way infuriated God.

• *Against those who are ungrateful:* Laban prospered from Jacob's twenty-year stewardship over his flocks, yet never thanked him. Instead he tried to lower Jacob's wages. In response, "Jacob became incensed and took up his grievance with Laban." (see Genesis 31:36–42).

• *Against those who commit slander:* Moses was outraged by the rebels Korach, Datan, and Abiram, and their false claim that he used his position to aggrandize himself (Numbers 16:15).

• *Against those who mistreat the poor:* The prophet Isaiah, speaking in God's Name, denounced those who oppressed society's most vulnerable members: "That which was robbed from the poor is in your houses. How dare you crush My people and grind the faces of the poor?" says the Lord, God of Hosts" (Isaiah 3:14–15; see also Amos 5:21–22).

• *Against those who worship false gods:* God is furious at King Solomon, who, in his later years, built idolatrous shrines in Israel. "The Lord was angry with Solomon because his heart turned away from the Lord, the God of Israel, who had appeared to him twice" (I Kings 11:9).

• *Against those who make false, and cruel, claims in God's Name:* God is angry with Job's friends for telling him that his sufferings were sent by God (Job 42:7).

That God, and people such as Jacob, Moses, and Isaiah all express anger indicates that this emotion, when expressed correctly and justly, is a moral one.

3. Maimonides regards those who never become angry, regardless of the provocation, as being corpselike. In other words, it is unnatural and inappropriate never to lose our temper.* We should aim rather "to be angry only for a grave cause that rightly calls for indignation, so that the like shall not be done again" ("Laws of Character Development" 1:4).

Maimonides' view of anger was probably influenced by Aristotle, of whose writings he was a lifelong student. In his *Nichomachean Ethics,* Aristotle wrote that "a person is praised who is angry for the right reasons, with the right people, in the right way, at the right time, and for the right length of time" ("The Virtue Concerned with Anger," 4:5).

Each of Aristotle's conditions can help us guard against inappropriate expressions of anger:

• *for the right reasons:* We should not become angry over petty matters.

• *with the right person:* If we are angry at our boss, we should not come home and take it out on our spouse or children. Also, we should not get upset at our supervisor for implementing an unfair order from our mutual boss (a phenomenon known in popular parlance as "blaming the messenger," and in psychological terms as "displacement").

• *in the right way:* Even when we are justifiably angry, we are still required to act fairly (see, for example, page 261; see also chapter 28 on fighting fairly).

• *at the right time and for the right length of time:* We shouldn't react immediately (unless we know we are calm). Right after something has taken place, our anger may be out of control, and it is better to wait until we are more composed. However, we also should not react long after the event has occurred. Finally, we must learn to let go of our anger once we

---

*An example of this is one of the most pathetic figures in Jewish literature, Bontsha Schweig (the character's name is the title of a short story by the great Yiddish writer, I. L. Peretz), a man who is incapable of expressing anger. Bontsha is repeatedly mistreated and humiliated, yet he never reacts with anger. Does he become an elevated person as a result? Hardly. When the judge in the heavenly court tells him that everything in paradise is his for the asking, Bontsha, whose unending suffering and repression of anger have caused him to lose the ability to dream, has but one wish: "to have every morning for breakfast, a hot roll with fresh butter." Such a person, it would seem, is conscious that he is but "dust and ashes," but not that "for my sake the world was created" (see page 239).

have expressed it. There are many families whose sense of cohesiveness is destroyed by members who hold on to their rage for years or even decades.

———

Aristotle's checklist is an important one for each of us to review when we are angry. Otherwise we will not hold our anger in check, believing, even when we are wrong, that we are justified. The Catholic theologian Saint Francis de Sales wrote, "[Anger] is nourished by a thousand false pretexts; there never was an angry man who thought his anger unjust."[2] In modern times, the most obvious exemplars of such an attitude are terrorists who justify the most heinous acts against innocent people.

———

4. The biblical law "You shall not hate your brother in your heart" (Leviticus 19:17) implies that not all anger should be repressed. The Bible does not forbid all hatred, but only that which you are keeping secret. Therefore it is best to tell the person who has offended you why you are angry, because doing so might lead to a change in the person's behavior or to an apology—and to reconciliation. Rashi, commenting on Numbers 12:9, suggests that you should not become angry at someone without first telling the person what he is doing that has upset you. Once you have done this (and your reason is valid), then, if the person does not alter his behavior, you have the right to be angry at him.

5. Even when anger is justified, such as when your children have acted badly and you wish to return them to the right path, you should strive to present yourself as angry, but "inwardly you should be calm." (Maimonides, "Laws of Character Development" 2:3).*

In other words, we should try to be like an actor who is playing the role of an angry person; the goal of our anger should not be to inflict punishment, but to prevent the problem from recurring (1:4).

6. Even when it is justified, anger needs to be expressed in proportion to the provocation. A defining characteristic of unjustified anger is that it is irrational, exaggerated, and unpredictable. If your anger is expressed in a disproportionate way, then it is better not to express it at all, or to wait until you have calmed down before you speak of the matter.

———

*If your anger is truly very great, it might be best to leave the house and walk around outside until you achieve some perspective and feel calmer.

One way to assess whether your anger is excessive is to ask yourself—and this requires self-discipline—whether you still feel compassion or concern for the person who has upset you. The prayer of the prophet Habakkuk contains a reminder that applies to all of us when angry: "In Your wrath, remember mercy" (3:2).* If the only emotion you can get in touch with is rage, then your anger is most probably excessive.

27

CONTROLLING ANGER

1. We can almost always control our temper. Many of us who don't behave well, or who say cruel things when irate, claim that we simply can't control ourselves. But unless we are suffering from certain types of brain damage or are taking mind-altering drugs, this is rarely true. Thus there is no one at whom the average person would feel greater rage than a mugger. We are walking along a street, when suddenly a man confronts us with a knife or gun and demands all our money. Although we are justifiably enraged at such a person, do we express to him anger and hatred? No, we almost certainly respond courteously, and do or say nothing to goad him further.† In other words, we can control our temper when we believe it important to do so.

Similarly, consider a situation in which we are fuming at family members (most manifestations of anger are exhibited toward our family), and there is a knock on the door. If it is our boss, a new client whose business we are trying to solicit, or anyone we are trying to impress, would we go on screaming in this person's presence? Of course not. Again, we can

---

*Rabbi Abraham Joshua Heschel comments on this passage: "Anger and mercy are not opposites" (*The Prophets,* page 283). Or, rather, they need not be opposites. While anger devoid of compassion might be an appropriate response to a Hitler, a Stalin, or a suicide bomber, in the overwhelming majority of instances the demonizing of the person at whom we are angry will lead us to act in a manner that we will come to regret.

†This, of course, is the prudent thing to do. In a tragic instance in New York City in February 2005, a young actress and her boyfriend were held up by a mugger who pointed a gun at them. The woman bravely, but unwisely, challenged him, "What are you going to do? Shoot me?" He did, and the woman died.

control our anger when we feel that the price paid for not doing so will be too high.

But then, one might counter, isn't it true that as soon as the person leaves, our rage will resume?

Even if this is true, the fact that we can control our anger for ten or fifteen minutes means that we can control it for far longer. And even if the anger resumes after a few minutes, it will probably be expressed in a less extreme manner. On the other hand, expressing anger when we are most angry generally causes our rage to escalate.

Furthermore, common sense indicates that almost all of us can control our anger for far longer than ten or fifteen minutes. If we have a bad temper and are told that if we reduce our outbursts by seventy-five percent over the next six months we will receive two million dollars, would we not quickly learn how to control our temper? What is sad is that in the absence of such a financial incentive, many of us destroy relationships with our closest family members, relationships worth far more than two million dollars.

Therefore the first step in learning how to restrain ourselves is to acknowledge that we are able to control our temper and not be controlled by it.

———

That human beings have control over their anger is underscored by a statement God makes near the beginning of Genesis. Aware of Cain's fury at his brother Abel, the Lord says to him, "Sin crouches at the door, its urge is toward you, yet you can be its master" (4:5–7). Disregarding God's words, Cain makes no effort to control his anger, and kills Abel, thus becoming the first murderer in history. However, God's words, "you can be its master," remain as an admonition to all of us who are tempted to act cruelly or violently when angry.

———

A psychiatrist told me of a patient whose wife claimed that she was incapable of controlling her temper, and who used to scream hysterically at him and even slap him. Yet she never expressed such anger in public. The patient learned that when she was screaming at him in their car, if he opened the windows, she would immediately desist for fear of being overheard. Her calmer behavior in public proved, of course, that she could control herself if she wanted to. She would not do so, however, and the couple divorced.

———

2. **Work on developing greater patience thirty minutes at a time.** The Jerusalem Mussar teacher, Rabbi Shlomo Wolbe, suggests that we try to figure out the half-hour each day during which we are most likely to become

impatient, then not allow ourselves to do so during that time. For example, perhaps our tensest half-hour is when we arrive home from work; often, in this situation, we find our young children screaming and crying, and our frazzled spouse yelling back at them.

Rabbi Wolbe suggests that we recognize the pattern, and resolve to be calm. We should enter the house calmly, speak kind words to our harried spouse, "then pick up the first child, hold him and hug him . . . and sing gently to him. Then do so with your next child until, with your patience, you have turned the half-hour that used to get you angry all the time into the half-hour when the house returns to quietude." As Rabbi Wolbe intuits, we can accomplish more with patience than with anger.

After some time, we will be so used to being patient during this half-hour that we will be ready to choose another half-hour during which to remain calm. We should keep expanding the time periods during which we strive to be patient.[1]

———

Physical factors can also cause impatience. A friend told me that he is far more likely to lose his temper when he is hypoglycemic (experiencing low blood sugar). Indeed, this is true of almost all people. My friend makes it a practice to delay all serious discussions with his wife and children until after he has eaten. He says, "Once I eat, my disposition improves dramatically."

———

3. *The Ethics of the Fathers* teaches, "Do not be easily angered" (2:10). Many people's annoyance is triggered by minor incidents. (One woman, for example, recounted how her father went into a rage when he couldn't find a sharpened pencil on the desk where he had left it.) Therefore, try, one day at a time, to remain calm over behavior that is not particularly significant (such as a child's refusal to take a bath or go to bed on time, or a spouse's lack of focus or enthusiasm when you are speaking to them). Rabbi Moshe Goldberger, author of *Guard Your Anger,* suggests adopting this rabbinic teaching as a kind of mantra to help internalize the need to respond to others in a nonaggressive manner. He suggests repeating the words "Do not be easily angered" (in Hebrew, *al tehi noach leekh-os*) ten times in a row several times a day, "and see if it does not start to have a calming effect on you."[2]

It might also be helpful to repeat these words to yourself when you realize that you are about to lose your temper. For many people, saying the words in Hebrew, even if they don't understand the language, is helpful, since it endows the statement with the feeling of sanctity many people associate with words they say in *lashon kodesh* (the holy language).

————

Rabbi Goldberger understands the entire statement in The Ethics of the Fathers *(2:10) in which the words "Do not be easily angered" appear, as providing a helpful guideline in overcoming anger: "Rabbi Eliezer said: 'Let your friend's honor be as dear to you as your own, do not be easily angered, and repent one day before you die.' If your friend's honor is as dear to you as your own, you won't explode in anger and say hurtful things, because you can't simultaneously honor someone and 'blow up' at them. Therefore, control your temper. Indeed, if you're aware that you might die tomorrow, you won't explode over petty things."*[3]

————

4. Don't react with rage to a matter that should, at most, cause annoyance. Rabbi Abraham Twerski notes that Rabbi Israel Salanter used to say that "people are frequently provoked to anger by items of relatively little importance, but which, at that precise moment, appear to be significant. If one observes an infant, one will note that if someone takes a brightly colored wooden block away from him, he may become very angry and cry. Obviously, the deprivation of the block of wood is meaningless to a mature mind, but to the juvenile mind, it means a great deal. So do we, even as mature adults, sometimes perceive trivia as being of great importance and react accordingly with rage. Rabbi Salanter pointed out that if a person were engaged in a major transaction where he stood to profit greatly, he would ignore irritating trivia. The overriding goal would obscure the minor irritations."[4]

————

Likewise, Seneca wrote of our tendency to overreact when we feel our honor is at stake: "Because you are given a less honorable place at the table, you begin to get angry at your host . . . [and] at the man himself who was preferred above you. Madman! What difference does it make on what part of the couch you recline? Can a cushion add either to your honor or your disgrace?"[5]

————

Limiting your anger

5. An important factor in resolving conflicts is our willingness to be appeased. *The Ethics of the Fathers* (5:11) identifies four kinds of temperaments, one positive, one neutral, and two negative. As noted, the best temperament, one the Rabbis describe as saintly, is "one whom it is hard to anger and easy to appease." Second best is one who is angered easily, but is also easy to appease. As the Rabbis put it, "His loss [namely, becoming angry easily] is canceled by his gain." The next temperament is one whom it is hard to anger, but also hard to appease: "his gain is canceled by his loss." And the fourth, the worst, is one "whom it is easy to anger and hard to appease; this is a wicked temperament."

The Rabbis make clear what is not at all obvious: the most serious problem is not being easily angered (as long as we do not do or say terrible things when enraged), but being hard to pacify—in short, being the sort of person who finds it difficult if not impossible to forgive. The inability to be appeased is more destructive to our relationships than being easily provoked (though this, of course, is an unfortunate quality as well). Therefore, this is what people with bad tempers need to work on first.

Most important, when we become angry with someone, particularly a person with whom we've previously been friendly, we should remind ourselves of good things this person has done either for us or others. If necessary, we should sit down and force ourselves to list the good things we know about him. If he is someone whom we have known for a long time, it shouldn't be difficult to summon up such memories and associations.

Also, in line with the biblical law "In justice shall you judge your fellow" (Leviticus 19:15), we should force ourselves to construct one or two positive scenarios that can account for why the person acted as he did. If we recall the person's good deeds and try to put a more positive "spin" on why he has now acted inappropriately, we might choose not to break off a relationship over a relatively insignificant issue.

———

The self-destructive nature of long-term anger is underscored in Ecclesiastes' teaching that "anger dwells in the bosom of fools" (7:9). A fool, in other words, is not one who, when provoked, feels anger (because the feeling—as opposed to expression—of anger is an emotion one cannot always control); rather, a fool is one who holds on to anger, and who doesn't relinquish it. This is particularly evident in family disputes, in which anger often causes people to remain on nonspeaking terms for many years. This is more than wrong; it is foolish, and someone who allows himself, except in the most extreme of situations, to remain angry for so long is a fool. In contrast, children, who are often quick to flare up, usually get over their anger far more quickly than adults do.

Aaron Lazare, author of On Apology, *recalls an episode related to him by a seventy-five-year-old machinist: "I worked at my machine for thirty years. One day, something happened between me and the fellow next to me. Some unpleasant words were exchanged. I do not remember what was said or who was at fault, but we stopped talking. We did not speak to each other for the next six years. One day, I turned to him and said, 'I have been a damned fool,' and I stretched out my hand for him to shake. We shook hands. The grudge was over. Several workers nearby came over and asked what was going on. I said, 'I do not have to be a damned fool all of my life.'"**

———

6. We all sometimes say unfair, hurtful things to others while incensed. Following one guideline will greatly lessen the chance that we will say something that causes irrevocable damage to a relationship: *No matter how upset you are, restrict the expression of your anger to the incident that provoked it.* While this isn't the easiest rule to follow, it isn't that difficult. As long as we keep our words focused on the one incident, we are unlikely to say anything that will destroy our relationship. When we depart from this rule, using words like "always" and "never" (see page 390 for a discussion of why these words can be so damaging), or start recalling every occasion on which the other person has enraged us, we say things that are unfair and that destroy friendships and marriages.

In short, we must watch our tongue when we are angry. Once harsh words are said, the other person, while perhaps willing one day to forgive them, probably won't ever forget them. Would you?

———

Why is it that what we say when we are angry can cause such hurt and alienation? Unfortunately, people generally assume that what others say when they are upset reflects what they truly feel. But all that such words generally reveal is what the person feels at that moment. When we are angry, we often feel and think unfairly. Few of us would want our parents, spouses, children, or friends to know every angry thought about them that goes through our heads. That is why

---

*Aaron Lazare, *On Apology,* page 142. This incident also illustrates that acknowledgment of one's being in the wrong, even without elaboration, can sometimes bring about an immediate reconciliation. The worker's simple statement, "I have been a damned fool," restored to the other party a sense of respect. (This, in turn, makes it easier, when appropriate, for the other person to own up to his responsibility as well: "Well, you know, you're not the only one who's at fault. I didn't behave well, either.")

most of us choose to keep such thoughts to ourselves. But once we release these often distorted thoughts into the world, others tend to assume that they represent our true feelings.

Therefore we should be guided by the words of Solomon ibn Gabirol, the eleventh-century Spanish Jewish philosopher and poet: "I can retract what I did not say, but I cannot retract what I have already said."

———

7. Similarly, even when you are enraged, don't spread embarrassing information about another, even if is true. As the Talmud notes, after you apologize and make peace, the person may even accept your apology, but "inside, he is still burning" (Jerusalem Talmud, *Peah* 1:1). It is when we are angry that we are most obliged to guard our tongues.

8. No matter how enraged you become, don't curse someone to her face: your words will never be forgotten. The Bible records that when King David was fleeing for his life from his son Absalom, a man named Shimi ben Gera, a relative of David's predecessor, King Saul, unleashed a series of curses against him. Avishai, David's general, wanted to kill Shimi, but David stopped him, arguing that if his own son Absalom wanted to kill him, how could he kill Shimi for cursing him? (II Samuel 16:5–8, 11–12). Nonetheless, these curses rankled David. Many years later, on his deathbed, he advised Solomon, his son and successor, to make sure that Shimi died a violent death (I Kings 2:8–9). And, in the Psalms, which Jewish tradition attributes to David, he wrote, presumably of Shimi, "He loved to curse, may a curse come upon him" (109:17).

9. Speak softly when you feel upset. The medieval ethical text *Orchot Tzaddikim* (*The Way of the Righteous*) advises people to be particularly conscious of their tempers during difficult times:

- when under financial pressure (work pressure as well)
- when not feeling well
- when fasting

10. While anger is sometimes justified, it is important to banish excessive anger and vindictiveness from our hearts (Ecclesiastes 11:10). To motivate us to reach this goal, the following prayer was inserted as part of the prayers before going to sleep at night (the bedtime *Sh'ma*): "Master

of the Universe, I forgive all those who have caused me to become angry, and all those who have sinned against my body, my money, my honor, or anything else that is mine . . . and no one should be punished because of me."

For most of us, this prayer will not work the first time we recite it. But repeating it night after night will help us to become calmer and gain perspective. We will be less likely to find ourselves consumed with grudges and anger, and more likely to feel forgiving toward, and less angry at, those who have hurt us.

See chapter 18 for a discussion of when Jewish law deems forgiveness obligatory or optional, and when forbidden.

Be aware of what you are feeling

11. Learn to become aware of what you are feeling. That way, when you are tense and likely to explode, you can guard against doing so. Unfortunately, many people with bad tempers are not aware of their emotions; when others accuse them of being angry, they deny it, often with a "snappish" tone. In truth, when you see a person accuse someone else of being angry, and the first person denies it, she *is* usually angry. Therefore, if you are accused of being angry, before you deny it, consider the possibility that you are. Realizing that you're upset, or even just nervous, will put you on notice to be more careful than usual in what you say and do. If necessary, when you are in a bad mood, try to minimize your contact with others.

12. Keep a journal focused on your anger. For those who are motivated to develop techniques to control their temper, psychologist Solomon Schimmel recommends keeping an "anger diary." At the end of the day, ask yourself the following questions about incidents that provoked you to anger:

- Could I have avoided the provocation?
- Was my response justified?
- Did my response accomplish its goal?
- What unfortunate side effects did my response have?
- What alternative response could I have made?
- Would I react otherwise if the incident were repeated?
- Am I to be blamed or praised for my behavior?[6]

If you continue to ask such questions, you will soon achieve much better control over your temper. In his essay "On Anger," Seneca wrote, "Anger will cease and become more controllable if it finds that it must appear before a judge every day."

13. When you are angry and need to confide in someone, choose a fair-minded person with a mild disposition, one who will be able to calm you ("Oh, he said that to you. Perhaps he didn't mean it the way you think"). Don't go to someone who is likely to make matters worse ("He said that? What are you going to do about it?").

Three antidotes to anger: humility, compassion, and charity

14. Humility can serve as an antidote to a bad temper. The thirteenth-century rabbi Menachem ha-Meiri wrote of a righteous king who had one serious flaw: he was quick-tempered. Wishing to overcome this tendency, he wrote down three thoughts on a piece of paper, then instructed one of his servants to show him the paper whenever he started to lose his temper. The lines read:

- Always remember that you are merely one of God's creations, and you yourself are not the Creator.
- Always remember that you are flesh and blood and will eventually perish.
- Always remember that there will be mercy for you in the future only if you have mercy on others.[7]

15. Have compassion for the one who is provoking you. Rabbi Abraham Twerski writes that he never saw his father express rage; instead, his father would say, "The person who is provoking me doesn't understand that what he is doing is very foolish. He thinks he is wise and right. I feel sorry that he is a fool. Pity and rage do not go together. You cannot be angry at someone for whom you feel sorry."[8]

This solution will not always work. If someone's actions threaten your well-being and/or cause you great anguish, your sense that the person is a fool might not mitigate your rage. However, this technique works for more-minor irritations, of the sort that often cause us to explode.

———

Rabbi Noach Weinberg points out that if we were standing on a street corner and someone knocked into us and pushed us into the line of traffic, we would understandably be furious. Yet, if we turned around and saw that the culprit was blind, our anger would evaporate. There are many times when we should realize that the culprit in our dispute is similarly "blind." And while we need to protect ourselves (as we would need to do if we were standing on a streetcorner), anger, particularly long-term anger, is an inappropriate response.

————

16. The *Reishit Chochmah (The Beginning of Wisdom),* a late-medieval Jewish text, suggests that if you are trying to achieve greater control over your anger, you should decide on a sum of money that you will give to charity if you lose your temper unfairly. Be sure that the sum you choose is sufficient to force you to think twice.

If you wish to utilize this approach, make a note of each time you lose your temper unfairly (either when there isn't reasonable provocation or when your response is disproportionate). After a specified period of time, fine yourself for each outburst. The amount should depend on your level of wealth. Of course, whatever you give to charity should be over and above what you would otherwise donate.

If this technique does not work for you, then fine yourself and give the money to a cause of which you otherwise disapprove. If you are Orthodox, give it to a Reform or Conservative temple's building fund; if Reform or Conservative, donate it to an Orthodox yeshiva. That way, at least your anger will serve the cause of Jewish unity.

————

Dr. Isaac Herschkopf, author of Hello Darkness, My Old Friend, *a comprehensive study of anger, comments on this suggestion that it is better to fine yourself immediately, since the effectiveness of adverse conditioning is directly proportional to the speed with which it is administered.*

————

A final thought

17. A rabbinic sage related that whenever he found himself becoming enraged, he would check in the *Shulchan Arukh,* the authoritative sixteenth-century code of Jewish law, as to whether he had the right to be angry in such a situation. He found that going to his library, taking down the book, and checking through it calmed him down. When you feel anger, perhaps you can read through the section in this book on justifiable anger (chapter 26), and assess whether you have a right to be angry. Even if you do, check to make sure that your anger is not excessive. May this act of checking help to calm you down.

28

FIGHTING FAIRLY

1. The rabbinic teaching "Do not be easily angered" (*The Ethics of the Fathers* 2:10) acknowledges that all of us are angered occasionally. We all have disagreements and arguments with other people. What is needed, therefore, is an ethic of arguing, strategies to ensure that arguments are conducted fairly and do not escalate into bitter fights.*

In a remarkable and infrequently commented upon passage, the Talmud teaches that "God is angered every day," but that his anger lasts but a "moment" (Berachot 7a; the Rabbis analyze the length of a divine moment and conclude that it is less than a second).

---

2. The American actress Lynn Fontanne was once asked the secret of her successful marriage to, and acting partnership with, Alfred Lunt, an equally renowned actor. She responded that they were never uncivil to each other. Respect and civility (in Hebrew, *derech eretz*) are the preconditions for a fair fight. This means that you internalize the talmudic admonition to "let your friend's honor be as dear to you as your own" (*The Ethics of the Fathers* 2:10), even when you're having a dispute. It also implies that you express your anger without seeking to destroy the other person.

3. Never use damaging personal information to invalidate your adversary's contentions, as incensed people commonly do. In Somerset Maugham's

---

*For an example of such a tragic fight, see the discussion on page 251.

classic novel *Of Human Bondage,* the protagonist, Philip, has a clubfoot. He has a low estimation of human nature stemming from the realization "that when his fellows were angry with him, they never failed to taunt him with his deformity." Similarly, someone annoyed at another's lack of consideration might make a reference to the other person's unhappy love life: "That's why no one loves you or wants to marry you." Even if you believe that there is a connection between the two, the time to point this out is not when you're feeling angry. In such a state, you will be incapable of phrasing your comments fairly, and the other person will hear your words as intended only to hurt and wound.

4. As noted earlier (page 267), the best way to keep your anger in check is to restrict your comments to the incident that provoked it. Remember, only anger that is proportionate to the provocation is fair.

5. When angry, if you say or do something that's unfair, apologize as soon as you realize that you've said something inappropriate. Do so even if you feel that you are more in the right than the other party; in such a case, you still owe an apology for what you did that was wrong. Part of the tragedy in David and Michal's fight (see page 251) is not just what they said, but also that neither of them made an effort to apologize.

6. Express your anger directly to the person who offended you. Many people, afraid to confront the other person, instead share their anger with others, thereby besmirching their opponent's good name. The Rabbis understood the law "Do not hate your brother in your heart" (Leviticus 19:17) as meaning that when you have a grievance, you should neither hold it in nor share it with others. Rather, you should go directly to the person and inform him of what he has done to hurt you.

There is much wisdom in William Blake's poem "A Poison Tree":

I was angry with my friend;
I told my wrath, my wrath did end.
I was angry with my foe;
I told it not, my wrath did grow.

As a general rule, it is wisest not to confront the person with whom you are angry when you are at the height of your rage, since it is difficult at such moments to express your anger fairly.

———

Obviously, we should also be cautious about expressing anger to someone in a position to do us harm; the goal of expressing anger is to improve our situation with the other party, not worsen it.

———

7. The Talmud teaches that acting fairly when angry is a world-transforming activity: "The world exists only on account of him who restrains himself in strife" (*Chullin* 89a). As Rabbi Harold Kushner has commented, "Only God can give us credit for the angry words we did not speak."[1]

Humiliating
Others

———

Whoever shames his neighbor in public,
it is as if he shed his blood.

Babylonian Talmud,
Bava Mezia 58b

29

THE GREAT EVIL OF HUMILIATION

1. The Talmud teaches, "Whoever shames his neighbor in public, it is as if he shed his blood" (*Bava Mezia* 58b). Indeed, when someone feels humiliated, the blood drains from his or her face.*

English, too, expresses this thought; we speak of "dying from embarrassment."

Taunting can also be emotionally devastating, as reflected in the biblical story of Hannah, one of two wives of Elkanah. Hannah was childless, but Elkanah's other wife, Peninah, had children, and she used to mock Hannah, claiming that "the Lord had closed her womb. This happened year after year. Every time she went up to the house of the Lord, the other would taunt her, so that she wept and would not eat" (I Samuel 1:6–7).

After Saul was anointed as Israel's first king, "some scoundrels said, 'How can this fellow save us?' and brought him no gift. But he pretended not to mind" (I Samuel 10:27). The words "he pretended not to mind" suggest, of course, that Saul did mind, even though he knew he had been appointed to his position by God. Mockery can be painful and distressing, even for a king.

---

2. Because public humiliation is so damaging (the victim often becomes insecure and embarrassed in the presence of others), Jewish teachings regard it as almost unforgivable. The Talmud declares that one who publicly humiliates another forfeits a place in the World-to-Come (*Bava Mezia* 59a); this applies even if the offender is an ardent student of Torah, and performs many good deeds (*The Ethics of the Fathers* 3:15). Fortunately, given that most of us have been guilty of this offense at least once, other sources teach that eternal

---

*Alternatively, the blood rushes to the person's face, causing him to blush.

punishment is exacted only from those who routinely engage in such behavior (see Maimonides, "Laws of Repentance" 3:14).*

———

Rabbi Israel Spira, the Chasidic rebbe known as the Bluzhover, was present at a synagogue service during which the guest cantor repeated words in the prayer book for the sake of the melody he was singing. Some of the congregation, noting that his repetitions violated Jewish law, banged with their fists, and shouted at the man to stop. At the end of the service, the man quickly rushed out. The rebbe said to those present, "Our Sages tell us that one who publicly shames his fellow man has no share in the World-to-Come. Nowhere, however, does it say that one forfeits his portion for repeating words of the prayer text."[1]

———

3. Humiliating someone is regarded as an offense against God as well as against the person shamed, for when you humiliate someone, you mock God in Whose image that person was created (see *Genesis Rabbah* 24:7).

4. Judaism's strictures against humiliating others are often violated in today's society when:

- Newspapers, magazines, and other media broadcast scandalous information about public figures that the public has no need to know, and thus, from Judaism's perspective, no right to know.
- Political candidates divulge embarrassing and irrelevant information about their opponents.
- People poke fun at another's physical or mental handicaps, or call someone by an unpleasant nickname.
- Fraternities impose hazing procedures on those wishing to join.
- Teachers ridicule students.
- Lawyers demean opposing witnesses and cast doubt on the veracity of their testimony, even when they have reason to believe it is true.[†]

---

*Maimonides enumerates several offenses that, if committed often, cause one to lose one's share in the World-to-Come (*she-ha-rageel ba-hem ein lo chelek be-olam ha-ba*): among these are inventing cruel nicknames for people or calling them by such names (see page 287 for an example of how this behavior can destroy someone's life), publicly shaming others, and disgracing one's teachers. Even so, he teaches that if you wholeheartedly repent, "you will merit the World-to-Come, for nothing can stand in the way of repentance" (Maimonides, "Laws of Repentance" 3:14).

†Such behavior is also a violation of the biblical command to "stay far away from falsehood" (Exodus 23:7).

5. Genesis gives two examples of heroic figures who avoided humiliating people guilty of moral wrongdoing. Although Tamar could have been burned at the stake on a charge of adultery, she did not expose her former father-in-law Judah as the man who had impregnated her. Instead she offered him the opportunity to acknowledge what he had done (38:25). Based on this, the Talmud concludes, perhaps somewhat hyperbolically, "It is better that a person throw himself into a fiery furnace than publicly shame his neighbor" (see *Bava Mezia* 59a and *The Gates of Repentance* 3:139). Later, Joseph revealed himself to his brothers, who years earlier had sold him into slavery and who now didn't recognize him. But he did so only after first sending everyone else out of the room, thereby sparing his brothers the shame of having their heinous act publicly exposed (45:1).

6. *The Ethics of the Fathers* teaches that the Golden Rule applies to the realm of dignity and honor: "Your friend's dignity should be as precious to you as your own" (2:10), and *The Fathers According to Rabbi Nathan* offers as an example that just "as a man would not wish an evil report spread about his wife and children, so he should not wish an evil report spread about his fellow's wife and children" (chapter 16). In short, just as we hate for ourselves and those dear to us to be humiliated, so must we take care not to humiliate others.

7. When Rabbi Elazar ben Azariah was about to die, his disciples sat before him, and asked, "*Rabbenu* [our teacher], teach us only one thing" (i.e., one fundamental final teaching). "He replied, 'My children, what can I teach you? Every one of you go and be very careful of the dignity of others'" (*Derech Eretz Rabbah*, chapter 3).

———

Preserving the dignity of others is so basic a Jewish value that the Talmud teaches that, on occasion, it overrides other prohibitions in Jewish law (Berachot 19b). For example, Jewish law does not permit performing marriages on the

---

*Preserving the dignity of orphans, and protecting them from hurt, is a deeply embedded Jewish value; for example, "You shall not afflict any widow or orphan. . . . If you afflict them in any way, so that they cry out unto Me, I will surely hear their cry. My anger will wax hot." (Exodus 22:21–23). Maimonides, in a twelfth-century form of affirmative action, rules that a teacher who has orphans among his students "should not treat them like others, but make a distinction

Sabbath. Yet, when the wedding of a female orphan* was delayed on a Friday afternoon, the sixteenth-century Rabbi Moses Isserles (known as the Ramah, Rabbi Isserles was one of the preeminent codifiers of Jewish law) performed the wedding ceremony a full hour and a half after the Sabbath had begun. He reasoned that having one's marriage postponed, particularly after all the guests had assembled, "would be a lifelong disgrace to her [the bride]," and "there can be no greater emergency than this case in which a grown orphan was being put to shame."†

———

8. In recognition of how seriously Jewish law regards preserving the dignity of others, the Talmud records a blessing that one rabbi bestowed on another: "May it be God's will that you don't humiliate another, and that you're never humiliated" (*Mo'ed Kattan* 9b).

9. An ancient Jewish text teaches, "It would be better for a person not to have been born at all than to experience these seven things: the death of his children in his lifetime, economic dependence upon others, an unnatural death, forgetting his learning, suffering, slavery, and publicly shaming his fellow man."[2]

The first six items on this list represent some of the worst fates imaginable (becoming a slave, losing a child, and Alzheimer's). Thus it is striking that the Rabbis included "and publicly shaming his fellow man." Note that they did not say, "being publicly shamed," but "publicly shaming his fellow man."

Judaism teaches that our mental capacities are God-given, and that God created us to do good: "The goal of wisdom is to engage in repentance and good deeds" (*Berachot* 17a). It is wrong to squander the gifts bestowed by God, but it is far worse to use them for an evil purpose.

---

in their favor. He should guide them gently, with the utmost tenderness and courtesy." ("Laws of Character Development" 6:10).

†As the Ramah ruled in the *Shulchan Arukh*: "Sometimes when they [the marrying couple] could not reach agreement about the dowry on Friday until the night, then the ceremony is conducted on the Sabbath night itself, because all the preparations had already been made for the feast and wedding and it would shame the bride and groom if they were not married" (*Orach Chayyim* 339:4). The Ramah cited as precedent for this behavior the minority views of two medieval rabbis, Rabbenu Tam and Moshe of Coucy, and argued "that we have these two exceptional opinions to rely on in times of emergency, for great is the principle of protecting the honor of human beings" (see his responsa number 125, and the discussion of this ruling in Solomon Freehof, *A Treasury of Responsa*, pages 113–117).

30

HOW TO AVOID SHAMING OTHERS

═══════

Don't use information as a weapon

1. Do not mention an incident that will embarrass the person about whom it is told. Maimonides writes, "Don't relate a matter that will bring another shame" ("Laws of Character Development" 6:8). This includes alluding indirectly to something only he will understand. For example, if someone you know was involved in a scandal in Cleveland, avoid talking about Cleveland in that person's presence. (What matters here is your intention; if there is a truly relevant reason to speak about Cleveland, you may do so.)

The Talmud goes so far as to prohibit mentioning any object or incident that may cause pain to someone else. If a man's relative was hanged, the Talmud instructs us not to mention the word "hanging" in the person's presence (as in "Hang up this [item] for me"; see *Bava Mezia* 59b), for, as Rashi notes, "the very word 'hanging'" conjures up unhappy associations for such a person.

———

A friend told me that he has close friends whose daughter committed suicide. Even though thirty years have passed, if the word suicide *is mentioned in their presence, the mother still dissolves in tears. When this couple is present and he senses that others might mention the word—perhaps there has been something about suicide in the news—he makes sure to switch the topic.*

———

2. Never mock someone's past behavior. The Talmud designates such mockery as *ona'at d'varim*, oppressing with words, and mentions, as an example, taunting a formerly uncommitted Jew with his violations of Jewish law: "If a person is a penitent, it is forbidden to say to him, 'Remember your early deeds!'" (*Bava Mezia* 58b).

A contemporary example is revealing the former criminal behavior of someone who is now leading an ethical, law-abiding life, or making it known so as to embarrass that person's relatives.

It is also wrong to ridicule another's undistinguished or disreputable ancestry: "Let not a man say to his fellow, 'My father was greater than your father'" (Mishnah Sanhedrin 4:5).

___

3. If you admonish someone for a wrong she has committed, never do so in the presence of others.

___

People who do this sometimes justify their behavior by claiming that it is the only way to make an impression on the offender. However, the Chaffetz Chayyim demonstrates both the falseness of such a justification and the great wrong of doing so:

"A young man has done something improper. One of the young man's companions announces to a crowd what he has done. Present at this announcement is the boy's father, who, understandably, is quite upset. He tells the one who publicized his son's iniquity, 'Had you rebuked my son in private, with no one else present, I would have been deeply grateful to you. But why did you have to make known his deed in public? What you have accomplished is to make him an object of ridicule and disgrace. It seems to me that your intentions were not honorable. You were not out to correct my son's behavior; rather, you sought to damage his reputation and rejoice over his disgrace.'"

The Chaffetz Chayyim goes on to say that God, Who is the Father of every human being, rejoices at people's joy and is pained at their suffering. When a person rebukes another in public, thereby humiliating him, God feels pain, not pleasure (Rabbis Shimon Finkelman and Yitzchak Berkowitz).[1]

___

4. Don't expose someone's ignorance publicly: "If a question is asked about some branch of knowledge, one should not say to someone who does not know the field, 'What would you answer to that?' or 'What do you think of that?'" (Maimonides, "Laws of Sales" 14:14).

Similarly, "When a rabbi is engaged in teaching a particular tractate, do not question him about another tractate, lest he not be conversant with it [and be embarrassed]" (*Shabbat* 3b; see also Maimonides, "Laws of Torah Study" 4:6). Also, don't ask a teacher about something that is not in his area of expertise (for example, in a course on ancient history, don't ask a question that goes outside the purview of that subject), and don't pose a question when the teacher has first entered the room, and his mind is not yet focused.

Likewise, don't ask a public speaker about a matter that she isn't currently discussing, lest she not know the answer and be embarrassed.

———

The guiding principle as to what sort of questions a student should raise is common sense. Thus the Talmud praises a disciple of Rabbi Yannai who raised challenges during his intimate lectures in the yeshiva, but refrained from doing the same thing at Rabbi Yannai's public lectures, in case the rabbi was not able to reply (Mo'ed Kattan 5a).

———

5. Do not reveal a sexual scandal if there is no reason for others to know about it (and there almost never is). Unfortunately, many people enjoy discussing information like this.

The Talmud records that a woman once appeared in the study hall of Rabbi Meir, and said, "Rabbi, one of your disciples here married me through an act of intercourse."* She now wished to be granted a divorce so that she could marry another man. Rabbi Meir issued the woman a get (a Jewish divorce) even though he had not been married to her, whereupon all the disciples present got up and did likewise, thereby guaranteeing both that the woman received a valid divorce, and that the man she was talking about was not exposed (Sanhedrin 11a); it is important to emphasize that what had been involved in this case seems to have been an act of consensual relations.

Rabbi Meir's behavior serves as a rebuke to journalists who often vie with each other to break news of prominent people's sexual improprieties, and to private citizens who gossip about the sexual peccadilloes of their friends and neighbors.

6. The sixteenth-century Maharam of Lublin (Poland) teaches that one who shames those "who sleep in the dust" has also committed a grave sin. For example, one should not offer unnecessary negative information about those who have died.

This teaching is routinely violated in contemporary society, when the deaths of prominent people are frequently followed by the publication of scandalous or even defamatory biographies and memoirs, often by their own family members and others who knew them intimately.

---

*Ancient Jewish law assumed that a man who slept with a woman did so with the intention of marrying her. Therefore, marriage could be effected by a mutually agreed-upon act of sexual relations if done with the intention of consummating a marriage; however, the rabbis opposed effecting a marriage in this manner, and felt that people who did so, though legally married, had committed a sin.

When dealing with those who are less powerful and affluent than we are

7. Don't yell at or harshly criticize someone who works for you, particularly if the person is not in a position to yell back at you. It is even worse if the screaming or criticism is done in the presence of others.

———

The Academy Award–winning actor Michael Caine advises, "Never, under any circumstances, shout at anybody who is lower on the ladder than you are"—in other words, a person who can't shout back at you. To do so, as Caine explains, is to take "a monstrously unfair advantage."[2]

———

8. According to the Talmud, if you've lent someone money and you know that he is having difficulty repaying it, you should avoid the person, so that your presence does not shame him (*Bava Mezia* 75b; see Rashi). As Rabbi Louis Jacobs counsels, "Imagine how you would feel to have to be indebted to others, and spare his feelings as much as you can."[3]

9. Wealthy people should not embarrass those poorer than themselves. In ancient Israel, affluent people were usually buried in beautiful garments, and consequently funerals became very expensive. Eventually "the expense of burying the dead became harder for a family to bear than the death itself" (Babylonian Talmud, *Ketubot* 8b). This situation persisted until the first century C.E., when Rabbi Gamliel (usually referred to by the honorific title Rabban Gamliel), the leader of his age and a wealthy man, left instructions that he be buried in a shroud. He did this so as not to shame the poor, who could not afford expensive funerals. Soon everyone followed his example and clothed their dead in simple linen garments. Ever since then, the Jewish tradition has been to bury rich and poor alike in an inexpensive ceremony.

This law might serve as a precedent to discourage wealthy people from spending exorbitant sums on weddings, as well as Bar Mitzvah and Bat Mitzvah celebrations. Those who can't afford to sponsor such elaborate affairs often feel shamed into spending too much. Tens of thousands of Jews would benefit greatly were a few prominent and wealthy Jews to learn from Rabban Gamliel's example and hold less grandiose celebrations.

———

The Talmud records that rich people used to bring food to houses of mourning in silver and gold utensils, while the poor would bring food in straw baskets. The

*Rabbis ruled that all should use straw baskets so that the poor might not feel embarrassed (*Mo'ed Kattan *27a).*

———

10. It should be a universal right for all people to have adequate and attractive clothing. In ancient Israel, there was a holiday known as *Tu Be'Av* (the fifteenth of the month of Av), when, contrary to wooing customs, young women would go out into the fields to look for potential husbands. Poorer girls would be loaned lovely dresses so that they would not be embarrassed and disadvantaged by having to go out in unattractive clothing (*Ta'anit* 26b).

This talmudic ruling would suggest that in schools with students of widely divergent economic backgrounds, it would be better to have school uniforms so as not to embarrass children whose parents cannot afford the expensive clothes worn by their peers.

11. Do not give a poor person money when others are present, if it is not known that she needs charity. The Talmud tells of Rabbi Yannai, who saw a man giving money to a poor person in public and told him that it would be better not to embarrass him (*Chagigah* 5a). Obviously, what matters here is context. If a person is begging, it is clear that she does not mind being given a donation in public and one should do so.

12. Never refer to other ethnic, religious, or racial groups by derogatory names. Obviously, to do so to a member of the group humiliates the person, and to do so in conversation with others dehumanizes the group. Evil behavior generally starts with verbal dehumanization. The Crusaders did not get up one morning and start massacring Jews. For centuries, enemies of the Jews stigmatized them with names such as "Christ-killers," and in this way made them seem less than human. Once this label took hold, it became easy to kill Jews.

———

Never allow yourself to participate in the public humiliation of members of another group. This is a characteristic feature of authoritarian and totalitarian governments, and is absolutely immoral and forbidden.

Hayim Greenberg, the great writer and philosopher of American Labor Zionism, lived in Russia during the years when the Communists came to power. He wrote of an incident he witnessed in Kiev in 1920, and which remained vividly in his consciousness: "On the main thoroughfare stand young men with thick cigarettes between their lips who draft passing women for work. They examine

*every woman's documents and if one cannot prove that she is the wife of a prole-
tarian, or that she is engaged in 'socially useful' work, she is sent to clean the toi-
lets in one of the barracks. The more intellectual a woman seems to be, the more
certain she is to be sent to this kind of work accompanied by the applause of the
soldiers. On that day, I heard one soldier brag before another that the toilet of his
barracks was cleaned by the wife of a [former] governor. The other soldier gloated
over the fact that that the toilet of his regiment was cleaned by a baroness. He
therefore considered himself a step higher on the social scale than his comrade. Af-
terwards they nearly murdered each other in the brawl that followed the discussion as to who is nobler, a baroness or the wife of a governor. They finally made
up. Whichever woman was nobler, they were both aristocrats."*

Nor was this a singular occurrence. Eighteen years later, in March 1938, the
Germans took over Austria, and Nazi soldiers rounded up distinguished Jews
and forced them to clean the streets—sometimes the Nazis would make Jews do
this work with toothbrushes—while crowds of Austrians jeered at them.

Greenberg offers a fascinating theory as to why totalitarian regimes publicly humiliate those they regard as their opponents: "Elementary rights are
taken away from everyone; it is therefore good that there still exists one stratum
of the population which has still fewer rights. The more they are spat upon, the
more favored the others feel. . . . There is no price too high which the man without self-respect would not pay for the . . . right to treat others as being lower than
himself."[4]

Don't shame children

13. The prohibition against publicly shaming others applies as strongly
to children as to adults (*Bava Kamma* 86a–b). Maimonides writes, "Do not
humiliate your fellow in public, whether he [or she] is a minor or an adult"
("Law of Character Development" 6:8). Indeed, children are more vulnerable
to all attacks, including humiliation. Therefore, if parents need to admonish
a child, they should do so in private, just as they would with an adult. Parents who are quick-tempered must guard against breaking this law, for example, by berating a child in public, or in the presence of his peers.

Unfortunately, many parents routinely violate this ethical norm. Some
even humiliate children for behavior that is beyond their control, such as
learning disabilities or other disorders. Thus, one man in his fifties recalls
his shame and rage when he was six years old and still a bed-wetter, and his
father said to him in front of the whole family, "We can't go on vacation and

stay in a motel or at friends' homes because you still wet the bed. You are ruining the summer for all of us!" Rabbi Abraham Twerski, a psychiatrist, comments, "This was a totally unfair rebuke, because he was unable to control his bed-wetting, and [the man] said that his father's vicious criticism drove a stake into his heart. What was even worse was that this was said in the presence of his siblings. Thoughtless remarks such as this can have untold impact on a child, with long-term residuals of acrimony."[5]

————

At the Yeshiva where Rabbi Aryeh Levine taught, it was customary for Bar Mitzvah–age students to contribute money to purchase religious texts for each boy as he turned Bar Mitzvah. One student, however, whose family was very poor, was not able to make a contribution. When the time came for this boy's Bar Mitzvah, the other students decided to retaliate and not give him a gift. Reb Aryeh heard about this, and he gave, as a gift from the class, a beautiful set of the books of the Torah. "Who knows," he told the other students, "how much anguish this boy would have suffered if he saw his classmates coming empty-handed to his Bar Mitzvah celebration. It would have been murder."[6]

Like adults, children are created in God's image and must be treated accordingly. Rabbi Chaim Reines says, "Ethically, respect for man implies that the individual should be treated not on the basis of his social position or the actual level of his intellectual or moral achievements, but in accordance with his ideal value as a human being."[7]

————

14. Teachers must be careful not to humiliate a student, even one who has done something wrong. The guiding principle should be the words of the Rabbis: "Let the honor of your student be as dear to you as your own" (*The Ethics of the Fathers* 4:12). This also means, for example, that a teacher should not publicly humiliate a student by asking him or her a question that the student will probably be unable to answer. In addition, teachers must take particular care not to humiliate children who have developmental problems.

15. Teach children not to taunt one another. When children make fun of another child, they usually say that they are "teasing," but, more often than not, this is simply a euphemism for "humiliating." Children who are humiliated by their peers often suffer their entire lives from this abuse.

Furthermore, such acts of humiliation are not confined to young children.

How many teenage girls suffer from being labeled as "tramps," and how many boys are ridiculed because they are unathletic or unable to prevail in a fight?

———

A father learned that on his nine-year-old daughter's school bus, some children had been taunting a boy who was overweight, making up rhymes to ridicule the boy. When the man sat down with his daughter to talk about the situation, he started to cry. He told her, "It's a terrible thing to humiliate someone. Every adult knows this, but if you can learn this when you are nine, you can become a very great person."

———

16. It is forbidden to call someone by a nickname he dislikes (*Bava Mezia* 58b and Maimonides, "The Laws of Character Development," 6:8). Teaching this to children is particularly important, since they often inflict cruel nicknames on their peers, which can cause lifelong suffering.

———

Some years ago, People *magazine reported on the suicide of an overweight teenage girl who had been taunted with cruel nicknames and comments by her peers. The article prompted this letter: "As a teenager, I too was tortured by my fellow students. I was an overweight teen and was abused constantly. I could not escape it. Teachers witnessed this over and over again and did nothing. The principal told me her hands were tied. I thought of suicide but luckily I never did it. . . . I wish all teenagers who tease others could have it happen to them so they could feel the pain and humiliation they inflict. I am signing this letter with the name they chose to torture me with for six years. How would you like to be known to an entire school as Big Bertha."*

———

Using moral imagination not to shame others

17. Use the full range of your intellectual and moral imagination to spare others shame, particularly poor people. The talmudic sage Samuel related a story of a laborer who had devised a way to avoid humiliating a co-worker: "Every day, all the other workers and I pool our food, and eat it. But today, I saw that there was one man who had no bread, and he was ashamed. So I told all the other men, 'Today, I will collect the food.' When I came to that man, I pretended to take bread from him, so that he should not be ashamed" (*Shabbat* 156b). It is as important to spare the poor from shame as it is to spare them from hunger.

A lack of such ingenuity characterizes an unhappy story related in the thirteenth-century *Sefer Chasidim:* "Reuben, an honest man, asked Shimon to lend him some money. Without hesitation, Shimon made the loan but said, 'I really give this to you as a gift.' Reuben was so ashamed and embarrassed that he never again asked Shimon for a loan. Clearly, in this case, it would have been better not to have given Reuben a gift of that kind" (paragraph 1034).

This passage reminds us that good intentions alone are not enough; we must perform an act of kindness in a way that will do the most good, which means making sure not to humiliate the recipient.

18. It is particularly praiseworthy to spare someone from embarrassment by assuming the shame yourself. The Talmud relates an incident in which Rabbi Judah was delivering a lecture and, annoyed by the strong smell of garlic, said, "Let the one who has eaten the garlic go out!" Immediately, Rabbi Chiyya, a distinguished sage, stood up and left. It was later revealed that Chiyya hadn't in fact been the culprit, but wished to spare that person, a student of lesser status, public embarrassment (*Sanhedrin* 11a).

———

A guest at the Shabbat table of the great German rabbi Akiva Eger (1761–1837) once spilled some wine on the clean white tablecloth. Rabbi Eger, seeing the man's stricken face, immediately nudged the table so that his cup spilled as well. "This table is unsteady," he commented to all those present.

When a maid would break an item in the home of Rabbi Yitzchak Elchanan Spektor (1817–1896), the renowned scholar of Kovno, he would tell the family that it was he who had broken the article, so that no one would yell at the maid.

———

19. Stand up and identify with the person being humiliated or attacked. Rabbi Neal Kurshan relates: "Jeff, the son of some friends of ours, rode a school bus with children going to a variety of schools, including one Jewish youngster from a Chasidic family. The other children teased the poor boy mercilessly. No one would sit with him. They made fun of his traditional side curls and simple white shirt and black pants. They accused him of sleeping with hair curlers like a girl and of having only one set of clothes. Each day the boy was reduced to tears. After several days of this, Jeff got on the bus and sat down beside the Chasidic boy, announcing, 'Don't pay attention to them. They are just saying stupid things. I'll sit with you.' From that day until the end of the year, the two boys sat together and became friends."[8]

————

In December 1993, in Billings, Montana, an antisemite threw a brick through five-year-old Isaac Schnitzer's bedroom window. It happened during the holiday of Hanukah, and the boy had put up a stenciled Menorah on the glass as part of his family's celebration. The antisemitic attack (a growing number of white racists, affiliated with the Aryan Nation, had come into the area) was reported in the local newspaper, the Billings Gazette, *and the boy's mother, Tammie Schnitzer, told the reporter that she was disturbed by the advice offered her by the investigating police officer, to remove from her windows any symbols of the holiday. She wondered how she would explain this to her son.*

A local woman, Margaret McDonald, was deeply touched by Mrs. Schnitzer's dilemma. She imagined what it would be like to have to explain to her children that they couldn't have a Christmas tree in the window because it would be dangerous. She called her minister, Reverend Keith Torney of the First Congregational United Church of Christ, and suggested that he have the children at the church's Sunday school make cut-out menorahs for their own windows. Reverend Torney agreed, and then passed on this suggestion to colleagues throughout the city. A few days later the Gazette *published a full-page drawing of a menorah, and invited residents to put it up. By the end of the week, more than six thousand homes were decorated with menorahs (the entire Jewish community of Billings consisted of a few dozen families).*

————

20. Inconvenience yourself, if necessary, in order to spare another person embarrassment. For many decades, Rabbi Joseph Soloveitchik taught the highest *shiur* (class) in Talmud at Yeshiva University. His lessons generally lasted two or three hours. One year, one of his students, Ezra Lightman, was diagnosed with Hodgkin's disease, for which he was receiving chemotherapy treatments. In those days, people kept such information to themselves. Rabbi Soloveitchik was a family friend and therefore knew of the illness, although none of the students in the class was aware of it. Rachel Wiederkehr, Mr. Lightman's sister, recalls, "Once a chemotherapy appointment meant that Ezra would have to leave the *shiur* early. Aware that my brother's departure would arouse the curiosity of his classmates, [Rabbi Soloveitchik] dismissed the entire class early that day so that Ezra would not feel conspicuous and so that his secret would remain safe."[9]

21. When soliciting a person for charity, don't ask a donor for more money than she can comfortably afford (*Shulchan Arukh, Yoreh Deah* 248:7); if you do, either the person will feel that her contribution will be regarded as paltry or, to avoid embarrassment, will feel compelled to give more than she can afford.

_____

My friend David Szonyi, who has worked for fund-raising organizations, questions the contemporary applicability of this Jewish teaching: "It's a rule of fund-raising to try to get a potential donor to 'stretch' and consider giving somewhat more than he or she 'comfortably' can give. Potential givers, in turn, often will appreciate being thought of as having a higher giving capacity than they do."

_____

22. Be particularly careful not to dishonor your parents, even when one of them has done something wrong. The Torah records an incident in which Noah became drunk, and fell into a stupor. His son Ham "saw his father's nakedness and told his two brothers outside"; the language of the text suggests that Ham ridiculed his father or worse. At that point Noah's other two sons, Shem and Japheth, took a cloth, placed it over their backs, and walked backward into the room, covering their father's nakedness as they walked. "Their faces were turned the other way so that they did not see their father's nakedness" (Genesis 9:22–23). Protect your parents' dignity, as Noah's two sons did.

23. Jewish law notes several instances in which guests and hosts must exercise care not to embarrass one another. For example:

- Don't ask a guest intellectually demanding questions unless you have reason to believe that he will know how to answer them; otherwise you will cause him embarrassment (*Sefer Chasidim*, paragraph 312).

- When reciting the *Birkat Hamazon* (Grace after Meals) in the presence of a poor person, lower your voice during the final paragraph, which includes the words "I have been young and am now old, but I have never seen a righteous man in need, or his children begging bread" (Psalms

37:25). Also, if you are wealthy, don't talk about your financial dealings in the company of less affluent people, lest you cause them to feel inferior, unsuccessful, or envious.

• When you are a guest, don't ask your host for something that he is unlikely to have, since an inability to comply with your request will discomfit him. Make sure to teach this to your children, since young people are more likely than adults to make such requests.

———

A friend notes the following: "Don't ask a guest who isn't fluent in Hebrew to make Kiddush. *Similarly, at our Passover* sedarim, *which invariably include such guests, as we go around the table reading from the Haggadah in both Hebrew and English, I make sure that I read in English first, and only then do I ask others to read in English."*

———

24. Take particular care not to humiliate someone even when you believe yourself to be in the right. The Rabbis of the Sanhedrin deposed Rabbi Gamliel, the Sanhedrin president, for violating this norm. When Gamliel learned that the number-two figure in the Sanhedrin, Rabbi Joshua, had expressed an opposing view in private, he publicly humiliated Rabbi Joshua by ordering him to remain standing throughout a session of the Sanhedrin.* The Rabbis were so horrified by Gamliel's act that they stopped his lecture and deposed him from office. However, the Rabbis did not wish to humiliate Gamliel, either, and so did not appoint Joshua in his stead, feeling that that would cause Gamliel excessive anguish. Nor did they force Gamliel to resign from the Sanhedrin, but allowed him to continue participating in its discussions. Gamliel was reinstated only after he went to Rabbi Joshua's house and begged forgiveness, making it clear that he would not act in this way again (*Berachot* 27b–28a).

When you have shamed someone

25. If you have humiliated someone, your first obligation is to beg forgiveness. Since begging is humiliating in itself, this inflicts on you a little of what your victim experienced (for more on this, see page 163).

———

*Rabbi Gamliel's behavior can be compared to a teacher making an unruly student stand in the corner, which, it seems to me, Jewish ethics would also forbid.

26. If the humiliation took place in the presence of others, make your apology in their presence, as well as in private. Otherwise the victim has the right to say: "You shamed me in front of others, and now you want to apologize to me in private. Bring me all the people who heard you embarrass me, and then I will accept your apology" (*Yalkut Shimoni,* Hosea 14).*

Final thoughts

27. Because many of us take pleasure in the embarrassment of our peers and competitors (although we might not admit it), we should solicit God's assistance to help us avoid doing so. The Talmud teaches that when entering the study hall, some rabbis used to pray, "May my colleagues not stumble in a matter of law, and I rejoice over them" [that is, laugh over the error they made; *Berachot* 28b).[10]

If rabbis who spent their lives studying God's laws felt the need to offer this prayer, how much more does it apply to all of us who see in our competitors' errors an opportunity for us to advance, or who delight in telling others about an embarrassing event in another's life.

———

The Talmud condemns "one who elevates himself at the expense of another's degradation" (Jerusalem Talmud, Chagigah *2:1). Rabbi Aaron Levine, a scholar of Jewish law and an economist, applies this teaching to the realm of business ethics, noting that while a seller has the legitimate right to point out to everyone the good qualities in his own merchandise, he should not mock deficiencies in rival models. According to Rabbi Levine, "This amounts to 'elevating himself at the expense of his friend's degradation'"* (Journal of Halacha and Contemporary Society *1:2, page 21).*

———

28. In summary, the most basic guideline in safeguarding the dignity of others is the dictum from *The Ethics of the Fathers:* "Your friend's dignity should be as precious to you as your own" (2:10). This rabbinic restatement of the Golden Rule can almost always guide us in our treatment of other people.

————————

*Obviously, what is required here is common sense; if offering your apology in public, perhaps years after the event, will humiliate your victim further, you should not do so.

31

IF YOU'RE TEMPTED TO HUMILIATE
SOMEONE

1. When you are tempted to spread information that will shame someone, ask yourself, "Can I think of an episode in my own life that would greatly embarrass me if it became publicly known?" If you can—and few of us can't—then consider how you would regard someone who learned about this episode and shared the information with others. Wouldn't you consider her to be cruel, or at least grossly unfair? Wouldn't you find it difficult, if not impossible, to forgive her? If so, then think long and hard, and restrain yourself before you reveal such information.

It is particularly important to guard your tongue when you are in a dispute with someone, or in professional, political, or social competition. During such emotionally charged periods, many of us behave in ways that we would normally abhor. For example, in political campaigns, candidates often try to uncover embarrassing but irrelevant information about their opponents. It seems to me that when a candidate we support reveals information intended to humiliate his opponent, we are morally obligated either to vote for the opponent or, at the least, "sit out" the election.* Only by doing so and making it known to the candidate we formerly supported why we are doing so, can we make it clear that we oppose "dirty" campaigning?[1] As Adlai Stevenson, the former governor of Illinois and twice a Democratic presidential candidate, said, "The hardest thing about any political campaign is how to win without proving that you are unworthy of winning."

What is true of politics is true of almost all areas in which we find ourselves in competition with others.

2. It is particularly unkind, though common, to poke fun at other people's physical shortcomings, and even people of good character sometimes

---

*In theory, I can envision "life or death" situations in which it is so important that a specific candidate prevail that one could justify overlooking his immoral campaigning. But while I can "envision" such a situation, I can't really think of many examples in which this has happened. Obviously, people with stronger political convictions than I will probably disagree; such people have a tendency to view each political race as of paramount importance. Unfortunately, it is this

do so.* The Talmud records that Rabbi Elazar ben Shimon, a young and renowned scholar, was once greeted by a truly ugly man. Instead of returning the man's greeting, the rabbi said to him, "Are all the people from your town as ugly as you?" The man replied, "I don't know. But go and tell the craftsman who made me, 'How ugly is the vessel that You made.'"

The Rabbi immediately realized what a dreadful thing he had said, and begged the man's forgiveness. But the man persisted, "I will not forgive you until you go to the craftsman who made me and tell him, 'How ugly is this vessel that You made.'" Only after many others pleaded with him did the man grant the rabbi a conditional pardon: "For your sake I forgive him, provided he does not make a habit of doing this" (Ta'anit 20a–b).

This story serves as a powerful reminder of how wrong thoughtless banter can be. And yet, how often we hear men say cruel things about a physically unattractive woman ("She's a real dog."). To compound the suffering of those who are unattractive is an almost unforgivable offense.†

This law applies with particular force to parents, teachers, and others working with young people. I know a woman who became quite overweight during adolescence. Her mother mocked her appearance to such an extent that, throughout high school, she was always the last to leave the class, so that no one would see her from behind. Another woman I know has suffered a lifelong fear of public speaking. Her phobia dates from the time that a second-grade teacher repeatedly—and in front of her classmates—made fun of her grammatical mistakes.

3. A Yiddish witticism teaches, "Who is a hero? One who suppresses a wisecrack." Those with a sharp sense of humor should consider their words carefully. Similarly, people who write critiques of others (for example, book, movie, and theater critics) must take care not to be clever at a writer's or performer's expense.

———

The novelist Rebecca Goldstein was haunted by a malicious review of one of her early novels that had appeared in an influential newspaper. A full decade later she met the reviewer, and recalls, "He approached me nervously and said, 'I ac-

---

mindset that causes many people to justify any campaign tactics that will help elect the candidate they prefer.

*See, for example, page 287 on not ridiculing others with nicknames.

†Even if we do not make the comment directly to the person, but only to others, the comment might well get back to that person, and cause great pain.

tually liked your book, but I was a young writer hungry to make a name for myself.'" As Goldstein recalls, "I stood there in shock. Legitimate criticism is fine—no work of art is perfect—but to selfishly exploit someone who slaved over a novel for years is beyond words."[2]

————

4. The sage Rabbi Yochanan taught that we should be careful not to publicize information that will cause innocent people suffering and humiliation. This applies even when we can cite Jewish law as a justification for making the matter known. For example, the Torah rules that a child born of an adulterous or incestuous union is classified as a *mamzer* (bastard); both the child and its descendants are forbidden to marry other Jews (Deuteronomy 23:3) unless, as the Rabbis explain, they too are bastards.* However, Rabbi Yochanan advocated that those who are aware of such children's status remain silent. He told his colleagues, "It is in my power [to reveal the families of impure birth in Jerusalem] but what shall I do, seeing that the greatest men of our time are mixed up therein?" (*Kiddushin* 71a). Apparently, Rabbi Yochanan reasoned, "Why should I destroy these people's marital prospects, and cause suffering to some very fine, innocent people?"

This teaching should serve as a reminder to all of us who casually pass on gossip and unflattering information about others. Either out of malice or the desire to be perceived as knowledgeable, many people share privileged information about others that can cause them great embarrassment and damage their reputations.

————

A rabbi was given a memoir to review, and asked to remove information that could cause others embarrassment. For example, the book mentioned an incident in which a prominent Jewish figure had an affair with a married woman over sixty years earlier. The author mentioned the name of both the woman and man, arguing, "Who's going to be embarrassed now? All the relevant characters are dead." The rabbi responded that, aside from the fact that there is no reason to blacken the name of the dead, each of the lovers might have surviving children and grandchildren who would be upset and humiliated by the revelation of such scandalous and unnecessary information.

————

————

*In Jewish law, the term *bastard* does not apply, as it does in Western societies, to a child born out of wedlock; under Jewish law such a child suffers no legal disadvantages.

Not humiliating others: The carrot and the stick

5. When the scholar Rabbi Nechuniah ben Hakane was asked to what he attributed his longevity, he answered, "I never did anything that would bring me honor by humiliating someone else" (*Megillah* 28a). When the same question was posed to Rabbi Zeira, he responded, "I never found pleasure in someone else's failures, and I never called another by an ugly nickname" (ibid.).

These observations show how common it was, and still is, is for people to rejoice in the humiliation of others, particularly if it raises their own status.

The fact that these rabbis attributed their longevity to fulfilling this Jewish law indicates how important they deemed it to be in the eyes of God.

6. From Judaism's perspective, humiliating someone is among the most self-destructive acts in which a person can engage. As the Talmud teaches, "One who elevates himself at the expense of another's degradation will have no share in the World-to-Come" (Jerusalem Talmud, *Chagigah* 2:1).

When public shaming is permitted: Three examples

7. The Talmud reports that when a father who refused to support his children was brought before Rabbi Chisda, he proclaimed, "Turn a mortar upside down in public, and have the delinquent father stand on it and declare: 'Even a raven cares for its young, but I don't care for my young'" (*Ketubot* 49b).

Apparently, Rabbi Chisda reasoned that a father who refuses to support his children forfeits his right to be treated as a normal human being. Rabbi Chisda also hoped that this threat would motivate the man to do his duty and provide for his children.

Today, thousands of fathers shirk the moral responsibility of providing for their children's needs. The Talmud believes that such men are not protected by the laws forbidding public embarrassment.

8. Similarly, if a Jewish court orders a man to grant his wife a *get* (a Jewish divorce), and he refuses to do so,* his cruel behavior may be made public

---

*Because Torah law vests the right of divorce in the hands of the husband, it is the husband who, according to *halacha*, must issue the *get*. If he doesn't do so, the woman becomes an *agunah* ("a chained women"), and is forbidden to marry anyone else. Though a woman can't issue a *get*, if she refuses to accept one, the husband is also forbidden to marry anyone else (except in rare instances).

and people may boycott and picket his business, and otherwise embarrass him until he grants the divorce.

9. Public humiliation is also permitted when there is good reason to believe that the fear of it will prevent an injustice. Thus, in 1624, the Jewish Council of the Four Lands of Poland ruled that when someone declares an unnecessary bankruptcy (for example, if there is fraud involved, or the person spent extravagantly or unnecessarily in the months preceding the bankruptcy), he should be excommunicated in the synagogue in the presence of his wife and children. The rabbis hoped that the desire to avoid this censure would discourage this type of fraud.[3] Before imposing this penalty, however, the communal leaders had to make certain that the bankruptcy was fraudulent; in cases where bankruptcy is unavoidable, it is forbidden to humiliate the debtor.

ENVY

———

And when [Joseph's] brothers saw that their
father loved him more than any of his
brothers, they hated him so that they could
not speak a friendly word to him.

Genesis 37:4

32

BIBLICAL AND TALMUDIC PERSPECTIVES

The destructive effect of envy

1. As many biblical stories make clear, envy often leads to family feuds, slander, cruelty, and even murder:

> • *Family feuds.* A recurring theme in Genesis is family envy and particularly, but not exclusively, sibling rivalry. In the worst instance, Joseph's brothers envy his status as their father Jacob's favorite son. In their resentment, they first decide to murder him (37:20), then relent and make do with selling him into slavery (37:27–28).

———

In another incident, both sibling and wifely rivalry permeated the relationship of two matriarchs, Leah and Rachel. The two women were married to Jacob.* Rachel, who was having trouble conceiving, was jealous of her sister Leah, who already had four children: "When Rachel saw that she had borne Jacob no children, she became envious of her sister" (Genesis 30:1). She therefore offered Jacob her servant Bilhah, who soon produced a child (in ancient society, when a woman's servant had a child with the woman's husband, it was credited to the woman as if the child was hers as well).† When a second child was born to Bilhah, Rachel declared, "A fateful contest I have waged with my sister, yes, and I have prevailed" (Genesis 30:8). Meanwhile, Leah was no less envious of Rachel than Rachel was of her. True, Rachel did not have children, but Jacob loved her more than he loved Leah. This infuriated and pained Leah, and provoked her envy (see, for example, Genesis 30:15).

———

---

*Although later Torah law permitted polygamy, it forbade two sisters from marrying the same man, unless one of them had died (Leviticus 18:18).

† As Rachel says to Jacob, "Here is my maid Bilhah. Consort with her that she may bear on my knees and that through her I too may have children" (Genesis 30:3).

• *Slander.* Envy and jealousy cause people to speak unfairly of others. Thus, Aaron and Miriam were the second and third most powerful figures in ancient Israel, and heroes to the entire Israelite community. But when they grew envious of their younger brother Moses—apparently for being accorded more prominence than they were*—they spoke unfairly of him among themselves, an act for which Miriam (who seems to have instigated the slander; see Numbers 12:1) was punished.

———

Envy makes it difficult if not impossible for people to think clearly about the person they envy. Often the conclusions envious people draw are the precise opposite of the truth. For example, Laban repeatedly tried to cheat his son-in-law Jacob, yet Jacob, favored by God, amassed wealth. Laban's envious sons responded to this by claiming that Jacob "owes everything he owns to our father. All his wealth is at our father's expense" (Genesis 31:1). In actuality, as the Bible makes clear, it was Laban who was blessed by Jacob working for him.

———

• *Cruelty.* In perhaps the most famous incident involving King Solomon, the Bible tells of two prostitutes who lived together and who gave birth to sons within days of each other. When one of the women accidentally smothered her child, she took the other mother's baby. The two mothers ended up before King Solomon, each claiming the live child as her own. Unable to discern who was telling the truth, Solomon ordered that the child be cut in two, and each mother given half. Horrified, the child's true mother said, "No, let her have the baby, only don't kill my child." However, the envious woman wanted the other mother to suffer the same fate as she had: "It shall be neither yours nor mine; cut it in two" (I Kings 3:16–28).

• *Murder.* The first homicide in history, the killing of Abel by his brother Cain, was the result of envy. Both brothers had brought gifts to God, but while Abel offered the Lord his most precious animals, Cain tried to get by with less. God preferred Abel's gift to that of Cain who, spurred by envy, murdered his brother (Genesis 4:3–9).

• *Criminal mischief.* Genesis reports that when the Philistines, among whom the patriarch Isaac dwelled, envied him his financial success, they stopped up his wells by filling them with earth (Genesis 26:12–15).

---

*Also, as my friend Daniel Taub points out, Moses had just appointed seventy elders, and perhaps they felt their status had been undermined.

The sin of coveting

2. Coveting, an offshoot or outgrowth of envy, is the only emotion (as opposed to action) outlawed in the Ten Commandments: "You shall not covet your neighbor's house; you shall not covet your neighbor's wife . . . or anything that is your neighbor's" (Exodus 20:14). While envy refers, among other things, to wanting what others have for ourselves, coveting—in the context of the Ten Commandments and the usage of this term in Jewish life—refers to desiring what others have so much that we start scheming to acquire it.

In the normal course of events, we might assume that those most likely to covet would be the underprivileged. However, the Bible describes two major incidents involving kings whose covetousness leads them to violate even more fundamental commandments:

King David is highly attracted to Bathsheba. Even after he learns that she is married to an officer in his army, he orders her brought to his palace and sleeps with her. Bathsheba becomes pregnant, and David summons her husband, Uriah, back from the front, with the hope that he will sleep with his wife and presume that she became pregnant through him. But when Uriah twice avoids going home to be with Bathsheba (perhaps he had heard rumors of her dalliance with the king), David realizes that the woman's pregnancy will result in a major scandal, and arranges to have Uriah killed in battle (II Samuel, chapter 11). Thus, what began with the seemingly not-so-serious violation of the ban against coveting led to violations of the prohibitions against adultery and murder.

For the even more serious offense committed by the covetous King Ahab and his wife Jezebel, see pages 48–49.

The self-destructive nature of envy

3. Envy destroys our ability to enjoy what we already have; instead, our joy is diminished or entirely eliminated by the fact that others have more—perhaps only one thing more—than us. The most prominent example is Saul, Israel's first monarch, who was a popular king, and whose army had triumphed over the Philistines. However, when Saul hears the young women of Israel extol David, who had killed Goliath, in song—"Saul has slain his thousands, David his tens of thousands"—he becomes very upset: "From that day on, Saul kept a jealous eye on David" (I Samuel 18:7–12). Like many envious people, Saul quickly loses all sense of proportion. He arranges for his daughter, Michal, who loves David, to become betrothed to him, simply so that he will be in a position to bring about David's death more easily (I Samuel 18:20–25). What father, other than one crazed with envy, would manipulate his daughter's deepest emotions in this way? And when his Saul's son Jonathan, who is David's closest friend, tries to protect David from his father's wrath, Saul attempts to kill him (I Samuel 20:33).

So poisoned is Saul by envy (and his increasingly paranoid hatred of David) that he ignores tangible evidence that David is not his enemy. Thus the Bible describes two incidents in which David finds Saul asleep and unprotected, but does not harm him (see, for example, I Samuel, 24:5–12). Unfortunately these incidents do not convince Saul for more than a few hours that David is not his enemy. After a very brief respite, he quickly resumes his campaign to kill David.

In addition to alienating himself from his son Jonathan and his daughter Michal, Saul's campaign against David is self-destructive in another way. By alienating David, his leading soldier, Saul placed himself in a much weaker position vis-à-vis the Philistines, Israel's historic enemy. It was they, and not David, who eventually succeeded in killing him and three of his four sons in battle. In other words, Saul's envy helped bring about his destruction.*

———

A medieval folktale highlights the self-destructive nature of envy. A king promised a man anything he wanted on condition that the man's neighbor, whom he envied, would receive double. Instead of being pleased by this extraordinary offer, the man, obsessed and disheartened by his neighbor's even greater good fortune, asked the king to pluck out one of his eyes, just so that his neighbor would lose both (a similar version of the story is found in Orchot Tzaddikim, "The Gate of Envy").

———

4. Both the Bible and the Talmud note the negative effects of envy: "A calm disposition gives the body health, and envy rots the bones" (Proverbs 14:30; see also *Shabbat* 152b). *The Ethics of the Fathers* (4:28) teaches that "envy . . . takes a person out of this world" [that is, it brings about a person's death]. Rabbi Abraham Twerski comments: "Ironically, there is a saving

———

*Nor was this envy inevitable. Saul's son Jonathan, the one who stood to lose most by David's success (if David became king, Jonathan would not succeed his father), loved David and did not envy him (I Samuel 18:1).

grace in alcohol or drug addiction, because eventually the condition precipitates some kind of crisis that shocks the person into reality. At this time, he may accept treatment for his condition and turn his life around. Unfortunately, with jealousy [or envy] . . . there is not likely to be any crisis that may bring a person to his senses. People may have this self-destructive trait for their lifetime, which may be shortened by this futile and endless pursuit."*

In short, envy destroys our chances for happiness. Since there will always be people with possessions or talents that we don't have, if we are envious, we will always be dissatisfied and unhappy.

33

REDUCING ENVY

1. Accept that a certain level of envy is natural, and cannot be entirely eliminated.† The Jerusalem Talmud (*Berachot* 4:2) records a rabbinic prayer "that the hearts of others not be envious of us, and our hearts not be envious of others." The fact that the Rabbis felt they needed God's assistance to achieve this suggests that they believed that we should all solicit God's help to avoid or minimize envy.

A second talmudic teaching is even more explicit: "Rabbi Joseph son of Choni said: 'A man envies everyone except his son and his disciple'" (*San-*

Visions of the Fathers, page 264. It should be noted that jealousy and envy are similar, but not identical. Envy involves two people, while jealousy often involves three (for example, a man who is jealous of his wife because he fears she is cheating on him is also jealous of the man he suspects is her lover). In addition, it has been noted that jealousy and envy prompt different sorts of aggressive and violent responses, one straightforward, the other surreptitious. The journalist Irma Kurtz has written, "Jealousy fights duels. Envy poisons the soup" (cited in Joseph Berke, *The Tyranny of Malice*, page 292, note 42). Unlike jealousy, which has no particular stigma, envious people are rarely willing to acknowledge to others, and perhaps to themselves, a trait they likely regard as shameful. Joseph Epstein distinguishes the two as follows: "One is jealous of what one has, envious of what other people have. Jealousy is not always pejorative; one can after all be jealous of one's dignity, civil rights, honor. Envy, except when used in the emulative sense mentioned by Aristotle, is always pejorative" (*Envy*, 4).

†A talmudic dictum declares that "if you try to grasp everything, you will grasp nothing" (*Rosh Hashana* 4b). In other words, if you aim for perfection, such as by trying to eliminate every trace of envy from your life, you are likely to fail.

hedrin 105b). While the child and disciple might not be envied, this rabbinic maxim assumes that other people will be.

This last statement, as Daniel Taub notes, also offers a clue to how to reduce envy. We don't envy our children or students because we have contributed to, and are invested in, their success. Helping others achieve success, and feeling a sense of personal involvement in it, is one way to diminish feelings of envy.

———

The Rabbis deduce that a father will not envy his son from the case of Solomon, son of King David. When Solomon was anointed king during his father's lifetime, David's advisers congratulated him and said, "May God make the renown of Solomon even greater than yours, and may He exalt his throne even higher than yours" (I Kings 1:47). That it did not occur to them that such a statement might upset or antagonize the king suggests the psychological truth that a parent is not generally jealous of a child, and rejoices when the child achieves greater success than did the parent.

The Rabbis also cite the case of the prophet Elisha, who was the disciple of Elijah. When Elijah was about to depart from this world, Elisha beseeched him, "Let a double portion of your spirit pass on to me" (II Kings 2:9). Although Elisha was requesting that he be granted the ability to become an even greater prophet than Elijah, Elijah was not upset or annoyed by the request. He responded, "You have asked a difficult thing. If you see me as I am being taken from you, this will be granted to you. If not, it will not." Indeed, Elisha does witness Elijah's ascension to heaven in a chariot of fire (II Kings 2:11–12), and is granted extraordinary prophetic powers.

It seems to me that while the rabbinic view that a parent will not envy a child is almost always true,* in the case of a teacher-disciple relationship, envy will not occur if the relationship is as close, or as idealistically based, as that of Elisha and Elijah, or if the student takes pains to credit his teacher for what he has learned. Otherwise it is quite possible that a teacher will envy a disciple who has achieved greater success.

That a certain amount of envy is a universal trait is reflected in a bitterly comic observation of Sholom Aleichem (1859–1916), the great Yiddish writer: "A man must always be considerate of the feelings of his neighbors. . . . So, for instance, if I went out to the fair . . . and did well, sold everything at a good profit, and returned with pockets full of money . . . I never failed to tell my neighbors

---

*Herod, the first-century B.C.E. king of Judea, intrigued against and murdered three of his sons, prompting the Roman emperor Augustus to say, "It is better to be Herod's pig than his son."

that I had lost every cent and was a ruined man. Thus, I was happy and my neighbors were happy. But if, on the contrary, I had really been cleaned out at the fair . . . I made sure to tell my neighbors that never since God made fairs had there been a better one. You get my point? For thus I was miserable and my neighbors were miserable."[1]

———

2. Focus on the good someone is doing or has done. The Torah teaches that when two Israelites received the spirit of God and started to prophesy, Joshua, Moses' assistant and successor, became alarmed, and asked Moses to restrain them. But Moses refused, saying, "Are you wrought up on my account? Would that all the Lord's people were prophets" (Numbers 11:26–29).

Rabbi Nachman of Bratslav (1772–1810) taught that an envious person should force himself to focus on the good traits of those whom he envies. "Don't look at the person whom you envy with an 'evil eye,'" Rabbi Nachman cautioned, and don't downplay or try to explain away any good that person has done. Rather, look upon that person with a "generous eye"; indeed, if you force yourself to appreciate her good actions, you may come to believe that her good fortune was deserved, which will help you to stop envying her.

———

The French poet and playwright Jean Cocteau (1889–1963) mocked the way envious people downplay the accomplishments of others: "We must believe in luck. For how else can we explain the success of those whom we don't like."

———

3. If you are a religious person, be aware that envy will make it impossible for you to fulfill one of the most important biblical commands, "Love your neighbor as yourself" (Leviticus 19:18). You can't both love someone and feel envy and hostility toward him (an occasional pang of envy is common). Therefore, as noted in the preceding paragraph, when you envy someone, focus on what it is in that person that you find good and lovable. If you are a relatively good person, it is unlikely that the person whom you envy is devoid of virtue; good people don't envy the Adolf Hitlers of the world, no matter how powerful, affluent, or otherwise "successful" they are. Also, try to counter your hostile thoughts (most envious people wish that those they envy will suffer a significant decline in fortune) by offering prayers to God on behalf of those you envy. At first, when you offer a prayer like this, it may be difficult to be sincere. Therefore, before you pray, spend a minute concentrating on your desire to fulfill the command to "love your neighbor as your-self." Offer the prayer on a daily basis for several weeks, or until you feel your envy start to decline.

4. Focus on the suffering endured by the person you envy. Arrogant people compare their successes with other people's weaknesses. Envious people do the opposite. They compare their lack of success with the successes of others, and believe that other people enjoy unmitigated happiness and ease. But this is never the case. As my mother, Helen Telushkin, of blessed memory, used to say, "The only people I know who are happy are people I don't know well." If you are going to envy the success of others, consider whether you would be willing to assume their suffering and problems as well.

——

The psychologist Solomon Schimmel was treating a patient who was writing a book on coping with suffering, at a time when a book on the subject had been published by a rabbi. The rabbi's book was extremely successful, and whenever the patient saw the book on the best-seller list or heard the rabbi on a talk show, he became upset.

Although his patient understood that the envy he was experiencing was irrational (it was the rabbi, after all, not he, who had written the best-selling book) and was hurting him, he still remained upset. Dr. Schimmel instructed him to reflect on the following: "You know that the rabbi's book on how to cope with suffering was based upon a profound and prolonged personal tragedy which he experienced. One of his children had been born with a debilitating genetic disease that entailed slow, progressive deterioration. [The rabbi and his wife had to witness their child's physical and emotional pain, and his early death.] The fact that [his book] became a bestseller testified to the sensitivity and wisdom that he had acquired and his ability to pass it on to others in need of solace. Now you, in your personal life, have never experienced suffering in any way comparable to the torment that the rabbi went through for so many years of his life. Can you really envy this man and his success as a writer? Would you be willing to undergo what he experienced even for millions of dollars? Don't think about his fame or fortune. Think rather of his pain and suffering. Even as a rich man, can his money bring his child back to life or erase the memories of his child's suffering from his consciousness?"

Schimmel concluded, "As my client began to focus his thoughts on the rabbi's misfortune in life, which engendered compassion, his envy subsided."[2]

——

5. Dr. Schimmel offers the following strategies to help curb our envy.[3] I have added brief commentaries that offer concrete examples of how to internalize these suggestions.

- Think about positive and valuable things you possess that the person you envy does not. It is unlikely that she has had greater success, skill, and contentment than you in every sphere, including professional or financial success, admiration of her peers, happiness with her spouse, children, parents, and friends, and various talents, such as athletic or musical ability, and good health.

- Compare yourself with those less fortunate than yourself, rather than with those more fortunate. If you are a middle-class American—the predominant readers of my books—you are living a more comfortable life than ninety-five percent or more of humankind. Therefore, it is absurd to compare yourself only with those who have things that you don't have, and to feel deprived and miserable as a result.

———

My friend Dennis Prager read about an actor who was earning millions of dollars for each film he made, yet who noted with envy that Arnold Schwarzenegger, the actor and now governor of California, was earning even more. As my friend wrote, "Had this actor compared his salary with that of, let us say, any of his high school classmates, he would have been deliriously happy at his extraordinary good fortune." Instead, he compared his income with that of one of the only actors in the world who was making more than he was, and therefore succeeded in making himself feel envious and unhappier.[4]

———

- Consider whether the person you envy deserves her level of success, and that there may be good reason why you do not. In other words, instead of asking yourself, "Why should she be more successful than I am?" (the implication being that the other person's success is undeserved), consider this question seriously. Maybe she has accomplished more because she works harder or more effectively than you do, or is friendlier to people and they therefore respond well to her. Instead of allowing yourself to wallow in self-pity, consider whether there is something you can learn from the more successful person that might improve your life.*

———

*Obviously this does not apply in all cases. If you envy the large inheritance a friend or acquaintance received, it is unlikely that you will find reasons that he deserved such an inheritance (except perhaps that maybe he was an exceptionally devoted child). But there are other questions

• Realize that your envy could lead you to do things that may harm others and yourself. As noted earlier, King Saul's envy of David caused Saul, who had once been humble, kind, and forgiving (see I Samuel 9:21 and 11:12–13) to become a murderer (see I Samuel 22:9–19).

———

In 1994, champion figure skater Tonya Harding grew obsessively envious of her rival, Nancy Kerrigan, who, it was widely assumed, would soon beat her to become the American figure-skating champion. Harding's ex-husband, Jeff Gillooly, with whom she remained close, began plotting to injure Kerrigan and thereby clear the path for Harding to become the champion. Harding informed Gillooly where Kerrigan trained, and he hired two men, who attacked her one day when she left practice. One of the attackers hit Kerrigan repeatedly with a baton, just above the right kneecap, and she was badly hurt and had to withdraw from the upcoming competition. Two days later Harding was crowned American champion at the national meet in Detroit. At the time she complained hypocritically, "It won't be a complete title without having competed against Nancy [Kerrigan]." Harding's role in the attack was subsequently exposed, and in March 1994 she pleaded guilty to hindering the prosecution. She was ordered to pay a $100,000 fine and, most significantly, was stripped of her coveted national title, and permanently banned from the U.S. Figure Skating Association. Aside from the suffering endured by Kerrigan, what was the price paid by Harding for her envy? "I lost my life, my career, and everything else."[5]

———

Don't provoke envy

6. We noted earlier the prayer offered by the Rabbis "that the hearts of others not be envious of us." This reminds us not to act in a manner that will incite other people's envy. For example, people are less likely to envy a wealthy person known as an unostentatious philanthropist.

So, if you have been successful, don't initiate conversations with others about your achievements, your famous friends, your honors, or the successes of your children. If, in a small group, people ask you about some area of success, answer honestly, but try to downplay, and certainly not exaggerate, the accomplishments' significance. Don't give others cause to feel less good about themselves and envious of you.

---

you could ask yourself. For example, if you love your parents, would you prefer to have had different, wealthier parents, just so that you could have received a large inheritance?

At social events, prominent people should make an effort to speak to those around them at least as much about *their* lives as about their own. This may not be easy, because people often prod famous people to speak about themselves. Therefore, one must make an extra effort to encourage others to speak about themselves.

7. Try to anticipate and forestall situations that will cause envy. The *Sefer Chasidim* teaches that "when two righteous men arrive in a city at the same time, but the people pay homage to only one of them, then the one who is shown honor should show respect to the other, so that he not become jealous, and also to cause the people to honor the other righteous man" (paragraph 359).

So, if you have achieved success, express your admiration and appreciation for those who might not be as well known. For example, I have long been impressed that Rabbi Harold Kushner, one of America's most popular writers, has often used his fame and success to help promote the writings of people far less known than he.

8. Parents should take care not to provoke jealousy among their children. This was the great flaw in Jacob's raising of his sons: "And when [Joseph's] brothers saw that their father loved him more than any of his brothers they hated him so that they could not speak a friendly word to him" (Genesis 37:4).* Parents have a moral obligation not to provoke envy.

Even on purely prudential grounds, a parent should act the same way toward all his children. Thus, if a parent truly does love one child more than the others, he does the child great harm by making that known and causing the child's siblings to envy him or her. One suspects that, during Joseph's days as a slave and prisoner in Egypt, he did not remember Jacob's favoritism with gratitude. Indeed, that might be the explanation for an action (or rather non-action) of Joseph's that is otherwise inexplicable. When he was elevated to a high position in Egypt, second only to Pharaoh, he made no effort to contact his father and inform him that he was alive and well. Was he perhaps feeling some anger toward his father, whose behavior had helped provoke his brother's animosity, and bring about their terrible crime of selling him into slavery in Egypt?

---

*The story of Joseph also shows that favoritism can be just as cruel to the favored child as it is to the others.

Is envy ever good?

9. The word *envy* is sometimes used in a manner that implies admiration or respect for another, and not ill will.* For example, "I envy him his cheerful disposition," or "I envy her her faith." To a certain extent, a cheerful disposition and faith might be natural inclinations or gifts from God, but for most people, both of these qualities have to be developed. Someone who is cheerful has, just like you and me, endured upsetting and perhaps devastating experiences, and yet has found a way to remain upbeat. The same applies to faith. So, even where envy has an element of admiration, don't just envy or admire that person. Rather, see if you can learn from him how to integrate these life-affirming values in your life.

Ask the cheerful person if she ever feels down or depressed, and how she deals with it. If somebody had developed a business technique that yielded great profits, you would want to learn how to apply it to your life. Why not do the same with personality qualities that will bring greater happiness and a sense of well-being into your life?

10. The Talmud says that envy among scholars leads to intellectual advances and breakthroughs: "The envy of scholars brings about greater wisdom" (*Bava Bathra* 21a). One can hope that at least part of the wisdom it will bring about is the realization that envy, if not held in check, is among the most destructive and self-destructive of traits.

———

Unfortunately, it is widely known that in the worlds of art and academia, envy often leads to pettiness far more than to greater wisdom. Joseph Epstein, the long-time editor of The American Scholar *and a faculty member at Northwestern University, laments that: "rarely, in my observations, do the top three or four people in any line of intellectual endeavor have kind words to say about the others. . . . How little it takes to make one academic sick with envy over the pathetically small advantages won by another: the better office, the slightly lighter teaching load, the fickle admiration of students. For years in universities, if a scholar wrote well and commanded a wider than merely scholarly audience because of the accessibility of his prose, he was put down as 'popularizer.' Pure envy talking, of course."[6]*

———

---

*Sometimes it implies just friendly goodwill. As Joseph Epstein writes, "One might say, 'I envy you your two-month holiday in the south of France,' without in one's mind plotting how to do the person out of it" (*Envy*, 6).

Hatred and Revenge

If you see your enemy's donkey lying
down under its burden and would refrain
from raising it, you must nevertheless
raise it with him.

Exodus 23:5

34

THE MOST DESTRUCTIVE EMOTION

1. Hatred, particularly when directed against a group, is the cause (along with untamed anger) of more suffering than any other human emotion, and is a violation of Judaism's most fundamental principles. As noted, when asked to define the essence of Judaism, Hillel said, "What is hateful unto you, don't do unto your neighbor, the rest is commentary" (*Shabbat* 31a). In other words, "the essence of Judaism . . . is not to act in a hateful manner" (Rabbi Nachum Amsel).[1] Yet that is exactly what hate-filled people do: treat others in a way that they would hate to be treated.

For the limited instances in which hatred is appropriate, see chapter 36.

2. As frequent victims of antisemitism, Jews know well the terrible consequences of unchecked hatred. Such enmity led to the Crusades, the Inquisition, pogroms, terror bombings against Israel, and, of course, the Holocaust. Indeed, the history of antisemitism and of racism—which led to crimes such as slavery, segregation, and lynching—is rooted in people doing unto others precisely that which they would regard as evil if done to them.

Hatred as self-destructive

3. The Talmud teaches that hatred *between* Jews can be as destructive as hatred *against* Jews. Thus the Rabbis attributed the destruction of the Second Temple (70 C.E.), the greatest tragedy of ancient Jewish life, to the sin of "groundless hatred" (*sinat chinam*): "Why was the First Temple destroyed [in 586 B.C.E.]? Because of three offenses committed [by the Jews of that period]: idolatry, sexual immorality, and murder. . . . But why, then, was the Second Temple destroyed, given that the Jews of that time studied Torah, kept the commandments, and performed acts of charity? Because groundless hatred was prevalent. . . . This teaches us that the offense of

groundless hatred is the equivalent of idolatry, sexual immorality, and murder" (*Yoma* 9b).*

Although this passage, one of the most famous in the Talmud, has long been the subject of rabbinic sermons, it would appear that few people have ever stopped hating others because of it. Perhaps this is because the Talmud limits its condemnation to "groundless hatred," and few people are willing to acknowledge that their hatred is without basis, or even exaggerated. In consequence, most people assume that the Talmud's condemnation applies to other people's hatreds, not their own. In actuality, even in instances in which hatred can be justified, if any part of it is disproportionate to the provocation and is therefore excessive, that excess is "groundless [and hence forbidden] hatred" (for more on this, see page 320).

―――

Rabbi Abraham Isaac Kook (1865–1935), the renowned Ashkenazic Chief Rabbi of Palestine, was profoundly affected by this text. During the 1920s and 1930s, at a time of great tension and animosity between Palestine's Orthodox community and the largely secular Zionist chalutzim (pioneers), Rabbi Kook taught: "The Second Temple was destroyed because of groundless hatred. Perhaps the Third will be rebuilt because of groundless love."

―――

4. An oft-recited rabbinic proverb teaches that "hatred makes the straight crooked" (see for example, *Sanhedrin* 105b). When people are consumed by hatred, they are unable to think clearly. For example, hatred commonly causes people to hate those they believe to be their enemies more than they love the people closest to them. This happens in many divorces; the exes' rage at each other sometimes overwhelms even their love for their children. A friend who has dealt with many divorcing couples spoke of how often neither spouse is willing to pay for camp, tutors, clothing, or Bar Mitzvah or Bat Mitzvah, because each insists that it is the other's obligation, and neither is willing to set this financial precedent. As a result, the child goes without.†

―――――――――――

*During the first-century Judean revolt against Rome, expecting a siege of Jerusalem, the Jews of the city stockpiled sufficient food for many years. But one of the Zealot factions, furious at those Jerusalem Jews who did not support the revolt, burned the entire supply, in the hope that destroying this "security blanket" would compel everyone to participate in the revolt. The deprivation and starvation that resulted caused suffering as great as any inflicted by the Romans, who soon destroyed the city and the Temple.

†On occasion, when the exes are not venomous, the divorce lawyers provoke animosity. A friend of mine consulted a lawyer who told him, "I'm an aggressive, no-holds-barred lawyer, the sort of peron you go to when you don't care whether you ever speak to your ex again."

This type of irrational hatred operates on the national level as well. Thus, in December 2003, a large earthquake hit Iran and killed some thirty thousand people. In the quake's immediate aftermath, there were people stranded inside and under buildings, and the Iranian government issued an appeal soliciting aid from the rest of the world, with one exception: the government announced that it would not accept help from Israel. Ironically, in part because of the long history of Arab- and Iranian-supported terror bombings directed against Israel, Israel has more experience than other nations in rescuing people from damaged buildings. And Israel, both because of its sensitivity to human life, and out of a desire to do something to break the pattern of hatred felt toward it in the Islamic world, was very willing to extend help to those trapped in the earthquake. But the Iranian government, terrified that Israel might save some lives and bring about a lessening of hatred for Israel and the Jews, preferred to see Iranians die rather than have them saved by Israelis.

5. "Hatred of one's fellow drives a man from the world" (*The Ethics of the Fathers* 2:11). The obsessive quality of hatred often makes it impossible for people to enjoy the good things they do have. Thus, King Ahasuerus elevated Haman to the second highest position in the Persian Empire, and granted him extraordinary power, wealth, and honor. Yet when Mordechai refused to bow down to him, Haman was overcome with rage. It was not enough that everyone else in Persia treated him with deference, Mordechai had to be punished for his disrespect. And not just Mordechai. In his hatred, Haman "disdained to lay hands on Mordechai alone. Having been told who Mordechai's people were, Haman plotted to do away with all the Jews, Mordechai's people, throughout the kingdom of Ahasuerus" (Esther 3:6). This obsession caused Haman to embark on a course of action that destroyed him. By the end of the Book of Esther, the Jews, whom Haman wished to murder, were alive and prospering. But Haman, who would have remained in power if he had reined in his hatred, was dead, along with his ten sons.

———

Hatred is self-destructive in less dramatic ways also. I know, for example, that on days when I am consumed by anger against someone, I rarely get worthwhile work done. Every time I begin something, the angry thoughts intrude and distract me.

———

On curbing hatred toward other groups and nations

6. Try to curb your animosity, even when you believe you can find a justification for hating another group or nation. Thus, the Israelites leaving Egypt—after having endured hundreds of years of slavery and, at one point, the drowning of their newborn male infants—could easily have justified hating Egyptians. And yet the Bible legislates, "You shall not abhor an Egyptian, for you were a stranger in his land" (Deuteronomy 23:8).

In other words, even in an instance as extreme as that of Egypt, the Jews must still remember that they had entered Egypt by invitation at a time of famine and desperation, had been provided with food, and given land on which to live (Genesis 47:1–6).

On the other hand, the directive against hating Egypt was not given when the Israelites were still being oppressed and killed by them, but only after the Egyptians had been struck with the Ten Plagues (and thereby punished for the evil they had committed), and the Israelites had been liberated.

———

To this day at the Passover Seder, a drop of wine is spilled at the mention of each of the plagues that befell Egypt. In Jewish tradition, wine symbolizes joy, and its spilling the diminution of joy.

In the twentieth century, modern Egypt became one of the State of Israel's most unrelenting foes, and Egyptian President Anwar Sadat orchestrated the 1973 Yom Kippur War, in which almost three thousand Israeli soldiers were killed. Prior to that, Sadat, who had been pro-Nazi during World War II, often preached to his army and people the crudest sort of antisemitism.[2] And yet, in 1977, when Sadat announced his willingness to make a full peace with Israel, Israelis treated him with great warmth and admiration. I recall reading an article at the time written by an Israeli Bible scholar on the commandment not to hate the Egyptians; the article was dedicated to the memory of the author's son, who had been killed during the Yom Kippur War.

———

7. The same verse that prohibits hating Egyptians, continues, "You shall not abhor an Edomite [a historic enemy of Israel], for he is your brother" (Deuteronomy 23:8). In this prohibition of hatred, we are reminded that many of those whom we regard as our enemies are also our brothers, fellow creatures who, like us, are created in God's image.*

---

*The Edomites were descended from Esau, Jacob's brother; hence, they were in a sense, the Jews' cousins.

———

This verse can help to check Jewish hostility to contemporary Arabs, many, but not all, of whom support the destruction of Israel. If the only emotion Jews feel toward Arabs—who are descendants of Abraham through Ishmael, and our "cousins"—is animosity, any future reconciliation will become impossible.

———

35

"IF YOUR ENEMY IS HUNGRY":
BREAKING THE PATTERN OF HATRED

═══════

Do your enemy a favor

1. What often intensifies animosity between people is the sense that the person we dislike dislikes us even more than we dislike him. This perception often causes us to feel justified in our own hatred ("It's not my fault. Look how much he hates me."). Therefore the Torah commands that we try to break the pattern by doing our enemy a favor: "If you see your enemy's donkey lying down under its burden and would refrain from raising it, you must nevertheless raise it with him" (Exodus 23:5). The Midrash explains how this single act can transform our relationship:

"Rabbi Alexandri said: Two donkey drivers who hated each other were walking on a road when the donkey of one lay down under its burden. His companion saw it, and at first he passed on. But then he reflected: Is it not written in the Torah, 'If you see your enemy's donkey lying down under its burden . . . ?' So he returned, lent a hand, and helped his enemy in loading and unloading. He began talking to his enemy: 'Release a bit here, pull up over there, unload over here.' Thus, peace came about between them, so that the driver of the overloaded donkey said, 'Did I not suppose that he hated me? But look how compassionate he has been.' By and by, the two entered an inn, ate and drank together, and became fast friends" (*Tanhuma, Mishpatim* #1).

This commandment also reminds us that even if we hate someone, we are forbidden to "take it out" on his suffering animal or, even worse, on the members of his family. Rabbi Abraham Isaac Kook was often attacked unfairly by the Neturei Karta, an ultra-Orthodox anti-Zionist group. On one occasion the daughter of a Neturei Karta leader, a man who had made some of the most extreme attacks on Rabbi Kook, fell ill with a serious and rare disease. The man learned that a doctor in another country was by far the best person to treat her. However, the doctor was very busy, and without some special connection, he would be unlikely to take her on as a patient; in addition, the physician's fee was far beyond anything the father could pay. But the man also learned that the doctor was a great admirer of Rabbi Kook, and if the rabbi asked him to treat the girl, he would do so. The Neturei Karta leader was in a quandary: How could he, who hated and had attacked Rabbi Kook, ask him to intervene with the doctor? In desperation, the man sought out Rabbi Aryeh Levine, a well-known friend of Rabbi Kook, and asked him to speak to the rabbi. Reb Aryeh did so, and Rabbi Kook responded, "Of course I am prepared to give the man a letter to the professor. What does this have to do with the difference of opinion between the girl's father and me?" Indeed, when Rabbi Kook wrote the letter, he depicted the father in favorable terms. He explained to Reb Aryeh that because he had reason to dislike the man, "I will let no personal bias influence me as I write this." Rabbi Kook even wrote a letter to a shipping line with whose directors he had warm relations, asking them to offer the man and his daughter a substantial discount.[1]

---

2. "If your enemy is hungry, give him bread to eat. And if he is thirsty, give him water to drink" (Proverbs 25:21). Often, when we view someone as an enemy, we hope that misfortune overtakes him ("He should drop dead," or "I don't care if he starves"). But, as the Bible teaches, even if we harbor such feelings, we must not allow ourselves to *act* upon them. The fact that we regard someone as our enemy does not mean that he deserves to starve, and if we feed him, he might no longer be our enemy.

3. To break the pattern of enmity, there are times when you should help your enemy before you help others, including friends. The Talmud legislates that "if the animal of one's friend is lying under its burden and needs to be unloaded, and the animal of one's enemy needs to be loaded, one is commanded to first assist the animal of one's enemy's in order to subdue one's evil inclination" (*Bava Mezia* 32b).

The talmudic commentary *Tosafot* (*Pesachim* 113b) asks the following: Assuming that the person who hates his enemy has good reason for feeling so (the despised party really has acted badly), then why should the person feel obliged to "subdue his evil inclination"? What is wrong with hating, and not helping, someone who deserves it? *Tosafot* answers that even when you are justified in feeling animosity toward someone else, the ill will tends to escalate, leading to an exaggerated and unjustified *sinah gemurah* (complete hatred): at that point it is the evil inclination that is fueling the hatred, and it must be subdued. As *Tosafot* recognizes, our hatred often becomes disproportionate to the provocation and needs to be reined in.

Additional ways to lessen and eliminate hatred

4. Try to find a way to think differently about your enemy. Before reading further, think of someone whom you thoroughly dislike. Can you think of any good she has ever done for you, or any evil she was in a position to commit against you yet didn't. Are you willing to acknowledge that at least some of your animosity (and possible demonization of her) may be excessive?

It also helps to try and understand why your enemy hates you. Even if you believe the reasons to be unjustified and inaccurate, by putting yourself into the other person's mindset, you will become more understanding of the hatred, and this understanding may provide you with the insight to end the enmity. For example, a friend confided to me the following: "Once I realized that Mark hated and insulted me because he thought his wife, an old friend, had once loved me, I was able to improve the situation by continually complimenting him in front of her on how well he looked." It would be nice if such strategies always worked, but they do sometimes.

5. Try to restrain your angry thoughts against those you dislike. This does not mean that you must force yourself to think kindly thoughts about them; just try to think fewer bad ones. As the Bible teaches: "If your enemy falls, don't exult; if he trips, let your heart not rejoice. Lest the Lord see it and be displeased" (Proverbs 24:17–18).*

On the other hand, is it always wrong to feel some pleasure when your enemy suffers? That depends on why you regard the person as your enemy;

---

*Therefore, if you dislike someone, resolve that when that person's name comes up in conversation, you will not speak about her, except in the rare instance that the people to whom you are speaking need the information you possess. Even then, remain quiet unless you are certain that you can speak about her in a precise and non-exaggerated manner; the fact that you dislike someone does not entitle you to lie about her.

is it because of undeniably evil acts the person has committed, or is it for a less substantial and more personal reason? Some years ago, a reader wrote to my ethics advice column: "Lately, several of the highest-profile people in my industry—known for their cruelty to employees (including me) as well as for their talent—have been failing miserably and publicly. Their staffs are deserting them in droves. I'm trying not to gloat—can you help me?"

I responded, "Your final words imply that you're feeling guilty. Yet if your letter is an accurate portrayal of what's happened, perhaps you shouldn't. What is wrong about feeling happy that people known for their 'cruelty to employees' are experiencing professional failure? The alternative—being happy at their successes—would also mean feeling happy at their opportunity to go on being cruel to others who are unfortunate enough to work for them.

"Does this mean that all gloating about the sufferings of those who have hurt us is okay? No. What exonerates you from guilt in this case is that you are experiencing happiness that these people's cruelty in the workplace is now being rewarded by the workplace being cruel to them. It would be wrong to gloat, however, if they were forced to resign their positions because, say, they needed to take care of a child stricken with a virulent disease. Or, for that matter, if they themselves were so stricken. In such a case you might be pleased that they no longer were in a position to hurt others, but it would be wrong to rejoice.

"When we dislike someone, we may be tempted to say, when suffering comes to them, 'Serves them right,' but I would hold my tongue. For undoubtedly there are people whom I've hurt, and who believe some terrible fate would serve me right.

"The question remains: How much gloating is okay? It seems to me that it's all right to express your pleasure to those friends and relatives who are aware of how much you suffered while working for the 'highest-profile people' who are now getting their comeuppance, and to other former fellow employees. But limit the number of people to whom you speak about the situation, and don't go out of your way to start relaying your experiences and your gloating to others who aren't already in the know. Gloating about the sufferings of others won't do much for your own reputation; people might conclude that you're a vindictive person.

"Also, now that these people have fallen, see if you can distance yourself from your anger and find room in your heart for some compassion. I stress both words, 'compassion' as well as 'some.'

"Finally, if you want some good to come out of your gloating, think through what it is that these people did that really hurt you and others—

and then make sure that you don't act similarly toward other people. A lot of us who are geniuses at recalling every slight we've experienced are far less insightful at noting the emotional suffering and cruelties we inflict on others."

6. When you start obsessing about someone you don't like, pick up a book or try to divert yourself with some other activity. A woman I know plays soothing music, and sometimes a taped recording of a babbling brook or a rain forest, when she starts to find herself consumed by anger; she says that it is impossible for her to hate others while this music is playing.

7. If somebody has treated you badly, don't keep your anger inside; confront the person and tell her what she has done wrong. This course of behavior is implied in the unusual wording of the Torah commandment, "You shall not hate your brother in your heart" (Leviticus 19:17). The Torah does not prohibit all hatred, just hatred in the heart. The medieval *Sefer Ha-Chinnuch,* an exposition of the Torah's 613 commandments, notes that one who makes known his hatred does not violate the biblical command against hatred (although such a person violates the law to "love your neighbor as yourself," and might well come to violate the Torah's prohibition against bearing a grudge [Leviticus 19:18]).

8. Don't generalize about groups you dislike; your statements will be unfair at best. During the time of the Talmud there was great animosity between the talmudic scholars and those whom they categorized as *amei ha-aretz* (the term literally refers to the common folk, but it also acquired the connotation of ignoramuses, and those hostile to study). In an unhappy passage, there were Rabbis who justified hating the *amei ha-aretz,* arguing that they were "vermin and their wives are insects," and that one who married his son or daughter to such a person was, in effect, marrying them off to a subhuman creature (see *Pesachim* 49b).

While there were undoubtedly *amei ha-aretz* who were very hostile to Jewish scholars and scholarship, rabbinic teachings like these helped exacerbate the conflict, while unfairly denigrating a whole class of people, among whom were people who were kind and generous. To counteract such a tendency, the Rabbis offered another, very different, teaching: "Let no one say, 'I love the scholars and hate ignorant people [the *amei ha-aretz*],' but let one's rule be, 'Love them all' " (*The Fathers According to Rabbi Nathan* 16:5).[2]

Hatred becomes particularly dangerous when it starts to deny the very humanity of those who are hated. That is why the use of terms such as "vermin" is so troublesome. In the 1990s the Hutus of Rwanda, who organized the murder of 800,000 Tutsis in a period of three and a half months, regularly referred to the Tutsis as "cockroaches," a designation intended to provoke repulsion and a desire to kill. Yehuda Bauer, the great historian of the Holocaust, told me that he never employs the commonly used phrase "the extermination of the Jews" to describe the Holocaust. That term, he explained, was itself a Nazi term, intended to make it sound like the Jews being killed were insects or rats.

Do not take revenge or bear a grudge

9. In the very verse in which the Torah issues the command to "love your neighbor as yourself," it issues two other commandments as well: "You shall not take vengeance or bear a grudge against your countrymen" (Leviticus 19:18).

10. What constitutes revenge? The Talmud offers the following example: A asks B to lend him a sickle, and B refuses. The following day, B asks A to lend him an ax, and A says, " 'I will not lend it to you, just as you refused to lend me your sickle.' This is revenge [and is forbidden by the Torah]" (*Yoma* 23a).

11. Maimonides writes that the desire for revenge is "a very bad trait," and that we must do our best to relinquish it. One way is to realize that many things that prompt our wrath are "vanity and emptiness and are not worth seeking revenge for" ("Laws of Character Development" 7:7).

The Psalmist asks rhetorically, and with pride, "Have I repaid those who have done me evil?" (7:5). The same thought is conveyed in Proverbs: "Do not say, 'I will do to him what he did to me; I will pay the man what he deserves'" (Proverbs 24:29).

12. What constitutes bearing a grudge? A asks B for an ax and B refuses. The following day, B says to A, "Lend me your garment," and A answers,

"Here it is. I am not like you, who would not lend me what I asked for." This, the Talmud concludes, is bearing a grudge (*Yoma* 23b).

While the Bible's and Talmud's standard (not even reminding someone who mistreated you of his mean-spirited behavior) seems beyond the capacity of most human beings, the fact that the Torah requires us not to bear a grudge means that Jewish law deems it within our capacity.

In addition, Rabbi Abraham Twerski, who has spent much of his life treating alcoholics and other addicts, notes that grudges can pose an even greater danger to those holding them than to others. Among addicts, grudges are "probably the single greatest factor responsible for relapse. One recovering alcoholic said it simply: 'Carrying resentments is like letting someone whom you don't like live inside your head rent-free.' Why would anybody allow that?"[3]

Grudges stir up anger. An alcoholic consumed by rage tries to divert himself by drinking, the rest of us by engaging in other types of self-destructive behavior (such as eating junk food, getting angry at the people with whom we live, or maybe even not moving forward in our careers, or not achieving what we are capable of, because of our preoccupation with the person or people at whom we are angry).

"Another possible approach would be for A to say, 'Of course you can borrow my ax. I am curious, however, why you wouldn't lend me your sickle yesterday.' Such an approach forces B to confront his own behavior, and might well increase the likelihood of B realizing he was wrong" (Dr. Isaac Herschkopf).[4]

13. If you go about spreading *lashon hara* about the person who offended you, then, in addition to violating the ban on speaking *lashon hara,* you are also violating the prohibition against bearing a grudge.

A final thought

14. While many people regard a hero as someone who vanquishes his foes, the Rabbis teach the opposite: "Who is a hero among heroes? One who turns an enemy into a friend" (*The Fathers According to Rabbi Nathan* 23:1; see a further discussion of this teaching on pages 206–207).

———

For the story of how a cantor in Nebraska practiced this principle toward a Nazi, and transformed him, see pages 182–183.

———

36

WHEN HATRED IS PERMISSIBLE

1. That hatred is not always wrong is a well-known teaching of the third chapter of Ecclesiastes—one of the most famous chapters in the Bible—which speaks of "a time for loving and a time for hating" (3:8). The same chapter notes that other activities generally associated with hatred are also not always wrong: "A time for killing and a time for healing . . . A time for throwing stones and a time for gathering stones . . . A time for war and a time for peace" (3:3,5, and 8).

———

The Midrash comments that the words "a time for hating" refer to "the time when a war is being fought" (Ecclesiastes Rabbah 3:8). The implication of both the biblical verse and the midrashic comment is that when the war is over, the hatred should end. As Winston Churchill said, "I oppose the pacifists during the war, and the jingoists after the war." This is consistent with what was noted earlier; after the exodus from Egypt—but not during the time Jews were enslaved there—Jews were instructed not to hate Egypt (Deuteronomy 23:8).

———

2. So, when is the appropriate time for hating, and against whom should hatred be directed? The Bible teaches that certain actions render people hateful to God (it does not say that human beings are required to hate such people); for example, murderers. The Lord hates "hands that shed innocent blood" (Proverbs 6:17). The same verse lists other actions that "the Lord hates," including the following:

- hatching evil plots
- bearing false witness
- inciting brothers to quarrel
- cheating others ("You must have completely honest weights and completely honest measures, if you are to endure long on the soil that the Lord your God is giving you. For everyone who does those things, everyone who deals dishonestly, is abhorrent to the Lord your God" [Deuteronomy 25:13–16].)

- telling falsehoods: "I hate and abhor falsehood" (119:163); the emphasis is on hatred of the act rather than on the perpetrator

3. On several occasions the Psalmist speaks of permitted hatreds—for example, hatred directed against

- evil: "You who love the Lord, hate evil" (97:10; the emphasis in the verse is on hating evil, not evil people). Similarly, the Book of Proverbs teaches that "to fear the Lord is to hate evil" (8:13). Thus, fear of God and love of God lead to the same result, the hatred of evil.
- those who hate God: "O Lord, You know I hate those who hate You" (139:21)

4. In addition to the biblical verses, a talmudic passage (*Pesachim* 113b) teaches that "there are three whom God hates":

- hypocrites: "One who says one thing with his mouth while meaning another with his heart"
- "one who knows testimony for his friend, but does not testify"
- one who sees his friend involved in some sexual transgression—there are no other witnesses—and testifies or spreads word about it

5. A talmudic passage also teaches that we are permitted to hate a Jewish sinner, for example, a Jew whom we have witnessed performing an immoral act (*Pesachim* 113b). Maimonides writes that "it is a commandment to hate such a person [namely, one who is immoral] until he repents and abandons his wickedness" ("Laws of Murderers" 13:14). But even in such a case, Maimonides rules that if you see the person in a panic and in need of help, you must extend aid, lest by not doing so, you put the person in danger.

In several seminal modern rulings, rabbis have ruled that these permissions to hate Jewish sinners, particularly those who violate Jewish ritual laws, are no longer applicable. The Chazon Ish, for example, explained that since God today is not as evident in the world as He was, for example, during the revelation at Mount Sinai, we no longer consider non-observant Jews as *apikorsim*, heretics, people who knew God and rejected Him.

6. In summary, it is permissible to hate those who do evil and incite others to do so. Consider the verse from Psalms cited earlier, "O Lord, You know I hate those who hate You. . . . I regard them as my own enemies" (139:21–22). In the twentieth century there were two powerful political move-

ments that hated God, Nazism, and Communism. Hitler declared his hatred against the "Asiatic God tyrant of the Jews and his life-denying Ten Commandments," while Lenin, who led the Communist revolution in Russia, wrote, "I hate God as I do my personal enemies."[1]

The Nazis, of course, embarked on the most extensive campaign in history to murder every Jew in the world, and though Lenin did not hate those Jews who shared his atheism and were committed to Communism, the movement he created in the Soviet Union made extensive efforts to destroy Judaism. In other words, those who hate God really do become enemies of the Jews. Such people also engage in additional evil and incitement to evil (for example, Lenin's successor, Joseph Stalin, murdered more people than Hitler).

This does not mean, of course, that Jews should hate atheists, but they should hate those who *hate* God and who, on the basis of this hatred, advocate evil behavior.

Similarly, we are permitted to hate so-called religious people who do evil in God's Name, for such people, in addition to the cruelties they commit, discredit God. In medieval times, such behavior was engaged in by Catholic religious officials who encouraged the Inquisition to torture Jews and others, and in the contemporary world such behavior is epitomized by leaders (and supporters) of organizations such as Hamas and al-Qaeda, who murder innocent people in the Name of God.

Jews are also permitted to hate those who intentionally inflict irrevocable damage on others. The Bible records that Amnon, a son of King David, became infatuated with his half-sister Tamar. He invited Tamar to his home, where he raped her, and then had his servant throw her out. From that moment on, Tamar's brother, Absalom, "hated Amnon, because he had violated his sister Tamar"(II Samuel 13:22). There is no implication in the text that Absalom was wrong for feeling such hatred.

The First Book of Samuel also records the prophet Samuel's hatred for the Amalekite king, Agag, a hatred that seems to have been fed by Agag's acts of murder. Before executing Agag, Samuel said to him, "As your sword has made women childless, so shall your mother be childless among women" (I Samuel 15:33). Three thousand years after this passage was written, Israeli president Yitzchak ben Zvi cited these words in turning down Adolf Eichmann's request for a commutation of his death sentence.

III

Fair Speech

THE JEWISH LAWS OF
FAIR SPEECH

Have you heard something? Let it die with
you. Be of good courage: it will not burst you.

The Wisdom of Ben Sirach 19:10

37

LASHON HARA AND WHY IT IS SO HARMFUL

===

Lashon Hara *and* Rechilut: *Two types of hurtful speech*

1. *Lashon hara* (literally "evil tongue") refers to true statements that harm, embarrass, cause financial damage to, or lower the status of the person being discussed.* The fact that a statement or incident is true does not mean that others have the right to know about it.

There are many unpleasant truths about ourselves that we understandably don't want made known to others, and we would regard those who spread such information as doing us a wrong. So, too, is it wrong for us to relate negative truths, or express critical opinions, about people to those who have no need for this information. Therefore, while speaking the truth is a legal defense in an American court against a charge of slander, it is no defense in Jewish law against a charge of *lashon hara*; rather, it is tantamount to an admission of guilt.

———

The following are examples of gratuitous comments people commonly make about others that Jewish law forbids:

- *"She is only interested in boys, and never spends any time studying."*
- *"When he was a boy, he was expelled from school for cheating."*
- *"He's not very bright; the only reason he got his job is that his father-in-law owns the company."*
- *"He cheated on his wife."*
- *"Let me tell you what I really don't like about her."*

---

*Rabbi Israel Stein defines *lashon hara* as a "mean-spirited truth." Untrue slanderous comments are called *motzi shem ra*, and constitute a more serious offense (see chapter 43).

In each of these cases, even if the facts are accurate, it is still lashon hara *and, therefore, constitutes impermissible speech.*

———

2. *Rechilut,* a particularly damaging type of *lashon hara,* occurs when we pass on to someone hurtful things another has said about him or her. While this may seem justifiable ("Shouldn't Ron know what Sam really thinks of him?"), almost all of us say unkind things about others, particularly, but not only, when we are annoyed at them. In speaking to close friends, husbands or wives will occasionally say harsh words about their spouses, parents will sometimes make angry remarks about their children, and friends will often make hurtful comments about each other (quite apart from the cutting remarks we sometimes make about those to whom we are not close). Passing on these comments can cause great anger, and stimulate an ugly fight, even a rupture, in a relationship. Blaise Pascal, the great seventeenth-century philosopher, wrote, "I lay it down as a fact that if all men knew what others say of them, there would not be four friends left in the world."

———

In one instance, a brother made some condescending remarks about his sister to a friend, who passed on the comments. The ensuing bitterness caused a rupture in the relationship between the brother and the sister that lasted twenty years. Obviously the relationship had been a troubled one even before these comments were made, but the transmitting of this lashon hara *exacerbated the situation (in addition, it caused both the brother's and sister's children, cousins, to break off contact), and broke the heart of the feuding siblings' mother.*

What was gained by the "friend" who relayed these remarks? Certainly nothing good, and a great deal of gratuitous pain. Should the brother have refrained from making the remarks about his sister? Definitely. But in this instance the "friend" who passed on the remarks inflicted the greater damage. As Mark Twain said, "It takes your enemy and your friend, working together, to hurt you to the heart; the one to slander you and the other to get the news to you."

———

3. If you suspect that a statement made by one person about another may cause trouble, don't repeat it. In the Torah, the eighty-nine-year-old Sarah, overhearing an angel of the Lord predicting that she will give birth to a child within the year, laughs to herself and says, "Now that I am withered, am I to have enjoyment, with my husband so old?" In the next verse, God asks

Abraham, "Why did Sarah laugh, saying, 'Shall I in truth bear a child, old as I am?'" (Genesis 18:12–13). Compare Sarah's words with God's, and you will notice that the Lord leaves out the words, "with my husband so old," presumably because these words might hurt or anger Abraham. On the basis of this verse, the Rabbis conclude, "Great is peace, seeing that for its sake even God modified the truth" (*Yevamot* 65b).

Teachings from the Torah on forbidden speech

4. A verse in Leviticus introduces the prohibition of *lashon hara:* "You shall not go about as a talebearer among your people" (19:16). The Hebrew word for "talebearer," *rachil*, derives from the same root as that for peddler (*rochayl*). The implication is that, just as a peddler goes from house to house buying from one and selling to another, so too does a gossip. There is a peddling mentality to most gossips. Thus, if we reveal something intimate or negative about someone (information we might have received in confidence), we expect to be told some equally intimate details about the same person or another. We "peddle" one intimacy for another.

————

Maimonides refers to one who speaks lashon hara *as a* meragel, *or "spy" ("Laws of Character Development" 7:1). People who spread gossip act like spies, pretending to be a person's friend (just as spies pretend to be loyal citizens) in order to procure information that can then be used to damage or destroy the person's reputation.*

————

5. Those who speak negatively of others also violate the commandment to "love your neighbor as yourself" (Leviticus 19:18). Since people do not want damaging information about themselves shared with others, gossips cannot claim to have even tried to fulfill this fundamental law.

Gossips also violate the Torah's Golden Rule by revealing and discussing people's greatest areas of vulnerability. If we entered a room and heard people talking about us, what aspects of our lives would we least like to hear them discussing? It would probably be our character flaws and the intimate details of our social life. Yet most of us, when gossiping, focus precisely on these two areas.

6. Gossips also violate Leviticus 19:15: "In justice shall you judge your neighbor." Jewish tradition understands this law as requiring us to judge others fairly, and to incline toward the more favorable assessment of their behavior when two views are possible. Yet those who speak *lashon hara* tend to attribute bad or selfish motives to those they are talking about (for a more comprehensive discussion of judging others fairly, see chapters 5 and 6).

7. Bible commentators understand the verse "Cursed is one who strikes his fellow man in secret" (Deuteronomy 27:24) as referring not only to someone who strikes his unsuspecting neighbor physically, but also to someone who injures another by speaking *lashon hara,* an activity that takes place behind the victim's back. The Psalmist promises God's vengeance on such gossips: "He who slanders his friend in secret, I will destroy" (Psalms 101:5).

One of the great evils of *lashon hara* is that because it does not happen in the victim's presence, he is unable to defend himself.

———

These biblical verses help explain why Jewish tradition regards the spreading of negative information about others as so heinous. The Talmud cites Rabbi Jeremiah ben Abba's view that among those who will not be greeted by the "Divine Presence [after they die]" are "those who are habitual speakers of lashon hara."* *The other verbal sins also condemned by the Talmud are scoffing (using one's tongue to mock), flattery (ingratiating oneself through insincere and usually false words), and lying (Sotah 42a).*

A tale told by Rabbi Aryeh Levine reinforces this teaching. Rabbi Chayyim Berlin was a close friend of Rabbi Yitzchak Blaser. Once, in Reb Aryeh's presence, the two men made a pact: whoever died first would appear to the other in a dream and relate what the experience of passing over to the next world was like. Ten days after Rabbi Blaser died, he appeared to his friend in a dream. When Rabbi Berlin asked him, "Well, what has it been like?" Rabbi Blaser responded, "The profundity of the Divine judgment is immeasurable. The sins of the tongue are worst. But those who are humble and lowly, forbearing and forgiving, receive special consideration."[1]

———

*Since almost everyone occasionally gossips unfairly about others, the Rabbis understood this punishment as applying only to those who do so habitually; see page 347.

8. Two instances of *lashon hara* in the Torah, both of which led to great suffering, remind us that we should be particularly careful not to speak ill of family members. The first case occurs in Genesis: "And Joseph brought bad reports of them [i.e., his brothers] to their father" (37:2). This tattling is the first of several details the Torah provides about Joseph's relationship with his brothers, who soon came to hate him.

The most obvious lesson is that parents should discourage their children from informing on each other. It is good for a child to report if he or she is being bullied or otherwise taken advantage of. But the verse implies that Joseph was steadily bringing back negative reports about his brothers' actions, something that should not be done unless the misbehavior is extreme.

The Joseph story reminds us that, in many families, members often speak ill of each other to a parent or a sibling. While a certain amount of such talk may be unavoidable—it is inevitable for there to be some friction among people who live in close proximity—such talk, if not held in check, may eventually destroy feelings of family loyalty. Because of thoughtless remarks, family members become categorized as "the selfish one," "the fool," "the bad-tempered one," or "the incompetent."

———

Lashon hara is often responsible for the common phenomenon of close relatives who are not on speaking terms. In many instances, these family feuds start with hurtful comments one relative makes about another. Almost invariably, the objects of the complaints eventually hear about the gossip, and from that point on the antagonism escalates.

———

9. A second instance of *lashon hara* in the Torah also occurs within a family setting: Miriam and Aaron, Moses' sister and brother, start criticizing Moses to one another, focusing on some incident between Moses and his wife. (Perhaps out of a desire not to encourage *lashon hara*, the Torah does not tell us what the incident was.) A verse later, the real reason for Miriam and Aaron's annoyance at their younger brother becomes clear: jealousy of Moses' greater standing in the community. "They said: 'Has the Lord spoken only through Moses? Has He not spoken through us as well?'" (Numbers 12:2).

This last comment represents a common feature of *lashon hara*. When people envy someone, but can't find an obvious fault with the person, they attack anything they can in the person's life (such as, "Look what a bad husband he is," or "Look how her children turned out").

God is outraged by Aaron's and Miriam's comments about Moses: "How then did you not shrink from speaking against My servant Moses?" (Numbers 12:8). Immediately after receiving this rebuke, Miriam is stricken with leprosy. Aaron, who, a few verses earlier, had been bragging with Miriam about how they were both Moses' equals (since all three of them were God's prophets), is now forced to beg Moses to intervene with God on Miriam's behalf.

Many readers might consider Miriam's offense as ordinary, even minor. But a later Torah passage commands Jews to remember this incident and Miriam's ensuing punishment: "Remember what the Lord your God did unto Miriam by the way as you came out of Egypt" (Deuteronomy 24:9).

As this verse makes clear, *lashon hara* offends not only the person gossiped about, but also God. Wouldn't your parents be deeply pained if they learned that you were going about criticizing your brother or sister behind their backs? Jewish tradition teaches that God regards human beings as His children and is therefore hurt when they denigrate one another.

Why lashon hara *is so difficult an offense for which to make amends*

10. *Lashon hara* often does incalculable damage to the good name of the person being discussed. Unlike a physical injury, where the full extent of the trauma is usually obvious, *lashon hara* is likely to be repeated by those who hear it, and they in turn will tell it to others, thereby causing an ever-expanding circle of harm. Even if the speaker eventually regrets the damage he has done to his victim's reputation, it is usually impossible to undo it by getting in touch with all the people who heard the negative report.

———

In a small town, a man who disliked the rabbi went about spreading malicious reports about him. Some were true, but nobody else's business; others were either untrue or exaggerated. At a certain point the man realized that what he had said was unfair and had immensely damaged the rabbi's reputation. Full of remorse, he confessed to the rabbi what he had done, and begged for forgiveness.

The rabbi, shocked at what the man had said, told him, "Go home and take a feather pillow, then go outside, cut it open, and scatter its feathers to the winds. After you have done that, come back to me."

The man thought the request bizarre, but, relieved that this act would gain the rabbi's forgiveness, followed the instructions precisely. When he returned, he asked the rabbi. "Am I now forgiven?"

"One more thing," the rabbi replied. "Now go and gather up all the feathers."

"But that's impossible," the man said.

"Precisely," the rabbi answered. "And just as you can never gather all the feathers, so too you can never fully undo the damage you have caused me."

———

11. Gossips often speak ill of so many people that it is hard for them to remember all those about whom they have said these things, and certainly not everyone they have spoken to. Just as a thief who has stolen money from many people may no longer remember all his victims, and therefore cannot perform complete repentance (by returning what he has stolen or the value of what he has stolen, and seeking forgiveness), so, too, a habitual speaker of *lashon hara* can never fully make amends.

The destruction wreaked by lashon hara

12. A talmudic passage (Jerusalem Talmud, *Peah* 1:1) teaches that a gossip can stand in Rome and cause a death in Syria; that is, he can cause evil at a great distance. At a time when King Saul had launched a campaign to kill David, Doeg, Saul's aide, informed the king that the priests of the city of Nob had provided David with a night's lodging. In retaliation, Saul had eighty-five of the city's priests murdered (I Samuel 22:9–13).

What Doeg said was true, but providing information to someone you have reason to believe will misuse it—Doeg also knew that the priests of Nob were not aware of the conflict between David and Saul—can turn one into an accessory to murder. Indeed, that is what Doeg became.*

Nowadays, the telephone and the Internet make it possible to spread damaging information halfway around the world in a matter of seconds.

———

The same passage likens lashon hara *to an arrow: Why an arrow rather than another weapon? Because, the Rabbis explain, other weapons can slay only those who are near them, while an arrow can kill from a distance (Jerusalem Talmud, Peah 1:1).*

Another rabbinic source notes a second comparison between lashon hara *and an arrow: "If a man takes a sword in hand to slay his fellow, who then pleads with him and begs for mercy, the would-be slayer can change his mind and*

———

*See Psalm 52, a polemic against Doeg and all those who use words to cause harm; when Saul's troops refused to carry out the king's command, Doeg murdered the priests.

return the sword to its sheath. But once the would-be slayer has shot an arrow, it cannot be brought back even if he wants to" (Midrash Psalms *120:4*).

The thirteenth-century Rabbi Jonah Gerondi identified a third way in which lashon hara *and an arrow are alike: "One who draws the bow often sends his arrow into a person without the latter's knowing who hit him"* (Gates of Repentance, *part 3, paragraph 207*).

———

13. The iniquity of *lashon hara* derives in large part from its unfairness. By focusing on one or more negative aspects of a person, it causes those traits to become other people's primary associations with the person.*

———

Someone once confided to me the following: "Whenever Sam's name was mentioned, my friend Jeff, who had business dealings with him, always commented upon Sam's cheapness, how in every financial dealing he would try to squeeze out every last penny. I unconsciously assimilated Jeff's negative assessment, and whenever Sam's name came up in conversation, I also started commenting on his penny-pinching ways. I did so without thinking, until one day my wife commented, 'I know Sam's wife, and I like her very much, and I know how much she loves her husband. So there must be a lot more to him than his cheapness, which you don't even know for a fact to be true. And even if it is true, that's only one part of him. It's wrong of you to harp on it, particularly to people who have no need of this information.'"

"Needless to say," my friend told me, "I never mentioned this aspect of Sam again. It really was unfair and nobody else's business, and gave a very one-sided and ugly view of him."

———

14. By damaging a person's reputation, *lashon hara* reduces and undermines the ability of its victims to do good. That is why Jewish tradition regards the spreading of *lashon hara* about a rabbinic or any other worthy leader to be a particularly serious offense.

———

The late Israeli prime minister Yitzhak Rabin described how lashon hara *was used to discredit and demoralize Israeli prime minister and defense minister*

---

*As philosopher Bertrand Russell put it, "Nobody ever gossips about other people's secret virtues."

Levi Eshkol in the days preceding the 1967 Six-Day War: "They mocked him and chipped away at his image and publicized his weaknesses and made false accusations and claimed that the country did not, in effect, have a defense minister in its most difficult hour. Eshkol was exhausted. The burden of the times and that slander campaign worked together to call his position into question. His authority was damaged in the eyes of a few ministers and those of senior officers as well. . . . With his wings clipped and his authority curtailed, he lacked the power to impose his will on the government."2

In England, a century ago, a disciple of the Chaffetz Chayyim assumed a pulpit in a small community. The synagogue president treated the rabbi with contempt, often speaking disrespectfully to and about him.

On one occasion, however, the president needed the rabbi's help. His daughter was about to marry a non-Jew and leave the Jewish community. The man asked the rabbi to try to influence his daughter to break off the relationship and remain a committed Jew. The rabbi tried to do what he could, but found that the girl was unmoved by whatever he said.

When the father learned of the meeting's failure, he said to the rabbi with ill-concealed annoyance, "So, even this you couldn't do for me?"

The rabbi, who had suffered the president's insults in silence for a long time, finally spoke up, and related a parable he had heard from the Chaffetz Chayyim:

In a certain province, a terrible epidemic that affected only children broke out. The doctors had no remedy, and many children died. Then, one day, a doctor appeared who claimed to have a cure. He started administering a potion to children, and to everyone's amazement, it cured each child who received it. The doctor went from town to town administering the potion, and wherever he went, long lines of parents lined up to see him.

One day, however, as he was traveling between towns, a band of highwaymen attacked him. They stole the doctor's money, took his suitcases, and told him to flee for his life. The man ran away, leaving behind his potions and the equipment to make them.

When the thieves opened the suitcases and found inside only clothing, some equipment, and a few jars containing medicine, they threw the suitcases, along with their contents, into the ocean.

The doctor arrived at the next town with nothing more than the clothes on his back. The following morning he went to the office that had been set up for him. A long line of children and parents awaited him. The doctor called in the first parent and said to him, "I don't want to make a public announcement and create a mass panic. But something awful happened to me, and I want you to go out and start passing the word to others. To my great regret, I have no potion with me. Last night a gang of thieves attacked me while I was coming here, and stole both the potion and the equipment I have for making it. It will take me many weeks to procure new equipment and to produce a new supply of potion. Unfortunately, by then it will be too late to help any of the children here who are suffering from the disease."

The father paled, and grasped onto a pole to keep from collapsing. He knew all about those highwaymen—he had sent them, he was their leader. Unwittingly, he and his men had thrown into the ocean the very materials that could have saved his child's life.

———

When people speak *lashon hara* of a rabbi, the Chaffetz Chayyim taught, they rob him of his "tools and potions, for others will now disregard his words."

"You have only yourself to blame," the rabbi told the president, "for my inability to have any impact on your daughter. All these years you have treated me with utter disrespect. This is no secret—I'm sure your daughter is well aware of how you speak about me. Is it any wonder, then, that my words are meaningless to her?" (Retold by Rabbi Shimon Finkelman.)[3]

15. In addition, speaking ill of a person's professional ability, as opposed to some other, less central quality, can destroy a person's livelihood. As Rabbi Israel Salanter explained, "If you say of a rabbi that he does not have a good voice and of a cantor that he is not a scholar, you are a gossip. But if you say of a rabbi that he is no scholar and of a cantor that he has no voice, you are a murderer."

As regards the limited situations in which critical observations about someone's professional abilities are permitted, see pages 366–367.

16. *Lashon hara* is a gratuitous act of wrongdoing. While we all acknowledge that stealing is wrong, we understand why the thief does it. His motive is not to inflict suffering, but rather to gain something for himself. In contrast, the gossip's primary motive is entirely negative: to cause another a loss of status or worse, without gaining any tangible benefit for himself (other than the feeling that his status has been raised by lowering that of the other). Since the gossip's behavior cannot be attributed to giving in to a base but self-serving instinct, it is, in a certain way, worse than a conventional sin, a sort of evil for evil's sake.[4]

———

The Talmud offers this parable: "In the future, all the animals will assemble and come to the snake and say to it: 'A lion claws its prey and eats it. A wolf kills its prey and eats it [that is, each of these animals derives benefit from its acts of aggression]. But you, the snake, what benefit do you derive from poisoning people and killing them?' And the snake will answer: 'And what benefit does one who speaks lashon hara *against others derive?'* " (Ta'anit 8a).

Shakespeare expressed a similar sentiment:

> *Who steals my purse steals trash . . .*
> *But he that filches from me my good name*
> *Robs me of that which not enriches him*
> *And makes me poor indeed. (Othello, Act 3, scene 3)*

———

For the most common reasons people gossip, and what this reveals about their character, see chapter 40.

Why lashon hara *is self-destructive*

17. Instead of seeing the divine image in others, gossips look at others' flaws intently and incessantly; as a result, they view many people as irritating, disappointing, and untrustworthy (Chana Nestlebaum).[5] By speaking ill of those around them, gossips come to find the world an inhospitable and often unhappy place.

Just as people who think and speak well of others are more likely to have an upbeat attitude and be pleased with their lives, those who speak ill of others are more likely to be unhappy and pessimistic. Thus, ceasing to speak *lashon hara* almost invariably increases our personal happiness and sense of well-being.

———

Dr. Antonio Wood, a psychiatrist, notes that when we speak badly of someone, we alienate ourselves from that person. Generally, the more negative our observations, the more distant we feel from the person whom we are discussing. Thus a person who speaks overcritically and unfairly of many people comes to distance

*and alienate himself from many individuals and, as Dr. Wood points out, alien-
ation is a major cause of depression, one of the most widespread and rapidly growing disorders in America.*

———

18. Ridiculing or denigrating others for not conforming to our vision of
how people should behave reinforces a gossip's sense of superiority. Thus a
gossip is rarely humble. And humility, as we know from the Torah's description of Moses (Numbers 12:3), is an important quality to possess.

19. Speaking *lashon hara* lowers other people's opinion of us. The Chaffetz
Chayyim notes that if a man habitually complains to his wife of offensive
things others have said and done to him (the emphasis is on "habitually"),
she will begin to believe that he is not well regarded by his peers, and will
probably come to lose respect for him.[6] Thus, constantly carping about others' behavior toward us can cause the opposite effect of what we intend, lowering the regard in which we are held more than it lowers the regard of those
about whom we are speaking.

———

*A woman told me how her husband complained to her each evening about how
unfairly other people treated him. Often he would start to weep in her arms. After
some time, noticing how often he himself criticized others—herself included—
she stopped feeling sympathy for him; ultimately, she came to regard him as hostile and a whiner. Not surprisingly, the couple eventually divorced.*

———

Lashon hara *as an act of self-destruction*

20. According to the Talmud, the regular speaking of *lashon hara* makes
a person unworthy of reward in the Afterlife (*Sotah* 42a). Rabbi Zelig Pliskin
explains: "A person can be successful in business and nevertheless end up
penniless. This is possible if he has expenses that devour his profits. The
same applies to [the commandments]. One can amass a large amount of merits from Torah study and good deeds, but will be left empty-handed on the
day of reckoning if he habitually slanders [and speaks ill of] others."[7]

Although the secular society in which we live generally regards speaking
unfairly of others as a minor vice, Judaism regards it as a heinous offense.

38

THE DUST OF FORBIDDEN SPEECH

1. The Hebrew term *avak lashon hara* ("the dust of forbidden speech") refers to both verbal and nonverbal stratagems that lower someone's reputation without seeming to violate the laws of *lashon hara,* for example, when we praise another, but do so in a manner that inevitably stimulates discussion about the person's weaknesses: "Who of us who knew Martin years ago would have guessed that he would achieve the success he now has?" Or, "I really like Ron. I don't care what anybody else says." Since such statements focus attention on the person's past or present shortcomings, they are forbidden.

2. Another, more malicious example of "the dust of forbidden speech" is to say, upon hearing someone's name, "Don't talk to me about Barbara, I don't want to say what I know about her," or, "Don't make me speak about him, since I'm trying to avoid *lashon hara*" (see Maimonides, "Laws of Character Development" 7:4). Obviously, such statements are invitations to *lashon hara.* Even in the rare instance in which comments like this don't prompt such a discussion, they will cause the hearer to become suspicious of the person spoken of.

3. It is wrong to praise someone if doing so will stimulate negative comments. Thus we should not extol a person in front of a group where there are people who dislike him or her. Such comments almost inevitably lead to *lashon hara,* particularly after we leave, since many people cannot tolerate hearing good things said about someone they dislike.

For a further discussion of this point, see page 138.

4. We should also refrain from extravagantly praising a businessman or a professional in the presence of that person's competitors or colleagues. Because most people's competitive instinct is strong, it will probably be difficult for those to whom we are speaking to refrain from offering critical com-

ments. A somewhat hyperbolic Midrash teaches that "every craftsman hates his fellow craftsmen" (*Genesis Rabbah* 32:2). Thus, for example, it is best to refrain from asking a doctor his opinion of another physician who practices the same specialty in the same city or neighborhood. If we need to get a fair assessment, we should ask a doctor in a related specialty, or one who practices the same specialty in a different city.

5. Don't praise someone in the presence of those who might use the information you provide to take advantage of the person. In such a case, the Talmud rules that it is permitted to lie—for example, by downplaying or even denying another's hospitality—in a situation in which telling the truth will prompt others to take advantage of the host's generous nature (*Bava Mezia* 23b–24a; see pages 434–435). In contemporary terms, it would be inappropriate, for example, to speak at length about another's financial generosity, thereby causing many people and organizations to solicit, and possibly pester, the person for contributions. What is required in such cases is common sense and discretion, telling those who might be inspired by the person's generosity, and not those who will take advantage of it.

The Talmud speaks of a well-meaning but naïve guest who stayed in a house where the host expended great efforts on his behalf. The next morning he told the townspeople, "May God bless so-and-so who did so much on my behalf." Whereupon, those who heard the man's report ruined the host by taking advantage of his generosity (Arachin 16a).

---

6. A particularly ugly type of *avak lashon hara* occurs when we cause someone trouble while pretending to have innocent intentions. The Talmud offers an example of such hypocritical and mean-spirited behavior: Several Jewish leaders in the city of Sephoris (in the Galilee) were summoned to a meeting at the royal court. One of the leaders, Yochanan, didn't go. Another leader, resentful that Yochanan was getting away with not coming, said in a voice loud enough for the Roman officials to overhear, "Let's visit Yochanan today." The Romans realized that Yochanan was absent, and had him summoned (Jerusalem Talmud, *Peah* 1:1).

Maimonides refers to people who engage in such ruses as those "who speak *lashon hara* slyly" ("Laws of Character Development" 7:4).

People sometimes do this by pretending to be concerned. For example, we might say, "I feel so badly for Laura. She's getting divorced. It seems she heard that her husband was cheating on her. Is that what you heard, too? What can we do to help her?" Only we know if our concern is really to help, or just to find out more details about this woman's tragedy. And if our concern is to help, do we really need more details?

7. Maimonides also condemns those who speak *lashon hara* in a frivolous manner, claiming that they are joking and intend no harm ("Laws of Character Development" 7:4). Whether or not their intentions are pure, however, there is a good chance that emotional harm will result. For example, some years ago a website published a parody interview with the popular singer Mariah Carey. In it, she spoke about her difficulties in staying thin: "When I watch TV and see those poor starving kids all over the world, I can't help but cry. I mean, I'd love to be skinny like that, but not with all those flies and death and stuff." Although Carey never made such a callous remark, many mainstream news sources, believing the interview had taken place, reported her alleged remarks as fact. For years Carey was forced to deny the quote, which had provoked tremendous and enduring anger against her.

8. Other instances of "the dust of forbidden speech" involve sarcasm, saying something positive about another person and then offering a sarcastic laugh ("Yeah, we all know he's a real genius. Ha! Ha! Ha!"). Equally wrong is rolling your eyes when a person's name is mentioned, or praising someone but then clearing your throat in a manner that indicates that you mean exactly the opposite of what you said.

9. It is forbidden to show people an unflattering photo of someone, even if you make no comment. If, after developing a roll of film, you find that some photographs make their subject look awful (and the person would be embarrassed to have other people see them), you should destroy the pictures, and certainly not share them with others.

Some newspapers, usually tabloids, keep in their files unflattering pictures of prominent people, then print them when they have occasion to report something negative about that person.

10. We are also forbidden to show others a letter in which a person has made spelling or grammatical mistakes, if our purpose is to cause people to demean the letter writer. What matters is intention. Thus we are permitted to show others a letter a child has written from camp that contains age-appropriate mistakes. But to subject someone to ridicule is wrong.

39

HOW TO AVOID SPEAKING
UNFAIRLY OF OTHERS

Getting started

1. The Talmud teaches that all of us, on almost a daily basis, say or imply unfair things about others (*Bava Bathra* 165a). Therefore the battle against *lashon hara* is one that we must fight one day at a time. Our goal should be to observe as much of these laws as we can, even if our efforts are not always successful.

Although some people are disturbed that Jewish law includes a commandment that cannot be fully observed, this is not the only law of which this is true. How many of us can claim that we never violate the Torah's most famous command, "Love your neighbor as yourself" (Leviticus 19:18)? Yet this law causes many of us to act on a higher ethical level than we would otherwise. In the same way, the prohibition against talebearing helps restrain us—even when tempted—from speaking ill of others; even if we do say something we shouldn't, we share it with fewer people.

———

Jewish law distinguishes between those who occasionally speak lashon hara, *and those who are* ba'alei lashon hara *(habitual speakers of* lashon hara*). In the preface to his book,* Chaffetz Chayyim, *the Chaffetz Chayyim (he was known in Jewish life by the name of his book) comments: "You will find that the study of these laws will make you more aware of* lashon hara *so that even if, God forbid, you should stumble, you will at least not be in the category of a habitual speaker* *of* lashon hara *who, our Sages say, will not merit to greet the Divine Presence [in the next world]"* (Sotah 42a).

———

2. Because it sometimes comes naturally to many of us to say mean things, spread rumors, and mislead people, we need divine help to refrain from doing so.

Thus, although Jews don't pray, "Please, God, help me not to steal," Jews who pray the traditional *Shmoneh Esrei* prayer daily conclude with the words, "God, keep my tongue from speaking evil, and my lips from speaking guile."

3. Rabbi Yossi taught, "I never made a statement for which I would have to turn around and check whether the person about whom I was speaking was present" (*Arachin* 15b). Rabbi Abraham Twerski advises, "Even if one does not have time to master all of the scholarly works on the subject [of proper speech], a reliable rule of thumb is to ask: 'Do I need to look behind me before I say it?' If the answer is yes, do not say it."[1] Indeed, this advice is reminiscent of a Yiddish proverb: "What is straight talk to your face is slander behind your back."

4. Choose one day, perhaps the first day of each month, as a Speak No Evil Day. For twenty-four hours, guard your tongue from saying anything negative *about* or *to* anyone. And, on the other days of the month, choose a two-hour period each day when you will be particularly careful to speak no *lashon hara*. Some people agree to do this, then jokingly resolve to carry out their commitment between 3:00 and 5:00 A.M. It is best to schedule the two hours during a period that includes a meal, for this is when many of us are likely to speak *lashon hara*.

———

If the above seems too demanding, try this: Over the coming week, make sure that at least once a day you resist saying a negative truth about someone.

———

5. We should make a particular effort not to speak *lashon hara* during the Friday-night Shabbat dinner, which, for most traditional Jews, is the longest, most leisurely meal of the week. Because there is more time for conversation than at other meals, this is often the meal at which the most *lashon hara* is spoken.

Avoiding *lashon hara* requires vigilance on the part of the meal's participants; for most of us, it is hard to refrain from speaking about other people's flaws or about the intimate details of their lives. It also can be difficult to reprove those who start speaking negatively of others. Many of us don't want to sound self-righteous by saying, "Please stop speaking *lashon hara*." Therefore, a family should institute a code word or phrase, such as "Let's speak of pleasanter things" when the conversation starts drifting into *lashon hara*.

6. One offense for which Jews repent on Yom Kippur is "the sin we committed before You by speaking *lashon hara*." Yet many people who say this don't follow through by making an effort to stop gossiping. Such a confession becomes as meaningless as a thief reciting during the service, "For the sin I committed before you by stealing," and then leaving the service and going out to steal.

This year, on Yom Kippur when we recite, "For the sin we committed before You by speaking *lashon hara*," we should stop and think of at least one negative comment we made about another to someone who had no need of this information. We should resolve not to make such comments (or to make many fewer of them) in the future. At the very least, we should make sure that we don't sully Yom Kippur by speaking *lashon hara*.

7. Even though we should judge ourselves more critically than we do others, we should not speak *lashon hara* about ourselves, either. The Torah verse that commands us to "love your neighbor as yourself" (Leviticus 19:18) implicitly mandates that we love ourselves. Just as we would not wish to hear others speaking ill of someone whom we love, so too should we not speak ill of someone we are supposed to love: ourselves.

———

The Chaffetz Chayyim frequently traveled to Jewish communities throughout Eastern Europe to give lectures, often on the subject of lashon hara *and fair speech. During one trip, a man sat down opposite him on the train. The two men started speaking, and when the Chaffetz Chayyim asked the man where he was headed, he answered, "I'm going into the city to hear the Chaffetz Chayyim speak. He's the greatest sage and saint in the Jewish world today."*

Embarrassed by the man's words, the Chaffetz Chayyim said, "People say very exaggerated things about him, things that aren't even true. I know the Chaffetz Chayyim very well, and he's not such a great scholar, and he's certainly no saint."

The man was incensed. "How dare you speak like that about such a great man?" he said, and slapped the Chaffetz Chayyim in the face.

That evening the man attended the lecture, where he saw, to his horror, that the man whom he had slapped was none other than the Chaffetz Chayyim. As soon as the speech ended, he rushed over to the rabbi, "Please, please, forgive me. I had no idea it was you."

The Chaffetz Chayyim smiled and responded: "You have no reason to request forgiveness. It was my honor you were defending. On the contrary, I learned from you an important lesson. For decades I've been teaching people not to speak lashon hara *about others. Now I've learned that it's also wrong to speak* lashon hara *about oneself."*

––––

There are times when we should acknowledge our weaknesses to others, to help inspire them to improve ("If I could overcome this, so can you"; see page 389), because we need to speak openly about ourselves to our spouse or to others with whom we are intimate, and also in a therapeutic setting.

Telephone conversations, letters, and e-mail

8. The telephone serves as one of the most popular vehicles for unfair speech. Some religious Jews keep a picture of the Chaffetz Chayyim near their phones to remind them not to speak ill of others. We can also attach a little sticker to our phone with the words "No *lashon hara*" on it.

9. Before sending a letter or e-mail, check the contents. Is there some comment or information in it that will harm someone's reputation? Ask yourself whether there is a legitimate need to share this information; if there isn't, delete it.

––––

Such care is particularly important in the case of e-mail. A friend told me of an incident in which someone he knew wrote something disparaging about another person's spouse and then mistakenly sent the note to his entire e-mail list instead of to the one person for whom it was intended. Similarly, be careful before you forward an article containing lashon hara. *Ask yourself: Does the person to whom I am forwarding this need the information?*

––––

On not slipping into lashon hara

10. We need to watch our words even when what we are saying is positive. As a clearly hyperbolic statement in the Talmud puts it, "Let no man ever talk in praise of his neighbor, for through talking in his praise, he will come to disparage him" (*Arachin* 16a). The Rabbis realized that even conversations that start positively can quickly deteriorate. Thus, if we were asked to spend twenty minutes talking to a friend about a person we know in common, it's unlikely that the two of us would spend the entire time exclaiming, "Oh, you know that story which shows how nice she is, I know an even nicer story." It is far more likely that we will soon start sharing negative observations and gossip about the other person.

Similarly, if someone says to us, "I love so-and-so; I think he's a great guy. There's only one thing I can't stand about him," we will probably spend the next fifteen minutes speaking about that "one thing."

What is usually most interesting about others is what's not so nice about them, what might even be a little scandalous. As Isaac Bashevis Singer, the Nobel Prize–winning Yiddish writer, used to say, "Even good people don't like to read novels about good people."

Commonly justified, but still forbidden, speech

11. Three frequent—and invalid—excuses people give for speaking *lashon hara*:

- "But it's true." (Irrelevant: Do you believe everybody has the right to know everything true about you?)
- "I didn't actually say anything bad about the fellow" (when you have hinted at a flaw; see the preceding chapter).
- "I did the same thing myself" (and maybe you don't mind if people know about it, but the other person might).[2]

12. Don't tell others about a good person's past misdemeanors. For example, don't inform people that someone whom you have good reason to believe is honest used to be known for his shady business practices. In the past, you would have been right to warn someone who was contemplating entering into a business relationship with this person, but to cast a shadow over the person now because of his past misbehavior (of which he has now repented) is, from Judaism's perspective, unfair and wrong. Yet many of us,

aware of something scandalous in another person's (or her family's) past, exercise no restraint over our tongues, and share this information with many others.

This is admittedly a problematic issue, and should not apply to all of someone's former wrongdoings. Thus, in the United States, convicted child molesters, even after they have been punished and released from prison, are still legally obligated to be registered and publicized as such. In effect, the law says that it would be more unforgivable, even when unlikely, to allow them to prey on unsuspecting neighbors. In addition, there are also many instances of con men convicted in one state, who are released from prison and go on to practice cons in other cities. Then, when caught again and released from prison, they go to yet another city. In cases like these, should not the community be warned? Yes. That's why each of these instances has to be examined on a case-by-case basis.

13. Because *lashon hara* refers to a verbal offense that can harm someone, it is also forbidden to speak *lashon hara* about another's merchandise. The Chaffetz Chayyim teaches, "To our misfortune, it is very common for a storekeeper to degrade the merchandise of his competitor, or to engage in similar practices out of jealousy—and this is full-fledged *lashon hara*, which the Torah prohibits."[3] Thus, while Jewish ethics protects the right of a business owner to promote his own product, it opposes denigrating a competitor's product (it would oppose such advertising as well).

14. Be particularly careful with your words when speaking of an adversary. Unfortunately, when speaking of those whom we don't like, we often permit ourselves to violate the laws of *lashon hara*, rationalizing that the person about whom we are speaking is so clearly in the wrong that she has forfeited the right to be protected by these laws. Yet the laws of fair speech are not intended to prevent only the defaming of ourselves and those we like, but are also meant to protect from defamation those we dislike or with whom we disagree.

———

Unfair and excessive denunciations have been a common feature of interdenominational Jewish conflicts. Marc Shapiro, the biographer of the great twentieth-century Orthodox scholar, Rabbi Yechiel Yaakov Weinberg, notes that in one of the rabbi's responsa, he expresses concern that no negative gossip be spread about a Reform rabbi, a view that Shapiro calls "surely an uncommon sentiment among Orthodox decisors."4 But such a sentiment shouldn't be uncommon. The fact that we think someone is wrong in one important area or another should not lead us to impugn or judge him unfairly. As I write this, Americans recently went through a bruising presidential campaign between President George W. Bush and Senator John Kerry. I repeatedly found supporters of both candidates who seemed to assume that there was something wrong either with the character or intelligence of anyone who supported the candidate whom they opposed.

When speaking of public figures

15. "He who blesses his neighbor in a loud voice in the morning, by the evening it shall be thought a curse" (Proverbs 27:14). Jewish tradition understands this verse as meaning that even when someone comes into the public eye for a good reason, he will be subjected to such public scrutiny that, eventually, incidents of a personal nature which he would have wanted kept secret will become known, and his reputation will be damaged. Everyone, including heroes and public figures, should be afforded areas of privacy. We must learn to accept that we do not have the right to know all the details of anyone's life. The refusal to abide by such a standard causes many good people to avoid entering public life. (For example, even if you have led an overwhelmingly virtuous life, would you wish to pursue public office if that would cause every embarrassing thing you've ever done to become publicly known?) Furthermore, the standard of full disclosure does not in any way guarantee that the character of those pursuing public office will be on a high level. As political commentator Charles Krauthammer has observed, "If we insist that public life be reserved for those whose personal history is pristine, we are not going to get paragons of virtue running our affairs. We will get the very rich, who will contract out the messy things in life; the very dull, who have nothing to hide and nothing to show; and the very devious, expert at covering their tracks and ambitious enough to risk their discovery."5

16. The next time a scandal is publicized, whether it concerns a politician running for office, or someone in our community, if we believe that the issue does not reflect upon the person's ability to do her job, we should resolve that this is one scandal we will avoid discussing. It takes great willpower to do so, but then, all acts of ethical transformation do.

———

During the 1988 presidential primaries, one candidate, a front-runner, was caught by journalists in an extramarital relationship. The news was publicized and the man was forced to withdraw from the race.

Over the years I have asked dozens of audiences, "How many of you feel that the public had no right to know that this man was engaged in an extramarital relationship?" Generally, more than eighty percent of the audience vote that the public had no right to this information. But when I ask the follow-up question, "How many of you, as a result of that belief, refused to read about this relationship, and turned off your television when it was announced that they would now show photographs of the woman with whom the candidate had been seen?" almost everyone laughs, and few people raise their hands.

It requires great self-control not to read about another's scandal. While not many of us can exercise such self-control all the time, we should make an effort to do so as often as possible, and refrain from reading about or discussing a scandal that is not our business or that of other people.

In deciding whether the public has the right to know about such matters, the following guideline seems appropriate: If a highly placed public figure publicly acknowledges that he or she engages in adultery, that is something the public has the right to know. Officials who hold high positions serve as role models, and if they believe that monogamy is not, and should not be, presented as an ideal, then people should know that before voting for them. Otherwise, civility dictates that human beings should have a sphere of privacy that remains respected, and that will not be invaded.

Even journalists who publicize such scandals know that. Indeed, not surprisingly, the very journalist who pressed this candidate on the matter of his alleged adultery was subsequently asked by a magazine the same questions he had posed to the candidate: "Do you consider adultery immoral?" and "Have you ever committed adultery?" The journalist answered "Yes" to the first question, and "None of your business" to the second. In other words, even those who spread lashon hara *don't want to be its victims.* *

———

*As regards the commonly voiced argument that a public official, such as a president, who cheats on his spouse cannot be trusted not to cheat elsewhere, there is, in my view, little evidence to support this belief. As far as we know, President Richard Nixon was a lifelong monogamist, but he nonetheless misused his office in other ways, his monogamy notwithstanding. We also know of several presidents who committed adultery, and one would be hard put to find a connection between their wrongful behavior and their leadership of the country. One of the great generals in the State of Israel's history was a man widely known to have been a far from model husband, but there is no reason to believe that he acted in any way other than honorably in overseeing the country's army, and in ably defending its citizens.

As to how we should respond if a candidate we support spreads *lashon hara* about his opponent, see page 293.

When you're tempted to speak lashon hara

17. Before saying something negative about another, ask yourself three questions:

- Even if what I am saying is completely true, is it fair?
- Does the person I am speaking to need to know this?
- Is there positive information about the person's actions and/or motives that I'm omitting?

18. Another method to stop yourself from spreading negative information about someone: Think about something that you would not like others to know about you, then think of how appreciative you would be if someone knew this information and didn't pass it on.

19. Before speaking *lashon hara,* imagine that you will have to approach the victim of your words afterward to beg for forgiveness. Visualize yourself going to the person and telling him or her precisely what you said. Consider how upsetting this would be.

———

Even if you do ask forgiveness, once someone learns that you have spoken ill of her, there's a good chance she will never be able to make a full peace with you; she'll always remember what you said. Wouldn't you?

The Rabbis note that even if you apologize to the person about whom you've spoken and even if he accepts your apology, "inside he is still burning" (Jerusalem Talmud, Peah 1:1).

———

Alan Morinis, a contemporary student of Mussar, comments, "Curbing our speech may be difficult, but it is certainly less difficult than indulging 'the evil tongue' and then having to clean up the mess we have created."[6]

———

Lashon hara *and non-Jews*

20. The law that states, "Do not go about as a talebearer among *your people*" (Leviticus 19:16; emphasis added) seems to be directed only toward Jews; in other words, don't bear tales or speak negatively and unfairly about your fellow Jews. In legal works on *lashon hara*, it is generally assumed that we are forbidden to speak *lashon hara* only of fellow Jews. In a democracy like the United States, however, Jews have full equality, and are regarded, both by themselves and by non-Jews, as part of the American people. Therefore the laws prohibiting *lashon hara* should apply as well to the non-Jews among whom we live (unlike, for example, medieval Europe or Jews living under Roman occupation). In short, American Jews, as Americans and Jews, belong to two people, and have obligations to both.

When lying is permitted

21. If a person asks, or even presses, us to relate what someone has said about him, and what the other said was negative, we are forbidden to answer the questioner. If our refusal to do so causes the questioner to believe that the other person spoke badly of him, then, in order not to cause conflict, we are permitted to mislead the questioner as to the other person's comments ("Oh sure, he feels good about you"). The Chaffetz Chayyim rules that, in the worst-case scenario, if there is no other possibility, "it is permitted to tell a complete lie (*sheker gamur*) because of peace" (*Chaffetz Chayyim*, "Laws of *Rechilut*" 1:8).

For instances when we should tell someone the negative things another has said, see page 369).

Between adults and children

22. Discourage children from speaking unfairly of others (but don't deter them from transmitting relevant negative information, such as if an adult has behaved inappropriately toward them). Rabbi Yehuda Siegel, the Manchester, England, Rosh Yeshiva, emphasized that such teaching must begin during a child's formative years: "If a child is permitted to speak whatever enters his mind, with no one to admonish him, he establishes a habit that is very difficult to change, so that even when this child matures and is made aware of these violations, he will find it extremely difficult to be on guard."[7]

———

Dr. Isaac Herschkopf has expressed strong disagreement with the above view. While I am not certain I fully agree with Dr. Herschkopf's critique, I feel it is important to include his objection:

"Because the relationship between parent and child is so critical to the child's development, we should want our children to tell us everything, so they feel they have someone to talk to. If my child sees his classmate cheating, and tells me about it, should I admonish him? True, it is lashon hara, *but it is also cathartic for him to talk about it. If I stop him, he will feel rejected by me, and scarred by the experience. Far better, therefore, to allow, indeed encourage, children to speak their mind and then to discuss with them why they feel that way and whether or not their feelings are fair, or healthy."*

In reading Dr. Herschkopf's critique, it occurs to me that perhaps the issue is age. Therefore, we should not stop a young child from sharing such information. But as children start to get older, they can usually distinguish between information they need to tell you (such as that some children got in trouble in school for some prank they played) from that which they don't (such as the names of the children involved). Thus, I noticed that by the time my children reached the fourth and fifth grades, they would not generally mention the name of a child who did something wrong in school because, as they said, "It's lashon hara.*"*

———

23. We should refrain from asking our children to tell us *lashon hara*, for example, by asking our son or daughter the identity of a child who did poorly on a test. Jewish law encourages children, when asked a question like this, not to answer, just as it encourages children whose parents ask them to violate the Sabbath laws not to do so.

We should also not say to a child, "Tell me what so-and-so said about me." In this case, too, the child should not answer (see the book *Chaffetz Chayyim*, "Laws of *Rechilut*," 1:5). Making a request like this puts a child in a very uncomfortable situation, which is why we should refrain from doing so, unless there is some valid reason for us to know.

———

Adhering to this law encourages children to develop a sense of conscience, by learning that they, like their parents, are obliged to obey a Higher Authority.

———

24. If we have a real need to know the identity of the child who has done something wrong (such as when our child or another child is being bullied), and our son or daughter is reluctant to reveal this information, we should explain that in such a case, but not in general, it is right to reveal the culprit's identity, since it may lead to less suffering and pain.

See chapter 41 for a discussion of when it is morally permitted to speak *lashon hara.*

25. Teachers should not ask children to "tattle" on one another ("Tell me who wrote that rude comment on the blackboard when I walked out of the room!"). Rabbi Moshe Feinstein, the twentieth century's most authoritative figure on questions of Jewish law, ruled that it is an "ugly thing" for a teacher to insist that students inform on one another, and that it will cause the children not to take the laws of *lashon hara* seriously.[8]

However, when a student comes to a teacher without prompting to tell her of improper behavior by a peer so that the teacher can influence that child, the teacher may listen to this information, and should not stop the student from speaking (for example, by saying, "I don't want to hear this. It's *lashon hara.*"). Only if the teacher senses that the student's motivation is to get the other child in trouble should she stop the student, and be cautious about accepting as true what she has been told.

26. Teachers should be careful about what they write in student evaluations, particularly if these assessments are sent to parents. For example, if a teacher knows that a child's parents are very strict, elaborating on the child's negative behavior can cause undue suffering.

The Chaffetz Chayyim, writing at a time when many children were orphans being raised by foster parents, noted that all adults, not just teachers, should take care what they say about a child's flaws, lest such remarks lead the foster parents to drive the child from the house.[9] Today, of course, there are fewer children in such circumstances, but because of the high rates of divorce and remarriage, there are many "blended families" in which one of the parents raising the child is a stepparent. Often, stepparents view a child's negative behavior more critically than biological parents. Therefore, teachers and other adults should be aware that speaking very critically of the child to a stepparent can have more negative consequences than are justified.

When people start to tell you lashon hara

27. Not only should we not speak *lashon hara;* we should also not listen to it. When we listen, we become like those who buy stolen goods from thieves; without such people, thieves would lose much of their motivation to steal. Similarly, without listeners, speakers of *lashon hara* would be less motivated to utter it.

Ideally, therefore, if someone starts to speak *lashon hara* to us, we should ask the person to refrain from doing so. If we don't feel close enough to the person to offer such a reproof, then we should do so in a nonconfrontational manner, for example, by changing the subject. If that too is impossible, and we find ourself in a group that is being told *lashon hara*, we should not let our facial expression show interest in, or approval of, what is being said. We should try to appear stern-faced or withdrawn, and resolve in our heart not to accept the negative gossip as true, or at least not as the whole truth. Obviously the best approach is simply to excuse ourselves when the *lashon hara* begins (ideally, we should also explain why we are leaving).

———

A well-known but rarely observed talmudic passage teaches, "Why do human fingers resemble pegs? So that if one hears something improper, one can plug one's fingers in one's ears" (Ketubot 5b). If you are comfortable doing this, such a gesture can show the speaker you don't want to listen to lashon hara, *without having to reprove him directly. However, several friends with whom I shared this suggestion argued that such an unusual action might be interpreted as so weird or hostile as to be counterproductive.*

———

28. We should consider carefully how we conduct ourselves with those friends with whom we spend a great deal of time. Some people bring out the good in us; with others we feel the need to act cynically, and speak critically of others. We should try to minimize our time with those acquaintances who have the tendency to attribute bad motives to others, and who routinely share *lashon hara* with us.

How to make yourself almost lashon hara–proof

29. We should train ourselves not to regard others in a critical manner (see chapters 5 and 6 on judging others fairly). One way is to spend less time thinking about other people's behavior, and more time thinking about our

own. For example, we should analyze why we are drawn to certain kinds of negative behavior (Do we have a mean temper? Are we completely honest in financial matters?). Rabbi Chaim Kramer writes, "When a person thinks about himself—how distant he is from perfecting his own personality, improving himself, and acquiring good qualities—he won't spend his time and efforts attempting to belittle and bring dishonor to another."[10]

Repenting for lashon hara

30. If we have spoken *lashon hara* about someone, we should try to undo the damage by seeking out the people we spoke to, and explaining that what we said, or at least some of it, was unfair. If we believe that what we said was accurate but should not have been shared with others, we should explain that it was wrong of us to pass it on, and ask the others to not repeat what we said. We should also apologize for having involved them in a transgression against Jewish law and ethics. Whenever appropriate, we should go out of our way to speak up on the person's behalf, citing positive things we know about him or her.*

As regards confessing to the person about whom we spoke *lashon hara* what we said, see pages 164–165.

The benefits of observing the laws of lashon hara

31. It is hard to be in possession of scandalous and damaging information about others—particularly when we know it will interest people and make us seem well informed—and not spread it. But, Jewish ethics teaches that this is something God wants us to do. Indeed, to paraphrase Rabbi Harold Kushner's insightful observation about anger (see page 274), "Only God can give us credit for the gossip we know and do not spread."

32. Learning to control our tongues, perhaps the most difficult faculty to control (the Chaffetz Chayyim used to lament that people are lazy in the

---

*If you can't think of anything positive to say about the person, then the chances are you are guilty of *sinat chinam,* hatred that is, at least in part, without cause. People guilty of such an offense invariably exaggerate the flaws of the person whom they dislike, and are blind to acts of goodness performed by that person. Therefore it becomes impossible for such people to speak about the person without violating the laws of *lashon hara.*

use of every organ except the tongue) will help us gain self-control in other areas as well, which is indispensable for being a good—and a successful—person. As we learn to govern our tongues, we will say fewer hurtful things to those around us, and our relationships will become more harmonious.

———

Throughout the day, we will have to consider what we are saying so that we don't cause pain or damage to others. Eventually this preoccupation with goodness, sensitivity, and ethical speech will become an important part of who we are (Chana Nestlebaum).[11]

———

33. Observing the laws of *lashon hara* demands good judgment—for example, an ability to realize that the same statement made about two different people can reflect differently on each of them. To say that a person of modest means donated $250 to a charitable cause praises that individual, but to say the same of a person known to be very wealthy is *lashon hara*. If you exercise good judgment, and anyone who observes these laws will have to do so frequently, you will become a wiser and fairer person.

If you are going to gossip anyway . . .

34. Limit the number of people with whom you gossip. Thus, if we hear something unusual and perhaps negative about a mutual friend, we will probably relate it to our spouse or partner, and perhaps one or two close friends. But we should make sure to stop there. Obviously, even this situation is not ideal, since our friends will probably share the news with their close friends.

The issue of whether we should share negative information and opinions about others with our spouse is a difficult one. On the one hand, Jewish law, as understood by the Chaffetz Chayyim, demands that all of us who learn personal information about others treat it with the same discretion that secular society demands from lawyers, physicians, and clergy; just as we expect such people not to share professional confidences with their spouses, so too does Jewish law demand the same from every individual. On the other hand, professional confidences are not usually about the people whom the professional and his/her spouse know in common. It is unrealistic to expect that most couples will not transmit any negative information and opinions about friends or relatives to each other. Nor, as I heard a friend argue, is that necessarily even desirable: "If you never speak about people with your partner, you're probably not very intimate with each other." One of the ways in which couples establish intimacy is by noting their reactions to ethical dilemmas, news events, plays and movies—and other people.

Therefore, how much should one speak about others with one's spouse? I leave this as an open issue, and ask only that those who do engage in such gossip adhere to the following guideline: If you are going to gossip (with a small number of people), develop a way of talking about others that is as kind and fair as you would want others to be when saying things about you that, although true, are not complimentary.

———

Psychiatrist Isaac Herschkopf, in a private communication to the author, offers a perspective on lashon hara *between a husband and wife, or with others with whom we are close, built around the following case:*

"Let me offer a real-life, disguised example, to which I was privy. Jack, an officer in a synagogue, discovers that his revered rabbi has impregnated a local high school girl. When Jack arrives home, agitated and upset, does he have the right to tell his wife why? I can't imagine a more therapeutic, cathartic conversation. The following Shabbat, the rabbi announces his resignation, explaining that he needs to devote his precious time and intellect to Jewish study, instead of being caught up in the many activities of a pulpit rabbi. At lunch, Jack's brother-in-law goes on and on about how they, members of the synagogue, were not worthy of so great a spiritual giant. Jack and his wife become increasingly frustrated at her brother's well-meaning, albeit ill-informed, tribute to their departing rabbi. Her brother decides that he will raise money to pay off the rabbi's mortgage, and asks Jack to match his very generous contribution. Must Jack and his wife suffer in silence, appear cheap and ungrateful, and allow their relationship with her brother and his wife to deteriorate, to protect the guilty?

"There are innumerable other examples. Does an incest victim have the right to explain to relatives and/or well-meaning friends why she won't invite her father to her family celebrations? There are too many examples where the inappropriate application of lashon hara *further penalizes innocent victims who have already suffered too much.*

"I realize that this is a slippery slope. How discreet will Jack's brother-in-law be? (There really is no reason for everyone in the synagogue to know what happened.) Also, what defines a close friend, and with whom can we share such information? Any time we disseminate information we are taking a risk. However, not sharing anything with anyone (except your therapist) is not a healthy recipe for marriage, or for life. As always, we have to balance the needs of the individual with the needs of society."

———

When gossip and slander are spread about you

35. How should we respond when we are the victim of unfair gossip and slander? For example, is it permitted for us to spread truthful but damaging information that will lower the status of the person spreading the false report? The *Sefer HaHinnuch,* a standard medieval exposition of the Torah's 613 commandments, rules that we are permitted to do what is necessary to protect our good name: "For there can be no doubt that a person is not obligated to endure injuries from the hand of his fellow, but rather has the right to [engage in self-defense and] save himself from the other's hand. Thus, likewise, a person may save himself from the words of the other's mouth, words that are filled with cunning and deceit, and he may do so with every means by which he can rescue himself" (commandment number 338). Therefore, if we are the victim of unfair speech, we should answer the calumnies and tell the truth of what has happened. If we know who is responsible for spreading the report, we are permitted not only to defend our name, but to say that the other person is lying. (If we have any reason to think it will help, we should first confront our accuser, and encourage him to retract what he has said.)

Even in defending ourselves, however, we should refrain from spreading any *lashon hara* about our opponent other than that which is necessary to protect our good name. Thus, if we can show instances where the person has lied about, or spoken unfairly of, us or others before, we should publicize this information.

Not only do we have the right to protect our good name, we have the obligation to protect the names of other people whom the slanderer, or spreader of *lashon hara*, might defame in the future.

———

Obviously, what should guide us in instances in which we are attacked is common sense. There are times when "starving a rumor" (or "starving" a true but negative report), and not discussing it—like starving a fire of oxygen—is the prudent thing to do.

———

Two final thoughts

36. We should treat the laws of *lashon hara* as seriously as religious Jews treat ritual offenses. Rabbi Zelig Pliskin, writing for an observant audience, teaches, "If you were told that the food you were in the midst of eating was unkosher, you would immediately spit it out. React similarly if you find yourself speaking *lashon hara*. Stop abruptly."[12]

37. "Have you heard something? Let it die with you. Be of good courage: it will not burst you" (Apocrypha, *The Wisdom of Ben Sirach* 19:10).

40

THE TEMPTATIONS OF GOSSIP

1. The most important reason we spread negative information and opinions about others is to diminish them and lower their status. Gossip, therefore, enables us to feel superior to others. That is why, as a rule, people gossip only about those whom they see as their social equals or superiors, and not about their maids and handymen, toward whom they already feel socially superior.

Jewish ethics encourages us to grow in humility by seeking out ways we can learn from others (see page 216), but speaking *lashon hara* reinforces our feelings of arrogance (Instead of thinking, "Look what I can learn from him," we think, "Look how much better I am than he is").

2. We also gossip so as to show that we know intimate details about people that others don't—in other words, to show that we are knowledgeable, well-informed people. Samuel Johnson observed, more than two centuries ago, that "the vanity of being trusted with a secret is generally the chief motive to disclose it." This desire to appear "in the know" causes many of us to become bad friends and betray confidences (a common occurrence if we are friendly with someone who is prominent, and know things about the person that others would be curious to learn).* Therefore, the desire to gossip is sometimes fed not by hostility, but by insecurity, and the craving to be regarded as an important person who knows things that others do not.

---

*"Prominent," in this case, does not refer only to a person who is known nationally; it could also refer to an instance in which a high school student gossips about her friend who is part of the "in crowd" or is captain of the basketball team.

Though understandable, such behavior is still reprehensible, particularly when it causes us to betray a friend's secrets.

3. We often speak *lashon hara* when we are angry at someone and want to damage that person's good name. Understandable as a desire for vengeance may be, Jewish law counsels those of us who have a grievance against someone to confront him directly, rather than to go about speaking ill of him. Many of us, however, lack the courage to do so (sometimes it can be risky to confront another—for example, when we are angry at our boss). Instead we take our revenge by denigrating the person and thereby diminishing the person's reputation.

This approach is both morally and tactically wrong. Morally, because it is unlikely that we will be able to speak fairly and accurately about the person with whom we are upset. Most of us exaggerate the wrong done by another when we are angry, and/or attribute evil motives to those who provoked our wrath.*

In addition, if we smear the person's name, he will probably learn what we have done, become enraged, and spread his version of what happened, which will lead to an escalation of the dispute. Therefore, the proper thing to do is either speak to the person with whom we are angry (but obviously not when we are most upset), or speak about the matter only to those who might help to bring about a resolution.

If neither alternative is feasible, and we feel the need to "let off steam," we should choose as our confidante a person who is likely to calm us ("I don't think he meant it the way you're thinking" or, "He was just upset and blew up. Don't take it so personally") rather than further provoke us ("He said that to you? What are you going to do about it?").

There are two additional benefits of learning to speak directly to those with whom we have a grievance. We will learn to be more courageous and forthright in our dealings with others. Also, we will grow in the process and be able to handle future confrontations better.

4. It is clear, then, that many of the primary motives for speaking *lashon hara* are undesirable character traits: the desire to feel superior to others, the need to be perceived as being important, and an inability to confront those with whom we are angry.

---

*Such vituperation is a common feature of fights that occur within Jewish communal life and within synagogues; indeed, an old Jewish joke claims that every Jew has one synagogue which he attends, and another in which he won't set foot.

These reasons, however, do not exhaust people's motives for gossiping about others, nor do all the motives reflect poor character on the part of those who gossip. We also gossip because people's lives are interesting, and are even more interesting when they have done something wrong, or even just surprising. It is interesting, for example, to know why a couple is divorcing, and to learn if the tensions in their marriage parallel tensions in our own. While we might find that speaking about the divorce with one or two people, such as our spouse, might help us in working on our own marriage, it is unfair and unnecessary to speak about it with others.

People also gossip at the workplace to be "in the loop," to know, for example, who might be losing a job, and who might be promoted. Again, the issue here has much to do with quantity—how many people we discuss the matter with, and how long we spend discussing it.

As a rule, in work settings no less than in more personal areas, the most important person on whom to focus is oneself. This is self-serving advice as well. People who are perceived as busybodies or gossips are unlikely to be the ones receiving the promotions, since such people are generally regarded as unsubstantial and untrustworthy. As a rule, they are.

41

WHEN *LASHON HARA* IS ALLOWED

1. Although it is almost always wrong to speak *lashon hara,* there is one time it is permitted to do so: when the person to whom we are speaking has a legitimate need to know something negative about another. In such a case we are permitted, and sometimes even required, to share this information. For example, it is permitted to speak *lashon hara le'toelet* ("for a purpose") when someone consults with us on whether or not she should hire a certain person for a job. Thus, if we are asked about a former employee who has applied elsewhere for a position, and we know that the person was often tardy, did not do the work as instructed, or was otherwise incompetent or dishonest, we are permitted, and perhaps even obligated, to give accurate answers about that person's work performance. True, doing so might damage our former employee's prospects for getting the job, but since hiring such a person

is likely to cause damage to the future employer, she has the right to this information.

2. In addition to being accurate, the information we convey must be specific. Thus we should not, for example, simply say, "Trust me, you don't want this guy working for you." Rather, we should tell the person what it is about the worker that was not good. For example, we might explain that the person could follow only precise orders, and did not show initiative. It might turn out that while for us this was a liability, the person to whom we are speaking might need someone who carefully follows orders, and does not improvise.*

Also, it is forbidden to exaggerate flaws. This can be hard to do. For example, employers who are frustrated by a worker's weaknesses often grow so annoyed that they overstate the person's faults (I once heard a man, upset by his housecleaner having placed some clothes in the wrong drawer, refer to her as "a moron who never gets anything right").

If we know that we are apt to exaggerate, it is better that we say nothing at all. Even when Jewish law permits us to speak "lashon hara for a purpose," it does not allow us to lie, and exaggerations that can cause damage to another are a form of lying.

3. We are also permitted to speak lashon hara in a therapeutic setting, when speaking, for example, to a psychologist or psychiatrist. In such a situation, the success of the treatment depends on a patient's ability to say whatever he or she is thinking or feeling. Also, because the person to whom we are speaking is obligated to keep what we are saying confidential, we don't need to fear that our words, even if unfair, will be repeated to others.

4. We are obligated to relate lashon hara to help an innocent victim who will suffer an injustice if the truth is not made known: "Know that incidents . . . such as those involving theft, robbery, damage, the causing of pain, shaming and wronging with words, may be revealed to others. Even a solitary observer [Jewish law normally requires two witnesses to establish the

---

*As regards the virtue of specificity, a doctor who serves on the faculty of a medical school told me, "I had a student who had no business becoming a doctor. I failed him as all his other professors had. On his evaluation, however, rather than simply writing, as the other doctors had, that he was perhaps our worst student, I cited the many potentially catastrophic mistakes he had made, listing all the relevant details. Of course, he was expelled. Shortly thereafter, he sued. I was told by our lawyers that it was only my detailed, damning evaluation that convinced his lawyers during discovery to drop the suit."

truth of a matter] should relate what he has seen, so as to assist him who has been wronged" (Rabbi Jonah Gerondi, *Gates of Repentance* 3:221).

Thus, in an infamous incident in New York some years ago, a rabbi who was the principal of a school was falsely accused of inappropriate behavior by a female employee, and was fired by the board. The principal, who denied the charge, sued the board. The court found that the principal was innocent, and that several members of the school board, who hated the man, had arranged with the woman to make a false accusation. In such an instance, whenever this man's name comes up, and it is apparent that some of those present have heard and believed the accusations against him, we should tell the truth of what happened, and make known, if necessary, the reprehensible behavior of the school board members and of the woman who made the charge.

5. The biblical law "Do not stand idly by while your brother's blood is shed" (Leviticus 19:16) obliges us to intervene whenever someone's life is endangered (such as helping one who is drowning). In addition, Jewish law has long understood this biblical ordinance as also mandating that we share information that may help save another from significant injury.* For example, if we know that one party in a romantic relationship is withholding information that would cause the other partner to reconsider the relationship (for example a serious illness, a sexually transmittable disease, mental instability, or serious past misbehavior), we have the right to make such information known to the relevant party.

———

My friend Rabbi Michael Berger cautions, "Be careful. Information we believe is important to know may not in fact be. Or there may be other ways to communicate the information—for example, by speaking to a rabbi whom the couple knows about the man's or woman's issue."

———

6. Even when it is permissible to reveal certain information, however, timing is very important. For example, while it is obvious that someone who is dating and has a serious disease is morally required to reveal his or her medical condition to the other party, what is not clear is when he, she, or others should do so. If one insists that such a revelation be made at the relationship's outset, the sick person's social life will be ruined; others who are made

---

*The Bible records that Mordechai overheard two officers at King Ahasuerus's palace plotting to kill him, and immediately made sure that this information was brought to the king (Esther 2:21-23).

aware of a person's condition, and who have little or no other knowledge of the person, may not even wish to meet the person for a first date. (Imagine if you were told, "There's a nice person I'd like you to meet. But you should know that he [or she] has a fairly serious chronic disease.") If, however, such knowledge is made known when the other party has come to appreciate other aspects of the person, the medical information will be one of a series of important things one person will know about the other, allowing for a fairer, more balanced judgment to be made.

7. Based on the law "Do not stand by while your brother's blood is shed," we should inform a person if another is going about besmirching her reputation; a person has the right to know of attacks being made against her good name. However, while a person has the right to know both who it is that is speaking against her, and to whom the *lashon hara* has been conveyed, as a rule this should be done only when there has been a significant effort to damage someone's name. Otherwise, if we hear a person say something negative about another, it is usually not wise or right to tell the victim what has happened (for example, if we hear someone call another person a "braggart" or "arrogant," or say, "She gets on my nerves"). Rather, we should try to dissuade the speaker from spreading this sort of mean-spirited *lashon hara*. We should not go around telling someone when minor *lashon hara* has been spoken about him or her, because doing so will cause unnecessary bad feelings.

When we feel that it is necessary to tell a person that someone is slandering her, we have the right to ask her not to reveal that we are the source of the information, since we don't wish to become the gossip's next victim.

8. "*Lashon hara* for a purpose" is permitted when someone is doing something very wrong, and there is reason to believe that publicizing this fact will pressure the person to change his behavior. For example, Jewish law, basing itself on Deuteronomy 24:1, invests the right to initiate divorce in the hands of the husband; therefore it is the man who must grant his wife a *get*, a Jewish divorce. If a man refuses to do so, the woman remains an *agunah*, "a chained woman," and is forbidden to all other men.* In instances in which a man refuses to give a *get*, and a rabbinical court has made it clear that he should do so, it is permitted to publicize this fact, and to exert a variety of pressures on the man, including publicizing his wrongful behavior in

---

*Since the tenth century, Jewish law has ruled that a woman must accept the *get* willingly. If she refuses to do so, then the husband is likewise forbidden to marry another.

newspapers (particularly Jewish newspapers), picketing his residence and/or place of business, and walking out of a synagogue service in which he is accorded any honor (such as being called to the Torah for an *aliyah*).

Even in such a case, however, we should abide by the rules of *lashon hara* and reveal only that information which the public needs to know about the case (thus, it does not seem right to reveal embarrassing information about the person that is extraneous to the issue of the divorce).

9. It would appear, based on several incidents described in the Bible, that it is permitted to discuss well-known cases of wrongful behavior in order to educate people not to do such things. Thus the Bible reveals negative behavior by some of its leading characters; its probable motive for doing so was to warn readers against such behavior. For example, the Bible tells us of an act of adultery committed by King David (II Samuel, chapter 11). The Bible could easily have omitted this information, yet it did not. Why? Obviously—and there might well be other reasons—it wished its readers to understand that no matter how prominent a person becomes, he must never stop working on his character; David might have thought he was immune to the temptation to act immorally, but he was wrong. We should all learn from this episode that if someone as great as David is not immune to committing a great sin, neither are we.

Similarly, although the matter was much less serious, the Bible details for us Moses' occasional bad temper, and how it caused him to be denied entry to the land of Israel (Numbers 20:1–13). Telling us about this in the Torah can perhaps likewise be designated as a kind of "*lashon hara* for a purpose."

In addition, as noted, Deuteronomy specifically enjoins us to remember Miriam's speaking *lashon hara* against Moses and the punishment she suffered as a result (Deuteronomy 24:9; see pages 336–337).

Obviously in all these cases the Bible felt that there was educational value in publicizing and studying the wrongful acts committed by others.

The Talmud continued this tradition. For example, it relates several incidents in which Rabbi Shammai's temper caused him to mistreat would-be converts to Judaism, and how these people, when exposed to the sweeter temperament of Hillel, chose to become Jews. Again, the Talmud could have simply related the converts' positive experiences with Hillel, but it did not do so. The educational value of what we are taught about Shammai's behavior is obvious: if you want to expose people to Judaism, you must learn how to control your temper. Similarly, the Talmud records that Rabbi Chanina ben

Gamliel's bad temper caused him to be served unkosher food.* The fact that the Talmud cited Rabbi Chanina by name, instead of relating the episode anonymously, suggests that the incident must have been known at the time, and the Rabbis thought it appropriate to alert others to the sin that might ensue from an angry disposition. In this case, mentioning the rabbi by name made the incident more memorable to readers: "If not controlling his temper could cause a man as great as Rabbi Chanina to be served unkosher meat," readers might reason, "it means I had better learn not to terrify the members of my household." If the rabbi in the incident had been anonymous, people would be more likely to forget about it, or regard it as a sort of "urban legend."

The Talmud rules that if a matter has become known to many people, it is no longer regarded as *lashon hara* (*Arachin* 16a).† Nonetheless, common sense suggests that when such incidents are mentioned to influence people to act more righteously, it might be best to use age-old incidents from the Bible and Talmud, rather than to cite current or recent incidents that will cause shame to the person who sinned, and to the person's family.

10. The most obvious instance in which we are permitted to solicit *"lashon hara* for a purpose" is when we are in practical need of such information. Jewish law defines this as applying in the following situations: If we are planning to:

- enter into a business relationship with another
- hire an employee
- go to work for someone
- become involved, or if we are involved, in a romantic relationship with someone

In such cases it is fair and appropriate for us to ask questions about the character and behavior of the person from those who have firsthand knowledge of him or her. Even when such permission is granted, however, we should restrict our questions to information that we need to know. Thus, if we are going to work for a person, we have a right to know if that person is fair to employees, appreciative, fully honest, and so on. We do not have a right to solicit gossip or information in areas that are not work-related. Also

---

*See page 254 for a discussion of how this came about (*Gittin* 7a).
†Even in such cases, we must be careful to say only what we know to be true; exaggeration still puts us in violation of the prohibition against slander (see chapter 43).

such conversations should be held one-on-one with the person who has the information, and with that person alone; there is no reason for others to be present.

———

Some people who might want to "check out" whether someone is suitable for a romantic relationship will not want the one whom they are questioning to be fully aware of their intentions. So they will mention the names of several people, and include among them the name of the one in whom they are interested. This is forbidden, as it causes the speaking of unnecessary, and therefore prohibited, lashon hara.

———

As regards the issue of *lashon hara* between a husband and wife, see pages 361–362.

42

RUMORS: WHEN PERMITTED,
WHEN FORBIDDEN

1. Even those of us who acknowledge speaking *lashon hara* believe that we never spread malicious lies. And yet, if we pass on rumors, we inevitably end up disseminating lies as well. That is because rumors, in general, are not positive ("Hey, did you hear that so-and-so is a wonderful person?"). Many, perhaps most, rumors are negative. If they also turn out to be false, then we have helped to pass on a damaging lie. "But I didn't know it was untrue," we will say. This, however, is not a valid defense. Someone who drinks alcohol before driving does not intend to go out and kill anyone with their car. Yet if a person routinely drinks and drives, he will, sooner or later, get into an accident and cause an innocent person grave injury. If we don't resist passing on rumors, then sooner or later—probably sooner—some of these rumors will be both negative and untrue. That we did not inflict the harm intentionally is as much of a consolation to the victim as is the claim of the drunk driver that he did not mean to maim his victim.

Transmitting a false rumor also puts us in violation of a specific biblical command: "You shall not carry false reports" (Exodus 23:1).

---

2. Therefore, when we hear a damaging rumor about another, we should not pass it on, tempting as it is to do so: "For just as a person dislikes any blemish on his own name, so should he refrain from damaging someone else's reputation" (*The Fathers According to Rabbi Nathan* 15:1).

3. Rumors inflict harm on groups as well as individuals. In the aftermath of the September 11, 2001, terrorist attacks on the Twin Towers in New York, antisemitic rumormongers—operating largely, and internationally, through the Internet—spread a report that four thousand Jewish (in some versions, Israeli) employees had been warned in advance to stay home from work that day. This was, of course, a lie (among the almost three thousand people killed that day, about four hundred were Jews), and yet it raced over the Internet and throughout the Arab world, and is today believed by tens of millions of people. Those who accept such rumors as true become inflamed against Jews, and are far more likely to support terrorist actions to hurt and kill Jews than are those who have not been exposed to them. In earlier centuries, similar sorts of rumormongers spread reports that Jews killed non-Jews in religious rituals and drank their blood (the infamous "blood libel"), a false report that led to the murders of tens of thousands of Jews in medieval Christian Europe, and is still widely believed in the Arab world.

4. Is one, therefore, obligated to disregard all rumors? No. If you hear a rumor from many people or, more significantly, from someone you know to be trustworthy (who presumably checked into the rumor's validity before passing it on), you should act with caution toward the person about whom the rumor is told, and investigate its truthfulness.

Thus, when Eli, the priest of Shiloh, heard "evil reports from [many] people" that his sons were stealing food at the temple and sleeping with women who came to pray and offer sacrifices there, he confronted them: "I hear evil reports about your doings from all the people" (I Samuel 2:23).

If a rumor appears to be true, this is the proper way to confront the person: "I hear that . . ." and then await the response. Many people, however, hear a rumor, accept it as true, and attack its object.

In a later biblical episode, a Jewish leader refused to believe a report he heard from a reliable source, and great tragedy ensued. In 586 B.C.E., after the Babylonians put down a Jewish revolt in Judea and destroyed the Temple, they installed Gedaliah ben Achikam as governor; most Jews saw this as a positive development, since having a Jew in a high position enabled them to retain some control over their affairs. However, some Jews, headed by Ishmael ben Netanya, regarded Gedaliah as a traitor and resolved to assassinate him. A soldier named Yochanan, along with his fellow officers, warned Gedaliah of Ishmael's intentions. "But Gedaliah ben Achikam would not believe them [and responded], 'What you are saying about Ishmael is not true'" (Jeremiah 40:13–16). He could not have been more wrong; some months later, Ishmael and his followers came to meet with Gedaliah and, at the meeting, murdered him. His death ended what little power the Jews still had in Judah (following the assassination, the province lost its separate identity) and has been regarded ever since as a tragedy; the day of Gedaliah's death (it falls on the day after Rosh Hashana) is still observed as a fast day, *Tzom Gedaliah*, in the Jewish calendar. This tragedy could have been averted had Gedaliah considered the possibility that Yochanan's warning was true. He would then have had a security force present when he received Ishmael.

Therefore, if you hear a rumor from several people or from a person whom you have reason to believe is trustworthy, do not reject it out of hand.

5. When you hear a rumor that you have reason to believe is true and that is important for others to hear, before transmitting the rumor to others, try to authenticate it. "If it is as clear to you as it is clear to you that your sister is forbidden to you, only then say it" (*Shabbat* 145b). If you cannot establish that the rumor is definitely true, but it is relevant for another to know, then tell the rumor to the concerned party or parties, emphasizing that it is a rumor and you are not certain it is true.

For example, if a friend of yours has invested, or is planning to invest, funds with a money manager, and you hear a report that the manager has in the past lost a great deal of money for his clients, you should first try to ascertain whether the rumor is true, but if that is not feasible or easily accomplished, tell your friend what you have heard, emphasizing that it is a rumor, and that he or she should investigate the matter.

6. If you hear a rumor that someone is planning or plotting to hurt another, and the rumor comes from a person whom you regard as at least somewhat trustworthy, pass it on to the person in need of the information. You must explain, however, that it is a rumor, and that you do not know it to be definitely true.[1]

In Tarasoff vs. California, a precedent-setting legal suit in the United States in the 1970s, the court ruled that a psychiatrist or psychologist is legally and morally obligated to violate confidentiality, the sacrosanct cornerstone of therapy, to inform a potential victim of a threat made against them. If the therapist doesn't do so, he is morally and financially responsible for any tragedy that might ensue. As Justice Matthew Tobriner, ruling for the majority in that case, opined: "The risk that unnecessary warnings be given is a reasonable price to pay for the lives of possible victims that may be saved. We would hesitate to hold that the therapist who is aware that his patient expects to attempt to assassinate the president of the United States would not be obligated to warn the authorities because the therapist cannot predict with accuracy that his patient will commit the crime."[2]

43

THE WORST FORM OF FORBIDDEN SPEECH

1. The worst form of unfair speech is *motzi shem ra* ("giving someone a bad name"), spreading lies about another. Although this offense is usually committed by an individual who is involved in a bitter conflict with, or is jealous of, another, it can also be committed by someone without malicious intent; thus, one who spreads a negative rumor that turns out to be false is also guilty of "giving someone a bad name" (see the preceding chapter). Destroying someone's reputation is committing a kind of murder, an idea conveyed in English by the expression "character assassination."

Throughout history, many people have been killed or have had their lives ruined because of slander. Thus, in the seventy-five–year period following the Civil War, several thousand African-American men were lynched in the American South, many on the basis of false charges of rape. The most famous such accusation was that directed against the "Scottsboro Boys." As is often the case with motzi shem ra, the case originated with a fight. In March 1931, a group of young African-American and white men were hitching rides on a Memphis-bound train in search of work. While the train was passing through Alabama, a fight erupted between the white and African-American youths, and the African-American men threw five of their white opponents off the train. One of the youths complained to the police, also mentioning that the African-Americans had been riding the trains with two white girls. The police issued an order "to round up every Negro on the train and bring them to Scottsboro," the largest town in the area. Nine African-American youths, aged thirteen to twenty, were arrested, along with two white females. The girls, fearing that they would be jailed as vagrants, accused the African-Americans of having gang-raped them. Within two weeks, and despite medical evidence indicating that the girls had not had relations on the day of the alleged crime, eight of the nine African-Americans were sentenced to death. Before the sentences could be carried out, it became apparent that no crime had been committed (one of the girls eventually acknowledged that no rape had occurred), but all of the arrested men spent at least five years in prison, and some of them far longer.

In literature, the most famous of Shakespeare's villains, Iago, accomplishes his evil through slander. When Othello, the Moorish general, bypasses him for promotion, Iago vows to destroy him, and does so by convincing Othello that his beloved wife, Desdemona, has betrayed him. The charge seems preposterous, but Iago repeats the accusation again and again, and arranges damning circumstantial evidence to destroy Desdemona's credibility. In the end, Othello kills Desdemona, only to learn that Iago's accusation was false. For Othello, as an old proverb teaches, "Hell is truth seen too late."

———

2. The victims of slanderers are not only individuals, but also groups. The difference between those who slander individuals and those who slander groups is that, in the case of groups, the victims can number in the tens and hundreds of thousands. Thus, during 1920 and 1921, Henry Ford, the most successful businessman in the United States, launched an attack against Jews. Promoting his campaign through the *Dearborn Independent*, a newspaper he owned, Ford published a series of ninety-one articles on "The International Jew: The World's Problem." The articles, based on the antisemitic forgery known as *The Protocols of the Elders of Zion*, charged that Jews were involved in an international conspiracy to control world finances and politics, that they had a plan to destroy every religion in the world except Judaism, and that they had no loyalty to the societies in which they lived. Even though Ford eventually issued a letter of apology to the Jewish community (there is reason to believe that it was issued only in order to end a libel trial then being conducted against him), the damage done by his campaign proved

irrevocable. The Nazis translated Ford's articles into German and distributed them widely. In the United States, Ford's antisemitic diatribes helped bring about the 1924 quotas restricting immigration (from Eastern Europe in particular). Historian Lucy Dawidowicz has commented on the murderous effects of such acts of *motzi shem ra*: "It is a paradox of Jewish history that the anti-Semitism propagated in the United States after the First World War wrought more damage to the European Jews than to the American Jews. The restriction of immigration . . . prevented hundreds of thousands of Jews from entering America in years to come when the difference was the difference between life and death."[1]

3. "Life and death are in the hands of the tongue" (Proverbs 18:21). The damage caused by words can do far more than inflict emotional distress on their victims, or lower their status. There is no evidence that Adolf Hitler killed a single one of the six million Jews who died in the Holocaust with his own hands. Yet his untruthful speeches and writings, and his eventual ordering of the Holocaust, created an environment in which Germans who, prior to Hitler, would have regarded murdering Jews as immoral and forbidden, now considered it not only permitted, but morally correct.

4. Because the damage done to a person's good name often cannot be undone (see pages 337–338), Jewish law regards slander as an offense that the victim is not required to forgive, even if sincerely requested: "One who gives his neighbor a bad name, can never gain pardon" (that is unless the victim chooses to forgive him; Jerusalem Talmud, *Bava Kamma* 8:7; see pages 199–200 for a further discussion of this issue). Therefore, before you make a negative statement about someone, be sure that it is accurate and that the people to whom you are telling it have legitimate need of the information.

5. If we hear someone say something nasty about another person, and we know that the statement is untrue or even just exaggerated, we are required to try to refute it, and thereby minimize the damage. The Golden Rule offers helpful guidance on how to act in such a situation. If someone was spreading lies about us, we would want those hearing the report to defend us, and deny what was being said. Therefore, we too, are obligated to protect our neighbor's good name.

6. The worst thing we can do in such a situation is to convey the impression that we accept what the speaker is saying as true. Rabbi Jonah

Gerondi, author of *The Gates of Repentance* (*Sha'arei Teshuvah*, one of Judaism's seminal works on repentance), teaches that one who does so has committed a serious offense, "for people will say that the report must be true since those who heard it agreed with it" (part II, section 212).

———

There is reason to believe that Rabbi Gerondi might have been motivated, at least in part, to write The Gates of Repentance *because of his involvement as a young scholar in an act of motzi shem ra against Maimonides. Rabbi Gerondi was part of a group of French rabbis who believed Maimonides' philosophical treatise,* Guide to the Perplexed, *contained heretical views (they were particularly bothered that Maimonides was influenced in his views by non-Jewish philosophers such as Aristotle and by his occasional attempts to synthesize aspects of Greek and Jewish thought). When the French Inquisition was established to censor and destroy heretical Christian works, Rabbi Gerondi, along with some colleagues, approached the Inquisition and asked it to ban the "heretical" writings of Maimonides as well. The Inquisition agreed to the request, but then, to the rabbis' dismay, soon started to investigate other Jewish writings; a few years later the Inquisition banned and burned the Talmud. At this point Rabbi Gerondi realized that his group's earlier request to ban Maimonides' writings had set this in motion. Overcome with remorse, he is reported to have stood up in his synagogue and proclaimed, "I undertake to prostrate myself at Maimonides' grave and confess that I spoke and sinned against his books." Rabbi Gerondi did not succeed in making this trip to Israel, but left behind as his legacy* The Gates of Repentance, *a book whose origins are likely shrouded in the evil that can come about when we slander the good name and works of another.*

———

CRITICISM

———

You shall rebuke, yes rebuke, your fellow,
and not bear sin because of him.

Leviticus 19:17

44

WHEN TO CRITICIZE

═══════════

1. The commandment "You shall rebuke, yes rebuke, your fellow, and not bear sin because of him" (Leviticus 19:17) means that we should not remain silent when we observe someone behaving badly.* Rather, we should speak to the person and point out what's wrong with his behavior (see the next chapter for ways to express criticism). The verse's second clause, "and not bear sin because of him," means that if we have the ability to influence someone who is acting improperly, and don't, then we share in the responsibility for that person's misdeeds.[1]

2. The greater your ability to influence others, the greater your responsibility to do so. The Talmud teaches, "Whoever can stop the members of his household from committing a sin, but does not, is held responsible for the sins of his household. If he can stop the people of his city from sinning, but does not, he is held responsible for the sins of the people of his city. If he can stop the whole world from sinning, and does not, he is held responsible for the sins of the whole world" (*Shabbat* 54b).

3. Because of the tendency to equate being religious solely with observing rituals, most contemporary writings on this commandment focus on rebuking another for violations of Jewish rituals (for example, if you see someone violating a Shabbat law). In reality, many people witness serious ethical offenses but remain silent, without first considering whether their speaking out might not have a positive effect. For example, you might:

- see friends of yours humiliating one of their children or routinely favoring one child over another

─────────

*This often overlooked commandment is so significant that the Talmud teaches, "Jerusalem was destroyed because its citizens didn't rebuke one another" (*Shabbat* 119b). Thus, no matter how elevated a society is—and Jerusalem has long been regarded as Judaism's premier city—if people don't effectively critique each other's ethical lapses, the society will deteriorate quickly.

- witness someone you know acting disrespectfully toward another, for example, berating an employee
- observe a friend being unfair or unkind to his or her spouse
- see someone who has drunk too much alcohol about to drive a car

4. Because the notion of "minding one's own business" is deeply instilled in our culture, the commandment to rebuke another makes most people uncomfortable. (It should; those who enjoy criticizing others are often motivated more by self-righteousness than righteousness.) Nevertheless, the belief that "all Jews are responsible for each other" (*Shevuot* 39a) mandates that we should try to prevent others from engaging in wrong behavior.

In societies such as the United States, where Jews are treated with full equality, it seems to me that we are also obligated to try to influence our non-Jewish friends and neighbors, and all those whom we have reason to believe will listen to our words (see paragraph 2).

5. "Love unaccompanied by criticism is not love" (*Genesis Rabbah* 54:3). In a relationship where two people never criticize each other, neither grows morally. Rabbi Abraham Isaac Kook was asked why he so loved the saintly Jerusalem scholar and teacher Rabbi Aryeh Levine. He responded, "For twenty years he has been frequenting my home and in all that time he has never flattered me . . . [yet] if he ever saw me do anything which he did not understand, he questioned it or commented on it."*

Rabbi Kook's observation is particularly important for wealthy and/or powerful people, many of whom are surrounded by those who are too much in awe of, or too frightened by, them to offer criticism. Yet we all need people we can trust to question and criticize us when we act wrongly.

Do you have at least one friend (it could be your spouse) who speaks honestly to you, and who criticizes you? If not, then you have no real friends.

6. The midrashic teaching that "love unaccompanied by criticism is not love" also applies to the parent-child relationship. The Bible tells us that during the last year of King David's life, his son Adonijah went around Jerusalem boasting that he would soon be king. Explaining his arrogant and disrespectful behavior toward his father, the Bible notes, "His father had never

---

*See Simcha Raz, *A Tzaddik in Our Time*, pages 85–86. Rabbi Kook offered two other reasons as well: "He never once told me of anything said by my fierce opponents, who were continually denigrating and defaming me, and whenever he asked a favor of me, it was never for himself but only for others." Rabbi Kook used to say, "If there were three Jews in our generation like Reb Aryeh, the Messiah would come."

scolded him [and said] 'Why did you do that?'" (I Kings 1:6). David's error apparently was in not criticizing and challenging Adonijah's bad behavior as it occurred.

The Talmud teaches that parents must critique and influence their children, particularly when they are young, and still under the parents' authority (*Kiddushin* 30a). Even when children are grown, they are still very open to the influence of their parents.

———

Criticism is important in the other direction as well. For example, many parents are able to stop smoking only when they are rebuked by their children, no matter how young.

———

7. The law "You shall rebuke, yes rebuke, your fellow" applies to all instances in which you become aware of a wrong and have reason to believe that your words can make an impact. Thus a teacher should admonish a student who is acting inappropriately, and a student should rebuke a teacher in similar circumstances: "How do we know that a disciple sitting before his Master [who is judging a case and] who sees that the poor man is right, and the wealthy man wrong, should not remain silent [if his teacher is wrongly favoring the wealthy litigant]? Because it is said, 'Keep far away from falsehood'" (Exodus 23:7; see *Shevuot* 31a).*

———

A man told me that as a child, in his second year of summer camp, he had a slow-witted counselor. He often would mock the fellow's lack of intelligence and incompetence. One day his counselor from the previous year, whom he idolized, overheard him, took him aside, and told him how disappointed he was in his behavior. From that point on, the young man never mocked his counselor again. As this first counselor understood, if you have reason to hope your words can have an effect, speak up.

———

8. Rabbi Yonatan Eibeschutz (died 1764) pointed out that a friend's rebuke can carry more impact than a rabbi's. One who is criticized by the latter may think, "If I were a rabbi, I also wouldn't do such a thing." But when a

———

*This would also apply if the teacher was unfairly favoring the poor litigant. Presumably the Rabbis cited the example of a judge favoring the rich litigant because that happened more often, certainly in the past.

friend tells you that your behavior is inappropriate, you may think, "If he is careful about this matter, I should be too."[2]

In short, all Jews, not just rabbis and scholars, are obligated to reprove anyone who is acting badly: "How do we know that one who sees his friend doing something ugly is obligated to rebuke him? Because it is written, 'You shall rebuke, yes rebuke, your fellow'" (*Arachin* 16b).

9. As noted earlier, the first part of Leviticus 19:17 reads, "You shall not hate your brother in your heart." Jewish law understands the words "in your heart" to mean that if someone has wronged you, you are forbidden to remain silent and nurse your hatred. You must either find a way to forgive the offender or make your grievance known by confronting him and asking, "Why did you do this to me?" "If the person admits his offense, and asks for forgiveness, you should be ready to forgive" (Maimonides, "The Laws of Character Development" 6:6).

10. When practiced properly, the commandment to rebuke another can often lead to a defusing of the anger. Perhaps you dislike someone because you suspect him of something that never happened; for example, you've heard that the person has slandered you. By speaking to the person, you may find out that what you've heard is untrue or exaggerated.[3] If it is true, your rebuke, if delivered properly, may help the person change his behavior, thereby helping him, while reducing your annoyance at him as well.

When not to rebuke

11. "Just as it is a mitzvah to say something which will be listened to, so too is it a mitzvah to refrain from saying something which will not be listened to" (*Yevamot* 65b). The rabbinic belief is that if you warn someone against sinning, and the person ignores you, then their sin becomes intentional instead of accidental, and therefore much worse. This applies only to minor sins.* However, when it comes to more serious offenses, such as dishonesty or malicious gossip, you should inform the sinner of the wrong he is doing, even if you believe that your warning will not be heeded.

---

*For example, rabbinic law extends the fast of Yom Kippur beyond twenty-four hours, and rules that one should start fasting earlier than actual nightfall (no prescribed length of time is specified). However, the *Shulchan Arukh* rules that those who eat and drink until darkness should not be admonished, lest they continue doing so consciously; it is better to allow them to remain unaware of this transgression than risk their willful violation of it (*Orach Chayyim* 608:2).

12. Rabbi Shneur Zalman of Liady (1745–1813), the founder of the Lubavitch movement, teaches that we are obligated to admonish only those with whom we have a close enough relationship so that the admonition is likely to have an impact (*Shulchan Arukh ha-Rav* 156:7). When you doubt that your words will have an effect (for example, you see someone acting rudely in the street or, at a restaurant, you see another patron failing to leave a tip), you are not required to voice your concern.

———

Don't be too quick to take advantage of this excuse not to rebuke. A woman came to her landlord, who had sent her family an eviction notice a week earlier. She told the landlord, who, like her, was an observant Jew, that her husband had not slept through the night since the notice had arrived. The landlord responded, "Tell your husband to take a sleeping pill." She leaned over the man's desk, looked him in the eye, and said, "Is that a nice way to speak?" The landlord did not apologize, but his subsequent behavior became more civil, and the two parties were able to reach a settlement. The woman knew that at the moment she rebuked her landlord, heir to a compassionate religious tradition, he realized that his remark had been unkind and he was ashamed.

———

13. You are also exempt from delivering a rebuke if doing so will endanger you or cause the other person to hate you.[4] The Book of Proverbs teaches, "Do not rebuke a scoffer, for he will hate you" (9:8). Thus, if a person is known for being testy, or for lashing out at those who criticize him, you are not obligated to rebuke him. (If you yourself have such a disposition, see page 395).

———

A friend told me about a college classmate who had observed a group of tough-looking motorcyclists at the beach, smoking and throwing their stubs in the sand. He rebuked them for littering, and in response, they beat him up.

———

14. To forgive the person who hurt you without delivering a rebuke is not only permitted, but is also regarded as a highly moral act (Maimonides, "Laws of Character Development," 6:9). Be certain, however, that your forgiveness is authentic and that you're no longer carrying a grudge. Sometimes we don't reprove another because we're too timid, or because we don't want to hear the other person's self-justification, and thus be deprived of "luxuriating" in our anger.

————

There is a risk in forgiving another without saying anything about the person's behavior: the person might keep on doing similar hurtful things to others. Sometimes it is worth saying something even if the behavior did not particularly bother you, but so as to protect others from being hurt.

————

Before offering criticism

15. Before rebuking someone for an offense, be sure that you yourself are not guilty of the same wrongdoing. The Talmud tells us that Rabbi Yannai had a tree whose branches extended beyond his private property onto a public road. Another man in the town had a similar tree that interfered with traffic, and some local townspeople, whose passage was obstructed by it, came to Rabbi Yannai to complain. He told them, "Go away now, and come back tomorrow." That night he hired workers to cut down his tree. The next day he ordered the man to have his own tree cut down. The man responded, "But you also have such a tree." Rabbi Yannai replied, "Go and see. If mine is cut down, then cut yours down, and if mine is not cut down, you need not cut yours down." Based on this incident, the Talmud concludes, "Correct yourself before you correct others" (*Bava Bathra* 60a–60b and *Bava Mezia* 107b).* If you don't, people won't accept your opinion or judgment.

————

A story, perhaps apocryphal, is told about Gandhi. A woman asked him to tell her husband to stop eating so much sugar because he was endangering his health. Gandhi told the woman to come back with her husband a week later. He then said to the man, "Stop eating sugar." When asked why he needed the week's delay, he said, "To stop eating sugar myself."

————

---

*The Talmud in *Bava Bathra* asks why Rabbi Yannai had allowed his tree to overhang public land. It explains, "At first he thought that passers-by were glad of it because they could sit in its shade, but when he saw that they objected [to the other man's tree], he had his own tree cut down."

Final thoughts

16. The Vilna Gaon teaches that if you influence someone to improve his behavior, you share in the credit for that person's subsequent good deeds.[5] For example, perhaps you know an affluent person who assists his needy parents less than he should. If you persuade him to be more generous, you share in the moral credit for the good that results.

17. Rabbi Yonatan Eibeschutz notes that admonishing another can have a positive effect on us; we may be prevented from committing the same transgression. When faced with temptation, we may say to ourselves, "I rebuke others for doing this; how can I do it myself?"[6]

———

A Jewish folktale tells of a man who lived in Sodom, who used to protest each day against the evil perpetrated there. A child once said to him, "No one listens to you. No one repents. Why do you keep shouting?" The man answered, "At first, I protested because I hoped to change them. Now I protest because if I don't, they will change me."

———

45

HOW TO CRITICIZE AND HOW NOT TO

═══════

The ability to rebuke others effectively (and also accept criticism graciously) is rare, and always has been. The Talmud cites Rabbi Tarfon's almost-two-thousand-year-old view: "I wonder if there is anyone in this generation who knows how to accept reproof," and Rabbi Elazar ben Azaryah's counter, "I wonder if there is anyone in this generation who knows how to give reproof" (Arachin 16b). As these rabbinic statements suggest, the two skills are related: People will accept rebuke only if it is offered in a way that is not threatening. Jewish law and teachings have therefore developed a series of guidelines on how to fulfill this difficult mitzvah. The following section contains both suggestions and anecdotes illustrat-

ing how Jewish sages have carried out the command to rebuke; these offer a variety of strategies to use when criticism is called for.

———

1. One who criticizes another should follow three guidelines. Deliver the rebuke

- lovingly and gently (for example, when criticizing a spouse or child, remember to use terms of endearment")*
- patiently (when reproved, none of us is able to acknowledge all his flaws and transform himself immediately, so don't expect the person to whom you're speaking to do so)
- privately, so as not to embarrass the other person (see Maimonides, "Laws of Character Development" 6:7)

2. Because someone who has acted badly is more likely to change his behavior when the rebuke is delivered gently, if you find yourself looking forward to offering the criticism, don't speak up. Your motives are probably insincere, and your words are unlikely to sound loving. However, if the thought of what you need to do pains you and you wish you didn't have to do it, then proceed. Your motives are probably sincere, and this will be clear to the person when you say something. Apparently, then, the commandment to admonish another is best fulfilled by those who least enjoy it.

3. Many people believe that an effective rebuke must be harshly or sternly worded. On the contrary; the Chaffetz Chayyim instructed a man who used to shout angrily at others to stop doing so: "When you put on *tefillin* or perform other commandments, you don't raise your voice. So, too, with rebuke."[1] Therefore, be careful how you voice your criticism, and speak in a fair and respectful way.

This is especially important when a child is admonishing a parent. Maimonides writes, "If one sees his father violating a Torah law, he should not say, 'Father, you have violated the Torah'; rather, he should say, 'Father, is it not written in the Torah?' as if he were asking a question, not delivering a warning" ("Laws Concerning Rebels" 6:11).

———

*See the discussion of this point in Isaac Steven Herschkopf, M.D., *Hello Darkness, My Old Friend: Embracing Anger to Heal Your Life,* page 240.

———

The Chaffetz Chayyim is reputed to have said, "I am not referring to anyone in particular, but if there is anyone here who thinks I mean him, I do mean him."[2]

———

4. The nineteenth-century rabbi Chaim of Volozhin taught that anyone who could not deliver a rebuke in a pleasant manner was freed from the commandment to admonish another, since an unpleasantly delivered criticism would antagonize the one being criticized.[3] Therefore, if you are unable to temper your remarks, and become harsh and perhaps even insulting, it is better to remain silent.

5. As noted, in order for a rebuke to be effective, it must be delivered in a supportive and not an antagonistic manner: "The righteous person comes with pleasant, gentle words and draws people to the Torah" (*Midrash Proverbs* 10:20).* For example, *The Ethics of the Fathers* tells us that Aaron, Moses' brother, "loved peace, pursued peace, loved people and drew them near to the Torah" (1:12). Aaron's open-hearted love enabled him to influence the behavior of anyone he talked to.

On expressing criticism gently

———

When some students of Rashi did something he regarded as forbidden, his response was a model of tactful criticism: "I am certain that . . . righteous people themselves surely don't cause damage. However, from now on you should not act this way, and may our Rock guide us in the path of truth and goodness."[4] Note that Rashi says, "may our Rock guide us," not "you." Because he identified with his disciples and didn't claim to be better than they were, he worded his response in a respectful manner that made it easier for them to accept his correction. On another occasion, Rashi gave this answer: "When you brought your proof . . . my beloved friend, you did not think it out properly. . . . I believe that you have confused what you learned."

The Rabbis believed that Aaron was sometimes capable of influencing sinners' behavior without even alluding to their misdeeds: "When Aaron would walk along the road and meet a wicked man, he greeted him warmly. The next day, when that man was about to go and commit a transgression, he would say

———

*Elsewhere, the Bible teaches, "The words of the wise, uttered gently, are accepted" (Ecclesiastes 9:17).

to himself: 'Woe is me, how could I ever raise my eyes and face Aaron? I would be too embarrassed by the man who greeted me so warmly' (The Fathers According to Rabbi Nathan, *chapter 12). This strategy might not work with most people, but apparently it does with some. Therefore, seek out opportunities where your willingness to be friendly might help motivate others to act ethically.*

Conversely, in Israel, some religious zealots throw stones at cars that drive in or near religious neighborhoods on Shabbat. This can cause a fatal accident and, in addition, such behavior is a desecration of God's Name (Chillul Hashem), *and provokes antagonism toward religious Jews.*

———

6. Acknowledge faults you share in common with those you are criticizing; this will make it easier for your listeners to accept the rebuke. When Rabbi Chaim Soloveitchik offered criticism during a lecture on *Shabbat Shuvah* (the Sabbath preceding Yom Kippur), he told the congregation that "Chaim is speaking to Chaim, but you can eavesdrop if you so desire."[5] Another rabbi would say to audiences: "Don't think that I am innocent of all the offenses I'm enumerating. I, too, have committed some of them. All that I am doing, therefore, is speaking aloud to myself, and if anything you might overhear applies to you also, well and good."

This is a good way to handle one-on-one situations. Admitting that you, too, have struggled with the same problem makes the other party less ashamed to admit wrongdoing, and may also prompt him or her to ask for your help.

———

This is also a valuable technique to use when talking to your children, since many children believe that their parents are perfect.

———

7. If someone seems unwilling to accept your criticism, don't keep insisting that she do so. Rather, consider her objections, and let her see that you are not rejecting her words out of hand. If necessary, wait for a more propitious time. The Chazon Ish once advised a young man on an important matter, and the man explained why he disagreed. After listening to the young man's reasons several times, the Chazon Ish extended his hand and wished him success. The young man left, thinking that his explanation had satisfied the Chazon Ish. But a few days later he received a letter from the rabbi, saying, "My precious one, I did not want to hurt your feelings while you were here, but I also did not want you to think that your explanation met with my approval. It is my obligation to apprise you of this."[6]

8. Don't make unrealistic demands of the person you are criticizing. When Rabbi Israel Salanter arrived in Memel, Germany, he learned that the city's Jewish longshoremen worked on Shabbat. He knew that if he told them to stop this practice, they would ignore him. Instead he met with them and asked them to avoid Shabbat violations that were not essential to their work (such as writing). A few weeks later he asked them to refrain from other non-essential activities. Eventually, many of the longshoremen became Sabbath observers.[7]

Rabbi Salanter's step-by-step approach also applies to ethical behavior. For example, it's unrealistic to ask someone who gives little to charity to start tithing, and your suggestion to do so will probably be rebuffed. Better to encourage that person to increase her giving gradually, perhaps by raising the percentage one percent each year (say, from four percent to five percent). Similarly, if a person gossips extensively, ask him to select several hours each day during which he won't say anything negative about anyone, and then try to influence him to gradually expand that period.

9. Confine your criticism to a specific act, for example, "I noticed you making fun of so-and-so," while avoiding blanket statements such as "You're always making fun of others." Critical generalizations demoralize the offender and make him defensive. (Who would be willing to admit, "It's true. I'm a cruel person. I always make fun of others"?)

10. Although it is generally forbidden to rebuke another in public (see page 392), if remaining silent will cause people to think that you are condoning unethical behavior, it is better to speak out. If you're in a group and someone starts speaking unfairly about someone not present, you should point out to the gossiper that such talk is unfair and forbidden. If circumstances make it very difficult for you to do so, try to defend the reputation of the person being defamed, or, at the least, change the subject.

11. The prophet Nathan serves as a model for how to rebuke. He learned that King David had slept with Bathsheba, the wife of his army officer Uriah, and later arranged to have Uriah killed in battle. Nathan realized that a direct

accusation of David would be met with denial or defensiveness, or perhaps he feared a violent response. Instead, he approached the king to solicit his advice on a supposed case of injustice that had been brought to his attention: "There were two men in the same city, one rich and one poor. The rich man had very large flocks and herds, but the poor man had only one little ewe lamb that he had bought. He tended it and it grew up together with him and his children: it used to share his morsel of bread, drink from his cup, and nestle in his bosom; it was like a daughter to him. One day, a traveler came to the rich man, but he was loath to take anything from his own flocks or herds to prepare a meal for the guest who had come to him, so he took the poor man's lamb and prepared it for the man who had come to him." David flew into a rage against the man, and said to Nathan, "As the Lord lives, the man who did this deserves to die!" Nathan responded to David, 'That man is you!'" (II Samuel 12:1–7).

By depersonalizing his critique (at least until the very end), Nathan enabled David to view the issue in its moral simplicity. He had taken another man's wife, just as the rich man had stolen the lamb that the poor man had loved. And once David declared his verdict—"The man who did this deserves to die" and Nathan responded, "That man is you!"—David had no choice but to acknowledge that he merited the same condemnation.

Because Nathan knew how to offer criticism, David learned how to repent.

12. If the person you criticize doesn't change quickly, don't become angry. Rabbi Simcha Zissel Ziv, a leading disciple of Rabbi Israel Salanter, noted that teachers often lose their temper with students who are admonished three or four times and don't reform. But the teacher should ask himself if he always corrects all of his own shortcomings by the third or fourth reminder.

———

The medieval Catholic theologian Thomas à Kempis observed: "Be not angry that you cannot make others as you wish them to be, since you cannot make yourself as you wish to be."

———

13. Rabbi Everett Gendler lists a number of behaviors to avoid:

• "Do not talk about the person to others." The commandment of rebuke obligates you to confront the sinner, not to destroy her good name.

What Rabbi Gendler is suggesting is, of course, very difficult to do. When we feel that someone has acted badly, particularly toward us, it is tempting to share our resentment with others. However, we should first confront the offender and allow her the opportunity to explain her behavior, and reform. Even if she doesn't, there is no reason to share our feelings about, and experiences with, the person with others, except in the rare instance in which they need to know about it (see chapter 42).

> • "Avoid harsh words or epithets or painful personal references which will embarrass the other. Such an approach will only aggravate the bad feelings between the two of you, and such infliction of hurt is specifically forbidden by the tradition."[8]

14. Before you admonish someone, ask yourself:

• Am I being fair or am I exaggerating?
• Will my words hurt the other person's feelings, and if so, how can I express myself without inflicting too much pain? (See paragraph 1 of this chapter.)
• How would I feel if someone criticized me this way?
• Am I enjoying the prospect of offering this criticism? (See paragraph 2.)
• Is my criticism confined to a specific act or trait? (See paragraph 9.)
• Are my words nonthreatening and, at least in part, reassuring? (See paragraphs 5 and 6.)

Don't speak up until you have answered these questions honestly.

Not shaming the person you are criticizing

15. The final words of Leviticus 19:17, "You shall rebuke, yes rebuke, your fellow and not bear sin because of him," can also be translated as "*but do not* bear sin because of him." The Rabbis understood the ambiguity in the Hebrew as meaning that, even when criticizing someone, you should not commit a sin by shaming him or her. As Rashi explains in his commentary on this verse: "Though rebuking him, you should not publicly embarrass him, in which case you will bear sin on account of him." To the question, "Should you rebuke one to the point that his face changes color?" the Talmud responds, "No" (*Arachin* 16b).

16. Shaming someone is both ineffective and immoral. If you're rebuking a person for a serious offense, shaming him will only make him defensive, and thus render your words less effective. And if you're rebuking someone for a small offense (as a parent might do to a child who has broken a plate), then shaming him is a greater sin than the offense itself.

17. The best way to avoid shaming a person is to deliver the criticism privately (see the opening paragraph of this chapter), "with soft language and gentle words" (see *Sefer Ha-Chinnuch*, commandment number 239).

For more on not shaming or humiliating another, see chapters 29 and 31.

46

WHEN OTHERS CRITICIZE YOU

1. The inclination to deny responsibility for wrongs we have committed is deeply rooted. According to the Bible, such behavior goes back to the first two human beings. Thus the Torah teaches that when God confronted Adam for disobeying His command and eating of the fruit of the Tree of Knowledge of Good and Evil, he blamed Eve: "The woman You put at my side—she gave me of the tree, and I ate" (Genesis 3:12); Eve, in turn, blamed the snake: "The serpent duped me, and I ate" (Genesis 3:13).

Always try to acknowledge your responsibility and, above all, refrain from blaming others. After all, if you deserve praise for the good you do, don't you deserve criticism for the wrong?

2. It is also vital not to point out faults in whoever is rebuking you, since this is irrelevant. It is also a common temptation. Rabbi Tarfon noted how common it was for people to respond defensively: "If one says to another, 'Remove the chip of wood from between your eyes,' the other responds, 'Remove the log from between your eyes'" (*Arachin* 16b).

3. When you are criticized, reflect on what the other person has said. Even if you believe the criticism to be overstated, ask yourself: Is there some truth in her words? If so, think of a way to avoid that behavior in the future.

4. Train yourself to feel gratitude, not animosity, toward your critics (unless you have reason to believe that someone is being malicious, or is always criticizing and never praising you; such a person should be avoided or ignored). Rabbi Simcha Zissel Ziv taught that we are all willing to pay a doctor for trying to heal us; should we be any less grateful to one who helps to improve our character?[1]

Rabbi Noach Weinberg expresses this with an even more concrete illustration: "Everyone is grateful to someone who tells him that in his carelessness he dropped his wallet with a large sum of money in it. That should be our attitude to constructive criticism."

———

Because the only way to become a better person is to overcome our faults, "you should appreciate it when someone points out ways you can improve. A person who is interested in becoming wealthy will utilize any tips and suggestions he hears if he thinks they will be financially beneficial. In the same way, utilize any tips and suggestions that can be spiritually beneficial" (Rabbi Zelig Pliskin).[2]

———

5. Refusing to listen to criticism cuts us off from the possibility of improvement. As Maimonides taught: "One who hates admonition does not leave himself a path for repentance. Admonition leads to repentance" ("Laws of Repentance" 4:2). Denial is a serious obstacle to repentance and self-improvement.

———

In the case of a nation, it is a catastrophe to have a leader whom people fear to criticize. Such was the case with Mao Zedong, the Communist leader of China, and one of the great mass murderers of the twentieth century. During the late 1950s, there were widespread food shortages in China. Mao insisted that no such shortages existed, and claimed that rich peasants who did not want to hand over their grain were spreading these reports. In truth, the 1959 grain harvest was at least 30 million tons less than the preceding year's, but officials, knowing how angrily Mao would react to such news, instead issued a report claiming large increases. Finally, one man, Peng Dehuai, the minister of defense, sent Mao accurate reports about the increasing danger of widespread starvation. With tremendous courage, Peng even wrote a letter to Mao, amplifying on what he had written.

Mao ignored the criticism, and denounced Peng as "an anti-Party element." Peng was placed under house arrest, and forced to write self-criticism denouncing himself. Several years later, during the Mao-inspired Cultural Revolution, Peng was tortured and killed. Meanwhile, his comments to Mao about the food shortages and starvation were accurate and, as he had predicted, enormous numbers of people died. As the philosopher and historian Jonathan Glover has written, "Mao's policies needed corrective feedback, but most people were too frightened to give it."[3]

———

6. As noted (page 384), people are not obligated to rebuke those who lash out at their critics. If you have a tendency to do this, you might be relieved that people no longer criticize you, but your defensiveness is not a trait of which you should be proud. The fact that the people around you have concluded that it's not worth pointing out your faults (since you're apparently incapable of changing) means that your life as an evolving spiritual and ethical being has ended. As Rabbi Nachman of Bratslav taught, "If you are not going to be better tomorrow than you were today, then what need have you for tomorrow?" And if no one ever feels comfortable criticizing you, the likelihood that you will be better tomorrow is small if not nonexistent.

Truth, Lies, and Permitted Lies

———

You shall stay far away from falsehood.

Exodus 23:7

47

TRUTH: "THE SEAL OF GOD"

═══

THREE REASONS WHY LYING IS BAD

God and the Bible despise falsehood

1. There are many acts prohibited in the Torah; for example, we are forbidden to steal or cheat (Leviticus 19:11), commit adultery (Exodus 20:13), or take advantage of the blind (Leviticus 19:14). But falsehood is the only sin that the Torah commands people to avoid actively: "Stay far away from falsehood" (Exodus 23:7).

2. Another Torah commandment explicitly prohibits lying: "You shall not lie to one another" (Leviticus 19:11). Although the Talmud understands this verse to be a ban on swearing falsely in monetary matters (*Bava Kamma* 105b), it also serves as a general prohibition of lying. Indeed, the Bible has an especial abhorrence of liars: "Lying lips are an abomination to the Lord" (Proverbs 12:22). The Talmud designates habitual liars as so hateful to God that "the speaker of falsehood shall not stand before My eyes" (that is, will be denied a place in the World-to-Come; *Sotah* 42a and *Sanhedrin* 103a).

———

Lying also reveals a fundamentally irreligious attitude. As Rabbi Reuven Bulka explains, "Lies are usually told to cover up or impress others whose attitude toward us is so important that we lie. But by doing so, we ignore the fact that God is also listening; we obviously care less about the impression we are making on God."[1]

———

3. The Torah notes that truth is one of God's thirteen attributes (Exodus 34:7), while the Talmud teaches that "the seal of God is truth" (*Shabbat*

55a; *Sanhedrin* 64a). Rabbi Louis Jacobs explains, "In ancient times, a man would append his seal to a document as evidence of its authenticity [a king, for example, would apply his seal to an enactment of which he approved]. This seal bore some distinguishing mark for identification purposes. Where truth is found, there is evidence of God's presence"[2]; conversely, a lie indicates a lack of God's presence.

An upshot of the teaching that "the seal of God is truth" is that we should never lie to, or about, God—for example by saying, "As God is my witness, I am going to . . ." and then not doing what we have committed ourselves to do. Need one add that it is a "profanation of God's Name" (*Chillul Hashem*; see pages 456–457) to say things such as "I swear to God, I'm going to kill that guy" (obviously, if you swear to do something that Jewish law prohibits, it is forbidden to carry out your oath).

An even worse offense is lying "in God's Name," an act commonly committed by religious extremists who carry out acts of terrorism and cruelty in the Name of God.

Rabbi Abraham Twerski comments that speaking or acting falsely in God's Name renders us guilty of "forging His seal," since we make it appear that God approves of something which He detests.

————

In one of the Talmud's most surprising and rarely commented-upon passages, the Rabbis teach that one should not offer a prayer or praise to God that does not reflect one's own experience of the Almighty.

Thus the Rabbis note that Moses described the Lord as "the great, the mighty, and the awesome God" (Deuteronomy 10:17), but that when Jeremiah described God he spoke of Him as "O great and mighty God" (Jeremiah 32:18), and omitted the word "awesome." The Rabbis imagine Jeremiah as reasoning to himself, "Aliens are destroying His Temple. Where then are His 'awesome' deeds?" Later the prophet Daniel spoke of God as "O Lord, great and awesome" (Daniel 9:4), and omitted the word "mighty." The Rabbis imagined that he reasoned, "Aliens are enslaving his sons. Where are His 'mighty' deeds?" Subsequently, the Men of the Great Assembly (the 120–man ruling body of the Jewish people during the early days of the Second Temple) restored Moses' original words to the prayer service. However, the Talmud expresses amazement that Jeremiah and Daniel had the temerity to abolish an expression used by Moses.* Rabbi Elazar

————

*Some people regard the Talmud's analysis as overstated, and assume that Jeremiah's and Daniel's respective omissions of "awesome" and "mighty" were happenstance, and unintentional. Perhaps, but unlikely. Moses' description of God was so well known that omission of any part *explained: "Since they knew that the Holy One, blessed be He, insists on truth, they would not ascribe false things to Him"*(Yoma 69b).*

Therefore, when we speak to God, we should not use words that are not a truthful expression of our own experiences.

In a similar vein, I once heard the late theologian Rabbi Eliezer Berkovits suggest that on Yom Ha-Shoa (Holocaust Memorial Day), Jews should gather in synagogues and say . . . nothing. While most Jews feel it appropriate on Yom Ha-Shoa to recite the Kaddish prayer in honor of the six million, Berkovits reasoned that since the Kaddish is a prayer that praises God,† it is more appropriate to offer no prayer at all, such silence constituting a form of protest against God for not using His power to stop the Holocaust.

———

4. Other biblical passages, as well, emphasize truthfulness and the avoidance of falsehood. According to the prophet Zechariah, God instructed him to go to the Jewish people to tell them that "these are the things you are to do: Speak the truth to one another . . . and do not love perjury because all these are things that I hate, declares the Lord" (8:16–17). The Psalmist offers as a guideline for anyone who wishes to lead a good life: "Keep your tongue from [speaking] evil and your lips from speaking guile" (34:13; see also Jeremiah 9:2–7).

———

Among the biblical characters who most epitomized the sin of "speaking guile" was Delilah, the beautiful lover of Samson.[3] When the Jewish strongman refused to tell her the source of his strength, Delilah, who had been promised an enormous payment of silver by Philistine authorities for betraying Samson, pressured him into giving her the information: "How can you say you love me when you don't confide in me?" Delilah's deception—convincing a man (or woman) for whom one has no feelings that one loves him, so as to betray him and be rewarded—is particularly cruel. She finally succeeded in wearing down Samson's resistance and, in the Bible's words, "he confided everything to her." His unshorn hair was the source of his strength: "If my hair were cut, my strength would leave

---

was probably intentional. The equivalent would be an American politician announcing that he was committed to "life and the pursuit of happiness." People would assume that his or her omission of the word "liberty" was intentional and significant.

*And because, in Jeremiah's life, God had not revealed Himself to be "awesome," and in Daniel's to be "mighty," they would not use these words in their statements to God, because, for them, this would constitute speaking falsehood to God;

†Its opening words, *"Yitgadal ve-yitkadash shmei rabbah,"* mean, "Magnified and sanctified be God's great name."

*me and I should become as weak as an ordinary man." Delilah promptly de-
livered this information to the Philistines, then lulled Samson to sleep on her lap,
and called in a man to cut off his hair. At that point, Philistine troops over-
powered Samson and gouged out his eyes. Unsurprisingly, Delilah's very name
has entered English, and other languages as well, as a symbol of betrayal (see
Judges 16).*

———

Lying leads us to commit other sins, while truth-telling will stop us from doing so

5. The *Pele Yoetz*, a nineteenth-century compilation (and commentary) of Jewish teachings on a large variety of subjects, cites a midrashic tale of a "very evil man" (*rasha gamur*) who decided to reform. He undertook to fulfill one commandment, not to lie under any circumstances. Through this commitment alone, he achieved full repentance and character transformation. Whenever he was tempted to commit an improper act, he reasoned, "If I am questioned as to whether I did this, what will I say? If I speak the truth, I will be disgraced [or worse]. If I lie, I will have violated the one rule I agreed to accept." Thus, by keeping only this one rule, the man became a true penitent.[4]

The nineteenth-century German rabbi Samson Raphael Hirsch also saw a commitment to truthfulness as the ultimate safeguard against wrongful behavior: "No one commits a breach of law without planning to save himself, in case of discovery, by lying. If you are unable to tell a lie, you will never listen to anyone who wishes to persuade you to do a misdeed. Truthfulness is a protective armor against criminality."[5]

———

*A psychiatrist told me of a patient who was a compulsive womanizer. In his
fifties, the man vowed one Yom Kippur to stop lying; he soon found that he could
no longer juggle several relationships simultaneously as had been his wont. As a
result he entered into his first exclusive, and fulfilling, relationship.*

———

Lying is self-destructive and a cause of unhappiness

6. Even in instances where lying can be justified (see chapter 50), untruth still introduces deceit into our relationships. Thus, although the text offers no criticism of the lie Jacob tells his blind father, Isaac, that he is Esau,

Isaac's firstborn son,* it does not seem to be a coincidence that no other biblical character finds himself on the receiving end of so many deceptions. His father-in-law, Laban, tricks him into marrying Leah instead of Leah's younger sister, Rachel, whom Jacob loves and who had been promised him (Genesis 29:21–30). Many years after this deception, Jacob's sons sell their brother Joseph, Jacob's favorite, into slavery. But first they remove the beautiful coat Jacob had given Joseph, dip it into the blood of a slaughtered goat, and show Jacob the bloody garment (Genesis 37:31–33), leading him to believe that Joseph had been killed by a savage beast. He who deceived *his* father is now deceived by his sons.

The narrative seems to suggest that sin and telling mistruths, even if they can be justified, bring an element of deceit into our relationships.†

Thus, if we find ourselves in a relationship, or a society, in which we must often lie, it is best to remove ourselves from such an environment as soon as possible. Even justifiable lies, if we tell them often enough, become a bad habit and can lead to a lack of truthfulness in all our relationships.

———

Boris Pasternak, the Nobel Prize-winning novelist and author of Dr. Zhivago, *lived in the Soviet Union, a totalitarian regime, and routinely had to lie to stay out of prison. Pasternak noted the toll it took to live in a state of continual untruth: "Your health is bound to be affected if, day after day, you say the opposite of what you feel, if you grovel before what you dislike, and rejoice at what brings you nothing but misfortune."*

———

7. "Such is the punishment of a liar that, even when he speaks the truth, no one listens to him" (*Sanhedrin* 89b). Once you become known as a liar (as in the children's fairy tale about the little boy who cried "wolf"), it is very difficult to change your reputation. And even if you get away with your lies, further punishment awaits: liars often end up not trusting others, since

———

*Genesis 27:6–19; Jacob told this lie in order to secure a special blessing from Isaac. It is clear from the biblical text that it was Jacob, not Esau (whose primary interest seems to have been hunting: Genesis 25:27–28), who was more worthy to receive this blessing, since the future of the monotheist ideal demanded that the most qualified son be chosen to carry on the tradition.

†See Nechama Leibowitz, *Studies in the Book of Genesis*, pages 317–324. We have no way of knowing whether Jacob's sons knew that he had lied to his father Isaac (there is reason to suspect that they might have, since the incident was known to several people, among them Isaac, Rebecca, and, of course, Jacob and Esau; the Midrash suggests that Leah, and by implication Laban and Rachel, knew about this lie as well; see *Genesis Rabbah* 70:19) but it seems evident that they had no compunctions about lying to Jacob.

they find it hard to imagine anyone else is telling the truth in a situation in which they know they would lie.

———

The ArtScroll commentary on Sanhedrin *89b notes that the term used for liar in the above passage is* baddai, *an Aramaic word that connotes "one who embellishes the facts, mixing false details into his stories and statements. Such a person's reports are always considered unreliable because he has effectively trained himself never to let an untainted reference leave his mouth." That's yet another reason why, even when a liar speaks the truth, people mistrust him.*

———

48

BECOMING MORE TRUTHFUL

═══════════

Make sure you speak factual truth

1. Avoid half-truths. A Yiddish proverb teaches that "a half-truth is a whole lie," because an admixture of truth and lies makes the lies more credible. For example, Haman's statements to King Ahasuerus in the Book of Esther about the Jews in the Persian empire started with a truth (that the Jews were scattered and dispersed throughout the Persian kingdom), and then shifted to a half-truth (that the Jews were regulated by different laws than the rest of his subjects). While it is true that the Jews did have some different laws, such as observance of the Sabbath, and the dietary restrictions of Kashrut, their different laws did not conflict with Persian regulations, although this was the impression Haman wished to convey. Finally, he shifted to an outright lie: "They don't obey the king's laws, [therefore] it is not in your majesty's interests to tolerate them" (Esther 3:8). Through the potent combination of truth, half-truth, and lies, Haman convinced Ahasuerus to issue an edict ordering the murder of all Jews.

Therefore, it is important that even when you make allegations against someone you dislike, you allow no exaggeration or partially true accusations to mix in with the true ones. For most people, such restraint is a challenging task: Can we speak pure truth—without exaggeration and half-truths—even about someone we dislike? If we can't do this, it is better to say nothing at all.

———

The recognition of the danger of partial truth is what seems to be behind the oath taken by witnesses in American courts to "tell the truth, the whole truth, and nothing but the truth" (emphasis added). Truth, to be true, has to be whole, not partial.

———

A New York Times *op-ed column reported on March 23, 2004, that in the aftermath of the September 11, 2001, terrorist attacks on the United States, Ari Fleischer, President George Bush's press secretary, had, at a press briefing, "ominously warned" Americans to "watch what they say, watch what they do." Fleischer's words, as the column cited them, do indeed have an ominous ring; an American president's press secretary warning Americans to "watch what they say."*

Did Fleischer indeed say these words? Yes. However, the column wrenched them out of context, thereby conveying the opposite of what Fleischer had conveyed. At a press briefing two weeks after September 11, Fleischer had been asked about a racist comment made by a congressman from Louisiana who said that if he saw a Sikh-American with a towel wrapped around his head, he would tell the man to get out of his state. Fleischer criticized the congressman's statement and noted that "the traditions of our country that make us so strong and so free [are] our tolerance and openness and acceptance." Then another press representative asked him about the statement made by a media figure who asserted that members of the American armed forces who fire missiles are cowards, while the terrorists who crashed their planes into the Twin Towers were not cowards. Fleischer answered, "It's a terrible thing to say, and it's unfortunate," and then went on to say that these sorts of comments are "reminders to all Americans that they need to watch what they say, watch what they do."

As Fleischer, who was pained by the distortion, wrote, "My remarks urged tolerance and openness and were addressed [in part] to those who made statements and threatened actions against Muslims or Sikhs in America."[1]

———

Be precise and accurate

2. Avoid making even minor alterations to the truth, or telling what you believe are insignificant lies. For a set period of time, follow the words of the nineteenth-century Rabbi Menachem Mendel Leffin, author of *Cheshbon Ha-*

Nefesh (Accounting of the Soul): "Do not allow anything to pass your lips that you are not certain is completely true."

For example, many people's voice-mail messages say, "I will call you back as soon as I can." Then they listen to a message, write it down, and wait a day or two before returning the call. They certainly have the right to do so, but then why say, "I will call you back as soon as I can"? Rather, say something more truthful, such as, "Please leave a message, and I will return your call."

———

Alan Morinis writes of how, while on a campaign to become more truthful, he became aware of the little deceits in which he, and many of us, commonly engage.

"I attended a lecture at the university given by someone whom I had known as a graduate student. Since then, he has continued in academia while I long ago wandered off [to other pursuits]. At lunch, he sat opposite me, and early in the conversation, he asked what I thought of a particular book. I had read it years before and couldn't recall a thing about it except the title and author. I hemmed and hawed until he came out with his opinion (which is actually what I think he wanted to do anyway). Why couldn't I have just been honest and said, 'To tell you the truth, I don't remember a thing about it'?"

———

3. Avoid not only outright lies, but also exaggerations that listeners might think are literally true. (This is implied by the wording of Exodus 23:7: "Keep far away from falsehood.") People often violate this command and try to prove a point through exaggeration. For example, I heard a talk-show host making the case for the superiority of the two-parent family. To bolster his argument, he said that 99 percent of teenage violent crime is committed by young males raised without a father at home. But this is not accurate; the percentage is substantially less.[3] The host feared, as many of us do, that the truth alone would not convince others; it needed to be "helped along." Such hyperbole is not only wrong, but also undercuts the speaker's credibility among those who are aware of the inaccuracy (see pages 449–450 for examples of when Jewish law views exaggerations as permissible).

4. Get into the habit of speaking with precision about even minor matters. For example, when a visitor to the Chazon Ish's home posed a question to the rabbi about a Jewish text, the rabbi responded that he had posed the same question, and marked it down in the margins of a book in his library. The Chazon Ish, who was in frail health, asked the visitor to go to his study

and bring the book. A few minutes later the man returned and said, "I looked for the book, but it's not there." The Chazon Ish corrected him, "Don't say, 'The book is not there,' for in fact it is there. Instead say, 'I could not find it.'" Indeed, a moment later, the Chazon Ish's brother-in-law, who was present, went to the room and came back with the book.[4]

5. We can also convey falsehood nonverbally, through nods and facial gestures. That is why the thirteenth-century rabbi Judah the Pious ruled that even nodding or shaking one's head in a manner that creates a false impression is prohibited (see *Sefer Chasidim,* paragraphs 47 and 1058).

Avoid common temptations to mislead and lie

6. Admit when you are wrong. On occasion, the Talmud cites a rabbi's view, and then notes that he later changed his mind.[5] But why didn't the Talmud just cite the rabbi's final view; why tell us that he altered his opinion? Maimonides explains that this was done to teach us that our rabbinic forefathers so loved the truth that they were willing to acknowledge when they were wrong (see the introduction to his Mishnah commentary on *Zeraim*).

Each of us must learn to follow the Rabbis' lead. For example, don't argue on behalf of a position you suspect might be wrong, either out of obstinacy or because you are unwilling to admit your opponent is right. And if you change your mind, don't hide the fact. Thus, Rashi, in responding to a legal query, wrote, "I used to permit this . . . but I was mistaken."[6]

Acknowledging errors is a characteristic of an honest person, and also of a smart one. *The Ethics of the Fathers* teaches that one of the attributes of a wise person is that he acknowledges the truth and admits when he is wrong (5:7); in other words, a wise person wants the truth even more than he or she wants to be right.

———

John Maynard Keynes (1883–1946), the renowned British economist, once delivered a speech in the House of Lords in which he took a different position from one that he had held earlier. When questioned about this inconsistency, Keynes answered, "Occasionally, after being presented with new information or arguments, I change my mind." He then asked his questioner, "And what do you do in such a circumstance?"

———

7. Acknowledge when you don't know something. Some people find it difficult to admit that they are ignorant about a subject. To counteract this, the Talmud instructs people, "Teach your tongue to say, 'I don't know'" (*Berachot* 4a).* If you don't know the answer to a question, don't try to turn the conversation to a topic with which you are familiar; rather, acknowledge the question, and say, "I'm sorry, I don't know."

————

Unfortunately, the desire to be thought of as intelligent and knowledgeable causes many people to pretend to know something that they don't. This applies to relatively minor areas as well. For example, tourists to certain countries often bemoan the tendency of locals to give directions, even when they are uncertain of the way.

————

8. Don't lie even on behalf of a good cause, not only because lying is wrong, but also because people will come to doubt the truthful things you say. Thus, God instructed Adam not to eat of the fruit of the Tree of Life in the Garden of Eden. But Adam, fearing that Eve would violate the edict, apparently told her that not only had God forbidden them to eat from the tree, but that He had also forbidden them to touch it (Genesis 3:3). A Midrash, picking up on the discrepancy between God's original words and Adam's, and Eve's claim to the snake that God had forbidden them to even touch the tree, teaches that the serpent pushed Eve into the tree. When she saw that no injury ensued, she assumed that Adam had likewise lied when he told her that God had forbidden them to eat of the tree. So Eve proceeded to eat the fruit, with disastrous results (Genesis 2:17, and 3:1–19).

From this we learn that even when our cause is just, we must be completely truthful. Thus, Jewish law forbids a person who is soliciting for a charitable cause to say that he gave a larger gift to the charity than he did, in order to influence the person whom he is asking to give a larger gift (see the commentary of the Maharsha on *Sukkah* 29b).

---

*The talmudic citation finishes, "lest you be caught in a falsehood." Rashi notes that this is self-serving advice as well; if you're caught in an untruth, you will lose your credibility. Therefore, when you offer advice or information of which you're unsure, tell people of your doubt. It is not just ethically appropriate, but will also prevent you from being exposed as untruthful or foolish if what you said turns out to be wrong.

———

During World War I, Allied propagandists, anxious to rally public opinion against Germany, concocted tales of atrocities carried out by German occupation troops. German soldiers were accused of tossing infants in the air and impaling them on their bayonets, cutting off children's hands, burning whole families alive, and raping nuns. The stories were widely believed, and helped unite the citizens of the Allied countries in the war effort and motivate the troops (in the United States, these reports occasionally provoked physical attacks on Americans of German descent). When the war ended, it soon became known that although German rule had been harsh and deserved criticism, the atrocities charged to German soldiers had not occurred. More than twenty years later, during World War II, stories of atrocities by German troops again began to circulate, only this time they were all too true. But many people in the West rejected the reports, citing the lies told during World War I, and claimed that this was once again untruthful anti-German propaganda. Thus, immoral lies told during World War I were a factor in discouraging people from believing true reports of Nazi atrocities.

The creators and disseminators of the World War I anti-German propaganda undoubtedly believed that it was justifiable to lie on behalf of a worthwhile cause. They were wrong, and two decades later, tens of thousands of innocent victims, whose suffering was ignored and disbelieved, may have paid the price for their moral error.

———

9. Don't lie or exaggerate in order to help someone at another's expense. Rabbi Jonah Gerondi condemns anyone who makes a recommendation, saying "So-and-so is trustworthy," when he does not in fact know this to be the case. As a result, the other person might entrust his assets to the one recommended and suffer greatly (*The Gates of Repentance* 3:194). Therefore, if you have reason to think well of someone, but are not *sure* of his or her character or competence, make that fact known. Say, "I have a high regard for him, although I don't know him that well," as opposed to, "You can trust him one hundred percent." Giving your honest impression is sometimes more easily done through verbal communication than in a letter of recommendation.

———

Some years ago the noted American writer Norman Mailer used his reputation to help bring about the release from prison of Jack Henry Abbott, a convicted murderer. Impressed by Abbott's writing ability, Mailer wrote strong letters on his behalf. He argued that, in addition to Abbott's writing talents, he was no *longer dangerous. Unfortunately, this was not the case. Within weeks of his re-lease, Abbott got into an argument with a waiter at a restaurant, and stabbed him to death.**

As I have heard it said, "Whereof one does not know, one should not speak."

---

10. As noted earlier, the Talmud teaches that the first question we will be asked in the heavenly court after we die is "Did you conduct your business affairs honestly? *(Shabbat* 31a). In line with this teaching, Rabbi Jonah Gerondi writes that the worst lies are those that are told to cheat in financial matters (*The Gates of Repentance* 3:178).

Even lesser lies, those not involving outright deception, should be avoided. Thus the *Sefer Chasidim* teaches that a would-be purchaser should not, as a bargaining strategy, unfairly denigrate the seller's merchandise, saying things such as "These goods are inferior, and are of little value" (unless they really are) in order to pressure the seller to lower the price. Rather, one should say, "This is what I want to pay you" (paragraph 925).†

"It is virtually certain that the lies which many businessmen employ are not even necessary to accomplish their goals. For example, why must a person lie about the price he paid for an item, when he could simply state, 'This is the price I am asking. I cannot accept less.'" (Chaffetz Chayyim, Sefat Tamim, chapter 2).

---

11. Don't teach your children to tell lies for your convenience. Unfortu-nately, it is quite common for parents to instruct children to lie and tell a

---

*Even subsequent to the murder, Mailer did not want to see Abbott sentenced to a long jail term: "I'm willing to gamble with a portion of society to save this man's talent"; see Carl Rollyson, *The Lives of Norman Mailer*, page 315.

†For one significant instance in which, it seems to me, it would be permitted not to be truthful, and even misleading, in a business negotiation, see Scott Rae and Kenman Wong, *Beyond In-tegrity: A Judeo-Christian Approach to Business Ethics.* The authors note that "the obligation to tell the truth is contradicted by the requirements of commercial negotiation. . . . if there are to be negotiations, rather than a fixed . . . price, there must be *room* for negotiations—call it a negoti-ating range. The range is defined by the highest price the buyer will pay and the lowest the seller will accept. Within those limits a deal can be struck. Now one or the other must make a state-ment, else the negotiations could not begin. The statement, however, must be misleading. If the buyer reveals the highest price he is willing to pay [at the very outset] . . . the deal will be made at that figure. Nor can the seller reveal the lowest price he will take. The *duty* of either is to make his opposite believe that the top (or bottom) of the possible range is lower (or higher) than it really is. And to mislead someone is, of course, to tell him an untruth or, at the least, let him infer what is not the truth. Truth in commercial negotiations is a casualty of the responsibility

cashier at a movie theater, for example, that they are eleven when children twelve or over have to pay adult prices. That is wrong, as it usually is to instruct children to tell a telephone caller the parent is not at home when he or she is;* these types of behavior can be injurious to the child's character. As Samuel Johnson wrote, over two hundred years ago, "If I accustom a servant to tell a lie for me, have I not reason to apprehend that he will tell many lies for himself?" Substitute "child" for "servant" and the contemporary relevance of the statement is clear. Thus, Rabbi Yaakov Kamenetsky never permitted his children to tell callers that he was not at home when he was; rather, he would instruct them to tell the caller that he would be at home at a certain hour, without making any reference to whether he was then at home. (Alternatively, the child can simply say the parent is unavailable.) Thus the children told no lies, and nobody's feelings were hurt.

———

The Talmud relates that Rav was constantly tormented by his wife. If he asked her to cook lentils for him, she would cook peas. If he asked for peas, she would cook lentils.

When his son Chiyya grew up, he would transmit to his mother his father's requests, but would reverse them. If his father asked for lentils, he would say that he wanted peas.

One day his father said to him, "Your mother has improved."

Chiyya answered, "That is because I reversed your messages."

Rav said to him, "Indeed, that is the expression people say, 'From your own children you learn reason.' Nevertheless, do not do so anymore, for the Bible [a higher authority than the people] says ,'They have taught their tongues to speak lies'" (Jeremiah 9:4; Yevamot 63a).

As Rav apparently believed, a parent's obligation to raise a truthful child overrides any convenience the parent might gain from the child's lies.

———

For a similar, but subtly different, case in which lying may be permitted by a child, see the ruling of Rabbi Shlomo Zalman Auerbach on pages 439–440.

---

of the participants to the business entity for whom they work" (page 160). That is why, for example, most of us would not regard a person who says during negotiations, "This is the lowest price I will accept," and who subsequently accepts a lower price, as a liar or as having acted dishonestly.

*I say it is "usually" wrong, because I am not an absolutist on this subject. Sometimes a parent has a very important reason not to take the call, and the child can understand the reason, and not be corrupted by lying on the parent's behalf.

Make sure that you speak with integrity

12. Don't say the opposite of what you feel. The Talmud teaches that among those whom God hates is "one who says one thing with his mouth, while meaning another thing in his heart," (*Pesachim* 113b); this is a form both of hypocrisy and lying. Rabbi Abraham Twerski offers a concrete example: "If you meet someone whom you dislike, it is not hypocritical to behave civilly and even smile. The Talmud says that we are to greet everyone with a pleasant countenance (*The Ethics of the Fathers* 1:15). However, if you say, 'I am so happy to see you,' or in any other way try to give the impression that you truly like the person, that is hypocritical."[7]

13. "You must fulfill what has crossed your lips, and perform what you have vowed" (Deuteronomy 23:24). As Maimonides explains: "By this injunction, we are commanded to fulfill every obligation that we have taken upon ourselves by word of mouth" (*Book of the Commandments*, Positive Commandment # 94). Although this verse seems to be speaking of someone who has made a formal vow to do something, subsequent Jewish law regards it as obligatory to fulfill whatever you have said you were going to do.

Therefore, keep your word, particularly if someone is relying on it, and even when it is inconvenient to do so. Not infrequently, we offer to do someone a favor. At the time we commit ourselves, we really intend to do it. Later, however, we realize that the favor is more inconvenient or time-consuming than we originally thought, and we are tempted not to follow through. Nonetheless, we remain obligated to carry out our word (see Rabbi Jonah Gerondi, *The Gates of Repentance* 3:183).

Rabbi Avrohom Ehrman notes that the responsibility to keep our word increases in proportion to the degree upon which it is relied. Thus he rules that if we tell someone, "I will take you to the airport" (a long drive), and a difficulty arises, "the speaker may back down from his word. However, if the passenger says, for example, 'I'm relying on you,' and the speaker responds, 'Yes, you can rely on me,' that is considered a promise, because the passenger [fully] expects the speaker to keep his word."[8]

One advantage of this is that you will be more cautious before promising to do something. Some people casually offer to do favors in order to be well thought of, but don't follow through, and incur far greater animosity than they would have done if they had not made the offer in the first place. Rabbi Aaron Levine summarizes this aspect of the Jewish tradition on truthtelling: "One should never make a commitment unless one fully intends to carry it out."[9]

———

When traditional Jews undertake to do something, they often add on the words, "bli neder" ("without taking an oath") to protect themselves from having lied in case they don't do what they said they would—for example, "I'm going to mail you that document tomorrow, bli neder."

———

Perhaps the most famous biblical example of keeping a long-standing commitment was Moses' taking Joseph's bones with him when he led the Israelites out of Egypt. Centuries earlier, Joseph had exacted an oath from his brothers, saying, "When God has taken notice of you [and brings you back to Canaan], you shall carry up my bones from here" (Genesis 50:25). On the day the Jews left Egypt, Moses was unquestionably very busy, and the commitment to Joseph had not even been made by him, but by his ancestors; nonetheless, the Bible tells us that he "took with him the bones of Joseph" (Exodus 13:19).

———

14. Similarly, abide by your word even when it is disadvantageous, and perhaps costly. The rabbis understood the Psalmist's words, "one who speaks the truth in his heart" (15:2), as referring to one who follows the truth even when it is known to him alone, and is disadvantageous in practical terms. The classic rabbinic example of a person who acted truthfully in such a circumstance was the fourth-century sage Rabbi Safra, who had an item for sale. A customer came in while the rabbi was reciting the *Sh'ma*, a prayer during which it is forbidden to interrupt, and made an offer for the item. The offer was fair, but since Rabbi Safra could not interrupt his prayer, he said nothing. Because of the rabbi's silence, the customer assumed that his offer was not high enough, and made a higher bid, and then another, still higher one. When the rabbi finished praying, he turned to the man and accepted his first bid. As he explained, "Since I knew when I heard you call out your offer that it was acceptable to me, it would be dishonest for me to accept your higher bid."*

———

The following question was sent to the ethics advice column I was writing: "My husband and I bought an apartment for investment purposes, and placed it with a broker. A couple came to look at the apartment, liked it, and told our broker that they accepted the $4,000 a month rent that we had requested. We were

———
*See Rashi on *Makkot* 24a; I have expanded on the words spoken by Rabbi Safra, and put into his mouth words that are only suggested in Rashi's commentary.

pleased, but the broker insisted that he should still show the apartment to a few other people, since there's always a chance that the first couple might renege on their commitment.

"The following day, another couple saw the apartment, loved it, and offered to pay $4,500 a month. The broker is advising us to take the second offer, since our agreement with the first couple was only verbal. But what do you think— am I obligated to stay with my original commitment, or should I accept the second offer, which amounts to an extra $6,000 a year, money we could really use?"

I responded, "You put something on the market at a price that you yourself specified. Someone agreed to the price, and you accepted their offer. Are you bound by this agreement or not?

"If you are asking a legal question, the answer is obvious. Because nothing was signed, you're not legally bound to abide by your commitment. If you are asking me a moral question, the answer is very different. It seems to me that it would be immoral for you to back out of this deal. The people who made the first bid relied on your word, and accepted the conditions you laid down. To paraphrase Samuel Goldwyn, we will be living in a pretty sad world if verbal agreements are not worth the paper on which they are not written.

"As a practical matter, I would notify the people whose offer you accepted that you have been made another, higher, offer, and that, therefore, in addition to their verbal commitment to rent your apartment, you wish them to immediately (let's say over a forty-eight–hour period) sign a lease. If they refuse to sign right away, then you have the moral right to enter into an agreement with the second couple. By making such a notification, you will be doing the fair thing, while also protecting your own interests."

———

Yet another example of speaking the truth in your heart: If, after hearing a charitable appeal, you resolve in your heart to give a certain amount to the cause, then you should carry this out even if you're tempted later to give less. Similarly, if you hear of a friend who is sick and resolve, "I really must go see her today," then be sure to do so, even if you find yourself running late, or the visit is inconvenient.

———

15. Don't put people off with false excuses: "Do not say to your fellow, 'Come back again, I'll give it to you tomorrow' when you have it with you" (Proverbs 3:28). Many people delay paying bills, arguing that they are short of the necessary funds when they are not. As this verse makes clear, such lies are forbidden; it is particularly wrong to tell such a lie to a working person who might well have little savings and who relies on prompt payment for his and his family's needs.

16. Never promise to give something to a child and then not do so, because the child will learn from your behavior that it is permissible to lie (*Sukkah* 46b). If you don't deliver on your pledge, the child will conclude that truthfulness is only for children, but in the "real world," one may lie.

————

A rabbi who had promised to take some young children on a car trip was asked a short time later by a prominent rabbinic scholar for a ride. The rabbi didn't have room to take them all, and assumed that Jewish law would dictate that transporting the scholar should take precedence. However, when he asked Rabbi Yaakov Kamenetsky, a twentieth-century rabbinic scholar renowned for his truthfulness, whether his reasoning was correct, the rabbi answered, "God forbid that you do such a thing. You will be teaching the children to be liars. They are too young to understand that [normally] an older person comes first. You promised them; you must take them" (Rabbi Shimon Finkelman).[10]

————

17. It is wrong according to Jewish ethics—though not, it would seem, according to American legal ethics—for a lawyer to try to make it appear that an opposing witness is lying when the lawyer has no reason to believe he is, and indeed believes that the witness is probably telling the truth. The more the lawyer feels that the opposing witness is speaking truthfully, the more he might feel it is vital to his case to impugn the witness's testimony. But influencing a jury to believe that a truthful person is a liar is an act of deception (it also violates Judaism's strictures against humiliating a person in public), and puts one in direct violation of the biblical injunction to "stay far away from falsehood" (Exodus 23:7).[11]

18. Basing itself on the biblical law "Stay far away from falsehood," the Talmud rules that if a judge suspects that witnesses are lying, he is forbidden to rule according to their testimony (in Jewish law, judges, not juries, determine guilt and innocence). However, if the judge can't disprove what the witnesses are saying, and therefore has no legal basis for invalidating their testimony, he should recuse himself. A judge who disbelieves the testimony he has heard is forbidden to reason to himself, "I will decide the case on the basis of their testimony, and let the guilt fall on their heads" (*Shavuot* 30b–31a and Maimonides, "Laws of the Sanhedrin" 24:3).

———

Throughout history, judges, particularly in non-democratic societies, have often, and knowingly, issued unjust rulings. The Italian writer Ignazio Silone recalls an incident from the town in which he was raised: "One Sunday, while crossing the little square of my native village with my mother leading me by the hand, I witnessed the cruel, stupid spectacle of one of the local gentry setting his great dog at a poor woman, a seamstress, who was just coming out of church. The wretched woman was flung to the ground, badly mauled, and her dress was torn to ribbons." The woman decided to sue the squire whose dog had attacked her. Because of the man's power, not a single witness would testify on the woman's behalf, and no lawyer would represent her. On the other hand, the squire brought in a well-paid lawyer, along with bribed witnesses who testified that the woman had provoked the dog. The judge acquitted the squire, and condemned the poor woman to pay the court costs.

A few days later the judge, who was a friend of Silone's family, visited them and explained, "It went very much against the grain with me. On my word of honor, I do assure you, I was very sorry about it. But even if I had been present at the disgusting incident as a private citizen and couldn't have avoided blaming him, still as a judge I had to go by the evidence of the case, and unfortunately it was in favor of the dog [and the squire who had set the dog on the woman]."*

Contrast this man's understanding of judicial ethics with that of the Torah and Talmud.†

Out of a concern for truth and justice, Jewish law ruled that if a student

---

*Ignazio Silone, unnamed essay in Richard Crossman, ed., *The God that Failed*, page 83. The judge's lack of decent character is further reflected in the fact that he made no effort to raise money to help the woman, though he believed she had been wronged. Compare his behavior with that of New York Mayor Fiorello La Guardia (1882–1947; he served as mayor from 1933–1945), as recorded by Bennett Cerf. La Guardia was presiding at the police court during the Depression when a poor man was brought in for having stolen a loaf of bread. The man acknowledged that the accusation was true, but claimed that his family was starving. La Guardia said, "I've got to punish you. The law makes no exceptions. I can do nothing but sentence you to a fine of ten dollars." La Guardia reached into his pocket and paid the fine out of his own pocket, and then declared, "I'm going to fine everybody in this courtroom fifty cents for living in a town where a man has to steal bread in order to eat." He had the bailiff collect the fines, and gave the man $47.50 (see Clifton Fadiman and Andre Bernard, *Bartlett's Book of Anecdotes*, page 329).

†In all likelihood, the judge was too afraid to confront the squire and rule against him. It was concerning such judges that the Torah ruled, "Fear no man, for judgment is God's" (Deuteronomy 1:17). In Maimonides' *Book of the Commandments*, he writes, "By this prohibition a judge is forbidden to be deterred by fear of a vicious and wicked evildoer from giving a just judgment against him. It is his duty to render judgment without any thought of the injury the evildoer may cause him" (Negative Commandment number 276). This is, of course, a courageous and difficult standard to live by, but one who cannot do so has no right to become a judge.

saw a rabbinic mentor judging a case and making an error, he should challenge him, and not fear that he was acting disrespectfully in doing so. Again, the Rabbis root this ruling in the verse "Stay far away from falsehood" (Shavuot 31a).

Encouraging others to be truthful

19. Don't cause others to lie. The extraordinary subtlety of Jewish ethics' concern with truthfulness is underscored in a ruling of Rabbi Judah the Pious, an admonition that we take care not to be the cause of another's lying. Thus we should not ask someone a personal question that she will probably not wish to answer, lest we cause her to lie. Similarly, if we see two people whispering, we shouldn't ask them to tell us what they're talking about, lest they, embarrassed to offer no answer—or unwilling to reveal the true one— give us an untruthful response (*Sefer Chasidim*, paragraph 1062).

I believe this standard would have been wise to abide by some years ago, when it was revealed that an American president had engaged in very inappropriate, but consensual, sexual misbehavior with a twenty-one-year-old White House intern. It seemed to me both unwise and unfair to subject the president under oath to questions about his sexual life, because many, and probably most, people cannot be expected to speak fully honestly about so private and personal a matter.

---

20. If your children do something wrong, forgive them without punishment as long as they admit the truth *(Pele Yoetz, page 32)*. One important reason that children should not be raised to fear their parents,* but rather to love and respect them, is that fear is the most common reason children lie to their parents, and end up becoming liars to others as well.

For more on this, see page 254.

---

*Many people assume that the Bible wants children to fear their parents. But the verse that often is translated as commanding fear more accurately means, "Let each man be in awe of his mother and father" (Leviticus 19:3). Awe is understood by Jewish law as mandating, for example, that a child not sit in a chair that normally is reserved for a parent, but not that the child be afraid of the parent.

49

DECEIVING OTHERS

1. *G'neivat da'at* (literally "stealing the mind") refers to deceiving others so that they will think more highly of you than you deserve, for example, by making them believe that you have done them a favor when you haven't. Judaism views this as theft, a "stealing" of another's goodwill.

The Talmud offers several examples of this: "Rabbi Meir used to say, 'A man should not urge his friend to eat with him if he knows very well that he won't. Nor should he offer him any gifts if he knows that he won't accept them'" (*Chullin* 94a; see Rashi's commentary). Another instance would include misleading a person into thinking that your recommendation was instrumental in getting him a job when it wasn't.

Rabbi Nachum Amsel offers an example of how some merchants try to secure undeserved goodwill: "If a store owner advertises that, in sympathy with all those who are suffering because of the recession . . . he is lowering prices, and the truth is that he is lowering prices because he has huge inventory or his competitor lowered prices, that is a violation [of the prohibition of *g'neivat da'at*] because the public will think better of him [although] it is not deserved."[1]

Similarly, Rabbi Avrohom Ehrman notes that it is forbidden for a storekeeper "to give all his customers a reduction from the listed price, yet tell an acquaintance that he is giving him the lower price 'because you are my good friend.'" It would be fine to say, "You're my good friend; I'm happy you came when the item is on sale."[2]

Rabbi Amsel notes, "In a famous advertisement a number of years ago, a coffee company advertised that one should drink their coffee because it is 'mountain grown.' It turns out that all coffee grows in a mountainous area. . . . No one knew that, and people began buying this brand because it was mountain grown. Since all coffee is mountain grown, this is clearly undeserved goodwill . . . and would be improper advertising from a Jewish perspective, even though it is perfectly fine according to American law since nothing false was said."[3]

---

2. The Talmud prohibits "stealing the minds" of non-Jews no less than Jews (*Chullin* 94a). Thus, Maimonides notes that it is forbidden for a Jewish butcher to sell a non-Jew unkosher meat and tell him that it is kosher. While non-Jews are permitted to eat unkosher food, the butcher, in declaring the meat to be kosher, is misleading the non-Jew into feeling grateful to him for selling him something special that would not normally be made available to non-Jews ("Laws of Character Development" 2:6). Rabbi Amsel notes that "in a modern example, a Jew would not be [permitted] to give away a delicious cake full of *chametz* (food forbidden on Passover) to his non-Jewish neighbor [just before] Passover without informing the non-Jew that because of the upcoming holiday he must get rid of the cake. Otherwise, the non-Jew would feel indebted, undeservedly so, and [might feel compelled] to do something good for this Jew in the future."[4]

3. Another form of "stealing the mind" is cheating on a test, thereby misleading the teacher into thinking that you are entitled to a higher grade. This can have extensive ramifications. Rabbi Moshe Feinstein ruled that if a person obtained a better-paying job as a result of having cheated on a test, the higher salary earned is regarded as a form of stolen money, since it is based upon a false premise.[5]

———

This type of "stealing the mind" is commonly engaged in by college students who hand in college papers that they have paid for and that were written by someone else.

———

Additional types of deception

4. Deceptive behavior, consisting of half-truths and outright falsehoods, is often practiced in commerce, by salespeople and by purchasers alike, and is forbidden. Thus it is common, but wrong, for a salesperson to tell a customer the advantages of a product, but remain silent about its defects: "It is both good and honest to do everything to show the buyer the real value of the beauty of the article. However, for one to cover and hide a defect is nothing less than deceit, and is forbidden" (Rabbi Moshe Chaim Luzatto, *Mesillat Yesharim*, chapter 11).

Jewish law imposes obligations upon consumers as well. Thus we may not ask a storekeeper the price of an item if we have no intention of buying it (Mishnah *Bava Mezia* 4:10). While comparison shopping is, of course, permitted, raising a storekeeper's hopes with questions about the price is a form of "oppressing with words" (*ona'at d'varim*), and is forbidden. For example, if you intend to buy a product over the Internet, but want to see the item first, you may not go into a store and pretend to be a potential purchaser so that the storekeeper will demonstrate the product for you. Such deceptions involve a person in one or more lies, and constitute a violation of the biblical prohibition "Keep far away from falsehood" (Exodus 23:7).

5. The Torah curses those who take advantage of another's naïveté or lack of knowledge: "Cursed is the one who leads a blind person astray" (Deuteronomy 7:18). Since each of us has areas of "blindness"—as well as areas of expertise that enable us to take advantage of others—we may understand this curse as being directed against all those who mislead and deceive others, who engage in acts of *g'neivat da'at*, "stealing another's mind."

Three particularly destructive lies

6. *Lies that promote evil, and make it impossible to distinguish between good and evil.* More than 2,500 years ago, the prophet Isaiah denounced "Those who call evil good, and good evil; Who present darkness as light, and light as darkness." (5:20).

What makes such lies particularly wrong is that they cause people to come to immoral conclusions, and perhaps support and engage in immoral behavior. For example, Arab protesters at anti-Israel rallies have repeatedly displayed signs stating, "Israelis danced on 9/11"; in fact, 9/11 was greeted with dancing in many parts of the Arab world; shortly after the terrorist attack, a poll showed that some seventy-three percent of the residents of Gaza supported the murder of almost three thousand Americans. In addition, the terrorist attacks of 9/11, directed against New York City and Washington, D.C., were carried out by nineteen terrorists, all of them Arab Muslims. Nonetheless, since September 11, it has been a prominent feature of Arab antisemitic propaganda that it was Israelis who carried out the attacks.

———

During the 1930s, the New York Times's *Moscow correspondent was Walter Duranty. Throughout his years there, Duranty served as an apologist for Stalin, the greatest mass murderer, along with Hitler, of the twentieth century. Duranty's favorite expression was "I put my money on Stalin." During the infamous "show trials" of the late 1930s, when Stalin tortured many of his close associates to force them to confess, Duranty wrote, "It is unthinkable that Stalin . . . and the court martial could have sentenced their friends to death unless the proofs of guilt were overwhelming." In addition, Duranty assured readers of the* New York Times *that there were no food shortages in Russia at a time when Stalin was carrying out a "planned and deliberate" famine, which led to the deaths of over ten million Russians.[6]*

———

7. *Lies that are told in a courtroom setting under oath.* Witnesses in court testify under oath and in God's Name ("so help me God"), or affirm, with the understanding that they are doing so in God's Name, that they are telling the truth.* Therefore, lies told in court constitute a *Chillul Hashem* ("profanation of God's Name), since they associate God with a lie: "And don't take an oath, then lie in My Name and profane the Name of your Lord" (Leviticus 19:12; the prohibition against bearing false testimony is also one of the Ten Commandments; Exodus 20:13).[7] Furthermore, since justice is so important a commandment (the Torah ordains, "Justice, justice you shall pursue"; Deuteronomy 16:20), thwarting justice undermines a society. It is bad enough that a society contains criminals and corrupt individuals. If, however, the justice system itself is corrupt, then there is no hope for the society to improve itself. Therefore, lying under oath undermines a society's hope of being, or becoming, just.

———

Biblical law exacts what is, as far as I know, a unique and uniquely fair punishment for false witnesses: "And you shall do to them what they schemed to do [to their victim]" (Deuteronomy 19:19). Thus, lying witnesses who make a false claim of $10,000 should themselves be fined $10,000, while Jewish law rules that witnesses who tried to have capital punishment inflicted on an innocent person pay that penalty themselves.

———

*Obviously, atheists do not swear or affirm in God's Name, but they are a very small percentage of the population.

A situation in which one can envisage a Jew being permitted by Jewish law to lie under oath occurs when the punishment to be imposed on the basis of the testimony is so enormously disproportionate to the crime committed as to be a worse offense than perjury. For example, in eighteenth-century England, convicted pickpockets were subject to hanging. It would seem to me that a person who saw an act of pickpocketing and was summoned as a witness would be morally obligated to lie under oath if his truthful testimony could result in a person being killed for an act of pickpocketing (it is better to lie under oath, if one cannot avoid testifying, than to be responsible for bringing about a nonviolent felon's death). While situations like this are unlikely to arise in contemporary democracies, offering truthful testimony in authoritarian and totalitarian states can still result in unjust (in the case of dissidents) or disproportionate (in the case of societies such as China, in which thieves are sometimes executed) punishments. It seems to me that a similar permission to lie under oath would apply in societies such as Saudi Arabia, in which thieves have a hand amputated, a punishment that Jewish law finds immoral and abhorrent.

A friend with whom I discussed this issue strongly disagreed: "This is a very dangerous precedent. If a witness has the right to judge the morality of the punishment, then those who oppose the death penalty will feel morally justified to lie to exonerate a defendant who might be executed. I believe this exact problem has occurred, as well as with jurors who vote to acquit someone they believe is guilty because they oppose the death penalty." I understand my friend's hesitations, but I do not accept that one should therefore feel obligated to offer truthful testimony in non-democratic *societies whose leaders will use such testimony to inflict immoral punishments (like prison camps or execution for dissidents), or in semi-democratic societies like eighteenth-century England, in which pickpockets were hanged. Telling the truth in such settings is, I believe, comparable to following Kant's directive to speak truthfully to a murderer inquiring as to the whereabouts of his would-be victim; the truth brings about much greater immorality than would a lie (see page 423).*

———

8. *Lies that destroy another's good name.* As noted earlier, Jewish law designates this sin as *motzi shem ra* (see chapter 43), and it is one of the few offenses for which the victim has no obligation to forgive the offender, even if he repents and begs forgiveness (Jerusalem Talmud, *Bava Kamma*

8:7).* The great wrong of such a lie is that the damage inflicted may well be irrevocable; even if you try later to reach all the people to whom you spoke, and tell them that what you said was untrue, it is very unlikely that they will reach all the people to whom they conveyed this misinformation. Therefore your defamation will go on being believed by many people.

This applies to destroying the good name of a whole people, not just individuals; in the case of a people, the damage inflicted can include murder. Thus the medieval Crusaders didn't wake up one morning and start randomly killing Jews. Rather, they and their ancestors had been conditioned for centuries to think of Jews as "Christ-killers," which they weren't. (Even if some Jews in first-century Israel had been involved in bringing about Jesus' death, how could their descendants be described as "Christ-killers"? At worst they could be called "descendants of Christ-killers." This characterization rendered Jews as less than human, and once it took hold, it became easy to kill Jews.

50

WHEN LYING IS PERMISSIBLE

1. Many influential figures in the Western world, both Christian and secular, have argued that lying is always wrong, no matter what the motive. Saint Augustine believed that telling a lie costs one eternal life. He reasoned, therefore, that lying, even when doing so could save another's life, was both unjustifiable and foolish: "Does he not speak most perversely who says that one person ought to die spiritually, so another may live? . . . Since, then, eternal life is lost by lying, a lie may never be told for the preservation of the temporal life of another." Catholic theology, influenced greatly by Saint

---

*While many rabbinic figures advocate the victim extending forgiveness in such a case, the mere fact that Jewish law does not require it suggests that all of us must be very careful before we repeat and transmit negative stories about another that might not be true.

Augustine, likewise holds that lying is always wrong.* Indeed, John Henry Cardinal Newman, perhaps the nineteenth century's best-known convert to Catholicism, and a renowned theologian, argued against lying in terms even more forceful than those used by Saint Augustine: "The Catholic Church holds it better for the sun and moon to drop from heaven, for the earth to fail, and for all the many millions who are upon it to die of starvation in extremist agony . . . than that one soul . . . should commit one venial sin, should tell one willful untruth, though it harmed no one.[1]"†

Immanuel Kant believed that telling the truth was a universal moral absolute that allowed for no exceptions. In his essay "On a Supposed Right to Lie from Benevolent Motives," Kant argued that if a would-be murderer inquires whether "our friend who is pursued by him has taken refuge in our home," we are forbidden to lie and mislead him.[2]

Unlike Saint Augustine and Kant, the Hebrew Bible and the Talmud present a more nuanced view of truth-telling. Both emphasize that, while telling the truth is very important, there are instances in which lying is permitted and, on occasion, even mandated. In other words, while truth-telling is an important but not an absolute value, in at least six circumstances, Jewish law permits, or even obligates, us to lie, exaggerate, or otherwise mislead another:

- lying to prevent future harm (for example, when life—either your own or someone else's—is at stake)
- lying in order to right a past wrong done to you (for example, when dealing with a dishonest or deceptive person or government)
- lying when the effect of telling the truth will cause unnecessary hurt

---

*The citation from Saint Augustine is found in "On Lying," in *Treatises on Various Subjects,* volume 14, R. J. Defarrari, editor. Because there are times when it becomes almost impossible not to lie (e.g., if your spouse asks you, "Do you still think I'm very attractive?" and you don't, or one of your children asks, "Do you think I'm as smart as my sister?"), Catholic law was forced to come up with an institution known as the "mental reservation." Through this device, a person is permitted, in effect, to lie to another by making a reservation in their mind. For example, if a very sick patient who is likely to die soon asks his doctor, "Am I going to make it, Doctor?" the physician is permitted to say, "Yes, you're going to make it," while thinking to himself, "for another few days"; for another example of mental reservation in Catholic law, see the footnote on pages 428–429). There are striking parallels to the notion of mental reservation within Jewish law, though I have never seen that term, or a Hebrew equivalent, used. Thus, for example, the Talmud granted permission to use a form of mental reservation to enable a Jew to avoid paying a discriminatory tax (see pages 428–429). Also, during the Holocaust, when the letters *RK* in a passport stood for "Roman Catholic," rabbis permitted Jews to forge such passports and construct in their own minds a different meaning to the letters (see page 474).

†Rabbi Dr. Aharon Lichtenstein, both a talmudic and literary scholar, comments on this passage:

(for example, when people's feelings are involved, and no advantage, but only pain, will come from speaking the truth)

- lying to create peace or otherwise do good (for example, lying to a poor person to encourage him to accept money he needs [see page 445])
- lying because a question invades your zone of privacy (for example, a woman who tells unwanted suitors that she is engaged or married)
- lying when exaggerating to make a point, and it is understood that you are exaggerating ("I was so upset, I thought I was going to explode")

LYING TO PREVENT FUTURE HARM

Lying about facts

2. The fact that lying is sometimes justified is illustrated by the one incident in the Bible in which God instructs someone to lie. It occurs during the reign of King Saul. Appointed at God's behest, and anointed king by the prophet Samuel, Saul disobeys a divine command; God thereupon instructs Samuel to go and anoint David in his stead. The prophet fears to do so: "If Saul hears of it, he will kill me." God tells Samuel, "Take a heifer with you and say, 'I have come to sacrifice to the Lord'" (I Samuel 16:1–3).

God does not promise Samuel that He will protect him. Instead, God tells him to lie,* thereby teaching Samuel, and, by implication, all Bible readers, that one does not owe would-be murderers the truth.

———

The prophet Jeremiah also lied to save his life. When the province of Judea revolted against Babylon, Jeremiah believed the revolt to be hopeless. He publicly and repeatedly aired his views, telling the people that only those who surrendered to the Babylonians would be saved. Not surprisingly, the Judean leadership viewed Jeremiah as a traitor; they had him arrested and placed in a muddy pit that contained no water.

King Zedekiah, acting at the behest of a servant, had Jeremiah raised from

———

"Contemporaries may find it difficult to believe this sentence was not written by a virulent critic of Roman Catholicism but by one of its leading nineteenth-century spokesmen—indeed, by one of its most *liberal* spokesmen. . . . The statement rings harsh if not cruel." (*Leaves of Faith: The World of Jewish Learning*, page 169).

*Some people argue that since Samuel did indeed offer a sacrifice on this trip, he wasn't really lying. In truth, this is a specious argument. Since ending Saul's reign as king was the reason for *the pit and incarcerated in someone's home, a form of house arrest. Later the king summoned the prophet to a private audience, at which Jeremiah reiterated what he had been preaching throughout Judea, that the revolt was hopeless. He even warned Zedekiah that he would be captured by the Babylonians and that Jerusalem would be burned down.*

Before they parted, the king, probably fearing that his officers would depose him if they learned that he had met with Jeremiah, said to the prophet, "Do not let anyone know about this conversation or you will die." He instructed Jeremiah that if any government officials learned of the meeting and asked him about their conversation, he should respond, "I was presenting my petition to the king not to send me back to the house of Jonathan (in whose house Jeremiah was held prisoner) to die there." Sure enough, the king's officials did question Jeremiah, who replied as the king had instructed him. "So they stopped questioning him, for the conversation had not been overheard" (and therefore Jeremiah could lie without fearing he would be caught; Jeremiah, chapter 38). Once again, the biblical narrative implies that one should lie, as did the prophets Samuel and Jeremiah, to save one's life.

If one is permitted to lie *when life is at stake, then of course one is permitted to* mislead *to achieve the same result. For example, when David, running for his life from Saul, fled to Gath, he feared that King Achish, the local monarch, would kill him. David therefore feigned madness, scratching marks on the city's gate, and letting saliva run down his beard. Witnessing this behavior, the king said to his courtiers, "You see the man is raving; why bring him to me [to be killed]? Do I lack madmen that you have brought this fellow to rave for me?" The ruse was successful, and Achish left David alone (I Samuel 21: 11–15).*

———

3. On several other occasions, when biblical characters lied to save their lives or otherwise avoid unfair punishment, the text makes it clear that God approved of their misrepresentations. In perhaps the best-known incident, the two midwives Shifra and Puah received a direct order from Pharaoh to murder all male Israelite babies at birth. However, the text tells us that because they feared God, they "did not do as the king of Egypt told them [and] they let the boys live" (Exodus 1:17). When Pharaoh demanded to know why the women hadn't carried out his order, Shifra and Puah did not respond, "Because we thought your order was wrong." Rather, they made up a false

---

Samuel's trip, the fact that he also offered a sacrifice was irrelevant; comparable to a woman telling her husband that she is going to Mexico for a vacation, when the real purpose of her trip is to establish residence so that she can file for divorce. Even if she does vacation while in Mexico, she can't claim that she didn't lie to her husband.

excuse: "Because the Hebrew women are not like Egyptian women; they are vigorous. Before the midwife can come to them, they have given birth."

Did God disapprove of the midwives' lies? Definitely not. The next verses inform us that "God dealt well with the midwives . . . and He established households for them" (Exodus 1:20–21).[3] Like Samuel, Shifra and Puah had reason to fear that if they told Pharaoh the truth, he would execute them. These episodes yield important and still relevant lessons, among them being that we do not owe the truth to persecutors, and we do not have to accept martyrdom when it can be avoided.*

———

The Talmud tells of Rabbi Elazar ben Parta, who, during a period of Roman persecution, was questioned by the authorities: "Why have you been teaching the Torah and why have you been stealing?" [both of which were capital crimes]. Rabbi Elazar denied both charges. In actuality, while he was not a robber, he did teach Torah.

"Then why do they call you teacher?" the Romans asked.

"I teach weaving," the rabbi replied, a statement that was untrue (Avodah Zarah 17b). *The Romans also asked him why he did not attend the idolatrous services at the meeting house, which Jews were required to attend. Rabbi Elazar answered, "I am an old man and I was afraid you [the Roman troops] would trample me under your feet"* (Avodah Zarah 17b).

———

For the exceptions, when Jewish law would dictate not lying to persecutors, see chapter 52.

4. There are two other biblical instances in which people lied and misled others to save another person's life as well as their own; both occurred during the reign of King Saul. Saul hated and wished to kill David, although his daughter Michal was married to David, and his son Jonathan regarded David as his closest friend. When Saul conspired against David, Michal not only planned David's escape, but also lied to her father, telling him that she had

---

*Had biblical morality insisted on the midwives acting as martyrs, by telling Pharaoh the truth and bearing the consequences, it would probably have discouraged many future readers of the Bible from risking their lives to save victims of governmental oppression. Instead, by teaching that God rewarded the midwives for their behavior, which included lying, we learn that not only should we save the lives of the persecuted, but also that, if caught, we should lie to avoid punishment.

helped David only because he had threatened to kill her otherwise (I Samuel 19:17). Clearly, Michal's lies were occasioned by fear of her father. Similarly, on another occasion, when the king plotted to kill David, Jonathan lied to his father as to David's whereabouts (I Samuel 20:28).

These incidents imply that it is permitted for children to lie to an abusive parent (and perhaps to anyone in a position of power) who will *misuse* the information given.

5. Three incidents in Genesis suggest that it is permissible to say something untruthful to save one's life, even when doing so puts an innocent person at significant, though not mortal, risk. Thus Abraham, upon entering Egypt, and fearing that its people will kill him to take his beautiful wife Sarah, tells her, "Please say that you are my sister, that it may go well with me because of you, and that I may remain alive thanks to you" (Genesis 12:12–13).* Sarah does not dispute Abraham's fears. She proceeds to tell the lie Abraham asked her to relate, and even stands by it when the king takes her into his home. Only when God sends a plague on Pharaoh's house does the Egyptian monarch learn that Sarah is a married woman, and he immediately releases her.

Abraham lies about this matter once again (Genesis, chapter 20), and his son Isaac acts in the same way (Genesis 26:6–11). On none of these occasions does God express displeasure with what Abraham or Isaac has done (since God communicates with the Patriarchs on other occasions, He could have easily expressed disapproval of their actions).

Therefore, should a man expose his wife to the possibility of adultery if the alternative is that he will be killed? The response in Genesis seems to be yes.† However, one great medieval Bible commentator, Nachmanides, sharply criticizes Abraham, asserting that "our father Abraham inadvertently committed a great sin" by urging Sarah to identify herself as his sister. Instead, Abraham should have trusted in God to protect him" (see his commentary on Genesis 12:10 and on 20:12).

A contemporary legal scholar, Daniel Friedman, views Abraham and Isaac's behavior more sympathetically: "Both Abraham and Isaac acted with a threat of death hanging over them, and it could be argued that a lie essential to pre-

---

*Interestingly, Abraham's instruction to Sarah to lie is the first time he speaks in the Bible.
†Later rabbinic law might regard this as a situation in which "one should permit oneself to be killed rather than transgress"; see *Pesachim* 25b.

serving life cannot be criticized. Neither Pharaoh nor Abimelech [the object of Abraham's second lie, and Isaac's as well] deserve much sympathy. They were rulers who took women from the families of shepherds who crossed their land and did not hesitate to use force to obtain them."[4]

Therefore, whether one should lie in such a situation remains an open question, although most commentaries on Abraham's behavior do not criticize it.

———

6. We are permitted to lie to, or otherwise deceive, unscrupulous people even if we only *suspect* that our lives may be in danger. The Talmud speaks of a case (in context it appears hypothetical) of a man who perceived during the course of a meal that his host intended to kill him, and said, "This dish tastes just like one I had in the royal palace." The host thought to himself, "So he knows the king. I had better not harm him" (*Sotah* 41b).

———

While visiting the Jewish community of Morocco, my friend Dennis Prager saved his life with a similar stratagem. During a walk with some teenage Jews, the group was attacked by a band of antisemitic Moroccans. Dennis kicked one attacker hard, knocking him to the ground. The man jumped up with a knife in his hand. Dennis, who was fluent in French, pointed to a nearby tree and said, "I am a friend of King Hassan, and if anything happens to me, you will hang from that tree." Men standing nearby warned the man with the knife that he must be a diplomat, and the attackers quickly dispersed. Needless to say, Dennis did not know King Hassan.

———

7. It is permitted to lie, and even swear falsely, to robbers. The Mishnah rules that a farmer may vow to robbers that the material or produce they are demanding from him "belongs to the royal house, even if it does not." (*Nedarim* 3:4) in order to make them afraid to take it.*

8. A Jew is permitted to lie to avoid paying a tax that discriminates against Jews. (By implication, a person from any group would be permitted

———

*Compare this pragmatic ethic with an episode related by Father Joseph Esper in *Saintly Solutions to Life's Common Problems*, a compilation of ethical and spiritual advice based on the lives of hundreds of Catholic saints: "One day, the holy fifteenth-century Polish priest Saint John of Kanty [a professor at the University of Cracow] was walking down a country road when he was stopped by some robbers; they took the money in his bag and demanded to know whether he had any more. John said no, and the robbers departed. Immediately after this, however, John remembered that he had some coins sewn into his cloak, so he hurried after the highwaymen, caught up with them, and, apologizing for his error, handed over the additional coins. The rob-to lie to avoid paying a discriminatory tax directed against the group from which she comes.) Thus, during the reign of Shapur II (309–379 c.e.), a form of fire worship became the national and state-supported religion in Persia. To win converts to the faith, the Persian government exempted fire worshippers from the poll tax. In a Jewish version of the concept of "mental reservation," (see the footnote on page 428), the rabbinic scholar Rava ruled that it was permitted to avoid paying the tax by appearing before Persian officials and declaring oneself to be "a servant of fire." While the officials regarded such a statement as an acknowledgment that one was a follower of their religion, the Jew making this statement was instructed to think to himself that he was a worshipper of the one God, whom the Torah designates as a "consuming fire" (see Deuteronomy 4:24 and *Nedarim* 62b).[*]

Obviously, in democracies that do not have antisemitic taxes, Jews are obligated to pay taxes like all other citizens.

9. During a war, one may deceive enemies. The Bible relates how Ya'el, a Kenite woman, invited the fleeing Canaanite general Sisera into her tent: "Turn aside, my Lord, turn aside to me; have no fear," she told him, before lulling Sisera to sleep and then killing him. In addition to Sisera's cruelty as a military commander, he and his troops were also rapists (Judges 5:30), an act that makes Ya'el's killing of him more morally explicable. The prophetess Deborah praised Ya'el for her deception of Sisera (Judges 5:24–26; see also Judges 4:17–21).

In a more modern example, during World War II, the Allies took extraordinary measures to deceive the Germans as to the date and destination of the D-Day invasion of Normandy, France. Fortunately, they succeeded in doing so, thereby affecting the outcome of the war. If not for this deception, Hitler would have prolonged the war, and murdered far more people.

---

bers were so amazed by his honesty that they returned everything they had taken from him" (page 65). Father Esper, though clearly impressed by Saint John's extraordinary commitment to not lying, nonetheless notes that such behavior is not expected of everyone: "While outright lying should be avoided, we're entitled to use mental reservations in answering unjust questions. For instance, when asked by robbers whether we have any money, we may add to our negative response the unspoken statement, 'At least not any that I wish to give to you" (page 66).

[*] In the *Shulchan Arukh, Yoreh Deah* 157:2, the Ramah (Rabbi Moses Isserles) rules that, in cases of danger, it is permitted to use ambiguous language to mislead idolaters into believing that you share their faith. However, at the beginning of this passage, Rabbi Joseph Karo rules that even when a Jew's life is at stake, it is forbidden to identify oneself explicitly as a believer in an idolatrous religion.

In short, in the proper circumstances, deception is not only tolerated, but applauded.

10. Jewish law normally opposes "sting operations" in which police or other government officials lie and attempt to bribe or otherwise induce a person to commit a crime; the presumption is that it is wrong to tempt a person to do an evil act in which he might not have engaged had he not been tempted.* However, the Bible does record a "sting operation" that was set up to catch only those who were engaging in behavior that Judaism regards as abhorrent: idolatry. Fifty-one of the Torah's 613 commandments oppose idol worship. During a spread of such worship in ancient Israel—a veritable life-and-death struggle between the God of Israel and the god Baal—King Jehu pretended to be a follower of Baal (as his father, Ahab, had been). The king then invited the priests of Baal to a large religious gathering. When they arrived, the Bible reports, "Jehu acted with guile in order to exterminate the worshippers of Baal" (II Kings 10:18–19).†

———

The Bible's implicit approval of a "sting operation" to catch idolaters might serve as an ethical precedent for justifying such operations to root out other serious evils, such as large-scale drug sales, organized crime, and murder. The key ethical issue, it seems to me, is that the "sting" not be set up so as to seduce people who would not otherwise engage in such behavior (for example, police disguised as drug dealers offering money to people to smuggle drugs, unless they have very strong reason to suspect that the person approached has already done so).

———

*It would be permitted to engage in such behavior if the officials had received credible reports that the person had been taking bribes, and sent an agent to offer a bribe to test whether the reports they had received were true.

†The Bible's hatred of idolatry was rooted not only in idolatry's rejection of monotheism, but in its support of child sacrifice (see Deuteronomy 12:31 and Leviticus 20:2), its widespread practice of both heterosexual and homosexual cult prostitution (see, for example, Deuteronomy 23:18–19), and its support of bodily mutilation (Leviticus 21:5). In the later books of the Bible, the prophets condemn the idolatrous nations surrounding the Hebrews for the moral atrocities they committed far more than for their erroneous theological beliefs (see Amos's condemnation of the horrific cruelties committed by the peoples of Damascus, Gaza, Tyre, Edom, Ammon, and Moab; chapters 1 and 2). Rabbi Louis Jacobs, a British theologian and religious scholar, concludes that "nowhere in the prophetic writings are the [non-Jewish] nations condemned for worshiping their gods, only for the ethical abominations such as child sacrifice associated with the worship." ("The Relationship between Religion and Ethics in Jewish Thought," in Gene Outka and John P. Reeder Jr., eds., *Religion and Morality*, page 159).

11. Similarly, it is meritorious to lie to save an innocent person from being hurt. Rabbi Chayyim Yaakov Levine, the son of Reb Aryeh Levine, tells how his father used to take a parcel from his house every *Rosh Chodesh,* the first day of the new month and a minor Jewish holiday. He never explained where he was going, but once, when they were walking on the street, a man came over and asked Reb Aryeh, "How is your relative getting along in the mental hospital?" Reb Aryeh answered, "Thank God" *(Baruch Hashem),* and continued on his way. The son asked his father, "What relative do we have that is in the mental hospital?" Reb Aryeh explained that some years earlier he had paid a visit to the hospital and had come across a patient who was being mistreated and ignored. The man had no relatives or friends to visit and advocate for him, and the orderlies acted harshly with him, knowing that there was no one to champion his cause. Reb Aryeh immediately made it known to the orderlies that this patient was his relative. From then on, to make sure that the orderlies remembered that fact and treated the man with greater care (and to bring pleasure to the man as well), Reb Aryeh would bring him gifts every *Rosh Chodesh.*[5]

12. As will be shown later (see page 437), Jewish law mandates praising an unattractive bride as beautiful so as to spare her from humiliation. One is permitted to lie to spare *oneself* from humiliation, as well. Although there is no explicit statement about this in the Talmud, it is the inescapable conclusion of a well-known talmudic tale. Rabban Gamliel, the autocratic leader of the Sanhedrin, believed that the evening *Ma'ariv* prayer service was mandatory, as were the morning *Shacharit* and afternoon *Mincha* services. However, when a student asked Rabbi Joshua his view of the service's legal status, the rabbi told him that he thought the evening service was optional *(reshut);* one, therefore, was not in violation of Jewish law if one did not say it.

A short time later, at a public session of the Sanhedrin, the same questioner arose and asked if the evening service was obligatory or optional, and Rabban Gamliel answered that it was obligatory, and then asked, "Is there anyone here who disputes this ruling?" Rabbi Joshua, who was Gamliel's second-in-command, said, "No." Gamliel turned to Joshua and said, "But it was reported to me in your name that the evening prayer is optional."

The highly embarrassed Rabbi Joshua said, "Were I alive and he [the questioner] dead, I would be able to deny my ruling."*

---

*Gamliel ignored Joshua's comment, and then went on to humiliate him by forcing him to stand up while he, Gamliel, continued lecturing.

Rabbi Joshua's admission that he would have lied if he could have gotten away with it, coupled with his reputation in the Talmud as a man of a saintly disposition, suggests that we may lie if we have to pay an unfair price for admitting the truth. In this case, Joshua knew Gamliel to be an intolerant man, and he lied to avoid being humiliated by him. Indeed, the other rabbis present do not seem to have been bothered in the slightest by Rabbi Joshua's admission that he would have continued in his lie if he could have; they were only bothered by Rabban Gamliel's disrespectful treatment of Rabbi Joshua, an act for which they deposed him from office (*Berachot* 27b).

———

According to the Torah, when a woman gives birth for the first time, and the child is a boy, a ceremony known as pidyon ha-ben *(redemption of the firstborn) is performed thirty days after the baby's birth.[6] Rabbi Ovadiah Yosef, the former Sephardic Chief Rabbi of Israel, was confronted with an unusual question concerning a* pidyon ha-ben: *A woman had given birth out of wedlock and had put the infant up for adoption. Many years later the woman became religious and married, but never told her husband about the prior birth. When the couple's firstborn was a boy, the husband and all his family prepared to make the* pidyon ha-ben *celebration. The woman asked whether she had to tell her husband the truth about her previous child (an act that could have had serious repercussions for their marriage). Rabbi Yosef gave permission for the* pidyon ha-ben *to proceed, even though, ritually speaking, it was a sham service.[7] The rabbi's reasoning would seem to be as follows: Better to conceal the truth and spare the woman humiliation in front of her husband, and both of them humiliation in front of his family and the community.*

———

Lying about your intentions in order to prevent harm

13. In a situation in which someone's life is at stake, it is permitted to offer money, even if you are not in a position to pay. For example, if someone is drowning, and you can't swim, and a person who can swim makes it known that he has no intention of going into the water, Jewish law permits you to promise the would-be rescuer a large financial reward, which you are not obligated to pay. The reason, presumably, is not only that one should do anything to save a life, but that the person who is refusing to save the life is obligated to do so, whether he wants to or not (as long as his own life is not put at risk), and whether he is paid for doing so or not.*

14. A talmudic anecdote (but not a law) suggests that one is permitted to deceive someone who is withholding information that can provide people with relief from great pain. Thus, Rabbi Yochanan swore to a gentile noblewoman and healer that he would not reveal the contents of a remedy she had shared with him to heal a serious tooth ailment from which he was suffering. The next day, despite his oath, Rabbi Yochanan disclosed the remedy to his students, obviously feeling that to withhold such medical aid from people was a more serious offense than lying to the noblewoman (*Avodah Zarah* 28a).†

Having related this admittedly problematic story, I don't know whether we can draw a contemporary lesson from it. For example, it seems wrong for a pharmaceutical company employee to break a confidentiality agreement and reveal to people in need how an expensive medication is made, although I do acknowledge that that does seem to be the implication of this talmudic narrative.

Robert Mass, a lawyer and careful student of legal ethics, argues that acceptance of Rabbi Yochanan's behavior as legitimate might open the door to much ethically questionable behavior: "For example, is it okay to bring cheap [legal] drugs into the U.S., lying to customs officials at the border, even if you are going to do something as philanthropic as distributing them to the poor?"

15. Many biblical and talmudic teachings that, in effect, grant permission to lie in special circumstances, occur within the context of anecdotes. Thus, although there isn't a specific talmudic dictum that says, "One is permitted to lie to those one suspects of being thieves," the Talmud does speak with approval of Rabbi Akiva's disciples, who, while journeying to the town of Chezib, were overtaken by men they had reason to believe were bandits.

Shulchan Arukh, Choshen Mishpat 264:7 rules that a person who is fleeing for his life can promise someone an excessive sum to save him, but is then obligated to pay only the sum that is reasonable for the effort expended by the other.

†The talmudic account reports that the noblewoman said to Rabbi Yochanan, "Swear to me that you will not reveal the remedy to anyone." He swore to her: "To the God of Israel I will not reveal it." The Talmud explains that Rabbi Yochanan's oath was intentionally deceptive: "To the God of Israel I will not reveal it," which implies, "but to his people Israel, I will."

When the robbers asked the disciples where they were going, they responded "Acco," a city beyond Chezib. The bandits accompanied them, but when they reached Chezib, Akiva's disciples announced that they would be remaining there. The bandits, who apparently had intended to wait until they were near Acco before robbing them, asked them, "Whose disciples are you?" and the men replied, "Rabbi Akiva." The robbers responded, "Happy are Rabbi Akiva and his disciples, whom no evil man will succeed in harming" (*Avodah Zarah* 25b).

The behavior of Akiva's disciples brings to mind King David's laudatory description of God: "With the pure, You show yourself pure, but with the perverse, You show yourself wily"(II Samuel 22:27). Jewish sources understand this verse as meaning, "With an honest person act honestly, and with a perverse person (a trickster) show yourself subtle." Thus, a talmudic passage (*Bava Bathra* 123a) depicts Rachel as asking Jacob, "Are the righteous permitted to act deceitfully?" He responds, "Yes, they are [when others are trying to deceive them]."

16. Deception is allowed in order to determine which litigant is telling the truth. This strategy was practiced by King Solomon when he found himself confronted with an infant and two mothers, each of whom claimed the infant was hers. There seemed no way to decide which woman was the real mother until Solomon ordered that a sword be brought, and the baby cut in two. That way, each woman would receive half. One of the women begged Solomon not to do so: "Please, my lord, give her the live child, only don't kill it," while the other insisted, "It shall be neither yours nor mine; cut it in two."

Solomon immediately perceived that the woman who wanted the infant spared was the true mother, a decision he made by pretending to do something he had no intention of doing (see I Kings 3:16–28). Thus, lying sometimes can and must be used in the service of justice and, ironically, truth.[8]

Lying about our opinion to spare someone, including ourselves, harm

17. The Talmud says one may alter the truth or, if necessary, lie to save a person from being exploited. For example, if you are a guest, are treated generously, and are subsequently asked how your hosts treated you, you are permitted to understate the truth, and say something such as "It was okay," if you have reason to believe that speaking candidly ("They were fantastic, so generous and caring") will cause others to exploit your host's generosity (*Bava*

Mezia 23b).* Indeed, the Talmud rules that this is an instance in which even a religious scholar (that is a model Jew), is expected to lie. Such cases require common sense and the ability to discern the character of the people who asked the question.

18. "It is permitted to flatter [and thereby lie to] the wicked" (*Sotah* 41b), but only if you do so out of fear of their causing you injury or loss. In all other instances it is forbidden to praise or otherwise speak well of wicked people (Rabbi Jonah Gerondi, *The Gates of Repentance* 3:199). In other words, lie when you must to preserve life or property, but refrain from lying when you don't have to, lest it become a habit and you lose the ability to distinguish between good and evil, and between truth and falsehood.

Lying in order to right a past wrong done to you

19. You may lie to people who have defrauded or stolen from you, in order to get your property returned. The Talmud tells of two rabbis who deposited their wallets on a Friday afternoon with an innkeeper with whom they were staying. At the Sabbath's conclusion, when they asked for their purses, the innkeeper said, "You never gave them to me." The rabbis noticed that the innkeeper had lentils on his mustache. Meanwhile, one of the rabbis plied the man with drink, while the other went to the innkeeper's wife and said to her, "Your husband said you should give us the two wallets, and the sign [that we were sent by him is that he told us] that you served him lentils for lunch." They got their wallets back and departed (*Yoma* 83b).

20. It would also seem to be permitted to deceive someone who has deceived you, in order to undo the damage. For example, the patriarch Judah did not wish to marry off his youngest son, Shelah, to Tamar. Her two previous husbands, Judah's two older sons, had died,† and according to an ancient tradition—which Torah law later incorporated—since both of Shelah's brothers had been childless at the time of their deaths, he was obligated to marry Tamar. Therefore, after the death of the second son, Judah said to Tamar, "Stay as a widow in your father's house until my son Shelah grows

---

*Obviously, if you respond in this way, you should tell your host what you said and why, lest the host hear about it and be insulted.

†The Bible emphasizes that they died because of their sins, not because of anything Tamar had done, though Judah perhaps thought she was somehow responsible.

up." However, the Torah makes it clear that Judah never intended to give Shelah to her in marriage. Tamar, who was legally forbidden to marry any other man, set out to deceive and seduce Judah into sleeping with her, by veiling her face and pretending to be a prostitute (Genesis 38:14–19). She did this because she did not want to be left both unmarried and forever childless. The biblical text clearly sees Tamar's act of deception as a legitimate act of self-defense on her part (indeed, Perez, the older of the twin sons who resulted from this act of deception, became an ancestor of King David, and thus of Judaism's messianic line). Judah himself recognized that Tamar's act was justified. When he learned of her deception, he declared, "She is more righteous than I."

21. One is permitted to lie in financial negotiations to protect oneself from unscrupulous people, and only from unscrupulous people. Thus, if, in the middle of a job, workers break their contract with an employer, and demand more money than they originally agreed to, the employer is permitted to deceive them by telling them that he will pay them a higher salary, and then compensate them with the originally agreed-upon wages (*Bava Mezia* 76b and *Shulchan Arukh, Choshen Mishpat* 333:5).

22. Biblical and other Jewish narratives about lying would support the conclusion reached by the seventeenth-century Dutch Calvinist theologian and jurist Hugo Grotius, that not all people have the right to the truth. Grotius argues, for example, that an extortionist has no right to the information that she seeks to obtain. Therefore, to tell such a person a falsehood should not be regarded as lying.[9] A statement should be considered a lie only if it denies the truth to someone who deserves it.[10]

———

Rabbi Avrohom Ehrman offers the following example: Mr. Gold owns two businesses, a real estate business and an insurance business. One of his largest insurance customers is the Smith Company. One day Mr. Smith sees a million-dollar mansion offered for sale by Gold's real estate company. As he is a good customer of Gold, he figures he can bargain him down considerably. After much negotiating, Gold agrees to reduce the price by ten percent, at which point Smith pulls out his hole card: "Give me that mansion for $650,000 or I will take my business elsewhere." Since Smith is using extortion to force Gold to sell at a loss, Gold is permitted to alter the truth. "I'm sorry," he may say, "we are just an agent for a private anonymous seller who is demanding a minimum of $900,000 for the mansion."[11]

———

Lying when your words will cause unnecessary hurt

23. The prophet Zechariah teaches, "Love truth and peace" (8:19), and *The Ethics of the Fathers* says, "On three pillars the world is sustained: on truth, on justice, and on peace" (1:18). While truth, as these teachings make clear, is a fundamental value, other values, such as peaceful relations between people, are also basic: "The problems arise when two or more of these principles come into conflict" (Rabbi Ari Zitofsky).[12]

The classic case of truth and peaceful relations coming into conflict, and one that has deeply influenced almost all Jewish writings on truthfulness, occurs within a talmudic discussion of appropriate etiquette at a wedding:

"Our Rabbis taught: 'How does one dance [and what words does one say] before a bride?' The School of Shammai says, 'The bride [is described] as she is.' The School of Hillel says, '[Every bride is described as] a beautiful and graceful bride.'

"The School of Shammai said to the School of Hillel, 'If she is lame or blind, does one say of her, "Beautiful and graceful bride"? Does not the Torah command, "Stay far away from falsehood"?' (Exodus 23:7).

"But the School of Hillel answered the School of Shammai, 'According to your words, if a person has made a bad purchase in the market, should one praise it to him or deprecate it? Surely one should praise it to him.'

"Therefore, the Rabbis teach, 'One's disposition should always be pleasant with people'" (*Ketubot* 16b–17a).

The *Shulchan Arukh*, Judaism's sixteenth-century code of Jewish law, codifies Hillel's position as binding: "It is a mitzvah [a commandment] to gladden the bridegroom and the bride and to dance before them and to say that she is beautiful and graceful, even if she is not beautiful" (*Even Ha-Ezer* 65:1).

———

As one reads the debate between the houses of Hillel and Shammai, one wonders if Shammai actually intended people to call out a bride's physical shortcomings as well as her strengths (this would seem to be the meaning of his words "The bride [is described] as she is"). It is hard to believe that he advocated doing this, since calling attention to a bride's weaknesses would violate Judaism's laws forbidding shaming another, particularly in public (see page 276). Therefore, the Tosafot, a standard commentary on the Talmud, argues that Shammai intended people to confine their praise to those features of the bride that were truly attractive, for example, "her eyes or hands if they are pretty." If Tosafot's understanding of Shammai is correct, we can understand Hillel's advocacy of a gen-

eral, though sometimes untruthful, formula for praising all brides. If wedding celebrants restricted their praise to one or two features—the bride's hands, for example—it would just remind everyone of her less attractive, though unmentioned, features. Therefore, Shammai's commitment to truth-telling could easily be seen as an insult, and undermine the joy of both bride and groom.

Similarly, the Maharam Schiff, a later talmudic commentator, raises the question of why, in the case of an unattractive bride, the celebrants don't simply remain silent about her looks. Doing so, he notes, "would be repulsive," since other brides are praised for their beauty. (When was the last time you attended a wedding in which you did not hear people tell the bride, "You look so beautiful!") Therefore, saying nothing about the bride's appearance is tantamount to calling her unattractive.

―――

24. The House of Hillel's comment that if a person has made a bad purchase in the market, nonetheless "one should praise it to him," suggests that it is permitted to lie only when telling the truth will be of no help (that is, after the person has already made the purchase). Thus, if someone comes over to you at a party, obviously upset, and says, "I look terrible. These clothes make me look fat, and my hair's terrible," it is best to reassure the person that she looks fine, even if you think she doesn't. If, however, before setting out for the party, a person makes a similar observation to you, or you realize that she is dressed unbecomingly or inappropriately, then you should tell her the truth. Doing so might be unpleasant and even cause pain, but saying nothing, or assuring the person that she looks fine, may well result in far greater hurt.

―――

A friend told me that he had been given a recently published book by an author whom he knew. After he read it, he pointed out to the author a number of weaknesses that he felt made the book flawed. The author responded, "Why would you point out flaws if there is obviously nothing I can do about it now?" As my friend concluded, "I never repeated that mistake. I agree with Hillel."

While pointing out flaws in a book is an insensitive thing to do when the book has been published, it might be wise to note those flaws at a later time, particularly if the author is preparing to write another book, or will be bringing out a new edition of the book.

―――

25. The Rabbis root their permission to alter the truth in an incident involving God Himself. In Genesis, angels came to Abraham to tell him that he and his long-barren wife, Sarah, would have a son within a year. At the time, Abraham was ninety-nine and Sarah ten years younger. When she overheard the angel's blessing, "Sarah laughed to herself, saying, 'Now that I am withered, am I to have enjoyment, with my husband so old?' "

A verse later, God appeared to Abraham, and said, "Why did Sarah laugh, saying, 'Shall I in truth bear a child, old as I am?' " (Genesis 18:12–13). God transmitted only a part of what Sarah said, and left out what Abraham might have taken as a denigrating comment about himself ("with my husband so old"). As the Rabbis concluded, "Great is peace, seeing that for its sake, God modified the truth" (*Yevamot* 65b). This divine statement became the basis in Jewish law for altering the truth when reporting a statement that might hurt and anger someone.

26. As noted (see page 356), the Chaffetz Chayyim, Judaism's foremost scholar on the laws of speech, rules that when a person asks you what another has said about him, and the statement was derogatory, then, "if one can formulate a reply which will not repeat the bad things which were said and will also not be an outright lie, one should reply in this way. However, if one knows that one's friend will not accept such a reply, then it is permitted to tell a complete lie, because of peace" ("Laws of *Rechilut*" 1:8). The Chaffetz Chayyim's position is based on the Talmud's teaching that, for the sake of peace, one can modify the truth, and on Maimonides' ruling, "[A scholar] does not alter the truth in his speech, not adding or subtracting, except in the interests of peace and the like" (*Mishneh Torah*, "Laws of Character Development" 5:7).

In English we have the expression "to be brutally honest." If being honest means that you will have to be "brutal," then you should reconsider your words.

27. It is also permitted to lie to maintain one's privacy in a situation in which telling the truth (for example, that one wants to be alone) will hurt another's feelings. Rabbi Shlomo Zalman Auerbach noted that one is not obligated to see a person against one's will. If a person knocks on your door without an appointment, you have no obligation to see him, nor do you have an obligation to tell him what you are doing and why you don't want to see him at that time. On the other hand, informing the visitor through a member of your household that you are home but unavailable might insult him; after all, he will reason, if the guest were prominent enough, surely you would break off what you were doing to see him. Rabbi Auerbach concluded, "With the aim of avoiding friction, you should therefore inform the person, through a member of the household, that you are not home. Since the latter response avoids a strained relationship, it constitutes a permissible lie, and is therefore an application of the principle of *darkei shalom* ("the ways of peace"), fostering harmony and good will."[13]

———

A friend who read this ruling of Rabbi Auerbach disagreed. "An improbable insult to an uninvited guest is far less harmful than asking your child to lie." Perhaps, but perhaps it is important to teach your child that it is better to alter the truth than to hurt someone's feelings gratuitously. Such an explanation will not cause the child to think that Judaism takes lying lightly, but rather that it takes hurting another's feelings very seriously.

———

28. It is permitted to lie to a host and tell her that you like the food, even when you don't. The Talmud relates that Rabbi Joshua ben Chananiah was served oversalted food at a host's house. When the hostess, noticing that he was not partaking of the meal, asked him, "Why do you not eat?" he answered, "I have already eaten earlier" (*Eruvin* 53b).

Obviously, cases such as this require common sense. For example, if the rabbi knew that the woman was planning to serve this same food to guests who would be arriving later, he should have told her that the food was oversalted; likewise, if he knew that she had an alternative, then he should have requested it. However, if she didn't have other food, and he didn't know her well, such a diplomatic lie was the appropriate thing to do.

Similarly, one should be even more willing to lie to save the cook, or other employees, from their employer's wrath. The Chaffetz Chayyim was once dining with another rabbi, when the innkeeper asked the men how they had enjoyed their meal. The Chaffetz Chayyim said that his meal had been excellent, but the other rabbi responded that the soup had been oversalted and he had not enjoyed it. When the innkeeper departed, the Chaffetz Chayyim said to the other rabbi, "What you said was terrible. Do you realize the problems you will cause to that poor cook?" The other rabbi protested that he had just offered his honest opinion, and that the Chaffetz Chayyim was exaggerating the negative effects that could ensue from his complaint. "Really?" said the Chaffetz Chayyim. "Well, then, let's go into the kitchen and see who's right." They walked quietly to the kitchen door and eased it open. Inside, they could see the innkeeper berating the cook, who was in tears. Only then did the other rabbi understand how careful you need be even when you're speaking the truth.

So, do we have the right to voice a complaint if the food is not well prepared? I suppose that if you are eating in a restaurant, you have the right to voice a complaint. Nonetheless, always be careful and consider the consequences before you do so. Thus, in this case, specifically because the Chaffetz Chayyim and his rabbinic colleague were such distinguished guests, he understood how much damage could be caused by him or his friend offering a complaint.

———

My friend and editor, Toinette Lippe, offers the following comment: "If you say nothing, particularly in a restaurant, the chef may continue to offer inedible food. I always speak up, but nicely. The point is not to raise your voice or be unpleasant."

This story about the Chaffetz Chayyim should also serve to remind us to be cautious before complaining to parents about their child's misbehavior, particularly if there is reason to believe that the parents are overly strict.

———

29. According to almost all older Jewish sources, it is permitted, and sometimes obligatory, to lie to a person with a serious, perhaps terminal, illness, and to tell the person that he is less sick than he is. Thus the Bible records that Ben Hadad, the ancient king of Aram, fell ill and sent to ask the Jewish prophet Elisha whether he would recover. Elisha told the messenger that Ben Hadad would die, but that the messenger should tell the king, "You shall surely recover" (II Kings 8:7–10). Commenting on this passage, Gersonides (1288–1344), the eminent Jewish philosopher, scientist, and biblical exegete, suggests that absolute candor can hasten a patient's death (and it is wrong to hasten the death even of one with a terminal condition). Thus, lack of truthfulness in such a case should be mandatory. Indeed, we find that in rabbinic rulings prior to the contemporary period, the dominant view is to withhold negative information from the patient, or even to lie about it, lest the patient be demoralized.

Rabbi J. David Bleich, a contemporary legal scholar, argues that the mere "possibility of adverse reaction is sufficient reason for eschewing a policy of full disclosure." Bleich notes that fear itself can bring on death. For example, medical researchers have noted that there is a higher rate of mortality than there should be among people who have ingested sublethal quantities of poison or who have inflicted minor, nonlethal wounds on themselves: "In these cases, the sole cause of death is simply the victims' belief in their impending doom."[14]

Another biblical passage, however, seems to make the case for full disclosure to a terminally ill patient. Thus the prophet Isaiah came to the ill King Hezekiah and said, "Thus said the Lord: Set your affairs in order, for you are going to die; you will not get well" (II Kings 20:1).

Why would God instruct Isaiah to deliver so demoralizing a message? Perhaps when dealing with a nation's leader, one must sometimes speak bluntly, so that the leader will provide for his succession, something he would not do if he thought that he would recover. Ironically, however, and despite the fact that Isaiah delivered this prophecy in God's Name, it did not come true. As soon as the prophet left the king's room, Hezekiah prayed fervently to God, and Isaiah returned to tell him that God had been moved by his prayers and would extend his life by fifteen years.

Dr. Avraham Steinberg, a leading contemporary Jewish medical ethicist, argues for a nuanced position on truth-telling to patients with life-threatening illnesses, one that involves neither automatic lying nor automatic truth-telling. Dr. Steinberg acknowledges that he has been influenced by the sea-change in Western society. As recently as 1961, ninety percent of American physicians opposed telling cancer patients their diagnosis. Sixteen years later, a new survey revealed that only two percent of physicians opposed doing so. Other studies have also shown an enormous increase in the percentage of *patients* who wish full disclosure about their illness.

Dr. Steinberg attaches two caveats to the policy of informing the patient:

One size does not fit all. Therefore, even if most patients want to know their diagnosis, and will profit from doing so, there are patients for whom this is not the case, and for whom disclosure, and certainly full disclosure, will be detrimental. Therefore, doctors must avoid thinking in slogans— "One must always tell the truth," or "One must conceal distressing information from the patient"—and base their decision on how much to disclose on their assessment of what is best for each patient. This is not that hard to ascertain because, as I once heard an oncologist explain, "Patients almost always make clear to doctors how much truth they wish to be told."* Obviously, in cases where a patient makes it clear that he wishes to be told the

---

*Dr. Isaac Herschkopf, related to me the following: "Many years ago, I was consulted by a mother at 2:00 A.M. regarding what to tell her son about his father, who, a very short time earlier, had committed suicide. I advised her to treat this like a discussion of sex. Answer his questions honestly, but don't volunteer information. It worked perfectly. The son asked the details of the death, but not the motive. Years later, he asked that question and received an honest answer. Years after that, he asked about his father's psychiatric history. People will always let you know what they're ready to hear."

truth, refusal to do so can inflict great suffering, making the ill person feel that he is being lied to by his doctor and loved ones.

On the other hand, patients, particularly those who ask few questions, are probably signaling their desire not to be told the whole truth. During the last stages of my mother's cancer, she asked my sister and me to discuss her condition and the treatments she should receive with her oncologist, and told us emphatically that she did not wish to participate in the discussion.

Even when delivering bad news to a patient, a doctor should never deprive a patient of all hope. Thus, while it is sometimes vital to alert a patient to the need to set his or her house in order (write or update a will, address family issues that need to be settled), a doctor should avoid issuing definitive pronouncements on life expectancy. One reason is that no one but God knows when someone will die. I myself had lunch recently with a woman who was told thirty-one years ago by her oncologist that she had a maximum life expectancy of three years. Even if this were true, and obviously it turned out not to be, what possible good can come from telling anyone something so definitive?

As Dr. Steinberg puts it, "Care should be taken that the style, content, and general approach should, on the one hand, be serious, but on the other hand, give hope." Steinberg also notes that in many instances the physician "should not disclose the entire truth with all its details, at least not during the first encounter." And certainly, "in all instances, one should encourage the patient by telling him that one will do everything possible in terms of therapeutic intervention to relieve pain and suffering."*

———

I once read of an incident in which a medical professor asked his class if they thought it appropriate to tell a person that he had an illness from which he would surely die. When the professor made known his opinion that a doctor should always leave a person some room for hope, one student argued that if there was no reason for optimism, the doctor should tell the patient the full and ugly truth. The professor told the student that such an attitude made him unfit to be a physician, and that he should immediately go to the dean's office and tell him that Professor

---

*Dr. Avraham Steinberg, M.D., "Disclosure of Illness to Patient," *Encyclopedia of Jewish Medical Ethics*, vol. 1, pages 317–328 (Dr. Steinberg is the author of all the articles in the encyclopedia's three volumes). In making the case for openness with patients, Steinberg notes that "the fear that results from lack of knowledge is sometimes worse than the truth itself, and situations of doubt are more difficult to tolerate psychologically than certainty and recognition of facts."

So-and-So asked that he be expelled. The devastated student started to leave, but after he had taken a few steps, the professor said, "You don't have to go to the dean's office. I just wanted you to experience for a moment the sense of pain, fear, and hopelessness your patient will feel if you tell him that he is going to die soon and there is nothing that can help him."

On the other hand, if a person is in an advanced state of a terminal condition and seems ready to make peace with her impending death, it would be foolish for caregivers and friends to assure her that she will soon recover.

Lying to create peace or otherwise do good

30. It is permitted to lie to people who are in conflict, and to tell them that the other party esteems them and wishes to make peace (*Yevamot* 65b); obviously, it is only worth doing so if you have reason to think that you will be believed. Many people do the opposite, and inflame a feud by passing on derogatory comments that their opponent has made about them. But, Maimonides rules, "One who makes peace between two people and adds or subtracts from the statements of each of them so as to make them feel affection toward each other is permitted to do so" ("Laws of Robbery and the Return of Lost Objects" 14:13).

When two men had quarreled, Aaron would go and sit with one of them and say, "My son, see what your friend is doing! He beats his breast and tears his clothes, and moans, 'Woe is me! How can I lift my eyes and look my companion in the face? I am ashamed before him, since it is I who offended him.'

Aaron would sit with him until he had removed all anger [literally, jealousy] from his heart.

Then Aaron would go and sit with the other man and say the same thing.

Aaron would sit with him, too, until he had removed all anger from his heart.

Later, when the two met, they would embrace and kiss each other (The Fathers According to Rabbi Nathan, *12:3*).

Though you might need to modify Aaron's techniques in cases of great animosity (where you are unlikely to be believed), an approach like this may often help in family feuds, where each party might be looking for reconciliation, but is reluctant to take the first step. Hearing an untruthful report about how much the other party regrets the feud and his earlier behavior can help motivate each side to make peace.

———

31. You may lie to a poor person too embarrassed to accept charity, and tell her, for example, that you have made a "windfall" from an investment, even when you haven't, and that you would like to share some of it with her. Take care to make sure that she doesn't discover the truth, particularly if this knowledge would upset her.[15]

———

"Reb Shlomo Zalman Auerbach assumed the responsibility for rearing an orphan who lived in his neighborhood. . . . When the boy was dating, he spoke to Reb Shlomo Zalman about the dilemma with which he was grappling. The relationship was getting serious and . . . the boy continued, he was short quite a bit from what her family held to be his share of the wedding expenses. He was reluctant to reveal to the rabbi the astronomical sum they were demanding. Reb Shlomo Zalman interrupted the troubled young man to apprise him of some good news. 'If you are already speaking about money,' he said, improvising, 'you should know that I have been overseeing a fund all these years on your behalf. This fund now totals $5,500.'

"The boy could not believe his ears. Not only was this 'fund' a windfall, but the amount of money in the account was precisely the sum that he was missing. This young man had never divulged to anyone, including his benevolent 'foster father,' the figure that he was expected to provide. And the benevolent foster father never divulged the fact that until the day of that conversation, the 'fund' was nonexistent" (Rabbi Hanoch Teller).[16]

———

Rabbi Paysach Krohn relates the story of an ingenious and compassionate rabbi who knew a struggling rabbinical student; both the man and his wife were too proud to take financial assistance. One day the rabbi called the student and told him, "I was down at the grocery and the owner told me that he just got in some cases of canned fish that are damaged. The food inside is fine, but the cans are badly banged up, and he fears that customers will be hesitant to buy them. He is selling them on a first-come, first-served basis for two-thirds off the regular price. I'm down here at the store, so if you want I can buy a whole case for you at a really cheap price." The young man was very grateful for this opportunity. "I certainly could use such a bargain," he told the rabbi.

The rabbi took the cans home and, along with his children, got out some hammers and banged them up; they even tore off a few labels so that the cans appeared truly damaged. He then gave the canned fish, valued at over sixty dollars, to the rabbinical student for twenty dollars.[17]

---

32. One may lie to spare another embarrassment. The Talmud relates an incident in which Rabbi Gamliel asked seven sages to join him the next day for the ritual purpose of declaring a leap year.[18] The following morning, when Rabbi Gamliel discovered that eight sages were present, he announced that whoever had come without permission should leave. Rabbi Shmuel ha-Kattan arose to leave and said, "I am the one who [came] without permission." In fact, the Talmud explains, Shmuel ha-Kattan was supposed to be there, but made a false confession so as to spare the unwelcome participant public humiliation (*Sanhedrin* 11a).

33. The most famous lie told in the Torah (Jacob telling his blind father, Isaac, that he was Esau, Isaac's firstborn son; Genesis 27:6:19) came about because of Rebecca's fear that her son Jacob, and all his descendants, would suffer unfairly if he did not lie to his father. Years before this, Jacob's twin brother Esau had sold Jacob his rights as the firstborn son. Later, when Rebecca learned that Isaac was planning to bestow his primary blessing on Esau (as one of the privileges of being the firstborn), she helped Jacob to disguise himself as Esau, and instructed him to lie to his father and tell him that he was Esau, to secure the blessing.

This instance is a difficult case, one that pushes the border between permissible and impermissible lies. Nonetheless, it would appear that the Bible is teaching that one may lie when an injustice, in this case a major injustice, will occur if one doesn't.

For a discussion of the negative effects this lie had on Jacob's life, see pages 401–402. My friend Robert Mass argues that this lie is a case unto itself, and should be regarded as sui generis, *and not serve as an example to guide any of our future behavior.*

---

34. As a summary principle, the contemporary educational philosopher Dr. David Nyberg applies the Golden Rule, and Hillel's definition of Judaism's essence (see page 10), to the realm of lying and hurt feelings: "Be untruthful to others as you would have others be untruthful to you."[19]

———

Nyberg notes the difficulty of raising young children to be truthful, and then having to explain to them as they get older that there are times when it is appropriate to lie. He cites a children's book, Honest Andrew *by Gloria Skurzynski, which tells the story of a family of otters. One night, Andrew Otter is caught lying; he has thrown away his supper because he didn't like it, but denied having done so (he didn't want to hurt his mother's feelings by explaining why he threw the food away). His father gives him a lecture about speaking honestly, and Andrew promises that from now on he will always tell the truth. The following day, a beaver asks him how he is, and Andrew offers a long, highly detailed response. After the beaver departs, his mother scolds him for talking so much and boring the beaver. Later, he and his mother encounter Mrs. Woodchuck and her baby, and when Andrew's mother asks him, "Isn't she darling?" he looks at the baby and says, "Darling? She's ugly. Her face is all wrinkled. She looks like she slid facedown on a mud slide."*

Andrew's mother is embarrassed and angry at him. That evening, Andrew's father scolds him for being rude and insulting. Andrew answers that he was only trying to be honest and truthful, and his father answers, "But you mustn't hurt other people's feelings." At this point, Andrew is fighting back tears as he explains, "Last night I was trying not to hurt Mama's feelings when I really hated crayfish. You got mad at me then because I didn't tell the truth." The father becomes confused; he does not know what to say. But Andrew summarizes what he thinks he has learned: "Papa, is this what I should do? Should I always tell the truth, but be as nice and polite about it as I can?" The father answers, "Yes! That's it! That's exactly what you should do."

Nyberg notes that this outcome is a truism, and perhaps appropriate for a children's book. But there are times when telling a lie is necessary to "avoid injuring a person, shattering peace, violating privacy, or ruining self-confidence." In Nyberg's view, people who are so proud of their virtue as truth-tellers "will suffer as surely as will the rest of us sinners, but they'll suffer for sins of vanity" (pages 159–61).* In short, when people's feelings are involved, there are times when telling the harsh truth is wrong, and tactful lying is right.

———

*Nyberg's statement about the "sins of vanity" of compulsive truth-tellers might sound overstated, but only to those who haven't met people like this. Dr. Diane Komp, a professor of

Lying because the question invades your zone of privacy

35. The Talmud specifies three areas in which scholars (i.e., model Jews) are permitted, and sometimes even expected, to lie:

To protect someone from being exploited. As noted, one can therefore downplay or deny a host's hospitality to save the host from unscrupulous people who will take advantage of his or her generosity (see page 345).

For reasons of modesty. For example, a scholar can downplay his expertise in an area of Jewish learning so as to not sound like a braggart.

To safeguard one's privacy. Thus, a scholar asked questions concerning his sexual behavior may lie, because revealing such information exposes one to humiliation (*Bava Mezia* 23b–24a). The implication of this teaching is that a scholar may lie to anyone who asks for confidential information that they have no right to know (obviously, it is better to avoid lying by just declining or refusing to answer, but that is sometimes impossible).[†]

We may assume that if Judaism's models of ethical behavior are permitted to deviate from the truth in these ways, other people are permitted to do so as well.

———

The Talmud relates the case of a beautiful woman who arrived in a town and was ardently courted by several men, all of whom she told, "I am married." But then she suddenly announced her impending marriage. When the town's rabbis asked the woman about her previous statement that she was married, she re-

---

pediatrics at Yale University School of Medicine, relates the case of H. Clay Trumbull, a Union chaplain who was captured during the Civil War. He and other prisoners planned their escape, but when it turned out that the escape's success depended on either killing a Confederate soldier or lying to him, Trumbull announced that it was always wrong, even in such a case, to tell a lie. The other soldiers challenged him: Would it not be more moral to preserve the enemy soldier's life by telling him a lie than to have to kill him? Trumbull replied that he had no objection to killing a man who stood in the way of his freedom, any more than he would not have hesitated to kill a Confederate soldier in battle. Trumbull recalled, "My friend then asked me on what principle I could justify the taking of a man's life as an enemy, and yet not feel justified in telling him a lie in order to save his life and secure our liberty. How could it be claimed that it was more of a sin to tell a lie to a man . . . than to kill him?" Trumbull responded that he did indeed think that telling the lie was a greater sin. What comes through in Trumbull's work on the subject, *A Lie Never Justifiable* (at least in the passages quoted by Komp), is a sense of vanity; a feeling that it would be beneath him to lie, and therefore preferable for him to kill an enemy soldier. For Trumbull, it apparently was irrelevant that the enemy soldier would undoubtedly prefer to be lied to than killed. No less important, how would his widow and fatherless child feel? (see Dr. Diane Komp, *Anatomy of a Lie,* pages 17–20).

[†]If possible, it is perhaps better to put the questioner on the defensive by asking, "Why do you ask?" More often than not, the person will back down.

sponded, "At first, when unworthy men approached me, I told them I was married, so that they would not bother me. But now that eligible men came to me, I arose and betrothed myself to one of them." The rabbis accepted her explanation, and permitted the marriage to take place: "[Since] she gave a plausible reason for her [untruthful] words," they explained, "she is believed [and is trusted to be speaking the truth now]" (Ketubot 22a).

———

36. One can mislead others so as to avoid sharing information with them that they have no need—and no right—to know. When Abraham was commanded by God to sacrifice his son Isaac, he set off for the mountain where God had instructed him to carry out the sacrifice, along with his son and several servants. When they arrived at the site, Abraham, who had no wish to share what he was planning to do with the servants, told them, "You stay here with the donkey. The boy and I will go up there; we will worship and we will return to you" (Genesis 22:5).

A short time later, God sent an angel to stop Abraham from carrying out the sacrifice (verse 12). But at the time Abraham told the servants, "we will return to you," he had every reason to believe this to be a lie. Abraham apparently reasoned that what would happen that day was between God, Isaac, and himself, and did not concern the servants. Perhaps he also feared that if he simply said, "The boy and I will go up there," and nothing more, they might follow along and thwart his intended sacrifice.

Lying when exaggerating to make a point, and it is understood that you are exaggerating

37. While we should avoid exaggerations that might be accepted by listeners as literally true, it is acceptable to exaggerate to make a point. Thus, in describing the Israelites' joy when Solomon was anointed king, the Bible says, "All the people then marched up behind him, playing on flutes, and making merry till the earth was split open by the uproar" (I Kings 1:40).

In noting certain fanciful talmudic exaggerations describing aspects of the Temple in Jerusalem, Rabbi Ammi commented that "the Torah, the prophets, and the Sages sometimes speak in exaggerated terms" (*Chullin* 90b). As Rabbi Ari Zivotofsky, in a survey of Jewish perspectives on truthfulness, notes, "The [Talmud] here implies that exaggeration is an accepted practice used by everyone and, where there is no fear of being misunderstood, it is permitted."[20] Thus, for example, a talmudic passage relates that Rabbah, while drunk on Purim, "arose and cut Rabbi Zeira's throat, then brought him back to life on the following day" (*Megillah* 7b). It is, of course, doubtful that such an event really occurred, as Rabbah, even afterward, is considered to be one of the Talmud's great figures; Rabbi Abraham, Maimonides' son, cites this as an example of a rabbinic exaggeration.

Why did the Rabbis tell such a story? Probably to discourage excessive drinking, by indicating that even a great person, when drunk, can do terrible things.*

38. One instance in which Jewish law unabashedly encourages exaggeration is during a funeral oration. At such times, exaggerations are allowed because of *k'vod ha-briyot* ("human dignity")—in this case, the dignity of the deceased and his or her family. Thus, the *Shulchan Arukh* rules that, while it is forbidden to tell outright, albeit complimentary, lies about the deceased, it is fine, and even mandated, to exaggerate the person's good attributes (*Yoreh Deah* 344:1). Alternatively, we can be diplomatic by being selective in what information we choose to communicate.

Final thoughts

39. Rabbi Yosef Chaim of Baghdad, author of *Torah Lishmah* (section 364) warns that although the Sages allowed a person on some occasions to deviate from the truth, one should "place the fear of the Lord before oneself so as not to be excessively lenient." In other words, we should be guided not only by those instances in which lying is permitted, but also by the general biblical and talmudic abhorrence of lying.

40. Even when lying is permitted, try, when possible, to minimize the untruth. Rabbi Daniel Feldman notes that the Talmud, when speaking of such exceptions (such as God's alteration of Sarah's words; see pages 333–334), uses the words *l'shanot* ("to alter the truth") rather than *l'shaker* ("to lie"), to underscore that one should minimize the lie;[21] one way to do so, for example, is to make an ambiguous statement (see page 429).

---

*Similarly, the most famous story Americans know about George Washington, that he didn't lie to his father but rather confessed to cutting down a cherry tree, never happened. The story was created many years after Washington's death in a children's biography of America's first president written by a Parson Weems. This story, though itself untrue, has long been used to teach American children not to lie.

—

In a humorous example, Cecil B. DeMille invited fellow director Billy Wilder to a private screening of his soon-to-be-released epic film The Greatest Show on Earth. *At the conclusion, he asked Wilder his opinion. Wilder, who had not liked the film at all, but realized that it would be cruel to say so, answered, "Cecil, this was the greatest show on earth."*

—

IV

LEADING
A HOLY LIFE

ACTING AS AMBASSADORS OF GOD

———

The purpose of this commandment is that we
are in duty bound to proclaim this true
religion to the world, undeterred by fear
or injury from any source.

MAIMONIDES,
Book of the Commandments,
Positive Commandment number 9

51

KIDDUSH HASHEM:
SANCTIFYING GOD'S NAME IN
DAILY LIFE

1. *Kiddush Hashem* ("sanctifying God's Name") has three meanings:

- A Jew should conduct his life in such a way that non-Jews will think, "If that is how Judaism causes Jews to act, then Judaism is a wonderful religion and Jews are good people."
- Non-observant Jews will witness the righteous behavior of religiously committed Jews and, as a result, be brought nearer to God and Judaism.
- Jews should be willing to die as martyrs if oppressors try to coerce them to give up their faith.

———

So important is the commandment of Kiddush Hashem *that twice daily, in the* kedusha *prayer of both the morning and afternoon prayer services, Jews pray that they be granted the opportunity to "make Your Name holy in the world"* (nekadesh et shimcha ba-olam).

———

2. *Chillul Hashem* ("desecrating God's Name") also has three meanings:

- a Jew acting in a dishonest or obnoxious manner in dealings with non-Jews causes them to view Jews and/or Judaism with contempt
- a religious Jew acting in a way that causes non-observant Jews to lower their opinion of Judaism and/or religious Jews
- Jews giving up their faith to avoid persecution or gain an advantage (such as Jews who converted in antisemitic societies to get a job)

Desecrating God's Name is, of course, a very serious offense (*Shabbat* 33a), and some Rabbis regard it as unforgivable;* (that is because, even if the person who has desecrated God's Name repents, the people who were negatively affected by his actions might remain alienated from God and Judaism).

The best (but still imperfect) repentance for anyone who has desecrated God's Name is to go to the opposite extreme and sanctify God's Name, so that people come to associate integrity and kindness with God and Judaism.

Sanctifying God's Name in the Torah

3. The commandments that mandate sanctifying and not desecrating God's Name occur in the same verse in Leviticus: "Neither shall you profane My holy Name, but I will be hallowed among the children of Israel."(22:32).†

In addition, the third of the Ten Commandments, "You shall not carry God's Name in vain, for the Lord God will not forgive one who carries His Name in vain" (Exodus 20:7), also relates to the commandment banning the desecrating of God's Name. In most translations of the Bible, this verse (which begins, *"Lo tissa . . .")* is rendered as "You shall not take God's Name in vain," and people often are taught that this commandment means that it is blasphemous to utter God's Name in a curse, or that we must write God as G-d. But the Hebrew word *tissa* means "carry," and what the verse seems to forbid is using (i.e., carrying) "God's Name" to justify selfish and/or evil behavior. For example, during the nineteenth century, it was common for American southerners to justify their practice of slavery as something approved of by the Bible and by God. But even though the Torah permitted slavery, it hedged it with many restrictions that were ignored and violated in the South, restrictions that made biblical slavery very different from that practiced in nineteenth-century America. For example, according to the Bible:

- Beating a slave to death was a capital offense (Exodus 21:20); in the South such an act generally went unpunished.
- A master who punished a slave so that he or she lost an eye or tooth had to set the slave free (Exodus 21:26–27); no such law existed in the South.

The Fathers According to Rabbi Nathan, chapter 39; *Yoma* 86a suggests that forgiveness might be granted, but only after repentance and the sinner's death.

†Despite the verse's emphasis on "being hallowed among the children of Israel," *Kiddush Hashem* has long been associated with sanctifying God's Name among non-Jews as well; thus, when a Jew acts among gentiles in a manner that reflects well on Judaism, Jews will say, "That was a real *Kiddush Hashem."*

- If a slave ran away, it was forbidden to return him to his master (Deuteronomy 23:16); in the South, it was a crime not to return him, and in the infamous Dred Scott decision of 1857, the Supreme Court ruled—in direct contravention of the Bible—that a runaway slave who had achieved freedom in the North could be forcibly returned to the South and to slavery.

Therefore, when Southern clergy tried to justify their practice of slavery with the claim that the Hebrew Bible (what Christians refer to as the Old Testament) and God would have approved of their behavior, they "carried" God's Name in vain, and associated God with heinous acts.*

From Judaism's perspective, it is a *Chillul Hashem* to associate God with evil; that may well be why God announces that He will not forgive those who violate the Third Commandment ("the Lord will not clear one who carries His Name in vain"; Exodus 20:7). The reason would seem to be obvious: when we commit an evil act such as murdering or stealing, we discredit ourselves, but when we do evil in God's Name, we discredit God and alienate people who might otherwise have become drawn to God and religion.

4. The biblical exemplar of *Kiddush Hashem* is Abraham, the first Jew, who made so positive an impression on his non-Hebrew neighbors that they said of him, "You are a prince of God (*nasi elohim*) in our midst" (Genesis 23:6).

There are two activities in particular that Jewish tradition associates with Abraham: teaching people about God's existence and practicing hospitality. Both are cornerstones of the mitzvah of *Kiddush Hashem*. Thus the Torah depicts Abraham as exceptionally hospitable; even on the hottest of days, he would go out to greet weary travelers and offer them food, drink, and a place to rest (Genesis 18:2–5); it was irrelevant to Abraham whether his guests shared his faith. According to the rabbinic understanding, when travelers thanked Abraham and Sarah for their hospitality, the couple would direct the guests' thanks to God, the ultimate source of food

---

*Throughout history, slavery has prompted hypocrisy in its practitioners. In the seventh century B.C.E., the prophet Jeremiah denounced those of his Jewish contemporaries who circumvented the biblical laws of slavery by emancipating their slaves when the Torah required them to do so, and then enslaved them again (34:16). In addition to being an ethical offense, Jeremiah condemned this behavior as a profanation of God's Name, in that those who did this, by claiming that Jewish law allowed them to act as they did, implicated God in their transgression.

(*Tanhuma Lekh Lekha* 12). Through such behavior, Judaism's premier patriarch and matriarch made people aware of God's existence and made God lovable to them.*

For Maimonides, Abraham's behavior should serve as a model for his future descendants: "Just as Abraham, being a lover of God . . . summoned mankind to believe, you . . . must love God and summon mankind to Him" (Maimonides, *Book of the Commandments*, Positive Command number 3), and promote knowledge of God among all men and women; indeed, when people speak of Jews as the Chosen People, this is the task for which Jewish tradition understands them to have been chosen: to make known to humankind that there is One God, Whose primary demand of human beings is ethical behavior (see chapter 1). Carrying out this mission is the ultimate act of *Kiddush Hashem*.

———

Concerning the command to sanctify God's Name, Maimonides writes, "The purpose of this commandment is that we are in duty bound to proclaim this true religion to the world, undeterred by fear or injury from any source" (Book of the Commandments, *Positive Commandment number 9).*

———

5. In Moses' farewell oration, in the Book of Deuteronomy, he assures the Israelites that their observance of the Torah's laws "will be proof of your wisdom and your discernment to other peoples, who on hearing of all these laws will say, 'Surely, that great nation is a wise and discerning people'" (Deuteronomy 4:6). This verse has at least two significant implications:

• Jews are required to make the world aware of the teachings in the Torah; after all, if non-Jews remain unfamiliar with Jewish laws, those laws can hardly serve as proof of Judaism's wisdom. Thus, when appropriate, a Jew should make known to non-Jews some of Judaism's distinctive laws. For example, the laws of *lashon hara* mandate that it is forbidden to reveal an ugly truth about another person unless the person to whom you are speaking needs the information (see chapters 37–43);

---

*Other midrashic tales focus on how Abraham and Sarah influenced people to believe in God. In addition, the Rabbis also understood Abraham as wanting to preserve God's "good Name" in the world. Thus Abraham protested to God that if He destroyed the innocent along with the guilty in Sodom (Genesis 18:25), people would believe that God treated evil and good people alike, and was therefore unjust (*Genesis Rabbah* 49:9).

in secular society, most people assume that it is forbidden only to tell a lie about another, but never forbidden to tell the truth. Such teachings, by revealing Jewish law's unusual sensitivity to issues of fairness, help promote respect for the God and people who promulgated such laws.

• Jewish law cannot permit the practice of laws that *unfairly* discriminate against non-Jews.* It is inconceivable that non-Jews will regard Jews as a great or wise nation if they practice unfair laws. (Would Jews be impressed with the wisdom of another religion that promulgated many impressive laws but also discriminated against Jews?) Hence, any discriminatory laws that have crept into the Jewish tradition (for an example, see paragraph 8) must be regarded as false to the spirit of this Torah verse (Deuteronomy 4:6).†

6. In addition to avoiding unethical behavior, Jews must avoid any behavior that will cast Jews and Judaism in an irrational or foolish light. Thus, during a cholera epidemic in Vilna in 1848, when people's resistance to disease was lowered, Rabbi Israel Salanter issued a ruling permitting Jews to eat on Yom Kippur. Rabbi Salanter's son, Rabbi Isaac Lipkin, explained that, in addition to wanting to save lives, this "was [because of] the desecration of the Divine Name which would come about from the Gentiles [who would say] . . . that this illness came upon [the Jews] because of the Jewish religion, heaven forbid."[1]

---

*I emphasize the word "unfairly," though not the word "discriminate." Unfair behavior is always wrong, discrimination is almost, but not always, wrong. Thus, not counting a non-Jew in a *minyan,* a Jewish prayer quorum, is not *unfair* discrimination, since a *minyan* is expected to consist of people who are Jewish and who believe in Judaism. Not returning a lost object to a non-Jew who lives in a society in which non-Jews are expected to return lost items to Jews is both unfair and discriminatory.

†In an unusual and infrequently cited passage, the Talmud tells of two non-Jewish scholars who were disturbed by an act of discrimination in ancient Jewish law: "The Roman government once sent two officers to the Sages of Israel, saying, 'Teach us your Torah.' They read it once, reviewed, and then studied it a third time. When they were leaving, the officers said to the Sages, 'We have carefully examined your entire Torah, and it is all true, except for that which you teach, "If the ox of a Jew gores the ox of a Canaanite, the Jew is exempt from payment. . . . If the ox of a Canaanite gores the ox of a Jew . . . the Canaanite pays full damages" . . . However,' the non-Jews concluded, 'we will not reveal this matter to the authorities [lest it jeopardize your welfare].'" (*Bava Kamma* 38a). The Rabbis who edited the Talmud and chose to include this story—one in which the moral heroes are gentile scholars who show both considerable learning and great sensitivity—were obviously also uncomfortable that Jewish law had allowed this discriminatory piece of legislation to creep in; one suspects that they would certainly have wanted to see such a law changed in a society, unlike that of Rome, in which Jews were treated with equality.

7. While sanctifying God's Name is generally thought of as a command-ment carried out in public, Jewish law teaches that it can be performed even when only one other person is present. The Talmud offers as an example Joseph's restraining himself in the face of Mrs. Potiphar's attempts to se-duce him (see *Sotah* 36b). Joseph's rejection of Mrs. Potiphar's proposal— "How then could I do this most wicked thing, and sin before God?" (Genesis 39:9)—was motivated by his fear of God and his desire to act righteously (he makes it clear to her that he does not want to betray her husband); this episode is what caused the Rabbis to refer to Joseph as *ha-Tzaddik* (the righ-teous one). Therefore, any time a Jews acts righteously in the presence of even one other person, he or she is sanctifying God's Name.

Sanctifying God's Name in our relationships with non-Jews

8. Jewish tradition regards a Jew who has dealings with non-Jews as rep-resenting not only himself but the whole Jewish people; therefore, when he acts in a particularly honest or gracious manner, it reflects well not only on himself but on the people as a whole.

This concept of *Kiddush Hashem* is reflected in the talmudic story of Rabbi Shimon ben Shetach, who earned his living selling flax. On one occa-sion his pupils bought for him a donkey from an Arab seller, and found a valuable jewel attached to it (perhaps in the saddle). They came to the rabbi with good news: "You will no longer need to work." When Rabbi Shimon asked what they were talking about, the students told him about the jewel.

He then asked them, "Does the seller know about the jewel?" The stu-dents answered no, and the rabbi insisted that they return it.

"But it's not stealing," they protested, arguing that since the seller had sold them the donkey (and by implication everything on it), and since Jews were not required to return lost items to heathens, the pearl, by all rights, be-longed to the rabbi.

Rabbi Shimon was unimpressed by his students' reasoning. "What do you think—that Shimon ben Shetach is a barbarian?" (In other words, any Jew who keeps an item lost by a heathen, even if he can find a basis in Jewish law for doing so, is a barbarian.) He returned the jewel to the Arab, who ex-claimed, "Blessed be the God of Shimon ben Shetach."*

---

*Jerusalem Talmud, *Bava Mezia* 2:5, and *Deuteronomy Rabbah* 3:3; there are slight variations be-tween the two accounts, and I have drawn from both. Thus, in the talmudic account, the story ends with Shimon ben Shetach saying, "[I] would rather hear the heathen say, 'Blessed is the God of the Jews' than have any reward this world has to offer." In the account in *Deuteronomy Rabbah,* he returns the jewel and prompts the remark cited above by the Arab.

In short, the laws of *Kiddush* and *Chillul Hashem* are based on the presumption that when a Jew has interactions with non-Jews, whether business or personal, his behavior has the potential to reflect on Judaism and on all Jews, both for good and bad.

Is this fair? No. But, fair or unfair, when we have a negative dealing with a member of a different racial, religious, or ethnic group, we often make derogatory remarks about the entire group. Before you dismiss this as an unfair generalization, think about whether you have been mistreated by a member of another group, and have said, or even thought, something ugly about that entire group.

———

Blu Greenberg, the well-known Orthodox feminist and theologian, relates the following early-twentieth-century tale of Kiddush Hashem:

"My grandfather Moshe Genauer came to America in 1905, at age twenty-six. . . . He was a peddler [in Seattle, Washington], buying and selling used clothing. One day he walked four miles to the [affluent] Queen Anne district to buy clothes from a man. He came back to his little room, laid the suits out on his bed, and found a diamond brooch in one of the pockets. So he turned around and walked all the way back to the house of the man who had sold him the suits.

A woman answered the door. "I'd like to speak to your husband," my grandfather said.

She saw a man with a beard and a hat, obviously Jewish, speaking with an accent. "You can't bother my husband," the woman said. "You were here already. What do you want?"

"I didn't buy a diamond from your husband," my grandfather replied. "I bought a suit."

Her husband turned out to be the president of Rainier National Bank, and he rewarded my grandfather's honesty with an unlimited line of credit. This enabled my grandfather to bring over his wife, my uncle, and my father (then aged two), and later open up a men's wholesale clothing business. And that is how I came to grow up in Seattle. . . . The business became successful and supported six families the next generation."[2]

As regards Jewish law's permitting Jews to keep the lost property of heathens, Rabbi Louis Jacobs comments: "The rule about the lost property of heathens has to be understood against the background of the time when these heathens were themselves thoroughly dishonest [and wouldn't return lost property to Jews]. The law, taking this into account, refused to demand the strictest standards of honesty in dealing with them. However, this story [concerning Shimon ben Shetach and the jewel] wishes to point out that a truly honest person, faithful to religion, will not wish to avail himself of any loopholes in the law."[3]

———

9. When you do a good deed, do it in a way that makes your Jewishness recognizable. For example, when you make a charitable donation to a non-Jewish cause, do so as a Jew. Since it is awkward to write something such as, "As a Jew, I want to help your cause," you could send a note with your check saying, "As the Talmud teaches, 'He who saves one life, it is as if he saved an entire world.'" You can even print this up on a business card, and send it along with all your charitable contributions.

Calling attention to our Jewishness applies to areas of social justice as well. In 1965, Rabbi Abraham Joshua Heschel, the highly regarded theologian and writer, marched with Martin Luther King Jr. in civil rights demonstrations, most notably the one in Selma, Alabama. The fact that Rabbi Heschel wore a head-covering when doing so (which he normally did) was widely perceived as a *Kiddush Hashem,* because it showed that Jews cared about righting the injustices committed against African-American people.*

On the other hand, care must be exercised to identify God and Judaism only with causes that are clearly just (as was the case with the civil rights battle to end segregation), and not run the risk of identifying Judaism with whatever our political preferences happens to be.

———

In the late 1960s, during a civil war in Nigeria, a massacre was directed against the region of Nigeria known as Biafra. The Jerusalem rabbi Aryeh Levine made a contribution to Magen David Adom, the Israeli equivalent of the Red Cross, to help bring food and medical relief to the Biafrans; as he explained, "for they too are created in God's image." When the Magen David Adom representative returned from Biafra to Israel, he went to see Reb Aryeh to report on the suffering he had witnessed, and the help the organization had been able to extend. Reb Aryeh answered, "You have sanctified God's Name in the world," and doubled his contribution.[4]

———

*Reform Rabbi William Braude, of Providence, Rhode Island, came back from a civil rights march during the 1960s and announced that from then on he would wear a *kippah* (yarmulke) at services (in many Reform synagogues at the time, men sat bareheaded during services). Braude had been impressed when he had heard African-American people call the *kippah* a "freedom hat" when they saw rabbis wearing it at demonstrations and in jail.

Rabbi Moshe Feinstein routinely made donations for medical research and causes that helped mentally and physically handicapped people; as he explained, in addition to being the right thing to do, it was important that non-Jews see that rabbis, whom gentiles might think concern themselves exclusively with Jewish causes, support general charities as well.

———

10. The words "entire House of Israel" imply that children are expected to observe this commandment, even though they are not normally bound by Jewish law. Hence it is important to teach children from a young age (perhaps seven or eight) that their actions reflect on all Jews, and must be conducted on a high level. For example, children who have Hebrew names, or who dress in a manner that identifies them as religious Jews, need to understand the importance of good manners, honesty, and graciousness in their interactions with others. This might be a lot to expect from a seven- or eight-year-old child, but if a child cannot live up to such standards, it is best to minimize his contact with non-Jews and non-observant Jews.

———

A former student of Reb Aryeh Levine recalled an occasion when students at the Etz Chayyim Yeshiva, where Reb Aryeh taught, became embroiled in a fistfight at the school's entrance. Reb Aryeh ran over, and escorted the boys to his study, where he began reading to them the passage in which the Talmud (Yoma 86a) details how serious a sin it is to profane and demean God's Name. The boys understood, even without any elaboration from Reb Aryeh, that when yeshiva students, who are expected to set an example of religious behavior, fight in public, God's Name is dishonored. The student recalled, "As he read the words and unfolded their meaning, the rabbi was seized by emotion, and he began weeping. 'I would rather be taken from this world than cause any insult or degradation of God's Name.' 'I need hardly add,' the former student recalled, 'that his words had a profound effect on us, and we wept with him.'"[5]

———

Avoiding the desecration of God's Name

11. Because *Chillul Hashem* is such a serious offense, it would be better if religiously observant Jews who act unethically also ceased to observe Jewish rituals. Why? Because when people see unethical Jews observing religious rituals, they conclude that if a person can be religious but unethical, that must mean that Judaism doesn't care about ethics. This belief, of course, breeds contempt for Judaism. The Bible itself teaches that "the sacrifice of evildoers is an abomination" (Proverbs 21:27); in other words, God hates sacrifices offered by unethical Jews. In ancient times, sacrifice was the primary expression of Jewish ritual; today, certain rituals, most notably prayer, play that role, and the implication of this verse is that the ritual observances of the wicked are an abomination to God.

———

Commenting on the depressing phenomenon of a person who steals wheat, grinds and bakes it, then sets apart the share for the priests, and follows all these activities with a blessing to God over the bread, the Rabbis say, "The robber who recites a blessing scorns God" (Psalms 10:3; cited in Sanhedrin 6b).

———

12. The *Tosefta* teaches that defrauding or stealing from a non-Jew is a more heinous offense than stealing from a Jew. That is because, in addition to violating the biblical prohibition against stealing, cheating a non-Jew also causes God's Name to be dishonored (*Tosefta Bava Kamma* 10:15). More than a thousand years after this text was composed, the thirteenth-century *Sefer Chasidim* warned that if a gentile makes an error in a business dealing with a Jew, and the Jew doesn't correct it, the non-Jew may subsequently become aware of it, "and so the Name of Heaven (i.e., God's good Name) will be desecrated by you" (paragraph 1080).

At about the same time, Rabbi Moshe of Coucy, France, author of the legal code *Semag* (*The Big Book of the Commandments*), wrote, "For if Jews cheat non-Jews, they will say, 'Look how God has chosen for His people a nation of thieves and deceivers. . . . Indeed, God dispersed us among the nations so that we could gather converts to Judaism, but if we behave deceitfully towards others, who will want to join us?" (page 152b); in other words, a desecrator of God's Name is responsible for alienating non-Jews from Judaism as well as from God.*

———

*In more recent writings, one is apt to find that the primary concern is that acts of dishonesty by Jews will provoke antisemitism. Thus we find a somewhat hyperbolic statement of the Chaffetz Chayyim: "Cheating non-Jews brings about the desecrating of God's Name, for the non-Jew will say that all Jews are liars" (see *Middos: The Measure of Man*, page 253).

The obligation, even when sinning, to avoid committing the additional sin of "desecrating God's Name"

13. Rabbi Ila'i the Elder, taught, "If a person sees that his evil inclination [in this case, sexual lust] is getting the better of him, let him go to a place where no one knows him and put on black clothes and wrap himself in them [the hope is that the humble attire will deflect attention from the individual] and let him do what his heart desires, but let him not desecrate the Name of Heaven openly" (*Moed Kattan* 17a and *Kiddushin* 40a).

In other words, if you are not capable of resisting a sexual temptation, then yield to it in a secret place. Obviously, the Rabbis are referring to a sin that doesn't involve a victim (rape is equally evil whether done in secret or in public), but to activities such as visiting a prostitute (one who has not been coerced into becoming a prostitute) or to a place that is inappropriate for a scholar (such as a striptease show or a pornographic film), behavior that is unholy, but not necessarily immoral.*

What this talmudic teaching also conveys is that it is preferable for a person to remain embarrassed by such behavior and therefore perform it in private, or where one is unknown.

———

On a less serious note, a religious Jew I know, who always wears a kippah, *stopped wearing it when he was driving, because he knew that he was not a good driver, and didn't want people, annoyed at his bad driving, to see his* kippah *and get angry at religious Jews. Conversely, another religious friend told me that wearing his* kippah *forces him to make sure that he drives with great politeness and civility.*

———

14. Those who swear falsely, in addition to violating the Ninth Commandment, also commit an act of *Chillul Hashem*. As the Torah commands, "And don't take an oath, then lie in My Name and profane the Name of your Lord" (Leviticus 19:12). Because oaths are taken in God's Name, perjured testimony associates God with a lie.

———

*On the streets of Manhattan, one occasionally sees Jews dressed in the garb of the highly Orthodox entering theaters showing pornographic films or striptease shows. It is people like this who should heed these words of the Talmud, and dress in very different clothing (of course, this would not fully solve the problem, since, in the case of men, their untrimmed beards would usually identify them as religious Jews). One of the reasons ultra-Orthodox leaders want their followers to keep their beards long and untrimmed is so that they will be embarrassed to enter inappropriate places.

The particular obligation of Jewish leaders to sanctify and not desecrate God's Name

15. The talmudic sage Abaye deduced from Deuteronomy 6:5 "And you shall love the Lord your God," that this commandment requires us to make God lovable to others (just as when we fall in love with our future spouse we want everyone else to find them lovable as well). How does one make God and Judaism lovable to others? The Talmud explains that a Jew, particularly a Jewish scholar, should behave in such a pleasant manner that people will say of him, "Happy is the father who taught him Torah. Woe unto those who do not learn Torah. This person who learned Torah, see how pleasant are his ways" (*Yoma* 86a). When people understand that you behave in this way because you love God, they may well come to love God also.

In short, a Jew must act in such a way that people will assume that being committed to God's teachings makes one a better person. Indeed, does anyone doubt that if people consistently equated religious Jews with exemplary behavior, more non-Jews would become Jews, and more Jews would become religious?

16. Maimonides argues that the greater and more prominent the scholar, the more careful he must be to act in an ethically appropriate manner: Thus, to cite several examples noted by Maimonides, scholars have a particular responsibility to:

- pay their debts promptly (see the following paragraph)
- never embarrass colleagues
- not overindulge in merrymaking in public and thereby make spectacles of themselves (see *Yoma* 86a, and Maimonides, "The Foundations of the Torah" 5:11)

17. The talmudic sage Rav offered the following as an example of a *Chillul Hashem*: "If someone like me [a highly regarded religious scholar] were to take meat from a butcher and not pay him promptly" (*Yoma* 86a); obviously, Rav's teaching applies only in a situation in which the shopkeeper expects prompt payment, and the butcher, and others who hear about it, will assume that the rabbi is trying to avoid payment.*

---

*Rashi offers an alternative explanation of Rav's words, not that the butcher will be outraged at the nonpaying rabbi, but rather will learn from this behavior that if a Torah scholar is not careful about cheating others, he need not be careful either.

The same passage in the Talmud offers other examples, all of which focus on the particular responsibility of rabbis and Jewish scholars—the people whom the general public perceives as Judaism's representatives—to conduct themselves in an ethically appropriate manner. Thus the Talmud notes that if a person is known to study Torah, but his business affairs are not conducted honestly, and his manner is unpleasant, people will conclude, "Woe unto the person who studied Torah. See how perverse are his deeds, how ugly his ways" (*Yoma* 86a). In other words, a person who desecrates God's Name by identifying God with ugly behavior alienates others from God and Judaism, and possibly even causes others to conclude that it's not worth giving their children a Jewish education ("Woe unto the person who studied Torah"); through such behavior, one who dishonors God's Name may exert a negative effect not only on his own generation, but on future generations as well.

———

A doctor, an Orthodox Jew, shared with me the following recollection: "As a medical student, I remember attending a guest lecture from a renowned rabbi discussing medical ethics. His remarks were incredibly harsh and insensitive. One could see the large audience squirming in discomfort. Reflexively, I surreptitiously removed my kippah as his remarks grew more virulent. At the end of the lecture, I noticed that all the other Orthodox male medical students, approximately a dozen, had done exactly the same."

———

Rabbi Elya Meir Bloch, head of the famed Telz Yeshiva, told his students that he had once been on a trip raising funds for the Yeshiva when he ran short of cash. When he asked his host to cash his personal check, the man said, "It's hard for me, I already gave to the Yeshiva." Rabbi Bloch wept as he told his students, "If the plumber or electrician had asked him to cash a check, would he have hesitated? But because it was a Rosh Yeshiva *[head of a yeshiva], he thought the check would not go through [presumably the man had had some bad experience like this before]. He was afraid that I would not honor my check. Can there be a greater* Chillul Hashem?"[6]

In other words, the cause of Judaism suffers badly when people come to regard rabbis as schnorrers, *takers instead of givers.*

———

18. Ultimately, the laws of *Kiddush Hashem* are rooted in the belief that the Jews are, so to speak, God's ambassadors to the world, chosen by God to make known both His existence and His demand that people act ethically.

When Jews act with integrity, they not only bring credit on themselves, but they draw people to God. This has been the mission of the Jewish people since the time of Abraham, the first Jew, and it remains the mission of the Jewish people today.

52

MARTYRDOM

1. When a Jew is murdered because of his faith, he is said to have died *al Kiddush Hashem*, "to sanctify God's Name." The most famous martyr in Jewish history is the second-century Rabbi Akiva, who continued to teach Torah even after the Romans had decreed that doing so was a capital offense. Akiva disobeyed the edict and was arrested. Even while in prison he continued to answer questions of Jewish law, and the Jewish community arranged for his answers to be smuggled out. The Romans tortured Akiva, and he died with the words *Sh'ma Yisra'el* ("Hear O Israel, the Lord is Our God, the Lord is One") on his lips (*Berachot* 61b); ever since, it has been a tradition for Jews, particularly martyrs, to recite the *Sh'ma* as they die.

Jewish history is filled with the stories of thousands of martyrs (going back to the time of the second-century-B.C.E. persecutions of Antiochus), most far less well known than Rabbi Akiva. The great historian of medieval Jewish life, Professor Haim Hillel Ben-Sasson, has concluded that "*Kiddush Hashem* [as an act of martyrdom] is an original contribution by the Jewish faith and culture to the whole monotheistic world . . . [It] expressed for the first time in human history the readiness of simple people to die for their faith and opinions."[1]

The Talmud records that when Rabbi Akiva was taken out to be executed, it was the time to recite the [morning] Sh'ma. The Romans were flaying his skin with iron combs, yet Akiva was accepting upon himself the yoke of heaven [by reciting the Sh'ma]. His disciples said to him, "Our teacher, even at this point [you continue to have the presence of mind and the total faith to recite the Sh'ma]?"

He said to them, "All my life I have been troubled by the verse [in the first paragraph of the Sh'ma, *which says, 'You shall love the Lord your God . . .] with all your soul,' which I understood as meaning even if He takes your soul. I asked myself, 'When shall I have the opportunity to fulfill this verse? Now that I have the opportunity, shall I not fulfill it?'" A few minutes later, Rabbi Akiva died while proclaiming the Oneness of the Almighty ("The Lord is One").* (Berachot 61b).

Although Jewish tradition normally associates martyrdom with religious Jews such as Rabbi Akiva, there has been no shortage of non-observant Jewish martyrs.

In eighteenth-century Germany, a Jew named Suss Oppenheimer served as finance minister to the Duke of Wurtemberg. After the duke's sudden death, Oppenheimer's enemies had him arrested on trumped-up charges and sentenced to death. A Pastor Rieger promised Oppenheimer that he would save him from execution if he became a Christian, but Oppenheimer, though not an observant Jew, refused: "I am a Jew and will remain a Jew. I would not become a Christian even if I could become an emperor. Changing one's religion is a matter for consideration by a free man; it is an evil thing for a prisoner." Like Rabbi Akiva, Suss Oppenheimer died with the Sh'ma *on his lips.*

Unhappily, the issue of martyrdom remains a current one. In January 2002, Islamist terrorists in Pakistan kidnapped an American Jew, the journalist Daniel Pearl, who worked for the Wall Street Journal. *After several weeks of captivity and torture, Pearl was murdered. Although not a religiously committed Jew, among Pearl's last words was the declaration, "My father is Jewish, my mother is Jewish, I am Jewish." Both Pearl's words and the slitting of his throat were videotaped by his murderers. The fact that Pearl was murdered because he was a Jew, and that his final words were a reiteration of his Jewishness, means that, according to Jewish tradition, Daniel Pearl died* al Kiddush Hashem, *as a Jewish martyr.**

————

2. The Zohar, Judaism's premier work of mysticism, teaches that when reciting the *Sh'ma*, we should have the intention in our mind to be willing to die to sanctify God's Name (Numbers 195b). One exercise to help achieve this goal is to imagine the mood in which Rabbi Akiva recited the *Sh'ma* as he was martyred.

---

*Some people would quibble at designating Daniel Pearl a martyr, arguing that even had he wanted to, he could not have denied his Jewishness (his captors knew his religion when they kidnapped him). However, the fact that a Jew is murdered for being Jewish, and does not disavow his Jewishness, is what determines his status as a Jewish martyr.

3. One who dies to "sanctify God's Name" is called a *kadosh*, a "holy one." Jewish tradition teaches that such people sojourn in a special place in the next world. The Talmud tells the story of Rabbi Yosef, who had a near-death experience. After he regained consciousness, he said that during his brief period in the hereafter, he heard it said, "As regards those executed by the Roman government, no other creature can stand in their place" [that is, they have reached a level of holiness that is beyond the reach of others] (see *Pesachim* 50a, and *Bava Bathra* 10b).

4. When, however, is a Jew required to be a martyr? According to Jewish law, we are normally commanded to violate all Jewish laws if doing so will enable us to stay alive (thus, for example, if fasting on Yom Kippur will seriously impair our health, we are forbidden to fast). The exceptions are the prohibitions against murder (you can't murder an innocent person even if doing so will enable you to remain alive), certain sexual transgressions (such as incest), and idolatry, particularly if one is commanded to engage in it in public (*Sanhedrin* 74a, and Maimonides, "Laws of the Foundation of the Torah" 5:2; also see the following paragraph). Since Judaism regards it as a form of idolatry for a Jew to forsake Judaism for another faith, Jews have long understood that they should submit to martyrdom if enemies arise and demand of them, "Convert or we will kill you."

5. The Talmud teaches that during times of religious persecution, a Jew should even be willing to lose his life for less serious commandments (*Sanhedrin* 74a). What the Rabbis wished to avoid was the demoralization that would result from a foreign oppressor forcing Jews to violate Jewish laws. Maimonides, therefore, rules that in times of persecution, a Jew should be willing to die even for a ritual offense (such as eating unkosher food; "Laws of the Foundations of the Torah" 5:3). In this, Maimonides is following the view of Rabbi Eliezer, who, supported by the majority of the sages, ruled that one should be a martyr and accept death, even if threatened in private. In contrast, Rabbi Ishmael taught that it is permitted to carry out an act of idolatry in private (*Sanhedrin* 74a), a view that strikes me as more compelling. Why should Jewish law grant an individual idolater or several idolaters the power to determine for a Jew whether he should live or die? And why should Jewish law assume that God, who regards humankind as His children, prefers to see one of His children die rather than temporarily engage, in a private setting, in an act of denying Him? Just as parents would rather their children *not* die for the parents' honor, so, too, we can assume that God wants His children to stay alive.

Even before rabbinic law had explicitly ruled that, during a time of persecution, a Jew should be willing to suffer martyrdom even for a less serious sin, the Bible had described the case of Daniel. During a period when the Persian king Darius issued an ordinance forbidding the offering of prayers to any being other than himself, Daniel disobeyed and continued to pray to God. He was caught, and thrown into a lions' den, but God protected him, and he emerged unharmed (Daniel, chapter 6).* Also, as noted above, Akiva, during a time of persecution, continued to teach Torah, as did the famous martyr Rabbi Chanina ben Teradyon (Avodah Zarah 17b–18a). During the Yom Kippur service, we commemorate the sacred memory of the Ten Martyrs (among them Akiva and Chanina) who were murdered by the Romans for teaching Judaism and practicing Jewish rituals. The Talmud also describes the death of Rabbi Yehuda ben Baba, who, during a period of Roman persecution, sacrificed his life in order to keep the institution of rabbinical ordination (semicha) alive (Sanhedrin 13b–14a).

---

6. If the non-Jew who threatens the Jew's life is not on a mission to destroy Judaism, however, but simply wishes the Jew to serve him, then one should violate Jewish laws. As Maimonides rules, "If anyone about whom it is said, 'Transgress and do not sacrifice your life,' sacrifices his life and does not transgress, he is held responsible for his death" ("The Foundations of the Torah," 5:4). The *Shulchan Arukh* rules that if the violations of Jewish law can be done in private, one should do so, and not sacrifice one's life (*Yoreh Deah* 157:1). On the other hand, the leading medieval scholars of the Jewish communities in Europe, the Tosafists, ruled that if one wished to suffer martyrdom even for a lesser offense (for example, violating the Shabbat laws), it is permissible (*Tosafot, Avodah Zarah* 27b; indeed, the same passage in the *Shulchan Aruch*—in opposition to Maimonides—likewise rules that it is permissible).

---

*The Second Book of Maccabees tells of Elazar, a Jewish leader and scholar who, during the persecutions of Antiochus, was ordered to publicly eat pig meat. Elazar was offered the possibility of bringing kosher meat with him, which he could consume, while the crowd watching him would assume he was eating the unkosher meat. Elazar refused the offer: "It ill becomes [my] years to lie, and thus lead many younger persons to assume that Elazar in his ninetieth year has gone over to a heathen religion . . . for the mere sake of enjoying this brief and momentary life. . . . I will . . . leave behind me a noble example to the young of how to die willingly and nobly on behalf of our holy laws" (II Maccabees 6:18–30). After making this statement, Antiochus's troops tortured him to death.

7. In medieval times, Jews were frequently forced to observe the laws of martyrdom. Starting with the First Crusade in 1096, Christian crusaders often surrounded Jewish communities and demanded that the Jews convert or be killed. Throughout France and Germany (the largest Jewish communities in Europe at that time), many Jews chose martyrdom; frequently, men would first slaughter their children and spouses before killing themselves. This was so common that in medieval prayerbooks we find, along with the blessings over food and drink, the blessing to be recited before dying *al Kiddush Hashem*: "Blessed are You, Master of the universe, who has sanctified us through His commandments and commanded us to sanctify His Name in public."

———

Was it morally right for Jews to kill their children rather than permit them to convert? There is no simple answer to this question, though it is worth noting that moral parents who live in totalitarian societies put their children at great risk when they encourage them to resist the immoral decrees of the society's leaders.

Terrible as it is to die for one's religion, many medieval Jews regarded it as a privilege. Thus, when the Nordhausen community [in Germany] was led to be burned on the pyre during the Black Death massacres in 1349, the Jews obtained permission to hire musicians, and went singing and dancing to their deaths.[2]

———

8. Martyrdom is a last resort, of course, and when Jews can resist their oppressors by fighting back, they should do so (e.g., the Maccabean revolt). It is appropriate to fight back even when chances of victory are slim or none. Thus the historical records we possess of Jews who were attacked by Crusader forces indicate that the Jews tried to fight off their attackers at the cities' gates and even at the entrances to their homes. Only when those efforts failed did they choose to kill themselves rather than be tortured and forced to convert to Christianity. The Warsaw Ghetto Revolt was likewise a hopeless cause, at least militarily. The Nazis had trained troops and an almost unlimited supply of weapons. In contrast, the Jews were starved, weak, and without arms. Yet they fought back with Molotov cocktails, a few rifles, and their hands, and are regarded as modern exemplars of Jews who died *al Kiddush Hashem*.

9. While we should do all that we can to avoid martyrdom, the *Shulchan Arukh* teaches that even at the risk of death, a Jew should not "say that he is

an idolater so that he will not be killed" (*Yoreh Deah* 157:2). On the other hand, it is permitted to offer ambiguous, intentionally misleading answers when an enemy asks our religion, and some Rabbis ruled that it was permitted to wear Christian garb to mislead antisemites (see Ramah *Yoreh Deah* 157:2; obviously, in a society such as the contemporary United States Jews are not endangered by Christianity).

It seems to me that the more lenient rulings on this issue should serve as guides, and that Jews should be permitted to conceal their Jewishness in instances when making such an acknowledgment will lead to their deaths.* What sanctification of God's Name will ensue from acknowledging one's Jewishness to people who wish to murder every Jew in the world (unlike the medieval antisemites who wished Jews to convert to their religion)? Can we not argue that the greatest sanctification of God's Name is ensuring that there remain in this world Jews who can teach the world that there is a God whose primary demand of human beings is ethical behavior—in other words, a God whose primary demand of human beings is not to be a Nazi or an Islamist terrorist?

———

Whether or not we may deceive a non-Jew about our religion remained a source of controversy, and a question of life and death, during the Holocaust. Rabbi Ephraim Oschry, author of Responsa from the Holocaust, *a collection of responses to questions posed to him during the war, forbade buying a forged baptismal certificate. On the other hand, the Jewish legal scholar and historian H. J. Zimmels noted that some rabbis were less categorical and more uncertain on the subject, and feared that not to use every ruse possible to avoid being murdered was to play into the Nazis' hands by surrendering to slaughter.[3]*

Even Rabbi Oschry did permit temporary, deceptive measures, for example, writing "RK" in a passport; this stood for "Roman Catholic" in Germany, but, Oschry argued, a Jew might give the letters a different interpretation in his own mind.

———

10. The American Reform movement issued the following ruling in November 1985 as a guideline to Jews who find themselves held hostage by anti-

---

*Obviously, two of the recent martyrs murdered by Islamist terrorists, Daniel Pearl and Nicholas Berg, were known to be Jews by their kidnappers, and did not have the option of denying their Jewishness. However, when contemporary terrorists, most of whom are also antisemites, hijack an airplane, the hostages might sometimes have the opportunity to hide, or even deny, their Jewishness.

semitic terrorists: "In the case of modern hijackings by terrorists, potential hostages can help Israel to avoid blackmail and guard themselves from additional danger by hiding their Jewish identity. It would, therefore, be appropriate for children and adults, if taken hostage by terrorists, to conceal their Jewish identity first through passive acts and then through any other way which is possible."[4]

11. One can die in a manner that sanctifies God's Name without being a martyr, by acting with bravery, kindness, and self-sacrifice. Such was the case with Abe Zelmanowitz, a deeply religious Jew who died on September 11, 2001, in the terrorist attacks against the United States. When the first Twin Towers building was hit by the airplane, the survivors inside the building fled down the staircases in an attempt to exit the building. Mr. Zelmanowitz was close friends with a non-Jew named Edward Beyea who was a quadriplegic (the two worked for the same company as computer programmers), and when Zelmanowitz called his brother after the plane hit, and his brother asked, "Why are you still in there?" he explained that he did not want to leave his friend alone. It later came out that Beyea had a full-time aide with him, but Zelmanowitz had insisted that she leave and save herself. The two men waited together for the rescue workers, who could not get there in time, and when the building collapsed, both men died. The incident became well known, and President George Bush spoke of Mr. Zelmanowitz's bravery and kindness in an address to the nation. Mr. Zelmanowitz's brother, Jack, said that this type of behavior was typical of his brother. "Had it been a casual acquaintance [and not someone he was as close to as he was to Mr. Beyea], he would have done the same thing. He could never turn his back on another human being."

In the years since 9/11, Zelmanowitz's action has been regarded as a poignant example of *Kiddush Hashem*.

———

Rita Lasar, Mr. Zelmanowitz's sister, said shortly after his death: "Abe accomplished nothing really, except to decide on September 11, 2001, as the twin towers of death and fear filled his twenty-seventh-floor office, just what kind of person he would be. We can't control death; it comes to us all in the end. Abe's choice we keep to the end: What kind of person will I be?"

———

V

GOD AND
ETHICS

GOD AND GOODNESS

———

The fear of God is the beginning of wisdom.

Psalms 111:10

53

GOD AS THE BASIS OF MORALITY

1. The Bible teaches that God created the world, and gave humankind laws by which to live. These laws, which include commands to pursue justice and love your neighbor (Deuteronomy 16:20 and Leviticus 19:18), and which forbid stealing and murder (Exodus 20:13), are binding because God so ruled.*

Indeed, without God, by what authority can one argue that certain activities should be permitted and others forbidden?† As Ivan Karamazov says in Dostoevsky's *The Brothers Karamazov,* "If there is no God, all is permitted." Dostoevsky's words have often been cited as a prophecy of the horrors of the twentieth century. But Dostoevsky was not being prophetic; he was simply stating a logical conclusion: If there is no God, then why should everything, including murder, not be permitted?

The perplexity into which a question like this thrusts moral secularists was articulated by Bertrand Russell, the most prominent atheist philosopher of the twentieth century: "I cannot see how to refute the arguments for the subjectivity of ethical values, but I find myself incapable of believing that all that is wrong with wanton cruelty is that I don't like it."[1] Though Russell lived well into his nineties, he was never able to produce a stronger argument against wanton cruelty than that he didn't like it. Unfortunately, a considerable number of people do like it.

2. As both the Bible and Bertrand Russell would agree, without God there is nothing higher in the universe than human beings. But from where, then, can an objectively binding morality derive? Different people will have different conceptions of what is moral (or even whether being moral is desirable), and there is no reason for one person to accept another person's notions of ethics as superior to his own.

---

*Many of the conclusions reached in this chapter were developed with Dennis Prager.

†Thus, those who refrain from criminal behavior only because of governmental regulations have no motive to exercise self-restraint when they have reason to believe they will not be caught; that is why we would fear to be in a city where the police had gone on strike.

Therefore, in the absence of God, all that people can express about morality are opinions. "You like vanilla, I like chocolate; Hitler liked killing people, I like saving them."*

3. Because the biblical ideals of charity, love of neighbor, and the sanctity of human life have for so long pervaded the Western world (influencing people such as Bertrand Russell),[†] people often don't realize that these notions came into the world through the doctrine of ethical monotheism introduced by the Hebrew Bible more than three thousand years ago. But take away the divine foundations for teachings such as "Love your neighbor as yourself" (the basis for the Golden Rule), and they make no sense. As John Locke wrote in 1690: "Should that most unshaken rule of morality and foundation of all social virtue, 'that one should do as he would be done unto,' be proposed to one who had never heard of it before . . . might he not without any absurdity ask a reason why?" *(Essay Concerning Human Understanding).*

———

The most famous statement in the Declaration of Independence is, of course, its ringing declaration: "We hold these truths to be self-evident, that all men are created equal, that they are endowed by their creator with certain inalienable rights; that among these are life, liberty, and the pursuit of happiness." Rabbi Jonathan Sacks has noted that "these truths, of course, are anything but self-evident. They have been implicitly denied by most societies at most times in history. They are self-evident only to someone steeped in the Hebrew Bible."[2†]

———

---

*Writing in the late 1940s, educator Oliver Martin noted that secular ethical teachings, even when well intentioned, cannot bring about a universally binding moral system: " 'Bad' people like Hitler and Goering simply carried out more or less consistently many of the ideas long held by respectable 'good' people. . . . How do good people deny morality? In many ways:

- 'I believe in morals but all morals are relative.'
- 'I have my own private moral code.'
- 'Morals are entirely a matter of opinion.'

Hitler or Mussolini could accept every one of these statements" (*Two Educators: Hutchins and Conant*).

[†]Thus, Russell, a lifelong political dissident, used to recall the words written on the flyleaf of his parents' family Bible, "Do not follow the majority to do evil" (Exodus 23:2).

[‡]Sacks goes on to note that of the three most important political revolutions in the last two and a half centuries, the American, French, and Russian, only the American Revolution was driven by religious values, and remained moderate, just, and non-murderous. The French and Russian revolutions were inspired by secular—and, in the case of Russia, avowedly atheist—values: "Precisely these two," Sacks notes, "inspired by visions of a secular utopia, ended in bloodshed, and the suppression of human rights."

4. Secularists generally respond to arguments like these with the claim that human reason can serve as the basis for morality. Dr. Brad Blandshard, a professor of philosophy at Yale University and a well-known humanist, used to advise his students that "rationality, or the attempt at it takes the place of faith. . . . Take reason seriously . . . let it shape belief and conduct freely. It will shape them right if anything can."[3]*

Unfortunately, the belief that reason will lead people to morality is itself unreasonable. Reason is amoral, and how can something amoral—something that can and has been used to justify good, evil, and amoral behavior alike (hence the word *rationalization*)—bring people to morality? Thus, to the reasonable men of ancient Greece and Rome, reason dictated that handicapped and unhealthy newborns be abandoned. The ancient Hebrews were alone, as far as is known, in regarding such behavior as murder (the lives of newborn infants were considered sacred because they, no less than any other person, were created in "God's image"), a belief that the first-century Roman historian Tacitus regarded as ridiculous.

Morality and reasonableness sometimes coincide (for example, it is both reasonable and moral to have lifeguards stationed on beaches where many people swim), but often they don't. When the Nazis ruled over much of Europe, it was moral, but not reasonable, to risk one's life to save Jews. Because it is unreasonable to endanger one's life, particularly to save a stranger, most Germans and Poles, even those who thought that murdering Jews was wrong, chose not to take that risk. Furthermore, those people who did save Jews did not do so because they felt commanded by reason, but because they felt commanded by a moral law higher than reason.

Reason is an indispensable tool in helping people who want to do good to accomplish their goals. It is, however, equally indispensable to people who want to do evil. That is why an intelligent person who is evil is a much more dangerous adversary than an unintelligent one.

5. If God is the basis of morality, does this mean that belief in God will make people moral? Not necessarily. Many people believe that God created

---

*Allied to the belief that reason will guide people to morality is the belief that education will do so as well. In *The Future of an Illusion*, Sigmund Freud's well-known critique of religion, he predicted that education would lead to the good society. Writing in Vienna in 1927, Freud concluded, "Civilization has little to fear from educated people and brain-workers. In them the replacement of religious motives for civilized behavior by other, secular motives, would proceed unobtrusively" (page 39). Ten years after Freud wrote these words, the Nazis occupied Austria, and Freud witnessed his fellow intellectuals showing no more moral strength than any other group in Austria and Germany. Many intellectuals supported Nazism and, as Max Weinreich's the world, but do not believe that God's most important demand of human beings is that they act humanely. Some theists, for example, believe that what matters most to God is that people have faith in Him. The best-known exponent of this view was the sixteenth-century founder of the Protestant Reformation, Martin Luther, who held that salvation in the next world depended upon faith in Christ, *and nothing else:* "Be a sinner and sin vigorously, but even more vigorously believe and delight in Christ who is victor over sin, death, and the world. . . . It is sufficient that we recognize through the wealth of God's glory the lamb who bears the sins of the world; from this, sin does not sever us, even if thousands, thousands of times in one day we should fornicate or murder" (letter to Philip Melanchthon, August 1, 1521).[4]

Unfortunately, this leads to a morally problematic conclusion: "It follows that those who share Luther's belief will be saved even if they are mass murderers, while the rest of mankind is damned and will suffer eternal tortures in hell, regardless of the excellence of their works" (Walter Kaufmann)[5]

6. The biblical and rabbinic vision of how people should live is to acknowledge that God created the world, that He is a universal God, and that His primary demand of human beings is ethical behavior (see chapter 1). Those who believe in such a God accept that there is a binding ethical standard, one that conforms to God's will. Determining what that standard requires in a given situation often necessitates much study and discussion,* but what is most important is to acknowledge that such a standard exists; everything is not just a matter of opinion.† Therefore, when ethical monotheists see a fellow believer doing something wrong, they can appeal to the person's belief: "Is this how God wants you to act?" On the other hand, ethical atheists who wish to influence unethical atheists have no argument more powerful than "I (and maybe Aristotle and Plato as well) think that what you are doing is wrong."

7. The phenomenon of murderous behavior by religious fanatics, ranging from the Crusaders to the Inquisitors, and to Hamas and al-Qaeda terrorists today, is well known, but does not negate the argument that God's existence is necessary for there to be a universally binding standard of moral

---

Hitler's Professors documents, quite a number participated in its atrocities. Education makes people educated, not moral.

*Even then, one might not come to the right decision.

†Thus, a Hitler is wrong even when a majority of Germans vote him into power and support his policies.

behavior. Rather, what such fanatics demonstrate is the evil that results when people believe in a God concerned solely with issues of faith and rituals, and not with morality.*

Because so much attention has been focused on evil performed by religious fanatics, few people realize that with the "death of God" announced by the German philosopher Friedrich Nietzsche in the late nineteenth century, the most murderous doctrines in humankind's history were unleashed upon the world.† Nietzsche, an atheist, helped pave the way for some of these new "post-God" ideologies: "The great majority of men have no right to existence, but are a misfortune to higher men. I do not yet grant the failures the right [to exist]."6 In contrast to Judaism and Christianity, which saw pity and compassion as among the most elevated virtues, Nietzsche rejected such behavior as unmanly: "The weak and ill-constituted shall perish: first principle of *our* philanthropy. And one shall help them to do so. What is more harmful than any vice? Active sympathy for the ill-constituted and weak—Christianity."7 In *The Genealogy of Morals,* Nietzsche predicted that with the approaching end of belief in God, "morality will gradually perish," something he acknowledged might have some negative results, but which he also regarded as "perhaps . . . the most hopeful of all spectacles." Nietzsche posited the existence of the *Übermensch,* the superman who, in the absence of God, could create and impose his own laws.

Jonathan Glover, a contemporary ethicist, has observed that many of Nietzsche's ideas "became background assumptions to much of twentieth-century life and thought . . . [including his rejection of] sympathy for the weak in favor of a willingness to trample on them."8 It is probably not coincidental that in Germany, where Nietzsche exerted his greatest influence, the German people voted into power a leader who decreed that whole categories of people, such as Jews, had no right to exist (Nietzsche himself did not preach antisemitism).

---

*There is almost no cruelty of which those who preach faith and disregard morality are not capable. Thus, in 1209, a Crusader army defeated the French city of Béziers, which contained, according to a bishop's report, 220 Christian heretics, known as Cathars. Unable to ferret out the heretics, the Crusaders asked the papal commander Arnaud Amalric, "Lord, what shall we do? We cannot distinguish the good from the evil." Pope Innocent III's representative ruled, "Kill them all. God will recognize his own." Fifteen thousand people were murdered in one day. The Pope had promised the Crusaders forgiveness of all sins, and safety from all creditors (see Otto Friedrich, *The End of the World*).

†As Erich Fromm, the psychoanalyst and disciple of Freud, commented, "In the nineteenth century the problem was that God was dead; in the twentieth century the problem is that man is dead."

Karl Marx (1818–1883), the equally influential atheist philosopher and inspirer of communism, agreed with Nietzsche's conclusion that morality should be determined solely by human beings, and not by a God in whom neither he nor Nietzsche believed. In Marx's view, "Right can never be higher than the economic structure of society. . . . We therefore reject every attempt to impose on us any moral dogma whatsoever as an eternal, ultimate, and forever immutable moral law." A few decades later, Vladimir Lenin*—the Soviet dictator and Marx's most important disciple—declared, "We do not believe in an eternal morality. . . . We repudiate all morality derived from non-human [i.e., God] and nonclass concepts."[9] When Joseph Stalin, Lenin's successor, ordered the dropping of "class enemies" into vats of acid, there was no possible Communist code of morality by which such acts could be condemned (as long as they served the society's economic interests). True, years after Stalin died, many Communists started to criticize his Nazi-like cruelty, and even claimed that he had perverted the teachings of Marx and Lenin. The more significant truth, however, is that during Stalin's lifetime, Communists in the West, who had freedom of speech (unlike those who lived under Stalin's rule), continued to revere Stalin as a true Marxist; their denunciations of Stalin's murders after he died had less to do with morality than with the fact that he was no longer in power.[†]

———

An earlier attempt to base a moral system on secularly derived values was undertaken by the eighteenth-century Immanuel Kant, perhaps the most eminent of all German philosophers. Though Kant, unlike Nietzsche and Marx, believed in God, he refused to base his ethics on God's existence or will; instead he tried to establish a secular basis for morality. Unfortunately, Kant defined certain people as unworthy of life, specifically children born out of wedlock: "A child that comes into the world apart from marriage is born outside the law (for the law is marriage) and therefore outside the protection of the law. It has, as it were, stolen into the community (like contraband merchandise) so that the commonwealth can ignore its existence (since it was not right that it should have come to exist in this way) and can therefore ignore its annihilation."[10] Kant stated this heartless conclusion in explaining why the state should not charge a mother who killed

---

*Famous for his statement, "I hate God as I do my personal enemies" (*New Life*, December 16, 1905).

†One of those who repudiated Stalin long before his death was the English writer Arthur Koestler, who, after disavowing Communism, embarked on a noble, but largely unsuccessful, campaign to convince Communists of the movement's evil; see page 183.

a child born out of wedlock with murder, though it should so charge a married mother who murdered her child. Indeed, Kant's comment that the state can "ignore its annihilation" suggests that he didn't think such a mother should be charged with any offense at all.

Thus, Kant and Nietzsche bequeathed to Germany the notion that there are categories of people—both drawn from the circles of the vulnerable and weak—whose existence should not be protected by the state, and that the state might well be better off if they were eliminated.

———

8. Does this mean that people who are atheists are evil? Of course not. There are many atheists and agnostics who are highly moral; however, this is not because of their atheism, but despite it. Because atheism is amoral, its amorality will eventually affect the behavior of most atheists, and certainly that of their descendants. As Rabbi Milton Steinberg wrote over a half-century ago, "In the end, how a man thinks must affect how he acts; atheism must finally, if not in one generation, then in several, remake the conduct of atheists in the light of its own logic."[11]

Moral atheists are therefore faced with an uncomfortable paradox. If they wish their children to continue to practice the virtues they hold to be laudable, their best hope is to teach them that the practice of such virtue is the will of a god in whom they don't believe. Atheists might be uncomfortable teaching their children a doctrine they believe to be untrue, but then they should accept that they are bringing children into the world without any adequate system for teaching them to be good.

Religious people who are moral but who believe that God is more concerned with faith than with acts of kindness are faced with an equally uncomfortable paradox. If they want their children to continue to practice the virtuous behavior they deem laudable, they must teach them that being a kind person is what matters most to God. Therefore, they should convey to their children that a good person who does not share their precise theological views is still deemed a good person by God, whereas an evil person who shares their theology is deemed an evil person by God.

54

LOVING AND FEARING GOD

═══════

Fear of God

1. The commandment to fear God (see, for example, Deuteronomy 6:13), with its connotation of an angry, punishing deity, is repugnant to many people today; they see this notion as primitive and one that should be discarded. However, an examination of the concept of fear, or awe, of God in the Bible reveals that it is intended to achieve three effects:

- to prevent us from fearing people more than we fear God
- to promote fair and compassionate treatment of society's weakest members
- to bring people to wisdom

———

The Hebrew word used for "fear" (from the root yareh*) can also be translated as "awe" or "revere"; in other words, the Torah commands us to revere God, and experience a feeling of awe at His grandeur. The medieval Jewish philosopher Joseph Albo offers the following example: "The God-fearing man is ashamed to transgress God's commandments just as a person is ashamed to do an unbecoming thing in the presence of . . . a respected and wise old man who has a reputation for learning, character, and dignity"* (Sefer Ha-Ikarim, [The Book of Principles of the Jewish Faith]).

That fear of God should be more akin to awe and reverence than to terror is also suggested by the contemporary Jewish theologian Rabbi Louis Jacobs: "The fear of punishment is not really fear of God, but fear of what He might do. It is a kind of self-interest in which wrongdoing is eschewed from the same motives for which insurance premiums are kept up to date . . . in its worst form [it] conceives of God as a tyrant ready to pounce on those guilty of the slightest infringement of His laws."[1]

———

_____

*I once came across the statement (I do not recall the source), "He who truly fears a thing flees from it, but he who truly fears God, flees unto Him."

To prevent us from fearing people more than we fear God

2. When Pharaoh ordered the midwives Shifra and Puah to kill male Is-raelite babies upon birth, the two women, "fearing God, did not do as the king of Egypt told them; they let the boys live" (Exodus 1:16). That this is the only explanation the Bible offers for their behavior suggests that it was this fear that prompted them to act as they did. Pharaoh then commanded the Egyptian people, who presumably did not fear God but did fear him, to participate in his campaign: "Then Pharaoh charged all his people, saying, 'Every son born that is born you shall throw into the Nile'" (Exodus 1:22).

That fear of God can liberate people from fear of others explains why a disproportionate percentage of political dissenters in totalitarian societies such as Nazi Germany and the former Soviet Union were God-fearers. Such peo-ple presumably feared their country's rulers (they did not want to die), but they believed that obedience to God's will was more important than any-thing, including life. On the other hand, people who do not believe in or fear God are far less likely to risk their lives, the most valuable possession they have, to defy a country's ruler, no matter how immoral his edicts.

———

Fear of, and reverence for, God is a trait that is, of course, not restricted to Jews. The Cuban poet Armando Valladares, a committed Catholic and a political prisoner for twenty-two years in Castro's Cuba, reported that in the early 1960s—while incarcerated at the Isla de Pino prison—he frequently heard Cas-tro's firing squads executing dissidents. The last words Valladares heard called out by many of those about to be shot were, "Long live Christ the King! Down with Communism!" Valladares reports that "the cries became such a potent and stirring symbol that by 1963 the men condemned to death were gagged before being carried down to be shot."[2]

———

3. When Rabbi Yochanan ben Zakkai was nearing the end of his life, his closest students gathered at his bedside and asked for a blessing. Rabbi Yochanan told them: "May your fear of God be as strong as your fear of human beings" (*Berachot* 28b).

"Is that all?" the students asked, disappointed by so modest a blessing. In fact, though, Rabbi Yochanan was acknowledging the truth that most people, including many of those who claim to be religious, fear the reactions and opinions of people more than they fear those of God. When people pre-pare to do something unethical, they check to see that they are not being ob-served; however, they don't seem to fear or care that God is watching. If people feared God as much as they feared other people, they would perform almost no wrongful acts.

———

The Chaffetz Chayyim was once given a ride in a horse-drawn carriage. The driver, unaware of the identity of his passenger, stopped the carriage near a grove, and stepped down. After instructing the Chaffetz Chayyim to "call out if any-body sees me," he started to gather fruit from the trees in the field. Within a mat-ter of seconds the Chaffetz Chayyim called out in an agitated voice, "We are seen, we are seen." The frightened driver dropped the fruit, rushed back to the wagon, and drove off in great haste. After he had driven for a minute or two, he turned around and saw that the road behind them was empty. He turned to the Chaffetz Chayyim in anger, saying, "Why did you yell out like that? There was no one watching me." The Chaffetz Chayyim pointed skyward: "God saw what you were doing. God is always watching."

———

To promote fair and compassionate treatment of society's weakest, most vulnerable members

4. As noted, the Bible presumes that people who do not fear God will have no compunction about mistreating, and even killing, those weaker than they are. Indeed, this was so taken for granted that when Abraham entered Gerar, he told the local monarch, Abimelech, that Sarah was his sister. Abim-elech soon arranged for the beautiful Sarah to be brought to his palace, but before he could consummate the relationship, God appeared to him in a dream, and warned him that if he failed to return Sarah to her husband, he, Abimelech, would die.

When the king brought Sarah back, he asked Abraham why he had lied to him. Abraham answered, "I thought, 'Surely there is no fear of God in this place, and they will kill me because of my wife'" (Genesis 20:11).

5. The Bible hopes that fear of God will protect the vulnerable from op-pression and exploitation. That is why the demand to fear God is so often added to commands concerning the weak (and not to other commands). For example: "You shall not place . . . a stumbling block in front of the blind; you shall fear your God" (Leviticus 19:14). The average person, even one with a sadistic inclination, is unlikely to trip another; even if he is stronger than his would-be victim, he will fear that the victim will tell others who might then seek retribution. But there is no reason for a cruel person to refrain from hurting a blind person. The victim will have no idea who caused his injury, and might not even realize that the act was done on purpose. Therefore, God appends to this prohibition a reminder to fear God, the one who sees all that we do.

———

Rabbi Aaron Levine presents God's warning even more graphically: "Don't imagine that you will escape punishment just because your misdeeds go unde-tected by your fellow man. No! Remember that it was I who distinguished in Egypt between the firstborn and those who were not firstborn."[3]

———

6. In several other instances, the Torah condemns mistreating the weak and adds the words, "you shall fear your God":

• "If your kinsman, being in [difficult] straits comes under your au-thority . . . do not exact from him . . . interest, but fear your God" (Levi-ticus 25:35–36). Not only do poor people find it very difficult, if not impossible, to secure interest-free loans, but lenders, knowing that the poor will not be able to secure loans elsewhere, often charge them higher than normal rates of interest. In contrast, the Jewish community—in response to this biblical law—has developed *Gemilut Chesed* societies, organizations that give interest-free loans to poor people. Today, hun-dreds of such organizations, providing loans for food, rent, education, and even start-up businesses, exist throughout Israel, the United States, and other Diaspora societies.

• "You shall not rule over him [a servant] ruthlessly; you shall fear your God" (Leviticus 25:43). Throughout history, mistreated servants in al-most all societies have had no recourse. The Bible therefore instructed employers to fear God, who identifies with the weak.

• "You shall rise before the aged and show deference to the old; you shall fear your God" (Leviticus 19:32). This verse is posted on buses in Israel to encourage people to give up their seats to older passengers.

———

When a distinguished rabbinic scholar was in his sixties, his children grown and gone, his aged and infirm mother-in-law continued to live with him and his wife, as she had for many years. The rabbi remarked, "If it were not for the fear of heaven, I don't think I would have the ethical conviction to keep my mother-in-law in the house. It is such a strain on my wife and on our relationship that it would be so easy to rationalize sending her to a nursing home. . . . But when I remember the final accounting, it strengthens my commitment."[4]

———

7. In short, when we are dealing with those who are weak, and of whom we can take advantage without fearing retribution,* we should remind ourselves that God identifies with the weak, and turns against those who hurt them. The Bible issues a particularly strong warning against anyone who takes advantage of orphans and widows: "If you do mistreat them, I will heed their outcry as soon as they cry out to Me, and My anger shall blaze forth. And I will put you to the sword, and your own wives shall become widows and your children orphans" (Exodus 22:22–23). While there is no evidence that God actually, and on a routine basis, exacts such punishment in this world, the verse's passionate language should be sufficient to frighten all God-fearers from taking advantage of the weak.

To bring people to wisdom

8. The most famous biblical statement concerning fear of God is the teaching in Psalms: "The beginning of wisdom is the fear of God" (Psalms 111:10; see also Proverbs 1:7); this verse is recited daily near the beginning of the morning prayer service. Without fear and awe of God, without acknowledgment that there is something greater than us in the universe, a person may have intelligence (as did men such as Nietzsche and Marx), but wisdom and humility depend on recognizing that there is a force higher than human beings: "The religious person knows he is not God, and therefore he might be wrong. The person [who does not believe in or fear God] is likely to think that he is 'the be all and end all,' the possessor of wisdom" (Rabbi Jack Riemer).[5]

Love of God

9. It is perhaps a sign of God's very lovability and "vulnerability" that He asks us to love Him, and not just fear Him. This command forms part of

———

*The twentieth-century Bible scholar Nechama Leibowitz wrote that the commandment to fear God refers as well "to those acts which are beyond the jurisdiction of an earthly court, for the simple reason that witnesses cannot be produced. Only the individual conscience can know whether the action was committed in good or bad faith" (*Studies in* Vayikra [Leviticus], pages 373–374). For example, if you give another person advice that turns out to be disadvantageous for them, only you know if your motive in offering the advice was pure or not.

the *Sh'ma* prayer and is recited twice daily: "You shall love the Lord Your God with all your heart, with all your soul, and with all your might" (Deuteronomy 6:5). Because God has given humankind free will, love is the most obvious gift that we can offer God.

10. Love of God is rooted in the belief that God is a personal God (not an impersonal force in the universe) and that, like a parent, He knows and cares for each of us. Thus the Book of Exodus records God's reaction to the Jewish sufferings in Egypt: "I have indeed seen the suffering of My people. I have heard how they cry out because [of the harshness] of their slave masters and I am aware of their pain" (3:7). It is the sense that God knows us, the perception that we each have a personal and unique connection to God* that is an important source of human love for God.

11. Love of God is likewise rooted in the belief that God loves us. As the Mishnah teaches: "Beloved is humankind, for they are created in the divine image. It is indicative of an even greater love [by God] that it was made known to them that they are in God's image, as it is said, 'God made humankind in the divine image'" (Genesis 9:6; *The Ethics of the Fathers* 3:14). Our creation in God's image, the ultimate source of human self-esteem (see chapter 23) is an act of love by God which evokes our love in return.

Gratitude to God: three guidelines

12. Thank God throughout the day: The first prayer in the morning prayer service is one of gratitude: "*Modeh Ani,* I am grateful to You, O living God, for restoring my soul to me." Minutes later, during the morning prayers, we thank God for clothing, for other basic needs that we take for granted, such as sight, and even for the ability to perform bodily functions without difficulty. After finishing the service, we sit down to breakfast, and bless God for the food that we eat. In traditional Jewish culture, a Jew is expected to utter one hundred blessings a day.

Judaism's concept of gratitude is rooted in the belief that we should take *nothing* for granted—not life, nor clothing, nor food. Those who do take these things for granted, go through life with a sense of expectation, entitlement, and disappointment. Indeed, when their routine is interrupted—they don't feel well, their clothes are dirty, or food is not prepared to their

---

*Epitomized in the Jewish joke about the prayer of a struggling businessman: "O God, you help complete strangers, so why don't you help me!"

liking—they experience anger and frustration. In contrast, the Rabbis teach: "For every breath that a person takes he should praise his Creator" (*Genesis Rabbah* 14:9).

———

Jewish law even ordains a blessing to be recited after going to the bathroom: "Blessed are You, Lord our God, Sovereign of the Universe, Who has formed man in wisdom, and created within him many openings and many cavities. It is obvious and known before Your throne of glory that if one of them were to be ruptured or one of them blocked, it would be impossible to survive and to stand before You. Blessed are You, God, Who heals all flesh and does wonders."

Dr. Kenneth Prager, an observant Jew, recalls that when he attended a Jewish day school as a child, this blessing was posted outside the bathroom, and provoked much laughter from him and his friends: "For grade-school children, there could be nothing more strange or ridiculous than to link the acts of [urination] and defecation with holy words that mentioned God's Name."

Years later, in medical school, when Prager studied the terrible consequences that could result from even minor aberrations in the function of the human body, he started to appreciate the blessing's profundity: "After seeing patients whose lives revolved around their dialysis machines, and others with colostomies and urinary catheters, I realized how wise Rabbi Abaye [the composer of the blessing] had been."

Indeed, this blessing, known in Hebrew as asher yatzar, *underscoring that no aspect of health should be taken for granted, is part of the morning prayer service. Dr. Prager had occasion to write about this ancient prayer in the* Journal of the American Medical Association, *and concluded his article with the story of a twenty-year-old man named Josh, who had suffered severe injuries during a car crash, and was improving slowly over a period of many months: "But Josh continued to require intermittent catheterization. I knew only too well the problems and perils this young man would face for the rest of his life because of a neurogenic bladder. The urologists were very pessimistic about his chances for not requiring catheterization. They had not seen this occur after a spinal cord injury of this severity. Then the impossible happened. I was there the day Josh no longer required a urinary catheter. I thought of Abaye's . . . prayer. Pointing out that I could not imagine a more meaningful scenario for its recitation, I suggested to Josh, who was also a yeshiva graduate, that he say the prayer. He agreed. As he recited the ancient* bracha, *tears welled in my eyes.*

"Josh is my son."[6]

———

13. Focus with particular attention, and *at least some of the time,* on your prayers to God. Many of us recite our prayers quickly, often swallowing the words. To ask people never to do so is unrealistic.* But all of us should try to recite our prayers slowly and with real feeling at least some of the time. Alternatively, choose one prayer each day to recite carefully, with concentration, and with a feeling of love and gratitude to God.

The *Sefer Chasidim* tells of an incident in which "a wise man overheard another man reciting the *Birkat Hamazon* in haste. The wise man said, 'You did not rush when you ate. Why do you rush when reciting the *Birkat Hamazon?*'" While most religious Jews do recite this blessing quickly on weekdays, many people, after the lengthy Shabbat meal, sing the prayer slowly and aloud.

14. Express gratitude and love to God by treating other people, all of whom God regards as His children, with kindness and fairness. And just as parents feel love and appreciation toward those who treat their children well, so does God feel great affection for those who treat His children well.

God as the ultimate guarantor of life's meaning

15. "In the final analysis, for the believer there are no questions, and for the nonbeliever there are no answers" (Chaffetz Chayyim).

---

*Jewish law ordains three prayer services a day (and the morning one is long), and the recital of the extensive *Birkat Hamazon* prayer after each meal.

Torah Study:
The Mitzvah That
Equals All the Others

———

The evil inclination does not mind if a Jew
fasts or sheds tears, and prays all day long,
as long as he doesn't study Torah.

Rabbi Israel Meir Ha-Kohen Kagan,
the Chaffetz Chayyim (1838–1933)

55

THE PREEMINENT COMMAND

1. According to the Talmud (*Shabbat* 31a), the second question posed to Jews after they die is "Did you set aside regular time for Torah study?" (that is, the study of the Bible, the Talmud, and other Jewish holy texts).* In another, even more far-reaching formulation, the Mishnah teaches that "the study of Torah equals in value all the other commandments" (*Peah* 1:1).

Torah study is necessary so that Jews know how Judaism and God expect them to behave. As Joshua (1:8) teaches, "Study it day and night so that you may observe all that is within it."

In addition, study, along with prayer, constitutes the primary way in which Jews connect to God. However, Torah study, as Rabbi Louis Finkelstein, the chancellor of the Jewish Theological Seminary, used to say, has one advantage over prayer: "In prayer, we speak to God, but in study, God speaks to us."

———

One frequently meets Jews who are passionately political—most often liberal,[1] but sometimes conservative. I ask them if they have ever studied Jewish texts that caused them to reconsider some aspects of their liberalism or conservatism. If they haven't, then their real belief system is their political ideology, and Jewish texts are studied and cited just to support beliefs they already have. However, the goal of Jewish study should not be only to reinforce what we already believe, but to challenge our thinking as well.

———

Who is obligated to study Torah?

2. The obligation to study Torah applies to all Jews for the whole of their lives: "Every Jewish man [regarding the obligation of women to study Torah,

---

*In traditional Jewish culture, the word *Torah* refers to all Jewish religious writings, as well as the first five books of the Bible. As regards the first question we are asked, see page 19.

see paragraph 3] is required to study Torah, whether poor or rich, healthy or afflicted with painful disorders, young, or old and feeble. Even the poor man who lives from charity and begs from door to door [must study Torah] and the one who is hard-pressed to support a wife and children must set aside definite times to study by day and by night. . . . Until when is a person obligated to study Torah? Until the day of one's death" (Maimonides, "Laws of Torah Study," 1:8,10).

———

Given Judaism's often practical bent, one might have expected poor people, and all those under pressure to support their families, to be exempt from this obligation. But, just as Jewish law insists that poor Jews, no less than wealthy ones, refrain from working on the Sabbath and Jewish holidays, so does it require that poor Jews, like wealthy ones, devote time to Torah study. Because knowledge of Judaism is a prerequisite for living a Jewish life, exempting poor Jews from the obligation to study would be tantamount to excusing them from having to be Jewish.

In the Talmud we find many instances of sages who lived in poverty. The Talmud cites the case of Hillel, who worked for many years as a woodchopper, as an example that obligates the poor to engage in Jewish learning.*

Similarly, wealth, and its often concomitant business and philanthropic obligations, does not free us from the obligation to study, even if we donate generous sums to charity. In addition, it is particularly important for people engaged in commerce to study the Jewish laws that apply to integrity in business.

When the Chaffetz Chayyim tried to influence a wealthy man to spend more time studying Torah and praying, the man told the rabbi that he would

———

*When a poor person's life is examined, he is asked if he studied Torah. "If he answers, 'I was poor and worried about earning my living,' they [i.e., the Heavenly Court] will ask him, 'Were you poorer than Hillel?' For it was told of Hillel that every day he used to work and earn one *tropaik* [a small amount], half of which he would give [as tuition] to the doorkeeper at the house of learning; the other half he would spend on his and his family's needs. One day he was unable to earn anything and the doorkeeper would not permit him to enter the house of learning. So he climbed up to the roof and sat upon the window to hear the words of the Living God out of the mouths of [Rabbis] Shmaya and Avtalion. That day was a Friday in the middle of the winter, and snow fell down upon him from the sky. "When the dawn rose, Shmaya said to Avtalion, 'Brother Avtalion, every day this house is light and today it is dark. . . .' They looked up and saw the figure of a man in the window. They went up and found Hillel covered by four feet of snow. They brought him downstairs, bathed and anointed him, and placed him in front of the fire" (activities that would not normally be permitted on the Sabbath; *Yoma* 35b).

like to, but had no time. The Chaffetz Chayyim answered, "If you have no free time, you are not a rich man but a pitiful pauper."[2] Indeed, if a wealthy person comes before the Heavenly Court and justifies his lack of Torah study with the claim that he was too busy managing his business affairs, the court will challenge him with the example of Rabbi Elazar ben Charsom, who, despite fabulous wealth, devoted himself assiduously to the study of Torah (Yoma 35b).

The library at the YIVO Institute for Jewish Research in New York (an organization that commemorates Jewish life in Eastern Europe) contains an old book saved from the millions of Jewish books burned by the Nazis. Inside the volume is stamped The Society of Woodchoppers for the Study of Mishnah in Berditchev *[the Mishnah is the earliest part of the Talmud]. That the men who chopped wood in Berditchev, a job that had little status and that required no study, met regularly to learn about Jewish law demonstrates how widespread the tradition of study was, and is, in the Jewish community.*

Women and Torah study

3. Throughout much of Jewish history, the Jewish community restricted the educational opportunities available to women, and therefore limited the ability of women—who comprise half of the Jewish population—to contribute to Jewish life.* While the Talmud's dominant, but not exclusive, view is that women are not obligated to study Torah, the sage Rabbi Eliezer went further and declared that "he who teaches his daughter Torah, it is as if he taught her obscenity" (Mishnah *Sotah* 3:4).† While this statement was often cited in the past by those who wished to limit women's education, it is rarely noted (particularly by those who cite this teaching) that Rabbi Eliezer's contemporaries found him to be of so uncompromising a nature that they excommunicated him (*Bava Mezia* 59b). Rabbi Eliezer died while still under a ban of excommunication, whereupon the Rabbis eulogized him for his great knowledge, and reaccepted many of his legal rulings. Nonetheless, why should

---

*Thus, Maimonides opened his section on "The Laws of Torah Study," with the statement that women are free from the obligation to study Torah (1:1). He later acknowledged that although "a woman who studies will receive [a divine] reward," nonetheless, a father should not teach his daughter Torah "because most women cannot concentrate their attention on study, and thus transform the words of Torah into idle matters because of their lack of understanding" (1:13).

†This comment denigrates all Jewish women (imagine how men would feel if a woman leader taught, "She who teaches her son Torah, it's as if she taught him obscenity").

the hostile comment of an excommunicated rabbi be binding on future generations?* Are there people today who truly believe that God regards the teaching of Torah to women as obscene?

In contrast to Rabbi Eliezer, Ben Azzai taught that a parent is obligated to teach his daughter Torah (Mishnah *Sotah* 3:4). Furthermore, even highly conservative elements within the Jewish community acknowledge that women must be taught the laws that apply to them (see, for example, the eighteenth-century *Shulchan Aruch ha-Rav*, "Laws of Torah Study" 1:4). For much of Jewish history, this ruling was interpreted restrictively, as if the only laws women need to know concern commandments such as lighting Shabbat candles or the prohibition of sexual, and all physical, contact between a couple during and after a woman's period. The truth is, however, that the large majority of Jewish laws pertain to men and women alike. Thus a woman who has not studied Judaism's interpersonal laws will not know the laws concerning charity, unfair speech, and judging others fairly. Similarly, women are obligated, as are men, to observe the Jewish holidays, recite blessings, fear and love God, and observe Kashrut; therefore they must learn these laws.

———

That study was more widespread among Jewish women in the past than is commonly thought is reflected in two documents of the twelfth century, written at a time when illiteracy among the Jews' neighbors, both Christian and Muslim, was the norm for both men and women. In the first instance, a monk, a student of the renowned French Catholic theologian Abelard, reported that "a Jew, however poor, if he has ten sons would put them all to letters not for gain, as the Christians do, but for the understanding of God's Law, and not only his sons but his daughters." A letter written in the same century in Egypt, by a Jewish woman who was dying, exemplifies Abelard's description: "I tell you, my sister, that I have fallen into a grievous disease and there is little possibility of recovering from it. . . . If the Lord on High should decree my death, my greatest wish is that you should take care of my little daughter and make an effort for her to study. Indeed, I know that I am imposing a heavy burden on you. For we do not have the wherewithal for her upkeep, let alone the cost of tuition. But we

---

*My attribution of hostility, even misogyny, to Rabbi Eliezer is not just based on the above teaching, but also on an incident in which a woman asked him a question about a passage in the Torah. Rabbi Eliezer not only ignored the question (the Talmud goes out of its way to emphasize that it was intelligent), but insulted her instead, declaring that "women have no wisdom except at the spindle." After the woman left, when Rabbi Eliezer's own son protested his father's behavior, Rabbi Eliezer said, "Let the teachings of Torah be burned rather than entrusted to women" (Jerusalem Talmud, *Sotah* 3:4).

*have an example from our mother and teacher, the servant of the Lord."
Haim Hillel Ben-Sasson, the historian of medieval Jewry, concludes, "Here is
an instance of a Jewish family that was certainly not well-to-do in which the
women of two generations were educated and saw to the education of their
daughters."*[3]

———

4. The late Professor Yeshayahu Leibowitz has persuasively argued that
freeing women from the obligation of study had a negative effect on their
Jewishness, whereas freeing them from certain ritual obligations, such as
wearing *tefillin* or *tzitzit*, did not. The latter need not impinge on the essence
of a person's Judaism. Thus Jewish males of priestly descent (*Kohanim*)
publicly bless the congregation on certain holidays, but the large majority of
Jewish men, who are not priests, do not feel disenfranchised by not being
permitted to do so. But study of Torah is not merely a significant commandment; it is, as noted, as important as all the other commandments combined. Therefore, restricting women from studying Torah, in effect, limits
their ability to be full Jews.

Children and Torah study

5. Teaching Torah to one's children is a fundamental parental obligation.
The Rabbis root this commandment in a biblical verse: "And you shall teach
them [the words of Torah] to your children" (Deuteronomy 11:19; see also
Deuteronomy 6:7).* According to the Talmud, a father is obliged to teach his
children, or to arrange otherwise for their Jewish education. Thus parents
should not move to a city that does not have adequate educational opportunities for children; if they do so, they bear full responsibility for their
children's Jewish education.

From Judaism's perspective, parents who do not provide for their children's Jewish education are as negligent as those who do not make the effort
to provide their children with other basic necessities. Just as a child deprived

---

*In Hebrew, the word translated here as "children" (*beneichem*) is written in the male form;
therefore, it can also be translated as "sons." This is how those who oppose Jewish education for
women understand this verse: "And you shall teach them to your sons." But the word *beneichem*
often refers to all children. My father, Shlomo Telushkin, noted that the same passage in the
Bible also promises that fulfilling these laws will cause God to extend our lives and the lives of
our children in the Land of Israel (Deuteronomy 11:21). Once again, the word used for "children"
is in the male form. But, my father would ask, does any reasonable person believe that only
males are rewarded by God for keeping His commandments? So, too, my father argued, we
should assume that the law to teach our children applies to all our children.

of essential material needs cannot function in society, a child deprived of Jewish knowledge will not know how to live and act as a Jew.

———

As early as the beginning of the Common Era, the Rabbis developed an educational system throughout ancient Judea. Every city was required to have schools (Bava Bathra 21a),* and no teacher was permitted to be assigned more than twenty-five students.

Just how seriously Jews have taken the commandment to educate their children is suggested by a nineteenth-century document written by a senior official in the Russian-controlled kingdom of Poland: "Almost every one of their [Jewish] families hires a tutor to teach its children. There are undoubtedly 25,000 tutors per 100,000 families. We [the non-Jewish population] do not have more than 868 schools in towns and villages and 27,895 pupils in all. They probably have the same number of pupils, because their entire population studies. Girls, too, can read, even the girls of the poorest families. Every family, be it in the most modest circumstances, buys books. . . . Most of those inhabiting the huts in our [non-Jewish] villages have only recently heard of an alphabet book."[4]

———

6. The Jewish community is obligated to provide a basic Jewish education to children whose parents cannot afford to do so. Some two thousand years ago, the Rabbis warned Jewish leaders not to neglect poor children, "for from them will come forth Torah" (*Nedarim* 81a).[†]

In the United States today, where tuition at Jewish day schools can consume thirty percent of the income of couples with three or more children, the definition of poor Jews must be greatly expanded. Thus one hears of many parents earning middle-class salaries for whom sending their children to a Jewish day school constitutes a financial hardship. Therefore, in line with the Talmud's injunction, it is an imperative for the Jewish community to find ways to make Jewish education more affordable.

7. So important is children's study that the Talmud rules that "we do not cancel children's classes even to build the Temple in Jerusalem" (*Shabbat* 119b).

---

*The creation of a school system was particularly intended to benefit orphans and children whose fathers were not sufficiently knowledgeable to teach them.

†Throughout history, a basic, though not an advanced, Jewish education was generally made available to all Jewish males, including the poor. As a result, within the Jewish community there were much higher rates of literacy than among their non-Jewish neighbors (among women as well, although women were discriminated against).

Unfortunately, the Talmud's priorities are not shared by many modern Jewish parents who do not give their children an adequate, or any, Jewish education because they fear that their children will lack sufficient time to play soccer or learn a musical instrument.

———

Regarding parents who offer young children a choice whether or not to study Judaism, Rabbi Norman Lamm, the former president of New York City's Yeshiva University, notes that in no other crucial area of their children's development do parents make such an offer: Do you wish to attend elementary school or would you rather stay at home? Do you want to brush your teeth, or would you prefer not to? . . . [But] a way of life that will determine whether existence has meaning, whether [the child] is rooted in history or not, whether morality is binding, whether hope and destiny are real or illusions—this any child may choose for himself.[5]

———

8. One reason the Rabbis emphasize teaching children is that it is easier to learn and retain material when we are young. *The Ethics of the Fathers* compares the study of children to ink written on a clean sheet, which remains clear and lasts a long time (4:20). Thus, for example, the ability to learn poems and other material by heart is strongest at a young age. So, too, the ability to learn another language, such as Hebrew.

———

This is, of course, consistent with most learned behaviors, including physical skills. If you learn to ski, dribble a basketball, or ride a bike as a child, your expertise will generally be superior to one who learned later, even if the latter practices for more cumulative time.

———

9. Because the amount of Jewish learning necessary to become a literate Jew is extensive, the most effective form of Jewish education is the Jewish day school, in which the curriculum is evenly split between Jewish and secular studies. Such schools, in which Jewish laws are observed as well as taught, and the school year revolves around the Jewish calendar, are particularly effective in conveying to students that Judaism is to be lived as well as studied.*

---

*In less intense educational settings (afternoon schools that meet once or twice a week), students have fewer opportunities to see Jewish laws being practiced. Jewish summer camps can also provide a setting in which campers can "live" Judaism, and play an important, and often underrated, role in inspiring Jewish commitment.

In the early years of Jewish day schools in America, many parents feared that students would receive an inadequate secular education and would not be able to interact comfortably with non-Jews. Such fears have long been put to rest by the countless instances of professional success achieved by day-school graduates (the school I attended, the Yeshiva of Flatbush in Brooklyn, New York, numbers two Nobel Laureates, Baruch Blumberg in chemistry and Eric Kandel in neurophysiology, among its alumni).

Indeed, because of the singular importance of day schools in creating a knowledgeable, vibrant Jewry, it is vital that tuition is affordable.

10. Encourage children to learn about Judaism. A man asked the nineteenth-century Rabbi Menachem Mendel of Kotzk (the Kotzker Rebbe) how he could best ensure that his children study Torah. The rebbe answered, "If you wish your children to study Torah, study it yourself, in their presence, and they will follow your example. Otherwise, they will not themselves study Torah, but will simply instruct their children to do so."

In addition to studying on their own, parents should also study Jewish texts with their children. It is a common custom to have a discussion on the weekly Torah portion at the Friday-night Shabbat table. In one family I know, the Torah portion is passed around and family members and guests read it aloud, and stop every ten verses or so to discuss it.

Many important, and applicable, life lessons can be found in the weekly Torah reading. For example, chapter 2 in Exodus relates three episodes in the life of Moses prior to God's choosing him to be a prophet and lead the Israelites out of Egypt. The first is when he sees an Egyptian overseer beating an Israelite slave, and he attacks and kills the overseer. The second is when he intervenes between two Israelites who are fighting and tries (unsuccessfully) to make peace. The third is when he stands up to protect young Midianite women from shepherds who are bullying them. That these are the only events that the Torah relates about the young Moses suggests that they are paradigmatic, and are intended to convey that a man chosen as a prophet must be one who is passionate about preventing injustice and conflict. They also suggest that a prophet of God is concerned about all injustice, not just injustice against his own people. Thus Moses acts when a non-Israelite oppresses an Israelite, when two Israelites act inappropriately, and when non-Israelites oppress other non-Israelites. These stories also teach that we should employ different strategies in different circumstances. On one occasion, when appropriate, Moses reacts with force, on another with words, and in the final instance he finds it sufficient to stand up and identify with the oppressed.

The Torah, through both its stories and its laws, can become a permanent in-fluence on how a person (adult and child alike) views the world, and on how he or she acts. Dr. Isaac Herschkopf offers one suggestion on how to achieve this: "Whenever I sit in synagogue and listen to the Torah reading, I imagine that, at its conclusion, I will be called upon to give a sermon on it, and I prepare accordingly, trying to find meaning in its message. I encourage my children in the same exercise in order to make the experience more thought-provoking."

Adult study

11. Just as we are commanded to teach our children, so are we com-manded to teach ourselves. Therefore, "a person whose father did not pro-vide him with a Jewish education is obligated to arrange for his own instruction" (Maimonides, "Laws of Torah Study" 1:3). Today, when many Jews have been raised without much Jewish education, adults who had no Bar Mitzvah or Bat Mitzvah ceremony as children sometimes choose to celebrate a Bar Mitzvah in their thirties or forties, or even older.* Such celebrations are generally preceded by months and sometimes years of study.

Yet another option now available to those who wish to further their Jewish education is the Internet, which contains hundreds of sites where one can study the weekly Torah portion, the Talmud, and Jewish ethics and philosophy.

Although Jewish parents have long had the reputation of putting great emphasis on their children's education, Maimonides rules that "if a father wishes to study Torah and he has a child who must also learn, the parent takes precedence." If the child is more insightful, however, the child takes precedence. Even so,

---

*Many Jews are unaware that, according to Jewish law, a girl automatically becomes Bat Mitz-vah upon turning twelve and a boy automatically becomes Bar Mitzvah upon turning thirteen, whether or not any ceremony is conducted (such as being called to the Torah for an *aliyah*). The terms Bat Mitzvah and Bar Mitzvah, "a child of the commandments," simply mean that at the ages indicated, a Jew becomes obligated to keep Judaism's commandments. Nonetheless, in popu-lar parlance, Bar Mitzvah and Bat Mitzvah refer to the public celebration of these events (as in the question, "Did you have a Bar Mitzvah?").

"the parent must not ignore his own study, for just as it is a mitzvah to educate the child, so too is the parent commanded to teach himself" ("Laws of Torah Study" 1:4).

————

12. The opening Mishnah of *The Ethics of the Fathers* commands Jewish leaders to "raise up many disciples." Although the School of Shammai (around the beginning of the Common Era) believed that the Torah should be taught only to the elite, as secular study was confined to the upper classes in Greece and Rome, Jewish tradition sides with the School of Hillel, who taught that "One ought to teach every man, for there were many sinners in Israel who were drawn to the study of Torah, and from them descended righteous, pious, and worthy folk" (*The Fathers According to Rabbi Nathan* 2:9). Therefore, just as there has been an enormous expansion of Jewish day schools in recent decades in the United States, so too must there be a similar expansion in opportunities for adult Jewish study.

What matters more: study or deeds?

13. "Rabbi Tarfon and the rabbinic elders were dining in the loft of [a man named] Nitzah in the city of Lod. The question was asked of them: 'Is study greater or is the performance of deeds greater?' Rabbi Tarfon replied: 'Deeds are greater.' Rabbi Akiva replied: 'Study is greater.' All of them [the sages present] said, 'Study is greater for it leads to deeds" (*Kiddushin* 40b).*

Without study, people act on the basis of their emotions, and usually without consistency. For example, a student of Jewish law learns that one should *always* give money or food to a beggar who says that she is hungry (Maimonides, "Laws of Gifts to the Poor" 7:6). Therefore, we should not respond to such a person's request, as many of us do, only when our hearts are moved.

————

Though the question discussed in the Talmud sounds theoretical, it wasn't. It was raised during a time of Roman persecution of Judaism, and the Rabbis wanted

————

*As Maimonides expresses it, "Study takes precedence over deeds for study brings about the performance of deeds. However, the performance of deeds does not bring about study" ("Laws of Torah Study" 1:3).

to establish the commandments for which Jews should put their lives at risk. The feeling seemed to be that Judaism's survival would be even more imperiled if Jews stopped studying Torah than if they temporarily stopped practicing Jewish ritual and other laws. For once the persecution ended, as it always has, knowledgeable Jews could return to observance. But if Jews had lost all knowledge of Judaism, they would not be able to resume practicing it.

———

Study, however, should not be the whole of one's life

14. The rabbinic ideal is to study Torah and practice a profession. As Rabbi Gamliel taught: "The study of Torah combined with a worldly occupation is an excellent thing, for the energy needed by both keeps sinful thoughts out of one's mind. Any study of Torah not accompanied by a trade must fail in the end and become the cause of sin" (*The Ethics of the Fathers* 2:2).

The goal of Rabbi Gamliel's teaching is that a Jew lead a balanced life, consisting both of earning a livelihood and studying God's law. The eighteenth-century rabbinic scholar Yaakov Emden taught that the reason the first question asked by the Heavenly Court is "Were your business dealings honest?' and the second is "Did you set aside time for Torah study?" is to underscore that Torah study should be preceded by gainful activity.[6] As the Rabbis taught, "If there is no bread [to eat], there will be no Torah" (*The Ethics of the Fathers* 3:17).

———

The Talmud records a dispute between Rabbi Ishmael, who taught that one should combine the study of Torah with a worldly occupation, and Rabbi Shimon bar Yochai, who argued that if people work at a job, "What will become of Torah study?" He therefore advocated that Jews ignore making a living and simply study Torah. The Talmud concludes, "Many followed Rabbi Ishmael and succeeded. Many followed Rabbi Shimon bar Yochai and did not succeed." (Berachot 35b).

———

A final thought

15. Rabbi Joseph Soloveitchik explained the power of Torah study to connect Jews to the entirety of the Jewish experience, and to link students to many of Judaism's greatest thinkers and personalities: "Whenever I start my lesson, the door opens and another old man comes in and sits down. He is older than I am. He is my grandfather and his name is Reb Chayyim Brisker, without whom I cannot teach Torah. Then the door opens quietly again and another old man comes in. He is older than Reb Chayyim. He lived in the seventeenth century. His name is Shabbetai ben Meir ha-Kohen, the famous 'Shach' who might be present when you study Talmud. And then more visitors show up. Some of the visitors lived in the eleventh century and some lived in the twelfth century, some in the thirteenth century—some even lived in antiquity. Rashi, Rabbenu Tam, Rava, Rashba. More and more come in. Of course, what do I do? I introduce them to my pupils and the dialogue commences. The Rambam (Maimonides) says something. Rava disagrees. A boy jumps up, he has an idea. The Rashba smiles gently. I try to analyze what the young man meant. Another boy intervenes and we call upon Rabbenu Tam to express his opinion, and suddenly a symposium of generations comes into existence."[7]

56

THE BENEFITS OF
TORAH STUDY

"It is related that a king once gave his servants buckets and instructed them to draw water from his well. When they began, they noticed that the buckets had many holes and the water leaked out by the time the buckets were drawn to the top of the well. They stopped. When the king later asked them if they had done as he had told them, they replied that they had stopped because of the holes. 'You should have continued,' the king said. 'I didn't ask you to draw water because I wanted the water, but because I wanted the buckets cleaned.' So it is with Torah. The substance of what one has studied may later be forgotten, but the process of studying itself is purifying" (Nathaniel Bushwick).[1]

Acquiring wisdom

1. It is generally thought advantageous to have a mentor, an older person whose judgment one values, and who can offer wise advice and life lessons; most people regard themselves as fortunate if they have one or two such mentors. But the student of Torah is provided with dozens of such mentors, and three thousand years of insight and guidance into how to lead a good life.

The following examples are drawn from four rabbis cited in just the first two chapters of *The Ethics of the Fathers:*

- *On avoiding sin,* Nittai the Arbelite taught, "Keep far away from an evil neighbor, and do not become friendly with the wicked" (1:7); and Rabbi Judah taught, "Consider three things and you will not stray into sin: Know what is above you—a seeing eye, a listening ear, and all your deeds are written in a book" (2:1).
- *On achieving a balance between self-centeredness and altruism,* Hillel taught, "If I am not for myself, who will be for me? And if I am only for myself, what am I?" (1:14).
- *On maintaining skepticism when dealing with government authorities,* Rabbi Gamliel, the son of Rabbi Judah, taught, "Be cautious with the [ruling political] authorities, for they do not befriend a man except for their own advantage; they appear as friends when it is to their benefit, but do not stand by a man in his time of distress" (2:3).

2. The study of Jewish texts, Talmud in particular, broadens our ability to think creatively, flexibly, and subtly. Rabbi Norman Lamm recalls an incident that occurred when he was a young man and a new student in Rabbi Joseph Soloveitchik's *shiur,* the most advanced class in Talmud at Yeshiva University. Rabbi Lamm was intimidated when "the Rav" asked him to summarize *Tosafot's* (a medieval commentary) approach to the passage they had been studying. Hoping to please his teacher, Rabbi Lamm repeated the explanation the Rav had offered the day before. Rabbi Soloveitchik "erupted like a volcano, and said to me, 'I know what I am saying. I do not need you to tell me! What do *you* think?'"

As Rabbi Lamm explains, "His greatness as a teacher was that he wanted a student to learn to think along the lines of his method, but not simply repeat his conclusions parrot-like. He valued a student who challenged him over a student who passively recorded the information. As a matter of fact, he got so angry with me that he added, 'They can sell you the Brooklyn Bridge. The problem is that you check your evil inclination (*yetzer hara*) outside the classroom door and come in with your good inclination. Next time, bring your evil inclination with you, and leave your good inclination outside.'"

Rabbi Lamm understood Rabbi Soloveitchik to mean that he wanted his students to use their aggressiveness and passion, and perhaps their rebelliousness and disobedience as well, to go deeper into the arguments raised in the Talmud, and not simply repeat what they had heard.[2]

Similarly, Rabbi Lamm recalls his grandfather, Rabbi Yehoshua Baumel, a Talmud scholar, telling him something that most Jews would not expect to hear from an Orthodox rabbi: "When it comes to learning, you have to be an *apikores* (heretic). One needs to challenge everyone, one needs to be a skeptic." Lamm insists that his grandfather's insistence on maintaining "a skeptical attitude" is the only way to true intellectual achievement.[3]

3. Learning Torah can help keep students mentally alert and vigorous throughout their lives. Many people find that, as they age, their lives are increasingly restricted to medical appointments and taking care of their health; not surprisingly, they complain that their minds are no longer challenged and active. But, as the Talmud remarks concerning scholars, "Even as they grow older their wisdom increases, while ignoramuses who grow older grow more foolish" (*Shabbat* 152a). In other words, the study of Jewish sources keeps us rooted in an intellectual tradition and therefore helps our minds, and also our souls, to thrive.

The moral benefits

4. Torah study provides, and inspires, us with models of righteous behavior. This applies, of course, to all students of the Bible, non-Jews and Jews alike. Thus, in 1941, a Dutch minister known as Fritz "de Zwerver," an anti-Nazi organizer, arrived in the city of Eibergen, Holland, and walked to the podium of the Protestant church. At that time the Germans had taken over Holland, and were deporting Jews to concentration camps. The reverend opened his Bible to Exodus 1:15–22 and read aloud the story of the Egyptian midwives who disobeyed Pharaoh's order to murder the newborn male Israelite babies, and saved them instead. Afterward, he said to the congregation, "Who is the Pharaoh today? The Nazis! Who are the babies who have to be hidden? The Jews! Who are the midwives today? We are! It is our job to outsmart the Pharaohs, to have the courage of the midwives, and to protect the

Jews and all those who need to be hidden." He then left the church, got on his bicycle, and went to the next village. During the war, seven families from this little church hid Jews and other anti-Nazi resisters.[4]

5. It is necessary to study in order to know how to act ethically: "An ignoramus cannot be a saintly person" (*The Ethics of the Fathers* 2:5). We need not only to have good intentions but to know the right thing to do. The Torah describes Lot, Abraham's nephew, as a generous host who invites two strangers (unbeknownst to him, they are angels) to his home as guests. When the citizens of Sodom surround the house, and insist that he turn the guests over to them to be raped, Lot does all within his power to dissuade them. But when his arguments are rejected, he offers his daughters to be raped instead (Genesis 19:8). Obviously, the spiritually unaware Lot believed that this was what hospitality to one's guests demanded of him.

6. Torah study influences its students to become more empathetic. For example, if we study the laws regarding employers and employees, we learn that the Torah mandates paying a worker as soon as his job is complete (Deuteronomy 24:15; see also Leviticus 19:13); as the text puts it: "for he is needy and urgently depends on it." In a different context, the *Tanchuma* (in its commentary on Exodus 22:25–26) notes: "It is like the case of a man who had bought a sheaf of corn which he placed upon his shoulder, and then walked in front of the donkey who was longing to eat it. But what did the owner do? When he reached home, he tied the sheaf high above the donkey so that the animal could not reach it. People said to him, 'You cruel man; the animal has been running the whole day for the sake of the sheaf, and now you refuse to give it to him.' So it is with the hired worker; the whole day he has been toiling and sweating, hoping for his wages and you send him away empty-handed" (*Mishpatim* number 10).

Throughout history, and in many societies, wealthy people not only underpaid laborers, but often paid them late; they knew that even if their employees complained, the law was unlikely to protect them. But how could anyone study these two texts and not feel concern for the needs of his or her workers? At the very least, these texts teach us that not treating our employees fairly and compassionately is an offense against humanity and God.

7. Torah study helps us to resist our evil inclinations. The Talmud imagines God as saying to the Jews: "I have created the evil impulse and I have created the Torah as an antidote to it; if you occupy yourselves with Torah, you will not be delivered into its power" (*Kiddushin* 30b).

In another passage, the Rabbis explain, "No man is truly free unless he occupies himself with the study of Torah" (*The Ethics of the Fathers* 6:2). This statement is counterintuitive in that many people believe that Judaism's extensive laws limit a person's freedom. Such a view is naïve. A person who works on his character is better able to resist his "evil inclination," just as someone who gives up time and personal freedom to practice the piano has the manual dexterity to play well. To be better at anything, whether it is a sport, an art, or developing our character, it is necessary to have a system. Torah study and Jewish laws are Judaism's system for achieving goodness.

8. Torah study cuts across social, professional, and age barriers, and enables us to connect with people of different backgrounds and ages. Thus loneliness, for example, is a well-known scourge of old age; as a person reaches her eighties and nineties, she loses friends and family members of the same generation. But Torah study establishes links that cross generational lines. My grandfather, Rabbi Nissen Telushkin, died at ninety, with his mind still clear and engaged. The night before his death, he gave a class in Talmud to about fifteen people. All the attendees were younger than my grandfather, and some were sixty years younger. But because of his knowledge of Torah, instead of regarding him as an "old fogey," they sought his wisdom and companionship.

Two goals to keep in mind when studying

9. Integrate some activity from what you have learned into your daily behavior. "When you are about to conclude your study session, search through what you have learned [and, in the case of a lecture, what you have heard] to determine whether there is anything you can apply in practice" (Nachmanides).

For example, if you are studying the Mishnah in *Bava Mezia* (4:10) that prohibits oppressing people with words (*ona'at devarim*; see page 280), you will learn that Jewish law derives from this principle the prohibition against asking a storekeeper the price of an item if you have no intention of buying it. From this ruling, many lessons can be learned, most obviously that it is wrong to raise anybody's (not just a salesperson's) hopes for no reason. A friend of mine who lectures for a living was questioned by a telephone caller regarding his speaking fees. He spent much time on the call, hoping, of course, that the inquiry would result in a lecture engagement. He later learned that the questioner merely wished to find out what he charged because she was planning to invite another lecturer, and wanted to have a sense of what the fee might be. Behavior like this constitutes a violation of the "storekeeper law."

My friend Dennis Prager has argued that many men violate this law when they tell a woman whom they don't love that that they love her, so as to persuade her to become physically intimate with them. Such statements are false, and are intended to raise the woman's hopes that if she sleeps with the man, it will deepen his feelings for her. As Prager puts it, "There are powerful ramifications to the principle that if you know you are not going to buy, don't imply that you might, i.e., don't raise expectations you know you won't meet. One such ramification was made clear to me when a young woman, who had heard me speak about this law in a speech, told me how she wished the men whom she dated would live by the storekeeper law—so often, men imply interest that is, in fact, not there. . . . [In short] the storekeeper law keeps you honest."[5]

The above examples illustrate Nachmanides' point: When you learn a new law, spend time working out how you can apply it in your life.

Furthermore, even the study of Jewish texts that offer no explicit laws or advice can provide us with guidance. The medieval Bible commentator Rabbi Abraham Ibn Ezra, reworking a rabbinic proverb, teaches, "The deeds of the Patriarchs are a guide to how the children should behave" (see his commentary on Genesis 9:18). This suggests that we can learn from the narrative, as well as from the legal portions, of the Torah how to live and how not to. We learn from Abraham the importance of being hospitable (Genesis 18:2–8), and of not being afraid to argue with anyone, even God, when we think an injustice is being committed (Genesis 18:23–32); from Judah, the need to acknowledge when one is wrong (Genesis 38:26); and from the prophet Nathan the obligation to criticize unjust behavior (II Samuel 12).

10. The Talmud teaches that "the goal of wisdom is repentance and good deeds" (*Berachot* 17a). Therefore, we should focus a significant part of our studies on those areas of Jewish learning that promote self-examination and self-improvement, and that inspire us to engage in good deeds, such as the teachings found in *The Ethics of the Fathers*.

57

LEARNING AND TEACHING TORAH

LEARNING TORAH

Getting started

1. If you are not engaged in regular Jewish study, start today (as you are doing by reading this chapter). Hillel taught, "Don't say, 'when I have time, I will learn,' lest you never have the time" (*The Ethics of the Fathers* 2:4).

Even if you have only a limited amount of time to study, begin now and don't delay. A man said to Rabbi Israel Salanter, "I have but fifteen minutes a day available for study. Should I devote it to the study of Torah and Talmud, or to the study of Mussar [the ethical writings that strive to inspire us to work on our character]?"

"Study Mussar," Rabbi Salanter answered.

"Why?"

"Because then you'll see that something is wrong with your life if you have only fifteen minutes a day for study."

A witty and penetrating response, but, in truth, even fifteen minutes a day, if done consistently, can bring about a great deal of personal growth.

————

A friend of mine resolved to read two chapters a day of the Bible, and read the Bible straight through in less than a year. On most days it took him between ten and fifteen minutes. Obviously, if we read the material so quickly, we cannot study it in depth. But, in addition to achieving an overview of the entire Bible, he often found insights into daily issues with which he was grappling.

————

2. To be effective and transformative, study must be ongoing. When it is, there are few limits on what can be achieved. Rabbi Akiva was an illiterate shepherd well into his adult years. A rabbinic story describes the transformation that led to his becoming the greatest rabbi of his age: "He was forty years old and had not yet learned a thing. Once, he stood at the mouth of a well and asked, 'Who hollowed this stone?' He was told, 'Is it not the water which constantly falls on it day after day?' Rabbi Akiva reasoned to himself: 'If soft water can wear away hard stone, how much more can the words of Torah, which are as hard as iron, carve a way into my heart, which is of flesh and blood?' Immediately he turned to the study of Torah" (*The Fathers According to Rabbi Nathan 6:2*).

Rabbi Salanter noted, "The waters carved the stone only because they fell drop after drop, year after year, without a pause. Had the accumulated water all poured down at once in a powerful stream, it would have slipped off the rock without leaving a trace."

3. The Rabbis of the Talmud, aware that the sheer quantity of Jewish learning—the Torah and all the books of the Bible, Mishnah and Talmud, Midrash, the various codes of Jewish law, Bible commentaries, philosophy, and more—could overwhelm a student, particularly at the outset, offered the following parable: Two men were confronted by a massive mound of earth that needed to be cleared. One said, "Who can ever clear away such a mound?" and gave up. The other man, a "sensible" man as the Midrash puts it, said, "I will clear away two basketfuls today and two basketfuls tomorrow until I have cleared it away entirely." In a similar manner, the Rabbis concluded, the intelligent student says, "I will study two laws today, and two tomorrow, until I have learned the entire Torah, all of it." (*Leviticus Rabbah* 19:2).

———

When my father, Shlomo Telushkin, who was an accountant, became very busy with his work, my grandfather became concerned that my father would neglect his Jewish learning. So he urged my father to study two laws from the Mishnah every morning, right after he recited his morning prayers. My father adhered to this schedule for the rest of his life, and succeeded in going through the entire Mishnah several times.

*The Talmud records that when Rabbi Acha bar Jacob was diverted from his daily study and had to perform another activity, he would make up the time lost by increased study at night (*Eruvin 65a*).*

*"Whoever studies Jewish laws every day may rest assured that he is destined for the World-to-Come" (*Niddah 73a*). The Rabbis reasoned that regular study serves as an inspiration to keep improving ourselves ethically and spiritually, and helps restrain us from behaving inappropriately. Furthermore, if you learn a law, you will become more conscious, certainly on the day you have learned it, to try to fulfill it.*

———

Where is a good place to start?

4. Start with the Book of Genesis. Although it is the Torah's longest book, and contains very few commandments (only three of the Torah's 613 laws are in Genesis), its stories draw in students of all ages, enabling them to see the depth in Jewish texts. Also, Genesis communicates the most basic Jewish teaching of all, that God is the creator of the world and humankind.

Another early priority should be the first half of Exodus, which tells how the Jews were forged into a people. It conveys the notion that God cares about people (as illustrated by the story of the liberation of the Israelite slaves from Egyptian slavery), and wants them to be free. Study closely, as well, Exodus 20, which contains the Ten Commandments, the most influential legal document in human history, and Leviticus 19, which contains some forty-eight, about eight percent, of the Torah's laws, including the commandment to "love your neighbor as yourself" (Leviticus 19:18).

Get into the habit of reading the weekly Torah portion. All Jewish denominations have fine commentaries on the Torah. In addition, the classic Bible commentators, including Rashi and Ramban (Nachmanides) are available in English translations.

5. "A person who cannot study very many Torah subjects should concentrate his attention on study which leads to deeds" (*Shulchan Arukh ha-Rav*, "Laws of Torah Study" 2:9). In ritual areas, for example, this would mean studying the laws of Shabbat and Kashrut and, in ethical areas, the laws dealing with fair speech (*lashon hara*), charity, business honesty, and good manners, all of which involve commandments that can be incorporated into our daily life.

How to learn

6. Be diligent, and don't waste time in idle conversation. Rabbi Aryeh Leib, the Chaffetz Chayyim's son, was counseled by his father never to interrupt his study for more than a few seconds. Aryeh Leib argued that if a friend or acquaintance came over, it would be rude to ask him to leave quickly. The Chaffetz Chayyim responded that on market days, when a merchant is interrupted by a relative he hasn't seen in a while, "Do you think he will engage him in lengthy conversation as the customers stand waiting? Certainly not. He will greet his relative and then beg forgiveness for being unable to converse at that time, and he will ask the relative to return after dark when the market is closed for the day. Then he will greet him more warmly and spend more time with him."[1]

7. Review what you have learned again and again. By doing so, the teachings will remain clear in your mind, and you will be prepared for any questions and/or challenges you may encounter: "The Torah should be sharp on your tongue, so that if someone asks you about anything [you have studied], you will have an immediate response" (*Kiddushin* 30a). Conversely, "words of Torah are forgotten only through inattention" (i.e., by not reviewing what we have learned; *Ta'anit* 7b, and Rashi's commentary there).

———

The Rabbis feared, with reason, that the moment they stopped reviewing, their knowledge would decline: "If you abandon study of Torah for one day, it will abandon you for two" (Berachot 9:5). Also, "A man can learn Torah for ten years and forget it in two" (The Fathers According to Rabbi Nathan 24:6).*

In addition, constant reviewing leads us to new insights and also enables us to draw connections between texts. That is why the Rabbis state that you cannot compare the achievement of one who has studied a text a hundred times with one who has studied it 101 times (Chagigah 9b).

When my grandfather, Rabbi Nissen Telushkin, had an operation at the age of eighty-five, he was given a local anesthetic. He told me that during the operation he passed the time reciting aloud chapters of the Mishnah that he knew by heart.

———

8. Be enthusiastic and aggressive in acquiring knowledge. *The Ethics of the Fathers* teaches that "one who is bashful will never learn" (2:5). If you are too timid to ask questions, you will never gain a deep understanding of the subject.

9. Also, be willing to admit that you have not understood something a teacher has said, and ask that the explanation be repeated. As the *Shulchan Arukh* teaches, "A student should not be ashamed if a fellow student has understood something after the first or second time and he has not grasped it even after several attempts. If he is embarrassed because of this, it will turn

---

*A physician with whom I discussed this pointed out that this is analogous to physical training. An athlete will notice a perceptible decline in his conditioning if he skips even two or three consecutive days of exercise. He will find himself winded just walking to the train at his customary pace. The same thing can happen when your intellectual powers are not used.

out that he will come and go from the house of study without learning any-thing at all" (*Yoreh Deah* 246:11).

Teaching Torah

10. "He who teaches Torah to his neighbor's child will be privileged to sit in the Heavenly Academy" (*Bava Mezia* 85a).[2] In today's world, in which many adult Jews are, in effect, Jewishly illiterate, this teaching also applies to those who impart basic Jewish knowledge to adult Jews. Furthermore, teach-ers do not affect the student alone, but also her family and perhaps her de-scendants. In this way, as has been said, a teacher affects eternity; he has no way of knowing where his influence extends.

———

By implication, this promised reward of a seat in the Heavenly Academy applies to those who give money to Jewish schools and help further Jewish education. Such gifts enable our "neighbor's child" to study.

———

Seven ways to be a good teacher

11. *Make the material interesting and enticing.* As the Talmud explains, "A person only learns Torah from a place that his heart wants" (*Avodah Zarah* 19a). Since the goal of a teacher should be to create a student who will study throughout his life, it is not enough to teach the student the material: the student must also come to love the process of learning.

———

*Teachers should motivate children by any appropriate means. The Talmud tells of a teacher whose merit was so great that whenever he prayed for rain, it fell immediately. When the great scholar Rav asked the teacher, "What is your ex-ceptional merit [that your prayers so influence God]?" the man answered that he taught the children of the poor without fee, then added, "I have a fish pond, and when I find a pupil negligent in his studies, I bribe him with fish so that he comes regularly to learn" (*Ta'anit 24a*).*

In modern terms, this story suggests that in dealing with recalcitrant stu-dents, the teacher should find activities they enjoy and, in effect, "bribe" them to learn Torah as well. When I was in high school, one of my Talmud teachers, Rabbi Ephraim Shach, used to attend ice hockey games with us. Rabbi Shach enjoyed the games, but he also realized that joining his students in an activity they enjoyed brought him closer to us, and motivated us to study Talmud with him with greater enthusiasm.

———

12. *Use humor to create a relaxed atmosphere.* "Before beginning his discourses to the Sages, Rabbah used to say something humorous in order to amuse them. After that, he sat down and with awe began to discourse on the law" (*Pesachim* 117a).

If the Sages, mature men who devoted their lives to study, needed to be enticed by humor, how much more so the typical modern student who comes to learn Torah. An unwaveringly solemn demeanor in the teacher creates an overly serious atmosphere, and such solemnity can easily lead to yawns. Humor and a relaxed manner of teaching are particularly necessary today, when attendees at lectures and study groups are likely to be people who watch television, where they are used to being continuously entertained. Torah is serious, but serious subjects are studied with much greater enthusiasm when they are presented in an entertaining and dynamic style.

13. *Identify, and appeal to, each student's greatest area of interest.* "Subject matter in which one person finds the answers to all his deepest questions can leave another cold" (Rabbi Adin Steinsaltz).[3]

The Talmud records that two young rabbinical scholars, Levi and Shimon (the son of Rabbi Judah), were studying with Rabbi Judah. After they concluded the study of one book of the Bible, they debated which book to study next. Levi wanted to study Proverbs, and Shimon Psalms, and Rabbi Judah decided to teach them Psalms. When he reached the book's second verse, "His delight is in the Torah of the Lord and he studies that teaching day and night," he explained that "A man learns well only that part of the Torah which his heart desires." At that point Levi arose and said, "Master, you have just now given me permission to get up and leave" (*Avodah Zarah* 19a).

14. *Feel gratitude to your students.* In what is one of the Talmud's most widely cited pedagogical insights, Rabbi Chanina taught, "I have learned much from my teachers, and from my colleagues more than from my teachers, and from my students more than from them all" (*Ta'anit* 7a). Rabbi Chanina understood what is not obvious: People do not reach a full understanding of a subject until they have to teach it to others (it is only when we have to lecture on a subject that we are forced to think fully through the implications of the material). Teachers, therefore, should feel grateful to students, who not only provide teachers with an opportunity to earn a living, but cause them to grow in wisdom.

15. *Love your students.* Until the last century, many pedagogues believed that the attitude that should exist between teachers and students was fear (teachers in the past frequently beat students). In truth, love, not fear, is the appropriate emotion. Thus, when the prophet Elijah ascended to heaven in a whirlwind, his disciple Elisha cried out, 'My father, my father!' (II Kings 2:12). Israeli official Baruch Duvdevani noted that Elisha did not call out, "My rabbi, my rabbi!" "My leader, my mentor!" or "My sovereign, my king!" All he could say was, "My father, my father!"[4] Indeed, the Rabbis teach that "students are called 'one's children'" (*Sifre, Va-Etchanan* 6:7).

16. *Treat all your students with respect.* Rabbi Elazar ben Shammua taught, "Let the honor of your students be as dear to you as your own" (*The Ethics of the Fathers* 4:12).* Jewish law rules that the prohibition against humiliating others applies to children no less than adults (Maimonides, "Laws of Character Development" 6:8). Therefore a teacher should not say anything derogatory to a student in the presence of others, or call upon a student who the teacher has reason to suspect does not know the material, just to embarrass her.

17. *Have great patience.* This is so basic and necessary a quality in a teacher that the Rabbis hold up as a model Rabbi Pereida, who had a student who needed to be taught a lesson four hundred times before he could master it, and on some occasions even more (*Eruvin* 54b; it is unclear whether the Talmud meant the number literally, or to emphasize that the need for patience can be almost unending). The Talmud records that for such behavior

---

*Unfortunately, Jewish educators did not always follow these guidelines, and Jewish law did not always insist that they do so. The Talmud itself, in a shocking passage (Mishnah *Makkot* 2:2) rules that a teacher who kills a student while disciplining him is not subject to punishment. Maimonides, who recorded the prohibition against humiliating a child, also codified this mishnaic ruling as still binding, at least as of the twelfth century, when he was writing ("Laws of Murder" 5:5). One can only wonder how many children with learning disabilities (at a time when disabilities such as dyslexia were unknown) were subject to beating and humiliation at the hands of teachers who accused them of being lazy and called them stupid. In modern times, there is little doubt that the harsh discipline in many Jewish schools caused tens of thousands of Jews to abandon Jewish learning and Jewish life. Fortunately, such severity is generally unknown today, but awareness of such mistreatment should serve as a corrective to those who tend to romanticize all aspects of Jewish life in the past.

Rabbi Pereida was rewarded with extra years in this world, and a portion in the World-to-Come.

———

Conversely, the Rabbis believed that bad-tempered people should not be teachers (see page 252). In this regard, it should be emphasized that anger or excessive strictness is not the same as being demanding. Anger and strictness create an atmosphere of fear. A teacher, however, can and should be demanding, and insist that students accomplish what they're capable of.

Rabbi Moshe Feinstein was asked by a teacher if he should waste class time on the sort of foolish questions that students sometimes asked. Reb Moshe answered, "The person asking the question never thinks of it as foolish."*

———

———

*Dr. Isaac Herschkopf, who teaches at the New York University School of Medicine, told me, "The very first day of class, I tell all my medical students that I detest stupid questions. They immediately look intimidated. Then I define a stupid question as the one they *don't* ask. They invariably look relieved, and smile. Questions are the life-blood of teaching."

APPENDIX

The Nine Most Important Commandments
According to the Rabbis

At various places in rabbinic writings, the Rabbis identified nine commandments as being of equal significance with all the other commandments combined. In some instances (e.g., number 2 below), the Rabbis were clearly speaking hyperbolically, and their words should not be taken literally:

1. Charity. Rabbi Assi taught that "The commandment of giving charity is equal to all the other commandments combined" (*Bava Bathra* 9a). This teaching is perhaps what motivated Maimonides' previously cited ruling that "We are to be more particular about the commandment of charity than about any other positive commandment" ("Laws of Gifts to the Poor" 10:1).

2. *Lashon hara* (unfair speech about another person). "For these acts they punish a person in this world, while the principal (i.e., eternal punishment) remains for the World-to-Come: for idolatrous worship, incest, and murder, and for *lashon hara*, which is worse than all of them together" (*Tosefta, Peah* 1:2). Gossip and unfair speech are great wrongs (see chapters 37–43), but can one seriously consider them worse than idolatry, incest, and murder? This would seem to be an exaggeration designed to emphasize the seriousness of an act that most people regard as minor.

3. *Tzitzit* (the ritual fringes commanded in the Book of Numbers). "The Lord said to Moses: Speak to the Israelite people and instruct them to make for themselves fringes on the corners of their garments throughout the ages. . . . look at it and recall all the commandments of the Lord and observe them, so that you do not follow your heart and eyes in your lustful urge. Thus you shall be reminded to observe all My commandments and to be holy to your God"; 15:37–40). Because this commandment reminds us to practice all the others, the Talmud taught that "the observance of this mitzvah *(tzitzit)* is equivalent to the observance of all the commandments combined" (*Menachot* 43b). However, we should note that the Rabbis mandated the observance of *tzitzit* as required only for Jewish men; it seems odd, therefore, that a commandment that "is equivalent to the observance of all the commandments combined" applies to only half of the Jewish people.

4. *Brit Milah*. "Great is circumcision, for it is equal to all of the commandments in the Torah" (*Nedarim* 32a; see also *The Midrash on Psalms* 6:1). Circumcision symbolizes the willingness to submit even one's sexual organ to the rule of God.

As is the case with *tzitzit,* this commandment applies to only half of the Jewish people.

5. *Shabbat*. "Rabbi Levi taught, 'If the Jews observe the Sabbath properly, even just once, the Son of David [i.e., the Messiah] will come. Why? Because the observance of the Sabbath is equal to all the other commandments combined" (*Exodus Rabbah* 25:12). Later, the same passage describes God as saying to the Jewish people: "If you . . . observe the Sabbath, I will regard it as if you kept all the commandments in the Torah, and if you desecrate the Sabbath, I will regard it as if you violated all the commandments." The Talmud also sees the violation of Shabbat as a singular evil: "Jerusalem was destroyed only because the Sabbath was desecrated there" (*Shabbat* 119b).*

6. **Settling the Land of Israel**. "Living in the land of Israel is equivalent to performing all the commands of the Torah" (*Sifre Devarim, parashat Re'eh* 28).

Chief Rabbi Abraham Isaac Kook (1865–1935) was influenced by this and similar teachings to view with great love and admiration nonreligious Jews who came to settle in the Land of Israel. After all, even secular settlers in Israel obeyed a commandment that some of the ancient Rabbis viewed as equal in importance to all the other commandments.

7. **Not worshipping idols**. So basic is the rejection of idolatry to Jewish identity that the Talmud teaches that "whoever repudiates idolatry is called a Jew" (*Megillah* 13a);† in another passage, the Talmud teaches that "Anyone who renounces idolatry is like one that acknowledges [the truth of] the en-

---

*The Talmud was speaking about the destruction of Jerusalem and the First Temple in 586 B.C.E.
†In the context of the quote, it seems to mean, "Whoever repudiates idolatry is called a member of the tribe of Judah," but the broader meaning of Judah (i.e., a Jew) is widely accepted, since the

tire Torah" (*Kiddushin* 40a). Maimonides instructs those who are dealing with potential converts to "inform them of the essence of the faith, which is the oneness of God and the prohibition of idolatry" ("Laws of Forbidden Relations" 14:2).

8. *Talmud Torah* (study of Torah). "The following are the activities for which a person is rewarded in this world, and again in the World-to-Come: honoring one's father and mother, deeds of loving-kindness, and making peace between a man and his neighbor. The study of Torah, however, is as important as all of them together" (Mishna *Peah* 1:1; see also *Kiddushin* 40a). On the reason for the importance of Torah study in Jewish life, see page 496.

9. Making interest-free loans. "He who lends money without interest [i.e., to those in serious need] is regarded as if he fulfilled all the commandments" (*Exodus Rabbah* 31:13).*

In a post-rabbinic source, the *Shulchan Arukh* rules that there is no *mitzvah* greater than *pidyon shvuyim,* "redeeming captives" (*Yoreh Deah* 252:1, based on Maimonides, "Laws of Gifts to the Poor" 8:10).

The laws concerning the redeeming of captives will be explained in volume 2 of this work.

---

overwhelming majority of the Jews at the time of the Talmud were assumed to derive from the tribe of Judah. The other tribes had been dispersed by the Assyrians in 722 B.C.E., and had disappeared.

*See also *Makkot* 24a, which speaks approvingly of not charging non-Jews interest (based on Psalms 15:5), even though biblical law permits one to do so.

NOTES

CHAPTER 1: JUDAISM'S ETHICAL ESSENCE

1. Spero, *Morality, Halakha and the Jewish Tradition,* 29.
2. See the rabbinic discussion of this passage in *Makkot* 24a.
3. A comprehensive chart documenting the offenses with which the prophets charged their fellow Israelites can be found in Bergren, *The Prophets and the Law,* 182–83.
4. See the discussion of commandment 611 ("The precept to emulate the good and right ways of the Eternal Lord") in the *Sefer Ha-Hinnuch.*
5. Dr. Samuel Belkin explains the reason for this omission: "[I]t is only God, who rules over jealousy, who is called a 'jealous God.' Man, who has no power to rule over jealousy, must rather imitate God in His attribute of kindness, and not in his attribute of jealousy" (*In His Image,* 29–30).
6. See Rakeffet-Rothkoff, *The Rav,* vol. 1, 94.
7. Cited in Soloveitchik, *Halakhic Man,* 91.
8. For an example of how Reb Chaim practiced these teachings in his daily life, see page 222.
9. Cited in Finkelman, *Reb Moshe,* 150.
10. Cited in Baker, *Days of Sorrow and Pain,* 205–6.

CHAPTER 2: FREE WILL AND HUMAN NATURE:
THE TWO QUESTIONS

1. Darrow's speech appears in Safire, *Lend Me Your Ears,* 327–335.
2. Maimonides wrote, "[If there is no free will] what place would there be for the entire Torah?" ("Laws of Repentance" 5:4). Maimonides notes that some people, eager to limit human responsibility for wrongful actions, point to biblical verses to support their argument that there is no free will. For example, Deuteronomy 31:16, prophesying a future age, says that "this nation [i.e., Israel] will arise and stray after the alien gods of the land [of Canaan]." It thus appears that God decreed in advance that Israel would serve idols. Maimonides answers that God never decreed that a specific individual would be the one to sin. Rather, each person who sins has it within his power not to do so: "The Creator merely informed [Moses] of the pattern of the world. To what can this be compared? To someone who says, 'There will be righteous and wicked people in the nation. Thus, a wicked

person could argue that because God told Moses that there will be wicked people in Israel, it is decreed that he will be wicked" ("Laws of Repentance" 6:5).

3. I am indebted for this insight to Professor Howard Kreisel's *Maimonides' Political Thought*, 321 n. 61.

4. Frankl, *Man's Search for Meaning*, 75.

5. Cited in Rakeffet-Rothkoff, *The Rav*, vol. 1, 239–240. On another occasion, Reb Chaim told his son, Moshe, "I was born with an impersonal and insensitive nature, but I worked on myself until I developed good character traits" (251).

6. Rabbi Nachman of Bratslav, *The Alef-Bet Book*, 233.

CHAPTER 3: DEVELOPING GOODNESS

1. Maimonides' commentary on *The Ethics of the Fathers* 3:19; see also the anonymous *Orchot Tzaddikim*, "The Gate of Magnanimity."

2. Rigler, "Of Angels and Poinsettias, 219–24.

3. Raz, *A Tzaddik in Our Time*, 106.

4. The "broken windows" theory was first articulated by James Q. Wilson and George Kelling in an article for the *Atlantic Monthly* in 1982. The idea has influenced police work since, and is regarded as responsible for much of the decrease in urban crime in the 1990s. See, for example, Kelling and Coles, *Fixing Broken Windows*.

5. A reworking of Deuteronomy 6:5, which instructs people to love God, "with all your heart, with all your soul, and with all your might."

6. *Even Shleimah*; cited in *The Vilna Gaon Views Life*, 1.

7. See Maimonides' discussion of this point in his "Laws of Character Development" 2:3. Elsewhere, Maimonides writes: "Whoever takes a vow in order to stabilize his temperament and correct his deeds is zealous and praiseworthy" ("Laws of Vows" 13:23).

8. Ariel and Lazewnik, *Voice of Truth*, 215.

9. Jacobs, *Jewish Theology*, 234.

10. Twerski, *The Enemy Within*, 189–91.

11. Josephson, *The Power of Character*, 10.

12. Schlessinger in ibid., 26–27.

13. Raz, *A Tzaddik in Our Time*, 321.

14. "Hear O Israel, the Lord is our God, the Lord is One" (Deuteronomy 6:4).

CHAPTER 4: KNOWING OURSELVES
AND GUARDING AGAINST OUR WEAKNESSES

1. Abramson and Tougher, *Mishneh Torah*: Hilchot De'ot: *The Laws of Personality Development*, 12.

2. Cited in Katz, *T'nuat Ha-Mussar*, vol. 1, 300.

3. Seneca, *On Anger*, 329.

4. Finkelman, *Chofetz Chaim: Lessons in Truth*, 242.

5. Finkelman, *The Gift of Speech*, 97.

CHAPTER 5: THE IGNORED COMMANDMENT

1. Ehrman, *Journey to Virtue*, 17.

2. Raz, *A Tzaddik in Our Time*, 86–87.

3. Bazyn, *The Seven Perennial Sins and Their Offspring*, 47.

4. Tannen, *You Just Don't Understand,* 121.
5. Pliskin, *Growth Through Torah,* 116.
6. Bunim, *Ethics from Sinai,* vol. 1, 149.
7. Samet, *The Other Side of the Story,* 133.
8. Prager, *Think a Second Time,* 17–24.
9. Bulka, *Best Kept Secrets of Judaism,* 142.
10. Tendler, "Pain, Halakha, and Hashkofah," 95–96.

CHAPTER 6: CHALLENGES TO JUDGING FAIRLY

1. Schimmel, *Wounds Not Healed in Time,* 32.
2. Cited in Poliakov, *The History of Anti-Semitism,* 491 n. 38.
3. See Fendel, *The Halacha and Beyond,* 51.
4. Schimmel, *Wounds Not Healed in Time,* 44.
5. Cited in Segev, *The Seventh Million,* 220.
6. Ibid., 24 n.
7. Ehrman, *Journey to Virtue,* 16.
8. Cited in Freudenthal, *AIDS in Jewish Thought and Law,* 2.
9. McGinniss, *Fatal Vision,* 617–18.
10. Cited in Zaitchik, *Sparks of Mussar,* 13.

CHAPTER 7: BECOMING A GRATEFUL PERSON

1. Douglas, *My Stroke of Luck,* 153–56.
2. A few years after the war, when Pfefferberg learned that Schindler was in difficult financial circumstances, he helped raise $15,000 for him, a large amount of money in the late 1940s.
3. Goldstein, "Personal Glimpses of the Rav," 176.
4. Cited in O'Toole, *Money and Morals in America,* 116.
5. Krohn, *Around the Maggid's Table,* 40–42.
6. Rosenblum, *Rav Dessler,* 161.
7. Ibid., 162.
8. Rabbi Soloveitchik's teaching is cited in Weiss, *Insights,* vol. 1, 66.

CHAPTER 8: WHY GOOD MANNERS MATTER

1. *Derech eretz* can refer to work as well (*Berachot* 35b).
2. Carter, *Civility,* 78.
3. Ephraim Zuroff, in a private communication with the author. Zuroff, a well-known Nazi hunter and author of *The Response of Orthodox Jewry in the United States to the Holocaust,* notes that one of the armed underground groups, the ZOB, was founded by the socialist Zionists together with the Bund, while the other, ZZW, was the armed underground group of Betar and the Revisionists. The socialists and Revisionists were bitter political opponents.
4. Baker, *Days of Sorrow and Pain,* 245.

CHAPTER 9: THE OBLIGATION TO BE CHEERFUL

1. Feuer, *The Tzedaka Treasury,* 371.
2. Finkelman, *Reb Moshe,* 155–56.
3. See Buber, *Tales of the Hasidim,* 240.

4. Carter, *Civility*, 33.
5. Finkelman, *Reb Moshe*, 156.
6. Carter, *Civility*, 60, 62, 75.
7. *Or Yisrael* (a compilation of the writings of Rabbi Salanter), 118. This episode is cited in Etkes, "Rabbi Israel Salanter and His Psychology of Musar," 219.
8. See the discussion of this point in Feldman, *The Right and the Good*, 128.

CHAPTER 10: BECOMING MORE CONSIDERATE

1. Twerski, *Lights Along the Way*, 136.
2. Raz, *A Tzaddik in Our Time*, 94.
3. Goldberger, *Master Your Thoughts*, 51.
4. Katz, *The Mussar Movement* (Hebrew), vol. 1, 355.
5. Kilpatrick, *Why Johnny Can't Tell Right from Wrong*, 247.

CHAPTER 11: WHY COMMON SENSE IS SO IMPORTANT

1. Gandhi, *Non-Violence in Peace and War.*
2. Will, *The Morning After*, 370.
3. Pliskin, *Marriage*, 238.

CHAPTER 13: WHO NEEDS TO REPENT?

1. See also I Kings 8:46 and II Chronicles 6:36.
2. Twerski, *Angels Don't Leave Footprints*, 92.
3. Wiesel, *Five Biblical Portraits*, 129.
4. Petuchowski, *Studies in Modern Theology and Prayer*, 15.
5. See also *The Ethics of the Fathers* 2:10, and Maimonides, "Laws of Repentance" 7:2.
6. The *Yalkut Shimoni* makes this point more explicitly: "As long as a person is alive, there is still hope [for his transformation and improvement]"; see comment on Ecclesiastes 9:4.
7. Cited in Sherwin, *Jewish Ethics for the Twenty-First Century*, 159.

CHAPTER 14: HOW TO REPENT

1. *Prager Perspective*, 1 October 1998. Similarly, the philosopher Mary Midgley argues against replacing the word *evil* with *sick*. Doing so, except in the rare instance of a psychotic who is out of touch with reality, removes those who are wicked from blame for the evil they have done. Engaging in these sorts of euphemisms, Midgley argues, removes all distinction between criminals (including murderers) and the mentally ill (*Wickedness*, cited in Sommers, *Vice and Virtue*, 47).
2. Soloveitchik, *On Repentance*, 253.
3. Cited in Finkelman, *The Chazon Ish*, 239.
4. Cited in Morinis, *Climbing Jacob's Ladder*, 182–83.
5. See Lazare, *On Apology*, 2–4
6. Ibid., 50–51.
7. See Raz, *An Angel Among Men*, 239–40.
8. I am indebted to Rabbi Eliyahu Touger's commentary on Maimonides, "Laws of Repentance," page 21, for this source.
9. Nachman, *The Alef-Bet Book*, 237.
10. Twerski, *Living Each Day*, 53.
11. *Pele Yoetz*, 32. The words *pele yoetz* mean "wondrous adviser."

CHAPTER 15: OBSTACLES TO REPENTANCE

1. Cited in Lazare, *On Apology*, 220–21.
2. Milgrom, *Obedience to Authority*, 149.
3. See Jacobs, *Jewish Theology*, 254.
4. Cited in Zaitchik, *Sparks of Mussar*, 142.
5. Meiri, *Chibbur ha-Teshuvah—The Book of Repentance*; see also Maimonides, "Laws of Repentance" 3:6, 10; 4:1.
6. Trapp's story is told in Watterson, *Not by the Sword*.

CHAPTER 16: WHEN A GREAT EVIL HAS BEEN DONE

1. Raz, *A Tzaddik in Our Time*, 309–10.
2. See Huppin, "The Compassion of a King," 191–93.

CHAPTER 17: ROSH HASHANA AND YOM KIPPUR

1. Sherwin and Cohen, *How to Be a Jew*, 59.
2. Twerski, *Angels Don't Leave Footprints*, 221–23.

CHAPTER 18: WHEN OBLIGATORY, WHEN OPTIONAL, WHEN FORBIDDEN

1. Pliskin, *Love Your Neighbor*, 83.
2. Riemer, "Forgive Me," unpublished sermon.
3. *The ArtScroll Daily Prayerbook*, 41.
4. Ibid., 288–89.
5. Cited in Twerski, *The Enemy Within*, 217.
6. *The Complete ArtScroll Machzor*, 41.
7. Cited in Schimmel, *Wounds Not Healed by Time*, 8.
8. Ibid., 65.
9. Ozick's response is printed in Wiesenthal, *The Sunflower*, 186–88.
10. Schimmel, *Wounds Not Healed by Time*, 66.

CHAPTER 20: WHAT HUMILITY IS, AND WHY IT IS IMPORTANT

1. Cited in Zaitchik, *Sparks of Mussar*, 8.
2. Feuer, *Iggeres Haramban/A Letter for the Ages*, 46.
3. Boteach, *Judaism for Everyone*, 129.
4. Cited in Weiss, *Insights*, vol. 2, 258.

CHAPTER 21: CULTIVATING HUMILITY

1. Twerski, *Visions of the Fathers*, 30–31.
2. Twerski, *Lights Along the Way*, 296.
3. Related by Rabbi Soloveitchik's grandson, Rabbi Mayer Twersky, "A Glimpse of the Rav," *Tradition* 4 (Summer, 1996): 107.
4. Tendler, "Pain, Halakha and Hashkofah," 89.
5. See Himelstein, *Words of Wisdom*, 88.
6. Nachman, *The Aleph-Bet Book*, 236.
7. Kramer, *Crossing the Narrow Bridge*, 19.
8. Lookstein, "Our Rebbe," 241.
9. Riskin, "My Rebbe, the Rav," in ibid., 269.
10. Raz, *A Tzaddik in Our Time*, 74.
11. Ibid., 96.

12. This anecdote was related by Rabbi Joseph Baer Soloveitchik, Rabbi Chaim's grandson, and cited in Rakeffet-Rothkoff, *The Rav*, vol. 1, 226.
13. Jacobs, *Helping with Inquiries*, 87.

CHAPTER 22: AVOIDING ARROGANCE

1. Schimmel, *The Seven Deadly Sins*, 42.
2. Ibid., 53–54.
3. Raz, *A Tzaddik in Our Time*, 101.
4. Orwell, *The Road to Wigan Pier*, ch. 2.
5. Twerski, *Lights Along the Way*, 301.
6. Told in Morinis, *Climbing Jacob's Ladder*, 90–91.

CHAPTER 23: THE MORAL NECESSITY FOR SELF-ESTEEM

1. Twerski, *Angels Don't Leave Footprints*, 27–28.
2. See Rabbi Chaim of Volozhin's commentary on *The Ethics of the Fathers* 4:1.
3. Reines, "The Self and the Other in Rabbinic Ethics," 167.
4. Cited in Finkelman, *The Chazon Ish*, 182.
5. Rabbi Hanoch Teller, *And From Jerusalem, His Word*, 323–24.
6. Twerski, *Angels Don't Leave Footprints*, 52.
7. Cited in Kirschner, *Rabbinic Responsa of the Holocaust Era*, 16 n. 6.

CHAPTER 24: UNTAMED ANGER

1. *New York Times*, July 18, 1997, A14.
2. Caldwell, *A Short History of Rudeness*, 24.
3. *Torat Avraham*, 440; cited in Weiss, *Insights*, vol. 2, 353.

CHAPTER 25: DEALING WITH ANGRY PEOPLE

1. Schimmel, *The Seven Deadly Sins*, 94

CHAPTER 26: JUSTIFIABLE ANGER

1. Heschel, *The Prophets*, 280ff.
2. See de Sales, *Introduction to the Devout Life*, 119–22.

CHAPTER 27: CONTROLLING ANGER

1. Rabbi Wolbe's technique is discussed in Morinis, *Climbing Jacob's Ladder*, 187–88.
2. Goldberger, *Guard Your Anger*, 34.
3. Ibid., 121.
4. Cited in Twerski, *Lights Along the Way*, 172.
5. Seneca, *On Anger*, 343.
6. Schimmel, *The Seven Deadly Sins*, 103–4.
7. *Sefer HaMiddot*, 239, cited in Feuer, *A Letter for the Ages*, 31.
8. Twerski, *The Enemy Within*, 45.

CHAPTER 28: FIGHTING FAIRLY

1. Kushner, *When All You've Ever Wanted Isn't Enough*, 187.

CHAPTER 29: THE GREAT EVIL OF HUMILIATION

1. Cited in Weiss, *Insights*, vol. 2, 107.
2. Rabbenu Bachya, quoted in *Encyclopedia of Torah Thoughts*, 210. He cites as his

source *Ma'asei Torah*, which he attributes to the third-century Rabbi Judah the Prince, although it was most likely written several centuries later.

CHAPTER 30: HOW TO AVOID SHAMING OTHERS

1. See Finkelman and Berkowitz, *Chofetz Chaim: A Lesson a Day*, 253.
2. Caine, *Acting in Film*, 115–17.
3. Jacobs, *Ask the Rabbi*, 60.
4. "From Bakhmut to Vienna," in Greenberg, *The Inner Eye*, vol. 1, 367–72.
5. Twerski and Schwartz, *Positive Parenting*, 223.
6. Raz, *A Tzaddik in Our Time*, 469–70.
7. Reines, in Kellner, *Contemporary Jewish Ethics*, 166.
8. Kurshan, *Raising Your Child to Be a Mensch*, 13–14.
9. *YU Review*, Winter 2003: 6
10. In an alternative version, the petitioner asks God "that I not err in a matter of law and my colleagues rejoice over the error I made."

CHAPTER 31: IF YOU'RE TEMPTED TO HUMILIATE SOMEONE

1. For a further discussion of this point, see pages 353–354.
2. *Lifestyles*, Summer 1999: 57.
3. See the discussion of this procedure in Tamari, *The Challenge of Wealth*, 30.

CHAPTER 33: REDUCING ENVY

1. Cited in Klagsbrun, *Voices of Wisdom*, 35.
2. Schimmel, *The Seven Deadly Sins*, 78–79.
3. These suggestions are found in ibid., 63–64.
4. Prager, *Happiness Is a Serious Problem*, 21–22.
5. See the discussion of the Harding/Kerrigan episode in Kohn, *American Scandal*, 166–67.
6. Epstein, *Envy*, 32–33.

CHAPTER 34: THE MOST DESTRUCTIVE EMOTION

1. Amsel, *Jewish Encyclopedia of Moral and Ethical Issues*, 91.
2. In a speech before Egyptian army officers on April 25, 1972, President Sadat said, "The most splendid things our prophet Muhammad, God's peace and blessing upon him, did was to evict them [the Jews] from the entire Arabian peninsula. . . . I pledge to you that we will celebrate on the next anniversary, God willing and in this place with God's help, not only the liberation of our land but also the defeat of the Israeli conceit and arrogance so that they must once again return to the condition decreed in our holy book [the Koran]: 'humiliation and wretchedness were stamped upon them.' . . . We will not renounce this."

CHAPTER 35: "IF YOUR ENEMY IS HUNGRY": BREAKING THE PATTERN OF HATRED

1. Raz, *A Tzaddik in Our Time*, 115–16.
2. The passage then goes on to justify hating "only heretics, apostates, seducers [those who seduce people away from Judaism to another faith] and informers."
3. Twerski and Schwartz, *Positive Parenting*, 171.
4. Dr. Isaac Herschkopf, in a private communication with the author.

CHAPTER 36: WHEN HATRED IS PERMISSIBLE

1. *New Life*, December 16, 1905.

CHAPTER 37: *LASHON HARA* AND WHY IT IS SO HARMFUL

1. Raz, *A Tzaddik in Our Time*, 339; emphasis mine.
2. Rabin, *Service Book* (Hebrew), 148.
3. Finkelman, *The Gift of Speech*, 87–89.
4. See Danziger, *The Sanctity of Speech*, 102.
5. See Chana Nestlebaum in overview to *Chofetz Chaim: A Lesson a Day*, xxxvii.
6. Segal, *Chofetz Chaim: A Daily Companion*, 142–43.
7. Pliskin, *Guard Your Tongue*, 184.

CHAPTER 39: HOW TO AVOID SPEAKING UNFAIRLY OF OTHERS

1. Twerski, *Growing Each Day*, 150.
2. Pliskin, *Guard Your Tongue*, 202.
3. See *Sefer Chaffetz Chayyim*, "The Laws of *Lashon Hara*" 5:7.
4. Shapiro, "Scholars and Friends," *The Torah U-Madda Journal*, 1997, 119n3.
5. *Time*, September 10, 1984.
6. Morinis, *Climbing Jacob's Ladder*, 165.
7. Cited in Krohn and Shain, *The Sanctity of Speech*, xii.
8. Feinstein, *Igrot Moshe, Yoreh Deah*, vol. 2, number 103.
9. See *Sefer Chaffetz Chayyim*, "Laws of *Lashon Hara*," 8:3.
10. Kramer, *Crossing the Narrow Bridge*, 177.
11. See Chana Nestlebaum, summarizing the teachings of the Chaffetz Chayyim, *Chofetz Chaim: A Lesson a Day*, xxiv.
12. Pliskin, *Guard Your Tongue*, 192.

CHAPTER 42: RUMORS: WHEN PERMITTED, WHEN FORBIDDEN

1. See Finkelman and Berkowitz, *Chofetz Chaim: A Lesson a Day*, 190.
2. An overview of the Tarasoff case, which involved a patient who confided to a psychologist an intention to kill his ex-girlfriend can be found in "Tarasoff vs. the Regents of the University of California," in Wasserstrom, *Today's Moral Problems*, 243–62.

CHAPTER 43: THE WORST FORM OF FORBIDDEN SPEECH

1. Dawidowicz, *On Equal Terms*, 9.

CHAPTER 44: WHEN TO CRITICIZE

1. See Nachmanides' commentary on Leviticus 19:17.
2. Rabbi Yonatan Eibeschutz, *Ya'arot Dvash*, part 1, section 2. The title of the book means "Beehive of Honey"; see I Samuel 14:27.
3. See Ibn Ezra's commentary on Leviticus 19:17.
4. See the *Sefer Ha-Chinuch*, Commandment no. 239 and the *Mishneh Berurah* 608:7.
5. The Gaon of Vilna, *Even Shleimah* 6:7
6. Cited in Pliskin, *Love Your Neighbor*, 292.

CHAPTER 45: HOW TO CRITICIZE AND HOW NOT TO

1. Cited in Pliskin, *Love Your Neighbor*, 285.

2. Cited in Jacobs, *Helping with Inquiries,* 96.
3. Rabbi Chaim of Volozhin, *Keter Rosh* no. 143.
4. *Teshuvot Chachmei Tzarfat—The Responsa of the Scholars of France,* no. 15.
5. Related by Reb Chayyim's grandson, Rabbi Joseph Soloveitchik; see Rakeffet-Rothkoff, *The Rav,* vol. 2, 47.
6. Cited in Finkelman, *The Chazon Ish,* 215.
7. Katz, *T'nuat ha-Mussar,* vol. 1, 184.
8. Gendler, *The Loving Rebuke,* 6–7; regarding this last point, see paragraphs 15–17 in this chapter.

CHAPTER 46: WHEN OTHERS CRITICIZE YOU

1. Ziv, *Chochmah U-Mussar,* vol. 1, 34.
2. Pliskin, *Growth Through Torah,* 378.
3. Glover, *Humanity,* 287.

CHAPTER 47: TRUTH: "THE SEAL OF GOD"

1. Bulka, *Best Kept Secrets of Judaism,* 179.
2. Jacobs, *Jewish Values,* 145.
3. Other noted deceivers in the Bible include Laban and Haman; see pages 402 and 403.
4. Papo, *Pele Yoetz,* 32.
5. Hirsch, *The Wisdom of Mishlei* [Proverbs], 102.

CHAPTER 48: BECOMING MORE TRUTHFUL

1. *New York Times,* letters to the editor, March 24, 2004.
2. Morinis, *Climbing Jacob's Ladder,* 108–9.
3. As Irving Kristol has written: "[A]lmost two thirds of rapists, three quarters of adolescent murderers, and the same percentage of long-term prison inmates are young males who grew up without fathers in the house" (*Neo-Conservatism,* 67).
4. Cited in Finkelman, *Chofetz Chaim: Lessons in Truth,* 79.
5. *Mishnah Eduyot* 1:12–14 records instances in which the School of Hillel first disputed, then accepted, certain rulings of the School of Shammai.
6. *Sefer Ha-Pardes Ha-Gadol,* no. 239.
7. Twerski, *Angels Don't Leave Footprints,* 175.
8. Ehrman, *Journey to Virtue,* 93.
9. Levine, *Case Studies in Jewish Business Ethics,* 27.
10. Cited in Finkelman, *Chofetz Chaim: Lessons in Truth,* 85.
11. See the discussion of this point in Rabbi Michael J. Broyde, "The Practice of Law According to Halacha," *Journal of Halacha and Contemporary Society,* Fall, 1990, 21–22.

CHAPTER 49: DECEIVING OTHERS

1. Amsel, *The Jewish Encyclopedia of Moral and Ethical Issues,* 5.
2. Ehrman, *Journey to Virtue,* 107.
3. Amsel, *The Jewish Encyclopedia of Moral and Ethical Issues,* 5.
4. Ibid., 5.
5. Feinstein, *Igrot Moshe: Choshen Mishpat,* vol. 2, responsa number 30.
6. See Johnson, *Modern Times,* 307; and Hollander, *Political Pilgrims,* 119, 164.

7. Because of the profanation of God's Name, the Bible regards perjury as among the worst of crimes and, in writing of the punishment inflicted on perjurers, appends, "And you shall wipe out the evil from your midst" (Deuteronomy 19:19).

CHAPTER 50: WHEN LYING IS PERMISSIBLE

1. The Italian novelist Ignazio Silone wrote of how Catholicism's unbending and, in his view, immoral opposition to all lying struck him as wrongheaded even as a child. Thus he recalled an incident from his confirmation class where the students were discussing a puppet show they had seen in which the devil was searching for a child. When the devil turned to the audience and asked the children where the child was hiding, they lied, "He's left, he's gone away." At the class, the priest expressed his unhappiness over their behavior. "One must never tell a lie."

    "Not even to the devil?" Silone and his friends asked.

    "A lie is always a sin," the priest replied.

    Silone kept pressing the point: "Ought we have told the devil where the child was hiding, yes or no?"

    The priest answered, "That's not the point. A lie is always a lie . . . it's always a sin."

    Finally, Silone, by this point mischievously desirous of provoking the cleric, asked, "If it had been a priest instead of a child, what ought we have replied to the devil?"

    As punishment for his impertinence, the priest forced Silone to spend the rest of his lesson on his knees. "Are you sorry?" the priest asked him at the lesson's conclusion.

    "Of course," Silone replied. "If the devil asks for your address, I'll give it to him at once." (in an untitled essay by Silone in Crossman, *The God that Failed*, 84–85.

2. See Beck (ed.), Kant, *The Critique of Practical Reason*, 346–50.
3. The word "households" is generally understood as meaning that God blessed them with large families.
4. Friedman, *To Kill and Take Possession*, 63.
5. Raz, *A Tzaddik in Our Time*, 129–30.
6. The ceremony is based on Exodus 13:13 and Numbers 18:16.
7. Cited in Feldman, *The Right and the Good*, 92.
8. See Brams, *Biblical Games*, 124.
9. *On the Laws of War and Peace*, Book 3, chapter 1.
10. See Dratch, "Nothing But the Truth," *Judaism*, Spring 1988, 219.
11. Ehrman, *Journey to Virtue*, 96.
12. Zivotofsky, "Perspectives on Truthfulness in the Jewish Tradition," *Judaism*, Summer 1993, 267.
13. Cited in Levine, *Case Studies in Jewish Business Ethics*, 19; but see pages 409–410 of this book on the general prohibition against telling a child to lie.
14. Bleich, *Judaism and Healing*, 27–33.
15. See the discussion of this point in Taub, *The Laws of Tzedakah and Maaser*, 25.
16. Teller, *And from Jerusalem, His Word*, 345–46.
17. See Krohn, *Around the Maggid's Table*, 75. Krohn heard this story from Rabbi Moshe Grossman.
18. Prior to the Jews having a set calendar, the Rabbis decided on a year-to-year basis whether the following year would be a leap year.

19. David Nyberg, *The Varnished Truth*, 137.
20. *Judaism*, Summer 1993: 282.
21. Feldman, *The Right and the Good*, 82.

CHAPTER 51: *KIDDUSH HASHEM*: SANCTIFYING GOD'S NAME IN DAILY LIFE

1. Cited in Etkes, *Rabbi Israel Salanter*, 172.
2. See Frommer and Frommer, *Growing Up Jewish in America*, 76.
3. Jacobs, *Jewish Law*, 49.
4. Raz, *A Tzaddik in Our Time*, 113.
5. Ibid., 318.
6. Scherman, "What Do They Say About Us?" in Wolpin, *The Ethical Imperative*, 438–39.

CHAPTER 52: MARTYRDOM

1. *Encyclopedia Judaica* 10:985.
2. Ibid., 10:984
3. Zimmels, *The Echo of the Nazi Holocaust in Rabbinic Literature*, 78. Of course, the ones who most ardently opposed Jews acquiring baptismal certificates were the Nazis, who had no interest in Jews becoming Christians, and who ruled that a Jew caught with a certificate stating that he was a Christian was subject to immediate execution (page 79).
4. Jacob, *Contemporary American Reform Responsa*, 104.

CHAPTER 53: GOD AS THE BASIS OF MORALITY

1. Cited in Bree, *Camus and Sartre*, 15.
2. From a speech by Rabbi Dr. Jonathan Sacks, Chief Rabbi of the British Empire, cited in *Talmudic Ethics: Timeless Wisdom for Timely Dilemmas*, 16.
3. *The Humanist*, November–December 1974.
4. Luther's letter is found in Kaufmann, *Religion in Four Dimensions*, 156.
5. Ibid., 156.
6. Nietzsche, *The Will to Power*, section 872.
7. Nietzsche, *The Antichrist*, section 2.
8. Glover, *Humanity*, 11.
9. In other words, "For Marxism there is no reason (literally no reason: our universe, the movement posits, is the kind of universe where there cannot conceivably be any reason) for not killing or torturing or exploiting a human person if his liquidation or torture or slave labor will advance the historical process [i.e., the collapse of capitalism and the rise of communism]; Smith, *Islam in Modern History*.
10. Kant, *The Metaphysics of Morals*, "The Doctrine of Right," 109.
11. Steinberg, *Anatomy of Faith*, 96. Steinberg goes on to note that "most irreligionists, Bertrand Russell included, are living by the Judeo-Christian morality which follows from Judeo-Christian theism. At the same time, they profess a world outlook which in all its implications denies the code to which they conform. Eventually, the contradiction between theory and practice must reveal itself. Then one or the other way will give way."

CHAPTER 54: LOVING AND FEARING GOD

1. Jacobs, *Jewish Values,* 36.
2. Valladares, *Against All Hope,* 17. At the same time that these murders were being carried out in Cuba, the renowned left-wing American writer Norman Mailer published an open letter to the man who was ordering these executions: "So Fidel Castro . . . you gave all of us who are alone in this country . . . a sense that there were heroes in the world. . . . You were the first and greatest hero to appear in the world since the Second War." ("Letter to Castro," in Mailer's *Presidential Papers,* 67, 68.)
3. Levine, *Case Studies in Jewish Business Ethics,* 4.
4. Cited in Morinis, *Climbing Jacob's Ladder,* 128.
5. Cited in *Moment* magazine, June, 1998.
6. Prager, "For Everything a Blessing," *Journal of the American Medical Association,* 28 May 1997: 1589. Abaye's blessing is found in the Talmud, *Berachot* 60b, and in the *ArtScroll Prayerbook* on page 14.

CHAPTER 55: THE PREEMINENT COMMAND

1. In a 1988 survey of Jewish life in the United States, Leonard Fein, a longtime observer of the American-Jewish scene, wrote: "Politics is our religion; our preferred denomination is liberalism" (*Where Are We?,* 224).
2. See Finkelman, *Chofetz Chaim: Lessons in Truth,* 61.
3. The monk's quote is cited in Smalley, *The Study of the Bible in the Middle Ages,* 52. The letter of the dying mother in Egypt, and the comment by Haim Hillel Ben-Sasson are both found in Ben-Sasson, *A History of the Jewish People,* 521.
4. Quoted in David Vital, *A People Apart,* 130.
5. Lamm, *The Royal Reach,* 310.
6. Cited in Levi, *Torah Study,* 27.
7. Cited in Grishaver, *40 Things You Can Do to Save the Jewish People,* 223.

CHAPTER 56: THE BENEFITS OF TORAH STUDY

1. Cited in Goldberg, *The Mussar Anthology,* 58.
2. Norman Lamm, "Knowing vs. Learning: Which Takes Precedence?" in Saks and Handelman, *Wisdom from All My Teachers,* 18n7.
3. Ibid., 19–20 n. 11.
4. Cited in Zion and Dishon, *A Different Night: The Leader's Guide,* 49, and their *Different Night* haggadah, 89.
5. Prager, *Think a Second Time,* 16.

CHAPTER 57: LEARNING AND TEACHING TORAH

1. Cited in Finkelman, *Chofetz Chaim: Lessons in Truth,* 228–29.
2. Yet another talmudic dictum teaches that "Whoever teaches a child Torah is as though he had given birth to him" (*Sanhedrin* 19b).
3. Steinsaltz, *Teshuvah,* 91.
4. Cited in Raz, *A Tzaddik in Our Time,* 381.

BIBLIOGRAPHY

A NOTE ON CITATIONS FROM JUDAISM'S CLASSIC TEXTS

When citing statements from the Hebrew Bible, the *Tanakh*, I have generally relied upon the translation of the Jewish Publication Society (Philadelphia, 1985), a scholarly yet highly readable rendering of the Bible into contemporary English. On occasion, however, I have translated the verses myself, or used other translations that seemed to me preferable for a specific verse.

There are three English translations of the Mishnah; the one on which I have relied most is Jacob Neusner's *The Mishnah* (Yale University Press, 1988). There is an older and still valuable translation of the Mishnah by Herbert Danby (Oxford: Clarendon Press, 1933). In addition, I have also frequently consulted Pinchas Kehati's excellent Hebrew commentary on the entire Mishnah, *Mishnayot Mevuarot* (Jerusalem: Heichal Shlomo, 1977), which has been translated into English as well (Jerusalem: Department for Torah Education and Culture in the Diaspora of the World Zionist Organization, 1988).

In quoting from the Talmud, I have generally relied on the ArtScroll translation, one of the great works of modern Jewish literature. ArtScroll, which is based in Brooklyn, New York, has recently completed a translation of the entire Babylonian Talmud into English (when people speak of studying Talmud, they almost always mean the Babylonian Talmud, and not the shorter and earlier Jerusalem Talmud), along with extensive explanatory notes. The ArtScroll translation is line-by-line, and anyone who has basic Hebrew skills can utilize this translation to learn the Talmud's vocabulary and methodology. I have also consulted the highly accurate and literal translation of the Soncino Press (London, 1935), and the Hebrew translation and commentary of Rabbi Adin Steinsaltz on most of the Talmud. In addition, Random House has brought out many volumes of Steinsaltz's Talmud in a very readable English translation (under titles such as *The Talmud, The*

Steinsaltz Edition, Volume 1: Bava Mezia Part I). Though I have repeatedly consulted these works, I have also translated many of the cited texts myself.

Yale University Press has published Judah Goldin's translation of *The Fathers According to Rabbi Nathan* (1955).

The citations from the *Midrash Rabbah* have generally followed the Soncino translation (London, 1983: ten volumes), although I have checked all translations against the original, and have often made some alterations. The *Mekhilta* has been translated and published in three volumes by the Jewish Publication Society (Philadelphia, 1933).

Yale University Press has published a multivolume translation of Moses Maimonides' *Mishneh Torah* under the title *The Code of Maimonides.* In recent years, Rabbi Eliyahu Touger has been bringing out a very readable translation of Maimonides' *Mishneh Torah,* with the Hebrew and English on facing pages (the set is not yet complete). In addition, Rabbi Touger provides extensive notes on Maimonides' text, and also cites the talmudic and other sources for Maimonides' rulings (the work is published by the New York–based Moznaim Publishing Corporation). I have also relied on the Hebrew language edition of the *Mishneh Torah* by Mossad HaRav Kook (Jerusalem), which contains the wide-ranging commentary of Rabbi Shmuel Tanchum Rubenstein.

The sixteenth-century code of Jewish law, the *Shulchan Arukh,* by Rabbi Joseph Karo, has, with the exception of a few sections, not been translated into English. The *Mishnah Berurah,* the Chaffetz Chayyim's comprehensive work on the laws of *Orach Chayyim,* the first volume of the *Shulchan Arukh,* has in recent years come out in a multivolume English translation (Feldheim).

The other Hebrew works that are cited are listed, along with the other books I consulted, in the following bibliography.

Aaron Ha-Levi of Barcelona, Rabbi. *Sefer ha-Hinnuch (The Book of [Mitzvah] Education).* Translated and annotated by Charles Wengrov. 5 volumes. Nanuet, NY: Feldheim, 1984.

Amsel, Nachum. *The Jewish Encyclopedia of Moral and Ethical Issues.* Northvale, NJ: Aronson, 1994.

Anonymous. *Orchot Tzaddikim (The Ways of the Tzaddikim).* Translated by Rabbi Shraga Silverstein. Nanuet, NY: Feldheim, 1995.

Ariel, Yaakov Aryeh, and Libby Lazewnik. *Voice of Truth: The Life and Eloquence of Rabbi Sholom Schwadron, the Unforgettable Maggid of Jerusalem.* Brooklyn: Mesorah, 2000.

Aristotle. *The Nichomachean Ethics.* New York: Oxford University Press, 1998.

Augustine, Saint. "On Lying," In *Treatises on Various Subjects,* vol. 14, Edited by R. J. Deferrari, New York: Catholic University of America Press, 1952.

Azikri, Elazar. *Sefer Charedim.* Jerusalem, 1989.

Bachya ibn Paquda. *Duties of the Heart (Torat Chovot HaLevavot).* 2 volumes. Translated by Daniel Haberman. Nanuet, NY: Feldheim, 1996.

Bachya, Rabbenu. *Encyclopedia of Torah Thoughts.* Translated and annotated by Rabbi Dr. Charles Chavel. New York: Shilo Press, 1980.

Baker, Leonard. *Days of Sorrow and Pain: Leo Baeck and the Berlin Jews.* New York: Oxford University Press, 1980.

Bazyn, Ken. *The Seven Perennial Sins and Their Offspring.* New York: Continuum, 2002.

Belkin, Samuel. *In His Image: The Jewish Philosophy of Man as Expressed in Rabbinic Tradition.* Westport, CT: Greenwood, 1979.

Ben-Sasson, Haim Hillel, ed. *A History of the Jewish People.* Cambridge, MA: Harvard University Press, 1976.

Bergren, Richard Victor. *The Prophets and the Law.* New York: Behrman House, 1975.

Berke, Joseph H. *The Tyranny of Malice: Exploring the Dark Side of Character and Culture.* New York: Summit Books, 1988.

Bialik, Hayim Nahman, and Yehoshua Hana Ravnitzky. *The Book of Legends: Legends from the Talmud and Midrash.* Translated from the Hebrew *Sefer Ha-Aggadah* by William Braude. New York: Schocken Books, 1992.

Bierman, Michael, ed. *Memories of a Giant: Eulogies in Memory of Rabbi Joseph B. Soloveitchik.* Jerusalem: Urim Publishing, 2003.

Bleich, Rabbi J. David. *Judaism and Healing: Halakhic Perspectives.* New York: Ktav, 1981.

Bloch, Abraham. *A Book of Jewish Ethical Concepts: Biblical and Postbiblical.* New York: Ktav, 1984.

Bok, Sissela. *Lying: Moral Choice in Public and Private Life.* New York: Pantheon, 1978.

Bonhoeffer, Dietrich. *The Cost of Discipleship.* New York: Macmillan, 1963.

Boteach, Shmuely. *Judaism for Everyone: Renewing Your Life Through the Vibrant Lessons of the Jewish Faith.* New York: Basic Books, 2002.

Brams, Dr. Steven. *Biblical Games: Game Theory and the Hebrew Bible.* Cambridge, MA.: MIT Press, 2002.

Breger, Marshall J. *Public Policy and Social Issues: Jewish Sources and Perspectives.* Westport, CT.: Praeger, 2003.

Broyde, Rabbi Michael J. "The Practice of Law According to the Halacha." *Journal of Halacha and Contemporary Society* 20 (Fall 1990): 5–45, esp. 21–22.

Buber, Martin. *Tales of the Hasidim.* 2 vols. New York: Schocken, 1975.

Bulka, Rabbi Reuven. *Best Kept Secrets of Judaism.* Nanuet, NY: Feldheim, 2002.

Bunim, Irving. *Ethics from Sinai: An Eclectic, Wide-Ranging Commentary on Pirke Aboth,* 3 vols. New York: Feldheim, 1966.

Caine, Michael. *Acting in Film.* New York: Applause, 1990.

Caldwell, Mark. *A Short History of Rudeness: Manners, Morals, and Misbehavior in Modern America.* New York: Picador, 1999.

Canfield, Jack, Mark Victor Hansen, Rabbi Dov Peretz Elkins. *Chicken Soup for the Jewish Soul.* Deerfield Beach, FL: Health Communications, 2001.

Carmy, Shalom, ed. *Jewish Perspectives on the Experience of Suffering.* Northvale, NJ: Jason Aronson, 1999.

Carroll, James. *Constantine's Sword: The Church and the Jews.* Boston: Houghton Mifflin, 2001.

Carter, Stephen L. *Civility: Manners, Morals, and the Etiquette of Democracy.* New York: Basic Books, 1998.

Castle, Rabbi Dovid. *Rashi and the Tosafists.* Vol. 6 of *Living with the Sages.* Nanuet, NY: Feldheim, 1996.

Chaffetz Chayyim: *Chofetz Chaim: A Daily Companion.* Arranged for daily study by Rabbi Yehudah Zev Segal. Brooklyn: ArtScroll/Mesorah, 1999.

———. *Chofetz Chaim: A Lesson a Day: The Concepts and Laws of Proper Speech Arranged for Daily Study.* Compiled by Rabbi Shimon Finkelman and Rabbi Yitzchak Berkowitz. Brooklyn: ArtScroll/Mesorah, 1995.

———. *Chofetz Chaim: Lessons in Truth: Daily Studies in Honesty and Fundamentals of Jewish Faith.* Translation and commentary by Rabbi Shimon Finkelman. Brooklyn: ArtScroll/Mesorah, 2001.

———. *Middos: The Measure of Man.* (Compiled anonymously, this book is an anthology of the Chaffetz Chayyim's philosophical and ethical insights, translated by Raphael Blumberg). Jerusalem: 1987.

———. *Sefer Chaffetz Chayyim* (Hebrew). Jerusalem: Mercaz Hasefer, 1998.

Complete ArtScroll Machzor: Rosh Hashanah. Translated with commentary by Rabbi Nosson Scherman. Brooklyn: ArtScroll/Mesorah, 1985.

Complete ArtScroll Siddur. Translated with commentary by Rabbi Nosson Scherman. Brooklyn: ArtScroll/Mesorah, 1984.

Crossman, Richard H., ed. *The God That Failed.* New York: Columbia University Press, 2001.

Dawidowicz, Lucy. *On Equal Terms.* New York: Henry Holt, 1982.

De Sales, Francis. *Introduction to the Devout Life.* Translated by John K. Ryan. New York: Harper, 1966.

Douglas, Kirk. *My Stroke of Luck.* New York: Little Brown, 2002.

Dratch, Mark. "Nothing But the Truth," *Judaism,* Spring, 1988, 218–28.

Ehrman, Rabbi Avrohom. *Journey to Virtue: The Laws of Interpersonal Relationships, in Business, Home, and Society.* Brooklyn: ArtScroll/Mesorah, 2002.

Elijah ben Solomon (the Gaon of Vilna). *The Vilna Gaon Views Life: Even Shleima, the Classic Collection of the Gaon of Vilna's Wisdom.* Translated and annotated by Chaim Dovid Ackerman. Jerusalem: C. D. Ackerman, 1974.

Epstein, Joseph. *Envy.* New York: Oxford University Press, 2003.

Esper, Joseph. *Saintly Solutions to Life's Common Problems: From Anger, Boredom, and Temptation to Gluttony, Gossip, and Greed.* Manchester, NH: Sophia Institute Press, 2001.

Etkes, Immanuel. "Rabbi Israel Salanter and His Psychology of Mussar." In *Jewish Spirituality: From the Sixteenth-Century Revival to the Present,* edited by Arthur Green. New York: Crossroad, 1994, 206–44.

———. *Rabbi Israel Salanter and the Mussar Movement: Seeking the Torah of Truth.* Philadelphia: Jewish Publication Society, 1993.

Fadiman, Clifton and Andre Bernard, eds. *Bartlett's Book of Anecdotes.* New York: Little Brown, 2000.

Fein, Leonard. *Where Are We?: The Inner Life of America's Jews.* New York: HarperCollins, 1989.

Feldman, Daniel Z. *The Right and the Good: Halakhah and Human Relations.* Northvale, NJ: Jason Aronson, 1999.

Fendel, Rabbi Zechariah. *The Halacha and Beyond.* New York: Hashkafah Library Series, 1983.

Feuer, Rabbi Avrohom Chaim. *The Tzedakah Treasury: An Anthology of Torah Teachings on the Mitzvah of Charity.* Brooklyn: ArtScroll/Mesorah, 2000.

———. *Iggeres Haramban/A Letter for the Ages: The Ramban's Ethical Letter with an Anthology of Contemporary Rabbinic Expositions.* Brooklyn: ArtScroll/Mesorah, 1989.

Finkelman, Rabbi Shimon. *The Chazon Ish: The Life and Ideals of Rabbi Avraham Yeshayah Karelitz.* Brooklyn: ArtScroll/Mesorah, 1989.

———. *The Gift of Speech: Refining the Way We Speak.* Brooklyn: ArtScroll/Mesorah, 2000.

———. *Reb Moshe: The Life and Ideals of HaGaon Rabbi Moshe Feinstein.* Brooklyn: ArtScroll/Mesorah, 1986.

Foner, Eric and John Garraty, eds. *The Reader's Companion to American History.* Boston: Houghton Mifflin, 1991.

Frankl, Dr. Viktor. *Man's Search for Meaning.* New York: Pocket Books, 1997.

Freehof, Solomon. *A Treasury of Responsa.* Philadelphia: Jewish Publication Society, 1963.

Fox, Marvin, ed. *Modern Jewish Ethics: Theory and Practice.* Columbus: Ohio State University Press, 1975.

Freud, Sigmund. *The Future of an Illusion.* New York: Norton, 1961.

Freudenthal, Gad. *AIDS in Jewish Thought and Law.* Jersey City: Ktav, 1998.

Friedmann, Daniel. *To Kill and Take Possession: Law, Morality, and Society in Biblical Stories.* Peabody, MA: Hendrickson, 2002.

Friedrich, Otto. *The End of the World: A History.* New York: Coward, McCann, 1982.

Frommer, Myrna Katz, and Harvey Frommer. *Growing Up Jewish in America: An Oral History.* New York: Harcourt, 1995.

Gendler, Everett. *The Loving Rebuke: Personal Confrontation and Human Harmony.* New York: National Jewish Resource Center, 1982.

Gerondi, Rabbi Jonah. *The Gates of Repentance* (Sha'arei Teshuvah). Translated by Shraga Silverstein. Nanuet, NY: Feldheim, 1967.

Glover, Jonathan. *Humanity: A Moral History of the Twentieth Century.* New Haven: Yale University Press, 2000.

Goldberg, Hillel, ed. *Mussar Anthology.* Hyde Park, MA: Harwich Lithograph, 1972.

Goldberger, Moshe. *Guard Your Anger.* Southfield, MI, and Nanuet, NY: Targum Press and Feldheim, 1999.

Goldstein, Dr. Allen. "Personal Glimpses of the Rav." In *Memories of a Giant: Eulogies in Memory of Rabbi Joseph B. Soloveitchik,* edited by Michael Bierman. Jerusalem: Urim Publishing, 2003.

Greenberg, Hayim. *The Inner Eye.* New York: Jewish Frontier Association, 1953.

Grishaver, Joel Lurie. *40 Things You Can Do to Save the Jewish People.* Los Angeles: Alef Design Group, 1993.

Grotius, Hugo. *On the Law of War and Peace.* Whitefish, MT: Kessinger, 2004.

Herschkopf, Isaac Steven, M.D. *Hello Darkness, My Old Friend: Embracing Anger to Heal Your Life.* Xlibris, www.XLibris.com, 2003.

Hertzberg, Arthur. *The French Enlightenment and the Jews: The Origins of Modern Anti-Semitism.* New York: Schocken Books, 1970.

Heschel, Abraham J. *The Prophets.* Philadelphia: Jewish Publication Society, 1962.

Himelstein, Shmuel. *Words of Wisdom, Words of Wit.* Brooklyn: ArtScroll/Mesorah Publications, 1993.

Hirsch, Rabbi Samson Raphael. *From the Wisdom of* Mishle *[Proverbs].* Nanuet, NY: Feldheim, 1976, 1998.

Huppin, Beth. "The Compassion of a King." In Canfield, Jack, Mark Victor Hansen, and Rabbi Dov Peretz Elkins. *Chicken Soup for the Jewish Soul.* Deerfield Beach, FL: Health Communications, Inc., 2001, 191–193.

Jacob, Walter. *Contemporary American Reform Responsa.* New York: Central Conference of American Rabbis, 1987.

Jacobs. Rabbi Louis. *Ask the Rabbi.* London: Vallentine Mitchell, 1999.

———. *Helping with Inquiries.* London: Vallentine Mitchell, 1989.

———. *Jewish Law.* New York: Behrman House, 1968.

———. *A Jewish Theology.* New York: Behrman House, 1973.

———. *Jewish Values.* London: Vallentine Mitchell, 1960.

———. "The Relationship Between Religion and Ethics in Jewish Thought." In *Religion and Morality: A Collection of Essays,* edited by Gene Outka and John P. Reeder Jr. Garden City, NY: Anchor Press/Doubleday, 1973.

Jacoby, Susan. *Wild Justice: The Evolution of Revenge.* New York: Harper and Row, 1983.

Johnson, Paul. *Modern Times: The World from the Twenties to the Eighties.* New York: Harper and Row, 1982.

Josephson, Michael and Wes Hanson, eds. *The Power of Character: Prominent Americans Talk About Life, Family, Work, Values, and More.* San Francisco: Jossey-Bass, 1998.

Judah Ha-Chasid. *Sefer Chasidim.* Jerusalem: Mosad HaRav Kook, 1969.

Kant, Immanuel. "On a Supposed Right to Lie from Benevolent Motives," In *The Critique of Practical Reason,* edited and translated by Lewis White Beck. Chicago: University of Chicago Press, 1994.

———. *The Metaphysics of Morals.* Edited by Mary Gregor. Cambridge, England. Cambridge University Press, 1996.

Karpin, Michael and Ina Friedman. *The Plot to Kill Yitzhak Rabin.* New York: Metropolitan Books/Henry Holt and Company, 1998.

Katz, Dov. *T'nuat Ha-Mussar (The Mussar Movement).* 5 vols. Tel Aviv, 1945–52.

Katz, Fred E. *Ordinary People and Extraordinary Evil: A Report on the Beguilings of Evil.* Albany: State University Press of New York, 1993.

Kaufmann, Walter. *Religions in Four Dimensions: Existential, Aesthetic, Historical, Comparative.* New York: Reader's Digest Press, 1976.

Kelling, George, and Catherine Coles. *Fixing Broken Windows: Restoring Order and Reducing Crime in Our Communities.* New York: Free Press, 1998.

Kellner, Menachem Marc, ed. *Contemporary Jewish Ethics.* New York: Sanhedrin Press, 1978.

Kilpatrick, William. *Why Johnny Can't Tell Right from Wrong.* New York: Simon and Schuster, 1992.

Kirschner, Robert. *Rabbinic Responsa of the Holocaust Era.* New York: Schocken Books, 1985.

Klagsbrun, Francine. *Voices of Wisdom: Jewish Ideals and Ethics for Everyday Living.* New York: Pantheon, 1980.

Kohn, George Childs. *The New Encyclopedia of American Scandal.* New York: Checkmark Books/Facts on File), 2001.

Komp, Diane M. M.D. *Anatomy of a Lie: The Truth About Lies and Why Good People Tell Them*. Grand Rapids, MI.: Zondervan Publishing House, 1998.

Kramer, Chaim. *Crossing the Narrow Bridge: A Practical Guide to Rebbe Nachman's Teachings*. Edited by Moshe Mykoff. Jerusalem and Monsey, NY: Breslov Research Institute, 1989.

Kreisel, Howard. *Maimonides' Political Thought: Studies in Ethics, Law, and the Human Ideal*. Albany: State University of New York Press, 1999.

Kristol, Irving. *Neo-Conservatism: The Autobiography of an Idea*. New York: Free Press, 1995.

Krohn, Rabbi Peysach. *Around the Maggid's Table*. Brooklyn: Mesorah, 1989.

Krohn, Rabbi Yisroel Kolman and Rabbi Yisroel Meir Shain, compilers. *The Sanctity of Speech: A Compendium of the Laws of* Lashon Hara, *Based on Sefer Chofetz Chaim*. Adapted into English by Rabbi Hillel Danziger. Lakewood, NJ: self-published, 1986.

Kurshan, Neil. *Raising Your Child to Be a Mensch*. New York: Atheneum, 1987.

Kushner, Harold. *When All You've Ever Wanted Isn't Enough*. New York: Pocket Books, 1987.

Lamm, Norman. *The Royal Reach*. New York: Ktav, 1970.

Lazare, Aaron, M.D. *On Apology*. New York: Oxford University Press, 2004.

Leibowitz, Nechama. *Studies in* Bereshit *(Genesis)*. The World Zionist Organization, Department for Torah Education and Culture in the Diaspora, 1981.

———. *Studies in* Vayikra *(Leviticus)*. Jerusalem: The World Zionist Organization, Department for Torah Education and Culture in the Diaspora, 1980

Levi, Yehudah. *Torah Study: A Survey of Classic Sources on Timely Issues*. Spring Valley, NY: Feldheim, 1990.

Levine, Aaron. *Case Studies in Jewish Business Ethics*. Jersey City: Ktav, 1999.

Lichtenstein, Rabbi Aharon. "Does Jewish Tradition Recognize an Ethic Independent of Halakha?" In *Modern Jewish Ethics: Theory and Practice,* edited by Marvin Fox. Columbus: Ohio State University Press, 1975, pages 62–88.

———. *Leaves of Faith: The World of Jewish Learning*. Jersey City: Ktav, 2003.

Lookstein, Rabbi Dr. Haskel. "Our Rebbe: A Sermon of Tribute to Rabbi J. B. Soloveitchik. In *Memories of a Giant: Eulogies in Memory of Rabbi Joseph B. Soloveitchik,* edited by Michael Bierman. Jerusalem: Urim Publishing, 2003, 236–47.

Lowin, Joseph, ed. *Jewish Ethics: A Study Guide*. New York: Hadassah, 1986.

Luzzatto, Rabbi Moshe Chaim. *The Path of the Just* (Mesillat Yesharim). Translation by Shraga Silverstein. Nanuet, NY: Feldheim, 1966.

Maccoby, Hyam. *The Philosophy of the Talmud*. London: RoutledgeCurzon, 2002.

Mailer, Norman. *The Presidential Papers*. New York: Berkley Books, 1976.

Maimonides, Moses. *The Guide of the Perplexed*. Translated with introduction by Shlomo Pines. Chicago: University of Chicago Press, 1963.

Mandelbaum, Yitta Halberstam. *Holy Brother: Inspiring Stories and Enchanted Tales About Rabbi Shlomo Carlebach*. Northvale, NJ: Jason Aronson, 1997.

Martin, Oliver. *Two Educators: Hutchins and Conant*. Washington, DC: Regnery, 1948.

McGinnis, Joe. *Fatal Vision*. New York: Signet Books, 1999.

Milgram, Stanley. *Obedience to Authority*. New York: Harper Perennial, 1983.

Morinis, Alan. *Climbing Jacob's Ladder: One Man's Rediscovery of a Jewish Spiritual Tradition*. New York: Broadway, 2002.

Murphy, Kenneth. *Retreat from the Finland Station: Moral Odysseys in the Breakdown of Communism.* New York: Free Press, 1992.

Nachman of Breslov, Rabbi. *The Aleph-Bet Book: Rabbi Nachman's Aphorisms on Jewish Living.* Translated by Moshe Mykoff. Jerusalem and New York: Breslov Research Institute, 1986.

Nyberg, David. *The Varnished Truth: Truth Telling and Deceiving in Ordinary Life.* Chicago: University of Chicago Press, 1993.

Orwell, George. *The Road to Wigan Pier.* New York: Harvest/HBJ, 1973.

Oshry, Rabbi Ephraim. *Responsa from the Holocaust.* New York: Judaica Press, 1983.

O'Toole, Patricia. *Money and Morals in America: A History.* New York: Clarkson Potter, 1998.

Ozick, Cynthia. "Notes Toward a Meditation on Forgiveness." In Simon Wiesenthal, *The Sunflower: On the Possibilities and Limits of Forgiveness.* New York: Schocken Books, 1997, 204–10.

Papo, Rabbi Eliezer. *Pele Yoetz Hashalem* (Hebrew). Jerusalem, 1986.

Peli, Pinchas. *On Repentance in the Thought and Oral Discourses of Rabbi Joseph B. Soloveitchik.* Jerusalem: Oroth Publishing House, 1980.

Petuchowski, Rabbi Jakob. *Studies in Modern Theology and Prayer.* Philadelphia: Jewish Publication Society, 1998.

Pliskin, Zelig. *Growth Through Torah.* Brooklyn: Benei Yakov Publications, 1988.

———. *Guard Your Tongue: A Practical Guide to the Laws of Lashon Hara, Based on Chofetz Chayyim.* Jerusalem: self-published, 1975.

———. *Love Your Neighbor: You and Your Fellow Man in Light of the Torah.* Brooklyn: Aish HaTorah, 1977.

Pliskin, Zelig and Avrohom Barash. *Marriage.* Brooklyn.: ArtScroll/Mesorah, 1998.

Plutarch. "On the Control of Anger." In *Moralia,* vol. 6, translated by W. C. Helmbold. Cambridge, MA: Harvard University Press, 1939.

Poliakov, Leon. *The History of Anti-Semitism: From Voltaire to Wagner.* New York: Vanguard, 1975.

Prager, Dennis. *Think a Second Time.* New York: Regan Books, 1995.

Prager, Dennis and Joseph Telushkin. *The Nine Questions People Ask About Judaism.* New York: Simon and Schuster, 1981.

———. *Why the Jews: The Reason for Antisemitism.* New York: Simon and Schuster, 1983.

Prager, Dr. Kenneth. "For Everything a Blessing." *Journal of the American Medical Association,* May 28, 1997.

Rabin, Yitzhak. *Service Book* (Hebrew). Tel Aviv: Maariv, 1979.

Rae, Scott B. and Kenman L. Wong. *Beyond Integrity: A Judeo-Christian Approach to Business Ethics.* Grand Rapids, MI: Zondervan, 1996.

Rakeffet-Rothkoff, Aaron. *The Rav: The World of Rabbi Joseph B. Soloveitchik.* 2 vols. Jersey City: Ktav, 1999.

Raz, Simcha. *An Angel Among Men: Rav Avraham Yitzchak HaKohen Kook.* Jerusalem: Kol Mevaser, 2003.

———. *A Tzaddik in Our Time: The Life of Rabbi Aryeh Levin.* Translated from the Hebrew, revised and expanded by Charles Wengrov. Jerusalem and New York: Feldheim, 1976.

Reines, Chaim. "The Self and Others in Rabbinic Ethics." In *Contemporary Jewish Ethics,* edited by Menachem Marc Kellner, New York: Sanhedrin Press, 1978, 162–74.

Riemer, Jack, ed. *The World of the High Holy Days*. Miami: Bernie Books, n.d.

———. "Forgive Me," unpublished sermon, sent to the author.

Rigler, Sara Levinsky. "Of Angels and Poinsettias." In Canfield, Jack, Mark Victor Hansen, Rabbi Dov Peretz Elkins, *Chicken Soup for the Jewish Soul*. Deerfield Beach, FL: Health Communications, 2001, 219–24.

Riskin, Rabbi Dr. Shlomo. "My Rebbe, the Rav," in *Memories of a Giant: Eulogies in Memory of Rabbi Joseph B. Soloveitchik*, edited by Michael Bierman. Jerusalem: Urim Publishing, 2003, 261–70.

Rollyson, Carl. *The Lives of Norman Mailer: A Biography*. New York: Paragon House, 1991.

Rosenblum, Yonason, *Rav Dessler, The Life and Impact of Rabbi Eliyahu Eliezer Dessler, the Michtav M'Eliyahu*. Brooklyn: ArtScroll/Mesorah, 2000.

———. *Reb Yaakov: The Life and Times of HaGaon Rabbi Yaakov Kamenetsky*. Based on the research of Rabbi Noson Kamenetsky. Brooklyn: ArtScroll/Mesorah, 1993.

Sabato, Larry. *Feeding Frenzy: How Attack Journalism Has Transformed American Politics*. New York: Free Press, 1991.

Safire, William. *Lend Me Your Ears: Great Speeches in History*. New York: Norton, 1992. The speech cited in this book, by Clarence Darrow, is found on pages 327–35.

Saks, Jeffrey and Susan Handelman, eds. *Wisdom from All My Teachers: Challenges and Initiatives in Contemporary Torah Education*. Jerusalem and New York: Urim Publications, 2003.

Salanter, Rabbi Israel. *Ohr Yisrael: The Classic Writings of Rav Yisrael Salanter and His Disciple, Rav Yitzchak Blazer*. Translated and annotated by Rabbi Zvi Miller, and edited by Rabbi Eli Linas. Southfield, MI and Nanuet, NY: Targum/Feldheim, 2004.

Samet, Yehudi. *The Other Side of the Story: Giving People the Benefit of the Doubt—Stories and Strategies*. Brooklyn: ArtScroll/Mesorah, 1996.

Schimmel, Dr. Solomon. *The Seven Deadly Sins: Jewish, Christian, and Classical Reflections on Human Nature*. New York: Free Press, 1992.

———. *Wounds Not Healed by Time: The Power of Repentance and Forgiveness*. New York: Oxford University Press, 2002.

Schlessinger, Dr. Laura. "Character, Courage, and Conscience." In *The Power of Character: Prominent Americans Talk About Life, Family, Work, Values, and More*, edited by Michael Josephson and Wes Hanson. San Francisco: Jossey-Bass, 1998, 23–29.

Segev, Tom. *The Seventh Million: The Israelis and the Holocaust*. New York: Hill and Wang, 1993.

Seneca. "On Anger." In *Moral Essays*, vol. 2. Translated by John W. Basore. Cambridge, MA: Harvard University Press, 1928.

Sherwin, Byron. *In Partnership with God: Contemporary Jewish Law and Ethics*. Syracuse, NY: Syracuse University Press, 1990.

———. *Jewish Ethics for the Twenty-First Century*. Syracuse, NY: Syracuse University Press, 1999.

Sherwin, Byron, and Seymour Cohen. *How to Be a Jew: Ethical Teachings of Judaism*. Northvale, NJ: Jason Aaronson., 1992.

Siegel, Marvin, ed. *The Last Word:* The New York Times *Book of Obituaries and Farewells*. New York: Quill, 1999.

Smalley, Beryl. *The Study of the Bible in the Middle Ages*. Notre Dame, IN: University of Notre Dame Press, 1970.

Soloveitchik, Rabbi Dr. Joseph B. *Halakhic Man.* Translated by Dr. Lawrence Kaplan. Philadelphia: Jewish Publication Society, 1984.

———. *On Repentance;* see Pinchas Peli.

Sommers, Christina Hoff. *Vice and Virtue in Everyday Life.* Belmont, CA: Wadsworth, 2003.

Spero, Shubert. *Morality, Halakha and the Jewish Tradition.* New York: Ktav, 1983.

Steinberg, Avraham, M.D. *Encyclopedia of Jewish Medical Ethics.* 3 vols. Nanuet, NY: Feldheim, 2003.

Steinberg, Milton. *Anatomy of Faith,* edited by Arthur Cohen. New York: Harcourt Brace, 1960.

Steinsaltz, Adin. *Teshuvah: A Guide for the Newly Observant Jew.* Northvale, NJ: Aronson, 1996.

Szasz, Dr. Thomas. *The Untamed Tongue: A Dissenting Dictionary.* Chicago, IL: Open Court, 1990.

Tamari, Meir. *The Challenge of Wealth: A Jewish Perspective on Earning and Spending.* Northvale, NJ: Aronson, 1995.

Tannen, Deborah, Ph.D. *You Just Don't Understand: Women and Men in Conversation.* New York: Ballantine, 1991.

Taub, Rabbi Shimon. *The Laws of* Tzedakah *and* Maaser: *A Comprehensive Guide.* Brooklyn: ArtScroll/Mesorah, 2001.

Teller, Hanoch. *And from Jerusalem, His Word: Stories and Insights of Rabbi Shlomo Zalman Auerbach.* New York: New York City Publishing, 1995.

———. *Courtrooms of the Mind: Stories and Advice on Judging Others Favorably.* New York: New York City Publishing, 1987.

Tendler, Rabbi Dr. Moshe. "Pain, Halakha, and Hashkofah." In *Jewish Perspectives on the Experience of Suffering,* edited by Shalom Carmy. Northvale, NJ: Jason Aronson, 1999.

Travis, Rabbi Daniel Yaakov. *Priceless Integrity: Exploring the Parameters of Truth and Falsehood—From a Torah Perspective.* Edited by E. Schachter and S. C. Mizrahi. Southfield, MI: Targum, 2001.

Twerski, Rabbi Abraham J., M.D. *Angels Don't Leave Footprints: Discovering What's Right with Yourself.* Brooklyn: Shaar, 2001.

———. *The Enemy Within: Confronting Your Challenges in the 21st Century.* Brooklyn: Shaar, 2002.

———. *Lights Along the Way: Timeless Lessons for Today from Rabbi Moshe Chaim Luzzatto's* Mesillas Yesharim. Brooklyn: ArtScroll/Mesorah, 1995.

———. *Living Each Day.* Brooklyn: ArtScroll/Mesorah Publications, 1988.

———. *Visions of the Fathers:* Pirkei Avos *with an Insightful and Inspiring Commentary.* Brooklyn: Shaar, 1999.

Twerski, Rabbi Abraham J., M.D., and Ursula Schwartz, Ph.D. *Positive Parenting: Developing Your Child's Potential.* Brooklyn: ArtScroll/Mesorah, 1996.

Valladares, Armando. *Against All Hope: The Prison Memoirs of Armando Valladares.* New York: Knopf, 1986.

Vital, David. *A People Apart: The Jews in Europe 1789–1939.* Oxford, England: Oxford University Press, 1999.

Volozhiner, Chaim. *Ruach Chaim: Rav Chaim Volozhiner's Classic Commentary on* Pirkei Avos. Translated by Chanoch Levi. Southfield, MI, and Nanuet, NY: Targum Press and Feldheim, 2002.

Wagschal, Rabbi S. *Guide to* Derech Eretz. Southfield, MI: Targum Press, 1993.

Wasserstrom, Richard, ed. "Tarasoff vs. the Regents of the University of California." In *Today's Moral Problems,* 3rd edition. New York: Macmillan, 1985, 243–62.

Watterson, Kathryn. *Not By the Sword: How a Cantor and His Family Transformed a Klansman.* New York: Simon and Schuster, 1995; Boston: Northeastern University Press, 2001.

Wein, Berel. *Living Jewish: Values, Practices, and Traditions.* Brooklyn: Shaar, 2002.

Weiss, Rabbi Saul. *Insights: A Talmudic Treasury.* 2 vols. Jerusalem: Feldheim, 1990, 1996.

Wiesel, Elie. *Five Biblical Portraits.* Notre Dame, IN: University of Notre Dame Press, 1983.

Wiesenthal, Simon. *The Sunflower: On the Possibilities and Limits of Forgiveness.* New York: Schocken, 1997.

Will, George. *The Morning After.* New York: Macmillan, 1987.

Wilson, James Q. *On Character: Essays.* Washington, DC: The AEI (American Enterprise Institute) Press, 1991.

Wolpin, Rabbi Nisson, ed. *The Ethical Imperative: Torah Perspectives on Ethics and Values.* Brooklyn: ArtScroll, 2000.

Yalkut Shimoni (Compilation of Shimoni). New York: Title Publishing Company, 1944.

Zaitchik, Chaim Ephraim. *Sparks of Mussar.* Nanuet, NY: Feldheim, 1985.

Zimmels, Rabbi Dr. H. J. *The Echo of the Nazi Holocaust in Rabbinic Literature.* Ireland: self-published, 1975.

Zion, Noam, and David Dishon. *A Different Night: The Family Participation Haggadah.* Jerusalem: Shalom Hartman Institute, 1997.

———. *A Different Night: The Leader's Guide to the Family Participation Haggadah.* Jerusalem: Hartman Institute, 1997.

Ziv, Simcha Zissel. *Chochma Umussar.* (Hebrew). 2 vols. New York, 1957.

Zivotofsky, Avi. "Perspectives on Truthfulness in the Jewish Tradition." *Judaism,* Summer, 1993: 267–88.

Zuroff, Ephraim. *The Response of Orthodox Jewry in the United States to the Holocaust: The Activities of the Vaad Ha-Hatzalah Rescue Committee.* Jerusalem: Hebrew University Press and Ktav, 2001.

INDEX

ABOUT THE AUTHOR

RABBI JOSEPH TELUSHKIN, spiritual leader and scholar, is the author of the acclaimed *The Book of Jewish Values* and also *Jewish Literacy*, the most widely read book on Judaism of the past two decades. Another of his books, *Words That Hurt, Words That Heal*, was the motivating force behind the 1996 Senate Resolution 151, sponsored by Senators Joseph Lieberman and Connie Mack, to establish a "National Speak No Evil Day" throughout the United States.

Rabbi Telushkin is a senior associate of CLAL, the National Jewish Center for Learning and Leadership, and the rabbi of the Los Angeles–based Synagogue for the Performing Arts, and serves on the board of the Jewish Book Council. He lives with his family in New York City and lectures regularly throughout the United States.

Visit www.acodeofjewishethics.com for more information and to download a study guide to key ethical issues raised in *A Code of Jewish Ethics*.

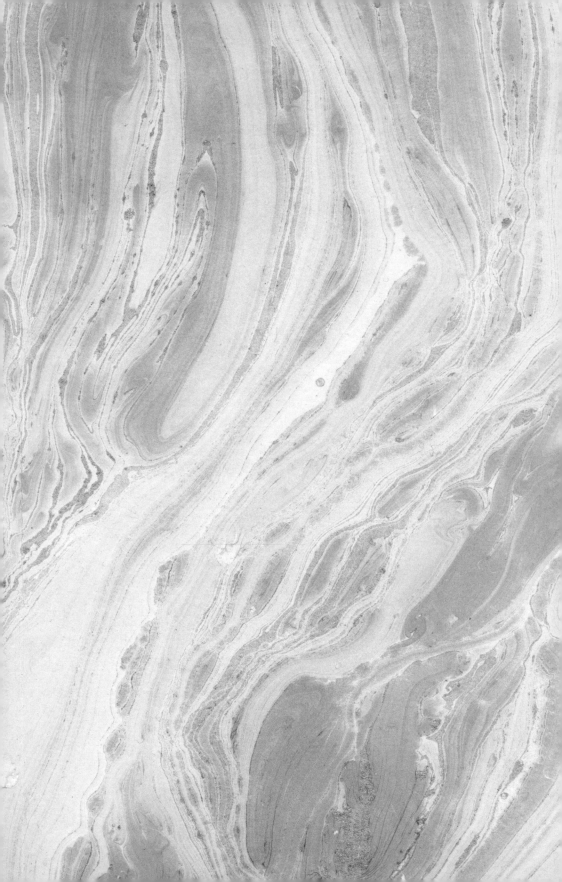